Novell® NetWare®:

The Complete Reference

Novell® NetWare®:
The Complete Reference

Tom Sheldon

Osborne **McGraw-Hill**

Berkeley New York St. Louis San Francisco
Auckland Bogatá Hamburg London Madrid
Mexico City Milan Montreal New Delhi Panama City
Paris São Paulo Singapore Sydney
Tokyo Toronto

Osborne **McGraw-Hill**
2600 Tenth Street
Berkeley, California 94710
U.S.A.

For information on translations and book distributors outside of the
U.S.A., please write to Osborne **McGraw-Hill** at the above address.

A complete list of trademarks appears on page 731.
Screens produced with Inset, from Inset Systems, Inc.

Pages were produced for this book by using Ventura Publisher
Version 2.

Novell NetWare: The Complete Reference

34567890 DOC 90

ISBN 0-07-881594-0

Acquisitions Editor: Jeff Pepper
Technical Reviewer: Novell
Copy Editor: Kay Luthin
Proofreaders: Julie Anjos, Barbara Conway, Jeff Green
Word Processor: Judy Koplan, Carole Latimer
Composition: Bonnie Bozorg
Production Supervisor: Kevin Shafer

CONTENTS AT A GLANCE

CONTENTS

Special thanks to Patti Heiser and Ed Cooper of Novell for their assistance and technical support. Additional thanks to Patrick Siefe and Steven Bottoms for technical editing, advice, and support.

A
C
K
N
O
W
L
E
D
G
M
E
N
T
S

Novell NetWare is a computer operating system designed to allow multiple computers to access multiple files and programs on one or more file-server devices. Such a system is known as a computer network or Local Area Network (LAN). Users of a LAN can easily share files and communicate with one another. Overall, the cost of software and hardware is often reduced. Sharable network versions of popular software can be purchased, and expensive hardware such as printers and hard disk storage units can be accessed by everyone on the network.

There is an increasing need for computer networks and information about them. In most cases, the personal computers required to build a LAN are already in place. By installing interface cards, cables, and network software, these systems can be connected into a sophisticated and productive communications system. This complete reference for Novell NetWare is designed to fill the gap in information for readers who are learning about NetWare and for readers who need a concise, readily available reference.

About This Book

This book brings together a wide range of information concerning the planning, preparation, management, and everyday use of a Novell network. The information provided in this book will get you started on the path to understanding NetWare and provide you with a resource you can use in day-to-day operations.

While much of the information covered in this book is also covered in the Novell NetWare manual set, many readers will find this book useful as a single source reference. Those familiar with NetWare know that it comes with up to ten separate manuals. These manuals may not always be available, may be too cumbersome to access, or may not cover topics in a useful way for beginners. System managers tend to keep the NetWare manuals to themselves. This book will provide readers with a handy reference to keep at their own desks.

INTRODUCTION

The topics in this book are arranged for beginning users who are learning about networks and Novell NetWare, as well as experienced users who require additional information. In general, Novell's manuals are designed for reference. Commands are placed in alphabetical order with the assumption that you know exactly what you are looking for. This book attempts to place commands and other topics under similar headings that relate to the tasks you might be attempting to perform. For example, the numerous commands and instructions for handling files are located under a single chapter heading related to files.

While this book can be opened to any page and used as a reference, chapters are written in an order that builds on the concepts, techniques, and commands covered in previous chapters. You may find this technique helps you learn and retain NetWare essentials more easily. Concepts are introduced and then reiterated in a different form later in the book. The many example exercises relate to how NetWare is used most often.

This book was also written for those planning the purchase and installation of NetWare. There is a tremendous amount of information to be gathered when researching and planning any network system. Hardware and software concepts must be grasped. This book is an attempt to bring together as much information as possible for readers who have not yet purchased the NetWare operating system and who do not have full access to the information they need to plan a good installation.

While an attempt has been made to make this book as complete as possible, it should be understood that no two network installations are ever alike. Keep in mind that the planning and configuration information in this book should never be considered the final answer for your installation. This book is designed to help you arm yourself with the concepts, terms, and products knowledge you will need to talk intelligently with consultants, dealers, or installers about your particular network needs.

How This Book Is Organized

This book is designed to help readers become familiar with Novell NetWare and the equipment required to establish a computer network under this operating system. There are four main topics of discussion that parallel the type of readers who may need this book:

- Planning
- Establishing a Network
- Managing the Network
- Day-to-Day Network Tasks

As mentioned previously, this book is organized to follow the procedures a system planner might follow when establishing a Novell network. The first few chapters familiarize the reader with network terms, many of which are specific to NetWare. The history of networks and an introduction to common industry terms is presented in Chapter 1. Chapter 2 moves on to a discussion of network hardware and software components. Chapter 3 then covers the range of Novell's network operating systems.

Chapter 4 gives readers a more thorough description of specific NetWare commands. Those familiar with DOS and other PC-based operating systems will be able to browse through this chapter to discover the tools and techniques available for managing and using a NetWare network. Others may wish to skip the chapter and use it for reference after the operating system and network have been installed.

Chapter 5 introduces readers to connectivity topics. Networks are advanced communications systems that can connect with other networks, minicomputers, and mainframes. The chapter discusses a wide range of Novell connectivity product offerings for those who will need to expand their networks beyond the basic local area network configurations.

Chapters 6, 7, and 8 are important chapters for those in the planning, design, and purchasing stages of their network. Chapter 6 covers the physical layout of a network and the components required to connect a system together. Chapter 7 discusses management and security issues that will need to be considered as part of the planning and design stages. Chapter 8 assists in the selection of network hardware and Novell software.

Chapters 9, 10, and 11 prepare and guide system installers through the actual setup of the network system and installation of NetWare. Chapter 9 helps installers gather pertinent information about the system that will be needed during the NetWare configuration and installation phases. Chapter 10 guides installers through the NetWare setup process. Chapter 11 then covers post-installation topics. NetWare ELS Level I users should refer to Appendix C for all installation procedures.

Beginning with Chapter 12 and proceeding through Chapter 15, new network supervisors are introduced to the management of a NetWare system. Topics include log-in procedures, loading software, adding users, setting up security, and other important topics.

The remaining chapters cover more specific network topics that are covered in an order important to the establishment of a properly functioning and efficient network. Chapters 25, 26, and 27 are concerned with network maintenance, monitoring, and improvement. These chapters are meant for network supervisors only, not the general user.

Conventions

You should find this book easy reading. Each chapter is split into several main topics that are listed at the beginning of the chapter. These topics are then divided into further sections.

Various exercises and examples are presented throughout the book. Commands you are to type are set off from the normal text and printed in bold. Listings from the computer are shown in a courier type that closely matches the screen display. In most cases, actual screen dumps are used for illustrations.

Keyboard keys are presented in small capitals, as in ENTER.

Additional Information

The author will be making additional information and publications available to readers. For more information write to

Tom Sheldon
1729 Roscoe Place
Cambria, CA 93428

Additional Help from Osborne/McGraw-Hill

Osborne/McGraw-Hill provides top-quality books for computer users at every level of computing experience. To help you build your skills, we suggest that you look for the books in the following Osborne/M-H series that best address your needs.

The "Teach Yourself" Series is perfect for beginners who have never used a computer before or who want to gain confidence in using program basics. These books provide a simple, slow-paced introduction to the fundamental usage of popular software packages and programming languages. The "Mastery Learning" format ensures that concepts are learned thoroughly before progressing to new material. Plenty of exercises and examples (with answers at the back of the book) are used throughout the text.

The "Made Easy" Series is also for beginners or users who may need a refresher on the new features of an upgraded product.

These in-depth introductions guide users step-by-step from the program basics to intermediate-level usage. Plenty of "hands-on" exercises and examples are used in every chapter.

The "Using" Series presents fast-paced guides that quickly cover beginning concepts and move on to intermediate-level techniques, and even some advanced topics. These books are written for users who are already familiar with computers and software, and who want to get up to speed fast with a certain product.

The "Advanced" Series assumes that the reader is already an experienced user who has reached at least an intermediate skill level and is ready to learn more sophisticated techniques and refinements.

"The Complete Reference" is a series of handy desktop references for popular software and programming languages that list every command, feature, and function of the product along with brief, detailed descriptions of how they are used. Books are fully indexed and often include tear-out command cards. "The Complete Reference" series is ideal for all users, beginners and pros.

"The Pocket Reference" is a pocket-sized, shorter version of "The Complete Reference" series and provides only the essential commands, features, and functions of software and programming languages for users who need a quick reminder of the most important commands. This series is also written for all users and every level of computing ability.

The "Secrets, Solutions, Shortcuts" Series is written for beginning users who are already somewhat familiar with the software and for experienced users at intermediate and advanced levels. This series gives clever tips and points out shortcuts for using the software to greater advantage. Traps to avoid are also mentioned.

Osborne/McGraw-Hill also publishes many fine books that are not included in the series described above. If you have questions about which Osborne book is right for you, ask the sales person at your local book or computer store, or call us toll-free at 1-800-262-4729.

Other Osborne/McGraw-Hill Books Of Interest to You

We hope that *NetWare: The Complete Reference* will assist you in mastering this fine product, and will also peak your interest in learning more about other ways to better use your computer.

If you're interested in expanding your skills so you can be even more "computer efficient," be sure to take advantage of Osborne/M-H's large selection of top-quality computer books that cover all varieties of popular hardware, software, programming languages, and operating systems. While we cannot list every title here that may relate to NetWare and to your special computing needs, here are several related books that complement *NetWare: The Complete Reference.*

The Practical Guide to Local Area Networks (ISBN: 0-07-881190-2) helps you decide which local area network is right for your needs. LAN specialist Rowland Archer guides you through the process of planning your LAN installation, pointing out the advantages and pitfalls every step of the way. Archer then applies the criteria he has developed to five of the most popular LANs available for the IBM PC and compatible computers: 3Com Ethernet, Corvus Omninet, Orchid PCnet, Novell NetWare, and IBM PC Network, and Token Ring.

If you're looking for the best way to get started in telecommunications or to get more out of the on-line services available today, see *Dvorak's Guide to PC Telecommunications* (ISBN: 0-07-881551-7). This book/disk package, written by the internationally recognized computer columnist John Dvorak with programming wiz Nick Anis, shows you how to instantly plug into the world of electronic databases, bulletin boards, and on-line services. The package includes an easy-to-read, comprehensive guide plus two disks loaded with oustanding free software and is of value to computer users at every skill level.

This book has been written to fill the need for a single source of information on the Novell NetWare operating system. You'll become familiar with the terminology and concepts of networks and how they relate to NetWare. You'll also become familiar with the features and requirements for each of Novell's NetWare product offerings, including ELS NetWare Level I, ELS NetWare Level II, Advanced NetWare 286, and SFT NetWare 286.

This book is of particular interest to the following:

- *Network planners*. If you are planning and designing a NetWare installation, this book will lead you through discussions of concepts, hardware components, management issues, NetWare features, and NetWare commands.

- *Network integrators and installers*. Those involved in network and NetWare installation procedures will benefit from the step-by-step instructions for getting NetWare up and running.

- *Network managers*. Network managers will benefit from topics that cover the planning, design, installation, and management of a NetWare system. This book is also a handy reference for day-to-day tasks.

- *Everyday users*. Users will find this book useful for day-to-day tasks, especially when considering that NetWare comes with only one set of manuals that are typically in demand by every user on the network.

Learn More About NetWare

Here is another excellent Osborne/McGraw-Hill book on NetWare that will help you build your skills and maximize the power of the network software you have selected.

If you are looking for a step-by-step, in-depth guide to installing NetWare, or need a handy reference to NetWare commands, see *NetWare Commands and Installation Made Easy* (ISBN: 0-07-881614-9).

Network Concepts

ONE

The Emergence of Networks
Mainframes, Minicomputers, and LANs
Networks Today
Reasons for Establishing LANs
Requirements of a LAN
Making the LAN Transition

It is often hard to pinpoint exactly what a network is—the concept is confusing. At first, it seems to be something physical: cables are strung through freshly drilled holes in the wall or hang from the ceiling tiles into the coffee maker. Then again, the network seems to be software: menus, mail systems, and special programs abound. Networks also introduce changes in the operation of a business: a network supervisor locks you out of programs, files, and directories, or the person sitting down the hall bumps your print job for someone else's.

In reality, a network is both hardware and software. The hardware consists of cables and interfaces that connect personal computers and peripherals together. The software manages the file and communications system. A network is most clearly defined as a communications system because it lets you communicate with other users, share files, and share peripherals. The telephone system is similar to a network in that it is a communications system above all else. When using it, we rarely think of the cables and hardware it is composed of. Instead, we think of the end result, which is useful and productive communications. In fact, a phone system with FAX machines to send documents and modems to send files can be compared to a network.

3

A local area network (or LAN, as it is commonly referred to) can be visualized as a sort of computerized phone system, but it is more appropriate to compare it to multiuser computer systems like the minicomputers and mainframes made by IBM, Digital, and other computer manufacturers. The most discernible feature of a LAN is its use of the *intelligent workstation* to accomplish a high level of "distributed" processing on each user's own personal computer. Unlike mainframes and minicomputers, which connect "dumb" terminals to a central processor, LANs allow individual PCs to retain and use their own processing power.

This chapter will explain how networks have developed, and how, in some cases, they have taken the place of mainframe and minicomputer systems. You will see how network systems operate and what features they offer to both users and managers.

The Emergence of Networks

One of the best places to begin a discussion of networks is to look back at the history of personal computers and see how networks and networking software have emerged. This history is strongly rooted in the need for users to maintain the "personal" aspects of personal computers and take advantage of the power already available on their desktops.

Operating Systems

The advent of the IBM Personal Computer in the early 1980s set a whole new standard in both business and personal computing. Along with the personal computer came a new computer operating system called *DOS*. The significance of any standard is that it stimulates growth of new products by providing software and hardware vendors with a development platform to build on. Needless to say, there are many incentives to follow a standard. DOS provided an easy programming environment for software vendors designing and marketing software. Operating systems provide an interface between the hardware of a computer system and its software applications programs. With a standard interface like DOS, problems with hardware compatibility diminish, because the operating system can mask incompatibilities at the hardware level with a layer of compatibility at the software level. Manufacturers can design their software to fit the software layer, rather than worrying about the differences in hardware.

Because this brought on an abundance of software, the use of personal computers increased. As more and more people began to use computers, it became obvious that a way of connecting them together would provide many useful benefits, such as printer and hard-disk sharing, especially when budgets became limited. Users who logged in to such networks could also transmit electronic mail and send files to each other.

Local area networks began to appear based on a particular hardware scheme, and as the concept of networking become more popular, each new year was heralded as the "Year of the Network." Vendors designed entire network systems with the hopes that their design would become a new standard. Although each piece of equipment and each type of network had its own advantages, users were often forced to choose one LAN over another based on the software that was available for it. Since each LAN vendor followed its own set of rules based on the hardware it had designed, applications software developers found it hard to write for each LAN type and often settled for only one.

Finally, a Standard

In 1984, IBM and Microsoft announced DOS 3.1 and NETBIOS (Network Basic Input/Output System). This operating system and the NETBIOS code provided a catalyst for changing the way networks were to develop. Suddenly, local area network standards were based on software rather than hardware. In this light, the LAN operating system became the critical factor in the development of LANs, rather than any hardware scheme. From this point on, LANs began to develop in more sophisticated ways. Features normally associated with larger mainframe and minicomputer systems, such as record locking, security features, and multiuser software, began to appear.

For the first time, applications running under DOS could make use of facilities to access networks and invoke file and record locking. Before DOS 3.1, networks in general tended to use proprietary access and locking schemes, requiring software manufacturers to design special drivers so their software would work on each of the available networks.

One of the first contenders in the post-DOS 3.1 network market was Microsoft Networks (MS-NET), which was introduced in 1985. Although up to 30 vendors pledged support for the program, that number dwindled, and today few versions of the program exist. One of those versions is known as the IBM PC Network Program. In the meantime, Novell was developing its product line, and it was this product line that soon became an industry standard and the basis for this book. There are many reasons why Novell's products have been accepted so well, as you'll discover in this book. One reason was Novell's break with DOS and the creation of a superior operating system that still allowed DOS applications to run. This enabled Novell to leap ahead of other operating systems and encroach on the minicomputer and mainframe world.

Mainframes, Minicomputers, and LANs

While personal computers were becoming more powerful through the use of advanced processors and more sophisticated software, users of mainframe and minicomputer systems were beginning to break with tradition—and from their information systems departments. It started to become clear that the personal computer could provide a more effective way to produce reports and maintain the information needed at a department level.

In the mainframe and mini environment, the data required by individual departments was often controlled by the management information systems or some similar department. This department controlled access to programs and data in the system. Each user was connected to the main system through a "dumb" terminal that was unable to perform its own processing tasks. Instead, the main system handled all of the processing, even though such systems could easily become overloaded.

The first breaks from the traditional systems and hierarchy began to appear in the early 1970s, when minicomputers began to replace larger mainframes in some businesses. These systems were inexpensive enough to be distributed to various departments within a single company and were controlled by the department managers. They could even be tied together through various communications methods, forming the first distributed

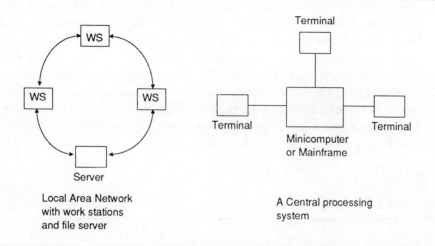

Local Area Network
with work stations
and file server

A Central processing
system

Figure 1-1.   LANs connect intelligent workstations together; central processing systems connect "dumb" terminals to a single system

processing systems. Department managers could now control their own
computing resources and have access to more computing processes. But
these systems still relied heavily on the use of dumb terminals that
accessed the central processor for their operations.

In the mainframe and minicomputer environment, processing and
memory are centralized. There are several reasons for this, including
expense, security, and management. The "host" computer became the
center of the computing environment and was managed by a team of
professionals whose sole task was to operate and manage the system.
Terminals attached to the system allowed other users to share the host
computers processing and memory. This type of *centralized processing
system* differs from the *distributed processing systems* used by LANs, as
shown in Figure 1-1. In a distributed processing system, most of the
processing is done in the memory of individual personal computers, which
are referred to as *workstations*. The *file server* or host system becomes a
place to store files and manage the network, as well as a place to connect
shared printers or other resouces.

Local area networks are now providing a new stage of development
that is changing the way people think about larger minicomputer and

mainframe systems. These systems are now playing a more equal role on local area networks—as powerful peripherals to be accessed by network users when required. In the old role, these systems controlled all users on the system and allocated processing time to them. Users can now choose to use the larger systems in the same way they might choose to use a network printer or some other device. The minicomputers and mainframes can thus be used to handle large processing tasks, such as accounting or intensive processing, while other tasks are distributed to individual PCs (see Figure 1-2).

Networks Today

There has been a slow and evolutionary development of network hardware over the last few years. Many of the old standards have given way to newer,

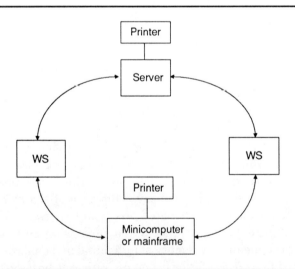

Figure 1-2.   Larger systems now share an equal role in a LAN, rather than a controlling role

faster, and more practical networking standards. Network systems and interface boards have become more reliable and support a wider range of networking features and functions. Because of this, networking is on the increase, and more and more software vendors are providing network-compatible software. In fact, the emphasis in the industry is on software, now that hardware standards have been met and exceeded. This section will describe some of the features that have developed over the last few years.

Communications Standards

A network can be a *closed system* that uses its own proprietary communications methods, which means that third parties can't add value to the system by creating add-on software. A network can also be an *open system* that makes its specifications available to third parties and includes programming "hooks" so developers can easily create add-on applications. An open system may abide by certain rules and methods that have become standardized in the industry or in the customer marketplace. Standardization helps vendors design products that work with other vendors products more easily.

Over the last few years, several network standards have taken shape, including the Open Systems Interconnection (OSI) model defined by the Open Systems Interconnection committee. The OSI model defines a network in layers, starting at the most basic hardware level with the cables and connectors and moving to the highest level, where network applications software runs.

Each layer in the OSI-defined guidelines provides a foundation of services and support for the layer above it. Because of this, the physical layer is listed at the bottom in the following list:

Application layer	Network software applications run on the network at this layer.
Presentation layer	Assists the user with tasks such as file transfers and program execution.
Session layer	Manages the connection between lower layers and the user; the user interface to the network.

Transport layer	Checks network data integrity and arranges data packets in correct order if necessary. Packet headers are also arranged to send packets of data to their destinations.
Network layer	Routes data over the network in packet form. Each packet is transferred through the two lower levels to its destination.
Data link layer	Manages input/output at the network interface. Raw data is organized and checked.
Physical layer	Defines the rules and protocols used in the network wiring and cables. This can include handshaking routines and transmission specifications. Cable types and connectors are also defined.

For the most part, network layers are invisible. The user should be involved in as little of the network's operation as possible. While network managers may control various aspects of the network at different network layers, users should be able to use software applications in an uncomplicated environment.

The Structure of Networks

Local area networks for personal computers come in several forms that can be grouped in the following ways:

Peer-to-Peer Systems   A peer-to-peer network allows any station on the network to become a server that makes its resources available to other workstations. Workstations can also become *receivers,* allowing them to access other workstation resources without sharing their own. Resource sharing is maximized on this type of network. The peer-to-peer network system may at first seem ideal, but it lacks security features and speed. In addition, a computer acting as a server may essentially become a system dedicated to running network operations as its memory is used. In this context, "dedicated" means that the system is so bogged down running as a server that no other DOS programs will run on it. The IBM LAN program and 3Com's 3+Share programs are examples of DOS-based peer-to-peer networks.

DOS-Based Systems   Although MS-DOS 3.1 provided the catalyst for industry network standards, in today's world it is not the best platform for a high-speed, secure, and efficient network. DOS is not designed to run multiple programs well, nor is it capable of handling requests from many users as a server would require. Vendors of DOS-based network software must often create special patches and fixes to keep the systems up and running. Networks in this category are generally peer-to-peer in nature.

DOS Emulating Systems   A DOS emulating system is capable of running DOS programs and responding to DOS commands, but does not operate under DOS. Instead, the operating system is often designed from the ground up to take advantage of the features of a particular microprocessor. For example, NetWare 286 is designed to use features of the 80286 that DOS does not use properly. LANs that take this approach offer design features similar to multiuser operating systems running on larger systems. Simultaneous requests are handled with ease.

Dedicated Server Systems   A dedicated server is one that cannot be used to run any end user programs. It acts only as a server facility, handling requests from workstations and managing the file system. A LAN operating system running in a true dedicated mode will allocate all of the resources of its processor, memory, and hard disk to network usage. The hard drives in such systems are given a special format that increases their efficiency compared to the DOS format, but it is not possible to read these drives when DOS is booted, a feature that adds to their security. Overall, dedicated server systems offer the best response time, security, and management functions. Novell NetWare can be used in the dedicated mode.

Nondedicated Server Systems   A nondedicated server system may offer all of the features of a dedicated system, as well as the capabilities to run the server as a workstation. The server essentially becomes two machines. While this may at first seem ideal, there is usually a trade-off in network efficiency. Novell ELS NetWare Level II and Advanced Net-Ware can be run in the nondedicated mode. Novell SFT NetWare can only be run in the dedicated mode.

LAN Features

Sophisticated LAN operating systems like Novell NetWare offer a complete range of features that were once only available on larger computer systems. Although not all of the features described here will be needed for every LAN system, most are considered essential components of the best LAN operating systems.

File Services   Files are what networks and file servers are all about. The manager as well as the users need to have good control over copying, archiving, and protecting their files. This may be done with menu-assisted commands. The system manager also needs to have the ability to "lockout" files and entire directories.

Resource Sharing   A lot has been said about the advantages of resource sharing. In peer-to-peer systems, any resource on the network can be used by any workstation. With dedicated systems like NetWare, shared devices like hard drives and printers are located at the file server or even at a special print server. On the other hand, printers can also be located at workstations and shared by other users when special software is used.

SFT   *System fault tolerance* is a feature available with Novell SFT NetWare that provides a certain amount of network survivability when various components of the server fail. The survival level depends on the level of SFT established in the first place. For example, you can install a second hard drive and then "mirror" all the data on the first hard drive to the matched hard drive. Information is written to both drives simultaneously, and the second drive can be used if the first fails.

Disk Caching   Disk caching improves hard disk speed by setting aside system memory to hold the file locations. The system then searches memory instead of the disk when looking for a file.

TTS   The *Transaction Tracking System* available with SFT NetWare is a method of protecting databases from corruption. If a transaction fails while data is being written to a database, the system backs out of the transaction and the database is restored to its last completed state. A transaction is a change in a record or set of records.

Security   Networks tend to locate files in a central place such as the file server. This can cause problems when snoopy people want to see your files or an untrained operator erases the payroll data. The more people who use a network, the higher are its security needs. A network manager will be required to assign access rights and passwords to users. Novell's dedicated server operating system is one of the most secure systems available. Once security is established, unauthorized persons cannot access the server or its files.

Remote Access   A good network system should allow access to users at remote sites through telephone communications lines, as shown in Figure 1-3. This may cause security problems, but a system with good security features will have no problem handling remote users.

Bridging   Bridging allows an existing network to tie into a new network or another existing network. This bridge may take place within the same building or through dedicated phone lines to remote LANs. A bridge must be transparent to the user.

Special Servers   Some systems allow applications programs to be run on dedicated servers rather than on workstations in special cases. This allows applications to take advantage of the superior file, memory, and processing resources of a server, if only temporarily.

Management Tools   Any network should have a complete toolbox full of useful utilities that allow users and managers to better use the system. These can include commands to view the status of the network or evaluate its current performance level. The tools should also allow managers to alter the system for better performance. Diagnostic tools should also be available so problems or potential problems can be serviced.

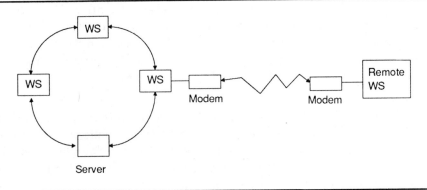

Figure 1-3.   Users at remote systems can become workstations on a LAN

User Communications   One of the added benefits of networks is that users can easily communicate with one another and send files over the network connections.

Print Spooling   Print spooling allows users to continue working immediately after sending a file to be printed. System memory, usually in the server or print server, is used to hold the unprinted document until it is printed. In this way, users can continue working on the systems. A good network will have a print-queue management system so that some print jobs can be given priority over others or can be printed at a scheduled time (after hours, for example).

Print Servers   A print server is a computer dedicated to the task of servicing the network printers. A number of printers may be attached to this computer, which has its entire memory dedicated to spooling the network print jobs. In most cases, it will be more desirable to share printers at workstations with other users using special software.

Availability of Applications

The quality and quantity of software available for local area networks and the way that software operates are often the most important considerations in selecting a LAN over other types of systems like mainframes and minicomputers. There tends to be a larger variety of software available in the PC DOS market than in the minicomputer or mainframe market. The price and availability of personal computers has created an entire "after-market" of software packages that fit just about every need. Many of these packages have been written to work in the network environment as well and have had significant feature and performance improvements.

Many of the available applications are also more sophisticated in operation and in their user interface, because PC applications tend to be written for equipment that is on the cutting edge of new technologies. A good example is graphics software written for high-resolution color displays such as the IBM VGA monitor. Applications written in the minicomputer environment for similar equipment are not as abundant and are expensive.

An application designed to run on a network can often be purchased in a single-user version or in a multiuser version. Multiuser versions are often purchased as add-on modules. Each add-on module allows several additional users to access the software. The access is controlled by a counter in the system so if too many users attempt to access it, they will be denied use until another user quits and the count is reduced.

Applications are run in the memory of individual workstations. When work is saved, it can be saved on the server, where other users can have access to the files. Files can often be shared simultaneously by two or more users, with some restrictions. *File lockout* occurs when a file is not marked shareable or cannot be shared. Shareable files include database files that provide *record locking*. A record lock prevents users who are sharing the same file from accessing the same record simultaneously. In this way, they can make changes to the file without affecting changes made by other users. For example, a company database holding client information could be used by several operators at the same time, but the record for a particular client might be accessible or changeable by only one operator at a time.

The Future

The current trend in network development is in the area of *interoperability*. This covers interfacing to a range of different operating systems, such as the Macintosh file system and UNIX. As hardware systems become more sophisticated, the ability to bridge different hardware systems through hardware emulation and translation becomes feasible. Novell has already established links to the Apple Macintosh systems. In the future, communications between NetWare, DOS, OS/2, Apple, UNIX, and many other systems will be transparent to the user.

Applications on workstations and servers usually run network-related programs. In some cases, it may be more efficient to run a disk or memory-intensive application on a dedicated machine other than the user's personal workstation. This machine can sit out on the network and make itself available to users who need to perform heavy number crunching or other highly intensive processing applications. Such dedicated servers are becoming more typical in network systems.

In some cases, an application may use several workstations. Highly intensive processing sequences are broken into smaller chunks that are then distributed and processed by several different stations. Processing time is decreased, since the workstations process simultaneously.

Reasons for Establishing LANs

One of the original reasons for establishing a LAN was to share expensive resources such as disk files, printers, and plotters. Although this aspect of networks has become less important now that peripherals are relatively less expensive, other more important reasons have emerged for using local area networks.

Availability of NetWork Software   A good selection of quality multi-user software that fits the needs of a company may be an important reason for selecting a LAN. On the other hand, the application itself may be the reason why a LAN is purchased. A point-of-sale system, for example, may be designed to work with a specific LAN system. Network software can also save costs if many copies of the software are required.

Proper Licensing   Software vendors are concerned that network users will not properly license the software used on their networks. A software package usually is licensed for only one person's use, but networks may allow several users to have access to a multi-licensed version of the package. If you are concerned about properly licensing the software within your company, purchasing network versions can help. When the maximum number of licenses for the network application are in use, no other users can have access to it.

Work Grouping   Tying personal computers together into networks allows work groups or teams of people involved in similar projects to communicate with one another more easily and share programs or files related to the same project. Novell NetWare supports work groups through its group naming feature. A group is first created, and then members are added to it. The group name can then be used to send messages or assign access rights to various directories.

Software Upgrade   Software upgrades are much easier if a package is stored centrally on the server. Instead of upgrading each user's individual PC, managers can upgrade the single copy stored on the server.

Data Backup   Backups are also simple, since data is centralized.

Data Management Benefits   Since data can be located centrally on the server, it becomes much easier to manage it, as well as to back it up. Files can be transferred between users through the network, rather than using floppy disks.

Organizational Benefits   Managers can benefit from new organizational concepts provided by a LAN. For example, members of work groups no longer need to be seated next to each other to share files and information among group members. You can now scatter group members wherever they might be more useful. For example, one member might be in the market research area, while another might be located in the management area. In fact, it may be beneficial to locate all managers together, rather than in their respective departments.

Sharing High-Quality Printers   Resource sharing has always been one of the benefits of a LAN, and while some peripherals are inexpensive enough to allocate to each user, others will remain expensive enough to share over the LAN. These include high-resolution laser typesetting machines and sophisticated plotters.

Distributed Processing

Many companies already operate as if they had a distributed processing system in place. If numerous PCs are installed around the office, these machines represent the basic platform for a network. Often a decision to install a network is based on the availability of existing PCs and the need for users to communicate with each other using PC-based applications, such as electronic mail or work group productivity software packages.

Electronic Mail and Message Broadcasting

Electronic mail allows users to communicate more easily among themselves. Each user can be assigned a mailbox on the server. Messages to other users can then be "dropped" in the mailbox and read by the user when they sign on to the network. It is also possible to alert users who have mail when they log on to the system. "Broadcasting" allows users or managers to send messages to other workstations. Meetings can be arranged, and schedules can be managed. Some add-on electronic mail and scheduling packages can track the schedule of an entire company. Users can schedule themselves and make requests in the schedules of other users.

Expanded PC Usage Through Inexpensive Workstations

Once a LAN is established, it actually costs less to automate additional employees. Diskless workstations or PCs without disk drives can be connected into the LAN to use the resources available at the server. These systems can be low in price and powerful in features.

Security

Security for data and programs can be achieved by using servers that are locked through both software and with physical means. Diskless workstations also offer security by not allowing users to download data that could be taken out of the building. These stations also prevent users from uploading unwanted software or viruses.

Requirements of a LAN

The hardware components of a local area network will be covered in detail in the next chapter, but there are certain features that every LAN should have. These features may involve either hardware or software.

Compatibility

First, a local area network operating system must provide a layer of compatibility at the software level so software can be easily written and widely distributed. This task is even more complex in a LAN, because the level of compatibility among all the machines and peripherals likely to be attached to the LAN is high. A network operating system that can provide these features, and become an industry standard, should be the most likely choice for your LAN software needs. Novell NetWare provides these features.

A LAN operating system must be flexible, which means that it must support a large variety of hardware. Once again, Novell NetWare is such an operating system. Although at one time NetWare only supported products made by Novell, its features and operations became so popular that most network hardware manufacturers designed their hardware to work with NetWare. At the same time, Novell has made sure they have the most compatible LAN package on the market.

Internetworking

One feature to emerge from the early days of LANs was a requirement to *bridge* different LANs together, thus forming one single network (see Figure 1-4). Users are able to access all workstations on the bridge network in a transparent way; no special commands are required to cross the bridge. This can be a difficult feature for a network vendor to incorporate because of the proliferation of hardware standards. A network operating system must be hardware independent, providing the same user interface no matter what hardware underlies the system.

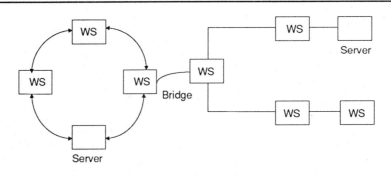

Figure 1-4.   Bridge connecting two or more networks with different cabling and protocol methods

Because new computer hardware, network interface cards, and networking topologies are always being introduced, hardware independence in a LAN operating system is even more important today. Network managers want to ensure that the equipment they buy today will be expandable in the future. Operating systems that support bridging must allow different types of networks to be connected. In this way, an established network can remain in place, while newer networks are added to it.

Protected-Mode Operation

An important feature in personal computer operating systems as well as LAN operating systems is the ability to operate in the protected mode of the 80286 and 80386 processors. Protected mode, as opposed to real mode, allows the processor to access up to 16MB of RAM memory (80286) and to gain more power from the microprocessor. Operating systems that use the real mode, such as MS-DOS, are limited to the traditional 640K RAM barrier. Various program fixes have attempted to overcome this, such as the Lotus/Intel Expanded Memory Specification, but a true multiuser operating system must operate in the protected mode. NetWare 286 provides this full compatability with the 80286 processor.

NetWare 386 is designed to take full advantage of the 80386 microprocessor and provides support for up to 250 concurrent users and 32TB (terabytes) of disk capacity.

File Servers

With the introduction of DOS 3.1 and the IBM PC Network Program, the *file-server-based* network became the most common network in the PC environment. Before this, *disk servers* were used as a centralized location for storing files. The operating system controlling a disk-server environment allocated one or more hard drives as a shared drive. Each workstation then considered this drive its own. The problem with disk-server environments is that file sharing is hard to maintain.

In the file-server environment, the entire file system on the server is managed by the file-server operating system. The sharing of files in a multiuser environment is easy to manage with this approach because file access is handled at the server, rather than by each individual machine. At the same time, file processing is distributed to the workstations so the server can allocate its resources to network tasks such as file transfers, printer management, and network communications.

Growth Path and Modularity

One of the most interesting aspects of local area networks is their *modularity*. A set of PCs can be converted into a LAN, which can then grow in size simply by adding additional workstations. If more storage is required, you can simply add another hard drive or add another server. If you need to connect with users on another LAN, you simply install a bridge. In addition, printers can be upgraded or added at any time.

Site requirements are easy to fill with LANs because network cables are usually easy to tap into and workstations can be placed almost anywhere. If a workstation is required beyond the capacity of the cabling system, a bridge or repeater can be used to extend the network.

System Reliability and Maintenance

All computers are prone to system lockups, power failures, and other catastrophes. If a centralized processing system goes down, all users connected to it are left without a machine to work on. If the server for a distributed-processing LAN system goes down, users can still work with their local PCs. Of course, if the power goes down, all stations will shut down unless suitable backup power is supplied to them also. These uninterruptable power supplies (UPS) can supply minutes or hours of additional power to a server and its workstations. The additional time may allow network managers to shut the system down properly so it can be brought back up with few problems, if any, when power is restored.

The bigger and more expensive the UPS, the longer managers will be able to work with the server, and users will be able to work at workstations. This may be essential in some installations, such as hospitals or law enforcement agencies. Not every workstation will need a UPS, but those used to shut down the server or perform tape backup should be connected to one.

Network operating systems now have sophisticated features for returning downed servers to a state of readiness with little or no file corruption. Files that were open when the power went out can be returned to their previous state with *Transaction Tracking Systems* like the one used in NetWare.

Making the LAN Transition

Installing a LAN will be covered in this manual, but preparing your work environment for a LAN will be entirely up to you. How well you prepare the future LAN users will make all the difference in the world.

It is doubtful that you will receive a lot of hostility for installing a LAN, because most users will benefit from it. Some, however, may complain about having to walk down the hall for printouts, or that the manager has locked them out of some applications, but for the most part, users will benefit from an increase in speed, the sharing of resources, and inter-network communications.

You may need to make procedural changes in the way things are done once the LAN is running, but even this can be positive in many situations. For example, backups can now be made by one person from the server and individual users will not need to bother with system backups. Physical changes may also be necessary. For example, systems may need to be moved to take advantage of network cabling. Printers may also need to be moved near the server.

If you are installing a network system in a multidepartmental company, expect the department managers to quibble about who has access to what on the network. Department managers may assume that they will lose some control when the network is installed. Instead, it should be explained that they will now have more control over the programs and data used by their departments while receiving the benefits of centralized services and internetwork connectivity.

The topic of who will perform system maintenance and provide help to users will also come up, especially in multidepartmental companies. Network support may be offered by a special group, or a network trainer may be assigned to assist users or managers.

The worst thing that can happen at any new installation is for everyone to misunderstand the purpose of installing a LAN in the first place: to increase communications and improve productivity. Attitudes may be negative, and the system installers or managers may "go on the defensive," creating a vicious circle of negative energy. Soon, the LAN is looked at with doubt or suspicion. "This is management's way of trying to control us," or "They want to track how productive we are," may be heard in the background. The best approach, of course, is to instill confidence in what the LAN will provide.

The next most important step for users will be training, training, training! As you read this book, keep "the transition" in mind. You will develop ideas and learn about ways to make it easier.

Components of a Network

File Servers
Workstations
Network Interface Cards (NICs)
Network Cabling
Network Layout and Topology
Bridges and Gateways

This chapter concentrates on the individual hardware components of a network running under Novell NetWare. The next chapter will cover each of NetWare's operating systems and their features, along with the hardware requirements and additional equipment you can use for each of the operating systems.

The four basic hardware components that make up a local area network are listed below and shown in Figure 2-1. Each of these components and its subcomponents will be discussed in the remaining sections of this chapter.

- File servers

- Personal computer workstations or other intelligent devices

- Network interface cards (NICs)

- Cabling

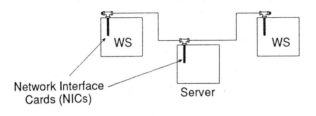

Figure 2-1.   Basic components of a local area network

File Servers

A network file server is a computer system used for the purpose of managing the network file system, servicing the network printers, handling network communications, and other functions. A server may be dedicated, in which case all of its processing power is allocated to network functions, or it may be nondedicated, in which case part of the server's functions may be allocated as a workstation or DOS-based system.

The network operating system is loaded into the server's hard-disk system, along with the system management tools and user utilities. When the system is restarted, NetWare boots and the server comes under its control. At this point, DOS is no longer valid on the NetWare drive, since it is running the NetWare operating system; however, most DOS programs can be run as normal. Part of NetWare's security comes from the fact that network hard drives can only be booted or logged to after starting NetWare, not DOS. The superior security features of NetWare then take over to keep unauthorized people out of the system.

The choice of a network server is critical to the performance and operation of a network. The primary task of a dedicated server is to handle the requests made by the workstations. These can be requests for disk usage, printer queues, or communications with other devices. Receiving, processing, and replying to these requests can take a considerable amount of time, which increases as additional workstations log on to the network. Since the server handles requests from all workstations, its load can be quite high.

Congestion can occur on a server as workstations continually make requests to it. Network traffic may become so high that some requests from workstations cannot be received. The workstations then continue to send additional requests until they receive a response from the server. This further increases the workload of the server because it must also process the retries by the workstations. In addition, the workstations themselves begin to slow down as they wait for a response from the server.

The larger the network, the more important it becomes to have a high-performance server. Larger amounts of RAM memory are required to support disk caches and printer queues. The server should be matched with the anticipated "throughput" as closely as possible. The throughput performance of a server is a combination of several factors, including the processor type, processor speed, wait-state factor, memory access channel size, bus size, and memory caching capabilities, as well as hard disk performance and other factors.

While most AT-class systems are satisfactory for NetWare, any improvements in the features just discussed will benefit the server's performance. An 80386 system is preferable if it fits the budget. The following recommendations are made by Novell:

Processor Type   An AT-class machine with an Intel 80286 processor is required, but an 80386 system is preferable if high network loads are anticipated.

Speed   This is the clock speed of the processor, which regulates the number of operations the processor performs. Clock speeds of 8MHz are standard on 80286 processors. Some manufacturers have increased this speed to 10MHz, 12MHz, or higher in some cases. The 80386 systems can run as high as 33MHz. The higher the clock speed, the faster the system.

Wait States   Wait states balance the performance of the processor with the rest of the system. The lower the better. Some 80386 systems have 0 wait states.

Memory Access Channel   A bus on a computer system is the "freeway" that connects each of the components in the system, such as the processor, memory, interface cards, and disk systems. The wider the bus, or the more lanes it has, the faster information can be transferred. 80286 systems have 16-bit-wide bus slots and 80386 systems have 32-bit-wide bus slots.

Bus Size   The bus extends out of the microprocessor to connect with external components. The 16-bit bus is standard on 80286 systems. However, many cards are only available in the older 8-bit bus design originally used on early PCs. Although these cards will fit in a 16-bit slot, they do not take advantage of the potential performance of the system's 16-bit bus slots. When selecting interface boards, it is preferable to purchase 16-bit cards. IBM Personal System/2 computers use a different type of interface known as the microchannel bus. This bus is superior in many respects to the standard AT bus but cannot use the same cards.

Memory Caching Capabilities   Cache memory determines the amount of data and the number of files that can be open on the network at one time. Cache memory also increases server throughput by placing disk-file information in memory to reduce disk searches. The more memory a system has, the more memory NetWare will make available to the cache.

Novell NetWare supports a wide variety of 80286 and 80386 systems, including the IBM PS/2 line, which uses the microchannel bus system. NetWare-compatible systems include those made by Acer, Compaq, Epson, Hewlett-Packard, Hyundai, Mitsubishi, NCR, NEC, WYSE, Zenith, and many others.

Hard-Disk Storage

Disk drives can reside in the server or be externally attached, but in order to be used as network drives with NetWare, they must be attached to the server. Most internal hard-disk drives attached to IBM or Western Digital controller boards are compatible. Internal hard disks in the IBM PS/2 systems attached to MFM and ESDI controllers are also supported.

Novell markets a disk interface, called the disk coprocessor board (DCB), which is designed to support disk subsystems. The DCB has been designed to interface the disk subsystem's input and output (I/O) with the file server's CPU (central processing unit). By specializing in this task, disk access time for NetWare servers can be reduced substantially. Disk I/O is one of the primary bottlenecks on a LAN. The DCB helps streamline the performance of disk reads and writes by relieving the processor of these tasks.

Hard-drive storage under NetWare is limited to a volume size of 255MB, with a maximum of 32 volumes per file server. If a hard disk exceeds 255MB, it must be divided into two or more volumes. This is done during NetWare installation.

Advanced NetWare and SFT NetWare can support up to five hard-disk channels, each controlled by a hard-disk interface board. Channel 0 is used by the internal hard disk of the file server. External hard disks can then be attached to channels 1 through 4 to expand the disk storage of the server. External hard disks are available from Novell or third-party manufacturers, but if Novell drives are used, they must be attached to disk coprocessor boards.

Uninterruptable Power Supply

The UPS has become an essential component of the server because it keeps the system running if the power goes down. Keep in mind that the workstation used to down the server in case of a power outage must also be attached to a UPS unless you use the server itself for this task. A UPS is also essential for the system performing tape backups, since it would be undesirable to have the server and tape system go down in the middle of a backup. Advanced NetWare and SFT NetWare also offer a UPS *monitoring* feature that informs users and managers when a power failure has occurred at the server. Most users know when a power failure has occurred because their own system has failed, but the UPS can warn those who are also operating on a UPS that the system will shut down in a certain amount of time. This gives users enough time to quit their applications properly until the power is restored. Also, the power may go down in a different building where the server is located.

SFT NetWare's Transaction Tracking System will protect database files from power outages. If a server or workstation goes down, the TTS will back files out to their previous state before the system went down.

Tape Backup

Tape backup systems for backing up the data on a network hard drive are another essential component of a network. Although other types of backup systems are coming into use, such as writable compact laser disks, tape backup systems still provide the most economical means of archiving data.

Most tape backup systems are placed in a workstation. The operator logs on to the server and begins backing up files over the network. At one time, only Novell tape backup systems could be mounted in the server itself; however, those drives are no longer available. Workstations with tape backup systems should also be equipped with an uninterruptable power supply so that tape backup can continue if the power goes down.

SFT NetWare provides the advantages of system fault tolerance, which means data is written to two separate drives simultaneously for backup purposes. The mirrored drive can then be put into service if the primary drive fails.

Peripherals

Part of any network are its peripherals—printers, modems, and other devices that may be shared by workstations. Under NetWare, up to five printers may be placed at the server, where they can be accessed by all users. Two printers may be assigned to the LPT parallel ports, and three serial printers may be assigned to the COM serial ports. NetWare for 80286 systems does not support the sharing of peripherals between workstations in a peer-to-peer method. Shared peripherals must be attached to the server unless third party software programs are used to allow peer-to-peer peripheral sharing.

Modems and other remote communications devices can also be shared by designating a station as a communications server. It is not recommended that the file server be used for this purpose since the communications processes can take a considerable amount of the server's time.

Workstations

Workstations are attached to the server through the network interface card and the cabling. The "dumb" terminals used on mainframe and minicomputer systems are not supported on networks because they are not capable of processing on their own. Workstations are normally intelligent systems, such as IBM or IBM-compatible personal computers with floppy disk drives or hard drives. The concept of distributed processing relies on the fact that personal computers attached to networks perform their own processing after loading programs and data from the server. This frees the server for network tasks. Files are then stored back on the server, where they can be used by other workstations or be included in the server backup. Networks help reduce the cost of desktop computing by reducing the hard-disk requirements at each workstation. These workstations use file storage available on the server so their cost is reduced, since internal hard-disk storage devices are not necessary.

The cost of individual workstations can be further reduced by using *diskless* workstations. A diskless workstation is a system without any disk drives but with the same computing power and memory of regular personal computers. Diskless workstations require special circuitry on the network interface card to access the server. Once these stations "locate" the server, they boot from its hard drive as if it were their own. A special file residing on the server looks to the diskless workstation like a disk drive. All of the startup files normally contained on a boot drive, such as the DOS system files, AUTOEXEC.BAT, CONFIG.SYS, and NetWare startup files, are contained in this single file. A boot file is created for each different type of workstation by the system manager after NetWare is installed.

Diskless workstations, like PCs, are equipped with microprocessors and memory so they can perform the same processing tasks as any similarly equipped personal computer, as long as they are booted from the server first. The network interface cards in these systems must be installed with a remote reset PROM that is normally available from the manufacturer as an add-on for about $50.

To connect a personal computer or workstation to a network, a network interface card and the appropriate cabling must first be installed. After the system boots, special network startup files created at the time of the installation are used to connect and log on to the server. These files are created specifically for the type of workstation and workstation interface card being used at each station. The NetWare startup files first link to the network hardware such as the cabling system and then provide a "shell" around the workstation's disk operating system (DOS) to allow it to interface with the NetWare operating system. In the case of diskless workstations, the shell files actually reside on the server.

There are few special requirement for operating a personal computer as a workstation. In fact, your basic, no-frills PC (mail-order for $500) can be used, as long as it has a way of booting, whether this be from a built-in disk drive or a remote reset PROM on the network interface card. However, the more powerful a workstation is, the better. Unlike dumb terminals attached to multiuser systems, network workstations do their own processing, so the bigger and faster the system, the better. It is recommended that any workstation have at least 640K of memory.

AT-class systems are the best choice for workstations because of their faster processors and because of the 16-bit bus interface, which can take advantage of new 16-bit network interface cards. Macintosh users can now connect into a NetWare network and have access to file services while retaining their familiar Macintosh icon-based file system.

There are two very good reasons why diskless workstations should be considered. The first is, of course, price. The second has to do with security. Since the stations do not have disk drives, sensitive data files cannot be downloaded to floppy disks and carried out of the building. In addition, users cannot upload data to the server, which may be important when a system manager wishes to keep users from filling the server with unnecessary files. Diskless workstations can also be used as a way to keep computer viruses out of the system. Viruses are small programs that can corrupt a computer filing system and are usually introduced when programs are copied from questionable outside sources.

Workstation Operating Systems

The power of the personal computer is increasing. When you use a PC as a workstation on a network, that power increases further. However, the operating system used by the local PC workstation may not be adequate to handle all of the things the system has the potential to do. For example, you may want to access a database or accounting package on the LAN, and then switch to a local application and perform other processing. A new multitasking operating system may solve the problem.

NetWare supports such multitasking operating systems as OS/2, PC-MOS, Windows/386, and Concurrent DOS. All of these programs allow multiple tasks to run in multiple windows on the workstation.

Network Interface Cards (NICs)

Network interface cards provide the connection for network cabling to servers and workstations. Because of the abundance of hardware design and development that took place before networking software became the standard on which to base network design, there are numerous types of cards that support many different types of cables and network topologies.

A network interface card first of all provides the connector required to attach the network cable to the server or workstation. The on-board circuitry then provides the protocols and commands required to support the type of network the card is designed for. Many boards have additional memory for buffering incoming and outgoing data packets, thus improving network throughput. A slot may also be available for the remote boot PROM, permitting the board to be mounted in a diskless workstation. Network interface cards also contain various switches and jumpers to select various hardware interrupts, input/output addresses, and other features that make the card compatible with the system it will be mounted in. Part of the NetWare installation process involves properly setting these switches and jumpers.

Network interface cards are available to fit the old style 8-bit bus, or the new, faster 16-bit bus. Cards made to fit the IBM PS/2 microchannel bus are also widely available for the most popular network types.

Hardware and software compatibility becomes an important issue when you consider the use of any network card. You will need to make sure that the card is capable of running in the intended workstation and that software drivers are available so the NetWare operating system can link to its protocols and board features. It is important to have the software drivers in hand during the NetWare configuration process, so make sure that the boards you intend to buy are compatible with NetWare. NetWare includes a large set of drivers for the most popular boards.

The specifics of each type of card will be discussed later in this chapter and in Chapter 6. The type of cable and the way the cable is laid out in an installation depends on the type of card used. This will be covered in the next few sections.

Network Cabling

Once the server, workstations, and network interface cards are in place, network cabling is used to connect everything together. The type of cable used (if cable is used at all) depends on many different factors and will be covered in detail in Chapter 6. Be sure you have made compatible decisions on the types of cards and cables you plan to use.

The most popular types of network cable are shielded twisted-pair, coaxial, and fiber-optic cabling. Telephone-type twisted-pair cabling is also becoming more popular. In addition, connections can be made through more exotic means like microwaves and radio signals. Each cable type or method has its advantages and disadvantages. Some are prone to interference, while others cannot be used for security reasons (radio). Speed and cabling distances are other factors that play a part in determining the type of cable used. The following section describes the advantages of twisted-pair, coaxial, and fiber-optic cabling.

Note: Cables and cards must match. Be sure to make your decisions wisely, preferably with the help of a competent dealer or a systems integrator.

Shielded Twisted Pair

Shielded twisted-pair wiring consists of two stranded copper wires that are insulated separately and twisted together. An outer layer of insulation covers the pairs. It offers the following advantages:

- Well-understood technology
- Minimal installation skills
- Quick and easy installation
- Minimal emanation of signals
- Some immunity to interference, cross talk, and corrosion

Coaxial Cable

Coaxial cable is composed of a copper wire conductor surrounded by a stranded shield that serves as the ground. A thick insulation material separates the shield from the conductor, and the entire wire set is protected by an outside covering. The cable is available in both thin and thick versions. Thick cable supports extended cable distances but is more expensive. Thin cable may be more practical for pulling through tight spots. Coaxial cable offers the following advantages:

- Both broadband and baseband communications support
- Useful for a variety of signals, including voice, video, and data
- Easy installation
- Well-understood technology
- May already be installed

Fiber-Optic Cabling

Fiber-optic cabling, although expensive, offers high speed in data transfer and is secure from tapping. Because the signal is carried by light, there is little chance of electrical interference or signal emanation. The cable consists of inner and outer optic cores that refract light differently. The fiber is encased in a protective cable and offers the following advantages:

- High transmission speed
- No emanation of electrical or magnetic signals that provide security
- Immune to interference and cross-talk
- Less expensive than coaxial cable in some installations
- Supports longer cable distances

Network Layout and Topology

The way network cables are physically laid out to connect with each of the workstations and servers is known as the network *topology*. The topology of a network looks similar to a map of the network on paper because cables can be traced to every workstation and every server in the installation. Topology is important because it determines where workstations can be placed, how easy the cable will be to run, and how much the entire cable system will cost. Although many different configurations are possible, five are briefly covered in this section, and then in more detail in Chapter 6.

A LAN is easily tailored to fit the requirements of almost any installation site. It can also grow from a small system into a system with a large number of nodes (workstations). The amount of flexibility a LAN has depends largely on its topology.

Star Topology

In a star topology, shown in Figure 2-2, a device is used as the central connection point for wires coming from the workstations. The central device may be the file server itself or a special wiring hub. The star is one of the earliest topologies, and resembles the phone system. AT&T's STARLAN and Novell's proprietary S-Net are examples.

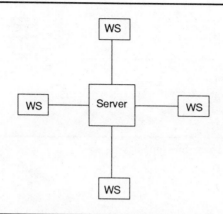

Figure 2-2.   Star topology

Diagnosing network problems is easy because workstations report through the central system. Node failures are easy to detect and cables are easy to modify. Data collision is impossible, since each station has its own cable, and the system is easy to expand. However, for large installations, cables from the workstations tend to cluster at the central unit, causing potential management problems. Large quantities of expensive cable may be required, as well as a dedicated server.

Linear Bus Topology

In a linear topology, shown in Figure 2-3, the file server and all workstations are connected to a main trunk cable. All nodes share this cable. The trunk must be terminated on both ends. Signals and packets travel up and down the cable with a destination address. Each node checks the addresses of packets on the network to see if they match its own address. Cabling can be snaked through the walls and ceilings of the installation site, and workstations can tap into it. Examples of this type of topology are Ethernet and G-Net.

Linear bus topology uses the least amount of cable, and the cable is fairly easy to install since it can be snaked through a building following

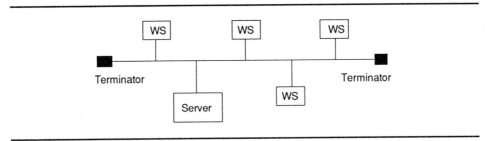

Figure 2-3.   Linear bus topology

the best possible routes. Total cable length will be much less than a star system because the cable does not have to extend from the server to each station, only from station to station.

Linear bus topology does have disadvantages. The trunk can become a bottleneck in high-traffic environments, since all workstations share the same cable. It is hard to isolate network cabling problems to any particular trunk segment or workstation, because all stations are on the same cable. A split in the cable will down the system.

Ring Topology

In a ring topology, shown in Figure 2-4, signals travel in one direction around a closed loop cable. Nodes pass signals to each other one node at a time. Data transmitted over the networks is assigned a specific address for each workstation.

With ring topology, networks can often be extended to long distances, and the total cabling cost will be less than a star system and possibly equal to a linear bus system. However, the complicated cabling must close back on itself. A break in the cable will down the system.

Combination Star/Bus Topology

In a star/bus configuration, shown in Figure 2-5, a signal splitter takes the place of the central device. The network cable system can take on the topology of either a linear bus or ring topology. This provides cabling

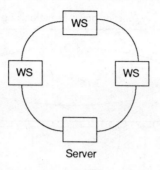

Figure 2-4.   Ring topology

advantages for buildings that have workgroups separated by long distances. Star/bus configurations have some of the advantages and disadvantages of both the star and bus topologies. ARCNET is an example of a star/bus topology. It offers a lot of flexibility for configuring the cable layout to easily fit any building. ARCNET also uses a token-passing communications protocol, which helps maintain a consistent throughput and avoids data collision problems like those that can slow an Ethernet linear bus system.

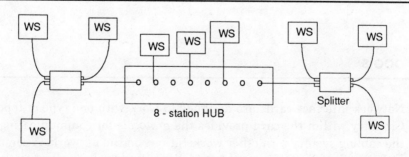

Figure 2-5.   The star/bus topology

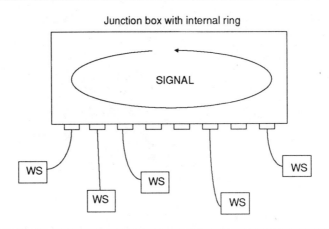

Figure 2-6.   Star/ring topology (exaggerated for clarity)

Combination Star/Ring Topology

In a star/ring configuration, shown in Figure 2-6, a communications "token" is passed around a central hub. Workstations then expand from this hub to increase potential distances. This configuration has some of the advantages and disadvantages of both the star and ring topologies. The IBM Token Ring system is an example of a star/ring topology. Its central hub is placed within a single box that then serves as a junction for workstations that radiate from it.

Protocols

Network interface cards are designed to work with one type of topology. Circuitry within the card provides the *protocols* for communicating over the cabling system with other workstations on the network. A communications protocol establishes the guidelines that determine how and when workstations can access the cable and send data packets. There are four commonly used protocols in network systems. These are differentiated by where control lies and how access is made to the cable.

Circuit-Switching Protocol

In this type of protocol, a node can demand to have access to the network. The controlling switch then gives that node access unless the line is already in use. As long as a line is open between two nodes, access is closed to other nodes.

Controlled-Access Polling

A central controller listens for node activity and gives access as needed. This method differs from the previous method because the controlling device determines which nodes have access, not the nodes themselves.

Carrier-Sense Multiple Access (CSMA)

This method is used on bus topology networks. Nodes constantly poll the line to see if it is in use or if data packets are addressed to them. If two nodes attempt to use the line at the same time, multiple access is detected and one node will halt access to try again later. On a high-traffic network, these data collisions can cause a slowdown in the system.

Token Passing

In a token-passing scheme, an electronic token or packet is sent around the network. Nodes can use the packet if it is not already in use to send data to other nodes. Because there is only one token, collisions are impossible and network throughput stays constant.

Although one type of topology and protocol system may seem superior to another, the best fit for any installation is usually determined by the site itself and the needs of the system. You should evaluate the placement of each workstation and determine how it will be cabled. The cost of the cable then comes into consideration. Chapter 6 provides a more extensive discussion of specific network hardware systems and topologies to help you make the best decision for your installation.

Bridges and Gateways

Part of any LAN installation may be a connection to another LAN, called a *bridge,* or a connection to another operating system, called a *gateway.* Gateways are usually connections made to mainframe and minicomputer systems. The process of making connections outside of the normal LAN topology is known as *internetworking.*

There are a wide variety of connection methods within the realm of internetworking. For example, a bridge can be made to a local LAN or to a remote LAN through a telephone connection. The same is true of gateways. A bridge between two LANs can also take place in the server, which is known as an *internal* bridge, or the bridge can be made at a workstation, which is known as an *external* bridge. The machine used to make an external bridge is often dedicated to enhance the performance of the interconnection.

One of the advantages of Novell NetWare is that bridges can be very transparent to the user, even though connected LANs may use entirely different network protocol methods and topologies. A user on the bridged network can access a server across the bridge with little knowledge of the lower-lying cable configuration and communications methods. Therefore, bridges are often established to connect an old existing LAN with a new LAN installation. Another reason for establishing a bridge is to overcome limitations in the cabling distance. Figure 2-7 illustrates how two LAN interface cards help extend the normal distance of a LAN. The first

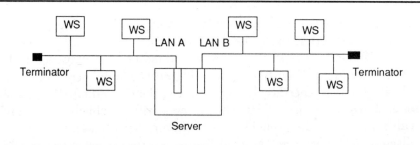

Figure 2-7.   Two LAN cards installed in the server can double the distance of a LAN

interface cards establishes a trunk out to the left; the second out to the right. The sum of both trunks doubles the normal maximum distance of the network.

Gateways under NetWare are extensive. For example, SNA gateways enable LAN workstations to access important information and applications on IBM SNA and compatible host computers. 5250 gateways enable workstations on a LAN to access similar information on IBM System/34, 36, and 38 minicomputers. There are many other possibilities, which will be discussed in Chapter 5.

The World of NetWare

Novell, NetWare 286 Product Overview
How NetWare 286 Works
Novell NetWare 386

Novell NetWare has been on the market since 1983, the same year IBM introduced the IBM XT personal computer and IBM PC DOS 2.0. These products set standards. The IBM XT was the first personal computer from IBM to include a hard drive. Simultaneously, IBM PC DOS 2.0 was the first PC disk operating system to support hard drives without special patches. Both created a standard environment for the growth of PCs into more sophisticated applications and environments. Advanced NetWare set the stage for the development of local area networks in the personal computer environment.

Novell originally developed NetWare as the operating system for the Novell S-Net, a network that uses the star topology and a proprietary server based on the Motorola MC68000 microprocessor. At about the same time, personal computers based on the 8088 microprocessor were booming. The announcement by IBM of hard-disk support with its PC XT system and DOS pushed the PC even further into business and other environments. Since NetWare was written in C, a so-called "portable" programming language, Novell was able to quickly port some of the code for NetWare to the 8088 environment.

As it turns out, the DOS/Intel 8088 environment is not the best environment in which to run multiuser applications, especially a multiuser operating system like NetWare. The BIOS (basic input/output system) designed for the original PC (and required for DOS) is designed only for single users. Novell decided to bypass the I/O system altogether and create an operating system that would run more effectively in multiuser mode.

45

Because of this, NetWare is written specifically for the hardware of 8088-based systems, rather than for DOS and its I/O system.

The trade-off for Novell in taking this approach has been the need to write hard-disk device drivers and a "DOS shell" interface for workstations to allow users to work with DOS and its commands in the normal way. But these problems have long been overcome, and NetWare is in many ways superior to DOS. Almost all DOS applications can be run from the NetWare operating system through the DOS shell. In addition, security features and fault tolerance features, which are impossible to design into the DOS file structure, have become a mark of excellence for NetWare.

Novell's early decisions to write software code directly for the processor rather than going through DOS has paid off. Novell is always the first to support new processors and DOS operating-system upgrades. Developers who have based their network operating systems on DOS have had to struggle with DOS's limitations and the need to stay compatible with it. DOS became like a ball and chain to these unfortunate vendors as newer, more advanced processors came on the market, since DOS was originally written for the old 8088 processor and still retains features locked to the limitations of that processor. As more advanced processors came out, DOS could not break its bonds with the older processors; thousands of users had made significant software and hardware investments that relied on DOS compatibility.

In the meantime, Novell began making significant advances that kept pace with microprocessor technology. NetWare 286 is capable of running in the more efficient protected mode on an 80286 processor. In 1989, Novell announced NetWare 386, the first operating system to take full advantage of the Intel 80386 microprocessor. The 80386 is especially adaptable to multiuser environments like local area networks. Novell has placed the new 386 operating system at the top of its product line, not only because it is the most powerful network operating system, but because the 80386 processor (and the 80486) is an ideal platform for network operating-system development. The 80386 and 80486 will play key roles in the shaping of future products developed by Novell.

Note: For those interested in NetWare 386 features, a special section at the end of this chapter provides a brief overview. The operating system is discussed in a separate book, *Novell NetWare 386: The Complete Reference.*

Through all of this, NetWare has remained compatible with DOS by emulating the DOS environments. A special program that runs when a workstation logs on to a NetWare system provides a shell so NetWare can translate and use DOS commands and programs. As new versions of DOS become available, the shell is upgraded to be compatible with the new DOS.

Novell NetWare 286
Product Overview

This section will discuss the features and benefits of the five products in Novell's 80286-based operating-system line. Because NetWare 386 is such a significant new product, it is discussed in a separate section.

There are five basic versions of NetWare. The Entry Level System (ELS) NetWare products provide solutions for small networks where cost is a concern. ELS Levels I and II provide support for single-server networks that do not need internetwork routing services and the reliability features of system fault tolerance (SFT NetWare).

ELS NetWare Level I supports a maximum of four users in a non-dedicated server mode. It is inexpensive (approximately $695) and easy to install. ELS NetWare Level II supports up to eight concurrent users on either dedicated or nondedicated servers and is priced in the $1995 range.

Advanced NetWare 286 provides support for up to 100 users. It is an internetworking system that supports both bridges to other networks and gateways to minicomputer and mainframe environments. Novell's top-of-the-line 80286 product, SFT NetWare 286, provides all of the features of Advanced NetWare 286 plus system fault tolerance. Advanced NetWare is approximately $3995, and SFT NetWare is approximately $4995.

Note: The above prices are suggested retail. Discounts may be available with a tradeoff in dealer support.

The remainder of this section describes each NetWare operating-system product. Since each product has features and benefits above the previous level's products, only the added features will be discussed for each package. You should therefore read the descriptions in order to learn about added features.

ELS NetWare Level I (Version 2.12 and Above)

ELS NetWare Level I is ideal for small businesses with only a few users who need to have access to multiuser programs and data. It is well suited to small business accounting, doctor's offices, and other environments where up to four workstations are required. ELS Level I is a nondedicated operating system, so the file server can also be used as a workstation.

One of the main reasons for installing a network is to share peripherals such as printers. ELS Level I allows network printer sharing as well as hard-disk sharing. The cost of the entire system can be kept at a minimum when workstations share the file services of the server. Workstations can be personal computers with a minimum configuration. A single floppy-drive system with a network interface card is adequate. Diskless workstations can also be used to reduce overall system price.

Features of ELS NetWare Level I

- ELS Level I is the easiest to install of any NetWare version.

- Multiuser, multitasking architecture enables ELS NetWare to perform many operations simultaneously.

- NetWare architecture enables some programs, such as databases, to actually run faster over the network than on a standalone PC.

- Restricted access can be used through log-in passwords.

- File-system security is offered through file and directory lockout.

- ELS Level I offers a maximum of four simultaneous workstations, one of which is the server itself. More than four users can have accounts.

- Virtually every DOS-based application program is supported.

- A built-in mail system is also available.

Hardware Requirements of ELS NetWare Level I

- The server must be an AT-class system (80286 processor) or an 80386 system.

- The file server must have 640K of base memory and a minimum of 512K extended memory.

- The following disk controllers are supported:

    IBM AT Western Digital internal controller

    IBM PS/2 MFM controller (model 50, 60)

    IBM PS/2 ESDI controller (model 70, 80)

    Note: There may be problems with Compaq 386 systems that use ESDI controllers; however, fixes are available through dealers.

- Only four network interface cards are supported by PC- or AT- class servers or workstations:

    NetWare Ethernet NE-1000

    3Com Etherlink 3C501

    NetWare RX-Net

    Standard Microsystems ARCNET

- IBM microchannel bus servers and workstations support the following cards:

    IBM PC Network II/A

    IBM Baseband/A

    Note: The following PC or AT bus cards complement the microchannel cards just listed:

    IBM PCN II

    IBM Baseband

ELS NetWare Level I can support up to four workstations, 200 to 1000 concurrent open files, 1 to 5 spooled printers, and 1 to 2 internal hard disks.

ELS NetWare Level II

ELS NetWare Level II expands on Novell's entry-level solutions. It is designed to provide the benefits of a multiuser, multitasking operating system to small businesses at an affordable price. Up to eight concurrent users are supported by the system. It expands on the features of ELS Level I by adding many features previously only available in Advanced NetWare. One significant new feature is support for the Apple Macintosh environment. Macintoshes and PCs can share files, messages, and printers. NetWare for Macintosh is server-based and gives Mac users full access to the NetWare server. NetWare is compatible with AppleShare network software and AppleTalk networks.

The ELS NetWare Level II operating system can be configured to work in dedicated or nondedicated mode on the server. The nondedicated mode allows the server to be used concurrently as a workstation, but dedicated mode provides significant increases in performance. The nondedicated mode does keep network cost down for those who cannot dedicate a server for network use.

The operating system is easily upgraded to Advanced NetWare and SFT NetWare.

Features of ELS NetWare Level II

ELS NetWare Level II has most of the features of ELS Level I, in addition to the following:

- Macintosh users can operate in the familiar icon-based file system they are used to. ELS Level II provides a functional connection to the AppleShare network system.

- Resources of the AppleShare network like the Apple LaserWriter PostScript printer can be made available to all users when Macintosh connections are made.

- It supports workstations running OS/2.

- It offers performance and functionality similar to that of small minicomputer systems for thousands of dollars less.

- Indexed file allocation tables (turbo FATs) allow file allocation tables on large files (more than 2MB) to be searched quickly.

- User account management allows log-in times to be established, as well as account expirations. User accounts can be temporarily disabled.

- Resource accounting allows companies or schools to charge for network resource use. Users can be charged for connection time, for bytes read or written to disk, for use of storage space on disks, or for the number of requests made by a workstation. Rates can vary by the hour or by the day.

- Duplicate directory structures prevent file loss and data mismatch.

- Level II offers Hot Fix (see the description later in this chapter).

- UPS monitoring feature allows the system to monitor the state of an uninterruptable power supply and warn the system manager. If the power goes down, the system can be downed in the proper way.

- Level II offers the USERDEF command for easily establishing new users on the system.

- Long-distance communications is offered through asynchronous remote bridge support.

- Most popular network adapters are supported.

Hardware Requirements of ELS NetWare Level II

Like ELS Level I, ELS Level II requires an 80286-based AT-class machine or an 80386-based system. Workstations can be PC, XT, or AT machines, as well as Macintosh systems.

- The network server must be an AT-class machine or any IBM PS/2 model except the model 25 or 30.

- Memory requirements at the server are 2MB or more for non-dedicated use or 1MB for dedicated use.

- Most network interface cards can be used.

- LocalTalk server adapters supported are the Novell NL1000 and NL/2. Others may also be compatible.

- EtherTalk server adapters supported include the Novell NE200 and 3Com 3C505.

- The AppleTalk or EtherTalk adapters must be installed in the server.

Features of Advanced NetWare

Advanced NetWare has many of the features of ELS NetWare Level II, including support for Apple Macintosh workstations and the ability to run the server in dedicated or nondedicated mode. Advanced NetWare also includes the UPS monitoring feature, resource accounting, and security enhancements.

Advanced NetWare will work with most network interface cards. It supports PC, XT and AT workstations, as well as the Macintosh. AT-class machines or 80386 machines are required for the server. In addition, Advanced NetWare has the following enhancements over ELS NetWare Level II:

- Advanced NetWare can be internetworked to other local area network systems through either internal or external bridges. Internal bridging is accomplished by installing up to four distinct network interface cards in the server. External bridging is accomplished by establishing a bridge at one of the LAN's workstations. An external bridge may also be a remote connection to another workstation or another LAN. Two remote bridge configurations are supported: X.25 and asynchronous. The software required to establish the bridges comes with Advanced NetWare.

- Up to 100 users can share the files and applications software stored on the file server's hard disk. Network users also share printers and other expensive peripherals.

Features of SFT NetWare

SFT (system fault tolerant) NetWare provides insurance against system downtime. It dramatically reduces the impact of network equipment failure with its duplicate directory structures, disk mirroring, and disk duplexing capabilities. In addition, the Transaction Tracking System (TTS) keeps information from being corrupted or destroyed if a system failure occurs during a database update.

SFT NetWare includes the features of the previous NetWare systems, including the external remote bridging capabilities of Advanced NetWare. Up to 100 users are supported.

Because of SFT NetWare's fault-tolerant features, it can only be run in the dedicated mode. The server cannot be used as a workstation.

How NetWare 286 Works

Each level of NetWare has features that increases its capabilities over previous levels. The features that will determine which level is right for your installation are related to the number of workstations or users to be supported, whether the server will be dedicated or nondedicated, whether you need to establish internetworks, and the amount of insurance you want for data integrity. This section will describe how NetWare 286 works and describe the operation of some of its features. Remember that some features may not be included in all versions.

Architecture

Recall from Chapter 1 that many network systems rely on the seven-layer Open Systems Interconnection (OSI) model as the basis for both hardware and software design. OSI increases the potential of interconnection among multivendor LANs. NetWare adheres to this model. But NetWare does not build its operating system around DOS, as others do. Instead, NetWare operates directly with the system processor and other hardware to maximize its performance. This provides a significant increase in speed. At the same time, NetWare retains its DOS compatibility by providing a DOS shell at the workstations.

Advanced NetWare 286 takes full advantage of the capabilities of the Intel 80286 microprocessor when you use an IBM PC AT or a compatible as a server. The operating system runs in the protected mode, as opposed to the real mode that DOS uses. This allows a network server to use up to 16MB of RAM and manage up to 2 gigabytes of disk storage, and it can boost the performance of the network because the amount of memory a network server needs is proportional to the amount of disk storage it must manage. Large networks with large amounts of storage need more memory, but more memory also allows additional users.

The Network Shell and IPX

NetWare uses four major software components. These are the workstation operating system (which is usually DOS or some form of it), the DOS shell interface, the file-server software, and the network utilities.

At the workstation, DOS is booted as usual. Any version of DOS 2.0 or above can be used. A command called IPX.COM is then executed. This is the Internetwork Packet Exchange program that allows workstations to communicate over the network. The IPX is customized during NetWare installation for each type of system and the network interface card used. The NetWare *shell* is then loaded as a program in the workstation. This shell provides the communications link between the DOS running on the workstation and NetWare. Applications that run under DOS also use the shell to communicate with the file-server software. The NetWare shell is where NetWare's DOS compatibility is established.

On nondedicated NetWare servers, a special relationship exists between the operating system that is servicing the network and the workstation side of the system. The DOS workstation actually runs as one of the tasks of the multitasking network operating system.

One of the unique features of the NetWare shell is that it can be easily modified and updated for new versions of DOS as they emerge. This gives Novell the ability to quickly provide support in NetWare for the added functions without making major changes to the operating-system code, as is the case with DOS-based network operating systems.

File-System Performance Features

NetWare uses a directory file system with a user interface similar to the hierarchical filing system of DOS 2 and above. At the same time, directories are referred to as drives, which is similar to the way the DOS SUBSTitute command works. For example, the directory \PUBLIC\APPS\LOTUS can be defined as drive H. Users can then log on to drive H to begin using the applications or data in the directory. At the disk-drive level, NetWare uses various schemes to achieve better performance from the server. These are outlined next.

Directory Hashing

Directory hashing reduces file scanning time by mapping a given file to an index and then searching the index instead of the entire directory. Net-Ware creates two tables for each volume's directory and keeps them in memory. The first table is a *hash table,* which mathematically groups directories and file names. Hash-table searches are not sequential and so are much faster, since searches do not have to start at the top and scan through the entire list. If a file is requested using the wildcard search method, where only part of the file name is given, the second table is used. This table groups file names so that wildcard searches are optimized.

Elevator Seeking

Elevator seeking is a technique used to optimize how files are read from the disk. NetWare assembles its current requests for the disk in an order of priority based on the current position of the disk head. In this way, the head does not have to jump around the disk to service requests. It reads the next available sector in the request list as the head moves over the disk surface, even if the sector is not in the requested order.

Disk Caching

Disk caching is a common technique used to increase the performance of a disk system by minimizing disk access. A block of data placed in memory is easier to read than one on disk, so a system with a read request will read additional data beyond the request in anticipation that it might be requested later. The requested data, along with the extra data, are stored in the cache memory.

During a disk write, the system will place data to be written to disk in a cache and hold it there until the cache is full or until there is a lull in disk activity. Data will then be written according to disk location to optimize the write procedures further.

Protecting Data

The failure of a server and its hard disk can be an especially serious problem on a LAN because of the number of users and the amount of data likely to be on the disk. If a network environment has been established using diskless workstations or PCs without adequate disk storage devices, users cannot continue working until the system is back up and running. Problems may also develop slowly. A hard disk may begin to lose the integrity of its magnetic surface over time, resulting in lost data. NetWare has several levels of protection to guard against these problems.

File Allocation Table Duplication

The location and size of files is kept in the *file allocation table* (FAT) of a hard drive. This table is usually located in one place on most hard drives. If data is lost in a disk's file allocation table area, entire files may be lost.

With NetWare, duplicate copies of the FAT are stored in different locations on the physical disk. If one of the FATs is corrupted, the other copy temporarily takes over. The corrupted table is repaired by using the backup. Defective blocks are marked as unusable, and new blocks with the correct FAT data are rebuilt elsewhere on the disk. All of this is managed by NetWare, so managers do not need to worry about making corrections, although they might want to be concerned about a disk that could possibly be failing.

Hot-Fix Redirection Area

Surface defects can become a problem on hard drives as they age. NetWare prevents data from being written to blocks that are unreliable by employing two complementary features, known as *Hot Fix* and *read-after-write verification*. These features enable a hard disk to maintain the same data integrity that it had when first tested and installed.

With Hot Fix, a small portion of the disk's storage area is set aside as the hot fix redirection area. This area will receive data blocks that are redirected from faulty blocks or blocks that the operating system has determined will go bad.

During read-after-write verification, a block of data is written to a hard disk; then the data is immediately read back from the disk and compared to the original data that is still in memory. If the data from disk matches the data in memory, the write operation is considered successful; the data in memory is released, and the next write operation proceeds. If the data does not match, the disk surface may be determined to be defective and the hot-fix feature will take over to correct it.

Disk Mirroring (SFT NetWare Only)

If a hard disk fails completely because of a mechanical failure, all data will be lost. Restoration can be made from tape backups if they are available, but the system downtime may not be acceptable to some users.

SFT NetWare provides a *disk mirroring* option that allows simultaneous duplication of the data on one drive to another. With disk mirroring, two drives on the same channel are paired together. Blocks of data written to the primary drive are duplicated on the secondary drive. The disks operate in tandem as files are updated. If one disk fails, the other disk can continue to operate without data loss or interruption of services. NetWare sends a warning message that a disk failure has taken place so mirroring can be reestablished.

Disk Duplexing (SFT NetWare Only)

Disk duplexing takes disk mirroring one step further by protecting against the failure of not only the disk drives, but also the channel between the disk and the file server. This channel includes the controller, power supply, and interface cable.

One advantage that comes from disk duplexing besides protection is known as *split seeks*. During a read request, the operating system will send a request to whichever drive can respond the fastest, and then read from that drive.

Transaction Tracking System
(SFT NetWare Only)

The Transaction Tracking System of SFT NetWare prevents database corruption if the system fails while data is being written to disk. The resulting file may be incompletely written, and the database can be corrupted and inaccessible. Often, database corruption of this sort may go unnoticed if the file can continue to be used.

SFT NetWare with TTS enabled views an entire sequence of database changes as a single "transaction" that must be completed or backed out of. If the changes are not completed and the system goes down, NetWare will restore the database to the state it was in before the changes were begun. The lost transactions must be reentered, but at least the database is not corrupted.

UPS Monitoring

An uninterruptable power supply (UPS) can provide battery backup to the server if the power goes down, as well as surge suppression and line filtering. When the power goes down, surges can often occur when it comes back up. Surges can also occur in industrial environments where, heavy-duty electrical equipment may cause fluctuations in the power. Low voltage can sometimes be as damaging as a surge of power.

NetWare 286 operating systems are capable of monitoring some UPS systems through cables and special boards. When the power goes down, the UPS begins to supply backup power for a certain amount of time. A signal is sent to the server that the UPS is supplying power, and a message that the server will go down in a predetermined amount of time is broadcast. This downtime is determined by the amount of time the UPS can keep the system running.

If commercial power is not restored, the server closes all files properly, writes all data in memory to disk, and shuts down. Keep in mind that each workstation may need its own UPS to completely protect user files or to allow users to continue working after the power goes down.

Resource Accounting

Government agencies, school and university departments, and work groups within large corporations must often keep strict records of their resource use. A good example is a research firm doing government work that needs to be tracked and recorded. Records may also need to be kept in order to make changes to the system according to individual or departmental usage.

The resource accounting features built into NetWare allow supervisors to monitor network usage and bill user accounts accordingly. The features of the system include the ability to set up a credit limit for each user, monitor the account balances of each user, and generate an audit trail of system usage.

Accounts can be charged for network usage based on the following:

Connection time to the server

Blocks read from disk

Blocks written to disk

Requests received from a workstation

Amount of disk storage used

System supervisors can set up user accounts and account balances for some or all users on the network. The use of print servers and database servers can also be charged.

Security Enhancements

Security in NetWare is based on user profiles. The network supervisor establishes a person as an authorized user on the network and grants various rights for use of the network resources, which can include the file system, network programs, and printers or other peripherals.

NetWare log-in security allows the system supervisor to prevent access to the system by unauthorized users. A password system can be utilized to prevent log-ins, and authorized users can be restricted from logging in to specific workstations, or from logging in outside of a set time range. These security aspects prevent users from using systems when supervisory personnel are not around. Accounts can also be closed or temporarily disabled for security reasons.

A network user's privileges to file-system directories are granted according to eight rights. These are Read, Write, Open, Create, Delete, Parental (control of subdirectories and rights), Search, and Modify (the ability to change file attributes). For example, users can change to directories besides their own, but if they don't have rights for the directory, it will seem empty when listed. The Search privilege must first be given to a user before he or she can begin to see the files, and then other privileges must be given before he or she can read and open the files or write new ones.

Directories can be flagged in various ways as well. The HIDDEN attribute hides directories from users, the SYSTEM attribute indicates directories used by the system, and the PRIVATE attribute establishes a directory that can only be viewed by the owner.

NetWare security features allow a system supervisor to

- Disable a user's account

- Specify an account expiration date

- Require a user to have a password

- Specify the minimum length of a password

- Specify that only the supervisor can change a password

- Force a user to change passwords periodically

- Forbid users from changing to a previously used password

- Restrict the times when a user can log in
- Restrict the physical station from which a user can log in
- Restrict the number of concurrent connections for each user
- Restrict the amount of disk space a user can have
- Keep an audit trail of all log-in and log-out requests
- Keep an audit trail of account lockouts
- Monitor intruder detection and account lockouts
- Check for security holes in the network

NetWare makes half-hour security checks to ensure that each user has the right to remain logged on the system. Warnings are given to log off five minutes ahead of an automatic log-off.

Many more features of NetWare will be covered in the chapters ahead. Many are installed during the installation process, while others are maintained on a continuing basis by a network supervisor or manager. It will be important to assign this role to a user or employee.

Novell NetWare 386

This chapter has so far traced Novell's NetWare 286 operating systems, from the Entry Level System to the system fault tolerant NetWare system. With the announcement of NetWare 386, increased server power and features are now available for up to 250 users at a time. But Novell's announcement of NetWare 386 goes beyond the normal features/benefits dialogue. Novell has made the announcement of NetWare 386 the basis for a whole new company strategy concerning network operating systems and their place in the computer environment.

Novell is basing all of its network computing solutions for the future on the 32-bit architecture of NetWare 386. Their aim is to develop operating systems optimized for the unique requirements of *network computing,* a term Novell has coined to describe the concept of linking many diverse components of a computing environment within a single network. These components may be DOS, OS/2, Macintosh, and UNIX workstations. They may also be systems based on larger operating systems, like DEC's VMS or IBM's VM and MVS.

Network computing goes beyond the older concept of "work group computing," in which DOS-based PCs were integrated into a network. Network computing provides integration of a much more diverse set of elements on a much broader scale. Network computing involves the integration of local and wide-area networks and the use of products from multiple vendors.

The one goal of network computing is to provide a transparent way of distributing data and computer services to users anywhere in the organization, no matter what type of workstation or system they are using. Novell has already had some success with this through its support of Macintosh workstations. Mac users can work on a NetWare network, using the familiar icon-based filing system they are used to rather than DOS commands.

Novell's attitude towards network resources has also changed. In the older work-group systems, resources and services were handled at the server. With network computing, the network itself becomes a platform for network services, and the services become available to anyone on the network. As network operating systems begin to support this type of computing, they will need systems that provide better performance. The 80386 (and 80486) environments with their 32-bit architecture will be essential.

NetWare Open Systems

Novell's new network computing strategy is guided by an architecture known as *NetWare open systems.* It is concerned with

- Providing NetWare services on expandable platforms

- Supporting key industry standards for connecting products from multiple vendors

- Providing integrated routing and wide-area network services

- Providing an open architecture to encourage development, and providing the tools for developers

The ultimate benefit of networks based on NetWare open systems is freedom of choice. NetWare open systems combines consistent services on a variety of platforms, across a variety of protocols, and to a variety of workstation operating systems with distributed system management.

Features of NetWare 386

NetWare 386 is not a modified version of NetWare 286—it is a completely new version written specifically for the 80386 and 80486 microprocessors. The NetWare file system has been redesigned to improve performance, capacity, and the operating system's ability to support a variety of client (workstation) operating systems.

NetWare 386 contains many of the same safety features of SFT NetWare, including Hot Fix, the Transaction Tracking System (TTS), disk mirroring, and disk duplexing. In addition, future versions of NetWare 386 will be able to mirror the entire network server. With SFT Level III, a system failure is completely transparent to the users. If a server fails, the operating system will use the mirrored server and users will notice no changes in system operation.

The following additional features have been added:

- Enhanced password encryption has been added so that password protection is enabled as soon as it is typed in.

- Back-end server applications are supported. A database "engine," for example, that runs in the background can process database requests rather than sending them to the workstation for processing. While this may at first seem to move away from the concept of distributed processing, the 80386 is capable of handling this type of task and still handle the network. The concept is especially useful in systems where only one 80386 system can be budgeted.

- NetWare 386 allows additional software components—NetWare loadable modules (NLM)—to be added to the network while the network server is running. In this way, third-party products such as applications, drivers, and utilities can easily be designed and added to the network.

- Installation is easier. A new server-based installation utility installs the basic operating system in minutes. Additional NLMs can be added at any time without downing the server.

- Applications loading can be locked so that only the supervisor has the right to add applications to the server.

- The storage capacity of NetWare 386 is vastly increased. Volumes, once limited to a single disk, can now span multiple disk drives. This means that large databases and applications (like those formerly stored on minicomputers and mainframes) can now be stored on the file server.

- The file system prevents wasted space by allocating to files only the amount of disk space they need. Deleted files are easier to salvage, and an optional feature allows the file system to retain deleted files until they are deliberately purged by the system manager.

- Printing has been expanded from the server to workstations as well. Multiple print servers, each supporting up to 16 printers, can be attached to the system. Print queues can also service jobs on a first-in-first-out basis, or give priority to those using a particular form.

NetWare 386 is designed to be a network operating system for the future. Its open and modular design allows network computing to take place. Future versions will include protocol independence, which allows different protocols such as IPX/SPX, AppleTalk, TCP/IP, SNA, NetBEUI, and OSI to be loaded and unloaded on the network server as needed. A third level of SFT, Level III, will extend the reliability of the operating system by allowing the entire network server to be mirrored to another server.

NetWare 386 will ship in two versions. Version 3.0 will provide the basic operating system, which will be the platform for all subsequent improvements to the product. Version 3.1 will then build on this platform by encouraging third-party applications development through an open interface. Novell is making a full set of development tools available to developers to encourage these applications.

FOUR

NetWare Menus, Commands, and Utilities

This chapter will give you a brief overview of the facilities available in Novell NetWare. The commands and utilities are listed according to the tasks they perform, so you can use this chapter for later reference once your NetWare system has been installed. If you don't have a NetWare system up and running at this time, the commands listed here will give you an idea of the tools available to NetWare managers and users.

Installation Commands

The following commands are used to install the NetWare operating system on the file server, to create workstation disks and boot files, and to create remote workstations.

SHGEN—SHell GENeration

The SHGEN program is used during initial installation and at any other time to create workstation startup files for the network.

NETGEN/ELSGEN—NETware or
ELS NetWare GENeration program

The NETGEN and ELSGEN programs are used to configure, install, and maintain a NetWare network.

DOSGEN—DOS remote
image file GENeration

When diskless workstations are used on a network, the DOSGEN command is used to create boot files for them in the LOGIN directory.

BRGEN—BRidge GENeration

The BRGEN program is used to configure an external local bridge or a remote bridge.

ARCONFIG—Asynchronous
Remote CONFIGuration

The ARCONFIG program is used to configure a remote workstation.

SETTTS—SET Transaction Tracking System

The SETTTS command ensures that SFT NetWare's Transaction Tracking System works with applications programs in tracking a transaction.

Menu Utilities

The NetWare menu utilities are designed to make both supervisor and user interaction with the operating system easier. Many of the functions on the menus described in this section have separate command-line counterparts, as described later in this chapter. The menus can be used to make alterations to a user session, alter directory and file attributes, and to monitor the system.

SYSCON

SYSCON is one of the most important and useful of the NetWare menu utilities. It can be used by both supervisors and users. The SYSCON utility topics are shown here:

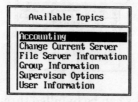

The following tasks are available:

- View current accounting information
- Work with other file servers
- View file-server information

- Display and alter groups

- Use special options for supervisors

- View user information

Only supervisors with the correct password can use the supervisor options. Supervisors can manage the accounting system, create and modify users, manage security features, manage access rights, alter the log-in script, and perform other tasks.

Users can use the SYSCON utility to view a list of other users on the system and to check current account balances (if accounting is installed), account restrictions, security equivalence, station restrictions, and other tasks.

SESSION

The NetWare SESSION menu utility is designed to make alterations to the current user's session. Changes are not saved for future sessions, nor do they affect the operating characteristics of other users. SESSION is designed to make the task of working with NetWare easier for both new and experienced users. The SESSION main menu is shown here:

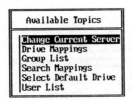

The following tasks can be handled through SESSION:

- View and change to additional file servers

- View, add, delete, and modify network drive mappings

- View, add, delete, and modify search-drive mappings

- Send messages to other users

- Change the current default drive

- Display user information such as log-in time, network address, node number, and a user's full name

FILER

The NetWare FILER utility is an important tool for managing both files and directories. FILER is designed for both network supervisors and network users. The FILER menu is shown here:

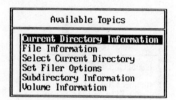

Network users can perform the following tasks with FILER:

- View such directory information as creation date and time, the directory owner, and the directory trustees

- View user rights in the directory

- List, delete, rename, and copy files. File attributes may also be altered, assuming the user has the right to do so

- View the current directory and change to other directories

- Set file and directory safety options so that files can't accidentally be erased or overwritten

- Manage subdirectories, which includes creating, renaming, and removing them if the proper rights exist

FCONSOLE

The FCONSOLE command is an extensive utility that can be used by managers to monitor the performance of the network and make appropriate changes to its operating characteristics. Novell describes the FCONSOLE command as a tool for "fine-tuning" the network. Although any user can use the FCONSOLE command, only the supervisor or other authorized users can access most of its "tuning" features. All other users will be unable to execute commands they do not have rights for.

Some of the features in FCONSOLE are designed for experienced users only, so anyone with access to the command should be familiar with NetWare networks or understand the functions they might be viewing or altering. FCONSOLE is also designed for programmers who might be writing special programs for the network. Information is provided that can help them write, test, and debug network programs. The FCONSOLE menu is shown here:

```
        Available Options
┌────────────────────────────┐
│ Broadcast Console Message  │
│ Change Current File Server │
│ Connection Information     │
│ Down File Server           │
│ File/Lock Activity         │
│ LAN Driver Information      │
│ Purge All Salvageable Files│
│ Statistics                 │
│ Status                     │
│ Version Information         │
└────────────────────────────┘
```

The following tasks can be performed with FCONSOLE:

- Broadcast messages to other users

- Change file servers

- View information about the current connection, such as who is on the system, record-locking information, names of files currently in use, and other information

- Down the file server, assuming the user is the supervisor

- View the current number of transactions being tracked by the Transaction Tracking System (TTS) and other TTS information

- View the current LAN driver information, such as the node address and hardware options related to its interrupt line, I/O address, and so on

- Purge salvageable files, which are files that have been marked deleted but not removed from the disk completely (can be recovered)

- View statistics on file-server performance; these statistics are quite extensive and can be used to evaluate and optimize the performance of the system

PRINTDEF—PRINTer DEFinition

The PRINTDEF menu utility is used to define the characteristics of various printers, plotters, and similar types of output equipment. Although Novell now supplies definition files for many popular devices, others may need to be created. This command provides the facilities for doing so. To create a new *print device,* the following must be defined:

- Define the device functions. Print functions are the Escape codes normally used to set such features on the printer as condensed printing or boldface.

- Define the device *modes.* Modes are sets of functions that define how a particular print job is initially set up, printed, and ended. Each device mode is given a descriptive name that can be selected in other printer menu utilities or commands.

PRINTCON—PRINT job CONfiguration

The PRINTCON menu utility is used to set up *print jobs.* A print job is a set of instructions that defines such things as the number of copies printed, the print queue to use, the device description defined in PRINTDEF to use, and the device mode (also defined in PRINTDEF) to use. This command is important if several printers are attached to the system and users need to send print jobs to one of the printers on a regular basis. Once a print job is defined, it can be saved for later use so the user doesn't need to redefine the job each time.

PCONSOLE—Print CONSOLE

The PCONSOLE command is a useful utility for managing the printer and print queues on a server. The supervisor has full control over printers and print queues, but may assign other users as queue operators. PCONSOLE is mainly used on busy networks where a continuous stream of print jobs are being sent to several different printers. The supervisor or queue operator can alter the priority of print jobs in queues with PCONSOLE, as well as change the destination printer or cancel print jobs altogether.

PCONSOLE is also used to create new print queues. New queues can be assigned to specific ports with specific print times. Users can then be assigned these queues to prevent them from using other printers on the server. A print queue can also be given a specific print time, such as after hours.

VOLINFO—VOLume INFOrmation

The VOLINFO utility displays information about volumes on the current file server. Up to eight volumes are displayed at once per page, but other pages can be viewed if available. The screen displays the total memory and the available memory for each volume. Total directories and available directories are also displayed.

MENU

The MENU utility allows you to create customized menus for users or system management. The menus are created with a text editor and executed with the MENU utility. An example is MENU MAIN, described next. Menus can be used to help untrained users.

MENU MAIN

A menu called MAIN can be executed by using the MENU command just described. This menu, shown here, is an example of a menu that you can create with the MENU command, but is also a useful menu utility you may want to use on a regular basis. Simply type **MENU MAIN** to display it.

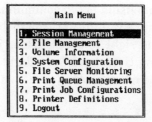

```
┌─────────────────────────────┐
│          Main Menu          │
├─────────────────────────────┤
│ 1. Session Management        │
│ 2. File Management           │
│ 3. Volume Information        │
│ 4. System Configuration      │
│ 5. File Server Monitoring    │
│ 6. Print Queue Management     │
│ 7. Print Job Configurations  │
│ 8. Printer Definitions        │
│ 9. Logout                    │
└─────────────────────────────┘
```

COLORPAL

COLORPAL is a menu utility that can be used to customize the color scheme for the rest of the menu utilities used by the system or the ones you create with a menu.

Help Commands

HELP

The HELP command is used to view on-line information for using the NetWare utilities. Information can be searched and retrieved. A related command is NFOLIO.

NFOLIO

NFOLIO is a database organizer that allows read-only capabilities. The NetWare HELP facilities now come in FOLIO-compatible files. The program allows easy search and display of information.

Security Commands

The security commands listed here represent the first level of security on a NetWare system. These commands are designed to keep unauthorized people out of the system using log-in commands and passwords. Security in the NetWare file system is fulfilled through directory and file privileges. Users are assigned the right to access a particular directory or file, as discussed in "Managing Users and User Rights" later. These commands may be entered at the system prompt or from a menu.

LOGIN

The LOGIN command is used to log in to a file server. The command will ask for a password.

LOGOUT

The LOGOUT command terminates a user's access to the file server and removes temporary drive mappings.

SETPASS

Users can use the SETPASS command to change their passwords on a file server.

SETKPASS—SET Keyboard PASSword (Console)

Set or change a password that "locks" the console keyboard. The LOCK VAP program must be installed on the file server before you can use this command.

SECURITY

The SECURITY command can be used to determine how secure a network is. The command checks for security weaknesses and displays a list of possible problems.

LOCK (Console)

LOCK is a value-added process that allows the supervisor or other users with proper rights to lock the console keyboard. LOCK is a command designed to improve security at the file server.

Managing Users and User Rights

The menu utilities covered at the beginning of this chapter can be used to create new users and assign them rights in directories. The commands shown here make the task of creating several users at once easier, or allow rights to be assign directly at the command line.

MAKEUSER (Advanced NetWare and SFT NetWare)

MAKEUSER is a command used to create and delete users. The command is especially useful when new users are common, as in an educational environment. The command displays a menu with options for creating, editing, and processing a special user file.

USERDEF (ELS NetWare Level II)

Used to create multiple users, the USERDEF command performs many of the same functions as MAKEUSER.

GRANT

The GRANT command is used to grant specific trustee rights to users or groups of users in a specific directory. A trustee of a directory is any user who has the access rights (granted by the supervisor) to use files in a directory. This command performs the same actions as the FILER and SYSCON commands. The rights that can be granted are: Read, Write, Open, Create, Delete, Parental, Search, and Modify. Right All can be used to grant all rights. No Rights revokes all rights. A related command is REVOKE.

REVOKE

The REVOKE command removes trustee rights for either a user or a group in a directory. The rights options are Read, Write, Open, Create, Delete, Parental, Search, Modify, and All, which revokes all rights.

REMOVE

The REMOVE command can delete a user or group from the trustee list of a directory.

RIGHTS

This command can be typed to view the current user's rights in the current directory or one that is specified.

WHOAMI

The WHOAMI command is used to view information about the file servers to which a user is attached. The user's name is displayed as well as the user's log-in time and date, groups belonged to, security equivalents, effective rights, and logical workstation addresses.

TLIST—Trustee LIST

This command displays the trustee list for a given directory.

USERLIST

The USERLIST command is used to display a list of current users on a particular file server. The command will also display the user's connection number, log-in time, network address, and node address.

Directory Commands

Although FILER is a comprehensive menu utility designed to make directory and file handling easier, as discussed earlier, commands typed directly at the keyboard are sometimes much easier and faster to use. These commands are covered here.

NDIR—Network DIRectory

Use NDIR to view information about files and subdirectories in a directory. The NDIR command is also used to list and work with files, as discussed later.

RENDIR—REName DIRectory

Use RENDIR to rename directories.

LISTDIR—LIST DIRectories

The LISTDIR command is used to list the subdirectories of a directory. The maximum rights mask, creation date, and subsequent directories may also be viewed.

FLAGDIR—FLAG DIRectories

The FLAGDIR command is used to view or change the attributes of subdirectories in a given directory. The attribute options are Normal, Hidden, System, and Private, which will be discussed later.

MAP

The MAP command is used to view current drive mappings, create new ones, or add them. MAP is also used to create search-drive mappings, which are similar to the DOS PATH command.

TLIST—Trustee LIST

TLIST displays the trustee list for a given directory.

SMODE—Search MODE

Use SMODE to assign a search mode to an executable file or to view the search mode already assigned to such a file. The SMODE command lets you establish how executable files search through the search drive structure (PATH).

File Commands

The FILER menu utility can be used to handle files on a NetWare system, or you can use the command-line utilities listed here. Many of the commands covered here take the place of some DOS command-line utilities and offer additional features.

NDIR—Network DIRectory

Use NDIR to view information about files and subdirectories in a directory. This command is also listed under the "Directory Commands" listing because it is just as important when working with directories.

NCOPY—Network COPY

NCOPY copies one or more files from one network directory to another, or to local floppy drives or hard drives.

FLAG

The FLAG command is used to view or change the file attributes in a directory. These attributes are Shareable, NonShareable, ReadOnly, ReadWrite, Normal, Transactional, Indexed, and Subdirectory. File attributes are used to share and protect files on multiuser LAN systems.

HIDEFILE

This command is used to hide a specified file or files so they do not appear in directory listings. A related command is SHOWFILE.

SHOWFILE

SHOWFILE is used to make files hidden by the HIDEFILE command visible again.

HOLDON

The HOLDON command is used to hold a file for personal use so others cannot access it until you release the file with HOLDOFF or reboot the workstation. This command prevents lost data and corrupted files by preventing file overwrites.

HOLDOFF

The HOLDOFF command reverses the effect of HOLDON. *See* HOLDON.

SALVAGE

Erased files may be recovered with SALVAGE unless PURGE has recently been used, which removes all salvageable files. Files must be salvaged immediately. If you log out, the files cannot be salvaged later. New files will write over erased files before they can be recovered.

PURGE

PURGE is used to permanently remove files marked for deletion. Before you issue this command, files can still be restored with the SALVAGE command.

Messaging and Broadcasting

Managers may need to send messages to users regarding the state of the network, and users may want to send messages among themselves. Messages can be addressed to a single user, a group of users, or all users. Note that third party software packages may be more appropriate when more complete mail and scheduling tasks are required. The following messaging commands are available to most users.

BROADCAST (Console)

The BROADCAST command can be used to send messages to all users who are logged in to a file server. It can be used to issue a message that the file server will be going down, or that some other activity will take place on the file server. The SEND command is used to send messages to specific workstations, whereas BROADCAST is used to send messages to all workstations. A related command is USERLIST, which is used to view current user names.

SEND

Whereas the BROADCAST command is used to send messages to all workstations, the SEND command can be used to send short messages from one user to another. The USERLIST command can be used to determine user names. SEND can also be used on the console.

USERLIST

The USERLIST utility displays the users who are signed onto the current file server or to other file servers on the network. The user name, connection number, log-in time, network, and node address are displayed. Note that this command is also covered under the "Security" heading earlier.

CLEAR MESSAGE (Console)

This command removes messages from the bottom of the file-server console screen.

CASTOFF

The CASTOFF command is used to block incoming messages from other users. Processes and programs that must run continuously and unattended can be interrupted if a message is received; the CASTOFF command prevents this.

CASTON

The CASTON command restores message receiving blocked by the CASTOFF command.

Printer Commands

Many of the printing tasks in NetWare can be handled by the PCONSOLE menu utility. In addition, the PRINTDEF and PRINTCON menu utilities are tools for defining new printers and print jobs. The following commands can be used at the command line to make printer handling even easier. Some of the following commands work in conjunction with the settings made in the print menu utilities.

CAPTURE

The CAPTURE command is used to "capture" printing normally directed to a local printer and send it to a printer attached to the server. ENDCAP ends CAPTURE.

ENDCAP—END CAPture

The ENDCAP command is used to restore printing to the local workstation printer after the CAPTURE command has been used to print on the server's printer. ENDCAP stops CAPTURE.

NPRINT—Network PRINTer

NPRINT is used to send files to a network printer, where they are entered in a print queue and then printed. Specific printers, jobs, queues, and other information can be included with the command.

PRINTER (Console)

The PRINTER command is used to control print jobs at the file server using the console.

QUEUE (Console)

The QUEUE command is used to control print queues and manipulate print jobs from the file-server console. Queues can be created, listed, prioritized, and deleted.

PSTAT—Printer STATus

The PSTAT command is used to view information about printers connected to the file server, such as their ready condition, active or stopped status, and form information.

Backup Commands

In most cases, backups should be made to tape drives or to another hard disk on a network system. However, there will be times when files need to be copied to a local workstation or archived to a special directory. The following commands can be used to back up and restore files for a NetWare network using directories and local drives. The commands are different than normal copy commands because they can be used to back up specific files in specific directories, such as those that have changed since the last backup.

LARCHIVE—Local drive ARCHIVE

The LARCHIVE command is used to archive DOS files to local disk drives such as floppy disks or hard drives. A related command is LRESTORE. A log of the archive is created with the name ARCHIVE.LOG.

LRESTORE—Local drive RESTORE

This command restores files from local drives such as floppy disks and hard drives to network drives. The restored files must be files archived with LARCHIVE.

MACBACK

MACBACK allows backup of Macintosh files.

NARCHIVE—Network ARCHIVE

NARCHIVE archives DOS files to network directories and creates a log report called ARCHIVE.LOG. A related command is NRESTORE.

NRESTORE—Network RESTORE

The NRESTORE command is used to restore archived files to a network drive. A related command is NARCHIVE.

Accounting

The SYSCON utility is used in most cases to handle the NetWare accounting system. The following commands provide additional features and convenience.

ATOTAL—Accounting services TOTAL

This command totals the accounting services usage on the network. It can only be run by the supervisor or someone with equivalent rights because it must be run in the SYS:SYSTEM directory, which has restricted access rights. The accounting feature must be installed.

PAUDIT—Print AUDIT trail

The PAUDIT command is used to view the system accounting records. PAUDIT must be run from the SYS:SYSTEM directory, which means that only supervisors or their equivalents can run the command. The accounting feature must be installed on the system.

Server Commands

ATTACH

The ATTACH command is used to attach to another file server while remaining logged in to the current file server. You can connect up to eight servers.

SLIST—Server LIST

SLIST is used to view the file-server list on an internetwork. Information about the servers is also displayed. The network address and node address of each server is displayed.

System Information

The following commands can be typed on the command line to display information about NetWare, the current file server, or other file servers on the network. Similar commands are available when using the SYSCON and FCONSOLE utilities.

TIME (Console)

Use TIME to view the time and date at the file-server console.

SYSTIME—SYStem TIME

This command displays the time and date for any file server on the network. It will also synchronize the date and time set on the workstation with that set on the file server.

NAME (Console)

NAME displays the name of the file server.

VERSION

The VERSION command is used to display the current version of a NetWare utility on the file server. Type **VERSION** followed by the name of the utility.

NVER—Network VERsion

NVER displays the version of software running on a file server and workstation. The current versions of IPX, SPX, NETBIOS, the LAN driver, the shell, the workstation operating system, and the file-server operating system are displayed for each file server on the system.

VOLINFO

The VOLINFO command displays information about volumes on the current file server as covered under "Menu Utilities."

CONFIG—CONFIGuration
(Console)

CONFIG is a console command that displays the hardware configuration for each network attached to the file server. The display will show the network address, hardware type, and hardware settings. The information can be used when installing bridges or other servers to avoid conflicts.

VAP—Value-Added Process
(Console)

Use the VAP command to display a list of value-added processes currently loaded into the NetWare operating system. VAP will also list commands used by the value-added processes.

Performance Monitoring

System managers and/or supervisors will be interested in monitoring the system to see who is logged on, to view the file server's performance, and to view other features that can help them manage the system. The following commands can be typed at the file-server console's colon prompt.

Additional commands for monitoring the performance of the server are covered in the next section.

CONSOLE (Nondedicated Servers Only)

The CONSOLE command is executed at the DOS prompt on servers running in nondedicated mode. It temporarily disables the DOS workstation and places the machine in NetWare console mode so console commands can be entered. To return to DOS, simply type **DOS** at the console colon prompt.

DOS (Nondedicated Servers Only)

The DOS command is used to switch a NetWare nondedicated file server from console mode back to workstation mode after the CONSOLE command has been used. The file server can then be used as a workstation.

MONITOR (Console)

The MONITOR command is used at the file-server console to display the activities of all workstations logged in to the file server. This display can be checked before downing the server to ensure that everyone is logged off. Programmers can use the display as a diagnostics tool. MONITOR can also be used to determine who is using a file and locking its access.

OFF (Console)

OFF is used to clear information from the file-server console display. Since some processing that could be used by the network is required to maintain the display, type **OFF** to clear the display, especially when MONITOR is running.

Disk Utilities

The following commands can be used to monitor the performance of a file server and its volumes. The statistics of a volume, such as its files in use and files remaining, can also be checked. Similar commands are also available in the SYSCON and FCONSOLE menu utilities.

CHKVOL—CHecK VOLume

CHKVOL is used to display information about a volume. This information includes the file-server name where the volume is located, the volume name, the total storage capacity of the volume, the number of bytes used, the number of files in existence, the number of remaining bytes, and the number of available directories.

DISK (Console)

The DISK command is used to monitor the status of network disk drives. It can be used to see which disks are functioning normally and which are not.

VREPAIR—Volume REPAIR

The VRPAIR utility will correct minor hard-disk problems on the file server without destroying the data on the drive. Problems are indicated by various error messages that appear on the screen. VREPAIR corrects directory and file allocation table (FAT) problems arising from defective media or unexpected power loss. Bad blocks are also located and added to the bad block table. Use COMPSURF as discussed next for major problems.

COMPSURF—COMPrehensive SURFace analysis

The COMPSURF utility checks and formats hard drives. It is normally used before installing a network to check new drives and mark bad blocks, but it can be used to check the condition or reformat malfunctioning drives. The command destroys all data on the drive, so be careful when using it.

MOUNT (Console)

Use MOUNT to add a removable volume to a file server. Removable volumes are disk-drive cartridges that can be removed from the server for security reasons. A related command is DISMOUNT.

DISMOUNT (Console)

This is used in conjunction with the MOUNT command to work with removable volumes, which are hard disk cartridges that can be removed and reinserted. Cartridges of this type can be removed to secure data from being accessed by other users.

UNMIRROR (SFT NetWare Console)

The UNMIRROR command is used to bring up a drive and turn its disk mirroring feature off. When a drive is unmirrored, the other drive in the pair continues to function.

REMIRROR (SFT NetWare Console)

The REMIRROR command is used to bring up a drive that has been shut down with UNMIRROR or has failed. When the command is executed, data on the operating drive will be copied to the newly restored drive.

Maintenance Commands

The following commands are used to maintain a NetWare file server or network. Managers or supervisors will want to ensure that users are aware when a file server will be brought down. Part of the commands listed in this section are used to notify users and prevent new users from logging on. The BROADCAST command should be used to inform users of possible system shutdown.

SET TIME (Console)

SET TIME is a console command used at the file server to set the time and date.

DISABLE LOGIN (Console)

This command can be used at the console to prevent users from logging in. If the system needs to be brought down, this command can be used to prevent new log-ins.

ENABLE LOGIN (Console)

This command can be used after DISABLE LOGIN has been executed to restore a user's right to log in to the server. If the file server was turned off after downing, it is not necessary to issue this command.

CLEAR STATION (Console)

This command clears all files open to a workstation and erases all internal tables the file server uses to keep track of that workstation. It is used when a workstation crashes and its files need to be released.

DOWN (Console)

The DOWN command provides a "graceful" shutdown for the file server. The BROADCAST command should be used to warn users, and the DISABLE LOGIN command should be used to prevent new users from logging on before the server is downed. The MONITOR command can also be used to see if users are on before the server is downed.

BINDFIX—BINDery FIX

The BINDFIX command is used to correct problems with the NetWare bindery.

BINDREST—BINDery RESTore

The BINDREST command is used to restore a previous version of the bindery files after the BINDFIX command has been run.

COMCHECK—COMmunication CHECK

The COMCHECK command diagnoses the communications links between workstations and servers. It is first used after the network cabling and interface cards are installed, but can be used at any time thereafter.

LCONSOLE

Use LCONSOLE to change the parameters of a remote connection while the bridge is running. The status of the connection can be viewed and terminated.

Miscellaneous Commands

NSNIPES or NCSNIPES

NSNIPES is a network game that can be played alone or with other network users. NSNIPES is used with monochrome monitors, and NCSNIPES is used with color monitors.

Connectivity

Local Bridging
Remote Bridges
SNA Gateways
Novell 5250 Gateway and Workstation Products
NetWare LU6.2 Software for Novell 3270 SNA Gateways

The term *connectivity* encompasses the whole range of communications activities, including connections to other LANs, minicomputers, mainframes, and remote workstations. This chapter will present local area network connectivity options available from Novell and assist you in the selection of those products.

Local Area Networks communicate over bridges, remote connections, and gateways. A *bridge* is a connection to another LAN. A *remote connection* is a communications link from a personal computer to a LAN, usually through the telephone lines. *Gateways* are communication links to larger systems with different operating systems.

Novell NetWare allows sophisticated bridging capabilities in servers or in external workstations. NetWare bridges can connect LANs with the same or different networking interface cards, protocols, and topologies. For example, an existing IBM Broadband network can be bridged with a new IBM Token Ring network by placing cards for both in the server. A bridge established in the server is known as an *internal bridge*. A bridge established in a workstation is known as an *external bridge*.

Bridges can also be *local* or *remote*. Local bridges connect LANs, usually within the same building, using either internal or external bridging. Remote bridges connect distant LANs, usually with telephone connections. Novell ELS NetWare Level II provides software to connect a remote bridge in the server or at a workstation. It does not support bridging to other networks.

The following sections will outline the various connectivity methods available with NetWare. Keep in mind that these methods are not available to users of Novell ELS NetWare Level I.

Local Bridging

Local bridges are the easiest to install, especially if they are installed internally in the LAN server. The operation of the bridge is completely transparent to the user. A new LAN is formed from the bridge, and users of both LANs are given transparent access to the resources of the server on both LANs.

One of the most important reasons for establishing a bridge is to extend the overall distance of the network workstations. LAN topologies that have limited distance can be doubled in size by installing a second network interface card of the same type in the server. The network then

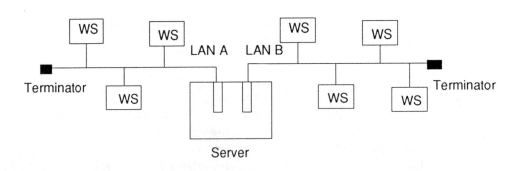

Figure 5-1. A LAN's total distance is extended by installing two network interface cards in a server

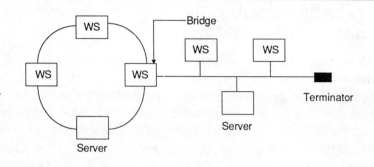

Figure 5-2.   An external bridge connecting two LANs within a workstation

extends off to the left and to the right, up to the maximum distance of the LAN, as shown in Figure 5-1. A LAN using this configuration will also have performance benefits.

A file server running under Advanced NetWare or SFT NetWare can support up to four similar or different network interface cards as an internal bridge. Each of these cards then forms one LAN that is referred to as LAN A, B, C, or D. Internal bridging can be cost-effective and maintenance-free once installed.

An external bridge is a connection between two similar or different LAN topologies. The bridge is installed in a workstation instead of the server itself. As shown in Figure 5-2, an external bridge is used to connect two separate file servers at a workstation located on the LAN. The workstation may be located at the most distant and common point between the two LANs to maximize the cable lengths.

External bridges can also be used to connect two dissimilar LANs and provide a suitable alternative if the bridge cannot be located in the server. It should be noted that if a high volume of traffic will cross the bridge, the workstation should be dedicated to provide its entire resources for handling the communications between LANs. The software required for external bridging is included with Advanced NetWare and SFT NetWare and is covered in Appendix B.

NetWare Bridge-Handling Techniques

Bridges are really an intelligent method for routing packets of data to nodes on the network. Novell uses the Internetwork Packet Exchange program (IPX) as a common protocol to connect each of the networks in the bridge. When a bridge is established, a router located in the server or bridge workstation handles the routing functions. A table of known network addresses is kept, and the packets are routed to the appropriate destination using this table. If multiple routes to a node exist, the NetWare routers are capable of determining which route will be the fastest. Multiple routes are also tracked so that alternate routes can be used if the primary route goes down.

Filtering is a technique that improves the performance of the internetwork by allowing the NetWare router to ensure that each network in the bridge is sent only the packets intended for it. The performance of the entire bridge network would be diminished if packets addressed for only one subnetwork were sent over the entire network. Filtering guarantees that each network only receives packets addressed to it. For example, a large network may be made up of several departmental networks tied together with bridges. Network traffic generally would stay within each department, with only a few messages going out over the internetwork from managers or other people coordinating interdepartmental activities. It wouldn't make sense for the network to send information meant for a single department outside of that department.

Novell NetWare bridges are generally high-performance bridges because of their filtering and packet-routing techniques, so it is possible to expand the networks with few problems. The departmental example can be used further. Since most network traffic on a bridged LAN stays within each departmental LAN, it is possible to bridge to even more LANs without adversely affecting the performance of the entire LAN. Novell estimates that only 10 percent of network traffic on a bridged LAN actually crosses bridges.

There are other advantages to using bridges besides those just described. Many have to do with topology. For example, the design of a building may require that a bridge be used to physically split the LAN. A bridge can also be used when the performance of a LAN is deteriorating because there are too many stations on one card. A second card can be added and half of the stations can be attached to it, thus providing a performance increase.

Remote Bridges

Technically, a remote bridge is used to make a connection to a network when the distance between the connection goes beyond the normal range of the cable or network topology. Connections are usually made with modems over the telephone lines. In this way, a local area network can become a *wide area network* (WAN).

Keep in mind that the connection at the local LAN can be either an internal remote bridge in the server or an external bridge at a local workstation. In some cases, an external bridge can be set up as a dedicated communications server. It is not wise to put communications devices in the file server, since overall system performance would diminish. The Novell Wide Area Network Interface Module Plus (WNIM+) overcomes this problems, however (you will learn more about it later).

When a LAN is connected to a remote LAN, a bridge must be established at both sides of the transmission. Even though establishing this bridge in dedicated communications servers will provide performance increases, there are additional ways to improve the internetwork performance when using remote connections. Although some users need low-cost communications for low-traffic applications, others need high-performance communications. Beyond this, multipoint connections, in which more than two LANs are connected, may be required.

Point-to-point communications may be established between two LANs by using character-based asynchronous communications techniques or by using faster block-transfer synchronous communications provided by the X.25 protocol. Asynchronous communication is fine for low-traffic situations, but X.25 may be required for more speed.

Communications Methods

There are two communications methods available when establishing a remote bridge: *asynchronous* and *synchronous*. Asynchronous communication is a character-based transmission method, whereas synchronous communication is a block-oriented method. The main difference is that synchronous communication is faster because it eliminates the need to transmit stop and start bits for each character.

Asynchronous communication transmits at speeds up to 2400 baud on voice-grade lines and up to 19.2K bits per second on dedicated telephone lines that are conditioned. Synchronous communications can transmit at up to 64K bits per second on direct connect lines. Novell uses the X.25 protocol standard for synchronous communications. Synchronous communication is best when connecting LANs to LANs in high-traffic situations, but its expense may make it prohibitive.

Novell Communications Hardware Products

Besides the standard asynchronous communications ports that come in most PCs, several Novell hardware products are used for communications. These are listed here.

Wide Area Network Interface Module Plus (WNIM+)

This board is a four-port asynchronous communications board for PC- and AT-type systems. Each board has four individual asynchronous ports that can communicate at speeds of up to 19.2K bits per second. A modem can be attached to each port. The WNIM+ has its own on-board processor to free the server or external bridge for other tasks. Figure 5-3 illustrates a WNIM+ connection.

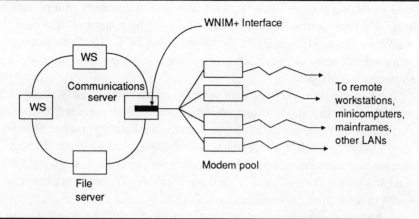

Figure 5-3.   Wide Area Network Interface Module Plus connection

Novell X.25 Adapters for PCs And IBM PS/2 Systems

The Novell X.25 communications interfaces are designed for PC- and AT-class machines, as well as the IBM PS/2 microchannel systems. The boards are used with several Novell communications packages discussed later. X.25 is a synchronous communications protocol. The boards have an on-board processor and 256K of memory to help minimize the use of resources in the attached system. The PC/AT board can provide throughput at up to 64K bits per second, and the PS/2 board can provide throughput at up to 19.2K bits per second. Up to 32 X.25 virtual circuits are supported. An X.25 extended adapter is also available for PC- and AT-class machines. It provides 512K of on-board memory and will support 254 X.25 virtual circuits.

Remote Workstation Software

A remote workstation is a single PC at a remote site that dials into the LAN using an asynchronous communications method. The workstation may be that of an employee working at home, a manager at a remote site, or a field representative who needs to check the company database. ELS NetWare Level II, Advanced NetWare, and SFT NetWare provide the required software to establish a remote workstation link, similar to that shown in Figure 5-4.

Since remote workstations operate much more slowly than normal workstations, the applications and utilities should be located on the workstation itself. Processing takes place at the workstation rather than at the server. Data or other server-based information must pass through the communications lines; however, the user will operate the workstation as if he or she were logged in to a local workstation. Transmission speeds will make this method only occasionally viable.

An asynchronous communications card must be available in the remote workstation as either COM1 or COM2, and a cable must be attached to a modem. Complete instructions for configuring the remote workstation software are given in Appendix B.

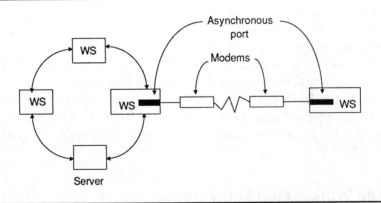

Figure 5-4.   A remote workstation link

Novell NetWare Asynchronous Remote Bridge Software

The NetWare Asynchronous Remote Bridge offers the same functionality as the remote-bridge software that comes with the Advanced NetWare and SFT NetWare software packages. In addition, it provides support for the Novell Wide Area Network Interface Module Plus (WNIM+). It is designed for occasional file transfers and access to shared data on the LAN. In addition, speeds of up to 19.2K bits per second can be realized with the proper equipment. When you use a WNIM+ board, it is possible to run the remote bridge in the server since the board has an on-board processor to free the file server for other tasks. The board also allows an external bridge to be used for other tasks.

The hardware requirements are a COM1 or COM2 port, or WNIM+ adapters. Up to two WNIM+ cards are allowed in external bridges, allowing up to eight remote LAN connections. Only one WNIM+ card is allowed in a server, providing up to four remote LAN connections.

NetWare Asynchronous Communications Server (NACS) Software

A personal computer workstation running the NACS software is a dedicated server used specifically for communications. The server allows up to 16 workstations to simultaneously call into or out of the LAN through the NACS server. There can be more than one NACS server installed on a single LAN. NACS supports the connection of the LAN to minicomputers and mainframes, and supports remote workstations calling in to the LAN.

NACS is Novell's software base for asynchronous communications to or from a NetWare network. It includes the NACS control program that runs in a dedicated communications server and the NetWare Asynchronous Services Interface (NASI) software that runs at a user's workstation. NASI provides the interface between terminal emulation and the asynchronous ports provided by NACS.

NACS requires at least one WNIM+ board for every four serial ports required, and up to four WNIM+ boards can be installed in each server. A dedicated IBM PC or compatible is recommended as the communications server. Since WNIM+ boards have on-board processors, the speed of the PC does not matter. Figure 5-3 shows what a NACS/WNIM+ configuration could look like.

Modems are attached to the WNIM+ boards in banks of what Novell calls *modem pools*. When a user calls out of the LAN, an appropriate non-busy modem is used. A set of commands and protocols for using a particular modem can be established and named. Users can then access these named services when they need to communicate outside the LAN.

Novell NetWare AnyWare

NetWare AnyWare is a remote connection software package that provides improved performance over the remote workstation software supplied with NetWare. NetWare AnyWare gives a remote user access to a workstation on the LAN so that programs and network commands can be run at that station rather than from the remote station. The user at the remote workstation uses the local PC as if sitting at its keyboard. File and database access are performed at LAN speeds, since all processing is handled by the local network workstation. Only keystrokes and screen displays are sent from the local PC to the remote workstation. The two machines function as one. Because this method does not perform any processing at the remote workstation, a dumb terminal can be used.

A NetWare AnyWare connection is often more useful than a standard remote workstation connection. The most important feature is that a dedicated communications server running the NACS program is required. This server can support up to 16 simultaneous connections, assuming four WNIM+ boards are installed. There must also be 16 local workstations to run the remote sessions. Each NetWare AnyWare package is licensed for four users. Figure 5-5 illustrates a typical connection.

The remote workstation starts a terminal program called ATerm, and then connects with the communications server through the modems. The communications server then transfers the call to a local workstation running the NetWare AnyWare program. Each remote workstation calling in and using this method must have its own local workstation to do the processing, which can become expensive. However, since the remote work-

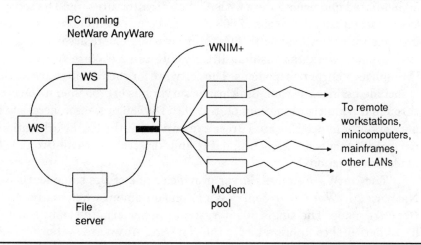

PC running
NetWare AnyWare

WNIM+

WS

WS

To remote
workstations,
minicomputers,
mainframes,
other LANs

Modem
pool

File
server

Figure 5-5.   NetWare AnyWare connection to multiple remote workstations

station can be a dumb terminal, costs can come down; many organizations already have unused dumb terminals from previously installed systems. Separate modems are required for each incoming line.

Novell NetWare ASCOM IV
Terminal Emulation Software

ASCOM IV terminal emulation software allows any workstation to access an asynchronous device over the network, rather than establishing an individual connection. Workstations can use this software to connect to host minicomputers, mainframes, and other asynchronous devices to transfer files and perform other activities. The software requires that the NACS software and a dedicated communications server be part of the network. Each ASCOM IV package is licensed for four users only.

NetWare Access Server Software

The NetWare Access Server provides a high-performance dedicated communications server for up to 15 remote users. The software runs on

80386-based microcomputers with AT-bus architecture only. The software takes special advantage of the 80386 architecture by dividing its processing time into 15 virtual 640K PCs for multiuser remote access.

Remote workstations dial directly into the NetWare Access Server through asynchronous modems. The software for the remote workstations is included. Since the communications server has established its own PCs through the multitasking capabilities of the 80386 processor, access to the network is enhanced because processing occurs at the local workstation at normal LAN speeds. Screen updates and keystrokes travel through the modem connection.

The NetWare Access Server provides some of the same features as NetWare AnyWare, with some savings on equipment when many connections are made. The single 80386 system can perform the same functions as 15 personal computers under the NetWare AnyWare system. In addition, local network stations are not tied up performing tasks for the remote users.

The software provides a *dial-back* security feature, which will call back a user who has just signed on to verify phone numbers and locations. Up to four WNIM+ boards may be installed in the communications server to access the 15 virtual sessions.

NetWare X.25 Point-to-Point Bridge Software

Point-to-point refers to communications between one location and another location. NetWare X.25 Point-to-Point Bridge software uses the X.25 synchronous protocols to establish connections between two LANs. The resulting LANs form a single, transparent internetwork. Dial-up lines or leased lines may be used to make connections, which are attached to the Novell X.25 adapter.

X.25 remote bridge communications is intended for applications in which point-to-point connections will bear a heavy traffic load. If large amounts of data are transferred between remote networks, the higher line speeds provided by this type of communications are necessary. Since X.25 protocols can be used on standard phone lines at high speeds, the costs associated with the use of public data networks (PDNs) can be avoided.

This adapter is available in standard PC/AT bus or IBM PS/2 micro channel bus systems. Transmission speeds can reach as high as 64K bits per second on the proper lines. A dedicated or nondedicated bridge workstation can be used, and up to two X.25 boards may be installed in the system. The software also supports IBM 3270 connectivity. If a NetWare SNA Gateway is installed, NetWare users can run 3270 LAN Workstation software on remote LANs to access their SNA host across the X.25 bridge. An upgrade package is available for those who want to switch to X.25 Multi-Point Bridge software, as covered next.

NetWare X.25 Multi-Point Software

Multipoint bridging allows multiple networks to tie together into a larger wide area network. Novell's X.25 Multi-Point software connects multiple NetWare LANs through an X.25 packet-switching network or X.25 public data network (PDN). Up to 11 remote LANs can be connected from each PC bridge at line speeds of up to 64K bits per second. Each LAN in the internetwork requires its own X.25 Multi-Point software package and X.25 adapter board.

The bridge operates as a NetWare external dedicated or nondedicated bridge in a PC- or AT-class machine, as well as PS/2 systems. Novell X.25 adapters are required. The system, once established, allows any number of workstations to access other remote LANs established in the connection. The software also supports X.75 connections, a protocol used by public data networks, and supports IBM 3270 connectivity in the same way as the X.25 Point-to-Point software just discussed.

SNA Gateways

Gateways are connections into minicomputer or mainframe systems that allow workstations on the LAN to emulate host terminals, use host programs and data, and download data. A gateway is essentially a connection between two dissimilar systems with different protocols. There are three elements to the gateway. The first two are in the gateway server, which has the interface board to the host system and runs the gateway software. The third element is the LAN workstation software, which is located in each of the PCs on the LAN that requires mainframe host access.

NetWare SNA Gateway software emulates a number of 3270 terminal models, including the 3278, 3279, 3179, 3178, and 3287 host-addressable printers. Any number of NetWare SNA gateway servers can reside on the LAN. The servers need not be dedicated and can be IBM PCs or compatibles. Workstations access the host by seeking a session from one of the gateway servers.

Novell gateway products are designed to operate using the peer-to-peer capabilities of a network to make the connections more reliable. Workstations and applications can communicate directly with other workstations, servers, or devices on the network. In this way, the LAN workstation software can communicate directly with the gateway server on the network to access and use the host system.

By moving the gateway server activities out of the server, Novell gateway products allow increased speed and less risk. Concentrating services in a file server or other single locations would introduce risks, since the failure of one service could jeopardize the rest. By distributing the services, overall performance of the LAN is not diminished. Most Novell gateways have on-board processors and memory so that programs can run on the board, for the most part, allowing the PC to be run for workstation functions. In addition, normal PCs (not AT or 386 computers) can be effectively used since processing speed is not important.

SNA Gateway Software Products

Novell's SNA Gateway software products can be used with ELS NetWare Level II, Advanced NetWare, and SFT NetWare. A separate version is available for ELS NetWare Level II. The gateway software products are designed to work in a workstation designated as a gateway server. This server must have one of the boards described in the "SNA Hardware Products" section later in this chapter. Workstations must use the 3270 Workstation software product.

Novell NetWare SNA Gateway

The NetWare SNA Gateway software allows up to 97 workstations on a LAN to communicate with an IBM or compatible host computer. The software can operate in dedicated or nondedicated mode on the gateway PC. Security features are available to control which workstations access the host system. The software also allows print jobs from the host to be redirected to a LAN printer.

There are five host connectivity options, as listed here:

- Token Ring. Up to 128 host terminal and/or printer sessions are supported. The gateway emulates a PU Type 2 controller connected with an IBM 37xx, 3174, or 9370 host Token-Ring interface.

- Coax. Up to five host terminal and/or printer sessions are supported with this type of connection. A Novell Coax Adapter or an IBM 3278/79 Adapter is required.

- CoaxMux. Supports up to 40 host terminal and/or printer sessions and requires a Novell CoaxMux Adapter.

- Remote. Supports up to 16 host terminal and/or printer sessions, accessed via modem connection to an IBM 37x5 communications processor. Requires either a Novell Synchronous Adapter (for PC type systems) or an IBM Multiprotocol Adapter/A (for PS/2 systems). Speeds of up to 19.2K bits per second can be realized.

- High-Speed Remote. Supports up to 128 host terminal and/or printer sessions, accessed via modem connection to a 37x5 communications processor. Requires a Novell Synchronous/HS Adapter or Novell Synchronous Adapter when used with an 80386-based computer. Operates at speeds of up to 56K bits per second.

Novell NetWare SNA Gateway ELS

The NetWare SNA Gateway ELS product is a lower-priced version of the SNA Gateway product. It provides the same features and functionality as the SNA Gateway but is designed for users who do not anticipate a growth in the need for host connectivity. The main difference is that the SNA Gateway ELS version provides only Coax or Remote host connections. The product will run on ELS NetWare Level II, Advanced NetWare, and SFT NetWare.

Novell NetWare 3270 LAN Workstation Software

The NetWare 3270 LAN Workstation software is designed to provide the workstation link to the SNA gateway server. It is licensed for the server, which means only one copy of the software is required to support all workstations that will make connections to the host.

The software provides up to five host display and/or printer sessions per workstation and includes both a file-transfer program and a keyboard mapping facility. Emulation of multiple 3270 terminals and 3287 printers is supported. It also supports Novell, IBM, and DCA application program interfaces (APIs).

Novell NetWare 3270 Token-Ring Workstation Software

NetWare 3270 Token-Ring Workstation software is a single-station terminal emulation product for a PC or PS/2 workstation on a Token Ring LAN. It provides access to up to five concurrent terminal and/or printer sessions on an SNA host. The connection is made directly to a 3174 cluster controller, an IBM 37xx communications processor, or an IBM 93xx host computer. Its features are similar to the NetWare 3270 LAN Workstation software.

SNA Hardware Products

The Novell SNA gateway hardware options listed here are designed to work with the NetWare SNA Gateway software products just described.

Novell Coax Adapter for PCs
And IBM PS/2 Systems

This is a coaxial interface board used to connect a PC or PS/2 to an IBM cluster controller. It supports a five-session LAN gateway with NetWare SNA Gateway or NetWare SNA Gateway ELS software and will attach to an IBM 3274 controller, an IBM 3174 controller, or an IBM 3299 Coaxial Multiplexer. Both boards support DFT-mode operation (one to five sessions).

Novell CoaxMux Adapter for PCs

A high-performance coaxial interface board with an enhanced 10MHz 80186 coprocessor and 512K of memory, this adapter is designed to connect to an IBM cluster controller. The device emulates a 3299 multiplexer connection and can support up to 40 concurrent DFT-mode mainframe sessions as a LAN gateway. The board works with the CoaxMux option of the NetWare SNA Gateway software. NetWare SNA Gateway ELS software does not support this board.

Novell Synchronous Adapter for PCs

This board has an RS-232C (CCITT V.24/V.28) interface. It connects a PC via synchronous modems to an IBM 37xx communications controller at speeds of up to 19.2K bits per second. If used in 80386-based PCs, the adapter will operate at speeds of up to 56K bits per second. When connected to an IBM 37xx communications controller, the board and NetWare SNA Gateway software appear as an SNA/SDLC IBM 3274 cluster controller. It works with NetWare SNA Gateway or NetWare SNA Gateway ELS software.

Novell Synchronous/HS Adapter for PCs

This is a high-performance version of the Novell Synchronous Adapter enhanced with a 10MHz 80186 coprocessor and 512K of memory. It is capable of communicating at externally clocked speeds of up to 56K bits per second.

Novell Synchronous/V.35 Adapter for PCs

This is a synchronous serial interface board with an RS-232 to V.35 interface. It connects a PC via synchronous modems to an IBM 37xx communications processor and operates at 64K bits per second when used with an 80386-based PC.

Novell 5250 Gateway And Workstation Products

Novell 5250 software products allow workstations on a LAN to access important information and applications on IBM System/34, 36, or 38 minicomputers. The products include the NetWare 5250 Gateway software package and the NetWare 5250 LAN Workstation package.

NetWare 5250 Gateway Software

The NetWare 5250 Gateway software enables a workstation on a LAN to access a System/3X minicomputer using a remote SDLC connection. The connection requires the use of the Novell Synchronous Adapter, which is described in the previous section. The software provides up to nine concurrent display or host- addressable printer sessions to PCs on the LAN, with up to five of those sessions available concurrently to any single workstation. Multiple NetWare 5250 gateways can also be installed on the same network. The system emulates either 5251 Model 12 or 5294 cluster controllers.

NetWare 5250 LAN
Workstation Software

The NetWare 5250 LAN Workstation software provides PC and PS/2 Models 25 or 30 with access to an IBM System/34, 36, or 38 minicomputer via the NetWare 5250 Gateway software. The software will emulate a variety of 5250 display stations. Any node on the LAN can access up to five concurrent minicomputer sessions and one DOS session. Any of those sessions can be allocated to a printer attached to the local PC.

NetWare LU6.2 Software
for Novell 3270 SNA Gateways

Peer-to-peer communications is the current trend in internetwork and gateway communications. PC-to-host and LAN-to-host communications are moving away from older terminal emulation methods to this more equal form of communication. Peer-to-peer communications is largely represented by the IBM Logical Unit 6.2 (LU6.2) specification.

There are several advantages to peer-to-peer communications besides the equality of mainframes and PCs. PCs can function as intelligent processing units on their own, rather than mimicking the host. Applications are also easier to integrate. The switch to distributed processing is already in full gear, but the use of minicomputers and mainframes will not come to an end. Their present role will change, however. Users are already realizing that minicomputers and mainframes can be used as highly efficient file servers or for processing highly intensive applications programs.

The NetWare LU6.2 application program interface (API) adds support for advanced program-to-program applications to a variety of 3270-series products. NetWare LU6.2 performs as a compatible alternative to IBM's Advanced Program-to-Program communications for the Personal Computer (APPC/PC) and provides a consistent peer-to-peer applications interface between personal computers, LANs, and mainframes using LU6.2 protocols.

SIX

Network Interface Methods
And Topologies

This chapter is designed to help you evaluate the Ethernet, ARCNET, and Token Ring network systems and determine which will be best for your installation site. Your decision should be based on cable, interface cards, topology, and the protocols used by the network system, as discussed in Chapter 2. This chapter will also help familiarize you with the components you will need to purchase for the selected network and give you a brief explanation of how each of these networks is connected.

First, each different type of cable is discussed so you can evaluate which might be best for your particular office layout. Next, an overview of each network type is given along with a discussion of minimum and maximum requirements for cables and workstations. An evaluation section then follows; the merits of each network type is discussed and comparisons are made to others. Following the evaluation, you will find a section that briefly discusses the installation steps of each network type. This discussion is designed to help you begin planning your installation. A final section discusses several topics you may find of interest if you are connecting large or multiple networks.

A network is a modular and adaptable communications system that can be customized to many different site requirements. Its modularity makes it easy to add new components or move existing ones, and its adaptability makes changes and upgrades easy. This is especially true when NetWare is used as the network operating system because Novell goes to great lengths to support and stay compatible with most PC-compatible network products.

Traditionally, Ethernet provides a linear bus topology with a CSMA/CD (carrier sense multiple access/collision detection) access method using coaxial cable. Token Ring provides a star/ring topology and a token-passing access method. ARCNET provides a star/bus topology with a token-passing access method. At one time, these networks were well established and used one type of cable; Ethernet used thin or thick coaxial cable, Token Ring used shielded twisted-pair cable, and ARCNET used coaxial cable. Today, telephone twisted-pair, fiber-optic, and other cable methods can be used as well, which increases the number of ways you can install the network.

There are four factors you should consider when purchasing network hardware:

- *Topology.* The topology allowed by any particular network system will determine how you can bend, shape, and expand the overall LAN to fit your installation. A *linear bus* lets you "string" cable through a building from one end to the other. A *ring topology* looks exactly like it sounds. A *star topology* has wires reaching to distant workstations from a single source. Combinations are also possible. The *star/ring* topology of Token Ring places the ring in a central box, and workstations then radiate out from this box on their own cables. ARCNET uses a *star/linear* bus topology that gives you great flexibility in wiring the network. Each of these methods is covered in Chapter 2. As you will see in a moment, the topology of a network system is partly determined by the cable access method.

- *Cabling.* Your choice of cable will in part depend on the cable performance, cost, ease of installation, and expandability. Performance is listed first because it is the most important factor in most cases. The performance of a cable determines how fast and how far it will transmit signals without degradation. Other factors also come into the performance factor, such as the cable resistance to outside interference, strength, durability, and so on. Some cabling systems are easier to install than others. For example, it is a simple matter to tap into some cables when adding another workstation.

- *Cable Access Method.* The access method of a cable is important because it plays a part in the actual throughput of a cable. While Ethernet has a high throughput of 10 megabits per second (10Mbit/sec), its access method can cause the throughput to drop during heavy network traffic loads. The access method of a network system also plays a part in the topology of the network. An access method using a token has a constant throughput, because there is only one token used to send and receive packets or exchange communications. In reality, an Ethernet system with high traffic may have the same throughput as a Token Ring or ARCNET system. A new 16Mbit/sec Token Ring System, available from IBM, provides a constant high-speed throughput using the token-passing method, but at great expense.

- *Network Interface Cards.* A particular network interface card is chosen after a combined decision is made on the rest of the elements just discussed. Interface cards are now commonly available to fit the 16-bit bus slots of AT-class 80286 systems, allowing faster throughput. Interface cards using 16- bit bus slots should be purchased whenever possible for 80286 systems if budgets can match their price.

Another Look at Cabling

Network cabling is chosen for its cost, performance, building code specification, ease of installation, expandability, and many other factors. This section will discuss several cable types for personal computer networks.

The electrical cables discussed here all suffer from some form of electrical interference, although shielded cables are less susceptible than twisted-pair cables. Copper cables can begin to act like antennas as their distance increases. They pick up energy from motors, radio transmitters, and other sources of electric power. In addition, metal cables have problems with grounding. All in all, metal cables can greatly modify the signals they are transmitting. To prevent these problems, you must limit distances or add expensive shielding. Metal cables also generate their own signals, which can be tapped. In fact, the signals emanating from a metal cable can be monitored to decipher the password codes entered by users, and some government agencies provide strict guidelines for installing cables in high-security installations.

An alternative to metal cable is fiber-optic cable, which will be discussed last. Although expensive, this cable provides for longer distances, faster transmission, and increased security. It is impossible to tap a light signal without actually cutting the cable, and this activity can be controlled by the network supervisors or installers by adjusting the amount of light through the cable. If a tap is made, the cable will fail because the system is not "tuned" for the addition of the tap.

Coaxial Cable

A coaxial cable consists of a single-wire conductor surrounded by an insulating core, then a woven ground wire, and finally an insulating jacket to protect the whole assembly. Coaxial cable is available for either baseband or broadband transmission.

Baseband

Baseband transmission passes digital signals from one workstation to the next over coaxial cable at speeds of 10Mbit/sec for distances of up to 13,000 feet. It is commonly used on Ethernet network. Baseband cabling may be easily spliced to add new workstations.

Broadband

Broadband cabling is capable of transmitting voice, video, and data signals, and is commonly used for television transmission. The cable supports several "channels" of radio frequency signals, which are analog in nature rather than digital. Because of this, network signals must be converted from digital to analog and then back to digital for transmission over the cable. This is done in the card or by an external device. Broadband cabling is often already installed at many sites, so existing cable can be used to reduce costs. Broadband can transmit at around 5Mbit/sec at distances of up to 36 miles. Because it is more expensive than baseband and requires complicated planning, broadband is recommended for long-distance LANs or as a network "backbone."

Twisted-Pair Cabling

Twisted-pair cabling is one of the most common types of cables used in telephone systems. The twisting in the cable helps eliminate a lot of the noise and interference associated with cabling systems. Much of the cabling installed for telephone systems is 25-pair cable in which only a few of the pairs are in actual use. In most cases, unused pairs can be taken advantage of to establish a network cabling system. It is important to check with the phone company or the owner of the cable before making such an installation. It is also important to check the specifications of the network interface board to make sure the cable is of sufficient quality for transmission. A higher- quality, shielded cable may be required. The distance of the cable may also be too excessive for use with a particular network board.

Unshielded Twisted Pair (Telephone)

Unshielded twisted-pair wire can offer an inexpensive alternative to network wiring problems. Although the wire lacks speed and is limited in distance, it is easy to install and may already be in place on existing telephone lines, as mentioned earlier. The cable will transmit at up to 1 megabit per second (1 Mbit/sec).

IBM requires 22- or 24-gauge wire with a minimum of 2 twists per foot when unshielded twisted-pair wire is used with its 4Mbit/sec Token Ring products. The workstations cannot be located further than 330 feet from the multistation access unit. Newer 16Mbit/sec IBM Token Ring cards do not support this cabling due to high throughput.

Shielded Twisted Pair

Shielded twisted-pair wire offers several advantages over unshielded wire in terms of speed and distance, but it is generally more expensive. Because the wire is constructed to more precise standards, the cable is able to transmit at higher rates over longer cable runs. IBM Token Ring Type 6 cable is shielded twisted pair that can have cable runs of up to 150 feet.

Fiber Optic

Fiber-optic cable transmits signals over glass-threaded wire using light beams. The light signals are immune to outside interference and do not emanate a signal beyond the cable itself. Because of this, fiber-optic cable is excellent for long cable runs that would normally pose major interference stumbling blocks for electrical cable, such as large machines, lighting equipment, and other devices. Since the cable does not emanate a signal, it is also excellent for high-security use.

It's interesting to consider that electrical signals travel down a coax cable at about the same speed as light travels through a fiber optic cable. Also, fiber cable doesn't provide any new exotic transmission scheme on the cable, such as parallel transmission. What's really different about fiber cable, and what makes it so attractive, is its security potential and the fact that data transfer speed can be increased without decreasing the reliability of the signal at the other end of the cable.

The reliability and transmission capabilities of fiber cable allow for increased distances. The glass in fiber-optic cable is so pure that two to three miles of it would be completely transparent if it were possible to view through one end to the other. A typical fiber-optic cable run can span up to two miles without repeaters. The reliability of fiber cable has to do with the fact that light is not susceptible to electrical interference and can carry extremely clean signals over the cable distance. Fiber-optic cable standards specify a data transmission rate of 100Mbit/sec, but it is possible to transmit at up to 1 gigabit per second although hardware is not currently available for this rate.

There are three types of fiber-optic cable: single-fiber monomode cable, multiple-fiber multimode cable, and graded-index multimode cable. The first has a wide band width but is difficult to splice. The second is easier to splice and comes in 2 to 24 fiber varieties. The third provides the fastest transmission rates over the longest distances, but of course is the most expensive.

The trade-off for fiber-optic cabling has always been its price. In recent years this has begun to change as the technology becomes more common and is offered by more vendors. In most cases, the cost of fiber cable is dropping, but high-data-rate fiber optics and the interfaces to support them can be expensive. Less expensive interfaces operate in the 10Mbit/sec range of Ethernet and provide all the benefits of fiber-optic cable. Fiber-optic cable may be a cost-efficient replacement for heavily shielded fire-retardant copper cabling.

An Overview of Popular Networks

This section will provide an overview of three of the most popular network types: Ethernet, Token Ring, and ARCNET. Several different cabling methods are also discussed.

Ethernet

Ethernet was originally developed by Xerox and DEC and has been available for over 10 years as a way to cable networks. The system was originally designed to use coaxial cable, but other cabling systems are now available. Ethernet has a throughput of 10Mbit/sec (megabits per second).

The topology of an Ethernet cable system is a linear bus with a CSMA/CD access method. Workstations are connected to a *trunk segment* of cable that is terminated on both ends. Trunk segments can be connected with *repeaters* to extend the total length of the network, known as the *network trunk*. A typical layout is shown in Figure 6-1.

Several different types of cable can now be used to form Ethernet networks. There are two types of Ethernet coaxial cable connections, referred to as *thick* and *thin,* which may be combined in a single network by using methods discussed later. Most Ethernet boards for coaxial cables have connections for either cabling system.

Ethernet cards are available from Novell, 3Com, Western Digital, Micom, AST, and Ungermann-Bass, among others.

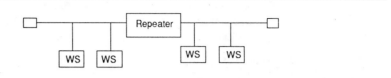

Figure 6-1.   An Ethernet trunk segment extended with a repeater

Thick Coaxial Ethernet

Thick Ethernet cable is often referred to as "standard Ethernet" cable or just "thick" cable. Figure 6-2 illustrates thick Ethernet cabling. The following rules and limitations apply:

- The maximum trunk segment length is 1640 feet.

- Transceivers are connected to the trunk segment.

- The maximum workstation-to-transceiver distance is 164 feet.

- The minimum distance to the next transceiver is 8 feet.

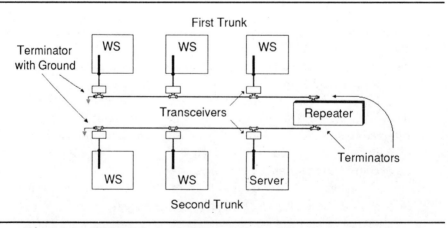

Figure 6-2.   Thick Ethernet cabling example

- Up to 5 trunk segments may be joined using 4 repeaters. Workstations are allowed on only three of the segments. The others are used for distance.

- The maximum network trunk length is 8200 feet.

- A maximum of 100 workstations can be on one trunk. Repeaters count as workstations.

- A terminator must be placed at each end of a trunk segment, and one end must be grounded.

Thin Coaxial Ethernet

Thin Ethernet cable is physically easier to handle and does not require the use of transceivers at the stations. Figure 6-3 illustrates a thin Ethernet network. The following rules and limitations apply:

- The maximum trunk segment length is 607 feet.

- T-type connectors are used to connect the cable to the network interface card.

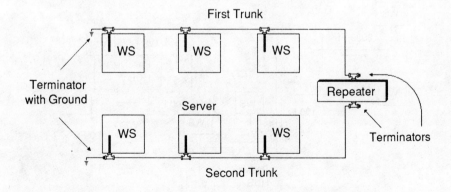

Figure 6-3.   Thin Ethernet cabling example

- Up to 5 trunk segments may be joined using 4 repeaters. Workstations are allowed on only 3 of the segments; the others are used for distance.

- The maximum network trunk length is 3035 feet.

- A maximum of 30 workstations can be on one trunk. Repeaters count as workstations.

- An ohms terminator must be placed at each end of a trunk segment, and one end must be grounded.

ARCNET

ARCNET is a baseband, token-passing network system that offers flexible topologies and generally the lowest price. Transmissions speeds are 2.5Mbit/sec. ARCNET combines the star and linear bus topologies to form a hybrid topology. Fiber-optic and twisted- pair cabling systems are also available from certain vendors. A typical ARCNET configuration is shown in Figure 6-4. The following rules and limitations apply:

- Up to 3 workstations can be grouped around a passive hub. Each workstation cannot be further than 50 feet from the hub.

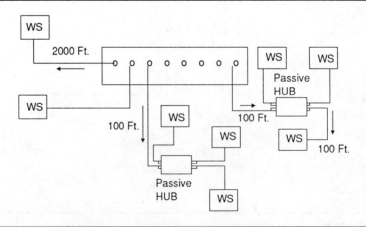

Figure 6-4. ARCNET cabling example

- Unused nodes on passive hubs should be terminated using a 93-ohm terminator cap.

- Passive hubs cannot be connected to other passive hubs. They can be attached to active hubs at a maximum distance of 100 feet.

- Active hubs have 8 nodes. Workstations on active hubs can extend as far as 2000 feet from the hub.

- The maximum number of stations is 255.

- The maximum distance between stations at opposite ends of the network is 20,000 feet.

- The maximum distance between two active hubs is 2000 feet.

- The maximum distance to or from any passive hub is 100 feet.

Token Ring

The IBM Token Ring network is a token-passing network with a star and ring topology. The network maintains a token-passing ring within a *multistation access unit.* Up to eight workstations then extend from this unit in a star configuration. Token Ring provides the advantages of a ring and a star in one design. A Token Ring network is shown in Figure 6-5. The following rules and limitations apply:

- The maximum number of stations is 96.

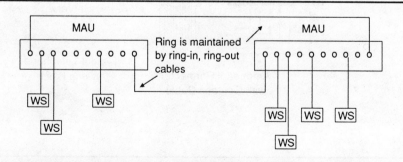

Figure 6-5.   Token Ring cabling example

- 8 workstations can be attached to a multistation access unit (MAU).
- Up to 12 MAUs may be included in the ring.
- The maximum distance between a workstation and a MAU is 150 feet.
- The maximum cable distance between two MAUs is 150 feet.
- The maximum patch cable distance connecting all MAUs is 400 feet.

Telephone Twisted Pair

The use of telephone twisted-pair wiring is now supported for Ethernet, ARCNET, and Token Ring. Simple-to-use RJ-45 jacks and standard telephone cabling can be used to create a basic network. In addition, punch-down blocks in wiring closets can be used to distribute the network wiring from a network concentrator or multistation access unit. Figure 6-6 shows how a telephone wiring block might be wired for a twisted-pair network.

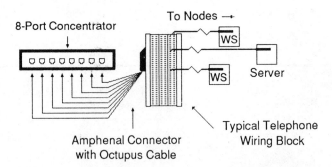

Figure 6-6. Telephone twisted-pair network with station interconnection occurring within the 8-port concentrator

The concentrator simply provides a connection between each of the plugs on its front panel. It is in this box that workstations communicate among themselves. The front-panel jacks are usually telephone RJ-45 connectors with wires leading off to a standard telephone block. This block then joins wires coming from the workstations through the walls or under the baseboards. Concentrators are available for 8 or more connections, with some units having up to 48 workstation connections.

Twisted-pair systems typically use a physical hub topology, so in the case of Ethernet twisted-pair system, the similarity to the original standard starts to fade. The hub topology will require more cable than a station-to-station wiring scheme, but each node has its own dedicated cable run. This provides an extra level of protection if a wire should be cut; only the station connected to that wire will lose its network connection.

The wiring closet can provide a place where different types of wiring schemes can be brought together. For example, a coaxial backbone may be used to connect two distant groups of PCs. Twisted-pair wiring is used at either end of the backbone to then cable out the short distance to each workstation from the wiring closet. The distances provided by twisted-pair wiring will depend on the manufacturer as well as the network type being used (Token-Ring, Ethernet, or ARCNET).

Evaluating the Choices

Recall that any decision on the type of network hardware requires an evaluation of the type of cable to be used, the topology, the access method, and the network interface board. This section will help you evaluate which system is better for your installation.

Methods for Evaluation

The following discussion ranks each network method according to cost, performance, and ease of installation. The following evaluations are based on coaxial cable ARCNET and Ethernet systems, and shielded twisted-pair (IBM Type 6) Token Ring systems.

Cost per User

High: Token Ring. Token Ring interface cards and cable are expensive. In addition, a multistation access unit is required for every eight users using the IBM system.

Medium: Ethernet. Interface cards are usually more expensive for Ethernet but the cabling cost is about the same as ARCNET.

Low: ARCNET. The cost per each workstation is lowest with ARCNET. Interface cards are generally cheaper, and cabling can take advantage of the linear bus or star topology, whichever fits into the installation better.

Performance

High: Ethernet. Transmits at up to 10Mbit/sec.

Medium: Token Ring. Transmits at 4Mbit/sec.

Low: ARCNET. Transmits at 2.5Mbit/sec.

Note: Token Ring is now available in 16Mbit/sec, making it the highest performer in some tests.

Ease of Installation

High: ARCNET. ARCNET is easy to install because cables can be configured in a linear bus or star topology. ARCNET provides the best of Token Ring and Ethernet when it comes to installation.

Medium: Ethernet. A single cable run connects all systems.

Medium: Token Ring. Token Ring is also in the medium category because it can be as easy to install as Ethernet under the right conditions.

Other Factors

Other factors that can be used to rank networks involve the number of supporting products like gateways, availability of installers, and support of new cabling technologies like fiber optics. For example, some IBM mainframe products now include Token Ring connections, which make the use of Token Ring interface cards a logical choice. Ethernet is an older, seasoned product that is well supported.

Evaluating Ethernet

Ethernet allows computers to be connected at various intervals along a main cable. This cable is usually made to fit the distances between each station. The cable can be spliced to add new stations. If the maximum number of nodes is reached on one trunk, a new trunk can be connected by using a repeater. Each node listens for signals on a bidirectional bus and receives the ones addressed to it. Since signals are traveling in both directions and any node can decide to send whenever it wants, there is a possibility of data collision in high-traffic conditions. Data collisions do not corrupt data, but the system throughput is reduced because the packets must be sent again.

The Ethernet system is economical and easy to install and expand. Cabling is reduced since a single trunk can be used. Each workstation does not have its own cable that extends from a central hub as does a star topology. Instead, cables are attached from workstation to workstation. A disadvantage to this is that a break or cut in the cable will down the entire system. A break or cut in a star-wired network will only affect the workstation connected to the broken cable run.

Because of its high throughput, Ethernet is often the best choice for high-volume applications, such as those in engineering or graphics environments, where large file transfers to printing, plotting, and storage devices may demand high speed. Twisted-pair Ethernet products are also available with new topological configurations.

One such configuration, available from Black Box (Pittsburg, PA), is known as a hierarchical star topology, and is shown in Figure 6-7. This configuration allows concentrator boxes to expand from other concentrator boxes in a hierarchical configuration. Workstations are also connected to concentrators.

Twisted-pair wiring is used in the configuration. An 8-station concentrator allows up to eight workstations or concentrators to be connected. The cable distance from a concentrator cannot exceed 360 feet. Each additional concentrator allows eight more workstations or concentrators.

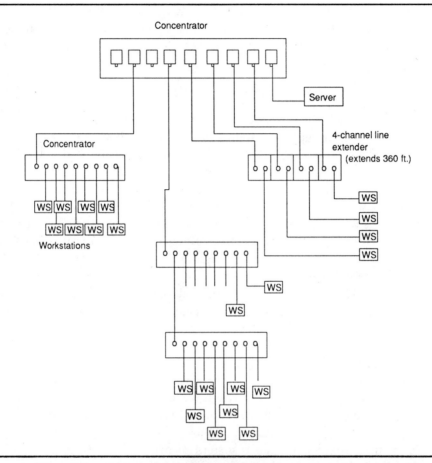

Figure 6-7.   A hierarchical wiring configuration using twisted-pair wiring and concentrator boxes (from Blackbox, Pittsburg, PA)

Evaluating ARCNET

ARCNET's price and topology options make it a natural choice for those with simple installations who don't want to spend a lot of money. ARCNET also has a safe and reliable token-passing access scheme, using a free-form topology that combines both a linear bus and star configuration. A linear bus configuration can be used when straight cable runs are required, and star configuration can be used to distribute workstations from a central point.

ARCNET is easy to install, expand, modify, and service. The wiring scheme used by ARCNET will not disable the network if a station goes down and fault isolation is easy. Workstations can be added or removed with little difficulty or configuration. It is almost impossible for ARCNET to cause a complete system failure due to a downed node. In fact, when a cable is cut, the system is reconfigured into two smaller systems.

Cost can be minimized if distances from a passive hub are kept under 100 feet. An active hub is required over this distance and allows workstations to extend to 2000 feet. A complete ARCNET system with multiple active hubs can extend as far as 4 miles. ARCNET is available for thin coaxial cable, unshielded twisted pair cable, and fiber optic cable.

Token Passing Versus CSMA/CD

The token-passing scheme used by ARCNET (and Token Ring) is not susceptible to the data collisions of the CSMA/CD access method used by Ethernet. A token passes through or is active on every station on the network, thus giving each station an equal time on the network. Collisions are avoided because a station can only send when it has the token. Throughput stays constant and collision-free, even with a great deal of network traffic.

Collisions occur on CSMA/CD LANs when two stations transmit messages at the same time. This is normally avoided under light use, but as the network traffic increases, the collisions require retransmission of messages, which slows the network. Collisions increase as the traffic load increases. The 10Mbit/sec throughput claim of Ethernet must be compared against the network loads you anticipate. If they are heavy, as would be the case when using a database system, an alternative cabling system might be preferable.

Configuring Star Topology
ARCNET System

A star topology is formed by linking workstations to a central passive hub, which normally has four connectors. Network expansion is performed by

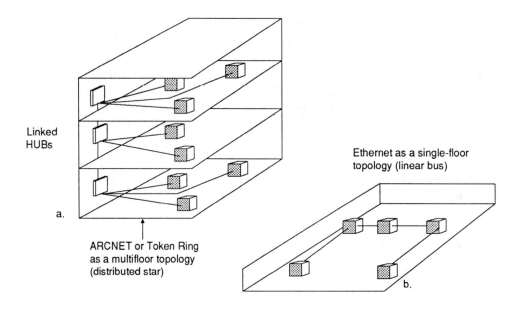

Figure 6-8. Layout of network cabling in a building: an ARCNET or Token Ring configuration (*a*); an Ethernet configuration (*b*)

linking an active hub and additional passive hubs to form a "distributed star" configuration. Site wiring is easy since hubs are placed in central locations and then linked together. If distances beyond 100 feet are required, an active hub should be used in place of the passive hub. Active hubs support eight workstations or support additional hubs. The multi-level office building shown in Figure 6-8 illustrates the advantage of a star configured ARCNET system. Note that Token Ring can be configured in the same way.

Configuring a Bus Topology
ARCNET System

An ARCNET cabling system can be configured in a linear bus topology in much the same way as the Ethernet system shown in Figure 6-8. The linear bus can branch directly off an active hub connected to a star topology network. T-connectors are used along the bus to connect workstations. Only eight workstations are allowed per cable segment. To expand further, active links can be added.

Evaluating Token Ring

The most common Token Ring network is that made by IBM, although several other vendors now offer it. The IBM Token Ring transmits at 4Mbit/sec, and a new version transmits at 16Mbit/sec. Token Ring uses a shielded twisted-pair wire to connect workstations to a central box known as the multistation access unit (MAU). In the IBM configuration, this box supports eight stations, but the MAU can be attached to other MAUs to form a loop. Other vendors offer more stations per MAU and allow other types of cable, such as unshielded twisted pair (IBM now offers this also).

Token Ring uses the token-passing access scheme (see "Token Passing Versus CSMA/CD" in the ARCNET section). Each node waits for the token before transmitting. As the token is passed around the network, it must be regenerated by each station (which is not the case with ARCNET), reducing its actual throughput slightly. Token Ring is still faster, and that is its main advantage over ARCNET. In general, Token Ring shares most of the features of ARCNET except for the linear bus topology, although this can be achieved by using various wiring schemes. Token Ring does suffer distance problems. The maximum distance between two stations using the IBM cabling system is about 700 feet.

The new 16Mbit/sec Token Ring cards from IBM offer the fastest throughput of any non-fiber-optic system but are expensive. They can be used in situations where high speed is essential, such as engineering or graphics environments. In fact, a bridge can be established in the server between a 16Mbit/sec network and a 4Mbit/sec network. Figure 6-8 illustrates how a Token Ring system might be installed in a multilevel office building.

Evaluating Unshielded Twisted Pair

Since unshielded twisted-pair wiring can be used on any of the systems just described, it is evaluated here as an option. Twisted pair is widely installed in phone systems and is now going through a resurgence as an inexpensive alternative to network wiring methods. Modern network hardware has noise- filtering and signal-conditioning features that make high-speed transmission over twisted-pair cable viable. New twisted-pair Ethernet systems can run as high as 10Mbit/sec.

Twisted-pair cable does suffer from distance and interference problems. Distance limitations are 350 feet. It cannot be used near fluorescent lights or electric devices that produce high electromagnetic and radio frequency interference. But because it is so inexpensive, using extra cable to route around these devices is not a problem. Problems may crop up if existing telephone twisted pair is used, since the cable runs may be near these devices. The majority of twisted-pair installations have been working with little problems, however, and usage is increasing.

When you use existing telephone twisted pair, moving workstations is easy if the new workstation location has an existing telephone. Simply tap into the extra pair at the new location and have it wired properly to the concentrator or MAU in the phone closet. Wiring is also simplified if the company moves, assuming the new location has twisted pair available. This will also reduce the cabling cost normally associated with moving a network.

Wiring a phone closet is not as hard as it may at first seem when you look in the closet. In most cases, a qualified installer can locate the lines coming from each phone, and then connect them to a wiring block, as shown in Figure 6-6. An "octopus" cable with a special block connector on one end and a multitude of cables on the other is then attached to the wiring block. The cables then correspond to each workstation attached to the block and are plugged in to the concentrator unit or MAU box. The concentrator then forms a loop or bus to connect the stations together.

Telephone wire and modular jacks are also much simpler to work with than coaxial cables or IBM Type 6 cable. Connections are a snap, and cables can be built with a simple, inexpensive tool.

Evaluating Fiber-Optic Cable

Fiber-optic cabling may be cheap or expensive, depending on what you want to use it for and what you are comparing it with. The fact that fiber optic cabling is considered a viable product for future use and expansion makes its consideration worthwhile now. With fiber-optic cable, network transmission rates in the 100Mbit/sec range are possible, so it may make sense to start a system now and expand it in the future.

Fiber-optic networks can reach miles with few repeaters. In some cases, fiber can take the place of existing techniques to span long distances, such as microwaves, buried cables, or telephone communications links, and fiber does not present the security problems typical of other methods.

Hardware Components And Installation Methods

This section will explain the equipment you need to purchase for each of the different network systems described in this chapter. When deciding on equipment and making purchases, you should talk with local network installation companies or distributors who market multivendor products. Black Box, of Pittsburgh, PA (412-746-5530) has an excellent catalog that lists many different network cabling options, software packages, and other related products.

Thick Ethernet

Network Interface Board   Most Ethernet boards will support either thick or thin Ethernet cabling. The board should have a female DIX-type connector for the attachment of the transceiver cable. A BNC connector for thin Ethernet connections will probably be on the board as well, but it is not used when installing thick-only cable systems. Combinations of thick and thin cabling are possible, as discussed later. Network interface cards are available in standard 8-bit bus design and AT-type 16-bit bus design.

The 16-bit boards provide faster network throughput. *Note:* If the Ethernet board will be installed in a diskless workstation, be sure to order a remote reset PROM.

Repeater   The repeater is an optional device used to join two Ethernet trunks together and to strengthen the signals between them. One transceiver will be required on each cable trunk to attach to the repeater. Cable should be included in the transceivers to attach to the repeater.

Transceiver   The transceiver is a junction box on the thick Ethernet cable where workstations can be attached. It has three connectors. Two are the thick Ethernet in and out connectors, and the third connector is used to attach the workstation to the transceiver using the transceiver cable.

Transceiver Cable   Transceiver cables usually come with the transceiver units. Male and a female DIX-type connectors are mounted on either end, along with slide locks to lock the cable to the network interface board and transceiver connectors.

Thick Ethernet Cabling   The cabling used for thick Ethernet is a 50-ohm 0.4-inch diameter coaxial cable. It is not the same type of cabling used in the transceiver cable. Thick Ethernet cable is available from many vendors, and most will have precut standard lengths ready to ship. Bulk cable can also be purchased, but N-series connectors must be mounted on the ends of the cable cuts. Connector mounting tools can be purchased from most cable distributors.

N-Series Male Connectors   These are thick Ethernet cable connectors to be installed on both ends of the cable. Preassembled cables will already have the connectors mounted.

N-Series Barrel Connectors   These are used to join two cable segments together.

N-Series Terminators   Each cable segment must be terminated at both ends with a 50-ohm N-series terminator. For each cable segment, order one terminator with a ground wire attached and one without a ground wire. The ground wire is usually 3 to 4 feet in length.

Cabling and Installing
Thick Ethernet Networks

When installing thick Ethernet networks, be sure to follow the rules and limitations discussed in the network overview section earlier in this chapter. These steps should only be performed after reading Chapter 10.

Cabling and installation of thick Ethernet cable is relatively simple. Start by installing and testing the network interface card after you have determined the correct switch setting. Switch settings can be determined when running the NetWare configuration programs and the cards should be installed after NetWare is configured.

Next, attach the transceivers and transceiver cables to the network interface cards at each station. Then string the assembled thick Ethernet cables between each station, and attach them to the proper connectors on the transceivers. At one end of the cable run, attach an N-series terminator with a ground wire attached to a suitable ground. At the other end, attach an ungrounded terminator.

If a repeater is being installed, it can be attached near the end of a cable trunk using a transceiver on each cable segment. The cable segment must still be terminated as normal, however.

Thin Ethernet

Network Interface Board   Most Ethernet boards will support either thick or thin Ethernet cabling. The board should have a BNC-type connector attached to the back, as well as a thick Ethernet connector. The thick connector is not used when installing thin Ethernet. A BNC T connector will be attached to a BNC connector on the back of the board to accommodate the in and out of the cable run. Combinations of thick and thin cabling are possible, as discussed later. Network interface cards are available in standard 8-bit bus design and AT-type 16-bit bus design. The 16-bit boards provide faster network throughput. *Note:* If the Ethernet board will be installed in a diskless workstation, be sure to order a remote reset PROM.

Repeater   The repeater is an optional device used to join two Ethernet trunks together and to strengthen the signals between them. One T connector will be required on each cable trunk to attach to the Repeater.

Thin Ethernet Cabling   The cabling used for thin Ethernet is a 50-ohm 0.2-inch diameter RG-58A/U coaxial cable. Thin Ethernet cable is available from many vendors who will have precut standard lengths ready to ship. Bulk cable can also be purchased, but BNC connectors must be mounted on the ends of the cable cuts. Connector mounting tools can be purchased from most cable distributors.

BNC T Connectors   T connectors are attached to the BNC connector on the back of the Ethernet interface cards. The T connector provides two cable connections for signal-in and signal-out. You will need a T connector for each workstation, plus two for each repeater being used.

BNC Barrel Connectors   These are used to join two cable segments together.

BNC Terminators   Each cable segment must be terminated at both ends with a 50-ohm BNC terminator. For each cable segment, order one terminator with a ground wire attached and one without a ground wire. The ground wire is usually 3 to 4 feet in length.

Cabling and Installing
Thin Ethernet Networks

When installing thin Ethernet networks, be sure to follow the rules and limitations discussed in the network overview section earlier in this chapter.

Note: These steps should only be performed after you have read Chapter 10.

Cabling and installation of thin Ethernet cable is relatively simple. Start by installing and testing the network interface card after you have determined the correct switch setting. Switch settings can be determined when running the NetWare configuration programs.

After running the NetWare configuration program discussed in Chapter 10, mount the board and attach the T connector. You can then string the assembled thin Ethernet cable between each station and attach them to the T connectors. At one end of the cable run, attach a BNC terminator with ground wire. At the other end, attach an ungrounded terminator. Be sure to attach the ground wire to a suitable ground such as an electrical outlet.

If a repeater is being installed, it can be attached near the end of a cable trunk using a T connector. The cable segment must still be terminated as normal, however.

Combined Thick and Thin Cables

It is possible to combine a thick and thin Ethernet cabling system. This is usually done to save money on cable, since thin Ethernet is usually cheaper than thick. Thick cable may be used to extend the distance between two thin Ethernet cable trunks by using a repeater. A repeater can also be used simply to join two existing trunks. The maximum number of trunk segments is five.

Combination thick and thin cable segments can be created using a BNC to N-series adapter, which is available with an N-series female or N-series male adapter at one end. Combination thick and thin segments are usually between 607 and 1640 feet long. The following equation is used to find the maximum amount of thin cable that can be used in one combination trunk segment:

$$\frac{1.640 \text{ feet} - L}{3.28} = t$$

where L is the length of the trunk segment you want to build and t is the maximum length of thin cable you can use.

ARCNET

Network Interface Board   ARCNET boards are available from many manufacturers. The board should have a BNC-type connector attached to the back. T connectors are normally not used in the ARCNET system; however, some versions allow linear bus-type cable runs in which T connectors are attached to the back of the interface boards. Network interface cards are available in standard 8-bit bus design and AT-type 16-bit bus design. The 16-bit boards provide faster network throughput.

   Note If the ARCNET board will be installed in a diskless workstation, be sure to order a remote reset PROM.

Passive Hub   The passive hub is a four-port connector with BNC jacks used as a wiring center for ARCNET cable coming from the workstations. Cable runs cannot exceed 50 feet unless an active hub is being used. Each unused port should be terminated.

Active Hub   The active hub is a network relay that conditions and amplifies the signal strength. Distances from active ports can be 2000 feet. Active hubs have eight ports. It is not necessary to terminate unused ports on an active hub.

ARCNET Cabling   The cabling used for ARCNET is a 93-ohm RG-62/U coaxial cable with BNC connectors on both ends. ARCNET cable is available from many vendors who will have precut standard lengths ready to ship. Bulk cable can also be purchased, but BNC connectors must be mounted on the ends of the cable cuts. Connector mounting tools can be purchased from most cable distributors. Cables from passive hubs cannot exceed 50 feet. Cable from active hubs cannot exceed 2000 feet.

BNC Terminators   BNC terminating plugs are used to cap passive hub ports not in use.

Cabling and Installing ARCNET Networks

When installing ARCNET networks, be sure to follow the rules and limitations discussed in the network overview section earlier in this chapter. Note the following:

- Passive hubs cannot be connected in series, but must be attached to passive hubs.

- If only two computers (a workstation and server) are wired, a passive hub is not required and the distance between them can be up to 2000 feet.

- A network with more than two stations must use a passive hub or an active hub.

- Do not create loops, which are formed when a cable wraps back around to form a connection into the hub of origination.

- Always terminate unused passive hub ports.

After setting the switches and jumpers on ARCNET boards according to the setting recommended during the NetWare installation as covered in Chapter 10, you may install them in the workstations. You may then connect the cables from the passive hubs to the workstations or from the active hubs to the workstations.

Token Ring

Token Ring Adapters   IBM Token Ring adapters are made for 8-bit and 16-bit bus structures, as well as the microchannel bus. New 16Mbit/sec boards are also available; however, these cards will operate at 8Mbit/sec if used on a network with 4Mbit/sec boards. Workstations using 16Mbit/sec cards should form their own network and be bridged in the server to 4Mbit/sec workstation networks. Be sure to order remote reset PROMs if cards are to be installed in diskless workstations.

Multistation Access Units   The IBM 8228 multistation access unit (MAU) is used to connect up to eight workstations using the network adapter cables. Up to 12 MAU devices may be connected together following the rules discussed in the next section. Each MAU is shipped with a setup aid, which is a small device that tests the ports of the MAU.

Token Ring Adapter Cable   The Token Ring adapter cable has a 9-pin connector on one end to attach to the network interface card and a special IBM cabling system connector (Token Ring connector) on the other end to connect into the MAU. Adapter cables are usually only 8 feet in length, but patch cables can be used to extend them. Standard IBM Token Ring cable is shielded twisted pair (IBM Type 6).

Patch Cables   A patch cable is made of IBM Type 6 cable and can be of any length up to 150 feet. Patch cables can be used to extend the distance of the workstation from the MAU device, or to cable two or more MAU devices together.

LAN Support Program   This software package will be required before you can run the IBM Token Ring network. It contains configuration files that must be installed using the CONFIG.SYS file. Authorized IBM dealers can supply this program.

Cabling and Installing
Token Ring Networks

When installing Token Ring networks, be sure to follow the rules and limitations discussed in the network overview section earlier in this chapter. Note the following:

- When you connect MAU devices together, the ring configuration must be maintained. This is done by connecting the ring-out receptacle on one device to the ring-in receptacle of another. If more than two MAU devices are used, a cable must run from the ring-out receptacle of the furthest device back to the first MAU device. The maximum cable distance between each MAU is 150 feet, and the total distance for all MAUs is 400 feet. Keep these rules in mind when ordering cable. Standalone MAU devices need not have their ring-in and ring-out receptacles connected.

- The IBM Token Ring connectors can be connected together by turning one connector 180 degrees. In this way, separate male and female connectors are not required.

- Some areas have restrictions against the use of IBM Type 6 cable. The cable should not be run in ducts, plenums, or other air handling spaces. Cable should not be run outdoors.

To begin installing the network, first configure the cards using the instructions supplied with the card. The NetWare configuration program may find line and interrupt conflicts, so its a good idea to run the NETGEN/ELSGEN installation programs first as covered in Chapter 10.

Once the cards are installed, test the ports on the MAU with the setup aid and follow the instructions that came with the unit. Connect the cable to the ports, making sure the connectors "snap in" properly. Note that the configuration files supplied on the IBM LAN Support Program disks must be copied to boot disks, and commands must be placed in the CONFIG.SYS file to activate them. Refer to the software instructions for more information.

Twisted-Pair Networks

If you wish to use twisted-pair cabling for your network, check with a dealer or distributor. There are various configurations available. In general, a media filter adapter will be required at the location where the twisted-pair network cable attaches to the workstation. A wire concentrator will be required in the wiring closet. For the IBM Token Ring system, the MAU unit can be mounted in the closet; however, other concentrators are available for Token Ring. Some support up to 48 workstations. Wires can be run directly from the wiring block in the phone closet to the concentrator, or an octopus-type connector can be used, as discussed previously.

Other Topics

There are a number of other network topics you need to be concerned with when connecting a LAN. These have to do with connecting more than one server, configuring a backbone cable, and establishing a wide area network (WAN).

Multiple Server Networks

NetWare allows a single network to have one or more file servers. In addition, a network can be bridged to another network and then have access to the file servers on that network. There is a difference between the two in how addresses are established, however. The analogy of street and home addresses is often used when explaining the addresses used by NetWare.

The *network address* is best thought of as the street. This address is an 8-digit hexadecimal number. Workstations are like buildings on the

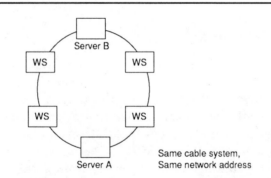

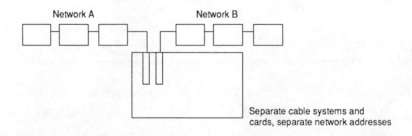

Figure 6-9. Network addresses

street, and each has a special *node address*. The file server uses these addresses to send information to each node over the appropriate address. If only one cable system exists, there will be only one network address (street). If the same network cable hooks up to another file server, both file servers share the same network address because they are on the same street. However, their node addresses will be different, as is shown in Figure 6-9.

If a network has two to four network interface cards installed, there must be two to four network addresses, even if the cards are the same type of cards. If servers on bridged networks attempt to share the same address, an error will occur and NetWare will need to be reconfigured for one of the networks with a different address.

Network Backbone Cabling

A *backbone cable* is nothing more than a cable that connects two networks together. This cable may run from an additional network interface card in one server to an additional network interface card in another server. The type of cabling and the distance between the servers is what makes a backbone cable unique.

The backbone cable may need to be established to span a long distance between two servers. At the same time, speed is important. Because of this, backbones may often be configured with a different type of cable and topology than the networks they are connecting. For example, Figure 6-10 illustrates a fiber-optic backbone cable connecting two Token Ring systems. The Token Ring system is inexpensive and efficient for the cable runs in each department. The fiber-optic cable system, while not inexpensive, is a fast and efficient link between the two networks. A company may find that fiber-optic interface cards are too expensive to place in each workstation on the network, but the cost is minimal when connecting only two distant servers.

In some cases, the backbone may be short to take advantage of various speed management and maintenance issues. In Figure 6-11, a short distance backbone cable connects three servers that are located in one room. Cables are then run from each server to the individual departments. The backbone cable may be a high-speed system like Ethernet that can handle the interserver (internetwork) traffic with little problem. ARCNET may then be used to cable to the workstations. ARCNET can provide the

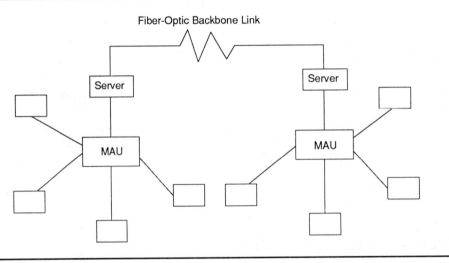

Figure 6-10.   Long-distance backbone connection using Token Ring

Figure 6-11.   Short-distance backbone connection

cable distance that may be required now that servers are centrally located, and it also provides a star topology to make cabling runs more efficient at the locations where workstations tend to congregate.

There are several advantages to using the short backbone. First, servers are located in one area where they can easily be serviced and upgraded by the system supervisor or manager. Servers are no longer locked in departments, where maintenance personnel may not be able to get to them when the department managers are away. Problems are more easily diagnosed; server performance can easily be compared when the network manager is viewing the screens of all systems at once. Each system can also share the same uninterruptable power supply, although the supply should be matched to the large load it would need to carry. Security is also enhanced, since the servers can be placed in a locked room with special fire-proofing.

As mentioned earlier, the short backbone may require additional cable to the workstations, but if expensive cable is used for the backbone, the cost of that cable will be reduced.

Wide Area Networks

A wide area network, or WAN, encompasses the connection of workstations and networks over wide areas with telephone, satellite, microwave, and other connections. WANs may be hundreds or thousands of miles apart. Many of the communications products covered in Chapter 5 are used to connect WANs together, but there are other methods, such as direct digital synchronous (DDS) lines for connecting networks.

Connections for WANs are often provided by public-switched networks or the local phone companies, and in some cases, by specially installed private lines. Typically, the phone system has provided the only means for networks to connect over long distances, but the quality of the services available for data communications has been limited and this kept many companies from establishing WANs. The highest quality modems can transmit at 19,200 bit/sec, but this is often limited because the phone lines are not of high-enough quality to reliably transmit at this speed. In reality, transmission is often set at 4800 bit/sec or less. When you consider that a typical LAN operates at 2Mbit/sec to 16Mbit/sec, you can see the limitations of the phone system.

For those who do need to connect WANs, there are several products available from Novell for doing so, as discussed in the last chapter. These include the NetWare Asynchronous Remote Bridge software for connecting LANs over voice-grade lines at up to 19,200 bit/sec. The NetWare X.25 Point-to-Point Bridge product can support transmission speeds of up to 64,000 bit/sec. Other connection methods are possible. Leased lines can provide digital quality at speeds of up to 56,000 bit/sec with little error. But even speeds provided by leased lines can be slow when compared to the requirements of a WAN.

The NetWare T-1 Bridge product line supports transmission speeds of up to 1.544Mbit/sec. This bridge can provide an excellent backbone-type configuration when several networks are connected. T-1 is a common telecommunications method often used to build private voice networks. T-1's band width is divided into 24 64,000 bit/sec channels, each of which can carry one voice or data transmission. With T-1, the local telephone company serves as a sort of hub for each network within a certain geographic area that is serviced by a central office of the local phone company. Networks at different company sites within the area serviced by the phone company (usually a metropolitan area) are then connected into the hub provided by the phone company. The area serviced by a phone company is known at its local access and transport area, or LATA. It is possible to connect to other LATAs by using links established by various "long-haul" carriers. You will then need to involve the local phone company, the remote phone company, and the long-haul carrier in your connection scheme.

SEVEN

Management and Security Issues For Network Planning

The System Manager
Tasks of the System Manager
Hardware and Software Support
Planning the System Security

This chapter discusses issues system planners, network supervisors, and network managers will need to consider as they plan a Novell NetWare system, prepare purchasing information, and plan the transition to the LAN. So far, this book has covered software and hardware products required to establish a LAN. This chapter discusses an equally important topic: the tasks of planning and preparing. As you read through this chapter, keep in mind that many of the topics discussed may not apply to every NetWare network, especially if it is small (3 or 4 nodes).

The System Manager

As soon as an organization begins to consider a LAN, it should begin to consider who will manage it. This manager will often be the very person who suggested a LAN in the first place or one of the people instrumental in its planning and installation. The system manager will be the most important person on site and should be knowledgeable enough to handle users' questions and emergencies when they crop up. A system manager may also be hired from an outside organization or may be a temporary consultant who will train in-house employees on the operation of the LAN.

The term *system manager* is used loosely in this chapter. It may in fact refer to several people who have been assigned the same responsibilities and who have the same access rights and privileges to the network server. Having two system managers provides backup and security on the human side of the LAN, since one person can handle the LAN if something happens to the other. You will see references in this chapter and others to the system manager as *supervisor*. This term comes from NetWare itself: the first person to sign on to a newly installed NetWare installation will be a user called SUPERVISOR. This person will be able to set the initial password to the system and will thus provide the first level of system security.

In some cases, a system manager may be different than the supervisor. It's possible that the *system manager* really manages the people who use the system and dictates how the system should be set up and run. The system manager then gives instructions to the *network supervisor,* who is a technically competent person capable of implementing the requests and policies of management on the system.

A system manager or supervisor should be wisely chosen. It doesn't make sense to train a person for the task if they might leave in six months. He or she should be trusted; once the manager or supervisor has the log-in rights, he or she has complete control over the system. A bitter and revengeful supervisor could lock everyone else out of the system prior to leaving the company. Without knowing the password, others would not be able to get in and change the access rights, and data might be impossible to access.

If new managers are brought in because the existing manager has been promoted or is leaving, it is best to break them in over a period of time. They should be shown the system logs, given a thorough tour of the building and its workstations, and be introduced to the users. The new manager should be updated on why various components are installed the way they are, or why certain people have special access rights on the system. Although an experienced manager can be hired from outside, it is often more beneficial to promote an existing employee who has computer knowledge and is familiar with the system.

Tasks of the System Manager

The job of the system manager (supervisor) is never done, if you consider the small list of tasks presented in the remainder of this section. Many of these tasks are required before the installation takes place, and in some cases should be part of the initial design and purchase stage. Other tasks are performed immediately after the system is installed. The majority of the system manager's tasks will take place on an ongoing basis, however. These tasks include managing users, implementing security, installing and upgrading programs, and backing up the system. The system manager also has a responsibility to other users to ensure that the network is kept up and running efficiently. Users have placed their trust in the manager's skills by allowing their personal data to be placed on the file server.

Managing the Transition to a LAN

When the time comes to make the transition from a non-network environment to a networked environment, planning is the best approach. New procedures will need to be implemented, and the staff will need to be trained. The system manager should work with personnel managers and department managers to establish how the system will be used by each department and each user. The manager should also plan the installation procedures around the schedules of individual department managers and their employees. Their schedules may be hard to adjust, and the network manager may need to plan to do the installation after-hours.

The manager will also need to plan for the software applications that will be installed and run on the server. Some of these applications will be used by all users, while others will be used by specific users in separate departments. NetWare gives the system manager or supervisor the means to organize users and the applications they will use into meaningful groups that can correspond to departments or to different levels of management. For example, a graphics department that uses drawing and CAD software can have a special group name and data directory especially for graphics. The accounting department can have its own group of users who will have access to the accounting software. Each different department can lock out their files to unauthorized users. An early part of planning for any network is to begin categorizing users according to the software and directories they will need access to and the groups they will belong to.

Users will need to understand that access to the system will be limited according to various rights assigned by the system supervisor. These access rights are often determined jointly by the supervisor along with the personnel or department managers. Department managers will be interested in what files their employees have or don't have access to on the system.

Users are often confused when they can't access files in a directory or when a program will not run, even though they know the files exist. Cryptic error messages appear and aggravate the user. It will be part of the supervisor's duty to provide each user with a list or description of the rights they have on the system or explain how they will access the system.

Document Everything

Network supervisors should keep a complete manual or log of everything done on the system. This is not only to avoid confusion in the future, but to provide a smooth transition path for future managers who may need to take over the system. Through logs, managers will be able to quickly locate resources on the network and determine the type of equipment used. Initially, planning logs will be useful when the system is being proposed and configured. Each personal computer that will become a workstation on the network should be documented. Log sheets should have information about users of the system, the installed hardware, and the software the system runs. User logs are important when defining the system security and how each user will access the system, and software logs are useful for planning a directory structure for the server.

A complete list of worksheets and logs is presented in Chapter 8, as well as in the back of the Novell documentation. If you haven't purchased NetWare yet, you can use the descriptions presented in Chapter 8 to develop your own worksheets. Alternatively, you can use the worksheet descriptions to build a computer database for your installation. This would

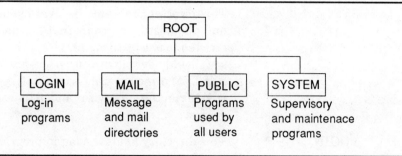

Figure 7-1.   Initial NetWare directories

be superior to a paper system, since the information can be indexed and searched. Reports can also be made easily from a computerized database.

Managing the NetWare File System

Once the NetWare server is installed and the system files have been copied to it as covered in Chapters 10 and 11, the network manager will be able to log in as the user SUPERVISOR. Initially, the system will not ask for a password, but the supervisor should establish one immediately, thus establishing the first line of security. From this point on, only the supervisor, logging on with the correct password, will have full access rights to the entire system, unless another user is made a security equivalent to the supervisor (however, this is not always recommended).

There are a number of tasks that need to be performed as soon as possible. These include creating directories, installing applications, and adding new users. These tasks will be covered in a moment.

Initially, NetWare creates the following directories on the main system volume. These are illustrated in Figure 7-1.

ROOT   The NetWare file system has a root directory
                            like DOS. All directories branch from the root.
                            Only the supervisors should ever have access
                            rights in the root directory.

SYSTEM

This directory contains NetWare supervisory and diagnostic programs that are usually restricted to use by the supervisor. The supervisor should never give other users access to the SYSTEM directory unless they will be authorized to run the supervisor and diagnostics programs.

LOGIN

This directory holds the log-in programs. It is the directory users are placed in when they switch to the server's hard drive after booting their workstations. The LOGIN directory also holds the boot files used by diskless workstations.

MAIL

The MAIL directory is used by the NetWare Electronic Mail System (an optional program) and other programs written by third-party developers. Each user will have a personal directory that branches from the MAIL directory that holds their personal log-in script as well as other files.

PUBLIC

The PUBLIC directory is the most important to users; it holds the menu programs and command utilities for NetWare. Network users will be given the ability to list and run the programs in this directory, but will not be able to write or delete files unless given rights to do so by the supervisor.

Other Directories

There will be other directories that need to be created by the supervisor. These will include personal directories for users and directories for programs and data. Figure 7-2 shows a typical directory structure for a NetWare system. Notice that directories for various types and versions of DOS branch from the PUBLIC directory. This allows workstations using different versions of DOS to locate DOS utilities and command files on the

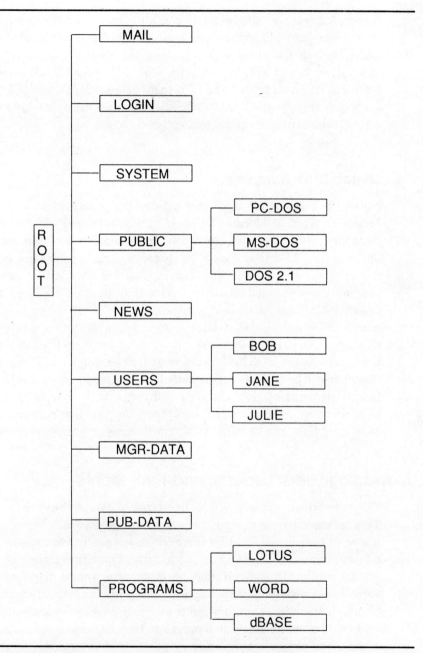

Figure 7-2.   Example of a NetWare directory structure

server. A directory called USERS contains "home" subdirectories for each user. Users can place their personal files in their personal directories, which are locked to other users. Also note the MGR-DATA and PUB-DATA directories. The PUB-DATA directory can be accessed by all users, but the MGR-DATA directory is locked out to all users except those that belong to a special group called MANAGERS. The supervisor assigns directory rights (called trustee rights) to users and groups.

Search-Drive Mappings

Notice in Figure 7-2 that applications programs such as Lotus and Microsoft Word are located in their own directories. When users access these programs, it should always be from another directory designed to hold the data files they create. In this way, data files are not mixed with the program files of the application. For example, users can run the programs while logged into their personal directories or while logged in to the PUB-DATA or MGR-DATA directories. NetWare uses a feature called *search-drive mapping* that allows programs to be run from other directories. A search drive specifies the location of program files to NetWare in the same way the DOS PATH command locates program files for DOS. The manager will be responsible not only for setting up search drives for users, but for giving users rights to work in directories. Unlike DOS, users must be given rights in any directory before any task, such as running a program or writing files, can be performed. These access rights are covered next.

Managing Users, Groups, and Their Rights

The network supervisor will be in charge of establishing each new user. This task involves assigning the new user a password, a log-in script, and a special user directory. Rights are then assigned to each user according to his or her need to access various programs and directories. These rights are determined by the system supervisor, department managers, and the security requirements of the system. As the network directory structure is planned, managers should begin to evaluate how each user will access the system. If users need to run a program, they should be given Read, Open, and Search rights in the directory where that program is located (these rights will be covered in detail shortly). If users need to have access to a data directory in which files are created and edited, they should be given the rights to create and write to files.

A "group" of users is a set of users that can be given access rights to a particular directory as a whole, making the supervisors task of assigning rights easier than doing so for each individual user. These users can share a particular directory or have access to various types of files. Messages can easily be sent to each member in a group by addressing the message to the group. A group might consist of several managers, or a group might consist of clerks. When a new member is added to a group, the rights in each directory assigned to the group are automatically given to that member.

As users are established on the network, special files called the *bindery files* keep track of information on users as well as the system resources. This information includes user names, user groups, passwords, server names, and the relations these have to each other. The bindery files are hidden files. Many third-party applications such as E-mail systems and group scheduling programs use the information in the bindery for their operation.

Establishing User Rights

Access to files and directories on the system is limited to users based on various security rights established by the system manager. These rights are directly related to the security features of NetWare. Security is important in a multiuser environment like a local area network to prevent users from destroying or corrupting important data files, and to allow users to maintain privacy or security with their own files and directories.

Note: Even if you feel that security is not an important issue with your installation, you will need to be familiar with the access rights of NetWare. By default, NetWare gives only the supervisor access to the entire system without restrictions. New users must be assigned access rights to directories as they are added to the system.

Security is managed on a NetWare system at four levels, as described in the following sections.

Log-in/Password Security   In order for a user to log in to the file server, the supervisor must first establish the user's account, which has a user name. The user may then be given a confidential password that must be typed every time he or she attempts to log in. Through the log-in/password security level, supervisors can establish various restrictions for users, such as a restriction to logging in on only one particular workstation, or to logging in before or after a set time. Users can also be prevented from logging on to another workstation simultaneously. One reason for this type of security is to prevent users from working on the network in areas where they are unsupervised.

Trustee Security   Users can be given the following *trustee rights* to work in a specific directory. Each user must be assigned these rights on an individual basis, unless the user is part of a group. Groups of users can be assigned the same rights as a whole. Supervisors can also use a shortcut method of assigning rights to users by giving them the same rights as another user, thus making them *security equivalent* to the other user.

Read right	Allows a trustee to see the contents of an existing, *open* file
Write right	Allows a trustee to change the contents of an existing, *open* file
Open right	Allows a trustee to open an existing file; note that trustees who wish to read or write a file must have this right
Create right	Allows trustees to create new files; the trustees can also create subdirectories if they have the Parental right
Delete right	Allows a trustee to delete a file; subdirectories can also be removed if the trustee has the Parental right
Parental	Allows trustees to create, rename, or delete subdirectories if they have the Create, Modify, and Delete rights; trustees with these rights can assign other trustees to the directories and assign restrictions

Search right

Allows trustees to list the files in a directory; without this right, the directory will appear empty when listed

Modify right

Allows trustees to modify the attributes of a file, such as its read or write status; trustees with this right can also rename directories and files.

Directory Security   Directory security is in some ways the opposite of trustee security, because it allows the supervisor to restrict one or more of the trustee rights in the directory so that no user can be assigned the right. For example, a supervisor may want to restrict the Parental right in a directory but give users the rights to do any of the other tasks just listed. When a supervisor limits a directory to specific rights, those rights are known as the *maximum rights* of the directory. A user's *effective rights* are a combination of his or her trustee rights and the maximum rights mask.

File/Directory Attributes   Individual files can be marked by the supervisor (or the owner, in some cases) of the file with the following attributes:

Execute Only

Prevents .EXE and .COM files from being copied, and can only be assigned by the supervisor; this option can also be used to prevent viruses from attacking executable files

Read-Only

Prevents a file from being modified

Read-Write

Users can read and modify files

Non-shareable

Only one user at a time can work with non-shareable files

Normal

Flags files as nonshareable and read-write

Hidden

Files do not appear in listings

Indexed	Indexes the FAT entry of large files to improve access from the hard drive
Modified	This attribute is set if the file has been modified since the last backup and is used in backup procedures to back up only files that have changed.
System	Files marked with the System attribute will not appear in listings
Transactional	Indicates that the file will be protected by the Transactional Tracking System of SFT NetWare.

With these rights in mind, supervisors should begin considering how they will establish the security and directory structure for the system. Remember that users will not be able to work in any directory or run programs from other directories until they are given the specific rights to do so. The task of assigning these rights to users is made much easier if users are placed in groups (MANAGERS, CLERKS, or TEMPS, for example). Part of the planning process is to determine the groups who will use the system, since it is easier to assign rights to groups.

Developing Work Groups

As mentioned, a group is a collection of users that have the same rights in specific directories. All users, including the supervisor, belong to a special group called EVERYONE. The EVERYONE group is automatically assigned Read, Open, and Search rights in the PUBLIC directory. Recall that PUBLIC contains NetWare menu utilities and command programs that users can access while logged in to the system. Since EVERYONE is a group that includes all users, it can be used to send messages to all users who are logged in. Every new user is also assigned to the MAIL directory, which is used to store messages sent by users if the Novell Electronic Mail package is installed.

In general, you should create groups when a specific set of users will share the same data or programs or have similar security needs. This is discussed in the next section. A group might consist of the staff of a particular department or a set of managers. A group might also be a set of clerks who have limited rights in a data directory, or a group of temporary clerks who should only have access to a database file they are updating. Planning groups ahead of time will help you determine how your system should be organized, because it helps you determine who will be using what applications and directories. Plan groups according to the task its users will be performing or the management level of users, thus determining the security access they should have to the system.

Planning for Applications and Data

When software applications are placed on the file server, the program files should be placed in a directory separate from the data files. In this way, users can be assigned rights to create and edit files in the data directory, and the program files can remain in a separate directory. Users are then given Open and Read rights to the program files so they can run the programs but not alter or delete them. Supervisors must establish the search drives to each of the program directories so users can access the programs from their data directories. Search-drive maps are usually established when the system first starts in the *system log-in script* or in the user's personal log-in script.

Supervisors and managers should design the directory structure for the software applications that will be used on the system and create log sheets that show how users will have access to those directories. Each software application should have a separate program directory and data directory with the following rights:

Program directory rights: Read, Open, Search
Data directory rights: Read, Write, Open, Create, Search, (Delete, in some cases)

It may not be wise to include the Delete right in some cases if inexperienced users have been known to accidentally delete important files. Instead, the supervisor or department manager should be placed in charge of deleting files. Some programs create temporary files that are deleted when the user is done with the program, thus the user will need the delete right.

In general, users will need to create files while logged into their personal directory, so they should be assigned all rights in that directory. They can then manage the files they create as they see fit. Users can also be allowed to create subdirectories in their personal directories. In this way, users can begin to create a file structure of their own on the server.

Preparing the Printers

When printers are attached to the network server, print jobs from workstations are placed in print queues before they begin printing. Since many different users may send print jobs to the printer, queues are used to help manage those jobs by stacking them in the order received to await printing. The order of the jobs in the queues can be rearranged, however, by the system manager or a user who has been given special print-queue operator status. Print jobs can also be completely removed from the queue if necessary.

Print queues and printer ports are normally established during the NetWare installation phase, which is covered in Chapter 10. Network managers may need to customize the printers at the server further by using several NetWare print utilities. These utilities are used if the default settings do not match the system requirements. For example, users can be assigned the use of one printer but not another. Forms such as those used for payroll checks or accounting can be set up and managed at the printer location. Users can request different forms, which are changed by the queue operators. When a form is changed, NetWare is informed of the form change so further print jobs not designed for the particular form are not printed.

Queues also allow print jobs to be routed to different printers if the primary printer is busy. In addition, some users can be given priority at a printer so their print jobs are automatically placed before those of other users. Some printers can be assigned more than one queue. In this way, low-priority jobs can be sent to a queue that is set up to send print jobs after hours.

Other Topics for Managers

The following topics are also of importance to network managers and supervisors who are planning or implementing a network.

Preparing for Emergencies

The system manager needs to develop contingency plans in case the network file server and other systems are damaged or cannot be used for some reason. Fires, electrical problems, downed equipment, sabotage, and many other things can bring a network down, along with the company that depends on it. The system manager should develop plans to keep the system up and running, to ensure adequate backup of data, and to ensure that adequate procedures for restoring a LAN to full operating condition are in place.

Part of these procedures should be assigned to another manager in case the system manager is not around. One or two additional people should know how to down the server to protect it during power fluctuations, earthquakes, fires, or other adverse conditions. Additional people should also know how to back the system up, and this should be done on a regular basis. Backup sets should go in fire-proof safes or be carried off-site (with proper security, of course). Procedures should also be written for restoring data to a system if that might ever be required. It's also a good idea to perform a trial system restoration, just to make sure that the procedure works and is understood by those using it. A backup and trial restoration should be performed as soon as possible before users start loading important data.

The system manager may want to establish an alternative backup method that can be used to bring a network back up if the primary server should fail. For example, a second file server can be added to the network with a file structure and user structure similar to the primary server. Backups can be made to this server from the primary during off hours. If the primary system should fail, the secondary server can be used. Data entered since the last backup may need to be reentered, but at least the network can be placed back in operation more quickly than if a wait is required while the primary server is repaired. Archive servers that maintain a constant backup may also be considered, but managers should have a plan for obtaining another server to restore data to it if the primary server goes down.

Many of these topics will be covered later in this chapter. System managers should be aware that they will play an extensive role in keeping the system up and running, as well as training users and assisting them when the need arises.

Network Management Tools

The larger a network is, the harder it is to manage. That seems obvious, but what isn't always obvious to some managers is that their network may be getting out of control "under the surface." Security may be lacking and potential problems may be lurking about, ready to spring forth at the most unfortunate time. Physical connections may also be failing, or the cables may be suffering from interference problems that cause data corruption. Other problems may be completely apparent: The system just doesn't work properly, but all the technicians and all the consultants can't get the system to work.

Network management tools can help. A whole range of software utilities and analyzing devices are now available to help any manager improve the performance of a network or isolate problems. Some LAN tools are only available by house-call from "LAN doctors"—technicians who arrive on-site to install expensive analyzing devices and locate the source of problems. Other tools can be purchased off the shelf.

Network management tools can be classified into several categories, as described in the following sections.

Network Performance Analyzers   The performance of a network can be monitored and analyzed to isolate problems or to locate bottlenecks with proper analysis tools. A good example is Sniffer, by Network General. This product monitors network traffic on the cables and can be used to inform management if a particular station is not responding because of a faulty interface card, cable, or workstation.

Network Monitoring   Networks can also be monitored to check their performance, which can sometimes be improved by making subtle changes to various settings. The NetWare FCONSOLE command can be used for this purpose.

Network Management Tools   Managers need software tools to help them manage users. These tools may provide convenient help menus to guide users through certain tasks, or may assist the manager in designing menu systems to fit the network environment.

Remote Workstation Management Tools   Often network managers will find themselves running around the installation site to assist users with simple requests or questions. Several available products allow a manager to log in to the user's workstation from his or her own workstation and operate the system as if sitting at the user's workstation. This can also be done through remote connections, which is extremely important when assisting users at locations on the other side of town or the other side of the country.

General Utilities   There are a number of utilities that improve overall network performance, assist users, or provide features not available with NetWare. For example, a package called SiteLock ensures that users do not use more copies of a software package than a site is licensed to use, which is important when you consider the fact that software companies are protecting their copyrights in court. Other utilities can be used to manage print spoolers or provide constant, on-line backup.

Hardware and Software Support

As networks grow, support for users and the hardware they operate becomes an increasingly important issue. Each new user may need to be trained in basic PC operations, as well as network usage. Deciding who will give this support is important on a large network. If the supervisor is left with the task of training new users or helping existing users, he or she will be drawn away from other network-related tasks, such as maintaining the efficiency of the network or the filing system.

Hardware support is also important. This support should be available as the network is being planned, during its installation, and after it is up and running. Hardware support should obviously come from the resellers or vendors of the products. These organizations should have a stable base of installed units and a competent staff of trained people. It's also helpful if they have a good stock of loaner equipment.

Authorized Dealer Support

Novell offers support for its products through a special network of dealers and distributors, as well as hot-line support numbers and bulletin board services. "Gold Authorized" dealers can often provide a high level of hardware support and, in some cases, user training. In turn, dealers rely on the authorized distributors they buy resellable Novell products from to provide them with additional assistance. Authorized distributors are required by Novell to maintain good response time to these dealers, so end users are not left hanging with uncorrected problems for long periods of time. This is especially true during the installation phase. Dealers and distributors often purchase special "support" packages from Novell that give them various call-back response times from 1 hour to 24 hours. To take advantage of these services, it is best to purchase from authorized dealers.

The same services can be purchased by end-users as well. For large installations, service contracts directly with Novell are often a must, at least through the initial installation and startup phase. Those with smaller installations may rely on their dealers. The Novell support lines maintain a complete database of known problems and bugs. This database is constantly updated as dealers and users call in with problems and as solutions are developed. In many cases, problem calls to Novell can provide immediate solutions. Although NetWare is generally bug-free, problems can occur when implementing third-party hardware and software.

User Training

The starting place for training most network users on the basics of NetWare will be the user training modules that come with the software. In some cases, however, this training may not be comprehensive enough to cover all of the features the users will need or tasks they must perform.

Network supervisors often find themselves involved in "random" support to users who have simple problems and hurdles to overcome. The supervisor may end up running around the office performing these missions while the network itself goes into disarray. User training is the key to eliminating these problems. Training can be drawn from outside the organization, but outside trainers may not always be familiar with the special needs of your organization.

Novell offers computer-based training (CBT) products that can be useful and productive in getting new users up and running on the system. Although NetWare comes with both user and supervisor training courses, other available CBT courses help train users and supervisors before the installation is in place.

Hardware Support

As networks grow in popularity, hardware components will become more widely available from a large number of vendors. Building networks from a wide assortment of these products can create hardware nightmares. In the early days of LANs, support usually came from one vendor because the whole of the network was purchased from that vendor. Novell NetWare, however, now supports a wide variety of products from other manufacturers, which encourages mix-and-match buying. For large networks, support during initial installation will be a necessity. After the installation, hardware support can often come from local dealers. Some large companies, however, have established their own in-house networking service and support facilities as an adjunct to the older information systems departments. These facilities may include a complete set of spare parts or backup systems to keep users and the network up and running, as well as a staff of trained personnel ready to help users.

The proper configuration of hardware can be determined before purchasing if you work with an experienced dealer organization or installer. These organizations may also have the tools needed to test networks after installation. Network analysis and performance monitoring equipment can be expensive, so you should look for a dealer or vendor that already has such equipment. As your network grows in size, you may need access to the equipment at some point.

Managing the Hardware

Networks have become increasingly diverse in the combination of equipment and interface boards that can be used. Internetworking increases the hodgepodge by allowing different types of LAN systems and topologies to become part of the same network. Managing these multivendor components in the network is not meant for the casual "only when needed" supervisor. The problem with maintaining any network is that it is usually in use by users. Bringing the network down may be either impractical or impossible. On the other hand, servicing the network while it is on line may also be impractical or impossible.

Fortunately, networks tend to be modular, unlike mainframe and minicomputer systems. One component can often be removed or temporarily replaced with a backup without bringing the entire system down. If a server does need to be downed, productive work can often continue at the workstations because many are fully operational, standalone PCs. Having a good service-support organization to fall back on is often the key. It will have backup equipment that can be borrowed until failing components are fixed or replaced.

As internetworking increases, the role of the network manager becomes more complex, and it becomes even more important to have one or more competent, well-trained managers or service assistants on hand. For example, bridges to other LANs over remote connections or gateways to minicomputer or mainframe systems may require a certain amount of continuous monitoring and maintenance. Emerging network trends involve the interfacing of more and more divergent hardware systems and operating systems, so the need for competent people will increase.

The network manager or service assistant must have the tools to keep the network running efficiently and to diagnose problems. These tools are beginning to become more widely available at a cost that is affordable to even those managing small systems.

Planning the System Security

Providing for the security of data on a file server is one of Novell NetWare's most important features. Not only can it be made difficult for a would-be snoop-to log in to the server, it can also be made difficult for those on the system to list files or look in other directories.

There are a number of reasons why network managers need to be concerned about the security of data on a network. Without file or directory locking, unknowing users could accidentally erase important files or cause other types of data corruption. Some files, such as the company payroll, should be locked so nosy employees can't view the contents. Some organizations need to be concerned about industrial spies. Fire is another concern that should be dealt with.

Another good reason to plan for proper security is the threat of computer viruses. A virus is a small program or piece of code written by a reckless programmer that corrupts data. It may be placed accidentally or intentionally on a disk filing system, where it begins to cause havoc. This can start immediately, or the virus may wait in the background ready to strike at a later time. Viruses are appropriately named; they can be as fierce and terrible as a living virus. They are sometimes located on disks obtained from bulletin boards. The danger of a virus is real. For example, a well-known software vendor recently shipped packages of its software with viruses on the disk sets, completely unknown to the vendor until it was too late.

Securing Data

Novell NetWare provides a set of tools for making your network installation more secure by using lockouts and assigning special privileges to each user. Security starts with the log-in procedure. Under NetWare, users can be assigned log-in names and passwords to control their access. The password can have certain characteristics. For example, as the supervisor you can force users to periodically change their password, or you can specify a minimum length for the password. Unique passwords can also be required in which the system will prevent users from using their last eight passwords.

Once a user is given access to the system, he or she will need a place to work. A special user directory can be created for each person with access to the system. Users can have complete access rights to their personal directory, including the right to create subdirectories branching from it. Beyond this point the supervisor has complete control over the directories and files the user has access to. A user might have access only to his or her personal directory, but at the same time be able to run programs stored in other directories. Each user's special directory is locked out to other users. Search drive mappings, similar to the DOS PATH command, are used to assign program usage to users.

The supervisor as well as department or personnel managers should work out a plan for how directories and files will be accessed by users. Part of this plan will establish where data files will be stored. Files that are sensitive can be placed in a secure directory, and public files can be placed in a directory that all users have access to.

Securing the Hardware

For security to be effective on the network, physical measures must be taken as well as software measures. The file server itself should be locked or placed in a secure cabinet or room. If the system is locked down or cannot be physically accessed, potential thieves cannot take the system or its hard drives. Systems equipped with a lock and key can be prevented from starting.

Security at the workstation is another matter. Users should log out as soon as they need to leave the system unattended. A potential snooper could simply walk up to a logged-in station and have access to the system with all the rights of the previous user. An industrial spy could walk up to such a system and download the company database to floppy disks.

Some amount of security can be obtained at the workstation level by using diskless workstations. Since these systems do not have floppy-disk or hard-disk drives, a user cannot download files to disk and carry them out of the building. Conversely, a user can't introduce viruses at the workstation without a disk drive to upload them. Diskless workstations are ideal for data entry and editing tasks where operators need to be limited to working with server-only files. It is also a good idea to place diskless workstations in high-traffic areas, or areas where supervisory personnel are not available to monitor the activity at the station.

The transmission of data on network cables is an area that can be potentially tapped by industrial spies. Cables can be physically tapped at locations unknown to the system manager. Signals travelling over the LAN cable can then be monitored and deciphered. More sophisticated equipment is even capable of monitoring and deciphering the signals your cabling system emanates to the environment. In the first case, detection of intruders is possible through special software that can sense abnormalities in the cable signal that might indicate a tap. Prevention of signal monitoring, the second case, can be achieved by using fiber optic cables or data encryption techniques.

Tracking User Activity

The NetWare accounting features can provide you with a log of user activity, including a user and intruder log for any workstation. The supervisor can establish various security restrictions that are based on expiration times, such as when a user's account expires or when a user's current session ends. For example, a session could be scheduled to end when the user normally leaves the building at the end of the day, just in case the user forgets to log off. Likewise, a session for a particular user can be scheduled to run only during certain parts of the day and only on a particular workstation. This ensures that the user can't come back into the building and attempt to log in from another station. A complete list of NetWare security features is presented in Chapter 3.

Securing Remote Connections

A remote connection is an off-site workstation, and the potential for intrusion is high. Thieves or vandals who break into your system from a remote connection are like invisible persons. Unless you can detect their presence through system monitoring, you may not know they are performing their devious acts. Intruders can sit in the comfort of their own homes or offices with little chance of being apprehended. However, there are steps you can take to protect your system.

NetWare provides log-in name and password security for its remote system software. To extend security further may require third-party packages. To prevent intruder break-ins from a remote site, a call-back system can be used. In this system, an authorized user calls the host system and then hangs up. The host then calls the user back at a predefined phone number, using the correct passwords.

To prevent the monitoring of signals that might emanate from cables or be broadcast during remote connections, data encryption techniques can be used. Using this method, data is encrypted before transmission. At the receiving end, a decrypting algorithm reconverts the file back to its readable state. Only authorized personnel will be given the decrypting algorithm.

Network Planning and Selection

Systems Planning Approach
Determining the Operating System Level
Identifying LAN Needs
Developing Logs and Worksheets

This chapter will help system designers and managers plan a network and purchase the components needed to begin the initial setup and installation. One thing to realize about planning and installing a LAN is that there will probably never be a final, set-in-concrete design. PC and LAN technologies are constantly changing and expanding, and at the same time, users and managers will request modifications to the plans. But a plan is still needed, and it should be developed in the most professional and responsible way, no matter what the size of the LAN.

There is an old saying in the computer industry that the right software should be found (or planned) before looking at hardware. This is especially true with personal computers, since users tend to order the most powerful equipment or the latest technology as if buying a home stereo system. Then they find that too much of the budget has been spent on sophisticated equipment and not enough on the applications or the support required to run them. It's best to get a good idea of exactly why an organization needs a LAN or the features it will provide before proceeding. It's also a good idea to make sure that everybody gives input on exactly what the LAN should provide. A LAN battleground can develop when users and managers don't see eye to eye on these requirements.

Systems Planning Approach

A certain methodology should be followed when planning, selecting, and installing computer equipment, designing programs, or establishing procedures. According to the American National Standards Committee, a *system,* in the data processing sense, is "a collection of men, machines, and methods organized to accomplish a set of specific functions." The function of a systems analyst, then, is to coordinate the activities required to develop a successful system or a plan for a system. Coordination requires planning. That is part of what this chapter is about.

To begin planning a network, an organization may want to hire a professional from outside the organization who is experienced not only with network hardware, but in the methods and procedures required to establish a network system. This systems analyst or consultant should be able to work among the users, the data processing people who will be running the system, and management. Users are familiar with their requirements and what they want the system to do. The in-house data processing staff may be familiar with computers but not with the needs of the users. Management must work with budgets and ensure that company requirements are met; they are interested in costs and benefits, return on investment, and development schedules. The systems analyst can help bridge the gap between these groups as an unbiased mediator.

Part of any network system will include technical specifications, such as the type of interface card to be used, server hardware requirements, and so on. At the user end, multiuser software programs will require new procedures, new personnel, and user training. The systems analysts can work with those familiar with specific aspects of the system and develop an overall system plan based on the information gathered.

The systems analyst must be able to translate the new system plan into one that management will accept. A classic methodology used by systems analysts to develop the overall system plan and complete the installation is described in the following steps.

Defining Current Problems

It sounds simple, but "problem" in the context used here should be defined. In most cases, individual users know a problem exists because they don't have enough storage or printing power. Managers know a problem exists because their staff is not productive enough. Data processing people realize that the system is not secure or that proper backups are not being made. The trick is to develop a problem definition that encompasses all of these. In doing so, everyone concerned will begin to develop an idea of what is needed, and the systems analyst will begin to understand more about how the organization operates. The familiar question "If I don't know what the problem is, how can I help?" really applies here. The systems analyst's job is to make sure that everyone agrees on exactly what needs to be resolved.

Feasibility Study

This stage is concerned with developing a feasible solution to the problem at hand. The systems analyst, along with other competent people such as the data processing staff and the managers of departments, begins to formulate ideas about how to solve the problems. Possible solutions are presented to users and management, along with estimated costs and other important facts, such as growth potential. It may be necessary to perform several studies and presentations until a suitable plan is developed. At this point, management will give the go-ahead to continue with the next phase or will stop the project altogether.

It is during this stage that the people working on the project may decide to develop a request for proposals (RFP). An RFP is essentially a request asking potential vendors or resellers to develop a solution to the problem with the hopes that they will be awarded the final purchase orders for hardware, service, or support. An RFP can be very specific, or it can describe the needs of the company in broad terms. Specific items might include a particular brand or model of server or a specific topology.

In some cases, a network system may not even be necessary. Instead, it may become clear that the processing power of individual PCs needs to be boosted, or that additional staff may be required to handle existing procedures. Companies tend to throw expensive hardware at problems without fully developing proper solutions. If a non-LAN solution comes out of the feasibility study, then the company has saved money on expensive hardware. You can pass this book on to someone else!

Analysis and Design

Systems analysis and design may be performed by the systems analyst or an outside vendor, depending on who is following through with the project after the previous phase. The in-house systems analyst continues with the project if he or she has been given the go-ahead by management, which has decided to commit funds for this stage. Specific types of equipment are brought into the plan and conferences are held to make sure the equipment will fit the needs of users, the data processing department, and management. Resource worksheets are developed to show the current system, and planning worksheets are developed to describe the new components. The types of systems and their specifications are defined, but not such things as the vendors or part numbers. This stage closes when all those involved decide that the solution is sufficient.

Detailed Design

The worksheets from the previous steps are used to begin collecting technical details and specifications for the systems. In this stage, all components, including connectors, drivers, software upgrades, and other "hidden" costs, are defined. The vendors are identified along with part numbers if possible. This stage provides information for purchasing, and it may involve a complete cost/benefits analysis so that management can decide on continuation of the project.

Acquisition

The purchasing department may begin to write a purchase order. More than likely, however, they will send out invitations to bid on the required equipment and for services such as installation and training if they have not already brought vendors into the project.

Installation

During this step, the system is installed and tested.

Maintenance

Maintenance involves ongoing monitoring of the system to ensure that components are running properly and efficiently. Maintenance logs are kept on all systems requiring service, new users are trained on the system, and improvements to the system may be made.

Documentation

Documentation is important through each stage. Not only will management want to know what the systems analyst is doing, it will also be concerned with why particular solutions have been chosen. Each stage should have an "exit criteria." For example, the problem definition phase ends when all involved have stated the problems they perceive and when all agree on the definition of the problems. The problems should be written down, but need not be more than one page in length.

The feasibility study is concerned with the cost of the system and whether it is even possible to develop a solution. Requests for proposals may be sent to vendors and resellers, who may then provide information for the next two stages. The analysis and design stage is the "blueprint" stage. Thorough drawings of the proposed systems, as well as worksheets defining existing systems, are the final product of this stage. A description of worksheets used in this stage is provided later in this chapter. The detailed design stage is then interested in specific parts and their numbers, pricing, and other factors. A cost benefits report may be given to management, and if the system is approved, detailed lists are given to purchasing.

From that point on, installation and maintenance of the system can proceed as components and parts are shipped, the system is fully tested, software is installed, and users are trained. The remainder of this book covers installation and post-installation activities for Novell NetWare and will provide useful information to systems analysts or others in the process of planning and designing a network system.

Determining the Operating System Level

As Chapter 3 described, Novell NetWare comes in several different levels designed to fit a wide range of environments. The Entry Level System series is designed for four users (Level 1) or eight users (Level II) and should be used in small offices or where budgets are limited. Advanced NetWare and SFT NetWare are designed for larger systems of up to 100 users. NetWare 386 is designed for advanced installations that require up to 250 users and high-speed processing, as well as growth to other operating system platforms.

The following should be considered when choosing the operating system level of NetWare:

- The number of workstations and the number of users who will operate those workstations

- Communications requirements

- Bridging to existing LANs

- Gateways to minicomputers or mainframes

- Requirements for the NetWare accounting feature

- Requirements for system reliability features such as disk mirroring and duplexing (SFT NetWare only)

- Large database usage that can take advantage of the Transaction Tracking System (SFT NetWare only)

- Future growth

Identifying LAN Needs

There are a number of reasons why a network system may be considered as a solution to a particular computing problem. In many cases, a network is a far better solution than a minicomputer or mainframe system, but in order to determine this, it is necessary to go through the steps of a systems analyst, as described earlier.

The following problems or problem-related solutions may have already been identified by users, managers, or data processing personnel:

- Insufficient storage capacity

- A multiuser software program is required

- Centralized backup of data is needed

- Sharing peripherals such as high-quality printers is needed

- Users need to communicate with electronic mail

- Departmental managers need to manage workgroups

As mentioned earlier, anyone trying to identify the LAN needs for an organization will need to know what the current problems are, as well as the current equipment being used. Identifying what needs to be done on a LAN or computerized system is also important and falls into the problem category if users can't do what they need to do with the existing system. The following is a brief outline that can be used to assess the current environment and determine problems and solutions.

Identify the Existing Equipment

Using the worksheets provided at the end of this chapter, write down any information known about the current in-house systems, such as the types of PCs and their storage devices, backup systems, printers, plotters, and communications equipment.

Map the Potential LAN Environment

Draw a map of the complete installation site, including the location of the systems and peripheral devices defined in the previous step. Since cable will need to be installed to connect all of these devices, take note of the best locations for the cables, along with wiring closets, existing cables, pre-drilled wall holes, and any other feature that might be of importance.

In some cases, drilling holes may be prohibited or not practical. For example, asbestos ceilings may present a potential health threat to employees if drilled or opened. Measure the distances between potential workstations so cable cost can be estimated. Be sure to include floor to

ceiling distances, if necesary. Determine the location of future workstations as well as the location of the nearest cable these stations can tap
into.

Evaluate Current Usage

Software on a network is as important as the hardware required to run it.
The current applications used by an organization should be determined.
Network versions of these packages will be required, or suitable alterna-
tives may need to be evaluated. The total number of potential users should
also be evaluated. This may be higher than the number of workstations
and could make a difference as to the size of the server's hard drive.
Multiple departments within a company may point to the need for elaborate filing structures and multiple software packages. This should be noted
so the system manager and department managers can begin to develop
directory structures, security, and access rights as discussed in the previous chapter.

Evaluate the Applications Requirements

One of the main reasons for installing a LAN is that management or
accounting has selected a multiuser applications program designed specifically for LAN use. Software purchased for LANs should be either "LAN-
aware" or designed specifically for LAN usage. Multiuser licenses should
also be available so several users can access the program simultaneously.
Often, a single-user version is purchased and then additional licenses are
added. LAN-specific software may monitor usage and prevent access when
the maximum number of licensed users have started the program, so it is
important to purchase the proper number of these licenses.

Keep in mind that some programs are "LAN ignorant." Although they
can still be stored on the LAN server and even used by several people, there
is a strong possibility that a file just edited by one person could be copied
over by another user as if that user saves changes. LAN-aware programs
keep track of how data files are being used and by whom, thus preventing
data from being corrupted.

As LANs become more popular, software developers are more moti-
vated to increase the quality and power of their LAN-based software.

Applications are now being developed that allow processing to take place in several machines at one time. Advanced CAD or modeling packages of the future may distribute their intensive processing out to several high-powered PCs to reduce the total processing time. For example, an engineer trying to simulate air flow around an aircraft might distribute chunks of the processing to workstations or to a dedicated processing machine like an 80486 system or a minicomputer. The whole process would be monitored and managed by a main program in the engineer's workstation or at the server.

A database program that uses a dedicated database server is another example of software that might be designed specifically for LANs. A user at a workstation can make requests to the database server, which then performs the processing with its own processor and memory, possibly much faster than the user's workstation is capable of processing. This allows the user to make use of the local workstation in other ways and still monitor the progress of the database server.

When selecting LAN-based programs, check the level of their "LAN awareness," or make sure the software designers plan to implement LAN support in the future. Also be aware of software licensing. You may need to purchase several versions of the software or simply an add-on LAN version.

Evaluate the Performance Needs

Network performance will be determined by the number and types of users on the system. Take a close look at what each user will be doing. The types of network interface cards and cabling system will play an important part in the speed of a system that has the potential for speed degradation. A high-speed server and workstation may also be essential. If bridges and gateways will be needed, the potential slowdown introduced by these devices should be a consideration. For example, it is not recommended that remote bridges or gateways be placed in the server. Instead, they should be placed in PC's dedicated for communications.

A bottleneck is a place or condition in the network environment that slows the entire network. The speed of a network is referred to as its *throughput,* which is the product of several different factors, including the cabling system, the performance of the server, and the performance of the workstation. However, if the system has a bottleneck, the throughput of the entire network could be affected. It is helpful to identify potential bottlenecks ahead of time and resolve them.

If a workstation appears to be running slower than it should on the network, but other workstations are running up to speed, then the problems are in the workstation and it may be necessary to replace it. Bottlenecks that can slow the entire system occur when large numbers of users are on the LAN at the same time and the cabling system, network interface cards, or server is not capable of handling the load. On the other hand, few users may be logged on the system, but a bottleneck can occur because one user is intensively using the server and, in the process, the cabling system (for example, if large data files were being uploaded by a CAD system). Large database applications can also slow a server. Such installations should use the highest-performance hardware.

If heavy throughput loads are anticipated, several solutions are possible:

- Increase the server memory, which increases the size of the cache and improves disk access.

- Upgrade the server hard drive to achieve better performance.

- Use a fast 80386 or 80486 system as a server.

- Use NICs with 16-bit interfaces.

- Use NICs with on-board data packet buffers.

- Use 10MB per second Ethernet cards and cable or 16MB Token Ring boards and cable.

- Consider fiber-optic cable with high throughput speeds.

- If the LAN is large, split it in two by using an internal server bridge.

- Add a second file server to distribute the file-server load.

The NetWare operating system uses extensive memory resources to increase its operating speed. Memory is used for cache buffers, communications buffers, directory caching, and various other tasks. It is recommended that 2MB of memory or more be installed in any server system to provide maximum performance.

Choosing Dedicated or Nondedicated Mode

You'll need to decide whether your server will act as a dedicated or nondedicated file server. Remember that a dedicated server operates more efficiently but cannot be used as a normal workstation. Nondedicated servers can be used for non-network tasks, but the network operating system will run slower while performing workstation tasks. SFT NetWare can only be run in dedicated mode, whereas ELS NetWare Level II and Advanced NetWare can be run in either mode. Keep in mind that a network may go down if the workstation side of a nondedicated server is running a DOS program that locks up (this is reason enough to dedicate any server).

The memory requirements for NetWare servers differ according to the NetWare version, whether you are running in dedicated or non-dedicated mode, and whether you plan to install Apple Macintosh compatibility. As a general rule, a server should always have 2MB of memory. If Macintosh support is being added, install an additional 1MB.

Evaluate Disk Storage Needs

A major factor that contributes to the overall speed of a network is the server hard drive. Coincidentally, the larger a hard drive is, the faster it will transfer data, due to the configuration of the internal components (number of disk platters and read/write heads). This makes the decision to buy large drives even more practical. In addition, Novell NetWare uses hard-disk storage much more efficiently than DOS, so an increase in the speed of a server hard drive will be realized when switching from a DOS environment to NetWare. In fact, some workstations can access a NetWare server's hard drive faster than their own.

Data storage requirements can be determined by the number of applications currently used by an organization and the number planned for future use. The disk storage required by these applications should be determined, as well as the size of the data files created with them. The number of data files will depend on the number of users, of course. Users may also place various programs, utilities, or data files in their personal directories, so this should also be accounted for. Once the total disk-usage space is determined, simply double or triple it to get an idea of future requirements.

Backup Systems

A backup system for the LAN server is extremely important and at the same time convenient because network data can be backed up at one location. There are a number of ways to back up the system, including tape backup systems, compact disk read/write systems, removable hard-disk systems, and even floppy-disk systems. Keep in mind that tape backup on Novell NetWare is not supported at the server on dedicated systems. At one time, this was supported by Novell tape drives, but the drives are no longer available.

A third-party tape backup system can be conveniently mounted in a workstation and used to back up the server during off-hours. Many tape backup systems come with software that can be set to perform a backup at a specified time. Tape backup systems are convenient because they provide a hands-off backup method—once the tape is installed and the software is running, an entire volume can usually be backed up to a single tape. Most tape software is capable of backing up only modified files or files with specific dates. A good tape system should also allow selective file restores.

Removable hard-disk systems can be installed in workstations and used as local hard drives when they aren't used to back up the system. This type of system offers several advantages over tape backup systems. Disks use random-access retrieval methods, so obtaining a single file from an archive is as simple as using any hard-drive system. Disks also have a speed advantage over tapes in retrieving a file, since tapes must be searched sequentially.

Selecting the Network Hardware

The type of network interface cards, the cabling, the protocols used on the network, and the topology all combine to make up the network hardware. Be aware of your cabling options so you can choose the best for your installation. The availability of qualified installers may be an important factor in deciding the type of cable you want to use. Ethernet cabling systems are easy to install but may be hard to debug. Token Ring is reliable and efficient but may be expensive. ARCNET is slower than Ethernet and Token ring but has many advantages, such as easy installation and expansion, plus flexibility.

Diskless Workstation Consideration

Diskless workstations are inexpensive computers that do not have either floppy drives or hard drives. They may be selected for price and for security. Since a local disk drive is not available, users of such a workstation are unable to download files from the servers. This adds to the security of the system.

Make sure the station has at least 512KB of memory and that the network interface card has a remote reset PROM available. These PROMs are usually available for less than $50. The PROM allows the workstation to boot from a boot file located in the SYS:LOGIN directory of the server. This file is created with the NetWare utility DOSGEN.

Printers

Up to five printers can be attached to the server under normal conditions. Three of these printers can be attached to parallel ports and two can be attached to serial ports, assuming the following:

- You may need to install extra ports inside the server.

- Parallel ports are referred to as LPT1, LPT2, and LPT3. Serial ports are referred to as COM1 and COM2. Note that IBM PS/2 systems allow additional comports.

- Adding additional ports may cause hardware conflicts that will require the custom NETGEN/ELSGEN installation method discussed in Appendix A.

- The maximum recommended distance a parallel printer can be placed from the server is about 12 feet.

- Serial connections allow extended cable distances from the server, which means that the printer can be placed away from the server or in an area that is more convenient to employees. This is a consideration if the server is locked in a room for security reasons.

- A printer attached to a serial port must have a serial interface connector. Some printers come with both parallel and serial connectors. If so, a switch inside the machine may need to be changed to select one or the other. If the printer doesn't have a serial port, make sure in advance that one can be installed.

- Serial ports may have 9-pin connectors or 25-pin connectors, so make sure to order cables that properly match the type of connections your system server has.

Cabling

A full understanding of the cable installation is important. The managers and installers should be familiar with the way the cable is assembled and connected to the various components, such as repeaters, hubs, and access units. A detailed map of the cable runs, including the location of all accessory components, should be drawn. Planning for growth is also important. Mark the locations where future stations might be added. If existing telephone twisted-pair wire is being used, it may be necessary to contact the phone company or the owner of the cable before using it.

Cable can be purchased in bulk from many different suppliers; 1000-foot rolls are common. Make sure the cable is the exact type required by the network interface cards and topology you have chosen. Be sure to purchase the connectors to fit on the ends of the cables if you are building your own. Special mounting tools may also be required. The cable supplier should be able to furnish installation and handling information. Cable can also be ordered in preassembled lengths from various suppliers if you have a good idea of the distances between workstations. Some cable can be "tapped" after it is strung through the building, which eliminates the need to estimate cable lengths between workstations.

If you are building your own cables, make sure to purchase the proper tools for mounting the cable connectors to the ends of the cables. Special crimping tools can be purchased from most cable suppliers or electronic stores. Instructions for using these tools should be followed so as not to damage the connector or cable. If necessary, order wall plates and other mounting brackets.

There are certain state and local codes that govern the type of cable that can be used in buildings. Cable that produces toxic gas when burned may be prohibited, or fire-retardant cable may be required. The code may also specify that cable be run through protective metal conduit. Plenum cable is fire retardant to some extent and may be used in place of cable requiring conduit protection, but its cost is higher than normal cable. The cost is usually less expensive than installing conduit.

System Protection Equipment

Don't forget to plan for the purchase of system protection equipment like uninterruptable power supplies, surge suppressors, line filters, and other equipment. Consider that workstations may need uninterruptable power as much as the server so users can continue working, at least long enough to save their files and exit from the network in a graceful way. The amount of time these units will run the system under backup power is an important consideration. A monitoring board will also be required in the server so it can determine from the UPS when the power has gone down or if the UPS is supplying power. Don't forget to order the cable that connects the UPS to the monitoring board.

Choosing the Right Vendor

As mentioned in Chapter 7, the vendor or reseller you choose to purchase products from should be reputable and should have experience with a number of similar installations. It helps if they also have loaner equipment, as well as expensive and sophisticated cable testing equipment. Price is also a factor, but be aware that resellers that give the best price probably can't afford to back up their service. You may want to purchase software and hardware from one organization and purchase installation, service, and support from another.

Developing Logs and Worksheets

This section describes various worksheets and logs that can be created while planning, installing, and maintaining a network. Keep in mind that the categories listed for the worksheets can just as well be used in an electronic database program to track your system. A database offers indexing, searching, and reporting advantages over a paper system.

Initial Planning Worksheets

Worksheets should be used during the initial planning stage of a network to collect information about existing equipment and the needs of users and management. The following worksheets are recommended.

Existing Equipment, Master Log

This log sheet is used to produce a master list for all equipment at the installation site. It cross-references to the workstation log, described next. List the following items, using one line for each existing system.

System number (to be assigned as required)

System (Brand name or other identifier)

Department

Location

User or users (optional)

System configuration information

Workstation Log

Fill out a workstation log for each existing system at the installation site and for each new system that will be added to the network.

System number (to be assigned as required)

System (brand name or other identifier)

Department

    Department manager

Location

User or users

Date installed

Primary vendor

System resources

> Floppy drives and hard drives
>
> > Software on hard drive
> >
> > Current backup procedures
>
> Monitor Type
>
> Printers
>
> Memory
>
> Communications adapters

Service information

> Service suppliers
>
> Previous repair log (if available)

Needs Assessment Worksheet

A needs assessment worksheet may be necessary for each user or potential user of the system. Alternatively, a single sheet may suffice as a master worksheet for each workstation. A needs assessment worksheet should also be worked out for each server. The assessment sheets should list the following items:

> Existing software used
>
> Required software
>
> Server storage requirements
>
> > Usage for programs
> >
> > Usage for data

Printing requirements

    Printer type or quality

    Forms

Network load estimates

Communication options

Other

NetWare Workstation Configuration Log

The workstation configuration sheet should be filled out and attached to the back of each workstation log. Note that the information required for this worksheet will be covered in Chapter 9.

Network information

    Name of file server

    LAN connected to: A,B,C, or D

    Network station address at file server

Network interface card installed

    Brand and model

    Option number

    Interrupt line used (IRQ)

    I/O base address

    DMA line

    RAM/ROM addresses

Additional resource sets

    Option number

    Interrupt line used (IRQ)

> I/O base address
>
> DMA line
>
> RAM/ROM addresses
>
> Information for remote workstations only
>
> > Network address
> >
> > Remote boot file name

LAN Workstation Log

The following worksheet is used to gather information for each of the LAN boards in the server (bridges). Fill out a complete log for each LAN (A,B,C, and D) using one line for each workstation or remote workstation from the following information:

> Workstation ID
>
> Type of computer
>
> DOS version
>
> LAN interface board
>
> Station (node) address
>
> > Decimal
> >
> > Hex
>
> Remote reset boot information

NetWare File-Server Configuration Worksheet

This worksheet should be filled out for the server. A workstation log can be used to gather additional hardware information about the server. The two can be attached together. Information for this worksheet will be covered in Chapter 9.

File-server name

System supervisor

NetWare operating system (ELS, Advanced, SFT)

   Version number

   Location of disks and manuals

File-server type

Memory

Disk drives

Hard disk information (fill out for each drive)

   Drive name

   Storage capacity

   Channel

   Controller

      Type

   Drive

   Hot Fix size (SFT NetWare only)

   Mirroring information (SFT NetWare only)

   Volume information (fill out for each volume)

      Volume name

      Size

      Number of directory entries

      Directory cached?

The following information should be collected for each LAN interface board in the system (LAN A,B,C, or D), each hard-disk channel (0 through 4), "other" drivers, and resource sets:

Option numbers

Interrupt lines (IRQ)

I/O base address

DMA line

RAM/ROM addresses

Installation Parameters

The information on the following worksheet should be collected and used during the NetWare installation phase.

LAN interface board addresses

Configuration parameters

Number of open files

Number of index files

Transaction backout volume

Number of transactions

Limit disk space (yes/no)

Number of bindery objects

UPS information

I/O address

Down time (minutes)

Wait time (minutes)

Battery low input setting (open/closed)

Battery on-line input setting (open/closed)

Network printer information

List type of printer

Connection method (serial/parallel)

Serial settings

(Baud rate, word size, stop bits, parity, Xon/Xoff)

Directory Structure Worksheet

The directory structure worksheet should be a map that shows all the directories and subdirectories of the system. Be sure to include the directories NetWare creates, which are SYSTEM, LOGIN, PUBLIC, and MAIL on the SYS drive. Also don't forget to add the directories for other volumes.

Trustee Security Worksheet

The trustee security worksheet is used to log the users and the users' rights in each directory. The worksheet is best if drawn as a matrix. Down the left side, list each directory on the system. Along the top, list each user or user group. In the corresponding boxes, list the security rights each user or user group has in the directory. Recall that these rights are Read, Write, Open, Create, Delete, Parental, Search, and Modify.

Resource List

The resource list is simply a log of user expertise that can be referred to by another user or the system supervisor when special assistance is required in a particular software package or procedure. List each user and the nature of the expertise he or she is willing to share.

Network Problems Log

Everything that happens on the network should be logged. The workstation logs have a place for problems occurring at the workstation, but if problems occur on the LAN they should be recorded in the network problems log.

Preparing to Install NetWare

Documenting the Installation
Site Preparation
Preparing to Configure and Install NetWare
Post-Installation Procedures

This chapter is designed to help you understand the steps involved in the installation of the NetWare operating system. The complete installation process could take some time, so don't plan on doing it in an afternoon. In fact, large wide-area network installations may take weeks to complete because hardware compatibility problems may arise or unexpected changes may need to be made. Cabling the network may take some time, and you may need to change or rearrange people and procedures. Smaller LANs located within a single building are usually easier to install and may take from one to three days to complete. In some cases a network can be installed in an afternoon if all goes well, so the best policy is to plan ahead.

Note: The network generation program for ELS NetWare Level II is called ELSGEN. The network generation program for Advanced NetWare and SFT NetWare is called NETGEN. These will be collectively referred to as NETGEN/ELSGEN in this and future chapters.

Once you have acquired the hardware and software you need for your network, you can begin the installation process. Novell recommends the following procedures in its installation manuals.

1. Acquire the equipment you will use in the installation. Have all the manuals ready so information about switch settings and other specifications can be easily accessed. The cable can be installed ahead of the NetWare configuration.

2. Generate the startup files for the workstations using the SHGEN (SHell GENeration) program.

3. Configure the network operating system using the NETGEN (NETwork GENeration) configuration program for Advanced Net-Ware and SFT NetWare or ELSGEN (ELS GENeration) program for ELS NetWare Level II.

4. Install the network interface boards and other equipment that requires special switch settings. NetWare will recommend the correct settings for the boards in some cases.

5. Install NetWare on the file server using the NETGEN/ELSGEN installation options.

6. Boot the file server.

7. Prepare and start the workstations.

Notice that the hardware installation specified in the fourth step should be completed after the software shells and operating system have been configured. There is a very good reason for this: The configuration programs help you locate conflicts with network interface cards and other hardware components before you tighten them down inside the systems. By locating these conflicts, you can make dip switch adjustments to the boards before installing them. Also notice that the NETGEN/ELSGEN programs are run in two phases. The first phase will be referred to as *configuration*, and the second phase will be referred to as *installation*.

You will learn more about the NETGEN/ELSGEN programs later in this chapter. Before proceeding, there are a few things you should do, as covered in the next section.

Documenting the Installation

One of the most important things to do as you begin to prepare your network is to keep a log of everything you have done. You should have already prepared various log sheets, as discussed in the last chapter, and should have a map of what your system will look like. Each workstation should have a separate log that describes its hardware components, location, type of interface card, and any other special configurations. Each station also should be assigned a physical location name or number so you can easily refer to it in the future. After installation, the NetWare operating system will give each workstation an address that can be used by the system manager for various activities.

Draw in the location of various network cabling components, like repeaters, multiple access units, and passive or active hubs. Do not forget to log the points where future expansions of the network might be possible.

Site Preparation

An installation as involved as a network is sure to disrupt the normal everyday environment of the installation site. Make sure that everyone concerned is familiar with what is happening. A schedule of installation activities can help workers and managers work with your schedule or make changes to it. It doesn't make much sense to perform an installation when the company is trying to get its payroll out, especially if you need to open machines to install cards and other components.

Preparing the Server

The file server you decide to use with ELS NetWare Level II, Advanced NetWare, and SFT NetWare must be an 80286 IBM-AT compatible computer or an 80386 system. Microchannel systems like the IBM Personal

System/2 computers are also supported. Be sure to install the video cards and other equipment necessary for the operation of the system and to back up any existing data. The installation of the NICs (network interface cards) can wait until after the NetWare operating system has been configured (as discussed in later chapters), unless you are sure that the switch settings on the boards will not conflict with other settings in the machine. If you are setting up an IBM Personal System/2 file server, you can install the interface boards if you run the SETUP program.

Note: Before closing the system cover, read the next section, "Hard-Disk Considerations".

Most AT-class systems and IBM PS/2 systems have a SETUP program used to set various features, such as the internal clock, memory size, drive types, and other specifications. You should locate this program and run it before going further. On some systems, you hold down a key while booting the system. On others, you press ALT-ESC. If an IBM PS/2 is being used as a server, the program is located on the IBM Reference disk. Cards installed in PS/2 machines will automatically avoid hardware conflicts, so you should install the cards and run the program before proceeding with the NetWare installation. Be sure to observe the following on IBM PS/2 systems:

- Novell recommends that you do *not* set a power-on password using the Set Features option of the IBM PS/2 reference disk.

- Do *not* choose "Set network server mode."

- Do *not* change the arbitration level of the MFM or ESDI fixed-disk driver from the factory default setting.

Hard-Disk Considerations

For the most part, ELS NetWare Level II supports the hard-drive controller in most AT-class and 80386 systems, as well as IBM PS/2 MFM or ESDI controllers. No other boards are supported. IBM and Western Digital controller boards are used in AT-class machines. Storage capacities of up to 255MB per volume are allowed. Drives exceeding the amount must be divided into two or more volumes with a maximum of 32 volumes. You will be given a chance during installation to divide large hard-drive systems into separate volumes. It may be necessary to prepare hard drives using the methods described next.

Running Disk-Surface Analysis

The NetWare COMPSURF (COMPrehensive SURFace analysis) program is designed to fully test and format your hard drives and will be covered in detail in Chapter 10. It can be run before performing the installation phase of NETGEN/ELSGEN, unless you are installing Novell hard drives or are upgrading from a previous version of NetWare. Novell hard drives are already tested extensively at the factory.

You should do the following before running the COMPSURF program:

- Find the bad blocks list. Most hard drive or systems manufacturers supply a list of bad blocks found during preshipment testing. This list is sometimes taped to the top of the hard drive or may be in the shipping carton. Be sure to write down the head number and cylinder numbers of any bad blocks while you have the server cover removed. Don't be too concerned if a list is not available; COMPSURF performs an extensive test itself and will map bad blocks on its own.

- It's a good idea to have a parallel printer attached to the system being tested so you can print the bad block list.

- Identify the drives. Use the SETUP utility supplied with your computer to identify your internal hard drives. Instructions for running SETUP should be included with your system.

- Know the *interleave* value. A correct interleave value helps the server's microprocessor and hard drive run more efficiently together by allowing data transfers to and from memory to keep pace with the rotating disk of the hard drive. Data is stored in block-sized chunks on sectors (pie-shaped wedges) of hard drives. As a block of data is read, a slight delay occurs as it is transferred into system memory. During this delay, the disk continues to rotate, and the next block may rotate out of range before it can be read. Interleave specifies that data is read or written from every other block (skips over blocks) to compensate for the spinning disk. If data transfer is fast, as it is on IBM PS/2 microchannel bus systems, sectors can be read sequentially, making an interleave value of 1 (no skips) possible. Novell servers and most IBM AT-type systems use an interleave value of 2. IBM PS/2 systems with internal drives should be set to an interleave value of 1. If you are not sure, check with the manufacturer in advance.

Workstation Considerations

A workstation can be any computer that can boot on its own from a floppy drive or a hard drive. A workstation can also be a diskless workstation with a remote reset PROM installed on the network interface card. Before a workstation can be connected to the network, it must first load DOS. Diskless workstations use the server hard drive as their boot drive, so the version of DOS required at the workstation will need to be copied to a subdirectory on the drive for use by the workstation during its network session.

The SHGEN program is used to prepare the files needed to connect a workstation to the network. If every workstation uses the same network interface board and is similar in configuration, you only need to run SHGEN once. If you are using several different brands of interface boards or must change the switch settings to avoid hardware conflicts in any machine, a separate run of SHGEN is required. In addition, if you are not using the same version of DOS on every machine, you should prepare a boot disk for each system that has a different DOS version. In general, have the following prepared in advance:

- A boot disk for each version of DOS

- A master shell disk to hold the startup files for each different type of interface card used

If a workstation boots from a hard drive, you do not need to create the DOS boot disks. You still need to run SHGEN to create the interface card drivers, however, and then copy the drivers to the root directory of the hard drive in each system, so a floppy disk will be required to copy the driver from the generating system to the hard drive of the workstation.

If you are preparing a diskless workstation, you still need to create a boot disk, and this must be done on a system that has a floppy drive. Start this floppy disk system with the version of DOS you want to use for the diskless workstation, and then format a new floppy disk using the FORMAT command's /S parameter, which places the system files on the disk. Other files, such as AUTOEXEC.BAT and CONFIG.SYS, are also placed on the disk. Later, you will run a program called DOSGEN that extracts the information on this disk to build the remote boot file. This file is then placed in the LOGIN directory of the server, where the workstation can locate and run it during its log-in process.

Important Advance Step for Diskless Workstations

If all your diskless workstations will use the same interface board and the same DOS, you can skip this section. If you plan to use different network interface cards or different versions of DOS in any of your diskless workstations, you must determine the *node address* of the card before installing the card in the diskless workstation. The node address is "burned" into the cards firmware; thus it can only be read by running the diagnostics program that comes with the card. To do this, you must temporarily place the card in a system with a disk drive, and then run the diagnostics. Refer to the instruction manual of the card for information on running the diagnostics program. The node address should appear on one of the screens. Write it down for later use when creating the diskless workstation boot files. You might want to place a sticker on the back of each card that displays the appropriate address.

Network Interface Cards and Drivers

When running the configuration phase of NETGEN/ELSGEN, be sure to have your network cards and their manuals available so you can make any necessary adjustments to the dip-switch setting for interrupt lines or I/O addresses, DMA lines, and memory addresses. It is more convenient to install the cards in the workstations and server after completion of the configuration phase of SHGEN or NETGEN/ELSGEN (for the server).

A LAN driver definition file must be available for the network interface cards you plan to install in the server and the workstations. Novell does a good job of supplying these drivers as new cards are introduced. If a driver for your network interface card is not included with your

NetWare package, you should contact your dealer or Novell for assistance in obtaining one. You can determine if your NetWare package contains the needed driver by running the NETGEN/ELSGEN configuration program up to the point where it displays a list of LAN drivers. Contact Novell or your dealer if you want to make sure ahead of time.

Cable Installation

Small networks can often be installed in little time simply by connecting short runs of cable, possibly within the same office. These networks are easy to install and maintain, since future connection problems between workstations and servers are easy to trace. The short distances between the stations makes it easy to trace cable problems.

For larger networks, it may be more convenient to schedule the cabling during off-hours if possible. Typically, installers step on top of desks, lift dusty ceiling tiles, drill holes in walls, and perform other activities that employees may find obnoxious while trying to make calls or catch up with their work before the weekend. It will be hard enough to make everyone happy with the new network without getting on their wrong side from the start. Coordinate a schedule with employees and managers for hardware installation ahead of time.

Using Cable Installers

It may be necessary to consider the use of an outside organization to install the cable, especially if the right tools are not available. Many white-shirt-and-tie employees don't want to be elected to climb through ceilings or under floors with cable in hand. A qualified installer will make sure the cable is fully tested and capable of transmitting signals by using proper test equipment. This can be important if cable is strung over long distances and through hard-to-get-at places. If a network problem occurs, you can always call the cable company back to test your cable. For example, a cable signal may be affected by lighting equipment or long distances. An installer is more likely to identify this type of problem. Many installers will work after hours so employees are not disturbed.

It's usually easy to spot a cable installation done by in-house person-nel: Cable is taped or tacked to the walls and draped over equipment. The primary concern was to get the system up and running rather than to be neat about the installation. An outside cable company can bid a cable job, including the installation of wall mounts and clean wire runs, at reasonable rates because they do it often and have the equipment, parts, and expertise.

Do-It-Yourself Cabling

If cable will be installed by in-house personnel, it is important that everyone understand the installation, wiring diagrams, and cable-handling procedures.

Although it's easy and less expensive to simply "drape" cable, there are various reasons why this should not be done. The first has to do with office decor—exposed cable simply doesn't fit in, and is dangerous. Exposed cable may be prone to stretching or breakage. Cables should be tacked neatly into baseboards if that method is to be used. Conduit or metal piping can also be used to protect cable in areas where environmental conditions justify it, such as outside the building. If a cable needs to cross a factory floor, special metal casings or plastic protectors should be used for the cable run. Be sure to check with your cable supplier for recommendations.

One of the most common methods for running cable is through drop ceilings. The ceiling tiles can be gently lifted in the appropriate place and the cable can be threaded through to the next office. In most cases, the walls between offices may only go as high as the tile ceilings. Clearance to the next office is usually available just above the tile. Take special care to keep certain kinds of unshielded cable away from fluorescent light fixtures commonly mounted in drop ceilings; electrical interference problems may result when cables are draped over these lights. Plan on using extra cable to stay clear of lighting fixtures, air conditioning units, heaters, or other electronic devices.

Handling the Cable

When running cable, make sure you do not nick it or bend it too sharply. Coaxial cable should never be bent. A kink in the cable can cause a change in its electrical characteristics and inhibit transmission. It is also important to prop cable up with fasteners, staples, or clamps, rather than letting it hang for long distances—cable is not necessarily designed to support itself. Be careful not to damage the cable when stapling or pounding fasteners in the wall. Also make sure not to stretch the cable when you pull it through openings or conduit. A stretched cable will lose its transmission properties.

Be aware that moisture not only corrodes cable but also changes its electrical characteristics and inhibits transmission. Cable should be protected in wet conditions by keeping it clear of moisture. Protective covering may be required, especially if the cable is making an outside run. You can also check with the supplier for cable that has higher water tolerance if moisture problems cannot be avoided.

Checking the Cable Installation

Cable runs can be tested with the Novell NetWare COMCHECK program, which establishes a proper connection between each workstation. This program cannot be run, however, until the network interface cards are installed in the workstations and the cables are attached. You must create a special startup file during the installation process as well. An alternative is to use an outside organization to test cable runs with special testing equipment.

Be aware of interference when running cable. The longer a cable run, the more likely you are of running into interference problems. Metal cables tend to act like big antennas, picking up stray fields and interference from devices along their paths. As cables grow in length, their signal reliability shrinks. Higher data transmission rates can also cause problems over long distances. If a certain workstation is having problems connecting to the network, check for large electrical devices in the area around the wire leading to the station, or see if the wire is lying over some other type of electrical transmission line. If two or more cables are running parallel to each other, there may some cross-talk interference occurring in the lines.

Cable that is well shielded usually causes few problems. Short cable runs are also fairly trouble-free. Be sure a cable run is properly grounded. In most cases only one side of the cable should be grounded to the electrical faceplate of a wall socket. This allows the cable to unload unwanted voltage peaks. If two ends of the cable are grounded, an unwanted loop may form, which causes other problems. In some cases disconnecting even the lone ground wire may eliminate problems you are having with a workstation's connections. If interference problems cannot be overcome, consider fiber-optic cable, at least for the cable run that is giving you problems.

Printers

Printers can be installed at the server and workstations at any time. If you are installing server printers, make sure you note the parameter settings of serial printers, such as Baud Rate, Word Length, Stop Bits, Parity, and XON/XOFF. It may be necessary to change a dip switch inside the printer to convert it from the standard parallel interface to the serial interface. Parallel printers can usually be attached without special considerations.

If additional interface cards are installed in a server to accommodate serial or parallel printers, hardware conflicts may occur with the network interface card. NETGEN/ELSGEN can be run in custom mode (see Appendix A) to resolve these conflicts before you install the network interface board.

Other Site Requirements

Always make sure that network equipment such as the server and workstations are connected to proper power sources. These must be standard three-wire outlets connected to an earth ground. Power conditioning equipment may be required in some areas or if the installation is near heavy electrical equipment. Fluctuations in the power can be damaging and cause the system to go down. An uninterruptable power supply (UPS) is the best protection in the case of surges, power downs, and noise filtering.

It may not be practical to place a UPS on each workstation, but protection should be provided by surge protection and line-filtering devices. Some devices indicate low-voltage states that can cause as much damage as surges. The operator is warned with an alarm or light signal during a low-voltage state and may have time to turn the system off.

You should also protect against static electricity. Various inexpensive devices provide a grounding pad that operators can touch before starting a system. Anti-static sprays and carpet covers are also available. Any type of grounding device should have a wire that connects to an earth ground.

Preparing to Configure
And Install NetWare

The rest of this chapter is concerned with preparing to run the SHGEN and NETGEN/ELSGEN programs. An overview of the process is necessary so you can be prepared with the proper information when performing the actual configuration and installation. The following section will help you decide which run method and level to use for the programs.

Copying the NetWare Diskettes

During the NetWare configuration phase, various files on the disk sets are gathered together and compiled into the operating system files. These files are then written back to disk so they can be carried to the server for the installation phase. Because files are written back to disk, you must make backup copies of the original disks. Never install Novell using the original disks.

When you make copies of the NetWare disks, do not use the DOS COPY command. Each disk contains an electronic disk label or volume name that matches the name shown on the outside of the disk. By using the DOS DISKCOPY command the disk label as well as the files are copied to the backup disk.

Copying the NetWare disks is one of the biggest chores awaiting you as you prepare for installation, so you should have access to a system that has two disk drives of the same size. This eliminates a lot of disk swapping during the copying process. NetWare is shipped on either 360K formatted 5 1/4-inch disks or on 720K formatted 3 1/2-inch disks. You can copy the disks to a higher capacity format, but the expense is not worth it since the extra disk space is not used.

There is one trick available for those who don't want to spend a couple of hours formatting and copying disks. If you use an installation method that makes use of a hard drive or network drive, as will be discussed later, and if you have a second system where you can format disks as needed, you can get by without copying all of the disks. NetWare only copies files back to several of the disks at the end of the configuration procedures. If you are running the hard-drive or network-drive method, NETGEN/ELS-GEN asks for each of these disks by name. As it asks for each disk, you can jump over to the second system and make a backup of the required disk before proceeding.

Since the disks required in the process vary for different versions and disk sizes and is subject to change, a list is not provided here. You must wait until the end of the configuration phase when NETGEN/ELSGEN asks for the disks before you can know for sure which disks to make backups of. Remember to have an extra system available for formatting if you plan to use this method, which will be covered in more detail in the next chapter.

Choosing the SHGEN And NETGEN/ELSGEN Run Levels

There are several ways to run the SHGEN and NETGEN/ELSGEN programs. The *standard floppy-disk method* runs completely from one or two floppy disk drives. You should avoid the floppy-disk method if possible, in favor of the other methods described here since numerous disk swaps are required. The *RAM-disk method* is available only for NETGEN/ELSGEN, not SHGEN, and uses a memory drive to improve the installation performance. This method is especially useful if your system has only one floppy drive. The *hard-drive method* is fast and easy but requires a hard drive with 1MB or more of available disk space. *The network-drive method* configures and installs the new server while it is logged onto a previously installed network as a workstation. This method is often used by systems integrators and installers who already have an in-house network in place.

If you use the hard-disk or network-drive method, SHGEN initially creates directories on your hard drive that branch from a directory called \GENERATE \NETWARE and that match the labels on the disks. It then copies the files on those disks to the hard drive automatically. Additional directories and files are created and copied during the NETGEN/ELSGEN configuration phase.

Note: Keep in mind that the \GENERATE \NETWARE directory on hard drives holds the installation files in case you want to run installation again. You will need to log to this directory to start the programs.

Each installation method is described in the following sections. You should choose the method that is best for the hardware configuration you have available.

Floppy-Disk Method

The following is a list of characteristics and requirements of the floppy-disk installation method:

- Use this method only if you do not have access to a hard-drive system with enough room to hold the SHGEN and NETGEN/ELS-GEN files.

- Two floppy drives will help prevent extraneous disk swapping.

- The system must have 640K of memory and be running DOS 3.0 or higher.

- Make sure the system is booted with the following parameters set in the CONFIG.SYS file: FILES = 20 and BUFFERS = 15.

- You must make a complete backup set of the NetWare disks.

The steps for the floppy-disk method are summarized here:

1. Make backups of the entire disk set using the DOS COPYDISK command.

2. Run the SHGEN program to generate the workstation shell disks. Create a disk and run SHGEN for each different network interface card.

3. Run the NETGEN/ELSGEN *configuration* program to determine the switch setting for boards in the server.

4. Set the switches for the boards in the server and install them in the server.

5. Run the NETGEN/ELSGEN *installation* program to install the operating system on the server.

6. Boot the server and perform the other post-installation procedures.

Ram-Disk Method

The following is a list of characteristics and requirements of the RAM-disk installation method:

- Use this method for NETGEN/ELSGEN only .

- It is advantageous if the system being used for NETGEN/ELSGEN has only one physical drive.

- This method requires 1MB of memory (640K of base memory and 384K of extended memory).

- Part of the computer's memory must be set aside as a RAM drive using a device driver such as VDISK.SYS, as discussed in DOS manuals.

- The CONFIG.SYS file on the boot disk must contain FILES=20 and BUFFERS=15.

- You must make a complete backup set of the NetWare disks.

The steps for the RAM-disk method are summarized here:

1. Make backups of the entire disk set using the DOS COPYDISK command.

2. Load the VDISK or other utility to create a RAM drive in system memory.

3. From the GENERATE directoy run the SHGEN program to generate the workstation shell disks. Create a disk and run SHGEN for each different network interface card.

4. Run the NETGEN/ELSGEN *configuration* program to determine the switch setting for boards in the server.

5. Set the switches for the boards in the server and install them in the server.

6. Run the NETGEN/ELSGEN *installation* program to install the operating system on the server.

7. Boot the server and perform the other post-installation procedures.

Hard-Drive Method

The following is a list of characteristics and requirements of the hard-drive installation method:

- This method requires 1MB of available disk space and 640K of memory.

- It also requires DOS 3.0 or higher.

- Make sure the system is booted with the following parameters set in the CONFIG.SYS file: FILES = 20 and BUFFERS = 15.

- You must have a disk drive that matches the size of the NetWare disk sets.

- This installation method is suited for resellers and installers who would like to keep the NetWare files on the hard drive for future installations.

- A complete backup set of the NetWare disks is not required if a second system is available to create the download disks as NetWare asks for them at the end of the configuration phase. Refer to page 204 for details.

The steps for the hard-disk method are summarized here:

1. Create a GENERATE directory on the hard drive to run the SHGEN and NETGEN/ELSGEN programs from.

2. From the GENERATE directory, run the SHGEN program first. Several additional directories are created on the hard drive and files are copied to them. SHGEN generates the workstation shells. Create a boot disk and run SHGEN for each different network interface card.

3. Run the NETGEN/ELSGEN *configuration* program to determine the switch setting for boards in the server. The program should be run on a hard-drive system other than the server, if possible. In this way you can regenerate the operating system at any time using the original hard-drive system. The first time NETGEN/ELSGEN are run, additional directories are created on the hard drive. After the program finishes, files are downloaded to disks. If you have another floppy-drive system, you can create the download disks as requested (to avoid making a complete disk set backup).

4. Set the switches for the boards in the server and install them in the server.

5. Take the disks generated during the configuration process in step 3 to the server and run the NETGEN/ELSGEN *installation* program to install the operating system on the server.

6. Boot the server and perform the other post-installation procedures.

Network-Drive Method

The following is a list of characteristics and requirements of the network-drive installation method:

- This method requires an existing network that is running NetWare 2.1 or higher.

- Make sure the system is booted with the following parameters set in the CONFIG.SYS file: FILES = 20 and BUFFERS = 15.

- The new server must be installed as a *workstation* on the existing network; therefore, a network interface card must be installed, and the system shell files (IPX and NET*x*) for the existing network must be executed.

- You must have a disk of comparable size to the NetWare disk set.

- This installation method is suited for resellers and installers who would like to keep the NetWare files on the hard drive for future installations. Installation to new servers is easily performed, since the necessary files are already located on a hard drive and they are transferred to the server through the network cabling.

- When using the network-drive method, SHGEN and the NETGEN/ ELSGEN configuration and installation phase are run while logged in to the existing server in a drive that is mapped to the directory holding the NetWare files. The configured files are then downloaded to the workstation and the workstation is converted to a new server.

- A complete backup set of the NetWare disks is not required if a second system is available to create the download disks as NetWare asks for them at the end of the configuration phase.

The steps for the network drive method are summarized here:

1. Attach the new server to the existing network as a workstation.

2. Create a GENERATE directory on the original server hard drive where the SHGEN and NETGEN/ELSGEN programs will be run.

3. Log in to the GENERATE directory on the server hard drive and run the SHGEN program from the workstation. Several additional directories are copied on the server hard drive, and files are copied to them. SHGEN generates the workstation shells. Create a disk and run SHGEN for each different network interface card.

4. Run the NETGEN/ELSGEN configuration program to determine the switch setting for boards in the server. The program should be run while logged into the server directory from the workstation. The first time NETGEN/ELSGEN are run, additional directories are created on the hard drive.

5. Set the switches for the network interface cards and install them in the server.

6. From the workstation that will become the new server, run the NETGEN/ELSGEN programs. The hard drive of the workstation

is configured as a server and files are copied to it over the network cabling from the original server.

Configuration and Installation Options

The NETGEN and ELSGEN programs have two steps. The first step, *configuration*, is used to specify all of the components you will install in your server. After running this phase of the program, you can install the components in the server, and then proceed with the second phase, *installation*, which installs NetWare on the server.

In both phases there are two methods you can select for installation: default and custom. The *default* configuration is the easiest. It uses default settings for the equipment and interface cards you are installing. In most cases, the default method can be used. The *custom* configuration and installation method provides more control during the installation with regards to the settings of NetWare features and switch settings on the hardware.

The default installation method is used in the next chapter as the preferred installation method for beginning users or those with simple installations.

In some cases, hardware conflicts may occur between some of the components in the server and those you are trying to install, such as the network interface cards. If a conflict occurs, you may need to use the custom installation method of NETGEN/ELSGEN to help you locate conflicts and alter the dip switches on the boards you are installing to a non-conflicting interrupt or address. In this way the custom installation method screens hardware conflicts before you actually install the boards and start the server.

A conflict occurs when two or more devices try to use the same interrupt lines, I/O addresses, DMA lines, and memory addresses of your server's microprocessor. This would be equivalent to the phone company giving you and another party the same phone number—it cannot be done. When running NETGEN you can pick from a list of interrupts and addresses for the interface cards you are installing. Dip switches determine the settings on the interface cards. Since NETGEN will show only a list of settings not already in use, you can change dip switches on your interface cards to match those available sets, thus preventing conflicts. As interrupts are selected, they are removed from the list. Once all of the dip

Device Resource	Base I/O Address	Interrupt
XT controller	320-32F	5
AT controller	1F0-1F8	14
Floppy controller	1F0-1F8 or 3F0-3F7	6
EGA Adapter	3C0-3CF	2
Monochrome Adapter	3B0-3BF	
Color Graphics Adapter	3D0-3DF	
Hercules Mono Adapter	3B4-3BF	
COM1	3F8-3FF	4
COM2	2F8-2FF	3
LPT1	378-37F	7
LPT2	278-27F	5
If LPT3 is used, then:		
LPT1	3BC-3BE	7
LPT2	378-37A	5
LPT3	278-27A	

Table 9-1.   Common Base I/O Addresses and Interrupt Lines

switches for your cards are set correctly, you can install them in the server and continue with the installation.

When the custom installation programs attempt to find conflicts, a list of known interrupts and address lines common on most standard AT class systems is used. If you are installing a system with additional components (extra LPT or COM ports, for example), you may need to include them in the list to avoid further conflicts. If this is the case, you can create your own resources or resource sets. A *resource set* is a collection of individual resources. For example, Novell makes available a resource set called AT Compatible File Server, which includes an auxiliary ROM chip, AT hard drive controller, and floppy-disk drive controller. To this you can add LPT and COM ports, UPS cards, and other devices.

A partial list of common Base I/O addresses and Interrupt lines is shown in Table 9-1. Compare the addresses and lines on this list with that used by your board. If there is a conflict, you must use the custom method to assist you in changing the board settings.

Keep in mind that resource management in the custom NetWare level is optional. It is designed to eliminate hardware conflicts before you proceed with the rest of NetWare's software installation and the hardware installation. Resource management is often used by systems integrators for configuring systems they sell often.

When to Perform Custom Installation

As with NetWare configuration, NetWare installation can be performed in the default mode or in the custom mode. If default mode is selected, the NETGEN/ELSGEN programs automatically select various settings for your file server. If you need to change any of these settings, use the custom installation methods described in Appendix A. In most cases you can refer to the programs and utilities you plan to run on your network for their requirements. The following sections describe the default settings and the need to run the custom installation method.

Number of Open Files

This parameter determines how many files can be open simultaneously. The default for ELS Network Level II is 60, with a minimum of 20 and a maximum of 1000. The default for Advanced NetWare and SFT NetWare is 240. There are 100 bytes per open file used. You can calculate the number of open files you may need by multiplying the average number of network users by the number of open files needed for the applications they will be running. A typical word processing program may require 20 open files per user, so that five users would require 100 open files. If Macintosh workstations are to be connected, allow 4 open files per station.

Number of Indexed Files

This parameter determines how many indexed files can be open simultaneously. A speed enhancement is realized since the file server creates a memory index of the files' locations on disk. The default for ELS Network Level II, Advanced NetWare, and SFT NetWare is 5, with a maximum of 1000. There are 1034 bytes used per indexed file. In most cases indexed files are files used by database programs. Determine how many indexed files need to be open at one time by the applications users and set the indexed file number slightly higher.

Disk Space Limitations

You can limit the amount of server disk space available to a user by entering **Yes** at the Limit Disk Space option. This prevents any one user from using a disproportionate amount of disk storage. The default is No in all versions. If you limit disk space, you must specify the amount to allocate to each user, and you must specify the custom installation options during the installation phase.

Hot Fix Redirection Area

The Hot Fix Redirection Area is the location on the server's disk where data can be redirected in case of media defects. The default is 2% of the drive. You may want to increase the size of the Hot Fix Redirection Area if you are installing an older, questionable drive. If this feature is to be changed, refer to custom installation options in Appendix A.

Hard Drive Volumes

A hard drive can be divided into one or more volumes, the size of which are measured in megabytes. Drives under ELS Network Level II, Advanced NetWare, and SFT NetWare can be divided into as many as 16 logical volumes. You must customize volume size if a hard drive is larger than 255MB or if you simply want to make several smaller volumes on a large hard drive. The minimum volume size is 10MB, and the maximum volume size is 255MB. Each volume must be given its own volume name during the installation process. The first volume is always SYS. Subsequent volumes then default to VOL1, VOL2, and so on.

Number of Directory Entries

During the installation a number that determines how many directories, subdirectories, and files that can be created on each volume appears as a default, based on the size of the volume. In most cases, the default number is sufficient.

Directory Caching

Directory caching increases the efficiency of the hard drive by keeping a copy of the directory in the memory of the file server. This is much faster than reading the directory table on the disk every time a file is requested. You can choose not to cache directories if you need to save memory space. In most cases the amount of memory used is insignificant, so you would leave this option on. Novell strongly recommends caching all directories to increase the efficiency of its operating system. Caching should only be deselected if your system has the minimum amount of memory required to run NetWare.

Printer Parameters

The default parameters for serial printers are as follows:

Baud Rate	9600
Word Length	8 bits
Stop Bits	1 bit
Parity	None
XON/XOFF	No

You can change these settings to match your printer or, in some cases, change the printer settings to match the NetWare defaults.

Post-Installation Procedures

The following sections describe some of the procedures and additional steps you may need to make after NETGEN/ELSGEN has completed.

Starting the Server

When NetWare is installed on the server, you can start it. Dedicated and nondedicated servers have different startup procedures. To start a dedicated server, simply set its on/off switch to on. NetWare goes through its startup procedure, and a colon prompt appears after the copyright messages indicating that the server is in the console mode. Nondedicated servers must be started from a DOS boot disk in the floppy drive. A file called NET$OS is then executed to start the server. You also need the NETx.COM file create by the SHGEN program to run the server as a workstation in DOS mode.

Keep in mind that a nondedicated system acts as if it were two separate systems. You can run DOS commands and programs on the system in the workstation mode. NetWare handles network tasks in the background. A slowness may be experienced when working at the workstation on the server, because NetWare is emulating a DOS machine.

Starting Workstations

Each workstation is started with the DOS boot disk you prepared during the SHGEN phase, or from the hard drive using the files created by SHGEN. These files, IPX.COM and NETx.COM, are executed to start the network. Recall that SHGEN should be run for each different type of network interface card. One IPX.COM file might be slightly different than another, since they are tailored to the type of network interface card placed in each workstation.

The SHGEN program creates two additional files that may be required on your startup disk under certain conditions. Use the NetWare NETBIOS emulator program, NETBIOS.EXE, if your workstation will be running applications written for IBM-type networks. A companion file called INT2F.COM is also created.

Starting Diskless Workstations

A special program called DOSGEN is used to create the boot files on the server for a diskless workstation. The boot files will be located in the LOGIN directory and are assembled from files located on a special workstation disk. This disk should be created from the DOS version you want to use on the workstation and should contain the IPX.COM and NETx.COM files that match the interface board and DOS version used on the workstation. You can also create CONFIG.SYS and AUTOEXEC.BAT files on the disk. When DOSGEN is run, it loads the files from the disk and compiles a single startup file for the workstation, which is placed in the LOGIN directory.

Creating the Startup Files

In addition to IPX.COM, NETx.COM, CONFIG.SYS, and AUTO-EXEC.BAT, there are several other boot files you can create to customize a workstation or server environment. These files may differ according to the NetWare version you have and can be created with the COPY CON command.

SHELL.CFG

The SHELL.CFG file is used to alter the shell configuration for work-stations. Some of the command options are used to alter the IPX.COM settings, and others are used to alter the NETx.COM settings. The file should be included on the boot disk or hard drive. It is read automatically during network startup.

AUTOEXEC.SYS

The AUTOEXEC.SYS file is used to set various printer configurations. This file is placed in the SYSTEM directory on the file server.

CONFIG.UPS or SERVER.CFG

The CONFIG.UPS file is created on the server in the SYSTEM directory and is used to set the parameters for an uninterruptable power supply. The parameters specify the type of UPS, the I/O address on the interface card, how long the UPS should run before the file server shuts itself down, and when to notify users. CONFIG.UPS is used in Advanced NetWare and SFT NetWare; SERVER.CFG is used in ELS Network Level II.

Installing Netware

Using the SHGEN and NETGEN/ELSGEN Menus
Phase 1: Running SHGEN, The Shell Generation Program
Phase 2: Running NETGEN/ELSGEN to Configure NetWare
Phase 3: Completing the Hardware Installation
Phase 4: Installing the Operating System on the Server

When the equipment required for your LAN is together, you can begin the NetWare generation process. Remember from Chapter 9 that there are different methods for installing NetWare:

- Configuring and installing with default or custom options

- Configuring and installing from floppy-disk drives or with hard drives

NetWare is supplied with various default settings made by Novell to match the most-used configurations. In most cases you can use the default settings. System installers and integrators may want to choose the custom installation method, which is covered in Appendix A. If you are new to the installation process, you should go through the default installation method covered in this chapter first to become familiar with the installation method. Then, if you find that custom features are required, you can refer to Appendix A to modify or reinstall NetWare.

The method you use to install NetWare can also depend on the way you work with the NetWare disks. The standard installation method involves configuring and installing from floppy-disk drives. One look at the number of disks supplied with NetWare will convince you that the floppy-disk installation method is not easy; you must swap disks many times.

Novell provides a configuration method for NetWare that uses a hard-drive computer system. If you have an existing Novell network already installed, you can even prepare the new server by attaching it to the existing network as a workstation and running the configuration and installation programs from the network drive, as covered in Chapter 9.

The installation procedure follows the steps outlined here, which is also how this chapter is organized:

Phase 1: Generate the workstation shells with SHGEN

Phase 2: Configure the operating system with NETGEN/ELSGEN

Phase 3: Install the remaining hardware

Phase 4: Install the operating system with NETGEN/ELSGEN

Phase 5: Start the NetWare network (covered in Chapter 11)

Note that the configuration and installation program for ELS NetWare Level II is called ELSGEN and that the configuration and installation program for Advanced NetWare and SFT NetWare is called NETGEN. Since their operation is similar, they will be referred to as NETGEN/ELSGEN. Also note that NETGEN and ELSGEN are run in both Phase 2 and Phase 4. Phase 2 is a configuration process and Phase 4 is an installation process. It is important to make a distinction between the two since configuration is involved with selecting the type of network you will use, possibly on a computer besides the server. Installation is performed at the server itself. It initializes the server and copies system files and utilities to the filing system.

Using the SHGEN and NETGEN/ELSGEN Menus

The SHGEN and NETGEN/ELSGEN menus have a few peculiarities that may take a little getting used to. You may be asked to press the ESC key to go to the next menu. This often is confusing at first, since most PC users consider the ESC key as a way of backing out or escaping from a task. Think of the NetWare menus as pop-up windows that stay on the screen until information is entered or options are selected. You then press ESC to close the window.

When a list of options is presented, you can use the arrow keys to highlight the option, and then press the ENTER key. This is referred to as *selecting* an item from the menu. If you need help, press the F1 key. Be sure to watch the abbreviated help screens that appear at the bottom of the screen. They offer help for the current menu.

Phase 1: Running SHGEN, The Shell Generation Program

SHGEN (SHell GENeration) is used to create the startup files IPX.COM and NETx.COM for the workstations. These files are placed on the boot disks or drives of each workstation. SHGEN is basically the same for ELS NetWare Level II, Advanced NetWare, and SFT NetWare.

Preparing the Master Shell Disks

SHGEN requires a disk on which to download the IPX.COM, NETx.COM, and other startup files after they are configured. Prepare one now for each different type of DOS-based system you will use as a workstation. The difference between workstations is basically determined by the type of network interface card installed. The disk must be formatted using the FORMAT /S command so that the DOS system files are loaded to the disk. Be sure to format this disk with the version of DOS you intend to use on the workstation. If you are installing a remote workstation to be used with ELS NetWare Level II, you should also create a boot disk for the remote station.

Assume you have five workstations. Two workstations will use AST Ethernode network interface cards and run AST DOS 3.3. One of these systems has a hard drive. Two other systems will use 3COM EtherLink cards and run Compaq DOS 4.1. One of these systems also has a hard drive. The fifth system is a diskless workstation that does not have a hard drive, but you will install an AST Ethernode card and run AST DOS 3.3 on it. The following disks should be created.

Example 1: AST Ethernode Disk   Create a disk formatted with AST DOS 3.3 and label it *AST Ethernode/AST DOS 3.3 NetWare Boot Files*. Run the SHGEN program and select the AST Ethernode LAN driver. Insert the disk at the end of the program to copy the completed startup files. Finally, copy the files to the boot disk of the floppy-drive Ethernode system and ROOT directory of the hard-drive Ethernode system.

Example 2: 3COM EtherLink Disk   Create a disk formatted with Compaq DOS 4.1 and label it *3COM EtherLink/Compaq DOS 4.1 NetWare Boot Files*. Run the SHGEN program and select the 3COM EtherLink LAN driver that fits the card. Insert the disk at the end of the program to copy the completed startup files to it. Finally, copy the files to the boot disk of the first Compaq system and the ROOT directory on the hard disk of the other.

Example 3: Diskless Workstation Disk   Since the diskless workstation will run AST DOS 3.3 and use the AST Ethernode interface cards, you can use the AST Ethernode disk to create the remote reset boot files in the server. It already contains the IPX.COM, NET3.COM, and other files that are required by the diskless workstation. You should add AUTO-EXEC.BAT, CONFIG.SYS, and SHELL.CFG file to this disk before generating the boot files, as discussed in Chapter 11.

Starting SHGEN

To start the SHGEN program, use the startup method that best fits your system. If you use the hard-drive or network-drive method, directories will be created on the hard drive and files will be copied to them, assuming this is the first time you are running the program. If SHGEN has already been run using one of these methods, you can skip the directory creation and file copying steps.

Using the Hard-Disk Method

Boot the hard-drive system and log in to the hard drive to which you want to copy the NetWare configuration files. If you are starting SHGEN for the first time, create a directory called GENERATE using the command

MD \GENERATE

Issue the following command to move to the GENERATE directory:

CD \GENERATE

To start the SHGEN program, insert the SHGEN-1 disk into the floppy drive, and enter the command

A:SHGEN -D

If you need to use drive B because its size correctly matches the disk size, replace A with B in the command. The D parameter specifies the default configuration mode. An N parameter can be used to specify a new session. If you previously ran SHGEN and do not wish to keep information from the previous session, use the N parameter.

Using the Network-Drive Method

The first step is to start the network and log in to the existing NetWare operating system. Create a directory called GENERATE on the network drive, and then map a drive to the directory using the NetWare MAP command. The mapped drive letter will be used later in the installation. Type the following command to start the program:

A:SHGEN -D

A can be replaced with B if that is the drive you plan to use. The D parameter specifies the default configuration mode. An N parameter can be used to specify a new session. If you previously ran SHGEN and do not wish to keep information from the previous session, use the N parameter.

Using the Floppy-Disk Method

The first step in this method is to start the computer you are using for the generation with DOS 3.0 or above. Then insert the disk and type this command at the DOS A: prompt to start SHGEN:

SHGEN -D

The D parameter specifies the default configuration mode. Use the N parameter to specify a new session. If you previously ran SHGEN and do not wish to keep information from the previous session, use the N parameter.

Generating the Shell

The SHGEN program may ask for disks as it runs, depending on the method you use and whether SHGEN has been run before. Insert each disk as requested. This is the first screen you will see:

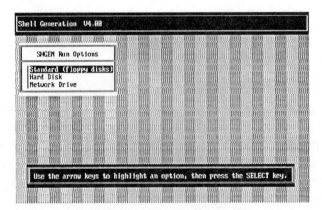

Use the arrow keys to select the run method you will be using and press
ENTER. If you select Hard Disk or Network Drive from the menu, SHGEN
requests the letter of the drive you wish to use as shown on the right in
this screen:

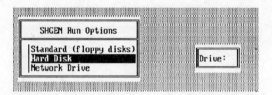

The drive you choose should be where the GENERATE directory was
created earlier. If you are running the network drive method, enter the
letter of the drive you mapped to the GENERATE directory.

The next screen to appear is the Available LAN Drivers menu:

Use the arrow keys to scroll through this list until you find the LAN driver
that matches the network interface cards installed in your workstations.
If you can not find the driver for your card, you must exit SHGEN by
pressing ESC, and then refer to Appendix A to run the custom level of
SHGEN.

Press ENTER on the LAN driver you select. The next screen displays
information about the LAN driver you selected and asks if you want to
continue with the generation process.

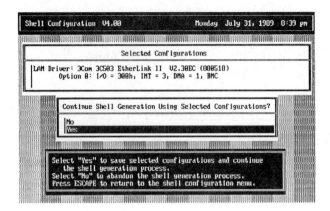

Notice that the screen displays the I/O, interrupt, and DMA settings it will use for your network interface board. You must compare this information with the current setting on your board, and then make dip-switch or jumper settings to match. The manual should list the default settings of the interface board or tell you how to read its switch settings. If your board cannot be configured in the same way as SHGEN's proposed settings, you must run the custom level of SHGEN, which is covered in Appendix A.

Be sure to record the information shown on the Selected Configurations screen to your network log sheets. The information also is copied to the file CONFIG.DAT on the SHGEN-1 disk or directory.

Select Yes at the Continue Shell Generation Using Selected Configurations option.

SHGEN then links the drivers you have selected with other modules to create the IPX.COM shell file. If you are using the floppy-disk installation method, you may need to make several disk swaps. Eventually the following screen message appears, indicating that the IPX.COM file has been configured:

```
A valid shell has been placed on SHGEN-1
          <Press ESCAPE to Continue>
```

The IPX.COM file is stored on the SHGEN-2 disk if you are using 5 1/4-inch disks and in the SHGEN-1 disk or directory if you are using 3 1/2-inch disks.

If you are running the hard disk or network-drive method, the following prompt appears on the screen:

Select Yes to download the files. The following message appears:

Insert the appropriate master shell disk that matches the network interface card driver you just selected and press ESC. The IPX.COM, NET*x*.COM, and other files are copied to it. Once the files are copied, the DOS prompt returns and you can proceed to the next step.

Before You Go Further

ELS NetWare Level II users who are installing remote workstations should run SHGEN again and select the IBM ASYNC (COM1/COM2) driver. After SHGEN completes, it asks for the master shell disk to download files to. Be sure this disk is the one you have labeled as the remote workstation disk. The IPX.COM and NET*x*.COM files copied to this disk are different than those copied to the local workstation master shell disks.

If your network uses several different brands or types of network interface cards that require different LAN drivers, run SHGEN again to create the IPX.COM and NETx.COM files for each card. Be sure to have a separate disk, properly labeled and ready to receive the downloaded files at the end of SHGEN.

The master shell disk also contains two files called NETBIOS.EXE and INT2F.COM. These files are NetWare NETBIOS emulators programs that allow workstations to run applications written for IBM-type networks.

Phase 2: Running NETGEN/ELSGEN To Configure NetWare

You are now ready to configure the NetWare operating system. Remember that this phase is concerned with configuration, not installation, so there is no need to move to the new server yet. Keep in mind also that this chapter covers only the default configuration mode. Refer to Appendix A for custom installations.

Starting NETGEN/ELSGEN

Use the appropriate method discussed in the next three sections to start the NETGEN/ELSGEN programs. Hard-drive and network-drive users should note that directories are created and files are copied if this is the first time the programs are being run. If SHGEN was run previously, you have already created the GENERATE directory and can skip that step.

Note: If you are using the hard-disk or network-drive method and this is not the first time you are running NETGEN/ELSGEN, you can skip the following steps since the files have already been installed. Enter **CD \GENERATE\NETWARE**, and then enter **NETGEN -ND** (for Advanced NetWare or SFT NetWare) or **ELSGEN -N** (for ELS NetWare Level II). Skip to the section called "Configuring the Operating System."

Using the Hard-Disk Method

Boot the hard-drive system and log into the hard drive to which you want to copy the NetWare configuration files. Move to the GENERATE directory created in the SHGEN phase with the following command:

```
CD \GENERATE
```

To start the NETGEN/ELSGEN programs, insert the NETGEN or ELSGEN disk into the floppy drive and type the command

A:NETGEN -D

or

A:ELSGEN

whichever matches your NetWare version. A can be replaced with B if that is appropriate for your system. The D parameter specifies the default configuration mode.

Using the Network-Drive Method

The first step is to start the network and log in to the existing NetWare operating system. Map a drive to the GENERATE directory using the NetWare MAP command. You will use this drive letter later in the installation. Enter the following command to start the program:

A:NETGEN -D

or

A:ELSGEN

The A can be replaced with B if that is the drive you plan to use. The D parameter specifies the default configuration mode.

Using the Floppy-Disk or RAM-Disk Method

The first step in using this method is to start the computer you are using for the generation with DOS 3.0 or above. If you are using the RAM-disk method, make sure this disk has a CONFIG.SYS file with the parameters previously described.

Insert the SUPPORT disk into a second drive if available. Type the following command at the DOS A: prompt to start NETGEN/ELSGEN:

NETGEN -ND

or

ELSGEN -N

The N parameter specifies that information entered during a previous run of the program should be kept, and the D parameter specifies the default configuration mode.

Configuring the Operating System

The first screen you see after completing startup is shown here:

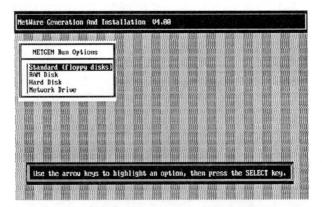

Use the arrow keys to select the NETGEN/ELSGEN run mode you have decided to use. If you select Hard Disk or Network Drive, the program asks for the hard drive or network drive to use for the installation, as shown in the following illustration.

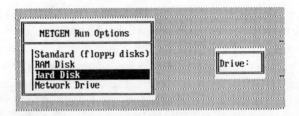

The drive you designate is where the GENERATE directory is located or mapped. You may be asked to insert several disks as the program loads.

This screen may appear, depending on your NetWare version:

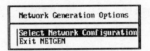

If you are installing ELS NetWare Level II, the first selection will be Operating System Generation. You can choose to go on with the installation or exit. Make the first selection at this time.

An Available Options screen appears next. These screens are slightly different for each version of NetWare. The Advanced NetWare Available Options menu looks like this:

The ELS NetWare Level II Available Options menu looks like this:

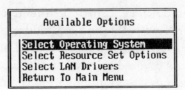

Each item on the Available Options menu will be selected one after the other until complete, so you can consider this menu your "home menu" until the final item is selected.

If you are running SFT NetWare, your screen will be similar to the Advanced NetWare screen, except the Set Operating System Options, which is used to select a dedicated or nondedicated operating system run mode, is not included for SFT NetWare because it runs in dedicated mode only. If you are using SFT NetWare, skip ahead to the "Selecting a LAN Driver" section of this chapter.

ELS NetWare Level II and Advanced NetWare users must select a dedicated or non-dedicated operating system. Choose the option for setting or selecting the operating system and press ENTER. The following screen appears:

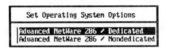

Use the arrow keys to select one or the other and then press ENTER. You will be returned to the Available Options menu.

If you are installing ELS NetWare Level II, proceed to the next section. If you are installing Advanced NetWare, proceed to the section called "Selecting a LAN Driver."

Selecting Resource Sets for ELS NetWare Level II

NetWare can fail to boot the first time if any components in the server attempt to "talk" to the systems microprocessor on the same lines or address. To avoid these conflicts ahead of time, you can supply NETGEN/ELSGEN with the line and address values already in use by your system. Although this is a topic covered under custom configuration in Appendix A, it is covered briefly here for ELS NetWare Level II users. Choose Select Resource Set Options from the Available Options menu to provide NETGEN/ELSGEN with the lines and addresses your system may be using. Press the ENTER key three times to get to the following menu. Use the arrow keys to scroll through the list of options.

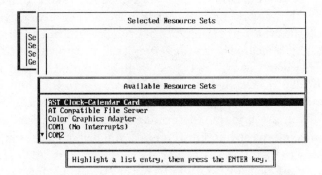

In most cases, you can select the standard resource sets such as AT Compatible File Server or IBM PS/2 Model 30 286 File Server as well as the COM1 and LPT1 port selections. You can then return to the Available Options menu to continue with the configuration process. If you are adding other boards to your server, such as those shown on the Available Resource Sets menu, be sure to select them as well. To select another resource, choose Select Loaded Item from the Available Options menu. Once you have made your selections, press ESC to return to the Available Options menu.

Selecting a LAN Driver

The next step for all versions of NetWare is to select a LAN driver. You should be able to find a LAN driver to match your network interface card in the list that NETGEN/ELSGEN presents, unless the card is too new or obscure to have been included in your version of NetWare. Advanced NetWare or SFT NetWare users need this step to specify bridges by selecting up to four LAN interface cards. ELS NetWare Level II installers will use this step to select both the LAN interface card and the IBM Async (COM1/COM2) interface for remote workstations.

Up to four network cards may be installed in a NetWare server running under Advanced NetWare or SFT NetWare. In this way you can bridge two or more different network systems together. For example, you can bridge an existing Ethernet network to a new Token Ring network by installing both network interface cards in the server or workstation.

Recall that there are two types of bridges: internal and external. An internal bridge is located in the file server itself and presumes that physical junction between the two networks will be located at the server. An external bridge is installed at a workstation where the connection point may be more convenient and where some speed enhancement may be realized. If you are bridging, determine whether an internal or external bridge will be more convenient. If an internal bridge is chosen, have both boards ready to install in the server.

Highlight Select LAN Driver from the Available Options menu, and press ENTER to display this screen:

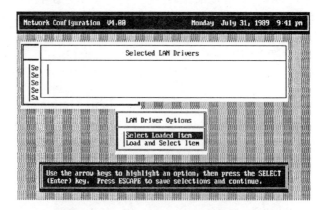

The Selected LAN Drivers menu is blank at this time since drivers have not yet been selected.

The current menu is LAN Driver Options. Choose Select Loaded Item to select from a list of LAN drivers that Novell supplies with NetWare. The Load and Select Item option is used to load a driver from a disk that may have been obtained from Novell or from a LAN card manufacturer. If you select the latter option, place a disk in the floppy drive containing the new driver file. Note that the disk must be labeled LAN_DRV_.003 (or higher).

Choose Select Loaded Item from the LAN Driver Options menu to display the Available LAN Drivers menu shown here:

You can scroll through this list using the arrow keys to select the LAN driver that matches your network interface card. Press ENTER at a selected item, and the Selected LAN Drivers menu displays your selection, as shown here:

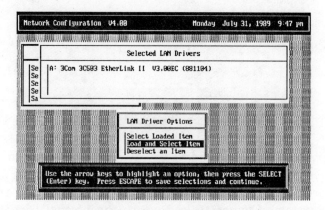

Advanced NetWare and SFT NetWare Users   Hardware conflicts may occur when installing more than two interface cards. You may need to refer to Appendix A to run NETGEN/ELSGEN in the custom mode so that these boards can be set to nonconflicting modes.

ELS NetWare Level II Users   Select the IBM Async (COM1/COM2) driver in addition to the LAN driver at this time if you are installing a remote workstation and the Async card will be in the server.

Macintosh Workstations   If NetWare for the Macintosh is to be configured, install an AppleTalk-compatible board in the file server and select the appropriate LAN driver. The AppleTalk network should be selected as LAN B.

Once you have selected the proper LAN drivers, press ESC to return to the Available Options menu.

Selecting Disk Drivers and Other Drivers

This section is for Advanced NetWare and SFT NetWare users only. If you are installing ELS NetWare Level II, proceed to the next section.

Choose Select Disk Drivers from the Available Options menu and press ENTER twice to display this menu:

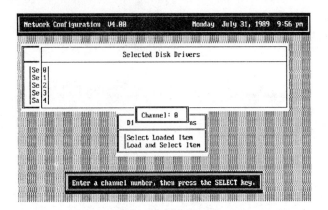

Advanced NetWare and SFT NetWare can support up to five hard-disk drive channels, which are numbered 0 through 4. Channel 0 supports the internal hard drive that comes standard with most AT-style systems and 386 systems. Channel 0 also supports the internal drives on IBM PS/2 systems. The other channels are used by Novell manufactured drives, so you should refer to Novell's documentation to determine which disk channels to use. In most cases, you should type **0** as a response. Press ENTER to display the following menu:

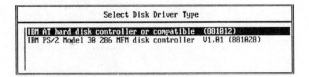

Select the option that best fits your system. If you have a new disk driver on disk that is not listed on the screen, you can choose Load and Select Item to load it from disk, assuming that the disk is labeled

DSK_DRV_.003 (or higher). Press ESC to return to the Available Options menu.

The Select Other Drivers option on the Available Options menu is used to load and select drivers that may be required for equipment you need to install in the server like streaming tape backup systems. This option is mainly designed for installing drivers that support Novell-specific tape backup systems, or Novell NetWare 286(T) or 386(T) file servers. Refer to the respective manuals for more information.

Generating the Operating System

The last option on the Available Options menu is used to save the selections you have made and generate the NetWare operating system installation files. ELSGEN displays the option Generate Operating System and NETGEN displays the option Save Selection and Continue. Both will display a File Server Information screen similar to this:

```
┌─────────────────────────────────────────────────────┐
│              File Server Information                  │
├─────────────────────────────────────────────────────┤
│ A: 3Com 3C503 EtherLink II  V3.00EC (881104)         │
│           Network Address: 1                          │
│ Non-dedicated Server DOS Process                      │
│           Network Address: 2                          │
│ Communication Buffers: 40                             │
└─────────────────────────────────────────────────────┘
```

Entering File Server Information

The information on the File Server Information screen reflects the options you have chosen in the last few steps. You must now assign a network address for the network interface cards you have chosen and, if you are running a nondedicated server, an address for the DOS process. In the case of a bridge, two to four network interface cards may require addresses. The best rule for assigning addresses is to start with 1 and count up for each address request. Never use the same address twice on the same server if multiple network cards are installed. If the file server is being attached to an existing LAN as an additional server, type the network address of the existing LAN. In the previous illustration of the screen, the 3Com board is given the network address 1 and the Non-Dedicated Server DOS Process is given the network address 2.

Note: Be sure to write this information in your log sheets because you will need it later.

The Communication Buffers setting lets you alter the amount of memory set aside by the server to hold "packets" of data arriving from workstations. A default buffer size is displayed by NETGEN/ELSGEN, but you can change this number if you wish. You may want to add one additional buffer for each workstation above the amount recommended by NETGEN/ELSGEN. Keep in mind that each buffer uses 1/2K of memory.

Press ESC when you are through with the File Server Information menu.

Reviewing the Settings

The next screen to appear is similar to the one shown here:

```
┌──────────────────────────────────────────────────────────────┐
│                    Selected Configurations                     │
├──────────────────────────────────────────────────────────────┤
│LAN A: 3Com 3C503 EtherLink II  V3.00EC (881104)                │
│        Option 0: I/O = 330h, INT = 4, RAM = C800, BNC          │
│        Network Address: 1                                       │
│Non-dedicated Server DOS Process                                 │
│        Network Address: 2                                       │
│                                                                 │
│OS Type: Advanced NetWare 206 / Nondedicated                     │
│                                                                 │
│Communication Buffers: 40                                        │
│                                                                 │
│Disk Chan. 0: IBM AT hard disk controller or compatible  (881012)│
│▼       Option 0: AT controller  I/O base = 1F0h, Interrupt = 14 │
└──────────────────────────────────────────────────────────────┘
```

It is important to review the information on this screen and compare the settings and other information to the equipment you are installing. Make sure the dip switches and jumpers on your hardware components are set as shown on this screen, otherwise NetWare may not boot properly. If your boards cannot be set to match these settings, refer to the custom installation section in Appendix A.

Press ESC to display the following continuation screen:

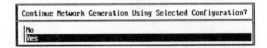

```
┌──────────────────────────────────────────────────────────────┐
│Continue Network Generation Using Selected Configuration?       │
├──────────────────────────────────────────────────────────────┤
│No                                                              │
│Yes                                                             │
└──────────────────────────────────────────────────────────────┘
```

Select Yes if the options on the previous screen are correct and you want to continue with the installation. If you need to make further changes, select No, and then select No again on the Abandon Network Generation and Exit! screen.

Note: ELS NetWare Level II users that return to the Available Options menu after exiting can select Configure Operating System to alter the setting of the server and choose a different set of lines and addresses for the LAN driver.

Proceeding with the Configuration

NETGEN/ELSGEN now proceeds to link and configure the operating system, if you selected Yes in the previous step. You must stand by and insert disks if you are running the floppy-disk or RAM- drive method. Don't be surprised if the process asks for the same disk more than once. The result of the link and configuration process is a file called NET$OS.EXE, which will be written to the OSEXE-x disk. If you are running the hard-disk or network-method, these files will also be located in the OSEXE-1 directory.

When the linking and configuration process is complete, you can begin the next phase of installation. The Network Generation screen appears as shown here:

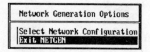

Exiting NETGEN/ELSGEN

Choose Exit NETGEN/ELSGEN from the Network Generation Options screen. If you are running the hard-disk method, the following screen appears:

Exiting NETGEN/ELSGEN

Choose Exit NETGEN/ELSGEN from the Network Generation Options screen. If you are running the hard-disk method, the following screen appears:

Choose Yes to download the needed files to floppy disk. You will be requested to place various disks in the floppy disk that will be used at the server during the installation phase. Those using the hard-disk installation method who have an additional system can format and diskcopy the appropriate disks as they are requested. Those using the Network install method need not download the files since they are automatically transferred through the network cable during installation.

Phase 3: Completing the Hardware Installation

The SHGEN and NETGEN/ELSGEN configuration steps covered in the last sections provided essential information for setting the dip switches and jumpers on the network interface boards. You now have the information you need to set the switch and jumpers and to install other hardware in your server or workstation.

Uninterruptable Power Supplies (UPS)

UPS units that are approved by Novell have UPS monitoring capabilities provided by special boards in the file server. These boards are the Novell SS Keycard with UPS monitoring or the Novell Standalone UPS Monitor board.

Switch settings need to be made on the board according to the type of UPS you have purchased. A UPS indicates a battery is low with an open contact (no current on cable) or with a closed contact (current on cable). The UPS manual should explain which setting it uses. The American Power and Elgar UPS systems use the closed setting discussed next. The jumpers on the board should be placed in the positions discussed in the following sections.

Standalone UPS Monitor Board

The boards can use I/O address 231h or 240h, but 231h should be selected since 240h is used by the Novell NL-1000 LocalTalk Card.

Battery Low Input—Jumper 1:

S1 = jump to specify open setting

S2 = closed setting (use for American Power and Elgar UPS)

UPS On-line Input—Jumper 2:

S3 = jump to specify open setting

S4 = closed setting (use for American Power and Elgar UPS)

I/O Address—Jumper 3:

S6 = jump for 231h (use this setting in most cases)

S7 = jump for 240h

SS Keycard with UPS Monitoring

Leave jumpers 2, 3, and 4 in their default setting of S4, S5, and S8, respectively.

Battery Low Input—Jumper 1:

S1 = jump to specify open setting

S2 = closed setting (use for American Power and Elgar UPS)

UPS On-line Input—Jumper 5:

S9 = jump for open contact

S10 = jump for closed contact (use for American Power and Elgar)

If you are using the mouse port on IBM PS/2 systems, you can simply attach the cable from the system to the UPS and proceed with the next step. Keep in mind that this will prevent the use of a mouse.

Network Interface Boards and Cables

To avoid confilicts, make sure the settings on your network interface boards are set according to the NETGEN/ELSGEN recommendations. Then proceed to install the boards in the server as well as the workstations. If the network interface cards were shipped with diagnostics routines, you should run them at this time according to the instructions supplied with the boards. Connect the cables to each of the workstations and the server. Make sure that all terminators and grounds are properly installed.

Running COMCHECK (COMmunication CHECK)

Once the network interface cards are in the system and the cables are attached, you can run COMCHECK to test the cable connections to each station (except the remote reset stations). COMCHECK is a useful way to verify that workstations are communicating over the LAN. If all stations have successfully COMCHECKed and problems crop up later after NetWare is running, you can probably eliminate cards and cables as the source of the problem. COMCHECK is also a useful management and diagnostics utility for isolating problems. It can help you locate bad network boards or cables after NetWare is up and running.

Note: If multiple LANs are being bridged by placing multiple network interface cards in the server, COMCHECK only checks workstations within each network, since the bridge is not established until NetWare is up and running.

To begin using COMCHECK, locate the DIAGNOSTICS disk in your NetWare disk sets. In addition you need the IPX.COM file you create for each workstation type. Make sure the IPX.COM file is the correct match for the network interface board in each workstation. You also need any drivers required by the network interface cards. For example, IBM Token Ring cards require several driver files that are loaded at boot time using the CONFIG.SYS file. The required steps outlined here should be performed on each workstation to be checked:

1. Prepare a DOS boot disk for floppy-drive systems or use the master boot disk created during the SHGEN process. If your system has a hard drive, you can start from the hard drive.

2. Create the CONFIG.SYS file if necessary, including the device commands required for the network cards in the system. Refer to the card manual for more information.

3. Make sure the IPX.COM file is on the disk. Or you can replace the boot disk with the disk holding IPX.COM. If the system has a hard drive, copy the IPX.COM file to the root directory.

Note: If IPX.COM does not load properly, the board interrupts and addresses may be in conflict with other system resources in that computer, in which case you will need to run SHGEN again, possibly in the custom mode as outlined in Appendix A. The board may also require special boot files loaded from CONFIG.SYS.

To start COMCHECK, simply switch to drive A or the drive holding the disk and type **COMCHECK**. Type a *unique* name for the station when requested. You then see a screen that lists the current workstation address (and possibly others), user name, and other information. Leave COMCHECK running and move on to the next station, following the same procedures, and continue this process until all workstations are running COMCHECK. Eventually, you begin to see other workstation names appear on the screen. Any stations that don't appear on other screens are having communications or cable problems and they should be checked in the following way:

1. Make sure COMCHECK is still running in the faulty machine.

2. Check the cable to the faulty station and make sure the cable connector is attached to the network interface card.

3. Make sure the station has a unique name.

4. Make sure the mode address is unique (refer to the interface card manual).

Once all stations have been checked, replace the DIAGNOSTICS disk and press ESC to exit COMCHECK. If you have further problems, the board or cable may be bad and you should contact your dealer.

Note: Be sure to log the network address and node address for each station on the worksheets. You will need these later.

Remote Workstation Configuration, ELS NetWare Level II Only

If you are installing a remote workstation under ELS NetWare Level II, the following steps are required to further prepare the disk for the station:

1. Locate the remote workstation master disk you created during the SHGEN phase for further preparation.

2. Use the DOS LABEL command to label the disk with an appropriate label, such as REM_STATION or CHICAGO.

3. Locate the UTIL-1 disk from your NetWare disk sets and log in to the floppy drive you will use. If possible, place the remote disk in the second drive, if one is available.

4. Type the following command at the A prompt:

   ARCONFIG volume_name:IPX.COM

   where *volume_name* is the label you gave the disk.

The following screen will appear

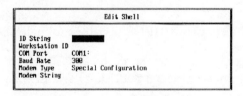

Enter the information as outlined here:

- The ID string is an optional nine-character uppercase name that should be exactly the same as the name specified for the remote workstation at the file server. Write this name down for later reference. The ID string is designed for security.

- The Workstation ID is a 2- to 45-character name that identifies the remote workstation. It is best to specify an easily recognizable name, such as the city or address of the remote workstation.

- Specify COM1 or COM2 as the modem communication port. You can press ENTER on the COM Port selection to see a list of choices.

- Press ENTER in the Baud Rate field to see the available baud rate selections.

- On the Modem Type field, press ENTER to select between Hayes Compatible or Special Configuration. If you select Hayes Compatible, you can enter the phone number of the remote location the modem will be calling. Press ENTER when done.

Press ESC to exit and select Yes to save the changes. The remote server configuration for the file server will be performed in the installation phase of NETGEN/ELSGEN.

Hard Drive COMPSURF (COMPrehensive SURFace Analysis)

The COMPSURF program is used to prepare hard drives for use with NetWare. The program performs a *comprehensive surface analysis* of the disk surface and provides initial disk information for the Hot Fix feature. It formats the disk, tests track zero, and runs sequential and random writes to locate bad blocks. Bad blocks are added to the bad block table.

There is no need to run COMPSURF on Novell hard drives or on IBM PS/2 machines. Novell drives are pretested at the factory. If your server is a PS/2 system, use IBM's own diagnostics software. You will see the following message if you need to run a surface analysis on the drive:

The drives listed above have not been tested by the surface analysis program COMPSURF. You must run this program for these drives before NETGEN will be able to continue. Press ESCAPE.

After you press ESCAPE, the Analyze Disk Surface option should appear on the menu.

Note: Do not run COMPSURF if you are upgrading from NetWare 286 v2.0 or above. The disks are already tested, and COMPSURF would destroy any existing data on the drives.

ELS NetWare Level II users should select Utility Programs from the following menu:

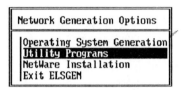

COMPSURF Requirements

As discussed in Chapter 9, you must locate the disk manufacturer's test printout that lists previously identified bad blocks. This list is usually attached to the top of the disk drive itself and may require the removal of the server's cover. You should also know the interleave value you want to use. This is normally 2 on AT-style machines and 1 on IBM PS/2s.

You should also attach a parallel printer to the LPT1 port of the system being tested, as COMPSURF will print the test results for future reference. COMPSURF may crash the system if you try to print without a printer attached.

Running COMPSURF

Select Run Disk Surface Analysis or Analyze Disk Surface from the menu. COMPSURF then requests the following information:

- Selection of the drive to COMPSURF.

- Whether to format the disk.

- The interleave value, if necessary.

- Whether you wish to supply the bad block list from the manufacturers listing, if available. Novell recommends that you enter blocks supplied by the manufacturer to ensure a more thorough test.

- The number of times you wish to run the Sequential Test. Each pass requires about 30 to 45 minutes per 20MB. Novell recommends you run the Sequential Tests at least three times.

- The number of reads and writes in the Random Test. You may accept the default unless you have reason to specify more or less.

When all the required information has been entered, you are asked for confirmation. If you select No, you may reenter the parameters. If you elected to enter bad blocks, an entry screen appears. Bad blocks are identified by head and cylinder number according to the listing provided by the manufacturer. Press INS or DEL to insert or remove bad blocks. Once the bad blocks have been entered, press ESCAPE. You are then asked to confirm the entries.

Testing and formatting begin immediately after selecting Yes, so make sure you want to proceed with COMPSURF. This process can take about 1 hour per 10MB. Once the drive has been tested, you are ready to begin Phase 4 of NetWare installation.

Disk Coprocessor Boards
(Advanced NetWare and SFT NetWare Only)

A Disk Coprocessor board is a circuit board that is installed in the file server to control external hard drives, such as the Novell NetWare Disk Subsystems (NDS2 and NDS4). If you are installing one of these drives, refer to the Novell or third- party documentation that comes with the drive for complete instructions.

If external hard disks are attached to one or more Disk Coprocessor boards mounted in the file server, the hard-disk configuration information for each channel must be programmed into the firmware of the channel's Disk Coprocessor board. This is done with the following steps:

1. Reenter NETGEN using the floppy-disk method, and select Configuration Utilities from the main menu.

2. Choose the correct configuration utility (Disk Coprocessor boards or third-party).

3. Run the configuration utility to indicate the number and types of hard disks and controller addresses of the controller boards.

The configuration utility must be run on the computer to be used as the file server after the boards and drives have been installed. The DISKSET option in the configuration utilities is used to program Disk Coprocessor boards. If third-party drives are being attached, refer to the configuration utility supplied by the manufacturer. Refer to your Disk Coprocessor board documentation for more information.

Phase 4: Installing the Operating System on the Server

The final phase of NETGEN/ELSGEN is the server installation phase. If you have been running the hard-disk method, you must now switch to the floppy-disk method on the server. Those running the network-drive method should now install NetWare on the hard drive of the server they have been using as a workstation.

This section describes the default installation method. Custom installation, covered in Appendix A, should be used when

- You need to reinstall the operating system after making slight changes in its characteristics and you don't want to reload the system and public files

- You need to create volumes on drives larger than 255MB

- You need to customize the printer options

- You need to modify the Hot Fix Redirection tables

Note also that if NetWare fails to load after installation with the default method, there may be interrupt or address conflicts that need to be corrected using customization procedures covered in Appendix A.

Reentering NETGEN/ELSGEN

Start the computer you will use as a server with DOS 3.0 or above and a CONFIG.SYS file that contains the line FILES=10. If you are using the network-drive method, attach the new server as a workstation on to the server where NetWare was configured. Then map a drive to the directory where the NETGEN/ELSGEN configuration took place and execute the commands shown here. All other users should insert the NETGEN or ELSGEN disk into the floppy drive where the program will be run and log to that drive. If a second disk drive is available, insert the SUPPORT disk.

Enter one of the following commands depending on the NetWare version you are installing:

NETGEN -D

or

ELSGEN

If you are running ELSGEN, select the default mode from the first screen to appear. The following screen, which appears for NETGEN, is similar to the ELSGEN screen that will appear after selecting the default mode:

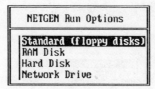

```
 NETGEN Run Options

 Standard (floppy disks)
 RAM Disk
 Hard Disk
 Network Drive
```

Select Standard (Floppy Disks) from the screen, unless you are running the network-drive method. Do not select Hard Disk at this time. Those who have installed a RAM drive can select RAM Disk.

The next screen to appear will be similar to the following:

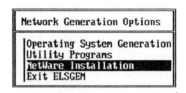

Advanced NetWare and SFT NetWare users should select the NetWare Installation option and jump ahead to the "NetWare Installation" section of this chapter.

Configuring the Remote Workstation, ELS NetWare Level II Only

ELS NetWare Level II users will see the Utility Program option on the NetWork Generation Options screen. Select this option, and you will see the following screen:

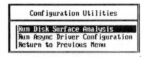

Disk Surface Analysis was covered in the last section. Select Run Async Driver Configuration if you are installing a remote workstation. The following screen appears:

Select the first item to configure the bridge. This option configures the file server and the line for the IBM ASYNC (COM1/COM2) LAN driver selected during ELSGEN configuration.

On the next screen to appear, you can enter the name of the bridge server, its ID string, and a password.

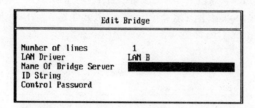

The ID string and the Control Password must be *exactly* the same as those specified when you configured the remote workstation. Be sure to type these in uppercase to ensure a proper match. Press ESC when the options are filled in.

If you select Configure a Particular Line from the main menu, the following screen will appear.

If you ran ARCONFIG before, many of the previously selected options appear. Specify the baud rate, modem type, dial mode, and other options as you did when configuring the remote workstation earlier in this chapter.

Note: The Auto Connect feature determines whether a file server automatically establishes a connection with a remote station when it is booted. The Life Class option allows the connection to be continuous or to have a time out. If you select Timed in the Life Class box, you can specify the time-out period after which an idle connection will be automatically terminated.

Once the settings are made, press ESC to return to the Network Generation Options menu, and continue with the next steps.

NetWare Installation

When you select NetWare Installation from the Network Generation Options menu, you are asked to verify the hard-disk configuration. A screen similar to the following will appear:

```
 Drive Name      Channel Controller Drive   Status
|IBM System2 MFM Hard►  0         0         0
```

Press ESC to confirm the drives, select Drive List Is Correct to accept the drives, and then move on to the next step. A screen similar to the following appears:

```
        Installation Options
Select Default Installation Options
Select Custom Installation Options
Continue Installation
```

The Select Custom Installation Options selection appears for those installing ELS NetWare Level II. These options are covered in the custom installation topics in Appendix A.

Note: Advanced NetWare and SFT NetWare users who must partition the server hard disk and install another operating system such as DOS or UNIX/XENIX in one of the partitions should refer to Appendix A.

Note: If two or more hard disks are installed in the server and you are running SFT NetWare, the Mirroring Options menu appears. You can choose to establish a mirror pair if you want to take advantage of NetWare System Fault Tolerance options. Drives can be paired for mirroring if they are on the same channel and duplexed if they are on different channels. These options are discussed in Chapter 9. Highlight Establish Mirror Pair from the menu, and then decide which of the listed disks will be the primary drive in the pair. Once two disks are paired together, they will appear as a single disk and assume the drive name and information of the primary disk.

The volumes you have selected appear in the next screen, similar to that shown here:

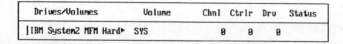

Record the information from this screen on your network log sheets. Press ESC to continue. The Fix Master System Table option may appear after you review the default volume names. If it appears, you must choose Yes to fix the table or else exit the program. This option appears if hard disks have been added or removed from the system.

You must now name the file server, using the following box:

A System Configuration box similar to this one appears next:

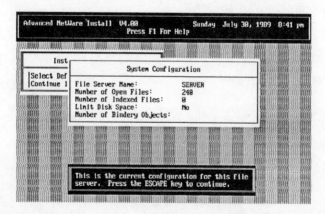

You can record these parameters on your installation log sheet.

The next few screens request information about the printers attached to your server. A screen similar to the following appears for each serial COM port attached to your system:

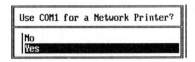

Answer Yes on these screens if you plan to use serial printers.

You then are queried about any parallel printers you intend to attach to the server. Answer Yes if you plan to use any of the parallel ports for printers. When the printer prompts have been answered, the printer configuration for your network is displayed on the screen. Press ESC to move to the next menu, which is shown here:

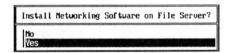

Select Yes to accept the changes you have made and to begin the installation of NetWare on your server. Then you are asked to insert various disks for file downloading. These files will be used to start the server, as covered in Chapter 11.

NetWare Startup and Post Installation Procedures

E
L
E
V
E
N

Part I
Starting NetWare at the Server and Workstations
Starting the NetWare Server
Starting a NetWare Workstation
Configuring Diskless Workstations
Part II
Post-Installation Procedures

The procedures in this chapter cover Phase IV of the installation as discussed in Chapter 10. Part I of this chapter covers starting the server and workstations. Part II covers the installation of a UPS (uninterruptable power supply) and the creation of the SHELL.CFG file. SHELL.CFG is used to make operational changes to workstation environments. An additional startup file, AUTOEXEC.SYS, is covered in Chapter 20.

If you are installing an uninterruptable power supply, be sure to refer to the UPS installation section later in this chapter. If you need to make changes to the shell environment for workstations (increasing buffers, files, machine names, and so on), refer to the section on creating the SHELL.CFG file. Keep in mind that the SHELL.CFG section will get a little technical and may not be for everyone. The file will be created in Part I of this chapter to include a single command. Other possible commands are discussed in Part II. Those needing to change the Internetwork Packet Exchange Program (IPX), NETBIOS, or the shell environment should refer to this section. In most cases, defaults already established during the installation will be sufficient, but they can be changed by adding statements to SHELL.CFG.

PART I

Starting NetWare at the Server and Workstations

This section will describe the various ways to start the NetWare server and its workstations, including diskless workstations. You do not need to read the entire section, only those parts that apply to your system. This section covers the following topics:

- *Starting NetWare servers.* Once NetWare is installed on the server, you will be able to start it. There are different procedures for starting dedicated and nondedicated servers. A dedicated server can simply be turned on. After NetWare starts, a colon prompt will appear after the copyright messages. Nondedicated servers must be started by booting DOS from a disk in the floppy drive, then executing he NETWARE startup drive.

- *Starting NetWare workstations.* Workstations are started with the DOS boot disk prepared when running the SHGEN program. The procedure to start a workstation is simple and requires few steps.

- *Starting NetWare Diskless Workstations.* Since diskless workstations can't boot DOS on their own, a special program called DOSGEN will be used to create the boot files in the LOGIN directory of the server. You will see how to prepare and run the DOSGEN program.

Starting the NetWare Server

Assuming that NetWare is installed properly, you are now ready to start the server and workstations. Since NetWare (except SFT) can be either dedicated or nondedicated, there are several ways to start the server. You will need to refer to the following section that is appropriate for your server.

If the server fails to boot using any of the methods described here, several things could be wrong:

- The wrong LAN driver was chosen during the NETGEN/ELSGEN configuration process.

- Nondedicated servers require at least 1.5MB of memory to start.

- The system may not be compatible with Novell NetWare. The incompatibility may be in the BIOS chip or the keyboard.

Starting a Dedicated File Server

A dedicated server may be started from either the hard drive or from a floppy disk. The floppy-drive method is only presented for those who do not have bootable hard drives which is rare.

Booting from a Hard Disk

If your system boots from the hard drive, simply remove any disks from drive A and restart the system (CTRL-ALT- DEL may be used). In a moment the NetWare file-server startup information will be displayed on the screen. The screen will keep you posted on the status of the startup and display messages if problems are encountered. The SYS volume is mounted, the bindery and queues are checked, and each LAN card in the system is initialized. In a moment, you will see the console colon prompt, where console commands can be entered. If the colon prompt appears, the network has successfully booted.

Once a dedicated server has been started, you can log in as the supervisor on one of the workstations, as discussed in "Starting a NetWare Workstation" later in this chapter.

Booting from a Floppy Disk

Start the system with a bootable DOS disk in the floppy drive that contains DOS version 3.0 or higher. When the DOS prompt appears, place the OSEXE-1 disk in the disk drive and type the following command:

NET$OS

You will be requested to insert the OSEXE-2 disk if you are using 5 1/4-inch disks. In a moment the NetWare file server startup information will be displayed on the screen. The screen will keep you posted on the status of the startup and display messages if problems are encountered. The SYS volume is mounted, the bindery and queues are checked, and each LAN card in the system is initialized. In a moment, you will see the console colon prompt, where console commands can be entered. If the colon prompt appears, the network has successfully booted.

You can now jump ahead to "Starting a NetWare Workstation" later in this chapter.

Starting a Nondedicated File Server

Since a nondedicated file server can also be used as a NetWare workstation, you must first boot DOS. If the server's hard drive has a DOS partition, part of the DOS boot and NetWare boot can take place from this hard drive after DOS is started. Follow these steps to create a non-dedicated-server boot disk:

1. Format a new floppy disk using the FORMAT command's /S parameter, which places the DOS system boot files on the disk.

2. Copy the NET$OS.EXE file from the OSEXE-1 disk or directory to the new disk. If you have a hard-disk DOS partition, copy this file to the root directory of the hard drive.

3. Copy the IPX.COM file, and appropriate NET*x*.COM to match your DOS version to the disk from the SHGEN-1 or SHGEN-2 disk or directory to the new disk. If you have a hard-disk DOS partition, copy this file to the root directory of the hard drive.

4. Copy the CONSOLE.COM file from the GENDATA disk to the new disk. This utility allows switching between DOS mode and NetWare console mode. If you have a hard-disk DOS partition, copy this file to the root directory of the DOS hard drive.

You are now ready to create an AUTOEXEC.BAT file on the boot disk using one of the following methods. For systems with hard disk DOS partitions, the boot disk and the AUTOEXEC.BAT file still must be created, because the system must initially boot from the floppy disk. The startup batch file on the floppy disk will switch to the hard drive and start the NetWare boot process from the DOS partition to increase speed.

AUTOEXEC.BAT File
For Floppy-Disk Startup

While logged into drive A, type the following to create the AUTO-EXEC.BAT file, pressing ENTER at the end of each line. Note that NET*x* should be replaced with NET2, NET3, or NET4, depending on the DOS version being used by the system. The last line is the CTRL-Z (or F6) end-of-file marker.

Note: If you need to execute other commands in the AUTO-EXEC.BAT file, enter them in this file.

```
COPY CON AUTOEXEC.BAT
PROMPT $P$G
NET$OS
NETx
F:
LOGIN
^Z
```

Note: The F: command switches to the first network drive and the LOGIN command starts the log-in process.

Once the file is created on the boot disk, you can reboot the system to start the server. The batch file will complete the log-in process at the server. When the system asks for a log-in name, type **SUPERVISOR** to log in for the first time. You will see the log-in screen, as shown in Figure 11-1.

You can now proceed to "Starting a NetWare Workstation" to start a workstation, "Creating the Startup Files" to continue with NetWare's configuration, or Chapter 12 to begin working with NetWare immediately.

AUTOEXEC.BAT File for
Systems with DOS Partitions

The following batch file should be created on the boot disk only if you have a hard disk DOS partition. The commands in the batch file switch to hard-drive DOS partition C, and then run the NetWare startup files from the hard drive for increased speed. Press ENTER at the end of each line. Note that NET*x* should be replaced with NET2, NET3, or NET4, depending on your DOS version. The last line is the CTRL-Z (or F6) end-of-file marker.

Note: If you need to run other commands on your system from the AUTOEXEC.BAT file, enter them in this file.

```
COPY CON AUTOEXEC.BAT
PROMPT $P$G
C:
NET$OS
NETx
F:
LOGIN
^Z
```

Note: The F: command switches to the first network drive and the LOGIN command starts the log-in process.

After creating the file, be sure to copy NET$OS.EXE and NET*x*.COM to the hard disk DOS partition before restarting the server. After the server restarts, type SUPERVISOR at the log-in prompt. You will then see the log-in screen shown in Figure 11-1.

You can now proceed to "Starting a NetWare Workstation" to start a workstation, "Creating the Startup Files" to continue with NetWare's configuration, or Chapter 12 to begin working with NetWare immediately.

Starting a NetWare Workstation

Use the following steps if you are logging in to NetWare from a workstation. Initially, anyone can sign on to the server as the supervisor until passwords and other access rights have been established. If the network supervisor

```
Good morning, SUPERVISOR
Drive A        maps to a local disk.
Drive B        maps to a local disk.
Drive C        maps to a local disk.
Drive D        maps to a local disk.
Drive E        maps to a local disk.
Drive F     := SB-SERVER/SYS:SYSTEM
Drive G     := SB-SERVER/SYS:LOGIN
DRIVE Y     := SB-SERVER/SYS:PUBLIC
           ------
SEARCH1    := Z:. [SB-SERVER/SYS:PUBLIC]

F>
```

Figure 11-1.   NetWare initial log-in screen

or installer has already established log-in names and passwords, you will need to use your assigned name and password to sign on to the system. This discussion will assume that the network supervisor is signing on for the first time. The next chapter will cover sign-on procedures for users in more detail. In addition, this section describes how to automate the log-in process with batch files.

Basic Log-in Steps

The log-in procedure at a workstation can be performed from a bootable floppy drive or hard drive. If a diskless workstation is being started, refer to the next section.

The steps for logging in are briefly outlined here:

- Start DOS on the workstation from the floppy drive or hard drive.

- Execute IPX.COM to initialize the network.

- Execute NETx.COM to start the DOS shell.

- Switch to the default network drive.

- Type LOGIN to start the log-in procedure.

In order to execute these procedures, follow these steps:

1. Start the system with the version of DOS you want to use. If you are booting from a floppy-disk-based system, place the DOS disk you want to use in the floppy drive. If you are booting a hard-drive system, make sure a disk is not in the floppy drive to ensure the system will start from the hard drive.

2. Next, get the disk that was used to download files during the SHGEN workstation configuration process in Chapter 10. Be sure to use the disk that was made for the network interface card you have in the system. There might be several different IPX.COM files, depending on the number of different interface cards used in the network.

3. Copy the files shown here from the SHGEN workstation disk to the new boot disk, or to the root directory of the hard drive. Remember that NET*x*.COM may be NET2.COM, NET3.COM, or NET4.COM, depending on the version of DOS used to boot the workstation.

   IPX.COM

   NET*x*.COM

4. If you are running applications requiring NETBIOS, copy the following files to the boot disk from the SHGEN workstation disk:

   NETBIOS.EXE

   INT2F.COM

5. Copy any additional files required by your network interface card or computer system. These files may be special drivers to activate the card. They are normally included on disks supplied with the card. If you are using the IBM Token Ring system, refer to the instructions in the IBM LAN Support Program package for installing the Token Ring driver commands in the CONFIG.SYS file.

6. If special drivers are used, create a CONFIG.SYS file with DEVICE commands to load the drivers in the root directory of the boot disk or hard drive.

7. Create a SHELL.CFG file to add a custom name to the system. SHELL.CFG is a special file used to customize the network environment and DOS shell configuration. It is covered in detail in Part II of this chapter. For now, you can create a basic version of the file to give your workstation a unique name that will be used by the NetWare log-in script. The DOS COPY CON command can be used to create the file in the root directory of the boot disk.

   Machine names help identify a particular workstation and the DOS version it is running to NetWare. The name will help establish the correct search path to the DOS directory on the NetWare volume and can also be used to provide customization for the workstation. There are two possible names. One is the *long machine name* and the other is the *short machine name*. The long machine name is of interest here. It is IBM_PC by default but can be changed to a six-character name that reflects the type of machine you have, such as COMPAQ or DELL.

   To create the SHELL.CFG file and include the command to assign the long machine name, type the following commands, pressing ENTER after each. Replace the machine name "DELL" with the name to be used by your system.

   COPY CON SHELL.CFG

   LONG MACHINE NAME = DELL

   ^Z (or press F6)

8. To start the network, type **IPX**, and then **NET**x (depending on the DOS version). If NETBIOS support is required, type **NETBIOS** and **INT2F**.

9. Switch to the network hard drive by typing **F:** at the prompt. If the workstation is booting with DOS 2, switch to one of the following drives:

   C: for two floppy drive systems

   D: if one hard drive exists on the workstation

   E: if two hard drives exist on the workstation

Note: The startup commands can be placed in a batch file such as NET.BAT for ease of use. They can also be placed in the AUTOEXEC.BAT file if you want the network to start every time you boot the system. This is covered in the next section.

10. Type **LOGIN** to start the log-in process, and enter **SUPERVISOR** as the log-in name. You will see the log-in screen shown in Figure 11-1. At this point you can proceed to the next chapter or continue with other topics in this chapter.

Starting the Network Automatically

If the network is to be started every time the workstation is booted, you can include the startup files in an AUTOEXEC.BAT file. Use COPY CON to create a new AUTOEXEC.BAT file or EDLIN to edit an existing file, and then include the following commands in the order shown:

```
PROMPT $P$G
IPX
NETx
F:
```

If NETBIOS support is required, include the commands NETBIOS and INT2F in the startup file after the NETx command. If DOS 2 is being used, change the F: command according to step 9.

Configuring Diskless
Workstations

Since diskless workstations cannot boot DOS on their own, remote reset PROMs are used to give them the capabilities of booting from the network server hard drive, as if the network drive were a hard drive built into the workstation. This section will describe the steps necessary to create the boot files. Before you create them, make sure the diskless workstations have remote reset PROMs installed on their network interface cards.

If you are using different interface cards, different interrupts and addresses, or a different version of DOS in any of your cards, a separate boot file will need to be created for each different diskless workstation. This will require additional steps to configure the boot file and will be covered in a separate section later.

In order to create a boot file for a diskless workstation, a boot disk must be created, even though the diskless workstation will never be able to use the disk. The boot disk is created on another system with a disk drive. Each startup command and file you want to run on the diskless workstation must be included on this "pseudo" disk. It must be formatted as a bootable disk with the DOS version you want to run on the diskless workstation, and it must include the NET*x*.COM for that version of DOS. The disk should also include the IPX.COM file for the network interface card in the workstation. You can also include other startup files such as SHELL.CFG and AUTOEXEC.BAT.

Once the disk is created, it is placed in a network workstation that has a floppy-disk drive, and the NetWare DOSGEN program is executed. DOSGEN reads the files on the disk and combines them into a new workstation boot file that is placed in the LOGIN directory of the server. This file then contains everything the diskless workstation needs to boot from the server and is called NET$DOS.SYS by default.

Creating Multiple Remote Boot Files

Typically, most workstations will use the same network interface card and DOS version. If not, you will need to run DOSGEN to create a separate file for each customized diskless workstation. A unique name is given to each customized file when you create it. You must then specify which custom workstation will be using which remote boot file by creating a match-up list in a file called BOOTCONF.SYS. This file will hold the network address and node address of each custom diskless workstation, and the name of the remote boot file each workstation is to use. Remote workstations that are not assigned to a custom file will use the standard file NET$DOS.SYS.

You should have written the network address down for each diskless workstation network interface card, as discussed in Chapter 9. If you don't have these addresses, you can determine them by running the SLIST command from the NetWare command line. The node address will also be required. This can be determined by placing the network interface card for the diskless workstation in a floppy-disk-based system and running the diagnostics or utility software that comes with the interface board. The diagnostics will display the node address assigned to the card. You should refer to the manual supplied with the card for more information. Keep in mind that the steps covered here are only required if you are using more than one type of remote reset network interface card; otherwise, the default NET$DOS.SYS file can be used.

Running DOSGEN

Once you have created the "pseudo" boot disk for the diskless workstations, you are ready to run the DOSGEN program. You will need to log in to the server as the supervisor before you can proceed with these steps. Refer to the previous two sections if you need help logging in to NetWare. The following steps create the NET$DOS.SYS file which will be the default remote boot file:

1. Once you are logged on to the server, type the following commands to map the network SYSTEM and LOGIN directories:

   MAP F:=SYS:SYSTEM
   MAP G:=SYS:LOGIN

2. Next, change to the SYS:LOGIN directory by typing:

   G:

3. Place the boot disk in drive A and type the following command:

   F:DOSGEN

   NET$DOS.SYS will be created and stored in the SYS:LOGIN directory.

4. Type the following command to make the file Shareable-Read/Write:

FLAG NET$DOS.SYS SRW

If you are not creating custom boot files, you can boot your remote workstations at this time. Continue with the next chapter or with Part II of this chapter to customize the system further.

Creating Multiple Boot Files

Perform the following steps to create additional custom remote boot files. These steps must be repeated for each custom file.

Type the following command, replacing *filename* with the name for the remote boot file. This name should reflect the machine type, DOS version, or interface board. For example, a boot file for a Western Digital interface board could be called WESTDIG.SYS.

F:DOSGEN A: *filename*.SYS

Once you have created a remote boot file for each different type of diskless workstation, you will need to create the BOOTCONF.SYS file. This file tells NetWare which files each diskless workstation should use, based on its network and node address.

Locate the network and node address for each system as discussed earlier. Make sure you are still logged in to drive F and the SYS:LOGIN directory, and then use the COPY CON command to create the BOOTCONF.SYS file:

COPY CON BOOTCONF.SYS

Create an entry for each diskless workstation as shown here:

0x[*network address*],[*node address*]=[*remote boot filename*]

For example, the following would be typed for the Western Digital boot file if its network address were 1 and its node address were 54321:

01,54321=WESTDIG.SYS

PART II

Post-Installation Procedures

This section covers the installation of an uninterruptable power supply and the creation of the SHELL.CFG file. You can read through this section now or return to it at another time if you want to continue with the following chapters.

Configuring the Uninterruptable Power Supply

The SERVER.CFG file is created on the server in the SYSTEM directory; therefore, it can only be created by the supervisor or the supervisor's equivalent when the network is up and running. Transfer to the SYSTEM directory and use the DOS COPY CON command to create the file. The commands that can be placed in the file are described next.

Hardware Type

The TYPE command specifies the type of UPS monitoring hardware that is connected to the UPS. Type the command shown here on a separate line in the SERVER.CFG file, replacing x with 1 if the hardware is a UPS standalone board, 2 if the hardware is an SS keycard, and 3 if a PS/2 mouse port is used.

TYPE = x

I/O Address

Place the following command on a separate line in the file to specify the I/O address you specified when setting the jumpers on the monitoring board in Chapter 10:

UPS IO = *xxx*

IBM PS/2 systems will not require this command. If you are using a standalone UPS monitoring board, specify 231 as recommended in Chapter 10 or 240 if you have reason to use this setting. If an SS keycard for UPS monitoring is being used, specify 230 as the address.

UPS Downtime

The DOWN command specifies the "downtime" for the UPS. This is the number of minutes users have to log out of the file server after the UPS begins supplying power but before the operating system brings down the file server. Replace *xx* in this command with the time you prefer.

DOWN = *xx*

The default downtime is 3 minutes. The minimum can be 1 minute, and the maximum can be 30 minutes. Enough time should be given so that users can log out but it should not be enough time to drain the power supply. The power supply may drain faster than rated if it is supplying power to many devices. If the battery drains before the time runs out, the system will automatically shut down 1 minute after it receives the "low battery" signal from the UPS.

UPS Wait Time

The WAIT command specifies the number of seconds to wait before notifying users that the power is off. This option is available because it may not be necessary to notify users every time there is a slight fluctuation in power. Type the following command, replacing *xxx* with the desired wait time:

WAIT = *xxx*

The default wait time is 15 seconds, but the range is from 15 seconds to 300 seconds (5 minutes). The wait time must be less than the downtime.

VAP Wait Time

The SERVER.CFG file has a command not related to the UPS called VAP WAIT. A VAP is a third party Value Added Process used to customize the network operating system. This command is used to specify how long the server should wait before automatically loading VAPs. In the following command, replace *xxx* with the wait time in seconds:

VAP WAIT *xxx*

The wait time can be from 10 to 360 seconds, with 10 being the default. Pressing a key during the wait time will abort the automatic loading.

The SHELL.CFG Configuration File

The default settings made for various NetWare operating features during the NetWare installation will be adequate for most installations. If you do need to make changes to them for any reason, however, Novell gives you the opportunity to do so with the SHELL.CFG file. This file is similar to the DOS CONFIG.SYS file because the commands in it are executed as NetWare loads. Commands in the file can be used to alter IPX.COM, NET*x*.COM, and NETBIOS.

As mentioned, most default settings will be adequate for IPX.COM, but there are a few settings for NET*x*.COM that you may find useful, so it may be beneficial to review this section before moving on. For this reason, the NET*x*.COM options are listed first.

The SHELL.CFG file needs to be located on the same disk and in the same directory as the NET$OS.EXE. The file is read when NetWare is started. Use the DOS COPY CON command to create the file.

Options for Altering the NetWare Shell (NETx.COM)

To specify any of the following options in the SHELL.CFG file, type each command on a separate line in the file.

CACHE BUFFERS = *number*   Sets the quantity of 512-byte buffers. The default is 5. This command improves network performance by providing a buffer for disk data during sequential reads.

FILE HANDLES = *number*   Sets the number of possible open files. The default is 40.

PRINT HEADER = *number*   Sets the size of the buffer holding the printer escape characters sent before a print job. The default is 65 bytes.

PRINT TAIL = *number*   Sets the size of the buffer holding the printer escape characters sent after a print job. The default is 16 characters.

EOJ = ON/OFF   Turns the end-of-job (closing of files, locks, semaphores, and so on) on or off. The default is ON.

LOCAL PRINTERS = *number*   Can be used to specify 0 printers at the local workstation to prevent system lock if SHIFT-PRT-SCR is accidentally pressed.

HOLD = ON/OFF   Sets file hold on or off. If set to ON, all files opened by a program are not usable by others until the program ends. The default is OFF.

SHARE = ON/OFF   Sets file-handle sharing. When ON, the child process inherits the file handle of the parent process. The default is ON.

LONG MACHINE TYPE = *name*   Assigns a 6-character name to a machine that is later used by the %MACHINE variable in log-in scripts to establish the operating environment for a specific type or brand of machine and the DOS version it is running.

SHORT MACHINE TYPE = *name*   Assigns a 4-character short name to the variable %SMACHINE that is used to specify the color palette for menu utilities. The default color palette short machine name is IBM. Setting the short machine name to CMPQ will set black and white mode.

LOCK RETRIES = *number* Sets the number of times the shell should attempt to get a lock on the network. The default value is 3.

LOCK DELAY = *number* Sets the amount of tick times the shell should wait before retrying to get a lock. The default is 1.

READ ONLY COMPATIBILITY = ON/OFF When this is set to On, the shell reverts to an older NetWare method of allowing read-only files to be opened with a write-access call. Any attempt to write to the file will fail, however.

SEARCH MODE = *number* Sets the way .EXE and .COM files search for needed files in the directory structure. The following search modes may be set, but the default is 1:

0	No search instructions
1	Search on the path specified in the executable file itself; if a path is not specified, search the default directory and then all search drives
2	Search on the default directory
3	Search only the path leading to the data file specified in the .EXE file itself; if a path is not specified and the executable file opens data files as Read-Only, search the default directory and then all search drives
4	Reserved
5	Search the default directory and all search drives whether or not the path is specified in the executable file
6	Reserved
7	Search the default directory and all search drives whether or not the path is specified in the executable file, if the executable file opens data files Read-Only

MAXIMUM TASKS = *number* Specifies the maximum number of simultaneous active tasks. The default is 31, the minimum 8, and the maximum 50.

PATCH = *byte offset,value* Allows an option in the shell to be patched with any value.

TASK MODE = *number*   This option determines the way in which the shell creates, switches, and destroys tasks. If you are using Windows 386 or any multitasking program, set the task mode to 1. If you are not, set the task mode to 0. The default is 1.

Options for Altering Internet Packet Exchange (IPX)/Sequenced Packet Exchange (SPX)

IPX SOCKETS = *number*   Specifies the maximum number of sockets, or "subaddresses," that IPX can have open at the workstation. The default is 20. Change if an application using IPX requests an increase in the default.

IPX RETRY COUNT = *number*   Sets the number of times a packet should be re-sent if packets are lost. The default is 20.

SPX CONNECTIONS = *number*   Specifies the maximum number of SPX connections that a workstation can use at the same time. The default is 15.

SPX ABORT TIMEOUT = *number*   Specifies the wait time before a session is aborted if responses aren't being received from the other side. The default is 540 ticks (30 seconds).

SPX VERIFY TIMEOUT = *number*   Sets the interval at which SPX will send packets to determine if a session is still active. The default is 540 ticks (30 seconds).

SPX LISTEN TIMEOUT = *number*   Sets the amount of time SPX waits for a session packet before a request for a session packet is made. The session is still valid if the request for a packet gets a response. The default is 108 ticks (6 seconds).

IPATCH = *byte,value*   Allows any location in the IPX.COM file to be patched with any value.

Options for Altering NETBIOS

The following options can be used to alter the NETBIOS environment if it is being used.

NETBIOS SESSIONS = *number*   Sets the number of sessions NET-BIOS will support at one time. The range is 4 to 100; the default is 10.

NETBIOS SEND BUFFERS = *number*   Sets the number of send buffers NETBIOS uses. The range is 4 to 20; the default is 6.

NETBIOS RECEIVE BUFFERS = *number*   Sets the number of receive buffers NETBIOS uses. The range is 4 to 20; the default is 6.

NETBIOS RETRY DELAY = *number*   Sets the delay (in ticks) between each packet sent when establishing sessions or registering names. The default is 10 ticks (.5 second).

NETBIOS ABORT TIMEOUT = *number*   Sets the amount of time NETBIOS will wait for a response before terminating a session. The time-out number is in ticks (18.21 per second on IBM compatibles). The default is 540 ticks (30 seconds).

NETBIOS VERIFY TIMEOUT = *number*   Sets the interval at which NETBIOS will send packets to determine if a session is still active. The default is 54 ticks (3 seconds).

NETBIOS LISTEN TIMEOUT = *number*   Sets the amount of time NETBIOS waits for a session packet before a request for a session packet is made. The session is still valid if the request for a packet gets a response. The default is 108 ticks (6 seconds).

NPATCH = *byte offset, value*   Used to patch any location in the NETBIOS.EXE data segment with any value.

Starting with NetWare

Logging in to the System
Exploring the NetWare Filing System
Drive Mappings and Search Drives
Initial Supervisor Tasks

If you logged in as SUPERVISOR in the last chapter, you are now a member of the NetWare "Fellowship of Supervisors." This is an unofficial group of people who have made it through the entire planning and installation phase and who have the opportunity to see the NetWare copyright screen and log-in message. Congratulations! All the hard work and planning were your initiation rights into this special group. You are now ready for the day-to-day task of managing the system.

Logging in to the System

If you are not currently logged in to the system, do so now by following the steps in the previous chapter. Your initial log-in screen should look similar to the one shown here. There may be a difference if you started the system with DOS 2 or a non-hard-drive system or if the system log-in script has already been modified.

275

```
Good morning, SUPERVISOR
Drive A      maps to a local disk.
Drive B      maps to a local disk.
Drive C      maps to a local disk.
Drive D      maps to a local disk.
Drive E      maps to a local disk.
Drive F   := SB-SERVER/SYS:SYSTEM
Drive G   := SB-SERVER/SYS:LOGIN
DRIVE Y   := SB-SERVER/SYS:PUBLIC
          ------
SEARCH1   := Z:. [SB-SERVER/SYS:PUBLIC]

F>
```

In this illustration, drives A through E are "mapped" to local drives. Even though the drives might not be physically present, NetWare reserves their drive letters. The first network drive is drive F, which is currently mapped to the SYSTEM directory. The PUBLIC and LOGIN directory are also mapped. Note that the PUBLIC directory is referred to as SEARCH1 in the illustration. This is explained in the following section.

Exploring the NetWare Filing System

Now that you are logged in to the network, you can begin exploring its file system, create directories, add applications, and establish users on the system. To start, it is important to understand the terminology used on a NetWare network when referring to its servers, volumes, directories, and files. These are described in the following sections.

Servers

Your network may have one or more servers. Each server is given a specific name so you can switch between one or the other during your network sessions. In the screen display above, the server name is listed as SB_SERVER. Your system will be different, depending on the server name you specified in NETGEN/ELSGEN.

You can use the NetWare SLIST command to view a list of available servers either before you log in or after. To log in to a different server, the server name is specified in the LOGIN command, as will be discussed later. You can also "attach" additional servers to your current session with the

NetWare ATTACH command. In this way, you can map directories on the additional servers for use. A mapped directory can be switched to simply by typing its drive letter and a colon, and then pressing the ENTER key.

You will be able to see your current log-in connections and status by typing the NetWare WHOAMI command. This command displays your log-in name and time, along with the servers you are attached to.

Volumes

A hard drive may be divided into several volumes, especially if the capacity of the hard drive is over 255MB. Volume names are also part of a directory name you can see by typing the MAP command at any time. In the previous illustration, the volume is SYS, which is always the first volume name. Other volume names will be VOL1 or VOL2.

The NetWare MAP command can be used to map directories on other volumes for use in your current session.

Directories

Once you are logged on to a NetWare server and in to a particular volume, you can begin to work with directories in the same way you would work with directories in the DOS environment. NetWare adds security features and menu utilities, of course, but for the most part, the DOS CD (Change Directory), MD (Make Directory), and RD (Remove Directory) commands can be used, assuming users have the proper rights to do so.

- The FILER menu utility can be used to work with directories.

- NDIR is used to list directories. The creation date and attributes of each file are shown, among other things.

- RENDIR is used to rename directories.

- LISTDIR can be used to display a map of directories and sub-directories.

- FLAGDIR can be used to change subdirectory attributes to Hidden, System, Private, or back to Normal.

The Complete Name of a File

The complete name of a file includes the server name, volume, directory, subdirectories, and the file name itself. You don't have to enter the complete name every time you work with the file, but keep in mind that the other information specifies exactly where the file is located. If you are working in one volume and need to work with a file in another volume, you must specify the volume name, directory name, and subdirectory name for the file you want to work with. Alternatively, you can map the directory where the file exists; then just refer to it by mapped drive letter and file name. The complete file name is shown here:

File Server Name/Volume Name:Directory/Subdirectory/Filename

Note that the file-server name and volume name are separated by a slash, and the volume name ends with a colon. As mentioned previously, you won't need to specify either the server or volume name in most normal file operations.

Looking at the SYSTEM and PUBLIC Directories

As the supervisor, you have complete rights to the entire system. In addition, the SYS:SYSTEM directory is reserved for use by the supervisor or the supervisor's equivalent. Switch to this directory now if you are not already there by typing its drive letter. You can type the following command to see a list of drive assignments:

MAP

Note: If the prompt is not showing the name of your current directory, type **PROMPT pg** at the command line. You can add this command to the log-in script, as described later.

The SYS:SYSTEM Directory

Once you change to the SYS:SYSTEM directory, you can type the following command to display the files in the directory.

NDIR

You will see a list of files in the directory, their size, modification dates, access dates, flags, and owner information. The supervisor is listed as the owner of these files. Commands in the SYS:SYSTEM directory are meant for supervisors only. Since the files are used to handle the system security and accounting, as well as system related activities, regular users should not have access to them.

The SYS:PUBLIC Directory

Now switch to the SYS:PUBLIC directory by typing the letter of the drive that has been mapped to it. If you are not sure, type the following command to display the drive listing:

MAP

Once again, type the following command to display a list of files in the directory:

NDIR

SYS:PUBLIC contains the menu utilities and command files used by all users of the system. When you create a new user, the user will be given a search drive to this directory by the default log-in script. As the supervisor creating new log-in scripts, you will need to make sure the new users have access to this directory with a search-drive mapping since the directory contains commonly used commands. The following command can be placed in the system log-in script to ensure that all users are search-drive mapped to SYS:PUBLIC:

MAP S1:=SYS:PUBLIC

The SYS:LOGIN and SYS:MAIL Directories

SYS:LOGIN is the directory users are placed in when switching to the network server from a local drive prior to logging in. The directory holds the LOGIN.EXE command file. The SLIST.EXE command is also located in the directory so users can view a list of available servers before logging in. If you have diskless workstations, the SYS:LOGIN directory holds the files created by the DOSGEN command, as covered in Chapter 11.

The SYS:MAIL directory is primarily used by the NetWare Mail program, which is available as a separate option. When a user is created, a subdirectory is created in the MAIL directory that corresponds to the user's ID. Each user's personal log-in script is also stored in the SYS:MAIL subdirectory assigned to the user.

Drive Mappings And Search Drives

The NetWare MAP command is one of the most-used commands in the operating system. Supervisors will use it to map directories to drive letters and to map directories as search-drive mappings. A full explanation of the command will be presented in later chapters. For now, you should become familiar with what it does and what it can be used for.

Drive Mappings

A drive mapping is a way of assigning a drive letter to a particular directory. The drive letter can then be typed on the command line to move into the directory, rather than having to type the complete name of the directory. This provides more ease of use for the NetWare filing system, since it is much easier to type a single letter than it is to type a long directory name.

Mapping a drive is similar to using the SUBST command in DOS. For example, you could execute the following MAP command to map a directory called SYS:PUBLIC\APPS\DBASE to the K: drive:

```
MAP K:=SYS:PUBLIC\APPS\DBASE
```

After the drive is mapped, you can type the following drive switch command to switch to the directory.

```
K:
```

Drive mappings can be personal, or they can be established in the same way for each user. In most cases, supervisors will want to establish the same drive mapping for all users from the system log-in script. In this way, the supervisor does not need to create and edit a personal log-in script for each user on the system. This also establishes a "generic" operating environment that will be much easier for the supervisor to manage. Users can create their own mappings, either by editing their own log-in scripts, by using the MAP command on the NetWare command line, or by using the SESSION menu utility, which will be covered later. Batch files can also be used to establish specific mappings before running a program.

All drive mappings are lost when a user logs out, but they can be reestablished every time the user logs in if the MAP commands are placed in the system log-in script or the user's personal log-in script.

Even if you don't specifically map a directory to a drive, simply switching to that directory will map it to the current drive, but the previous drive map will be lost. This is often confusing to new users who (inadvertently) change the assigned drive maps set by the system or a log-in script by using the CD (Change Directory) command. For example, assume the current default drive is K and it is mapped to SYS:PUBLIC/APPS. Now assume the user changes to the SYS:PUBLIC directory using the DOS CD command. Drive K is now mapped to PUBLIC, but so is drive F, which was mapped in the log-in script. When the MAP command is typed to display the current mappings, PUBLIC will be mapped twice, as shown here:

Drive F: = SM-SERVER/SYS:PUBLIC
Drive K: = SM-SERVER/SYS:PUBLIC

What the user should have done was simply type **F:** instead of the DOS CD command to get to the PUBLIC directory. This would have retained the drive K mapping to SYS:PUBLIC/APPS.

Note that any available drive can be used to map any available directory, but the MAP command should first be used to view the current mappings to see if a directory is already mapped. If an existing drive letter is used, the new mapping replaces the old mapping.

Each user can have his or her own set of drive mappings. For example, Bob may map a data directory called PUB-DATA to his drive K, while Jane maps the same directory to her drive R. If Bob tells Jane that he has just placed a file in R, Jane should be aware that her drive K is where the file is located.

Search Drive Mappings

In addition to mapping directories to drive letters, directories can be mapped as search drives. The supervisor can then specify search paths for directories that contain executable program files so that programs can be run while working in other directories. The DOS PATH command performs a similar function in DOS. For example, the following command creates search drive S3, which is mapped to the SYS:PROGRAMS directory:

MAP S3:=SYS:PROGRAMS

A search map is a pointer to a directory that contains executable programs required by system users. A search-drive mapping should always be set up for the SYS:PUBLIC directory so users can have access to the menu utilities and other commands stored there. Search-drive mappings should also be assigned to the directories in which software applications are stored, so users can access them from their personal directories or the directories used for data storage.

If you map a search drive to a program directory for a user, you will also need to give the user trustee rights in the directory so the user can execute the programs. These trustee rights include the Read, Open, and Search rights and can be assigned to a user with the SYSCON or FILER menu utility. Also keep in mind that users who need to create and edit files will need the Create, Write, Read, Open, and Search rights. The order and drive letters given to search drives can be confusing. They are assigned starting with S1 and counting up. When the search drive assignments are listed with the MAP command, S1 will be Z, S2 will be Y, S3 will be X, and so on. Sixteen search drives are allowed, but this number is limited by the number of regular drive mappings, which start with A, then B, then C, and so on.

Initial Supervisor Tasks

Before continuing on to the next chapter, there are few things the system supervisor will need to handle, as outlined in the following sections.

A Word About Security

Security is an important built-in feature of NetWare, with capabilities that go far beyond what DOS systems can offer. NetWare security can keep intruders out of the system and keep users from looking at or deleting other people's files. But many new users of NetWare feel that the security features are unnecessary for their business. Many small businesses feel that all of their employees can be trusted and that security features such as passwords would be a nuisance. Although keeping intruders out is always important, NetWare security goes beyond that. It also helps to keep users working in the areas they are assigned to and keeps weary users from deleting valuable data files accidentally.

Supervisors and users should realize that NetWare is a multiuser operating system. In a way, each user is given a part of the server for his or her own use. Since the server is shared by everyone, there needs to be a way to keep each user's data separate from those of other users. The security features help do this, and also keep intruders out. The password features are not only important for making sure that only authorized users are allowed to use the server, but for making sure that each user is identified properly for the purposes of running specific log-in scripts and for logging the user in to the directory that holds their personal files.

When considering the effects of an infection by a computer virus, it would seem that no user should have the capability to add files to the system. NetWare's ability to prevent file uploading or to protect executable files from viruses make its security features worthwhile. Preventing file uploads is not always practical, however, since users may need to transfer files between non-network systems. One solution is to provide floppy-disk-based systems in supervised areas and diskless workstations in all other areas. Users will then not be able to upload files to the server. Another solution is to flag all executable programs as Execute Only. A virus normally attempts to attach itself to an executable program and then, through that program, corrupts other files. By marking such files as Execute Only, you can prevent disaster.

Note: Use caution when flagging files as Execute Only: corruption has occurred in some cases and versions of NetWare. Always have a good backup set before doing so.

Changing the Log-in Password

Until the user supervisor is assigned a password, anyone can sign in as the system supervisor and have complete access to the entire system. This may not be a problem at first on a new system, since applications and important or private files don't yet exist, but the supervisor should immediately establish system security by assigning a password to the user supervisor.

Once the password is established, only the actual supervisor will be able to log in as the supervisor. All other users will need to log in with the log-in names and passwords assigned by the supervisor. In this way, the supervisor will have complete control over the system. Management will probably want to make sure that at least one other person has knowledge of the supervisor password or has access to the system as a supervisor-equivalent user, in case something should happen to the supervisor.

To establish a supervisor password, you can issue the command shown here at the NetWare command prompt. Make sure you are logged in as the supervisor before doing so.

SETPASS

The first request will be for your old password. Since you haven't yet assigned a password, simply press ENTER. You will then be asked to type your new password and then to type it again for verification. The command will then ask if you want to "synchronize" the password across all servers. If you have more than one server, you can type **Y** (or press ENTER) to use the same password when logging on to any other server. To use different passwords, type **N** and refer to the next paragraph. Your display will look similar to the following:

ENTER your old password:
ENTER your new password:
Retype your new password:
Would you like to synchronize your passwords on all attached servers?

If other servers are attached to the network, you can specify the use of the same password by answering Yes to the synchronize request.

To create supervisor passwords for other servers, type the command shown here, replacing *server* with the name of the other servers, and then follow the instructions just given.

SETPASS *server*

Note: To log in to other servers using the LOGIN command, type **LOGIN** **server/user name**, where *server* is the name of the server and *user name* is the name of the user logging in.

Using the Console

The NetWare console is a command area on the server (dedicated and nondedicated) where a limited number of commands can be used to monitor and regulate the file server's resources. Console commands can be used to send messages to users, manage printers and print queues, and down the server. The console can also monitor the activities of various workstations. Commands are also available for handling mirrored drives and mounting or unmounting removable disk packs.

If the server was set up in nondedicated mode, the console can be reached from the server workstation by typing the following command:

CONSOLE

The console colon prompt will appear. If the server is dedicated, it is already running in console mode, and the colon prompt should appear on the screen. If not, type the following command:

OFF

If you have access to the LOCK VAP, which may be included on a separate disk in your NetWare disk set, you can install keyboard locking on the console. In this way, the keyboard can be locked out to those without the proper password. The SETKPASS command is used to assign the console password. The installation of the LOCK VAP and use of SETKPASS is covered in Chapter 24.

To return to the DOS workstation of nondedicated servers, type the following command:

DOS

Check the Network Printers

You can check to make sure your network printers are working by issuing the commands in this section. Before doing so, make sure any local printers at workstations are operating by typing the following command, which assumes that local printers are on the parallel LPT1 port. Press ENTER at the end of each line, and then press the F6 key to close the file and send it to the printer. Note that this procedure may not work on the server workstation, since the CAPTURE command (discussed shortly) needs to be entered first.

```
COPY CON LPT1
This is a test
<F6>
```

Once you are sure the local printers are working, issue the following command to "redirect" printing from the workstations to the printers attached to the network. Note that x in the command should be replaced with the network printer number, which may be 0 through 4. Start with 0 if you are not sure.

```
CAPTURE P=x
COPY CON LPT1
This is a test
<F6>
```

Repeat this procedure for each printer on the server. If a printer does not function from the workstation, you should check the printer for problems first, and then check your installation routine to make sure the printer was set up properly.

The CAPTURE command will be a common way to redirect workstation printing to the network printers. The command can be issued in each user's personal log-in script so you can assign the user the use of a specific printer, 0 through 4 if available. As the supervisor, you can assign the use of a specific printer to each user, depending on the user's needs. For example, the accounting department can be assigned a high-speed dot-matrix printer for printing reports, whereas public relations might be assigned to use a high-quality laser printer.

To restore the local printing at a workstation, type the command ENDCAP (END CAPture). Other commands used in printing are NPRINT (Network PRINTer), which directs printing of a file on the network printer, even though local printers are currently the default printers. PSTAT (Printer STATus) can be used to check the status of network printers. The PRINTDEF, PRINTCON, and PCONSOLE menu utilities can also be used to manage printers. These commands are covered in detail in Chapter 20.

DOS Directories on the Server

You will need to create directories on the server to hold the DOS system and command files for each of the workstations. If every workstation is using the same version of DOS, only one DOS directory needs to be created. If workstations are using different versions of DOS (PC DOS or MS-DOS, version 2, 3, or 4) then you will need to create a separate directory for each.

The Long Machine name in the SHELL.CFG file (see Chapter 11) is used to create a DOS-directory search drive mapping for each workstation. The log-in scripts you create later in this book will contain commands that take advantage of the Long Machine name to map a search drive to the correct DOS directory on the server for each workstation logging in. For example, assume IBM workstations need to have access to IBM PC DOS in the SYS:PUBLIC/IBMDOS directory, and that all IBM machines are using the same DOS version. Also assume that the SHELL.CFG file on the boot disk of every IBM machine contains the command LONG MACHINE TYPE = IBMDOS. The following command, placed in the system log-in script, will set a search drive to the proper DOS directory:

MAP S2:=SYS:PUBLIC/%MACHINE

Note that systems using other types of DOS will have different %MACHINE names. For example, a Compaq workstation might be given the machine name CPAQ. A SYS:PUBLIC/CPAQ directory would then need to be created.

To create each individual DOS directory, issue the commands shown here, replacing *machine_name* with the name that you are assigning to the machines with the LONG MACHINE TYPE command in the SHELL.CFG file.

MD SYS:PUBLIC*machine_name*

Next, copy the files from the correct DOS disk to the new directory. You must also mark the files in the directory as Shareable so more than one user can access them simultaneously. Also, the files should be marked Read-Only as a protective measure. Type the following command, replacing *machine_name* with the name of the DOS directory:

FLAG SYS:PUBLIC*machine_name* *.* SRO

The naming system can get quite elaborate if you have many different versions of DOS. For example, NetWare is able to determine the DOS type and version number and assigns these to the variables OS and OS_VERSION. If a workstation logged in using MS-DOS version 3.2, OS would be equal to MSDOS and OS_VERSION would equal 3.2. You can then create a map command in the log-in script that sets the search path to the DOS directory. An example is shown here:

S2:=SYS:PUBLIC/%MACHINE/%OS/%OS_VERSION

The S2 search drive would then be mapped to the SYS:PUBLIC/AST/MSDOS/3.2 directory.

For practical purposes, it is best to update all of your workstations to the same version of DOS to avoid multiple DOS directory mappings. This is not always possible because some machines must run with the version of DOS supplied by the manufacturer.

Tasks Ahead for the Supervisor

As the system supervisor, you will need to perform various tasks to manage the operating system, file system, users, and groups. The system security will also need to be managed. These topics, outlined here, will be covered in the next few chapters.

Defining and Establishing Users, Groups, and Operators

You will need to establish each user on the system. This also includes establishing yourself as a user as well as the supervisor. In most cases, it's a good idea to log in as a regular user if you are using the system like everyone else. You can then establish various log-in scripts and directories for your own use. This lets you work in a normal way on the system without accidentally issuing a command (with full supervisor privileges) that you might regret.

User groups can also be established. You will want to plan these groups around the tasks that each user will be performing. Using the worksheets described earlier, map out the exact work group and directories each user will be assigned to. This will help you begin planning your directory structure and the system security you will need.

The next few chapters will show you how to create a new user so you can see how it is done manually. Chapter 18 describes the NetWare MAKEUSER utility that can make the task of creating a large group of new users easier. MAKEUSER is often used in academic environments, where whole sets of student accounts need to be removed or established at various times during the school year.

Managing System Security

System security starts with the log-in procedure. If you create a password for the supervisor, you have already established the first line of security. The next step is to create new users and require that they use passwords when logging in. Users can then be given trustee rights to the programs and directories they will be working in. You can also assign them to groups to make the management of users easier.

Creating Directories and Loading Applications

You'll need to design a directory structure that fits in with the applications you plan to use, the users and groups that will access them, and the security of the system. Make sure that programs are stored in directories that are separate from the data directories. Also make sure that Read, Open, and Search rights are given to appropriate users in the program directory and Create, Write, Read, Open, and Search rights are given to appropriate users in the data directory. Rights will be discussed in future chapters.

Log-in Scripts

Log-in scripts can be used to display messages and execute various commands when users first log in. There are two types of log-in scripts, the system log-in script and the user's log-in scripts. The system log-in scripts contain commands that are to be issued for everyone logging in. User log-in scripts can be assigned to each user and may contain commands that you want to set for each specific user. Users can edit their own log-in scripts, but not the system log-in script.

Accounting

If you plan to establish the accounting feature on your network, you will need to read through Chapter 23. The accounting feature must be activated before it can be used. You can then perform the following:

- Track user log in
- Charge users for system resources used, such as disk storage and printer time
- Charge users for the amount of time they use the system

Alternatively, the accounting feature can be used simply to keep statistical information about the use of the system by users, without charging them for it.

Network Hierarchy and Security

Hierarchy of a NetWare System
Network Security
Security and Access Rights for NetWare 386

NetWare provides system managers with a full set of tools and features to control access to information on the server. Users are given rights to programs and information based on needs determined by the user, the supervisor, and management. A user may request access to files in a particular directory; the supervisor then establishes the access to the directory as if unlocking the door to it. This chapter will cover the hierarchy of users on a NetWare system and how security can be administered to control those users.

Keep in mind that NetWare servers are devices used by many different people. Each user needs to be able to create files that can be kept secure from other users. At the same time, the system supervisor needs to keep the system files secure from users and "busybodies" who might accidentally erase files or look at files they have no right to see. You will see how users can secure their own files and directories and even their own rights in other directories if the supervisor gives them such access.

The supervisor needs to be aware of the needs of users and must respond to their requests in a reasonable fashion, while maintaining both the security and functionality of the system. At the same time, users must feel confident in the supervisor's ability to properly manage and maintain the network. After all, they are keeping their valuable data on the server and expect the network to be operational on a continuing basis. It is the supervisor's responsibility to make sure that data is safe, secure, and accessible at all times.

Hierarchy of a NetWare System

The NetWare file system has a hierarchy that gives some users more rights than others. This hierarchy is established by the network supervisor as users are created and changes are made in personnel. Often, various network maintenance and management tasks are relegated to other users. Outside this environment will be the management structure of the company, which dictates how the supervisor should establish the users and the hardware of the network. The hierarchy of a network is discussed here, along with the access rights given to each type of user.

System Supervisor

You are already familiar with the role of the system supervisor if you've read through the previous chapters. The supervisor has full access to the system files and control over the security system. The supervisor can establish various security levels and features, such as workstation restrictions, user restrictions, accounting, and various other features.

Part of the supervisor's responsibility is to add new users to the system and remove those who should no longer have access. In this role, the supervisor may need to interact with department managers and the users themselves. Users may request access to certain files or directories, and the supervisor may need to get approval for this access from the department manager before assigning those rights to the user.

Supervisors who manage large networks will no doubt be kept busy as they train users, answer questions, and "extinguish fires." Maintaining the network filing system and its associated hardware are also part of their task. Supervisors will probably find it necessary to assign some maintenance tasks to other users to help free up their own work load for more important management activities. These assigned tasks may include the following:

- System and file backups

- File archiving and purging

- Management of print queues and the printers

- Disk management and optimization tasks
- Emergency activities such as system shutdown

In addition, supervisors may find it necessary to assign the training of users to an internal training staff or an external training company. User training is crucial to the proper operation of a network. Questions are bound to come up at any time, and it is usually the supervisor who gets called. The best supervisors make sure that all of their users are well trained to avoid such situations.

Work-Group Managers

A *work-group manager* is a new class of user in NetWare 386. The work-group managers have additional rights to the system that give them some of the capabilities of supervisors without compromising network security. With non-NetWare 386 versions, the supervisor and the user comprise the two main groups. While some users might be given a few additional rights as discussed in the previous section, it is sometimes necessary to give the users the same rights as the system supervisor in order to relieve the supervisor or provide adequate backup.

Work-group managers under NetWare 386 can be created in a way that does not compromise the system security. Work-group managers have supervisor control over any user or user group they create, as well as their associated resources. This allows the supervisor to assign department managers the special rights of the work-group manager, while still maintaining control over the system as the supervisor with the proper security features.

Although it is not possible to create a user with the rights of a work-group manager under non-NetWare 386 systems such as ELS Net-Ware Level II, Advanced NetWare, and SFT NetWare, the concepts of a system user who is responsible for a group of users is still appropriate. While it may be necessary to give these users some of the rights of the supervisor, their task will be to relieve the supervisor of the job of managing a large number of users. The work-group manager may be in charge of deleting group files or determining which employees in the manager's group will have access to what files. The work-group manager is equivalent to a department manager in this sense.

If a user on a non-NetWare 386 system is assigned the equivalent role of work-group manager, it is important that this person be trusted and well trained to handle the tasks. This user should already have some management and employee responsibilities.

Users

Users are created by the supervisor or supervisor equivalent as needed. Users may also be created on a large scale with the MAKEUSER utility, as will be discussed in Chapter 18. A user is a person who has limited rights to the system, and these rights are controlled by the supervisor or work-group manager.

Users as Directory Trustees

A directory trustee is a user who has been given rights in a particular directory. For example, a new user might be assigned the right to read, write, open, and create files in a data directory. Once assigned the rights, that user becomes a trustee of the directory. Initially, users have no rights in any directories. They must be individually assigned by the supervisor or work-group manager. Once a user is assigned rights to a directory, a drive mapping to that directory should be established in the user's log-in script so the user can easily access the directory.

Remember that rights are assigned by the supervisor (or a designated manager) to a user in a single directory at a time. However, rights are carried into subdirectories. If the user creates subdirectories (they must have the rights to do so) in the directory, the same rights will be effective in the new subdirectory. This assumes that the supervisor or manager has given the user the rights to create subdirectories.

In most cases, a personal directory will be created for each user on the system and will branch from a directory called SYS:USERS. The name of the directory, however, is completely up to the supervisor or system planners. USERS is only recommended as a name. The NetWare manuals often recommend creating user directories that branch from the SYS:PUB-LIC directory; however, you may find that this complicates your directory structure. Each user can be given full rights to his or her own personal directory. For example, the users John and Jane would have separate user

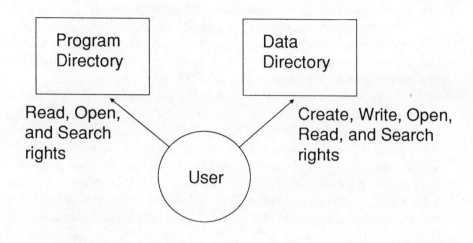

Figure 13-1.   How user rights should be set in program and data directories

directories called SYS:USERS\JOHN and SYS:USERS\JANE, respectively, and they would be given full rights in these directories.

Users are assigned rights in other directories if they need to access files or run programs. Typically, programs are stored in one directory, and the data files created by those programs are stored in a separate data directory. A user who needs to run the programs and access the data will need the rights illustrated in Figure 13-1. The supervisor or work-group manager will need to first establish the Read, Open, and Search rights for the user in the program directory so the user can execute the programs, and then establish the Create, Write, Open, Read, and Search rights in the data directory so the user can create and edit files. Note that some programs may also require the delete right.

The User GUEST

The user GUEST can be used by anyone needing temporary access to the system. GUEST is automatically a member of the group EVERYONE, as will be discussed later, and has all of the rights of that group. The rights usually include the ability to read files and list directories.

The supervisor can change the passwords for GUEST as necessary, since the person signing in as the guest will probably change often. If a GUEST user should no longer have access to the system, the supervisor can simply change the password for GUEST.

The supervisor may need to change the access of the GUEST user as necessary. For example, if a consultant or programmer is the guest, it may be necessary to assign additional rights. If a temporary data input person is the guest, it may be necessary to limit rights. If the supervisor has a lot of guest activity, it may be preferable to establish special users who have the rights needed by each different type of guest. For example, the supervisor might create a user called TEMP; this user will have the rights to run a data entry software program and edit files in a special data directory.

Operators

A network operator is a regular user who has been assigned additional privileges. These privileges are not the same as the Trustee Rights discussed earlier. Instead, a special status is given to the user through one of NetWare's menu utilities. These are discussed here. Typically, an operator is given the privilege to use the FCONSOLE utility, which among other things can be used to down the server.

FCONSOLE Operator   The FCONSOLE operator is capable of running the FCONSOLE utility, which can be used to monitor the activity and efficiency of the network and make adjustments to it. FCONSOLE is typically used by maintenance personnel who are enhancing or repairing the system, or programmers who are developing special applications. The FCONSOLE operator status is given to a user by the supervisor using a special option in the FCONSOLE menu utility.

Queue Operators   A queue operator is given the right to control the activities of a print queue. A print queue is like a "waiting line" for print jobs at the printer. Each job sent to the printer is stacked in the queue. The queue operator has the power to rearrange the jobs in the queue or remove jobs. Queue operators are assigned by the supervisor for each queue that exists, using a special menu option in the PCONSOLE menu utility. Typically, each printer will have one queue. However, a printer might have more than one queue to receive print jobs from different sources at a different print-job priority. A queue can also service more than one printer. In this way, if one printer is busy, the queue sends the print job to another printer.

Console Operators   The console is the special command area of a dedicated server, or the non-DOS, NetWare side of a nondedicated server. Users who have access to the console can issue special commands to the operating system. These commands can be used to broadcast messages, disable log-ins, mount or unmount removable disk packs, monitor or alter printers and queues, and down the server. Console operators are established by first running a utility that locks the keyboard at the console and then allows access only through password entry.

Operators should be chosen wisely. They should be trusted and be aware of the responsibilities of managing the server. For example, if the power goes out or the system is threatened by fire, an operator should have the responsibility and knowledge to down the server properly and take it elsewhere if necessary. Queue operators may need to prepare for awkward situations should they need to bump one user's print job for another.

Groups

Groups are exactly what they describe: groups of users. Typically, a group is created after users are created. Users are then added to groups. Because groups allow managers to more easily manage the system, and because groups typically correlate to real work groups or department groups, both supervisors and department managers should think of users in terms of the groups they belong to whenever possible. The reasons for this will become clear as you establish the network and its users, program directories, and data directories. In terms of directory trustee assignments, it is easier to assign rights to a whole group than to each individual user one at a time.

When the activity of groups is considered, the structure of the system itself becomes more easily definable. Almost every user will belong to a group and is placed in a group according to the type of information and the

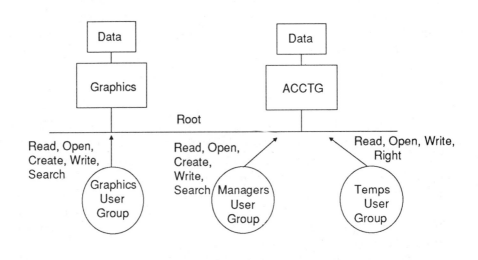

Figure 13-2. Group rights for three different groups

applications the user will use, as well as the departments for which the user works.

Groups make the supervisor's job easier, but groups can also make it easy for users to communicate among themselves. In the first case, it's easier for a supervisor to assign an entire group the rights to a directory rather than to assign each user rights one at a time. In the second case, messages can be addressed to an entire group rather than sent to each user individually.

As an example, consider the groups shown in Figure 13-2. The staff of the graphics department is placed in a group called GRAPHICS. The group is then given rights to use the programs in the GRAPHICS directory and the data directory branching from it. Another group called MANAG-ERS is given access rights to a directory called ACCTG and the data directory that branches from it. These rights allow them to create new files if necessary. A third group called TEMPS is given rights in the ACCTG directory and its data subdirectory, but those rights are limited to editing.

Once the groups are created and given the proper rights to each directory, the supervisor can add new members to the group or remove old members as necessary. When a member is added to a group, he or she is given all of the rights already established in a directory for the group.

The EVERYONE Group

All users belong to the group EVERYONE. Each user is assigned to this group when initially created as a user by the supervisor or supervisor equivalent. Supervisors can use the EVERYONE group to grant rights to all users in specific directories at the same time. Since everyone is automatically assigned Read, Open, and Search rights in the PUBLIC directory and their personal mail directories, all new users automatically have the rights to use the programs or read the files in those directories.

Group Manager

A group manager is a person who normally has supervisory control over a group of employees in the structure of the company. On the network, this person might be given control over the access rights and files of the same group. The supervisor can give these work-group managers rights to directories so they can control other users in the directory, thus freeing the supervisor from the tasks of managing the directory. For example, the manager of the accounting department might be given full rights to the directory ACCTG in Figure 13-2, including the right to delete files, modify file flags, and create subdirectories.

Network Security

Security on a network is administered in four different ways. The first has to do with how users log in to the system and the restrictions they have once they log in. The restrictions, called *log-in rights,* determine the amount of time they can stay logged in and whether they can log in to additional stations. Other restrictions can also be applied, as you will see. The remaining security methods regulate how users access a server filing system. Users can be granted rights, called *trustee rights,* in a certain directory, or they can be locked out of directories in one of three ways by the supervisor through the use of a rights mask. At the file level, special attributes can be given to files to prevent users from reading, editing, and deleting them. Other file attributes are also available.

This section will describe each of the security methods and how the supervisor can take advantage of them to protect a server, a directory, or files.

Log-in Rights

The first level of security has to do with the log-in process and the restrictions placed on a user after logging in. Users must specify their log-in name and an optional password as described here.

User name   The user name is the identity of a user and is used to identify the user's personal account on the system. The supervisor defines the user name when creating the new user. This name is also used when creating the users personal directory that branches from the SYS:USER directory. In most cases a user's name will be his or her common name, but other names like CLERK01 or SALESMGR can be used.

Password   A password is an optional access keyword that is known only to the user. The supervisor has the ability to change a user's password at any time. Although passwords are optional, it is recommended that they be used.

The LOGIN command is used to gain access to a server. As mentioned in the previous chapter, a user wanting to log on to a server from a workstation must first connect to the network on that station by running the IPX.COM and NETx.COM commands. The user then switches to the LOGIN directory by selecting the first network drive letter, which is drive F for DOS 3 and above. The commands for logging in to the network reside in the SYS:LOGIN directory. These files include the LOGIN command as well as SLIST, which displays a list of available servers.

Users can type **LOGIN** and the operating system will ask them for their user name and password; or users can type **LOGIN** followed by their user name, and the system will ask for the password. If a user enters the wrong user name or password, he or she is denied access to the system. The user can, of course, try again. The supervisor can regulate how often a user can attempt to log in to the system by using the *intruder lockout feature*. In this way, unauthorized users can't try several different names and passwords in an attempt to gain access; after a while, the system will lock out their attempts.

When a user gains access to the system, the system log-in script is executed, as well as the user's personal log-in script if available. The supervisor is responsible for creating and updating the log-in script to include commands for establishing the network environment such as drive mapping commands. Supervisors can also alter the user's personal log-in script, or this can be done by the user.

Password Options (Account Restrictions)

There are a number of ways the supervisor can control the password log-in procedure. These are described next. The SYSCON menu utility is used to create users and establish the restrictions described here. They will be covered in more detail in Chapter 18. The screen for changing these options, called Account Restrictions, is shown here and is available in each user's User Information window. Note that the supervisor can set default restrictions for all users under SYSCON Supervisor Options window.

```
┌─────────────────────────────────────────────────┐
│        Account Restrictions For User NEWUSER     │
├─────────────────────────────────────────────────┤
│Account Disabled:                      No         │
│Account Has Expiration Date:           No         │
│   Date Account Expires:                          │
│Limit Concurrent Connections:          No         │
│   Maximum Connections:                           │
│Allow User To Change Password:         Yes        │
│Require Password:                      Yes        │
│   Minimum Password Length:            5          │
│Force Periodic Password Changes:       No         │
│   Days Between Forced Changes:                   │
│   Date Password Expires:                         │
│   Limit Grace Logins:                            │
│      Grace Logins Allowed:                       │
│      Remaining Grace Logins:                     │
│Require Unique Passwords:              No         │
└─────────────────────────────────────────────────┘
```

Allow User to Change Password   This option is used to specify whether users will be able to change their own password or not. The GUEST account should not have this right, since you wouldn't want one guest locking another guest out by changing the password. Most user accounts should have this right, however.

Require Password   A password can be required for a specified user. If Yes is selected in the option, values can then be specified for the remaining options described here.

Minimum Password Length   The supervisor can specify the minimum length of a password to increase security. It wouldn't make much sense to have one-character passwords, since breaches to security might be possible. NetWare requires a minimum of five characters, but passwords can be up to 128 characters long.

Force Periodic Password Changes   To improve security, the supervisor can force periodic password changes for periods specified in days. The default is to force changes every 40 days if the option is selected.

Limit Grace Log-ins   Grace log-ins are the number of times a user can log in with an expired password. This gives them a chance to change the password. The default is six times if the option is chosen.

Require Unique Passwords   If this option is set, the system will not let users specify a password used as one of their eight most recent passwords.

Station Restriction

The supervisor can restrict the physical station a user logs in to. You might use this option to keep temporary personnel from logging in to a disk-based system where they might download valuable data files. It can also be used to keep the same users from logging in to a system in an unsupervised area of the building. Station restrictions are set for individual users in the

SYSCON menu utility by specifying the station number the user will be assigned to.

Time Restrictions

Time restrictions can be set up for individual users or all users. For example, you may not want anyone using the system after 5:00. Default time restriction can be set by the system manager for all users on the system, and individual user time restrictions can be set for each individual user. Time restrictions are specified in the SYSCON menu utility using a screen similar to that shown here. Only the headers on this screen differ between the supervisor's Default Time Restrictions and individual user's Default Time Restrictions screen. The example shows default log-in times set for 7:00 A.M. to 6:00 P.M. except Wednesday, when, for example, the time is extended for system maintenance.

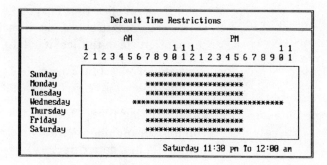

Intruder Detection and Lockout

Intruder detection makes it possible to control how often a user can make an attempt to log in to the system. The screen shown here is available in the Supervisor Options area of the SYSCON menu utility. When Yes is selected in the Detect Intruders field, the feature is activated. The threshold number of attempts is specified, which is the number of times an intruder can attempt to access the system before being locked out. The system will prevent further attempts beyond this number and for the amount of time specified in the menu.

```
┌─────────────────────────────────────────────────────────────┐
│                 Intruder Detection/Lockout                  │
├─────────────────────────────────────────────────────────────┤
│Detect Intruders:              Yes                           │
│                                                             │
│Intruder Detection Threshold                                 │
│Incorrect Login Attempts:      7█████                        │
│Bad Login Count Retention Time: 0  Days    0  Hours    30 Minutes │
│                                                             │
│Lock Account After Detection:  Yes                           │
│   Length Of Account Lockout:  0  Days    0  Hours    15 Minutes │
└─────────────────────────────────────────────────────────────┘
```

Trustee Rights

Recall that a trustee is granted certain rights in a particular directory. Once the trustee is given these rights, they *extend into subdirectories until redefined at another level*. The supervisor is assigned all rights in all directories. The rights that can be granted to individual users are summarized here:

Read	Read from an *open* file. This right is required to run programs in a program directory or view the contents of data files in a data directory.
Write	Write to an *open* file. This right is required to change the contents of a file in a data directory.
Open	Open existing files. This right is required to run a program in a program directory or open a data file in a data directory.
Create	Create new files. This right is required to create new files in a data directory and to create subdirectories within the current directory.
Delete	Delete files. This right is required to remove files and subdirectories. In some cases, it must be included in program directories if the program creates and then deletes temporary files.
Parental	This right is required to create, rename, and erase subdirectories, as well as to set trustee and directory rights for users in the directory or its subdirectories.

Search   Allows files to be listed.

Modify   Allows trustees to modify file attributes.

Note: It is important to understand that while these rights can be assigned to users, the supervisor can also assign the same access rights to the directory as a *maximum rights mask.* The combination of a user's trustee rights in a directory and the maximum rights mask applied by the supervisor are the user's *effective rights,* which are covered in a moment.

The trustee rights can also be granted to an entire group of users. In this way, the supervisor can make quick work of establishing the rights for a group directory. All users should understand the significance of trustee rights; otherwise they may attempt to create, write, or copy files in directories where they don't have such rights. Users will become confused and frustrated, and the supervisor will need to explain to them why they can't do what they are attempting to do.

Note: Trustee rights are enhanced for NetWare 386. Those connecting to NetWare 386 systems should refer to the final section in this chapter for details.

Security Equivalence

Another quick method the supervisor can use to give users rights to a directory is to copy the rights of one user to another. This is known as making a user *security equivalent.* There are two ways to make a user's rights equivalent to others. The first method is to add the user to a group that already has rights in a specific directory. The user will automatically inherit those rights. The second method is to use the SYSCON menu utility, which has an option for assigning security equivalence to a user under the User Information menu.

Directory Access

While individual users can be restricted in what they can do inside a directory through trustee rights, the supervisor can assign rights and attributes to directories that override individual rights. There are two sets of security options for directories, as discussed next. The first set limits all users rights to a directory. The second set hides directories from users.

Directory Maximum Rights

The supervisor or trustee manager can exclude any of the rights listed earlier under "Trustee Rights" to the directory itself. In this way users, no matter what their individual rights may be, cannot override the rights given to a directory itself, unless the user has Parental rights (as explained later). These rights are referred to as the maximum rights mask for the directory.

When a directory is first created, it has no rights or restrictions itself. Security is put into place when the supervisor begins removing some of these rights. (Keep in mind that users must still be given trustee rights to use the directory.) For example, the supervisor may decide not to allow anyone to delete files in a directory. The Delete right is removed from the directory's maximum rights mask using the SYSCON menu utility. Now, even if a user has the Delete right, he cannot delete files in the particular directory because the supervisor has removed the right from the directory itself.

Anyone that has the Parental trustee right in a directory actually has the right to alter the maximum rights mask set by the supervisor. The supervisor should take care when assigning the Parental right to a user, since the user could restore any directory rights originally revoked. Note that maximum rights apply to only one directory. They do not carry down through the directory structure as do trustee rights.

Directory Attributes

Directories can be given the attributes listed here by those who have the Modify and Parental rights in the parent directory. The FLAGDIR command is used to assign these attributes.

Normal	Indicates no attributes have been set. This attribute corresponds with the Public folder in the Macintosh environment.

Hidden	Hides the directory so it cannot be seen in a directory listing by any users. Users can still change to the directory, however, if they know its name.
System	Indicates the directory is used by the system and will not appear in a directory search.
Private	The contents of a directory cannot be viewed unless a user has the Search right.

Effective Rights

The *effective rights* of a directory are a combination of the maximum rights mask and the trustee rights of a user. Figure 13-3 illustrates how to determine the effective rights of a directory.

The effective rights of a user are important to understand and be aware of when working in a directory. If a particular task can't be executed, it is probably because one of the rights is missing.

	Read	Write	Open	Create	Delete	Parental	Search	Modify
Trustee Rights	R		O		D	P	S	
Maximum Rights Mask	R	W	O	C			S	
Effective Rights	R		O				S	

Figure 13-3.   A user's effective rights mask is a combination of the trustee rights and the maximum rights

Important Effective Rights

In most network environments, users work with applications from a data directory, not in the directory where the applications programs reside. That means that users will need to have different rights in both the data directory and in the program directory, as listed here:

Program directory	Users must be able to execute the files in the program directory that is mapped as a search drive from their data directory. The minimum rights for running programs are Read, Open, and Search.
Data directory	Since files need to be created and altered in the data directory, users must have the Read, Write, and Open rights. The Delete and Create rights may also be important, depending on the type of user.

Table 13-1 lists the required effective rights to perform various tasks on a NetWare operating system. Note that this table does not account for individual file attributes, which are discussed in the next section.

File Access

The files in a directory can be protected in various ways by changing file attributes. File attributes can prevent accidental erasures or changes in specific files. Files used by several network users at once should be marked Shareable. The complete list of file attributes is shown here. These attributes are assigned with the FLAG command or with the FILER utility.

Execute Only	Prevents EXE and COM files from being altered or copied and can only be assigned by the supervisor.
Read-Only	Prevents a file from being modified.
Read-Write	Allows users to read and modify files.

Activity	Right
Read from a file	O,R
Write to a file	O,W
Create and write to a file	W,C
COPY or NCOPY files into a directory	D,W,C
Make a new directory	C,P
Remove an empty subdirectory	P,M,D
Search a directory	S
Change files from SRO to SRW	M,S
Rename a file	R,W,M
Change maximum rights mask of directory	P
Change trustee rights	P
Delete a file	D

Table 13-1.   Required Rights for Various NetWare Activities (Refer to the section "Trustee Rights" for an explanation of the letter)

Non-shareable	Only one user at a time can work with non-shareable files.
Normal	Flags files as Non-shareable and Read-Write.
Hidden	Files with this attribute do not appear in listings.
Indexed	Indexes the FAT entry of large files to improve access from the hard drive.
Modified	This attribute is set if the file is modified since the last backup. Used in backup procedures to back up only files that have changed.
System File	Files marked with the System attribute will not appear in listings.
Transactional	Indicates the file will be protected by the Transaction Tracking System of SFT NetWare.

Security and Access Rights for NetWare 386

NetWare 386 access rights are slightly different than those of NetWare 286. They are listed here for those who may be interacting with the operating system. Access rights in NetWare 386 have been enhanced to improve the capabilities of network managers to implement effective and transparent network security. The rights can be assigned to users of directories, subdirectories, and files in any combination, allowing users to have access to resources without compromising security. The rights are listed here and are assigned on two levels: to directory trustees and to file trustees.

Read	Directory trustee: The user can open and read a file in the assigned directory and subdirectory.
	File trustee: The user can open and read to the assigned file.
Write	Directory trustee: The user can open and write to files in the directory and subdirectory.
	File trustee: The user can open and write to the assigned file.
Create	The user can create new files and subdirectories.
Erase	Directory trustee: This right can be assigned to a trustee of the directory, who can remove files and subdirectories.
	File trustee: This user can delete the file to which he or she is assigned.
Directory Scan	The user can see this directory name when scanning the parent directory.

File Scan	The user can see the file names of the files in the directory when scanning the directory. Users who are file trustees can see the file names of only the files they are assigned trusteeship to.
Access Control	Directory trustee: The user can modify the trustee list and inherited rights mask of this directory and of all child subdirectories and files, but the user cannot grant rights to themselves that they don't already have. File trustee: The user can modify the file's trustee list and inherited rights mask.
Supervisor	Directory trustee: A user has all rights to this directory and all child subdirectories and files. The user can grant supervisor rights to other users in this directory and child subdirectories and files. The user's rights override all inherited rights masks in child subdirectories and files. File trustee: The user has all rights to the assigned file.
Modify	Directory trustee: A user can change the name and attributes of a directory and all child subdirectories. File trustee: A user can change the name and attributes of the assigned file

NetWare Menu Utilities

This chapter will give you an overview of the NetWare menu utilities used by both supervisors and users. You should become familiar with their use, since they make many tasks easier to perform. In the next few chapters, the menus to be used as users, directories, and security are established on the system.

Using the NetWare Menu Utilities

The figures throughout this chapter show the major portion of each NetWare menu utility. Not shown is the information that appears at the top of each screen. This information includes the name and version of the utility in use, the date and time, and other information about the utility, such as the current directory name.

Once a utility is loaded, you can access help information by pressing the Help key, which is the F1 key. Information about the currently selected option will be displayed. Pressing F1 twice in a row will display the list of

313

```
The function key assignments on your machine are:

ESCAPE          Esc             Back up to the previous level.
EXIT            Alt F10         Exit the program.
CANCEL          F7              Cancel markings or edit changes.
BACKSPACE       Backspace       Delete the character to the left of
                                the cursor.
INSERT          Ins             Insert a new item.
DELETE          Del             Delete an item.
MODIFY          F3              Rename/modify/edit the item.
SELECT          Enter           Accept information entered or select
                                the item.
HELP            F1              Provide on-line help.
MARK            F5              Toggle marking for current item.
CYCLE           Tab             Cycle through menus or screens.
MODE            F9              Change Modes.
UP              Up arrow        Move up one line.
DOWN            Down arrow      Move down one line.
LEFT            Left arrow      Move left one position.
```

Figure 14-1.   The menu utility help screen

function-key assignments. These are listed in Figure 14-1 for your convenience and explained in the following paragraphs.

The Escape key (ESC) can be used to "back out" of a menu, and ALT-F10 can be used to quickly exit from a menu. The F5 key is the "mark" used to highlight multiple items from a menu. Simply scroll to each item and press F5 until all items are selected, and then press ENTER to continue with an operation. The F7 key is used to cancel markings made with the F5 key or to edit changes. The Backspace key is also used to edit items on the same line.

The Insert key (INS) is an important key in the menu utilities and is often referred to as the "lazy-man's" key. You can press it to display a list of options that can be inserted in a blank window instead of typing those options yourself. For example, when you need to specify a directory, you can often press the Insert key to display a list of directories to choose from. The Delete key (DEL) can be used to remove highlighted items from windows, such as user names or directories. Be aware of what is selected and what will be removed when using the Delete key. NetWare will always ask if you want to continue with a deletion.

The F3 key can be used to rename, modify, or edit a selected item. For example, a current drive mapping or search mapping can be selected, and then altered with the F3 key. ENTER is used to execute a selection.

The TAB key can be used to "circle" through menus or screens on some menu utilities, and the F9 key can be used to change modes.

Selecting Options

Options can be selected from menus by using the arrows keys to scroll up or down. Another method is to begin typing the name of the option until the highlight lands on the option. In most cases, the option becomes highlighted after you type the first letter, but two or three letters may be required if an option starts with the same first letters as another. You can also press the first letter repeatedly. Multiple options can be selected from a menu using the F5 Mark key as described in the previous section. Marked items appear in boldface or another color on the screen. Press F7 to unmark items.

Some options may extend below the screen display, in which case an arrow will appear at the bottom of the screen. You can use the arrow keys or Page Down keys to move through the list, or use the first-letter selection method. In long lists, such as those that display the files in a directory, it is better to type the first letter of the file you are searching for to get close to the target, and then use the arrow keys to highlight the exact file.

Changing Information

Some screens have fields that can be selected and changed. The arrow keys or the ENTER key can be used to move between fields. When the correct field is located, the ENTER key must be pressed to change the contents of the field. When all fields have been changed, the Escape key is pressed and changes will be saved if Yes is selected in a confirmation box.

NetWare Main Menu

NetWare has a main menu that can be accessed by typing the following command on the NetWare command line:

MENU MAIN

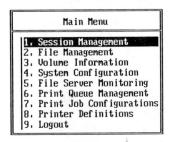

Figure 14-2. The main menu displayed by typing **MENU MAIN**

The menu in Figure 14-2 will appear and can be used to access all other menu utilities. MENU MAIN is actually an example menu system that demonstrates how the MENU command is used. The MENU command is covered Chapter 22.

System Console: SYSCON Menu Utility

The SYSCON menu utility is used to create users and define users' trustee rights. It is also used to create the system log-in script and users' log-in scripts. Most of the tasks performed in SYSCON require supervisor rights, although users will find the utility useful for displaying information about their status on the system, changing their log-in scripts, and displaying

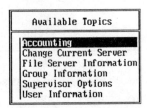

Figure 14-3. SYSCON Available Topics menu

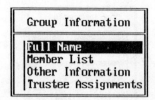

Figure 14-4. SYSCON Group Information menu

other useful information. Figure 14-3 shows the SYSCON Available Topics menu.

The first option is used to install or access the NetWare accounting features. The second option can be used to switch to another file server. The third option will display information about the current file server, such as the NetWare version, the number of current users, and the network address and version serial number, among other things. Users can select the User Information option to view information or change options on their personal accounts. They can also view limited information about other users but cannot change any options for other users.

The last three options on the menu are used mainly by the supervisor. These options are used to create and maintain users and groups, and to set and maintain various operating system features. The submenu for the Group Information options is shown in Figure 14-4. Groups can be created or altered, and trustee rights can be assigned by the supervisor. Other users can view these settings.

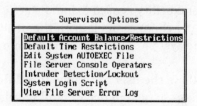

Figure 14-5. SYSCON Supervisor Options menu

Figure 14-6. SYSCON User Information menu

The menu for Supervisor Options shown in Figure 14-5 is available only to the supervisor. It provides options for setting default restrictions on the network and for creating special console operators, as well as for creating or editing the system log-in script.

The User Information window shown in Figure 14-6 is used to create and edit user accounts. Options are available for setting users' account, workstation, and time restrictions. These settings can be altered only by the supervisor, but can be viewed by users. User log-in scripts can also be created or altered by both the supervisor and user.

Note: Keep in mind that help is available when setting or altering most options by pressing the F1 Help key.

Session Manager: SESSION Menu Utility

The SESSION menu utility is used to handle activities and settings in the current session. Any changes made with the utility will be lost when the user logs out of the system. The SESSION main menu is shown in Figure 14-7.

SESSION allows the user to change to a different server; view, add, or modify drive maps or search drives; and to select a new default drive. Users can also view user or group lists and send messages to any user or

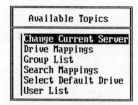

Figure 14-7.   SESSION Available Topics menu

group in the list. This list will consist of users currently logged in to the system.

SESSION can be used to add or modify drive mappings by selecting Drive Mappings from the main menu. A list of currently mapped drives appears, as shown in Figure 14-8. A mapped drive can be changed by selecting it and pressing the F3 key. The Insert key can be pressed to add new search drives. Search drives can also be modified by selecting Search Mappings from the main menu. As shown in Figure 14-9, the user selects a search drive to modify and then presses the F3 key. The Insert key is pressed to insert new search drives.

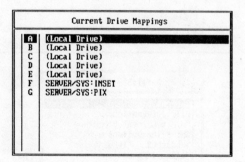

Figure 14-8.   SESSION Current Drive Mappings menu

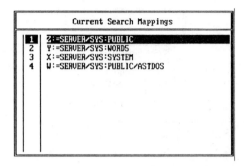

Figure 14-9.   SESSION Current Search Mappings menu

Be aware that mapping commands can be placed in the system log-in script or a user's log-in script in order to make them active every time a user logs in.

File Manager: FILER Menu Utility

The FILER menu utility is used to work with volumes, directories and files. Supervisors can use the utility to create directories and assign security. Files can be listed, deleted, renamed, and copied, and their attributes can be changed. Users will not have as much control in FILER as the supervisor

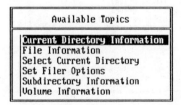

Figure 14-10.   FILER Available Topics menu

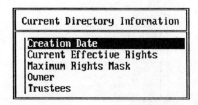

Figure 14-11.   FILER Current Directory Information menu

but will be able to view useful information about various directories and files. The FILER main menu is shown in Figure 14-10.

The first option displays information about the current directory. Supervisors can modify the maximum rights mask and the trustees of the directory. Supervisors and users can view the other information available from this menu, such as the directory creation date, its owner, and the effective rights of the current user as shown in Figure 14-11.

Each user may have different effective rights within a directory, based on the maximum rights mask assigned to the directory by the supervisor and the trustee rights given to the user in that directory by the supervisor. Users can select Current Effective Rights from the Current Directory Information menu to view these rights, as shown in Figure 14-12.

Supervisors and users may want to set various options when working within a directory. These options can prevent files from being accidentally deleted or from being overwritten. Directory listings can also be "filtered"

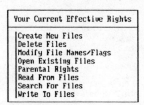

Figure 14-12.   FILER Current Effective Rights menu

Figure 14-13. FILER Filer Options Settings menu

so that certain files don't appear in the listing. This can be done with file exclude patterns. The Filer Options Settings menu is used to set these options, as shown in Figure 14-13.

Information about any volume as shown in Figure 14-14 can be viewed by selecting Volume Information from the main menu.

File-Server Console Utility: FCONSOLE

The FCONSOLE menu utility is a supervisor's utility used to view information about the network and to analyze and fine-tune its performance. Supervisors have full access to the features and functions of FCONSOLE. Users can view information about the system with the utility. The super-

```
            Volume Information

Server Name:              SERVER
Volume Name:              SYS
Volume Type:              Fixed
Total Bytes:              52,420,000
Bytes Available:          41,975,000
Maximum Directory Entries:      3,712
Directory Entries Available:    3,268
```

Figure 14-14. FILER Volume Information menu

Figure 14-15.   FCONSOLE Available Options menu

visor can give another user rights to the FCONSOLE utility by making them a console operator, which means they will have rights similar to those of the supervisor. The FCONSOLE main menu is shown in Figure 14-15.

The first option allows the supervisor to broadcast messages from the utility menu. This is important if the supervisor intends to bring the server down and needs to warn users to log off. The FCONSOLE operator can also switch to a different server with the second option. Connection information can be viewed also, as shown in Figure 14-16.

Much of the information and options available in FCONSOLE are intended for more experienced network users and programmers. For example, information about the Transaction Tracking System can be viewed using the File/Lock Activity option, as shown in Figure 14-17. Information about each LAN card installed in the server can be viewed by

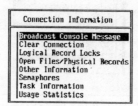

Figure 14-16.   FCONSOLE Connection Information menu

```
┌─────────────────────────────────┐
│        File/Lock Activity        │
├─────────────────────────────────┤
│ File/Physical Records Information │
│ Logical Lock Information          │
│ Semaphore Information             │
└─────────────────────────────────┘
```

Figure 14-17.   FCONSOLE File/Lock Activity menu

```
┌────────────────────────────────────────────────────────────────┐
│                      LAN A Configuration                         │
├────────────────────────────────────────────────────────────────┤
│ Network Address: 00454E44    Node Address: 640400454E44          │
│ LAN Board Type:  AST-EtherNode                                   │
│ Configuration:   0                                               │
│ Hardware Option: IRQ = 2, IO = 300H, No DMA, ROM = CC00:0        │
└────────────────────────────────────────────────────────────────┘
```

Figure 14-18.   FCONSOLE LAN Driver Information menu

```
┌─────────────────────────────┐
│     File Server Statistics   │
├─────────────────────────────┤
│ Cache Statistics             │
│ Channel Statistics           │
│ Disk Mapping Information      │
│ Disk Statistics              │
│ File System Statistics        │
│ LAN I/O Statistics           │
│ Summary                      │
│ Volume Information           │
└─────────────────────────────┘
```

Figure 14-19.   FCONSOLE File Server Statistics menu

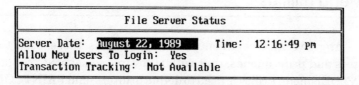

Figure 14-20.   FCONSOLE File Server Status menu

selecting LAN Driver Information from the menu. This information is helpful when trying to determine the network and node address of each card or the board settings, shown in Figure 14-18.

Statistics about the file server can also be viewed by selecting the Statistics option from the main menu. The Filer Server Statistics menu is shown in Figure 14-19. Experienced network users can use the information available from this menu to fine-tune the system and monitor its activities.

The status of the currently selected file server can be viewed by selecting Status from the main menu. A screen similar to the one in Figure 14-20 appears. Finally, Version Information can be selected from the main menu to view information about the current NetWare version. A screen similar to the one in Figure 14-21 appear.

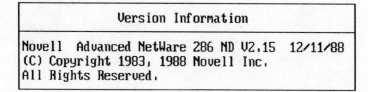

Figure 14-21.   FCONSOLE Version Information menu

Other Menu Utilities

There are several other menu utilities, such as those used to control printers and print queues, that will be covered in separate chapters. The PRINTDEF menu utility is used to define printers, and PRINTCON is used to specify which printers to use for different types of print jobs. The PCONSOLE command can be used to control the print queue.

Introduction to Managing Users, Directories, and Files

Creating New Log-in Scripts with SYSCON
Creating a New User with SYSCON
Creating Directories with the Group Method
Creating Groups
Assigning Maximum Rights to Directories
Considerations for Installing Applications Software

This chapter will help you as the system supervisor establish the first users on the system, as well as the personal directories for those users. Through these exercises, you will become familiar with the process of establishing new users and directories. Keep in mind the steps described here use the SYSCON and FILER menu utilities. Other methods for establishing users and directories include keyboard commands and the MAKEUSER utility.

The first step will be to create a new system log-in script. Then you will create the new users and their personal directories. Finally, you will create directories used by all users.

Creating New Log-in Scripts with SYSCON

Recall that a log-in script can be used to execute various NetWare commands when a user first signs on to the system. These commands can be used to map directories to drives and to establish search drives. There are a number of other commands you can include in the log-in scripts; they will be covered in Chapter 21. For now, you should be interested in establishing a fundamental log-in in script that can be expanded later.

There are two types of log-in scripts. The system log-in script is the log-in script executed for all users, including the supervisor. The user log-in scripts are executed after the system log-in script. User log-in scripts are created individually for each new user and are optional.

Creating a New System Log-in Script

To begin creating the system log-in script, type **SYSCON** from any directory. SYSCON will store the new script in the PUBLIC directory with the file name NET$LOG.DAT. Note that you must be logged in as the supervisor or supervisor equivalent to create or edit the system log-in script. At the SYSCON main menu, highlight Supervisor Options (you can type **S** to select it) and press ENTER. At the subsequent menu, highlight System Login Script by typing **S** or using the arrow keys, and then press ENTER.

You will see a blank screen with the heading System Login Script. Type the log-in script shown here. For best results, press the CAPS LOCK key when editing log-in scripts, since some command options must be in uppercase. You can use the arrow keys to move around the display for editing.

```
                              System Login Script

SET PROMPT = "$P$G"
MAP F:=SYS:USERS\%LOGIN_NAME
MAP G:=SYS:PUB-DATA
MAP INS S1:=SYS:PUBLIC
MAP INS S2:=SYS:PUBLIC\%MACHINE
COMSPEC = S2:COMMAND.COM
MAP INS S3:=SYS:SYSTEM
PCCOMPATIBLE
```

The commands shown in this illustration are recommended for your first system log-in script. In the future, you may want to change these commands or add others, as will be discussed in Chapter 21. The commands perform the following tasks in the order shown:

- The SET PROMPT command sets the NetWare prompts to display the current directory the user is logged in to.

- The first MAP command will map the users personal directory (which branches from the SYS:USER directory). This directory, which will be created later, must have the same name as the user name of each user logging in to the system. The variable %LOGIN_NAME in the command holds the username specified by the user when logging in. Thus, if a user logged in with the name John, the command would take the form

MAP F:=SYS:USERS\JOHN

Note: Drive F will be the default drive for the user unless another command is used to switch to a different drive.

- The second MAP command maps a directory called PUB-DATA to drive G. This directory will be created later and is a shared data directory accessed by all users. It is not required by NetWare but is used in this book for various examples.

- The third MAP command assigns search drive 1 (S1) to the SYS:PUBLIC directory. All users should have this search drive mapping, since SYS:PUBLIC contains the NetWare menu utilities and command-line utilities that users will access on a regular basis. Remember that commands in search drives can be executed from other directories.

Note: MAP INS is used to "insert" NetWare search drives or "paths" into your existing DOS paths. Without INS, the DOS paths established at the DOS level would be lost. This will be important at workstations that run programs from a local hard drive as well as the network drive.

- The fourth MAP command assigns search drive 2 (S2) to the DOS directory you created in Chapter 12. This DOS directory holds the version of the DOS files your are running at the workstation. The %MACHINE variable is replaced with the variable you assigned to LONG MACHINE TYPE in the SHELL.CFG file of the workstation boot disk or hard drive. For example, if the command LONG MACHINE NAME = IBMDOS were placed in the SHELL.CFG file, the MAP command would be as follows:

MAP S2:=SYS:PUBLIC\IBMDOS

- The fifth MAP command allows the workstation to locate a proper copy of COMMAND.COM on the server. This is important when exiting some programs that must reload COMMAND.COM. Without this command, the workstation would crash in some cases. Note that the command uses S2, assigned in the previous step, as the location for COMMAND.COM.

- The last MAP command is used to map the SYS:SYSTEM directory. This mapping is mainly used by the supervisor, since other users should not be able to run the commands in SYS:SYSTEM. Access can be denied to other users by removing trustee rights to the directory.

- The PCCOMPATIBLE command is necessary if you specified a long machine type other than IBM_PC. It informs the system that a non-IBM system is being used and allows the log-in script command EXIT to be used, which will be covered in Chapter 21.

When you have finished entering the command, press ESC. Answer Yes when asked if you want to save changes. You will be returned to the Supervisor Options menu. Press ESC again to return to the Available Topics menu.

Creating a New User with SYSCON

The log-in script just created will establish the drive mappings and search-drive mappings used by most users, including the supervisor. This log-in script will initially work for most systems until you have a chance to read through Chapter 21, which will help you customize the log-in script for your system. You can now create users who will be able to use the system, since a search drive is mapped to the SYS:PUBLIC directory.

To begin creating a new user, choose User Information from the SYSCON Available Topics menu. The User Names menu will appear; it may only include GUEST and SUPERVISOR. Press INS to add a new user.

For this example, the name NEWUSER is typed as the user name, but you should add yourself as a user by typing your own name in this box. The name you type can be used as your log-in name when logging in to the system for nonsupervisor activities. Press ENTER when done, and the name will appear in the User Names box.

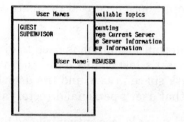

Modifying the User's Account

Each user has an account that is modified in various ways. Highlight the new user's name and press the ENTER key. The following screen appears.

You can use this screen for various tasks:

- The Account Restrictions option can be used to set security options such as the requirement for a unique password, forced periodic password changes, and minimum password length. Note that these settings will only be made for the currently selected user. Default settings can be made in the Supervisor Options menu.

- The user's password can be changed by selecting Change Password.

- A full name can be specified by selecting Full Name.

- Users can be added to groups by selecting Groups Belonged To. Note that users can only be added to groups that already exist. Groups are created under the SYSCON Group Information heading.

- The Intruder Lockout Status option is used to lock a user's account and to set how many times the user can attempt a log-in before being locked out.

- The Login Script option is used to create or edit the user's log-in script.

- The Other Information option is used to display user information, such as the user's last log-in date, console operator status, the amount of disk space in use, and the user ID. The user ID is also the name of that user's personal directory in the MAIL directory.

- The Security Equivalences option is used to make a user's security equivalent to another user's.

- The Station Restrictions option is used to assign a user to specific workstations.

- The Time Restrictions option is used to assign specific times a user can and cannot use the system.

- The Trustee Assignments option is used to make a user a trustee of a directory.

Creating the User's Log-in Script

Log-in scripts can be made for each user. In some cases this will be beneficial, but on large systems it may become too cumbersome for the supervisor to attempt to create personal log-in scripts for each user. The option is best left for the users, who may want to include additional log-in commands to fit their own needs. Supervisors should attempt to place commands in the system log-in script that establish systemwide mappings and other options.

Supervisors should be aware that each log-in script requires a minimum of approximately 4K of disk space. This may restrict the use of personal log-in scripts on large networks that have limited amounts of disk space. For example, it would be a waste of disk space to create personal log-in scripts in an educational environment, where hundreds of users may have temporary accounts at one time.

For those systems that do require the use of personal log-in scripts, an example is shown here. From the User Information window, type **L** to highlight the Login Script option and press ENTER. Type the command shown here, remembering to type log-in script commands in uppercase.

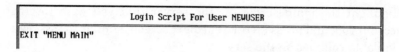

This command will display the main menu that was discussed in the previous chapter and will be discussed in more detail in Chapter 22. When the user's personal log-in script executes, the main menu will be displayed to assist the user with the system. After reading Chapter 22, you may want to create other types of menus that can be started from the user's log-in script.

Press ESC after typing the command, and answer Yes to save the request.

Creating the User's Personal Directory

From the User Information menu, select Trustee Assignments to create the user's personal directory. The goal is to create a new directory with the user's personal name that branches from the USERS directory. The user should have full trustee rights in this directory unless the supervisor wants to limit the user's activities. The following will appear on the screen:

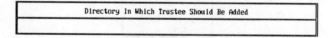

You can type the full name of the directory, including the server and volume name, or you can have NetWare do it for you by pressing INS. Try pressing INS. You will see a screen similar to this which should show a list of possible servers on your network:

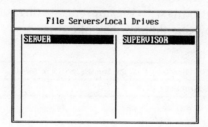

Highlight the main server, or the server that you wish to create user accounts on, and press ENTER. The next screen, similar to this, will list the available volumes on the server:

Highlight the volume you wish to use (SYS for this example) and press ENTER. At the Network Directories screen, which will be similar to the one shown here, you can type **U** to select the USERS directory if you created it as outlined in Chapter 12:

You will need to type the remaining information unless a directory already exists for the user, in which case you can select it from the list on the menu. Press ESC to type the remaining portion of the directory name. In the following example, NEWUSER was typed at the end of the name, but you can replace this with the appropriate directory name for your user. The upper window should now look like this:

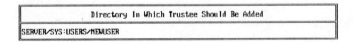

NetWare will ask if you want to create the new directory if one doesn't yet exist. Highlight Yes and press ENTER.

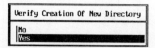

You are now returned to the Trustee Assignments menu, and the new directory is now part of the user's assignments, as shown here:

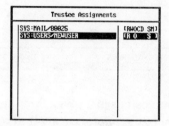

Granting User's Trustee Rights to Directories

Now that the user has a personal directory, you can assign him or her various trustee rights to the directory. Remember that the trustee rights you assign to the directory will carry over to any subdirectories created by the user, assuming you give the user rights to create subdirectories. In most cases, users should have full trustee rights in their own directories unless you want to limit the number of subdirectories they create.

While still in the Trustee Assignments menu, highlight the user's personal directory you just inserted and press ENTER. The Trustee Rights Granted menu will appear, as shown on the left in the next illustration. Press INS to see the Trustee Rights Not Granted menu shown on the right. You can press ENTER on any item in the right menu to add it to the left menu, thus granting the right to the user. Press INS and ENTER repeatedly until the user has all rights in his or her personal directory.

Once you have assigned all the rights, you can return to the Trustee Assignments menu. Note that the directory now displays the complete set of rights, as shown on the right in this illustration:

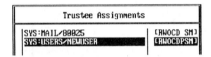

You can repeat the steps just given for other users at this time if you wish. The remainder of this chapter covers the creation of a public directory and directories used by applications programs. The Delete key can be used to remove rights if necessary.

Note: Keep in mind that you will need to go through the steps just presented for each directory you want to make the user a trustee of. In some cases the directory will be program directories, and users will only be given Read, Open, and Search rights. In other cases, users will be given additional rights.

Assigning a Password to a User

Each user should have a password to improve system security although it is complete optional. At the User Information menu, select Account Restriction. Arrow down to Require Password in the menu that appears, and type **Y** in the field as shown in the following illustration. This will turn password security on for the user. The first time the user logs on, he or she will be asked for a password that will then become their permanent password until changed. You can assign a password now by selecting Change Password from the User Information menu.

```
┌──────────────────────────────────────────────┐
│     Account Restrictions For User NEWUSER      │
├──────────────────────────────────────────────┤
│ Account Disabled:                No            │
│ Account Has Expiration Date:     No            │
│   Date Account Expires:                        │
│ Limit Concurrent Connections:    No            │
│   Maximum Connections:                         │
│ Allow User To Change Password:   Yes           │
│ Require Password:               [Yes]          │
│   Minimum Password Length:       5             │
│ Force Periodic Password Changes: No            │
│   Days Between Forced Changes:                 │
│   Date Password Expires:                       │
│   Limit Grace Logins:                          │
│     Grace Logins Allowed:                      │
│     Remaining Grace Logins:                    │
│ Require Unique Passwords:        No            │
└──────────────────────────────────────────────┘
```

Creating Directories with
The Group Method

Directories can be created in NetWare with the SYSCON and FILER utility, as well as the MD (Make Directory) command like that used in DOS. Although any of these method may be used, you will find it more beneficial to use SYSCON; you can more easily assign user and group trustee rights to the newly created directories in just a few steps, rather than going through several separate procedures. This becomes obvious when you consider that any directory you create will usually have a user or group trustee. Thinking in terms of directory trustees will help you set up and manage your system more efficiently. Recall that you, as the supervisor, can create a maximum rights mask over a directory to block certain rights for all users; however, this discussion will be concerned with the process of assigning rights to user groups, not directories themselves.

If you create a group of users, it becomes a simple matter to create a directory and assign the group as a trustee of that directory. Then every member of that group holds the same rights in the directory. For example, assume an accounting department has five clerks and a manager, all of whom are placed in a group called ACCTG. You can then use the Group Information option on the SYSCON main menu to create a directory called ACCTDATA with the group ACCTG as the trustees. All members of the group can then use the ACCTDATA directory based on the rights you assign.

Creating a Data Directory for The Group EVERYONE

The system log-in script created earlier in this chapter has a command that maps drive G to a directory called PUB-DATA. You can create this directory now and make it usable by everyone that logs in to the system. The job of assigning rights to this directory is as simple as assigning the group EVERYONE as one of its trustees and then defining the groups trustee rights in the directory. The following example explains how to do this.

Type **SYSCON** to open the SYSCON menu utility if it is not already running. At the main menu, select Group Information. The object is to create a new directory for the EVERYONE group, so select EVERYONE from the Group Names menu and press ENTER. The Group Information menu will appear, as shown on the right:

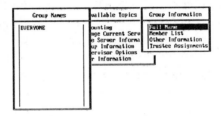

Select Trustee Assignments from the menu, and the following screen appears.

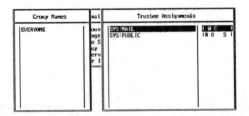

Groups can be assigned directories in the same way you assigned a directory to a user earlier in this chapter. Press INS at the Trustee Assignments menu. A screen appears, in which the full name of the directory can be typed. Recall from the previous section that you can press

INS to insert the server and volume names, or you can just type them by hand. Type **PUB-DATA** for the new directory as shown here, and press ENTER.

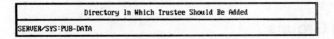

The new Trustee Assignments menu appears, similar to the following. Note that NetWare automatically gives the directory the Read, Open, and Search rights.

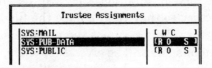

Highlight the new directory and press ENTER to add more rights. Press INS at the Trustee Rights Granted menu, highlight each new right you want to add, and then press ENTER. It is not recommended that you give EVERYONE the Parental, Modify, and Delete rights, but that is up to you. The final screen will look similar to this:

Now users in the EVERYONE group will be able to create and edit files in the PUB-DATA directory. You can consider this directory a place where users can store files that others may want to use. If you didn't assign the Delete right, only the supervisor will be able to erase files in the directory. This protects the files from accidental erasure by a user. You could also give a single user such as a department manager additional trustee rights to the directory by adding the directory to the user's personal Trustee Assignments list. After doing so, the user would have a combination of rights in the directory through the EVERYONE group, as well as through his or her personal trustee assignment.

Creating Groups

Groups are created not only to make the job of the supervisor easier when creating directories, but to help users work among themselves. In this section, a set of managers will be added to a group and assigned their own special data directory. In addition, they will be given full rights to the PUB-DATA directory so they can manage the file activities of the other users in the directory. This assumes the managers normally oversee the other users. The managers will be given the Delete, Parental, and Modify attributes in addition to the other rights so they can control the files and subdirectories of PUB-DATA.

You can substitute any group name or user name in the example shown here to fit your own needs. To begin, start the SYSCON program if it is not already loaded and select Group Information from the main menu. A screen similar to the following will appear. Press INS to enter a new group, and type **MANAGERS** as shown or the name of your own group.

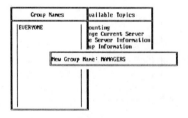

After creating the new group, press ENTER on its name to display the Group Information menu shown next. You can enter a full name for the group by making the top selection on the menu, as has been done in the illustration. The Full Name window appears at the bottom-right of the screen. Full names are useful for identifying groups in various reports and system management functions.

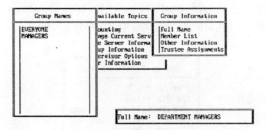

Next, select Member List from the Group Information menu and select the users you want to add to the group. In this example, Jane, John, and Sally are added by repeatedly pressing INS, selecting a name, and pressing ENTER, as shown here:

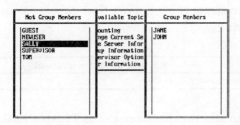

Once the members are added to the group, you can select Trustee Assignments from the Group Information menu to create a new directory for the managers. When you create a new directory, a blank window will appear in which you can type the full name of the directory, or you can press INS to choose from server and volume-name options. Press INS and select a server and volume, and then press ESC to enter the final directory name. In the following example screen, the new directory MGR-DATA is created:

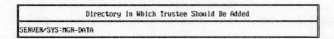

The new directory will appear in the Trustee Assignments menu with the Read, Open, and Search rights. Press ENTER on the directory name to begin adding the remaining rights. This is a process of pressing INSERT, highlighting the right to add, and pressing ENTER. Do this repeatedly until all rights are active for the directory, as shown here:

The last thing to do is give the MANAGERS group the remaining rights to the PUB-DATA directory. Press INS at the Trustee Assignments menu, and use the INS key to select a file server, volume, and the PUB-DATA directory from the windows that appear. Your screen should look like the following:

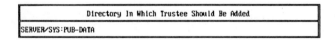

Press ENTER to add the directory to the Trustee Assignments menu, and then press ENTER on the new selection to begin adding rights. Follow the "INS-highlight-ENTER" process as you did previously. When done, the screen should look similar to the following, indicating that the MANAGERS group has all rights in the MGR-DATA and PUB-DATA directories.

You may want to map the MGR-DATA directory to a drive letter so

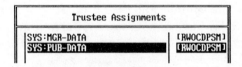

the managers can easily switch to it when necessary. The following command can be added to each manager's personal log-in script; here, H is the next available drive, but another drive may be the next available on your system:

MAP H:=SYS:MGR-DATA

Note that if you created the directory on another server or volume, the "SYS:" in this command would be replaced with another server and volume name.

Assigning Maximum Rights To Directories

You may decide as the supervisor that you don't want any user to have Parental rights in a directory, even though some users have already been assigned this right. The FILER menu utility allows you to assign the maximum rights mask to a directory, which will override any previous user rights.

For example, assume you want to remove the Parental right in the PUB-DATA directory to prevent anyone from assigning trustee and directory rights in the directory or its subdirectories. The managers in the MANAGERS group currently have this right from the last exercise. Removing the right from the maximum rights mask will remove it from the managers' effective rights in the directory.

Start the FILER utility and choose Select Current Directory from the main menu, as shown here:

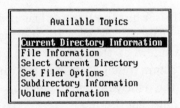

At the Current Directory Path menu, enter the name of the PUB-DATA directory and press ENTER.

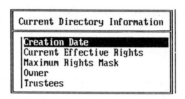

Next, highlight Current Directory Information to display the following menu:

Select Maximum Rights Mask and at the Maximum Rights menu, highlight the Parental Rights option, as shown here, and then press the Delete (DEL) key.

```
          Maximum Rights
       Create New Files
       Delete Files
       Modify File Names/Flags
       Open Existing Files
       Parental Rights
       Read From Files
       Search For Files
       Write To Files
```

Now, only the supervisor has the Parental right in the directory. If you log in as another user, you will be able to see this change in the Current Effective Rights window of the FILER command. You can also type **RIGHTS** from the command line while in the directory to see the current effective rights for the user you have logged in as. Be sure to log back in as the supervisor before continuing.

Considerations for Installing
Applications Software

When installing new software applications on the server, you will need to consider who should use the applications and where you want to store the data. In most cases, the program files should be stored in one directory and the data files in another. In this way, you can give the program files the Shareable and Read-Only attributes with the FLAG command. The data directory can then be assigned to a group of users authorized to work on the data files created by the application.

Assume that a special management program called Management Motivator is purchased for the MANAGER group discussed earlier. The first step would be to create a program directory for the software. This can be done in the SYSCON utility using the Group Information selection. You would select the MANAGERS group, and then give the group trustee rights to a new directory called something like MGR-MOV. The Read, Open, and Search rights can then be assigned to the directory. No other rights are necessary for the managers, since this directory holds program files only.

Note: Some programs may require additional rights before users can run them. For example, if temporary files are created and deleted during the program's execution, users will need write and delete rights in the directory.

The next step would be to create a data directory for the managers. The steps for doing this were outlined earlier when the MGR-DATA directory was created. The rights for the directory should be Create, Open, Read, Search, Write and possibly Delete. Finally, the log-in script for each manager will need to include a search-drive mapping to the MGR-MOV directory and a normal drive mapping to the data directory used to create and edit files when running the program.

Working with Servers
And Directories

This chapter will provide useful and detailed information for those working in directories and subdirectories, as well as those working on networks with multiple servers. The NetWare menu utilities will be covered in more detail with regard to the directory options. Command-line utilities for handling directories and subdirectories are also discussed. Some of these utilities are also covered in the next chapter, since they are used for handling files as well as directories.

File-Server Activities

A network system may have several file servers attached to it. A workstation will log itself in to the first available server unless the user decides to log in to another server. This can be done with the LOGIN command. In addition, the ATTACH command can be used to attach a workstation to another server once log-in has already been established at another server. The SLIST command can be used to view any servers on the network. Note that the SYSCON, SESSION, and FCONSOLE menu utilities can be used to switch to another server.

Listing Available Servers Before Logging In

The SLIST command is located in the LOGIN directory, so users can type it to get a list of available servers before logging in. This is convenient for users who can't remember the server names. SLIST will display a listing similar to the following:

```
Known NetWare Filer Servers    Network    Node Address
SERVER-1                       454E44     640400454E44  DEFAULT
SALES                          454E44     640401454E44
```

Logging In to Other Servers

The LOGIN command can be used to specify the server to be used when logging in to the system. The command takes the form

LOGIN *server/user options...*

where *server* is the name of the file server to log in to, *user* is the user name for the file server, and *options* are additional options that can be used by IF...THEN statements in the log-in script.

In order to log in to another server, the server name and user name must be specified together, separated by a backslash. If a backslash is not typed, the text string following LOGIN will be interpreted as the user name. To log in without specifying a user name, you would type

LOGIN *server/*

where *server* is the name of the server to log in to. The command will ask for the user name and password.

Note that the LOGIN command can be included in the AUTO-EXEC.BAT file of the boot disk or hard drive along with the IPX.COM and NETx.COM commands, as covered in Chapter 11. Note also that passwords can be synchronized for all servers a user may log in to, assuming the user uses the same user name on all servers. When the SETPASS command is executed, the user will be asked if he or she wants to synchronize the passwords.

Attaching to Another Server After Logging In

The ATTACH command is used to attach to other file servers after logging in to one file server. The command takes the form

ATTACH *server / user*

where *server* is the name of the server to attach to and *user* is the user name for the server. The file server name can be included in the command without the user name, but ATTACH will ask you for the user name.

Once attached to another server, you will need to create drive mappings for the directories you want to work in. This can be done with the MAP command or the SESSION utility. If a server is used often, it may be preferable to use the LOGIN command previously described to connect to the server. Log-in scripts can then be used to map drives automatically.

Viewing Server Information

You can view information about any server with the SYSCON command. Start the menu utility and select File Server Information from the main menu. A screen similar to the following will appear:

```
┌─────────────────────────────────────────────────┐
│           File Server Information                │
├─────────────────────────────────────────────────┤
│ Server Name:           SERVER                    │
│ NetWare Version:       Advanced NetWare 286 ND V2.15│
│ OS Revision:           2.15 Revision 0           │
│ System Fault Tolerance: Level I                  │
│ Transaction Tracking:  No                        │
│ Connections Supported: 100                       │
│ Connections In Use:    2                         │
│ Volumes Supported:     32                        │
│ Network Address:       00454E44                  │
│ Node Address:          640400454E44              │
│ Serial Number:         00920947                  │
│ Application Number:    0000                       │
└─────────────────────────────────────────────────┘
```

Mapping Directories

As mentioned earlier, drive maps are used to make access to NetWare directories easier. You can also map volumes and directories on other servers to a drive letter. Mapping is also used to create search drives, which specify the path the operating system should follow to find program files from other directories. Search drives are equivalent to using the DOS PATH command.

All maps are temporary and are lost when a user logs out. Map commands can be placed in log-in scripts so they are reassigned every time the user logs in. Drive mappings and search-drive mappings can be created with the MAP command or with the SESSION menu utility. Both are covered in this section.

In most cases, permanent maps will be created by the supervisor in the system log-in script or in individual user log-in scripts as one of the steps in creating new users or groups. These steps are outlined here:

- Create users and assign them to groups

- Create directories for the user or groups, or install applications software in directories

- Grant rights to users or groups in a directory

- Create search drives or drive maps for the directory in the system log-in script or user's log-in script

The process of installing any software package will usually include the steps to create mapped drives or search drives to the applications or data directories of that software for each user that will be using it. In addition, most data directories will be mapped for each user as required.

The MAP and SESSION commands may seem of little use if most users already have the necessary maps and search drives, as established in the log-in script. However, there will be occasions when a user needs access to another directory that is not mapped, and that is when the commands come into use. The following discussion will show you how to create temporary mappings at the NetWare command line. These mappings are temporary because they are only maintained during a user's current session. Keep in mind that any discussions of the MAP command can also be applied to log-in scripts to make the mapping more permanent.

Using SESSION to Map Drives

The SESSION manager can be useful for viewing and mapping drives. Type **SESSION** on the command line, and the following screen should appear.

Select Drive Mappings from the menu to see a list of current drive mappings similar to the following list. You can highlight any drive and press ENTER to see its effective rights, which are shown on the right in the illustration. Note that effective rights may be different for each user.

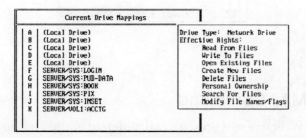

From the Current Drive Mappings window, you can press the INS key to create new drive mappings. Simply enter the drive letter and then the server, volume, and path for the new drive map.

Press ESC to return to the SESSION main menu and select Search Mappings. A screen similar to the following will appear. You can select any search drive and press ENTER to see its effective rights. You can also press the INS key to create additional search-drive maps.

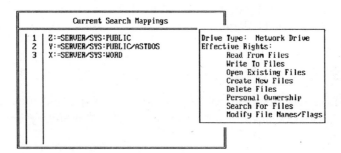

Return to the SESSION main menu and choose Select Default Drive. A screen similar to the following will appear. Simply select any drive and press ENTER to make it the current default drive.

```
                 Select Default Drive
     ▲ B │ (Local Drive)
       C │ (Local Drive)
       D │ (Local Drive)
       E │ (Local Drive)
       F │ SERVER/SYS:LOGIN
       G │ SERVER/SYS:PUB-DATA
       H │ SERVER/SYS:BOOK
       I │ SERVER/SYS:PIX
       J │ SERVER/SYS:INSET
       K │ SERVER/VOL1:ACCTG
       X │ SERVER/SYS:WORD
       Y │ SERVER/SYS:PUBLIC/ASTDOS
       Z │ SERVER/SYS:PUBLIC
```

Using the MAP Command

The MAP command takes several different forms, as discussed in the following sections. The *drive* option is the drive letter you want to assign, and *path* is the path to the directory to be assigned. Note that the path may include the server and volume name and that the drives are letters starting with F. Search drives are referred to as S1, S2, S3, and so on, and are typed in the drive-letter option.

Display the Current Maps

To display the current drive mappings and search-drive mappings, type the MAP command by itself as shown here:

    MAP

If you want to display how a particular drive is mapped, type the command as shown here, where *drive* is the letter of the drive map to view:

    MAP *drive*:

Note that the current directory is displayed as part of the operating system prompt if you include the command SET PROMPT = "PG" in the system log-in script.

Remap the Current Drive

All drives will have a current mapping, even if that map is for the root directory of the file system. To assign a new directory to the current drive, use the form

    MAP *path*

where *path* is the new path to map. The path can include a server and volume name as well. Note that you can use the DOS CD command to simply switch directories while logged in to a NetWare drive. The destination directory will become the new mapping.

Map a New Drive

The main form of the MAP command to create a new drive mapping is shown here. The *drive* parameter specifies the drive you want to assign, and *path* is the directory to assign to it. The path can include server and volume names.

MAP *drive:=path*

For example, the following command maps drive J to the SYS:PUB-LIC\APPS\LOTUS directory:

MAP J:=SYS:PUBLIC\APPS\LOTUS

If the directory were on the ACCTG server in the VOL1 volume, you would type

MAP J:=ACCTG/VOL1:PUBLIC\APPS\LOTUS

You can easily map another drive to the same directory by using the existing mapped drive letter in the MAP command. For example, to map drive L to the LOTUS directory just shown, you could type

MAP L:=J:

If you were already in drive J assigned to LOTUS, and you wanted to map drive L to the same directory, you could simply type

MAP L:=

Mapping Search Drives

To map a search drive, you may need to type the MAP command to see what the next available search drive is. For example, SEARCH1 and SEARCH2 may be mapped to a directory. You would then assign SEARCH3 to a directory called SYS:LOTUS by typing the following command:

MAP S3:=SYS:LOTUS

If you are not sure of the current mapping and want to insert a new drive without removing any others, you can use the INSERT option. For example, the following command reassigns an existing SEARCH3 drive to SEARCH4:

MAP INS S3:=SYS:LOTUS

Removing Search Drives

The first example shown here removes a network drive mapping. The second example removes a search-drive mapping. You cannot remove the mapping of the default drive.

MAP DEL H:
MAP DEL S3:

Directory Activities with FILER

The FILER utility can help you create and manage directories. Keep in mind that some of the features in FILER are repeated in other menu utilities, such as SYSCON. For example, supervisors can assign trustees to directories in both menu utilities. This is often confusing to new users, who assume that similar functions in each utility perform some different task. In reality, some of the menu options represent different ways of doing the same thing. NetWare groups many similar functions within the same menus so you don't have to jump from one menu utility to the next. This section will describe some of the ways you can use the FILER utility to work with directories.

Note: FILER is also useful when working with individual files, as will be covered in the next chapter.

Type **FILER** on the command line and press ENTER. The following screen will appear:

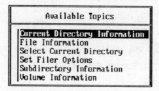

Select a Work Directory

One of the first things you should do when working with FILER is to set the directory you want to work with. If you were already logged in to the desired directory, FILER will be set to work with that directory. If you want to work with another directory, choose Select Current Directory from the menu. The following screen will appear:

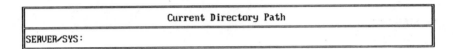

Type the name of the drive you want to work with in the menu, and press ENTER. Note that when you exit FILER, you will still be in your current directory. FILER does not change the default drive to the directory you selected with the Select Current Directory option. You can use the SESSION manager if you want to switch to a different default drive or to define a new drive mapping.

Viewing or Changing Directory Information

You can now select Current Directory Information from the menu to see information on the selected directory. The options on this screen, as shown here, will be familiar if you read Chapter 15.

As usual, supervisors and users have different access rights to the features and functions of FILER as well as other menu utilities. FILER allows both supervisors and users to view the creation date and effective rights. The effective rights displayed when Current Effective Rights is selected from the menu pertain only to the currently logged-in user. Users can view the maximum rights mask and trustees of a directory but cannot change them. Supervisors can change these options, as discussed next.

Changing the Maximum Rights Mask of a Directory

Supervisors can add or remove rights from the maximum rights of a directory using the Maximum Rights Mask option on the Current Directory Information window. To change the rights, highlight Maximum Rights Mask and press ENTER. The Maximum Rights window shown in the following illustration will appear:

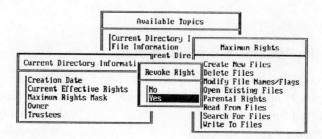

A supervisor may want to remove one or more of the maximum rights in a given directory, thus removing those rights from all users. For example, if a user is assigned the Create right but that right is not in the maximum rights mask, the user will not be able to create files.

Note: Keep in mind that users must have the Open and Read rights to read files or run programs in a directory, and they will need the Open, Read, Write, and Create rights to create and edit files.

The effective rights of any user are a combination of the maximum directory rights granted by the supervisor and the trustee rights given to the user in the directory. Figure 16-1 illustrates how rights are combined to form effective rights.

	Read	Write	Open	Create	Delete	Parental	Search	Modify
Maximum Directory Rights	R	W	O	C			S	
User /Group Trustee Rights	R	W	O	C	D		S	M
Effective Rights	R	W	O	C			S	

Figure 16-1. Effective rights: a combination of maximum rights in a directory and user's trustee rights

Managing the Trustees of a Directory

If you select Trustees from the Current Directory Information screen, you will be able to add or remove trustees from the selected directory or change the rights of the trustees. This option is similar to the user's options in the SYSCON utility. However, with SYSCON you start by selecting a user, and then you select a directory. With FILER, a directory is already selected—you then add, remove, or alter the rights of a user or group in the directory.

When Trustee is selected, a list of existing users and groups appears on the screen. You can highlight any user or group and press Delete (DEL) to remove them as trustees of the directory, or you can press ENTER to alter their trustee rights. New users and groups can be added as trustees of the directory by pressing INS. You can then edit the rights of the user or group by highlighting the new name and pressing ENTER.

Managing Subdirectories

From the FILER Available Topics menu, you can select Subdirectory Information to view a list of subdirectories for the current directory. By highlighting an existing directory, you can perform most of the operations on that directory that were discussed in the previous section. This illustration shows the subdirectory menus:

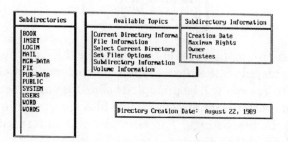

New subdirectories can be created by pressing the INS key, and old subdirectories can be removed by highlighting them and pressing the DEL key. When the INS key is pressed, the following screen appears. Simply type the name of the new subdirectory.

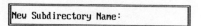

When DEL is pressed to remove a subdirectory, the following screen appears. If you choose Delete Entire Subdirectory Structure, the entire subdirectory, its files, and its subdirectories will be removed. If you choose Delete Subdirectory's Files Only, only the files within the subdirectory are removed. The subdirectory itself is left intact.

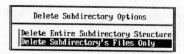

Setting FILER Options

Press ESC to return the FILER main menu, and then select Set Filer Options from the menu. The Filer Options Settings menu will appear, as shown here:

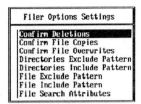

You can use this menu to set options for the FILER utility, many of which will be discussed in the next chapter. For example, if you set Confirm Deletions to Yes you will be prompted before files are deleted. The include and exclude patterns for directories and files are similar in use to wildcard characters in file listings. For example, you can specify in Directory Exclude Pattern that directories starting with ARC not be included in the Subdirectory Information listing. The same technique holds for files. The opposite is to specify the pattern you want to list by using the Include options.

When selecting one of these options, press the INS key to insert a new include or exclude pattern.

NetWare Commands for Working with Directories

The commands described in the remainder of this chapter can be used to work with directories on the NetWare command line. Some of the commands covered here can be used when handling both directories and files. The file features will be covered in the next chapter.

DOS Directory Commands

The DOS directory commands can be used in NetWare to create directories and subdirectories from the command line. These commands are often the easiest way to create a directory. Keep in mind that trustee rights and other security features will need to be applied through the menu utilities or some of the commands listed later. The DOS directory commands are shown here.

MD Make Directory   MD is used to create a directory that branches from the current directory. Simply type **MD** followed by an eight-character directory name.

CD Change Directory   The CD command is used to move to a directory. Specify the path to the directory after the command.

RD Remove Directory   The RD command is used to remove a directory. The directory must be empty before it can be removed.

Listing Directories with NDIR

The NDIR command is equivalent to the DIR command in DOS, except that it is much more extensive, as you will see by the options described in this section. NDIR can be used to display information about files as well as directories. This section will explain NDIR's directory-specific options.

One of the first things you can do with NDIR is to list its help screen. This can be done by typing the following command:

NDIR HELP

A screen listing of NDIR's options will appear. This information may appear cryptic until you understand how NDIR works. From any directory, type the following command to see a listing of files and subdirectories for that directory:

NDIR

Any directory can be listed by specifying its path. In the following command, the PUBLIC directory is listed using the path to the directory:

NDIR SYS:PUBLIC

The mapped drive letter of a directory can also be used to display the contents of a directory. The following example assumes that the PUBLIC directory is mapped to drive G. It produces the same listing as the previous command.

NDIR G:

What NDIR Displays

The NDIR listing displays a sorted list of files in a directory, and then finishes with a listing of subdirectories of the requested directory. NDIR will page the listing one screen at a time unless you type **C** to request continuous scrolling. The examples in this section will cover the listing of subdirectories only, not files. A typical screen might look like this partial listing:

```
SYS:
Directory Name Created          Max Rights Eff Rights Owner
-------------- --------------   ---------- ---------- -----------------------
BACKUP         9-07-89  8:46a [RWOCDPSM] [RWOCDPSM] SUPERVISOR
BOOK           8-21-89  8:28a [RWOCDPSM] [RWOCDPSM] SUPERVISOR
CRFC           9-04-89 10:58p [RWOCDPSM] [RWOCDPSM] SUPERVISOR
DATA           9-04-89 10:55p [RWOCDPSM] [RWOCDPSM] SUPERVISOR
DBASE          9-04-89 10:57p [RWOCDPSM] [RWOCDPSM] SUPERVISOR
DOC            9-04-89 10:56p [RWOCDPSM] [RWOCDPSM] SUPERVISOR
LOGIN          8-00-80  8:00a [RWOCDPSM] [RWOCDPSM] SUPERVISOR
MAIL           8-00-80  8:00a [RWOCDPSM] [RWOCDPSM] SUPERVISOR
MGR-DATA       8-23-89  7:01a [RWOCDPSM] [RWOCDPSM] SUPERVISOR
```

At the top of the screen are column headers that describe the information in the listing. This screen is only listing directories; if files were also listed, each file name and its size would be listed first, along with file access date information. The subdirectory name and creation date are shown, along with the maximum rights mask. The effective rights mask is also displayed, but it may be different for each user who lists the subdirectories since users may have different rights in the directory. The owner of the directory is also listed.

NDIR Options for Directories

NDIR has a large set of optional parameters that can be typed on the command line after the command and path or file name. Refer to Chapter 17 for a complete list of options, since only those useful for subdirectories are listed here.

The NDIR command takes the form

NDIR *path / filespec option...*

where *path* or *filespec* might include the path to a directory, a file name, or a path and file name. The options are typed last and more than one option can be specified on the command line. The following is a list of possible options you can use with the NDIR command when working with directories:

DO	Directories Only. The DO option can be used to view only directories and subdirectories, not files.
SUB	Subdirectories. The SUB option will include all subdirectories of the specified directory in the NDIR command.
OW	Owner. Directories owned by a specific user can be listed. A NOT option is available to exclude an owner from a listing.
CR	Create. Include the CR option to view directories created before, on, or after a specified date. A NOT option is also available to exclude directories created before, on, or after the specified date.

The following examples illustrate the use of these options.

To view only the subdirectories of a directory and not its files, specify the DO option. In the following example, the subdirectories of drive H are listed:

NDIR H: DO

If you want to see the subdirectories branching from drive H, type the following command:

NDIR H: DO SUB

To list another volume, specify the volume name in the command. The following command lists the directories and subdirectories on the VOL1 volume:

NDIR VOL1: DO SUB

To list directories on other servers, specify the server name also. The next example list directories and subdirectories in the SYS: volume on the server SALES:

NDIR SALES/SYS: DO SUB

The complete path to a directory can also be specified. For example, to list the subdirectories of user John's directory, the following command would be typed:

NDIR SYS:USERS\JOHN DO SUB

Since the listings display the maximum rights and users' effective rights for each directory, users can type the NDIR command with the DO and SUB options to view the rights they have in directories. The entire directory structure for the current volume can be viewed by specifying the root directory in the NDIR command, as shown here:

NDIR \ DO SUB

or

NDIR SYS: DO SUB

Note: The backslash character (\) can be used to indicate the root directory, as with DOS.

The OW (owner) option can be used to list the subdirectories owned by a particular user. The following command displays all subdirectories owned by John:

NDIR \ DO SUB OW JOHN

To list all owners' subdirectories except John's, the following command can be typed:

NDIR \ DO SUB OW NOT JOHN

All directories not owned by the supervisor can be listed by typing

NDIR \ DO SUB OW NOT SUPERVISOR

The CR (Create) option can be used to list directories created before, on, or after a certain date, or the NOT option can be used to get the opposite listing. The BEF (Before) and AFT (After) options are used to specify how the listing should treat the specified date. For example, the following command would display all directories created before 6-20-89 in drive H.

NDIR H: CR BEF 6-20-89 DO

To view files after the date, replace BEF with AFT. To view all branching subdirectories, include the SUB option.

The CR option can be used to filter the NDIR listing so that it doesn't include directories created on a certain date. The following command would list all directories and subdirectories in the volume except those created on 6-20-89:

NDIR \ CR NOT 6-20-89 DO SUB

The next command may be more elaborate than most users will care to type, but it illustrates the power of the NDIR command combined with the right options. The command lists all directories on the volume except those created on 6-20-89 and those created by the supervisor.

NDIR \ CR NOT 6-20-89 DO SUB OW NOT SUPERVISOR

Flagging Directories with FLAGDIR

The FLAGDIR command is used to flag a specified directory with one of the following attributes, which have been discussed in previous chapters as part of NetWare's security features.

(H)idden	The H or Hidden option is used to hide a directory so users cannot see it in a directory listing. User can still switch to the directory and list its contents if they have the rights to do so.
(S)ystem	The S or System option is used to flag a directory to be used by the system. Directories flagged with this option will not appear in a directory search.
(P)rivate	The P or Private option prevents users from viewing the contents of a subdirectory. Users must have the Search right to view the listing of the subdirectory from its parent directory and to view the contents of the subdirectory itself. The Private attribute corresponds to the Private (gray) folder in the Macintosh environment.
(N)ormal	The N or Normal option is used to cancel the other directory attributes assigned with the FLAGDIR command.

Users must have the Parental and Modify rights in the parent directory before they can change subdirectory attributes. The FLAGDIR command is typed on the command line in the following form:

FLAGDIR *path option*

where *path* is the path or drive letter of the target directory and *option* is one of the options just discussed.

Viewing Directory Attributes

The command can be typed by itself to determine the status of the current directory. The following command can be used to view the status of any subdirectories that branch from the current directory:

FLAGDIR *

To view the attributes of other directories, the name or mapped drive letter of the directory must be specified. In the following example, the directory attributes of drive K are displayed:

FLAGDIR K:

To view the subdirectory attributes of drive K, the following command would be typed:

FLAGDIR K:*

The asterisk is a wildcard character that lists all file names that don't have extensions, which is normal for directory names. If a directory is not mapped to a letter, you will need to specify the full path to the directory. For example, the following command lists the attributes of subdirectories that branch from the \USER directory:

FLAGDIR SYS:USER*

Changing Directory Attributes

To change the attributes of the current directory, simply type the FLAGDIR command followed by the attribute. Normally, the P and H attributes are assigned together to both hide a directory in file listings and to prevent users from viewing its contents. The following command makes the SYS:PUBLIC PROGRAMS directory both private and hidden:

FLAGDIR SYS:PUBLIC\PROGRAMS PH

If the directory were mapped to drive K, for example, the following command could be typed to assign the P and H attributes:

FLAGDIR K: PH

It is possible to assign the P and H attributes to all subdirectories of the current directory by typing the following command in the parent directory:

FLAGDIR * PH

To assign the P and H attributes to the subdirectories of a directory other than the current directory, specify the path or mapped drive letter of that directory. For example, if the current directory is SYS:SYSTEM and drive K is mapped to SYS:PUBLIC\PROGRAMS, the following command would assign the P and H attributes to all subdirectories in K:

FLAGDIR K:* PH

To flag directories on other volumes, be sure to specify the volume name or the server name if necessary. For example, the following command assigns the P and H attributes to the TRAINING directory on VOL1:

FLAGDIR VOL1:TRAINING PH

Renaming Directories with RENDIR

The RENDIR command is used to rename a directory and has a relatively simple format, as shown below:

RENDIR *oldname* TO *newname*

The *oldname* field is replaced with the complete pathname to the directory to be renamed. The *newname* field is replaced with the new directory name. It is not necessary to specify the complete path for the *newname* field. Those attempting to use RENDIR must have the Modify right within a directory to rename its subdirectories. Directories can only be renamed on the current server. To change directory names on other servers, you must first log in or attach to that server.

To rename the current directory, the period is used to represent the current default directory. The following command renames the current directory to TESTING:

RENDIR . TO TESTING

The TO in the command is optional, so the following could be typed to rename the directory TEST2:

RENDIR . TEST2

To rename directories other than the current directory, the full name of the directory should be specified in the RENDIR command. If the directory is already mapped to a drive, the RENDIR command will be much easier. For example, assume the SYS:USERS\TRAINING directory is mapped to drive L. Either of the following commands will rename the directory to TUTORIAL:

RENDIR SYS:USERS\TRAINING TO TUTORIAL
RENDIR L: TO TUTORIAL

Directory Trustee Commands

The following commands are used to display a list of directory trustees, and trustee rights, grant trustee rights, and revoke those rights. The trustee rights used by the commands described below are summarized here for your convenience.

Read	Allows a trustee to see the contents of an existing, open file
Write	Allows a trustee to change the contents of an existing, open file
Open	Allows a trustee to open an existing file
Create	Allows trustees to create new files
Delete	Allows a trustee to delete a file or directory
Parental	Allows trustees to create, rename, or delete subdirectories if they have the Create, Modify, and Delete rights
Search	Allows trustees to list the files in a directory
Modify	Allows trustees to modify the attributes of a file, such as its read or write status

TLIST

The TLIST command is used to view the trustee list for any directory. Only users who have the Parental right for a specified directory may use the TLIST command to view the trustee list for that directory. Only trustee lists for directories on the current server may be viewed.

The command takes the form

TLIST *path* USERS GROUPS

where *path* is the path or mapped drive name for the directory to be viewed. If USERS is included, only the user trustees of a directory will be listed. If GROUPS is included, only the group trustees of a directory will be listed.

To view the trustees for the current directory, type

TLIST

Information similar to the following will be displayed:

```
User Trustees:
    JOHN    [RWOCDPSM]      (JOHN JONES)
    ―――――
 Group Trustees:
    EVERYONE [RWOC  S ]
    MANAGERS [RWOCDPSM]      (DEPARTMENT MANAGERS)
```

If no users or trustees exist, the display will say so. The trustee rights in the directory are listed next to the user's names.

You can view the trustee list in any directory by specifying the full path to the directory or by using a mapped drive letter if one has been established. In the following examples, drive K is mapped to the SYS:PUBLIC\PROGRAMS directory:

```
TLIST K:
TLIST SYS:PUBLIC\PROGRAMS
```

Both commands produce the same listing of the trustees for the directory.

To view only the user trustees of the current directory, the following command can be typed:

TLIST . USERS

To view only the group trustees of the current directory, the following can be typed. A mapped drive letter or directory path can be typed instead of the period to specify another directory.

TLIST . GROUPS

RIGHTS

The RIGHTS command is used by any user to view their current rights in any directory. The command takes the form

RIGHTS *path*

where *path* is the full directory path or mapped drive letter of the directory for which you want to display the rights. To display the rights for the current directory, type

RIGHTS

To view rights in other directories, simply specify the path or search drive. Either of the following commands display the users' rights in the SYS:PUBLIC\PROGRAMS directory, which is mapped to drive K:

RIGHTS SYS:PUBLIC\PROGRAMS
RIGHTS K:

Keep in mind that the rights displayed for users are the effective rights they have in the directory, which is a combination of the maximum rights mask assigned to the directory by the supervisor and the trustee rights assigned to the user for the directory.

Note that the NDIR commands for listing directories (described earlier) may be more beneficial to users who are interested in viewing their rights for the entire directory structure.

GRANT

The GRANT command can be used in place of the SYSCON and FILER utilities to assign trustee rights to users and groups, assuming those users and groups have already been created by the SYSCON utility. The rights that can be granted to users and groups are listed at the beginning of this section. In addition, the GRANT command has a NO RIGHTS option, which revokes all rights to the user. Those attempting to grant rights to other users in a directory must have the Parental effective right.

The GRANT command takes the form

GRANT *option*...FOR *path* TO [USER *or* GROUP]

where *option* is the first letter of the rights as listed earlier. FOR is used to designate the directory where trustee assignments are to be granted. TO is used to designate the user or group to be granted the rights. Two additional options not shown here are ONLY and ALL BUT, which can be used to grant only the specified right or all but the specified right. These options are placed in front of the rights designators.

Note: USER and GROUP are optional and are used when a user or group share the same name.

The GRANT command must be issued for each user or group to be granted rights. To grant rights in the current default directory, type the command followed by the letters of the rights to grant and the user name. For example, to grant Read, Open, and Search rights to John in the current directory, type the following:

GRANT ROS TO JOHN

To grant rights in another directory, the full path to the directory must be specified, or the directory must have a mapped drive letter. In the following two examples, the SYS:PUBLIC\PROGRAMS directory is mapped to drive K and John is granted Read, Open, and Search rights:

GRANT ROS FOR SYS:PUBLIC\PROGRAMS TO JOHN
GRANT ROS FOR K: TO JOHN

To grant all but certain rights, the ALL BUT option can be used. Assume you want to grant John all rights except Parental and Modify in the current directory. The following command is typed:

GRANT ALL BUT PM TO JOHN

To grant specific rights and revoke all others, the ONLY option is used. To grant John the Search right only in drive K, the following is typed:

GRANT ONLY S FOR K: TO JOHN

To grant all rights to John in drive K, the following is typed:

GRANT ALL FOR K: TO JOHN

To revoke all rights in drive K for John, the following is typed:

GRANT NO RIGHTS FOR K: TO JOHN

Granting rights to groups is the same as granting rights to users. If a group and a user have the same name, you must specify whether the name used in the command is the user or the group. Precede the user name or group name with USER or GROUP in the command.

The GRANT command "enrolls" users or groups into the trustee list of a directory. The next two commands can be used to revoke the rights of a user in a trustee list and to remove the user from the trustee list altogether.

REVOKE

The REVOKE command is used in place of the SYSCON and FILER utilities to the revoke trustee rights of users and groups, assuming those users and groups have already been created by the SYSCON or MAKEUSER utility. The rights that can be revoked for users and groups are listed at the beginning of this section. Those attempting to revoke the rights of other users in a directory must have the Parental effective right.

The REVOKE command takes the form

REVOKE *option...path* FROM [USER or GROUP]

where *option* is the first letter of the rights as listed earlier. FOR is used to designate the directory where trustee assignments are to be revoked. FROM is used to designate the user or group whose rights are to be revoked. An additional option not shown here is ALL, which can be used to revoke all the rights of a user or group.

Note: USER and GROUP are optional and are used when a user or group shares the same name.

The REVOKE command must be issued for each user or group whose rights will be revoked. To revoke rights in the current default directory, type the command followed by the letter of the rights to revoke, and then the user. For example, to revoke the Read, Open, and Search rights for John in the current directory, type the following:

REVOKE ROS FROM JOHN

Don't forget to include FROM in the command. To revoke rights in another directory, the full path to the directory must be specified, or the directory must have a mapped drive letter. In the following examples, the SYS:PUBLIC\PROGRAMS directory is mapped to drive K and the Read, Open, and Search rights are revoked for John.

REVOKE ROS FOR SYS:PUBLIC\PROGRAMS FROM JOHN
REVOKE ROS FOR K: FROM JOHN

To revoke all rights, the ALL option can be used. Assume you want to revoke all rights for John. The following command is typed:

REVOKE ALL FROM JOHN

To revoke all rights for John in drive K, type

REVOKE ALL FOR K: FROM JOHN

Revoking the rights of groups is the same as revoking the rights of users. If a group and a user have the same name, you must specify whether the name used in the command is the user or the group. Precede the user name or group name with USER or GROUP in the command.

The GRANT command "enrolls" users or groups into the trustee list of a directory. The REVOKE command revokes the rights of a user in a trustee list. The next command is used to remove a user or group from the trustee list entirely.

REMOVE

The REMOVE command is used to remove a user or group from the trustee list of a directory. The command is different than the REVOKE command, which revokes a user's rights in a directory but does not remove the use from the trustee list. The command takes the following form:

REMOVE *user or group* FROM *path*

The *user or group* option is used to specify the name of the user or the group to remove. If a user and group have the same name, precede the name with USER or GROUP to indicate which to use. Only those users who have Parental effective rights in a directory can remove users in that directory.

To remove a user from the current directory, specify the name of the user. For example, to remove John from the current directory, you would type

REMOVE JOHN

A similar command is used to remove a group.

To remove a user or group from another directory, the full pathname of that directory must be specified, or the directory must be mapped to a drive. The following example would remove John as a trustee of the SYS:PUBLIC\PROGRAMS directory:

REMOVE JOHN FROM SYS:PUBLIC\PROGRAMS

If the directory is mapped to drive K, the following command can be typed:

REMOVE JOHN FROM K:2

Working with Files
And Applications

Using FILER
Listing and Copying Files
Changing File Attributes at the Command Line
Salvaging Deleted Files

NetWare allows security and protection on several levels, as discussed in the last few chapters. Users can be given trustee rights so they can work in certain directories, and supervisors can protect those directories by applying maximum rights masks. Individual files can also be protected by using such commands as FLAG, HIDEFILE, and HOLDON, as will be discussed in this chapter.

The FILER utility is also used extensively when working with files, not only to provide security and protection attributes, but to help supervisors and users list, copy, delete, and modify files. FILER is covered first in this chapter, and then the command-line utilities are covered in their various forms for those who prefer to work outside of the menu systems. The command-line utilities are the only method for performing some file tasks, so readers should review all sections in this chapter.

Using FILER

NetWare's FILER menu utility offers a number of features and functions for handling directories and files you won't find in DOS. As described in

377

the previous chapter, you can easily create new directories, assign trustees to those directories, and control the rights of those trustees. FILER is also useful for working with files. As the following examples will illustrate, you can select a directory to work in and then select a file to work with. Once the file is selected, you can view its attributes, creation date, owner, size, and contents. Files can be copied to another directory or duplicated to another file name. The supervisor or a user with the Modify attribute can change the attributes of the file.

FILER also allows multiple files to be selected for modification or deletion with the F5 Mark key. You can also set FILER options so only specific files in a directory can be viewed. Note that most operations involving modifications can only be performed by the supervisor. Users will be able to view file information, however, and change files they have created or to which they have been given access.

To start working with FILER's file options, type **FILER** on the command line in the directory you want to work with, or select the directory after you get into FILER. To select a new directory, highlight Select Current Directory from the FILER menu, as shown here. A blank Current Directory Path window will appear. You can type the names in this window, or press the INS key to insert the names of the server, volume, and directory you want to work with. Press ENTER when the full directory name is specified.

Note: If you want to follow along with the examples presented here, select the PUBLIC directory.

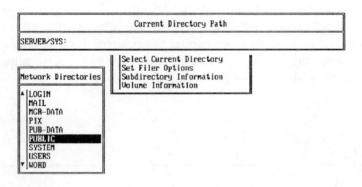

Accessing File Information

Files can be managed by selecting File Information from the FILER main menu. A list of files similar to the following will appear.

Highlight any file and press ENTER to display the File Information screen, shown here. The options on this screen allow you to view or change the file's attributes and perform other tasks.

By highlighting the Attributes option, you can view or change the attributes of a file.

Note: Only supervisors or those given the Modify right in a directory will be able to change the attributes.

The screen on the left in the following illustration shows the current attributes of a file. When you press INS, the Other File Attributes screen appears as shown, which allows you to add the Hidden, Indexed, or System attributes. These attributes are discussed in Chapter 13. Note that some files may have additional attributes listed in the window. For example, executable files can be given the Execute Only attribute, which makes them read-only and unchangeable as a protection against computer viruses.

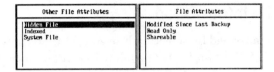

The options available from the File Information window are described in the following paragraphs. Remember that a supervisor or user with the Modify right in a directory is allowed to alter these options. In most cases, you can give users the right to modify attributes in their own personal directories.

Note: NetWare 386 allows users to be given the Modify right for their personal files within any directory, even though they don't have the Modify right for the entire directory.

Attributes   Changes the attributes of a file, as discussed in the previous paragraph.

Copy File   Files can be copied from the current directory to a specified directory using this option. The F5 Mark key can be used to select multiple files for copying.

Creation Date   The creation date of a file can be viewed and altered if needed. It is sometimes convenient to alter a creation date if you want to list files according to a particular date.

Last Accessed Date, Last Archived Date, Last Modified Date
These options will display the appropriate dates. Such information is often useful when backing up files.

Owner   The owner of a file can be viewed and modified.

Size   The size of a file can be viewed.

View File   The selected file can be viewed, but only in its ASCII format. Files created by applications that introduce formatting codes may not appear properly on the screen.

Setting FILER's Options

By selecting Select Filer Options from the main menu, you can gain more control over FILER's operations. The selections are shown in the following illustration. The first three options allow you to add protection to file operations that might delete or copy over existing files; however, starting with version 2.1 of NetWare, multiple copies are no longer allowed, so the Confirm File Copies option no longer works. Selecting Confirm Deletions, as shown in this illustration, can provide you with protection against accidental deletion of files. FILER will ask if you really want to remove a file. The third option is useful for preventing file overwrites when copying files that might already exist. DOS does not give you this protection.

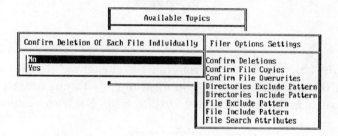

The last three options in the Select Filer Options menu can be used to control how FILER displays files in the File Information window. You can exclude or include certain patterns, and you can turn on the display of hidden or system files by selecting the menu shown here:

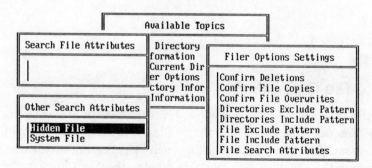

Some files are both hidden and system files, so you should select both options when choosing the File Search Attributes option. This option lets you view the NetWare hidden bindery files in the SYSTEM directory, as shown here. Use the INS key to insert both options in the menu.

In most cases, you may want to exclude files from a listing so you can more clearly see the remaining list of files. In the following illustration, .COM, .DBD, .EXE, .HLP, .OVL, and .PDF files are excluded from the file listing in the PUBLIC directory.

The file listing that results from these exclusions is shown next. Without using the exclusions, you would need to page through many extraneous files, such as those for the menu utilities and NetWare commands.

Multiple File Operations

At the Files window, you can select several different files with the F5 Mark key. You can then perform multiple file operations. For example, you can delete multiple files by highlighting each file, pressing F5 on each, and then pressing the DEL key. You can also display the Multiple File Operations menu, shown in the following illustration, by selecting more than one file and pressing ENTER.

Multiple file operations include setting file attributes, changing the creation date, changing the last accessed and last modified dates, and changing the owner of the selected files.

Listing and Copying Files

The commands presented in this section have equivalents in the DOS environment and can even be used in the same way as DOS commands to some extent. You will find in reading the following sections that the commands are quite powerful, and for good reason. A network manager may be faced with managing thousands of files created by many different users. The more control the supervisor has over these files, the better. The listing and copying commands can be used to list specific files or exclude others. Files can be listed by owner or by creation date. It will be beneficial to any supervisor to become familiar with these options for future use.

Listing Files with NDIR

The NDIR command is equivalent to the DIR command in DOS, except that it is much more extensive, as you will see by the options described in this section. NDIR can be used to display information about files as well as directories. This section will explain NDIR's file-specific options. The previous chapter explained NDIR's directory-specific options.

Note: The NDIR command is an important tool for viewing files on the entire system owned by a single user or created before a specific date. The owner of the files or the supervisor can use this information to "clean" the filing system or to find out where files are located. It is recommended that you read through and try the examples in this section to fully understand the importance and usefulness of NDIR.

One of the first things you can do with NDIR is list its help screen. This can be done by typing the following command:

NDIR HELP

An incomprehensible help screen of NDIR options will appear. This section will help you understand how to interpret this screen.

The NDIR command takes the form

NDIR *path/filename options*

where *path / filename* is replaced with the directory path, file name, or directory path and file name to list. The *options* are special filters you can use to control the sort order, date, owner, and other information about files.

The simplest form of the command is its solo mode, as shown next. From any directory, type this command to see a listing of files and subdirectories for that directory. The contents of the subdirectories are not listed.

NDIR

Any directory can be listed by specifying the full path. In the following command, the PUBLIC directory is listed, using the path to the directory:

NDIR SYS:PUBLIC

The mapped drive letter of a directory can also be used to display the contents of a directory. The following example assumes that the PUBLIC directory is mapped to drive G. It produces the same listing as the previous command.

NDIR G:

For clarity, mapped drive letters will be used in most examples for the remaining part of this section.

What NDIR Displays

The NDIR listing displays a sorted list of files in a directory, and then finishes with a listing of subdirectories for the requested directory. The display will page a display full of files at a time, unless you type **C** to request a continuous listing.

At the top of the screen are column headers that describe the information in the listing. The file name and its size are listed first. The date of last modification is then listed, followed by the last access date. Modified and accessed files are different, since a file may not be modified or changed every time it is accessed or opened by a user. The file creation date is also listed, which can be useful for managing the file system. For example, you may want to delete files prior to a certain date. The flags set for each file are also displayed along with the owner.

Note: A supervisor may need to view the modified date or access date of a file for security reasons or to determine the last time the file was used. A file that has not been accessed for some time may be a candidate for deletion.

Subdirectories are listed at the end of the NDIR display. The subdirectory name and creation date are shown, along with the maximum rights mask. The effective rights mask is also displayed, but it may be different for each user who lists the subdirectories because users may have different trustee rights in the subdirectory. The owner of the directory is also listed.

NDIR Options

The following options can be used to control NDIR's display. This control can be categorized in six ways.

- *Basic file information options* These options control how a file is listed in relation to its file name, owner, last accessed date, last update date, creation date, and size. The NOT option is used with these options to specify a listing of files that do not have the specified feature.

- *File attributes options* Files can be listed if they have an attribute or if they don't have an attribute. The NOT option is used with the attribute letter to specify a listing of files that do not have the attribute.

- *Sorting options* Files can be sorted in alphabetical or reverse alphabetical order on the file name, owner, last-accessed date, date of last update, creation date, and size. The REVERSE option is used to reverse the order.

- *View options* The view options are used to view only files or only directories. They are also used to view only subdirectories or Macintosh files. A Brief option will list only the size and last update for each file. Some options can be combined, such as the Directories Only and the Subdirectories options.

- *Archiving options* The archiving options can be used to view the archived (backup) status of files.

Each option is described in the following sections with examples of its usage. Note that each option has a name abbreviation. You can use the abbreviation, which is listed first, or the full option name.

Basic File-Information Options

FN (FILENAME)   The FILENAME option is typed after the directory path or drive letter. It produces a list of files that match the file name specified. Wildcard characters can be used to specify the files to list. The option takes the following form, where *file* is replaced with the file name. Note that asterisk wildcard characters can be used in the file name.

NDIR *drive or path* FN *file*

NDIR *drive or path* FN NOT *file*

Or the command can take the form of the DOS DIR command

NDIR *drive:file*

OW (OWNER)   The OWNER option lists files owned by a specified user or can be used to exclude files owned by the user. The option takes the following form, where *name* is replaced by the owner's name.

NDIR *drive or path* OW *name*

NDIR *drive or path* OW NOT *name*

AC (ACCESS)   The ACCESS option lists files accessed on, before, or after a specified date. The BEF (BEFore) and AFT (AFTer) options are used to specify listings before or after the specified date. The NOT option is used with the AC command to specify dates not within the range. The option takes the following forms:

NDIR *drive or path* AC *mm-dd-yy*

NDIR *drive or path* AC NOT *mm-dd-yy*

NDIR *drive or path* AC BEF *mm-dd-yy*

NDIR *drive or path* AC NOT BEF *mm-dd-yy*

NDIR *drive or path* AC AFT *mm-dd-yy*

NDIR *drive or path* AC NOT AFT *mm-dd-yy*

U (UPDATE)   The UPDATE option lists files updated on, before, or after a specified date. The BEF (BEFore) and AFT (AFTer) options are used to specify listings before or after the specified date. The NOT option specifies dates not within the range. The option takes the following forms:

NDIR *drive or path* U *mm-dd-yy*

NDIR *drive or path* U NOT *mm-dd-yy*

NDIR *drive or path* U BEF *mm-dd-yy*

NDIR *drive or path* U NOT BEF *mm-dd-yy*

NDIR *drive or path* U AFT *mm-dd-yy*

NDIR *drive or path* U NOT AFT *mm-dd-yy*

CR (CREATE)   The CREATE option lists files created on, before, or after a specified date. The BEF (BEFore) and AFT (AFTer) options are used to specify listings before or after the specified date. The NOT option specifies dates not within the range. The option takes the following form:

NDIR *drive or path* CR *mm-dd-yy*

NDIR *drive or path* CR NOT *mm-dd-yy*

NDIR *drive or path* CR BEF *mm-dd-yy*

NDIR *drive or path* CR NOT BEF *mm-dd-yy*

NDIR *drive or path* CR AFT *mm-dd-yy*

NDIR *drive or path* CR NOT AFT *mm-dd-yy*

SI (SIZE)   The SIZE option lists files according to their size, or it can be used to exclude files less than or greater than a certain size using the GR (GReater than) or LE (LEss than) option. The NOT option can be used to exclude files of a specified size. The option takes the following form, where *nnn* is replaced with the file size in bytes:

NDIR *drive or path* SI *nnn*

NDIR *drive or path* SI GR *nnn*

NDIR *drive or path* SI NOT GR *nnn*

NDIR *drive or path* SI LE *nnn*

NDIR *drive or path* SI NOT LE *nnn*

File Attributes Options

SY (System)   Listings can include only those files with the System attribute or exclude files with the attribute (using the NOT option). The option is placed in the NDIR command behind the drive or pathname in one of the following forms:

NDIR *drive or path* SY

NDIR *drive or path* NOT SY

H (Hidden)   Listings can include only those files with the Hidden attribute or exclude files with the attribute (using the NOT option). The option is placed in the NDIR command behind the path or file name in one of the following forms:

> NDIR *drive or path* H
>
> NDIR *drive or path* NOT H

M (Modified)   Listings can include only those files with the Modified attribute or exclude files with the attribute (using the NOT option). The option is placed in the NDIR command behind the path or file name in one of the following forms:

> NDIR *drive or path* M
>
> NDIR *drive or path* NOT M

EO (Execute Only)   Listings can include only those files with the Execute Only attribute or exclude files with the attribute (using the NOT option). The option is placed in the NDIR command behind the path or file name in one of the following forms:

> NDIR *drive or path* EO
>
> NDIR *drive or path* NOT EO

SHA (Shareable)   Listings can include only those files with the Shareable attribute or exclude files with the attribute (using the NOT option). The option is placed in the NDIR command behind the path or file name in one of the following forms:

> NDIR *drive or path* SHA
>
> NDIR *drive or path* NOT SHA

RO (Read Only)   Listings can include only those files with the Read Only attribute or exclude files with the attribute (using the NOT option). The option is placed in the NDIR command behind the path or file name in one of the following forms:

NDIR *drive or path* RO

NDIR *drive or path* NOT RO

RW (Read Write)   Listings can include only those files with the Read Write attribute or exclude files with the attribute (using the NOT option). The option is placed in the NDIR command behind the path or file name in one of the following forms:

NDIR *drive or path* RW

NDIR *drive or path* NOT RW

I (Indexed)   Listings can include only those files with the Indexed attribute or exclude files with the attribute (using the NOT option). The option is placed in the NDIR command behind the path or file name in one of the following forms:

NDIR *drive or path* I

NDIR *drive or path* NOT I

T (Transactional)   Listings can include only those files with the Transactional attribute or exclude files with the attribute (using the NOT option). The option is placed in the NDIR command behind the path or file name in one of the following forms:

NDIR *drive or path* T

NDIR *drive or path* NOT T

Sorting Options

SO FN (SORT FILENAME)   Files can be listed in file-name order using this option. The REV (Reverse) option can be placed in front of the SO option to reverse the order. The options are placed in the NDIR command behind the path or file name in one of the following forms:

NDIR *drive or path* SO FN

NDIR *drive or path* REV SO FN

SO OW (SORT OWNER)   Files can be listed according to their owner using this option. The REV (Reverse) option can be placed in front of the SO option to reverse the order. The options are placed in the NDIR command behind the path or file name in one of the following forms:

NDIR *drive or path* SO OW

NDIR *drive or path* REV SO OW

SO AC (SORT ACCESS)   Files can be listed according to their access date order using this option. The REV (Reverse) option can be placed in front of the SO option to reverse the order. The options are placed in the NDIR command behind the path or file name in one of the following forms:

NDIR *drive or path* SO AC

NDIR *drive or path* REV SO AC

SO U (SORT UPDATE)   Files can be listed according to their update date using this option. The REV (Reverse) option can be placed in front of the SO option to reverse the order. The options are placed in the NDIR command behind the path or file name in one of the following forms:

NDIR *drive or path* SO U

NDIR *drive or path* REV SO U

SO CR (SORT CREATE)   Files can be listed according to their creation date using this option. The REV (Reverse) option can be placed in front of the SO option to reverse the order. The options are placed in the NDIR command behind the path or file name in one of the following forms:

NDIR *drive or path* SO CR

NDIR *drive or path* REV SO CR

SO SI (SORT SIZE) Files can be listed according to the file size using this option. The REV (Reverse) option can be placed in front of the SO option to reverse the order. The options are placed in the NDIR command behind the path or file name in one of the following forms:

NDIR *drive or path* SO SI

NDIR *drive or path* REV SO SI

View Options

FO (Files Only) The FO option is typed on the NDIR command line to specify that only files should be listed.

DO (Directories Only) The DO option is typed on the NDIR command line to specify that only directories should be listed. This is often used with the SUB option to display the entire directory structure, as discussed in the previous chapter.

SUB (Subdirectories) The SUB option is typed on the NDIR command line to include subdirectories in the listing of the specified directory. This is often used with the DO option to display the entire directory structure, as discussed in the previous chapter.

BR (Brief) The Brief option lists only the size and last update of each file.

MAC (Macintosh) The MAC option lists files created in the Macintosh environment for the specified directory.

Archiving Options

BACKUP   The BACKUP option can be included in an NDIR command to show the last modified date and the last archived date. By comparing these dates, you can determine whether a file has been archived since it was last modified. The command takes the form

   NDIR *drive or path* BACKUP

WIDE   The WIDE option can be included to use the normal file display format rather than the BACKUP format, which is automatically used by the ARCHIVED, CHANGED, and TOUCHED options.

   NDIR *drive or path* WIDE

ARCHIVED   The ARCHIVED option is used to view all files that have been archived. The NOT option can be used to view all files that have not been archived. The command takes the following form:

   NDIR *drive or path* ARCHIVED

   NDIR *drive or path* NOT ARCHIVED

AD (Archived Date)   The Archived Date option can be used to view all files archived before, on, or after a specified date. The BEF (Before) and AFT (After) options can be used to specify a list of files before or after the date.

   NDIR *drive or path* AD *mm-dd-yy*

   NDIR *drive or path* AD BEF *mm-dd-yy*

   NDIR *drive or path* AD AFT *mm-dd-yy*

CHANGED   The CHANGED option is used to view files updated (changed) since the last archive, or files that have never been archived (new files).

NDIR *drive or path* CHANGED

AB (Archive Bit)   Think of the archive bit as a switch. When files are archived, the switch is turned off. If it is still set, files have not been archived. To see a list of files that have not been archived, use the AB option by itself. To see a list of archived files, the NOT option is used with the AB option.

NDIR *drive or path* AB

NDIR *drive or path* NOT AB

TOUCHED   The TOUCHED option is used to view files modified since the last archive. This option checks both the archive date and time and DOS archive bit.

NDIR *drive or path* TOUCHED

NDIR Examples

While most of the command options just listed can be used by themselves in NDIR commands, you will find that many can be combined in exotic ways to produce exactly the kind of file listing you want. This section will concentrate on combinations of NDIR options. Keep in mind that these examples represent a small sampling of possible combinations.

Note: Chapter 23 will show you how to place long, extensive, hard-to-remember NDIR commands on menus similar to the NetWare menu utilities, making them much easier and more practical to use on a regular basis.

The following example lists file on drive K that include *.DOC in their file names (FN *.DOC) and that are owned by John (OW JOHN).

NDIR K: FN *.DOC OW JOHN

The next example lists files on drive K that include *.DOC in their file names (FN *.DOC) and that have a size greater than 3000 bytes (SI GR 3000).

NDIR K: FN *.DOC SI GR 3000

The next example lists files on drive K that include *.DOC in their file names (FN *.DOC) and that are owned by John (OW JOHN). The list is then sorted in file-name order (SO FN).

NDIR K: FN *.DOC OW JOHN SO FN

The next example lists files on drive K that include *.DOC in their file name (FN *.DOC), that are owned by John (OW JOHN), and that were created after 12-25-89 (CR AFT 12-25-89):

NDIR K: FN *.DOC OW JOHN CR AFT 12-25-89

The next command lists all files in the SYS volume owned by John (OW JOHN). All files in all subdirectories (SUB) are listed.

NDIR SYS: OW JOHN SUB

The following command lists all files in the SYS volume owned by John (OW JOHN) in all subdirectories (SUB) with a size greater than 3000 bytes (SI GR 3000).

NDIR SYS: OW JOHN SUB SI GR 3000

The next command lists all files owned by John in all subdirectories of SYS that have a size greater and 3000 bytes. The list is sorted in file-name order (SO FN) and files only (FO) are listed.

NDIR SYS: OW JOHN SUB SI GR 3000 SO FN FO

The next command lists all files in the SYS volume owned by John (OW JOHN) for all subdirectories (SUB) with a size greater than 3000 bytes (SI GR 3000). The list is sorted in file- name order (SO FN), files only are listed (FO), and file names ending in EXE are excluded (FN NOT *.EXE).

NDIR SYS: OW JOHN SUB SI GR 3000 SO FN FO FN NOT *.EXE

This NDIR command lists all files in drive K that are shareable (SHA) and excludes all files that end in EXE (FN NOT *.EXE).

NDIR K: SHA FN NOT *.EXE

The next NDIR command lists all files in drive K that have Shareable (SHA) and Read Write (RW) attributes and that were accessed after 12-25-89 (A AFT 12-25-89).

NDIR K: SHA RW A AFT 12-25-89

The last example lists all files in the SYS: volume that have Shareable (SHA) and Read Write (RW) attributes. The list is displayed in reverse sorted order by creation date (REV SO CR) for all subdirectories (SUB). Only files are listed (FO).

NDIR SYS: SHA RW REV SO CR SUB FO

Pattern Matching with NDIR

Wildcard characters can be used with NDIR to specify a range of files. For example, *.DOC is used in the previous examples to specify all files with the .DOC extension. NetWare also allows you to use the asterisk when trying to locate files that have a certain pattern within the file name itself. For example, assume the files ACCT16-1.DAT, SAL16-1.DAT, and MKT16- 3.DAT exist in a directory. Each file has the string "16" in common, but this string does not hold the same place in each file name. To list the files, the following command can be used.

NDIR K: FN *16*

The PUBLIC directory contains a number of files that have the dollar sign in their names. The following command can be used to list these files.

NDIR SYS:PUBLIC FN *$*

Other NDIR Operations

The output of the NDIR command can be sent to a file or to a printer. There may be several reasons for doing this. A file listing sent to a file can be further edited and used as a road map of the file system for a user or group. If the directed file listing extracts a certain user's files, the list can be invaluable to users as a way to find their way around. The supervisor or users who want to clear old files from the server can print a list of files filtered for a particular owner and for dates previous to a specified date. The date filtering allows the user or supervisor to list only those files that might be old and of no use.

The redirection symbol (>) is used to direct the NDIR listing to a file. In the following example, all files owned by John on the SYS: volume are sent to the JOHNFILE file for further editing.

NDIR SYS: OW JOHN SUB FO > JOHNFILE

It may be necessary to edit the file to remove the comments that normally appear on the screen during a listing.

In the next example, the same list is sent to the printer LPT1.

NDIR SYS: OW JOHN SUB FO > LPT1

This command assumes that a proper CAPTURE command has been executed to direct printing to the server printer, if necessary.

Copying Files with NCOPY

The NCOPY command, like the DOS COPY command, is used to copy files between drives and directories, as well as to make duplicates of existing files with new names. The NCOPY command works with Macintosh files as well and will copy both the data and resource "forks" associated with those files.

The NCOPY command is superior to the DOS COPY command in that it transfers groups of files in a much more efficient way. When a file is copied, it retains the last date and time of the original file; however, the date and time at which the new file was created and accessed will change. The wildcard characters * and ? can be used in commands to designate sets of files. These characters can act as placemarkers when you are targeting sets of files that have parts of their file name in common.

The NCOPY command takes the following form:

NCOPY *source filename* TO *destination filename* /Verify

Where *source filename* is the file or group of files to be copied and *destination filename* is the destination directory. Both the source and destination file names may include the path or mapped drive letter of the files. Files can be renamed during a copy by specifying a new file name in *destination filename*. Note that the TO option is not required in NCOPY commands but can be used for clarity.

The following commands show examples of copying files between directories. In the first command, the full path of the directories is used in the command

NCOPY SYS:PUBLIC\PROGRAMS*.DAT TO SYS:PUBLIC\DATA

If PUBLIC\PROGRAMS is the current default directory, only the names of the files need to be specified.

NCOPY *.DAT TO SYS:PUBLIC\DATA

Assuming that drive K is mapped to SYS:PUBLIC\PROGRAMS and L is mapped to SYS:PUBLIC\DATA, the following command will copy files from K to L.

NCOPY K:*.DAT TO L:

Copying Between Servers

Files can be copied between file servers. In the following command, files are copied from the server MKTG-1 to MGTG-2. The directories holding the files are specified in the commands.

NCOPY MKTG-1/SYS:PROJ-1 TO MKTG-2/SYS:PROJ-1

Assuming that drive S is mapped to MKTG-1/SYS:PROJ-1 and T is mapped to MKTG-2/SYS:PROJ-2, the following command would copy files between the servers.

NCOPY S:*.DAT TO T:

Renaming While Copying

In the following command, the YOURFILE.DOC file is duplicated in the same directory by using NCOPY to copy it to another file name. Two files will reside on the disk after you execute the command.

NCOPY YOURFILE.DOC TO MYFILE.DOC

Files can be copied and renamed between directories and servers using a similar command, but you must insert the mapped drive letter or full pathname of the source or destination directory.

Verifying After Copying

The V option is used to specify that you want to verify the integrity of files that have been copied. NCOPY will compare the contents of the copied file to the original. The following command illustrates the use of Verify.

NCOPY YOURFILE.DOC TO MYFILE.DOC /V

Changing File Attributes
At the Command Line

The following commands are used to change the attributes of files at the command line, rather than using the FILER utility. The FLAG command is the most commonly used to change attributes. Other file attributes include the ability to prevent a file from being used by another user until you are done with it. Files can also be hidden so they don't appear in directory listings.

The FLAG Command

The FLAG command is used to assign attributes to files outside of the FILER utility. The following attributes can be assigned to files with the command:

S   Shareable. The file may be used by more than one person at a time

NS   Nonshareable. The file may only be used by one person at a time.

RO   Read Only. The file may only by read and not changed.

RW   Read-Write. The file may be both read and written to.

N   Normal. The file is given the Nonshareable and Read-Write attributes.

T   Transactional. For SFT NetWare only. Assigns the Transaction Tracking System status to the file.

I   Indexed. The files location is indexed in memory for quick access. You would normally want to assign this file to databases or other large files.

The SUB option is used in the FLAG command to specify that the attributes assigned to files in a directory are to also be assigned to files in its subdirectories.

The NOT option can be used to specify that a file or group of files should not have the specified attribute. The NOT option cannot be used with the SUB option or the N (Normal) attribute.

Note: FLAG does not allow files to be marked with the System, Modified, Execute-Only, and Hidden attributes. You must use FILER or refer to later sections in this chapter.

Users who will be flagging files must have the Search and Modify trustee rights in the directory. Users must also be attached to the server where the files are located.

Viewing File Attributes

Type the following command to view the file attributes for all files in the current directory.

FLAG

To view attributes for specific files, type the file name or use wildcard characters to specify a group of files. For example, the following command would list the attributes of the .EXE files in the current directory.

FLAG *.EXE

The attributes of a single file can be listed by specifying its file name, as in the following:

FLAG MYFILE.DOC

If the files reside in other directories, the mapped drive letter to those directories or the complete directory path must be specified. For example, this command displays the attributes of the .DOC files in John's user directory.

FLAG SYS:USERS\JOHN*.DOC

If this directory is mapped to drive F, the following command will perform the same operation.

FLAG F:*.DOC

Changing File Attributes

The attributes of files can be changed by specifying the name of the file to change followed by the attributes to assign to the file. Wildcard characters can also be used to specify a group of files. For example, the following command would change the attributes of the .EXE files in the current directory to Shareable and Read Only.

FLAG *.EXE SRO

Note: The command just shown will be used often. Most program files used on a network should be marked with the Shareable and Read Only attributes. You should use a command similar to this after installing applications in a directory.

The attributes of a single file can be changed by specifying the file's file name and attributes. The following example changes the attributes of MYFILE.DOC in the current directory to Read Only.

FLAG MYFILE.DOC RO

Note: Files should be marked Read Only if you don't want them to be altered or erased by other users.

If the files reside in other directories, the mapped drive letter or the complete directory path to those directories must be specified. For example, this command changes the attributes of the DOC files in John's user directory to Normal.

FLAG SYS:USERS\JOHN*.DOC N

If the directory is mapped to drive F, the following command will perform the same operation.

FLAG F:*.DOC N

All files in a directory can be marked by specifying the asterisk (*) in the FLAG command. For example, the following command assigns the Shareable, Read-Write attribute to the files in the PUB-DATA directory.

FLAG SYS:PUB-DATA* SRW

Flagging Program and Data Files

When a program is installed, one directory should be created for the program files and another for the data files. The files in these directories should be flagged differently, as described next.

Program Files   The program files for the application should be marked as Shareable, Read-Only. In this way trustees of the directory can use the files but not alter them. The following command would change the program files in the DBASE directory to Shareable, Read-Only.

FLAG SYS:DBASE*.* S RO

Remember that anyone using program files in a directory will need to have at least the Read, Open, and Search directory trustee rights. Some programs that create temporary work files may require that the user also have the Write and Delete rights.

Data Files   The data files used by programs should be marked as Shareable, Read-Write files so users can share the files and make changes to them. Be careful when marking files Shareable, however. Some non-database applications do not support shareable files. One user could write over the file that has changes just made by another user. In most cases, files used by database programs such as dBASE III and dBASE IV are shareable because each user only works on one record at a time and not on the record being used by another user. This is referred to as *record locking.* Some applications support *file locking* and will not let two users have access to the same file. If an application does not support file locking, assign the Nonshareable attribute to your data files.

Executable Files

Executable files can be made Execute Only by using the FILER utility. Files marked with this attribute can only be opened and run as a program.

They cannot be changed, which provides protection from viruses. A virus usually tries to attach itself to an executable file and then proliferates through the system, using the file as a carrier. Assign this attribute to .COM and .EXE files whenever possible, especially if users are uploading files from disks at their workstations. Files from public domain utility floppy disks or bulletin boards are a common source of virus corruption. Always make sure to have a good backup set of the .COM and .EXE files since the execute flag may not work in some cases.

Assigning Search Modes
To Executable Files with SMODE

The SMODE command is used to assign a search mode to an executable file or to view the current search mode of a file. Executable files (program files) have the extension .EXE or .COM. Some of these files need to access data files when they run, and if these files are in the same directory, the executable files will not have any trouble finding them when necessary. However, if the data files are stored outside the executable file's directory, you will need to take steps to supply a search path for the data files. The SMODE command is used to assign one of the search methods described here to executable files.

0   Mode 0 is the default setting; it specifies no special search instructions. Instead, the executable file will look for instructions in the SHELL.CFG file, as discussed in Chapter 11. The command SEARCH MODE = n is placed in CONFIG.SYS, where n is equal to modes 1 through 7 as described here.

1   The executable file uses a path of its own, or if that path is not specified, searches the default directory and the current search-drive mappings.

2   The executable file will search only the default drive.

3   The executable file uses its own path; or, if such a path is not defined and if the executable file opens read-only data files, the default directory and the current search-drive mappings are searched.

4   Reserved.

5   The executable file searches the default directories and
         search drives.

6   Reserved.

7   If read-only data files are used by the executable file, it will
         search the default directory and all search drives.

The command takes the form

SMODE *path-or-filename option*

where *path* can be a mapped drive letter or the full path to a directory, and
filename is the name of the file to assign the mode to. *Option* is one of the
modes just described. For example, the following command assigns mode
5 to the START.EXE file in a directory called SYS:PUBLIC\PROGRAMS.

SMODE SYS:PUBLIC\PROGRAMS\START.EXE 5

To view the search modes of files in a directory, type the command in a
form similar to this but do not specify a search mode.

Holding a File

The HOLDON command lets a user gain single-user access to a file and
prevent other users from accessing that file while it is in use. The HOLD-
OFF command is used to release held files so others can access them.

   When a file is accessed with a program, it should be held open until
the user is finished with the file or leaves the program. If files are not held
open, other users can access the file simultaneously, with the possibility
that one user's changes to the file will be overwritten by another user.

HOLDON

The HOLDON command is designed to be used for programs that do not
hold a file open when a user accesses the file, which means that others

could possibly access the file simultaneously and corrupt it. To hold any files accessed while running a program, issue the following command before entering the program.

HOLDON

Files will be held open until exiting from the program or rebooting the workstation.

HOLDOFF

The HOLDOFF command is used to reverse a HOLDON command. The command is typed as

HOLDOFF

Protecting Files

Files can be protected in a number of ways. The FLAG command can be used to make a file read-only to prevent other users from changing the contents of the file. Files can also be protected at the directory level with the trustee rights granted by the supervisor. Trustee rights can prevent other users from accessing and deleting files in other user's directories or in shared directories not assigned to the user.

Files can also be archived to floppy disk, tape, other hard drives, and writeable digital disk media. NetWare has a set of archiving utilities that can be used to archive files to other drives. These utilities will be discussed in Chapter 25.

Hiding and Unhiding Files

The following commands are supervisor-only commands located in the SYS:SYSTEM directory. Since only the supervisor should have access to this directory, only the supervisor or supervisor equivalent can run the commands.

HIDEFILE

Files are hidden so they won't show in directory searches and cannot be deleted or copied over. Hidden files also cannot be copied to other directories. Hidden files are still accessible with commands and programs, however, and they can be backed up and restored with the BACKUP and RESTORE utilities of NetWare.

Note: The HIDEFILE utility hides files by setting the DOS Hidden and System file attributes.

The HIDEFILE command takes the form

HIDEFILE *drive or path* *filename*

where *drive or path* is the mapped drive letter or the complete pathname of the directory holding the file, and *filename* is the name of the file to hide. For example, to hide the MYFILE.DOC file in the SYS:USERS\JOHN directory, the following command would be typed.

HIDEFILE SYS:USERS\JOHN\MYFILE.DOC

If the directory were mapped to drive F, the following command would be typed.

HIDEFILE F:MYFILE.DOC

Wildcard characters can also be used to hide groups of files. For example, if John wants to hide the .DOC files in his personal directory, which is mapped to drive F, he would type

HIDEFILE F:*.DOC

After the command was executed, the display would show the hidden status of the file, but it would no longer appear in directory listings unless the SHOWFILE command were used to unhide it.

SHOWFILE

The SHOWFILE command is used to make files hidden by the HIDEFILE command visible again. Files will once again appear in directory listing and can be copied and deleted. The SHOWFILE command takes the form

SHOWFILE *drive or path* \ *filename*

where *drive or path* is the mapped drive letter or the complete pathname of the directory holding the file, and *filename* is the name of the file to make visible. For example, to make the MYFILE.DOC file in the SYS:USERS\JOHN directory visible, the following command would be typed.

SHOWFILE SYS:USERS\JOHN\MYFILE.DOC

If the directory were mapped to drive F, the following command would be typed.

SHOWFILE F:MYFILE.DOC

Wildcard characters can also be used to make groups of files visible. For example, if John wants to make the .DOC files in his personal directory visible, which is mapped to drive F, he would type

SHOWFILE F:*.DOC

Salvaging Deleted Files

Files can be deleted with the DOS DEL or ERASE command. It is often the case that an inexperienced or weary user may accidentally erase the wrong files. This is not a serious problem if the files are recovered as soon as possible with the RECOVER command. Files cannot be recovered under certain conditions. The following applies to erased files that you may want to salvage.

- Do not log out of the file server. Logging out eliminates the possibility of restoring the erased files with RECOVER.

- Do not create or erase any more files on the volume where files were erased. SALVAGE cannot recover a file once another file has been created or deleted on the same volume.

- Do not issue a PURGE command, which would render all erased files irrecoverable.

- Only files deleted by the current workstation can be salvaged. Activities on other workstations will not affect the salvageable status of the deleted files on the current workstations.

- The SALVAGE command must be issued at the workstation where files were originally deleted.

The SALVAGE command should be typed immediately after accidentally deleting files. The command can be typed as shown here to recover the most recently deleted files in the current directory.

SALVAGE

To recover files in other directories, type the mapped drive letter or full path of the directory where the files were deleted. In the following example, files are salvaged in the SYS:USER\JOHN directory.

SALVAGE SYS:USER\JOHN

Purging Files with PURGE

In some cases, you may want to completely remove files that have been deleted without any chance of recovering them. This is often the case where security is a concern and you don't want someone possibly salvaging the files you have just erased. The PURGE command will remove the possibility of recovering any files that were deleted by your workstation. The command does not affect files deleted by other workstations. To render all previously erased files unrecoverable, issue the following command.

PURGE

Creating and Managing Users

Setting Default Restrictions
Steps to Creating New Users
Console Operators
Command Utilities for Managing Users
The MAKEUSER and DEFUSER Utilities

Chapter 15 provided an overview of the initial steps a supervisor would go through when setting up a NetWare system. This includes adding users, directories, and system security. This chapter will provide more complete information on creating users, including an overview of the MAKEUSER (Advanced NetWare and SFT NetWare) and USERDEF (ELS NetWare Level II) utilities, which make the task of creating multiple users in educational or large system environments easier to perform.

Setting Default Restrictions

While the supervisor can set password, time, station, and other restrictions for each user individually, default restrictions that apply to all users also can be set. These restrictions can be set in the Supervisor Options menu of the SYSCON menu utility, as shown in the following illustration. The options are discussed next.

411

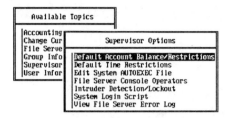

Setting Default Account Restrictions

The Default Account Balance/Restrictions menu, shown next, allows the supervisor to set the defaults shown for every user on the system. However, the default settings can be further modified for individual users by accessing a similar menu in the SYSCON User Options menu.

```
┌──────────────────────────────────────────────────┐
│       Default Account Balance/Restrictions         │
├──────────────────────────────────────────────────┤
│Account Has Expiration Date:      Yes               │
│   Date Account Expires:          September 1, 1990 │
│Limit Concurrent Connections:     Yes               │
│   Maximum Connections:           1                 │
│Require Password:                 Yes               │
│   Minimum Password Length:       5                 │
│Force Periodic Password Changes:  Yes               │
│   Days Between Forced Changes:   40                │
│   Limit Grace Logins:            Yes               │
│      Grace Logins Allowed:       6                 │
│Require Unique Passwords:         Yes               │
│Account Balance:                  1000              │
│Allow Unlimited Credit:           No                │
│   Low Balance Limit:             10                │
└──────────────────────────────────────────────────┘
```

The options on the Default Account Balance/Restrictions menu are covered in the following sections.

Account Expiration Date

The entire set of system accounts can be set to expire on the date specified in the second line of the menu. When the expiration date is reached, no one will be able to log in except the supervisor. The accounts are not removed from the system. The supervisor can add new expiration dates to accounts or remove accounts no longer needed. To set expiration dates for individual users, refer to the User Information menu selection.

Limit Concurrent Connections

Users can be limited to logging in to a certain number of stations at a time by setting the Limit Concurrent Connections field to Yes. Set Maximum Connections to 1 or the number of connections you want to allow.

Require Password

If you set the Require Password field to Yes, all users will need to enter a password to log on to the system. This field should normally be set to Yes when the system is initially being set up. The Minimum Password Length field is used to specify the number of characters in a password; the more characters, the better the security. Users will be required to create new passwords that meet or exceed the length when changing their passwords.

Force Periodic Password Changes

The supervisor can force users to change their passwords at the specified interval to enhance system security. Select Yes at the Force Periodic Password Changes field, and then specify the number of days between changes. The Limit Grace Logins field is used to limit the number of times users can log in with an expired password. You would normally want to allow several log-ins to give users a chance to change their password. Specify the number of grace log-ins in the Grace Logins Allowed field.

Require Unique Password

If the Require Unique Password field is specified, you can require all users to specify a password that has not been used in the last eight password changes.

Account Balance

The accounting feature of NetWare will be discussed in Chapter 23. You can use the last three fields of the menu to:

- Specify account balances for all users

- Specify whether they have credit

- Specify low balances

Default Time Restrictions

The Default Time Restrictions window is used to specify the times that all users will be able to log in. You can use the F5 (Mark) key to mark the times you *do not* want users to log in, and then press the DEL key to remove the asterisk characters from the marked area. Times that do not have asterisk characters are times that no users will be able to log in.

Intruder Detection Lockout

The intruder detection lockout feature is designed to set conditions for recognizing intruders. Intruders are users attempting to log in with unrecognized user names and passwords. For example, assume intruders are trying to break into the system using Joe's user name. They assume that Joe might be using the name of one of his kids as a password and attempt to log in with each name, one after the other. If Intruder Detection/Lockout is set to 3, the intruders will not be able to attempt log-in after the third attempt, assuming they haven't guessed the password.

The Intruder Detection/Lockout menu is shown here. Select Yes on the Detect Intruder field to enable the feature. You can then set the detection threshold and the length of lockout in the remaining fields. The initial threshold level is set to 7, but you can change this to any level you wish.

The Bad Login Count Retention Time field is set to the amount of time the operating system will keep track of incorrect log-ins. After the time has been exceeded, the incorrect log-in count will be reset to 0. The Lock Account After Detection field is used to specify the amount of time an account will be locked after an intruder has been detected.

In some cases, a user may find his or her account locked when he or she needs access to it. This is possible if the user forgot his or her password and attempted to log in using the guess method. To unlock a user account that has been locked, select User Information from the SYSCON main menu and then select the user that needs access to his or her account. Select Intruder Lockout Status and change the Account Locked field to No.

Steps to Creating New Users

There are a number of steps you should perform when creating new users. These steps will ensure that a user can access the system properly and use the applications they need to use. MAKEUSER/DEFUSER are described at the end of this chapter and can be used to perform most of the steps described here for a large number of users. If you are establishing a new network or a new group of users, you should refer to these utilities now. Supervisors running a school network that changes its network users every semester or quarter will want to use the utilities for defining new users.

The following can be used as a guide when creating new users with commands other than MAKEUSER/DEFUSER. Note that topics related to the SYSCON User Information selection are further discussed in "Defining User Information" later.

1. Add the User

The SYSCON utility must be used to create new users if the MAKE-USER/DEFUSER utilities are not used. Select User Information from the SYSCON main menu and press INS to begin adding new users. Type the new user's name and press ENTER. The name will appear in the User Names window. Press ENTER on the new name to display the User Information window. Select Full Name and type the user's full name in the window. Press ENTER.

2. Assign Account Restrictions for Users

From the User Information window, select Account Restrictions to assign password and sign-on restrictions to the user if necessary. Recall from the previous section that these restrictions may have been set using the supervisors default options for the entire system.

3. Assign Station and Time Restrictions to Users

Station restrictions can be added by selecting Station Restrictions from the User Information window. Time restrictions can be added by selecting Time Restrictions from the User Information window.

4. Assign Trustee Rights

New users must be assigned trustee rights in all directories they will work in, except the PUBLIC directory, which is already assigned to the user as members of the group EVERYONE. Select Trustee Assignments from the User Information menu and press INS to begin adding new directories.

You can create a personal directory for each user by specifying a path from the SYS:USERS directory with the user's personal name. Make sure this name is the same as the user's account name. You will be asked if you want to create the new directory. After the directory is created, select it and assign the user full rights by using the INS, select, and ENTER method. The system log-in script you may have created in Chapter 15 contains commands for logging users in to their personal directories.

Add additional directories to the user's Trustee Assignment window by using the INS key. You will need to make users trustees of the program and data directories they will use in their network sessions. Be sure to specify at least the Read, Open, and Search rights in program directories, and the Read, Write, Create, Open, and Search rights in data directories.

Note: Remember that it is easier to assign users rights by making users members of groups and assigning trustee rights to the group. This would be the case when you were assigning rights to public program and data directories.

5. Add Users to Groups

New users automatically belong to the EVERYONE group. They can be added to other groups, thus giving the new user the same trustee rights as the group. Select Groups Belonged To from the User Information window and press INS to select a new group.

6. Create Log-in Scripts

Log-in scripts can be created for each user, if necessary, by selecting Login Scripts from the User Information menu. Log-in scripts will be discussed in Chapter 21. In most cases, supervisors will want to execute as many commands for users as possible in the system log-in script rather than attempt to manage user log-in scripts for every user on the system. Users can then use their personal log-in scripts for their own use.

The NetWare Tutorial

Once users have been added to the system, they can run the NetWare tutorial to orient themselves on the system. The tutorial can be run from any directory as long as search drive is mapped to the SYS:PUBLIC directory. The following command is typed to start the tutorial:

TUTOR

Instructions for running the tutorial are contained within the program itself, so busy supervisors will find this program useful.

Defining User Information

The SYSCON menu utility contains most of the commands for creating and defining the parameters for users. When User Options is selected from the SYSCON main menu, a list of names appears. Pressing ENTER on any name will display the User Information menu shown in the following illustration.

```
 User Information
┌──────────────────────┐
│Account Restrictions  │
│Change Password       │
│Full Name             │
│Groups Belonged To    │
│Login Script          │
│Other Information      │
│Security Equivalences │
│Station Restrictions  │
│Time Restrictions     │
│Trustee Assignments   │
└──────────────────────┘
```

The options on this menu are used to define special parameters for each user. When Account Restrictions is selected, the menu shown here appears.

```
┌─────────────────────────────────────────────────┐
│      Account Restrictions For User JOHN          │
├─────────────────────────────────────────────────┤
│Account Disabled:               No                │
│Account Has Expiration Date:    Yes               │
│  Date Account Expires:         January 1, 1990   │
│Limit Concurrent Connections:   Yes               │
│  Maximum Connections:          1                 │
│Allow User To Change Password:  Yes               │
│Require Password:               Yes               │
│  Minimum Password Length:      5                 │
│Force Periodic Password Changes: Yes              │
│  Days Between Forced Changes:  40                │
│  Date Password Expires:        October 11, 1989  │
│  Limit Grace Logins:           Yes               │
│    Grace Logins Allowed:       6                 │
│    Remaining Grace Logins:     6                 │
│Require Unique Passwords:       Yes               │
└─────────────────────────────────────────────────┘
```

The Account Restrictions menu is used to set log-in and password rights for the user. Most of the options are discussed in the previous section for the default settings. These setting can be further customized from the default settings for each user. Refer back to the previous section for further explanations. The Account Restrictions menu has most of its options set to non-default settings. The default settings for the menu are as follows:

- Account is not disabled

- Account has no expiration date

- There is no limit on concurrent connections

- Users are allowed to change password

- Passwords are not required

If default settings are changed, the supervisor will need to supply additional information. For example, if Require Password is set to Yes, the supervisor will need to enter values in the fields just below it.

Other options in the User Information window allow the supervisor to change the password for the user, supply a full name, add users to groups, change a user's log-in script, and display information about the user. The Other Information screen is shown here:

```
Last Login:                      August 31, 1989  8:02:24 pm
File Server Console Operator:    Yes
Disk Space In Use:               0K
User ID:                         000C0035
```

The User Information window is also used by the supervisor to define security equivalences, station restrictions, time restrictions, and trustee assignments for the user.

Console Operators

The console operator is a user who has been given rights to access and use the FCONSOLE menu utility in more ways than regular users. The supervisor is allowed to assign FCONSOLE rights to the user. The following lists rights for both users and console operators.

- Users can use FCONSOLE to change file servers, view current user connection information, view a file server's LAN driver information, and view the version of NetWare currently running on the server.

- Console operators have additional rights to broadcast messages, purge salvageable files, view more detailed current user connection information, view file and lock activity, see and alter the status of the file server, and view statistics about the file server's performance.

- Supervisors are the only operators who are given the right to down the server from the FCONSOLE utility.

To assign a console operator, supervisors should start the SYSCON menu utility and select Supervisor Options from the main menu. The following screen will appear.

Select File Server Console Operators from the menu. A screen will appear, and you can press INS to see a list of users and groups. Select a user or group and press ENTER to add them to the list. In the following display, the groups CONSOLE-OPERATORS and MANAGERS are inserted as console operators.

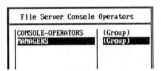

Command Utilities for Managing Users

Most of the commands utilities listed in this section have already been discussed in Chapter 16. They are briefly covered here to describe their usefulness in managing users from the supervisor's perspective. Supervisors should refer to Chapter 16 for more details.

Recall that users can be given the following trustee rights within a directory.

Read

Write

Open

Create

Delete

Parental

Search

Modify

Viewing the Trustee List with TLIST

The TLIST command can be used by supervisors to view the current trustee list for any directory. Only trustee lists for directories on the current server may be viewed.

To view the trustees for the current directory, type

TLIST

Information similar to the following will be displayed:

User Trustees:
    JOHN   [RWOCDPSM]   (JOHN JONES)
    ‾‾‾‾
Group Trustees:

EVERYONE [RWOC S]
MANAGERS [RWOCDPSM]   (DEPARTMENT MANAGERS)

If no users or trustees exist, the display will say so. The trustee rights in the directory are listed next to the trustee's names.

You can view the trustee list in any directory by specifying the full path to the directory or by using a mapped drive letter if one has been established. In the following examples, drive K is mapped to the SYS:PUB-LIC\PROGRAMS directory.

```
TLIST K:
TLIST SYS:PUBLIC\PROGRAMS
```

Both commands accomplish the same operation, which is to list the trustees for the directory.

Supervisors will want to use the TLIST command to determine who is using a directory and the rights that these users have in the directory. If users are having trouble accessing programs or files, it could be they don't have the proper rights. The supervisor can use TLIST to determine exactly what their rights are, and then use the GRANT utility to assign additional rights.

Viewing Current Users with USERLIST

The USERLIST command can be used to view the currently logged system users and their connection information. The command is useful for supervisors who need to see the user's connection number, log-in time, node address, and network address. The command is also useful to assist in sending messages, since it will list the name of each user on the system. The command takes the form

USERLIST *server* / *user* /A

where *server* is the optional name of the server to list, and *user* is the optional name of the user to list. If the /A (ALL) option is specified, the node and network address of each user will be displayed. This information is useful to supervisors who need to know where a particular user is working. Also, supervisors may need to shut a system down with the console CLEAR STATION command and will need to know the station number of the workstation to clear.

To begin using the command, simply type the following on the command line.

USERLIST

A screen similar to the following will appear.

Connection	User Name	Login Time
1	• SUPERVISOR	12-25-89 7:00 am
2	John	12-25-89 9:00 am
3	Jane	12-25-89 10:00 am

Note that an asterisk appears next the current user's name. To view information for only one user, type the user's name. For example, information about John's connection is listed with the following command:

USERLIST JOHN

The /A option can be used to list network and node address information about a user. In the following example, network and node information for John are displayed.

USERLIST JOHN /A

To view the user list of another file server, the name of the file server must be specified in the command. In the following example, users on the ACCTG server are listed.

USERLIST ACCTG/

To view information about the user Tim on the ACCTG server, the following command would be typed.

USERLIST ACCTG/TIM

To view node and network information for the user Tim on the ACCTG server, the following command would be typed.

USERLIST ACCTG/TIM /A

GRANT

The GRANT command is used in place of the SYSCON and FILER utilities to assign trustee rights to users and groups, assuming those users and groups have already been created by the SYSCON utility. The GRANT command takes the form

GRANT *option*... FOR *path* TO [USER *or* GROUP]

where *option* is the first letter of the rights listed earlier. FOR is used to designate the directory path where trustee assignments are to be granted. TO is used to designate the user or group to be granted the rights. Two additional options not shown here are ONLY and ALL BUT, which can be used to grant only the specified right or all but the specified right. These options are placed in front of the rights designators.

Note: USER and GROUP are optional and are used when a user or group shares the same name.

The GRANT command must be issued for each user or group to be granted rights. To grant rights in the current default directory, type the command, followed by the letter of the rights to grant, followed by the user name. To grant rights in another directory, the full path to the directory must be specified, or the directory must have a mapped drive letter.

You can refer to Chapter 16 for further discussion of the GRANT command. The supervisor can use the GRANT command to assign rights to users "on-the-fly." It may be necessary to assign a user a right temporarily so he or she can alter files in a particular directory or make other changes. The supervisor can then use the REVOKE command to take back the granted rights. In some cases, it may be necessary to create accounts for temporary help. These accounts can be customized quickly to match the directories and files the temporary help will use. When the help leaves, the supervisor can revoke rights from the accounts using the REVOKE command.

Supervisors can use GRANT instead of SYSCON or FILER. In most cases, granting rights will be quicker and easier than using the menu utility, but supervisors will need to be familiar with the syntax of the command.

The GRANT command "enrolls" users or groups into the trustee list of a directory. The next two commands can be used to revoke the rights of a user in a trustee list and to remove the user from the trustee list altogether.

REVOKE

The REVOKE command is used in place of the SYSCON and FILER utilities to revoke the trustee rights of users and groups, assuming those users and groups have already been created by the SYSCON utility. The REVOKE command takes the form

REVOKE *option*... FOR *path* FROM [USER *or* GROUP]

where *option* is the first letter of the rights listed earlier. FOR is used to designate the directory path where trustee assignments are to be revoked. FROM is used to designate the user or group whose rights are to be revoked. An additional option not shown here is ALL, which can be used to revoke all the rights of a user or group.

Note: USER and GROUP are optional and are used when a user or group shares the same name.

The REVOKE command must be issued for each user or group whose rights will be revoked. To revoke rights in the current default directory, type the command followed by the letter of the rights to revoke, and enter the user name. Refer to Chapter 16 for more details.

Supervisors can use REVOKE to remove user's trustee rights quickly in various directories. It may be necessary to prevent a user from accessing a file if the user has changed positions in the company. If temporary help is used, rights can be removed from temporary user accounts in various directories according to the type of work and the directories the users will need.

REMOVE

The REMOVE command is used to remove a user or group from the trustee list of a directory. The REMOVE command is different from the REVOKE command, which revokes a user's rights in a directory but does not remove the user from the trustee list. REMOVE takes the form

REMOVE *user or group* FROM *path*

The *user* and *group* options are used to specify the name of the user or the group to remove in the directory specified by *path*. If a user and group have the same name, precede the name with USER or GROUP to indicate which to use. Only those users who have Parental effective rights in a directory can remove users in that directory.

To remove a user from the current directory, the name of the user is specified after the command. To remove a user or group from another directory, the full path name of that directory must be specified, or the directory must be mapped to a drive.

Checking the System Security

The supervisor can use the SECURITY command to determine how secure the network is. The command must be run from the SYS:SYSTEM directory, or a drive must be mapped to the directory by the supervisor.

The SECURITY command is extremely useful, not only for locating holes in security, but for determining what steps still need to be completed to establish a user on the network. SECURITY lists each user or group one-by-one and reports on the conditions described next. Note that users and groups are referred to as "objects" in this discussion and in discussions of other more advanced NetWare commands.

Password Assignments   If an account does not have a password, anyone can sign in under that account name and use the system with all the trustee rights assigned to the account. The SUPERVISOR account should always be given a password, as should those users who have rights to valuable or sensitive data. The SECURITY listing will help you find holes in password security and fix them. You may want to use the Default Account Balance/Restrictions menu from the Supervisor Options selection in the SYSCON menu utility to specify that passwords are required by all users, as discussed in the first part of this chapter.

Unsecure Passwords   Unsecure passwords are passwords that might be easy to guess or that do not require periodic changes. The following password options are checked by SECURITY.

- Passwords similar to the log-in names

- Accounts that can use passwords of less than five characters

- Accounts that do not require password changes at least every 60 days

- Accounts that have unlimited grace log-ins

- Accounts that do not require new and unique passwords when passwords are changed

Supervisor Security Equivalence   SECURITY will list all accounts that are equivalent to the supervisor. In most cases, only one supervisor should have these rights. If the rights are given to another user, they should only be temporary.

Root Directory Privileges   Users should never have privileges in the root directory. Users with Parental rights in the root directory can grant themselves rights in all other directories under NetWare 286.

No Login Scripts   Users who do not have personal log-in scripts are listed.

Excessive Rights   SECURITY will list objects with excessive rights in the SYSTEM, PUBLIC, LOGIN, and MAIL directories. Only the supervisor should have rights in SYSTEM. Users should normally only have Read, Open, and Search rights in PUBLIC and LOGIN, and only Write and Create rights in MAIL.

Using the SECURITY Command

The SECURITY command is located in the SYSTEM directory; therefore, only the supervisor can use it if logged in to the directory or if a search drive is assigned to the directory. The command is typed as

SECURITY

Since the screen scrolls by quickly, press the Pause key.

It may be beneficial to redirect the output of SECURITY to a file for printing or viewing. The following command redirects the listing produced by SECURITY to a file called SECUR.DOC.

SECURITY > SECUR.DOC

To print the file, type the command

NPRINT SECUR.DOC

To view the file in paged mode, type the command

MORE < SECUR.DOC

Clearing a Connection

In some cases, it may be necessary for a supervisor to clear a user's connection. This will usually be necessary when a workstation crashes but the server has not yet released its files. In other situations—when a user is no longer welcome on the system or an intruder has managed to gain access—the supervisor may find it necessary to shut the workstation down. The CLEAR STATION command can be used from the console to perform these tasks. The command should be used with caution, since it clears all file-server resources allocated to the specific workstation.

Before using the CLEAR STATION command, you will need to determine the station number to shut down. Type the following command to help determine this:

USERLIST

If the station is locked up, you may need to use the MONITOR command in the console mode to determine the station number. To use the MONITOR and the CLEAR STATION commands, get into console mode by typing the following command:

CONSOLE

In console mode, type the following command to determine the number of the workstation, or refer to the next command if you already know it.

MONITOR

To clear a station, type a command similar to the following, which clears station 3.

CLEAR STATION 3

The MAKEUSER and DEFUSER Utilities

The MAKEUSER command is an Advanced NetWare and SFT NetWare command used to create or delete users from the system. The DEFUSER command is an ELS NetWare Level II command used for the same purpose. Both commands are designed to make the supervisor's task of creating a large number of users easier. These commands are especially useful in corporate or educational environments, where large numbers of users are either added when the system is first established, or at regular intervals, as would be the case with students enrolled in computer-related classes.

MAKEUSER is covered here first; this section should only be read by users of Advanced NetWare and SFT NetWare. Users of ELS NetWare Level II should jump ahead to the DEFUSER section.

The MAKEUSER Command

The MAKEUSER command allows you to create or edit a *script file* that contains various commands for defining new users, setting up their accounts, assigning them to groups, assigning log-in scripts, and other common tasks. The script file is then processed by MAKEUSER, which

establishes each user. The MAKEUSER main menu is shown here.

As you can see, a new script file can be created or an existing one can be edited. The last option is used to process the file. When a new script file is created, MAKEUSER will ask you to name the file. It is then saved on disk with the file name you specified and the extension .USR.

Creating a .USR File

The .USR file will contain a list of users you want to create, along with the rights and restrictions to be assigned to each user. Special keywords (covered later) are used to define each users parameters.

To begin creating users, type the command

MAKEUSER

In a moment, the MAKEUSER main menu will appear. Select Create New USR File from the menu and press ENTER. The MAKEUSER editing screen will appear. All of the commands and keywords required to create a user can be typed on separate lines in the editing screen. When the .USR file is complete, the ESC key is pressed and the operator is asked to name the new .USR file. Since .USR files are created in the default directory, it is suggested that you create a special directory for running the MAKEUSER utility so that all .USR files are stored in one place.

The keywords used in .USR files are listed here and then explained in detail further in this section. Each keyword is typed on a separate line. A set of keywords that define specific user parameters is typed on separate lines. These keywords are then followed by one or more CREATE keywords to assign the parameters to one or more users. To create additional users with different parameters, the CLEAR command is typed and a new set of keywords is started. These are followed by one or more CREATE statements to create users with the preceding parameters. Similar statements are typed for each user or set of users to be created. If a .USR file is being created to delete users or sets of users, the CREATE keyword is replaced with the DELETE keyword.

A .USR file might look like the following:

```
#REM File to create clerks
#PASSWORD_REQUIRED
#PASSWORD_LENGTH 5
#UNIQUE_PASSWORD
#CONNECTIONS 1
#HOME_DIRECTORY SYS:USERS
#GROUPS CLERKS
#CREATE Henry;Henry Jones;kokomo;;SYS:PUB-DATA ROSCW
#CREATE Jane;Jane Beach;plymouth;;SYS:PUB-DATA ROSCW
```

The first keyword is a remark. The next six keywords set up various parameters to be assigned to users. The last two keywords create the users Henry and Jane with the parameters in the previous lines and the parameters on the CREATE keyword lines, which include the user's full name, initial password, and the directory the user will be a trustee to.

Processing .USR Files

Once the .USR file has been created, it can be processed by selecting Process USR File from the MAKEUSER main menu. You will be asked to specify the name of the file to process, which should be the name you used in creating it. The processing phase of MAKEUSER first scans the file to determine if any commands are incorrect or typed incorrectly. If so, an error message will appear with an appropriate description. You can then select Edit USR File from the MAKEUSER main menu to make the required changes to the file.

Once the file is correct, processing will continue normally. MAKEUSER creates a report file with the same name as the .USR file and with the extension .RPT. You should scan this file to determine if any other errors occurred during processing. The TYPE command can be used to view the file.

MAKEUSER Keywords

The CREATE and DELETE keywords are covered first here since they are required to define or remove any user. The keywords also have special options that you should know about before learning the other options.

CREATE   The CREATE keyword is used to create users and specify information about them. It takes the following form:

#CREATE *username,fullname,password,group...;directory[rights]*

The variables are described here. Note that the *username* variable must be specified, but all others are optional.

username	The name to be given to the user.
fullname	Defines the full name of the user.
password	Assigns a password to the new users.
group	Defines the groups the new user will belong to. Several groups can be specified.
directory	The directory option is used to specify a path to a directory that the user will have trustee rights to. The trustee rights are typed within the square brackets. ALL can be used to specify all rights. The default rights are Read, Open, and Search.

The following rules must be followed when using the CREATE command.

- Separate all fields with a semicolon.

- If a field contains more than one variable, separate each variable with a comma.

- If the command reaches the end of the line, type a plus sign (+) to extend the field to the next line.

- A user name can only be used once per .USR file.

- The semicolon must be used as a placeholder for fields that are not used. A caret (^) is used to terminate a line at any point. For example, to specify a user name and password, but not a full name, you would type the following:

  #CREATE JUNE;;OKIDOKI^

DELETE   The DELETE keyword deletes users and related information. It can be used to remove a set of users and can be used in the same file that contains a CREATE statement. The keyword takes the form

  #DELETE *username;username...*

where each *username* is specified after the DELETE command. User names must be separated by a semicolon. This command is useful in an academic environment, where a teacher may want to delete the names of a previous class. Since the command can be used in the same file as a CREATE keyword, old students can be removed while new ones are created.

The CLEAR or RESET command must be used to separate statements used with the CREATE keywords from those used with the DELETE keywords. It may also be necessary to include the HOME_DIRECTORY and PURGE_USER_DIRECTORY keywords before the DELETE keyword in order to remove the users' special directories.

ACCOUNT_EXPIRATION   This keyword specifies when a user's account will expire. If it is not used, the account will never expire. The keyword takes the form

  #ACCOUNT_EXPIRATION *date*

where *date* is specified in the full, formal date format, such as June 15, 1990. The keyword will apply to all users until a CLEAR or RESET keyword is encountered.

ACCOUNTING   The ACCOUNTING keyword specifies the amount of accounting services a user can use. The account balance and low balance limits are specified. The server must support the accounting system, which can be selected in the SYSCON menu and is discussed in Chapter 23. The keyword takes the form

#ACCOUNTING *balance,lowlimit*

where *balance* and *lowlimit* are numeric values. Both must be specified, and *balance* cannot be less than *lowlimit*. The keywords affect all users until a RESET or CLEAR keyword is encountered.

CLEAR or RESET   The CLEAR or RESET keyword starts a new set of keywords in the same .USR file. Using the keywords is equivalent to starting a new file. Any keywords previously entered no longer have any effect on new CREATE or DELETE keywords.

CONNECTIONS   The CONNECTIONS keyword is used to specify the maximum concurrent connections each new user can have. If not specified, each user will be able to have as many concurrent connections as possible on the network. The keyword takes the form

#CONNECTIONS *x*

where *x* is the number of concurrent connections.

GROUPS   The GROUPS keyword is used to assign users to groups. The groups must have already been created in SYSCON. The command takes the form

#GROUPS *group;group;...*

where the name of each group is specified after the keyword. Several groups can be specified, but each must be separated by a semicolon.

HOME_DIRECTORY   The HOME_DIRECTORY keyword creates home directories in a specified directory path with the user's name. The command takes the form

#HOME_DIRECTORY *path*

where *path* is the home directory. Be sure to specify the full path, including the volume name. The user's name is used to create a subdirectory of the home directory for the user. If a path is not specified, a user directory will be created that branches from the root directory. The keyword automatically assigns all rights to the user's home directory.

If the HOME_DIRECTORY command was used when creating the user, it must be used again to delete the user. To do this, type it before the DELETE keyword.

LOGIN_SCRIPT   The LOGIN_SCRIPT keyword specifies the log-in script for each user; the log-in script must already exist. The keyword takes the form

        #LOGIN_SCRIPT *filename*

where *filename* is the name of the log-in script. The script can be created with the SYSCON utility or a text editor. The log-in script will be stored in the MAIL directory under the new user's ID number.

MAX_DISK_SPACE   The MAX_DISK_SPACE keyword specifies the maximum amount of disk space available to a user. Disk space is allocated in blocks of 4K each. If not specified, users will have unlimited disk space. The command takes the form

        #MAX_DISK_SPACE *x*

where *x* is the number of disk blocks. The specified value will always be rounded up to a multiple of four, since disk space is allocated in 4K units.

PASSWORD_LENGTH   The PASSWORD_LENGTH keyword specifies the minimum length of a new user's password. The length must be between 1 and 20 characters, with a default of 5. The command takes the form

        #PASSWORD_LENGTH *x*

where *x* is the length of the password. Password length can help in keeping the system secure by preventing passwords that might be easy to guess.

PASSWORD_PERIOD   The PASSWORD_PERIOD keyword is used to specify the number of days between password expirations. The command takes the form

#PASSWORD_PERIOD *days*

where *days* is the number of days between expiration periods. If the keyword is not used, the password will never expire. The range is from 1 to 365 days.

PASSWORD_REQUIRED   The PASSWORD_REQUIRED keyword is used to specify that users must have passwords. The command is typed without parameters in the .USR file above the CREATE keywords.

PURGE_USER_DIRECTORY   The PURGE_USER_DIRECTORY keyword is used with the DELETE keyword to specify that the user's special home directory be deleted along with their account. The keyword must be placed before the DELETE keyword.

REM   The REM keyword is used to place comments in the .USR file. All text after the REM keyword are ignored during processing.

RESTRICTED_TIME   The RESTRICTED_TIME keyword is used to specify when the user cannot log in to the file server. The command takes the form

#RESTRICTED_TIME *day,start,end;...*

where *day, start,* and *end* are normal day and time formats, as shown in the following example:

#RESTRICTED_TIME mon,8:00 am,2:00 pm

STATIONS   The STATIONS keyword is used to specify the stations the user can log in to. The command takes the form

#STATIONS *network,station...*

where the network and the station on the network can be specified. More than one station can be typed for each network, and more than one network can be typed. Each station in a network set is separated by a command, and each network set is separated by a semicolon. The addresses must be the hexadecimal addresses of stations created during installation.

UNIQUE_PASSWORD   The UNIQUE_PASSWORD keyword is used to force users to create unique passwords when they change their passwords. A unique password is one that is not the same as the last eight passwords.

Defining Users with USERDEF

The USERDEF command creates users in ELS NetWare Level II. The utility can be used to create multiple users, to provide simple log-in scripts, and to set up home directories, as well as to set up minimal log-in/password security, account restrictions, and print-job configurations.

The following steps will need to be completed by the supervisor before running USERDEF.

- Install the accounting option in SYSCON if the feature is to be used.

- Create additional user groups in SYSCON if groups other than EVERYONE will be required.

- Create the applications directories for the programs you will install.

- Create the USERS directory (or suitable equivalent) where the users personal directories can be created.

USERDEF has a default installation mode and a custom installation mode, both of which will be described here. You will need to select one of the modes when the utility first starts.

Running the Default Mode

To start the program, type the following at the command line:

USERDEF

You may be requested to place the DOS disk in the floppy drive of the workstation. If so, follow the screen prompts. When the Available Options menu appears, you can follow these steps.

1. From the Available Options menu, select Add Users and press ENTER.

2. Highlight Default and press ENTER at the Templates menu.

3. When the Users menu appears, press INS to create a new user.

4. Type in the full name of the user and press ENTER.

5. A log-in name will be suggested. Type a new name or press ENTER to accept the suggested name.

Repeat these steps for each new user you wish to create. If you make a mistake for one of the users, you can highlight the user's name and press DEL, then create the name over again using the steps just given. Once you have finished creating the users, press the ESC key.

The Create New Users Using Template Default screen will appear. Select Yes and press ENTER. The USERDEF utility will suggest a password for each user that should be written down before pressing ENTER. These passwords are the initial passwords you can give to each user. They are only good the first time the user logs on, since the users will be requested to change their passwords the first time.

After each suggested password has been displayed, the utility will create the new users. Any errors encountered while processing will be indicated on the screen. When the process is complete, the MakeUser Results screen will appear. It contains information about the new users. You can press ESC to leave USERDEF.

Running the Custom Mode

To start the program, type the following at the command line:

USERDEF

You may be requested to place the DOS disk in the floppy drive of the workstation. If so, follow the screen prompts. When the Available Options menu appears, you can follow the steps listed here.

1. Highlight "Edit Template" in the Available Options menu and press ENTER.

2. The Templates screen will appear. Press INS to create a new template.

3. You will be requested to enter the name of the new template. Use a name that will be appropriate for the types of users you are creating, such as CLERKS or TEMPS. Press the ENTER key when done.

4. On the next screen, select Edit Parameters and press ENTER.

5. The Parameters for Template screen will appear. Enter the information you wish to assign to the users or groups of users being created. Use the DOWN ARROW key to move to each field that is described here.

   - *Default Directory*. This is the directory that user's personal directories will branch from. It may be SYS:USERS or SYS:HOME.

   - *Copy PrintCon From*. This field allows you to specify where to copy print-job configurations from. Type **SUPERVISOR** in the field. Print jobs will be covered in Chapter 20.

   - *Groups Belongs To*. Press ENTER on the field, and then press INS to enter the groups the users will belong to. When done, press ESC to return to the menu.

   - *Account Balance*. If accounting is installed, the Account Balance option will appear. Enter the number of services a user can use. The default setting is 1000 charges.

   - *Limit Account Balance*. The default setting is no limits, which means that depleted accounts can still be used. To limit a user's credit, change the setting to Yes. The Low Limit setting is used to specify how low the account balance can go.

- *Limit Concurrent Connections.* No limitations on concurrent connections is the default setting for users. Type **Y** in the limit field and enter the number of connections in the Maximum Connections field.

- *Require Password.* The default setting is that users will require a password. You can change this to No, then skip ahead to Limit Disk Space. If a password is required, you can change the minimum number of characters in the Minimum Password Length field.

- *Force Periodic Password Changes.* The default setting is that passwords must be changed at fixed intervals. You can change this field to No. If the default setting is used, you can change the interval by changing the Days Between Forced Changes field.

- *Require Unique Password.* Unique passwords are passwords that haven't been specified by a user for the last eight changes. The default setting is Yes but can be changed to No.

- *Limit Disk Space.* This field can be used to specify whether a user has limited disk space and the amount of disk space they will be limited to. Disk space is allocated in 4K blocks.

When changes have been made in the parameter window, you can press ESC to return to the template menu. At this point, you can select Edit Login Script to create an initial log-in script for the user. Refer to Chapter 21 for information on log-in scripts. A default log-in script will appear, which you can edit to fit your needs. When you are done editing the script, press ESC to return to the template window.

Press ESC again to return to the Available Options menu. You will be asked if you want to save changes. Press ENTER to save, and then press ESC to return to the menu.

At the Available Options menu, follow these steps to complete the creation of the new users.

1. From the Available Options menu, select Add Users and press ENTER.

2. Highlight the new template you just created, and press ENTER.

3. When the Users menu appears, press INS to create a new user.

4. Type in the full name of the user and press ENTER.

5. A log-in name will be suggested. Type a new name or press ENTER to accept the suggested name.

Repeat these steps for each new user you wish to create. If you make a mistake for one of the users, you can highlight the user's name and press DEL, then create the name over again using the steps just given. Once you have finished creating the users, press the ESC key.

The Create New Users Using Template Default screen will appear. Select Yes and press ENTER. The USERDEF utility will suggest a password for each user that you should write down; then accept by pressing ENTER. These passwords are the initial passwords you can give to each user. They are only good the first time the user logs on, since users will be requested to change their passwords the first time.

After each suggested password has been displayed, the utility will create the new users. Any errors encountered while processing will be indicated on the screen. When the process is complete, the MakeUser Results screen will appear, which contains information about the new users. You can press ESC to leave USERDEF.

Topics for NetWare Users

NetWare Menu Utilities for Users
Command-Line Utilities for Users
Communicating with Other Users
Playing Games

This chapter discusses the normal daily tasks and commands performed or used by NetWare users. The network supervisor can have users read through this chapter as a way to become more familiar with a NetWare network.

NetWare Menu Utilities for Users

All of the menu utilities can be accessed by users, but the functions available to those users is limited compared to the supervisor. The utilities can be used to view connection information, who's on the system, trustee rights, and other system features. Each menu utility is covered here except the printing utilities, which are covered in Chapter 20.

SESSION for Users

The SESSION utility helps users manage their current log-in sessions. They can change servers, drive mappings, and search mappings. Users can also view the current group list and send a message to a group or view the current user list and send a message to a user. Users can perform the following actions from the main menu.

Change Servers   Users can select Change Current Server to switch to another server. A server is picked from a list by highlighting the server name.

Add Drive Mappings   The Drive Mappings option can be selected to insert additional drive mappings by the user. When the INS key is pressed at the Drive Mappings window, a new drive can be added. The next available drive is suggested, but the user can type any available drive letter. After ENTER is pressed to select the drive letter, the INS key can be pressed again to insert the names of servers, volumes, and directories.

Send Group Messages   The Group List option is selected to display available groups. By selecting a group and pressing ENTER, the user can type a short message to send to each member of the group currently logged on. This option is covered later in this chapter.

Add Search Mappings   The Search Mappings option can be selected by the user to insert additional search-drive mappings. When the window appears, the INS key can be pressed to add another search drive. The next available drive is suggested, but the user can type any available drive number. After pressing ENTER to select the search-drive number, the INS key can be pressed again to begin selecting local drives, other servers, volumes, and directories.

Select Default Drive   Users can choose the Select Default Drive option to switch to another mapped drive. A list of currently available mapped drives will appear on the screen.

Send Messages to Users and Display User Information   If you select User List from the menu, information about currently logged users can be displayed. Short messages can also be sent. This option is covered later in this chapter.

FILER for Users

The FILER utility can be accessed by users who want to work with files and directories. The features available in FILER are based on the user's trustee rights in a given directory, however. If a user has rights, he or she will be able to view and copy files, create new subdirectories, select and view files, change file attributes, and perform other useful tasks with the ease provided by NetWare's menu system.

The first task any user should perform when displaying the FILER menu is to choose the Select Current Directory feature to switch to the directory in which he or she wishes to operate. The options described here can then be selected.

Display Current Directory Information
The creation date, current effective rights, maximum rights mask, and owner of any directory can be displayed. Users can only change the maximum rights mask if they have the Parental right.

Work with Files
Users can select the File Information option to work with files in the directories they have rights to, based on those rights. The following menu appears when a file from the Files menu is selected.

Users can change files attributes if they have the Modify right in the directory. They can also copy or duplicate files, assuming they have the Create right in the destination directory. Other options allow the user to view specific information about files or to view the contents of the file. File options are covered in Chapter 17.

Select Directories
Users can select any directory using the Select Current Directory option but are limited to what they can do in the directory based on their access rights.

Set Filer Options   Options can be set to control the way FILER operates, such as confirmation of copies and deletes, and inclusions and exclusions in directory and file listings.

Create Subdirectories   The ability of users to create subdirectories in the FILER utility is completely based on the rights they have within the current directory or the directory they have selected.

Volume Information   Users can view volume information using the Volume Information option.

SYSCON for Users

The SYSCON command is important for users who want to find out about their rights on the system, as well as their disk usage, last log-in time, and station restrictions. The amount of information users can view about the system is limited, however. Users can also change their password and customize their own log-in scripts.

SYSCON can be used to view the full name of other users and the groups they belong to. This information can be important when working in shared directories or sending messages to groups of users.

Change Current Server   Users can switch to another server from the SYSCON menu utility as well as from the SESSION and FILER utilities. By selecting Change Current Server from the menu, the user will be able to choose from a list of servers. You may have noticed this feature is available in most NetWare menus.

Viewing File-Server Information   Users can select this option from the menu to view information about a particular server. They are first given a list of servers to choose from. The server information includes the NetWare version, network address, and node address, as well as other information.

Viewing Group Information   Users can select Group Information from the SYSCON main menu to view information about any group. A list is presented to choose from. Users can view the members of the group and its trustee assignments, which can be useful when sending messages or creating or copying files.

Viewing and Changing User Information   The following tasks can be performed by users who select the User Information heading. Users are limited in what they can view about other users and in what they can change about their own log-in status.

- View but not change their account restrictions

- Change their password

- View the groups they currently belong to

- View and change their log-in scripts

- Use the Other Information option to view their last log-in date; their console operator status, if they have it; the disk space they are using; and their user ID, which is also the name of their personal directory in the MAIL directory

- View their station and time restrictions

- View their trustee assignments

Users will be interested in viewing the trustee assignments to determine the data and program directories they have access rights to.

Command-Line Utilities for Users

Users may be interested in the current connection information, who is logged on the system, the system's time, or its volume and version information. The commands listed here can be entered on the command line.

Viewing User Information with WHOAMI

The WHOAMI command is used by network users to view who they are and their status on the network. The command displays a user's log-in name and the file server he or she is logged in to. It also displays the log-in date and time. With special options, the command will display the groups, security equivalences, and effective rights in every directory on the network.

The command takes the form

WHOAMI *server options*

where *server* is the name of the server the user wishes to view information about. Since a user may log in to each server with a different name and will have a different log- in status on each server, the command requires the user to specify which server to list. The *options* for the WHOAMI command are listed here:

/G	Groups. The /G option is used to view membership in groups on the current server.
/S	Security. The /S option is used to view security equivalences on any file server.
/R	Rights. The /R option is used to view rights in the directories of the file server.
/A	All. The /A option is used to view the combined information of the /G, /S, and /R options.

If the command is typed by itself, information regarding the current user's name and server connection is displayed. In the following example, George types the command

WHOAMI

and the following information appears:

You are user GEORGE attached to server STARSHIP connection 3
Login Time: Friday September 1, 1990 11:25 am

To view information on another file server, include the name of the file server. In the following command, George views his status on the ACCTG server.

WHOAMI ACCTG

The following information is displayed.

You are user GEORGE attached to server ACCTG connection 5
Login Time: Friday September 1, 1990 11:30 am

Viewing Group Membership

To view membership in a group, use the /G option. In the following example, George views his group membership on the STARSHIP server.

WHOAMI STARSHIP /G

A display similar to the following might appear.

You are user GEORGE attached to server STARSHIP connection 3
Login Time: Friday September 1, 1990 11:25 am
   You are a member of the following Groups:
      EVERYONE (group)
      ENGINEERING (group)
      BRIDGE (group)
      COMMUNICATIONS (group)

The following command is typed to view group memberships on all file servers.

WHOAMI /G

Viewing Security Equivalences

The /S option is used to view security equivalences. The file- server name is specified if a list for a particular server is required. If the server name is left out, security equivalences will be displayed for all file servers.

In the following command, George views his security equivalences on STARSHIP.

WHOAMI STARSHIP /S

A screen similar to the following might appear.

You are user GEORGE attached to server STARSHIP connection 3
Login Time: Friday September 1, 1990 11:25 am

You are security equivalent to the following:
    EVERYONE (group)
    OFFICERS (group)

Viewing Effective Rights

The effective rights of a user can be viewed by using the /R option. This is an extremely useful command for users trying to determine which directories they can use. The file-server name is specified in order to view the list for a particular server. If the server name is left out, effective rights will be displayed for all file servers.

In the following example, George views his effective rights on the STARSHIP server.

WHOAMI STARSHIP /R

A screen similar to the following might appear.

You are user GEORGE attached to server STARSHIP connection 3
Login Time: Friday September 1, 1990 11:25 am

You have the following effective rights:
[W C   ] STARSHIP/SYS:MAIL
[RWOCD SM] STARSHIP/SYS:MAIL/A005D
[R O   S] STARSHIP/SYS:PUBLIC
[RWOC S] STARSHIP/SYS:PUB-DATA

The Pause key or CTRL-S key may be required to pause the screen listing if a long list of rights appears.

Viewing All Rights

The /A option can be used to view all rights for the default server or the rights for a specified server. In the following command, George requests to see all rights for the STARSHIP server.

WHOAMI /A

Viewing Current Users with USERLIST

The USERLIST command can be used by users to view who else is on the system, their current connection number, and their log-in time. This is helpful when sending messages or working with specific files. The command is covered in detail in Chapter 18.

To see a list of current users, type the command

USERLIST

A screen similar to the following will appear.

Connection	User Name	Login Time
1	SUPERVISOR	12-25-89 7:00 am
2	JOHN	12-25-89 9:00 am
3	JANE	12-25-89 10:00 am

To view information about one user, type the user's name. For example, information about John's connection is listed with the following command:

USERLIST JOHN

The option /A can be used to list network and node address information about a user. This information is more useful to the supervisor, however. In the following example, network and node information for John is displayed.

USERLIST JOHN /A

To view the userlist of another file server, the name of the file server must be specified in the command. With the following example, users on the ACCTG server are listed.

USERLIST ACCTG/

To view information about the user Tim on the ACCTG server, the following command would be typed.

USERLIST ACCTG/TIM

To view node and network information for the user Tim on the ACCTG server, the following command would be typed.

USERLIST ACCTG/TIM /A

Viewing the Current Rights
With RIGHTS

The RIGHTS command can be useful to users who would like to view their current rights in a particular directory. The command is typed as follows if the rights for the current directory need to be viewed.

RIGHTS

To view rights in other directories, specify the mapped drive letter or full directory path of the directory to view, as in the following examples:

RIGHTS F:
RIGHTS SYS:USERS\JOHN

Communicating with Other Users

There are a number of menu utility options and commands users can take advantage of when communicating with other users. NetWare comes with a simple message broadcasting system. An optional mail system is also available from Novell but not covered here. In addition, third-party mail packages are also available.

Sending Messages
To Users and Groups

The SESSION menu utility provides an easy way for users to send messages to other users or groups. The main menu of the SESSION utility is shown in the following illustration.

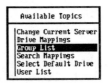

You can select Group List from the menu to send messages to any group or select User List to send messages to any user currently logged in to the system. For example, in the following display, Sally is sending a message to the group EVERYONE.

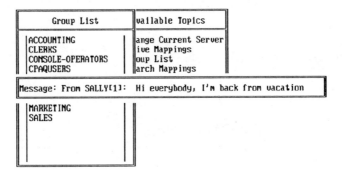

Messages will appear on the bottom line of user's screens, along with the name of the person who sent the message. The message can be cleared by pressing CTRL-ENTER.

Sending Messages With the SEND Command

The SEND command can be used in place of the SESSION menu utility to send messages to other users or groups. The message sent by SEND cannot exceed 45 characters, minus the number of letters in your user name. The command takes the following forms.

SEND *message* TO USER *server / user*...

SEND *message* TO GROUP *server / user*...

SEND *message* TO USER *server / user*... GROUP *server / user*

The first form is used to send messages to users. The second is used to send messages to groups. The third is used to send messages to both users and groups. The message must be enclosed in quotation marks. More than one user or group can be specified with the command, as indicated by the ellipses. The USERLIST command can be used to determine the names of users currently logged in to the system, as discussed previously. The USER and GROUP options in the three forms can be excluded if no users or groups share the same name.

 The following example illustrates how a message would be sent to John by the current user.

SEND "John, can we meet today at 2:00?" TO USER JOHN

Since it is unlikely that there are groups named JOHN, the USER option can be left out, as in the following command:

SEND "John, can we meet today at 2:00?" TO JOHN

A message similar to the following will appear on the sender's display.

Message sent to SERVER/JOHN (station 7)

 To send a message to a user or group on a different file server, the name of the file server must be specified before the user name. In the following example, a message is sent to the group CLERKS on the ACCTG server.

SEND "We're closing at 3:00 today!" TO ACCTG/CLERKS

To send a message to several users or groups, specify each user or group on the command line. In the following example, the message is sent to the user John and the group MANAGERS on the current server and the user Bert on the ACCTG server.

SEND "This is a stickup..." TO JOHN MANAGERS ACCTG/BERT

Note that users and groups on the current server do not require the server name in the SEND command.

Blocking Messages

The CASTOFF command is used to block any messages that might be sent to a workstation, and for good reason. Some applications are left to run unattended until a job is finished. This is common when running program compilers, recalculating a spreadsheet, or sorting and indexing a database. It is possible that a message sent from another user might interrupt the processing. When the user returns to the station, he or she may find that the machine has been sitting idle for some time, waiting for them to read the message.

To block messages sent from other workstations, issue the command

CASTOFF

The following message will appear on the screen.

Broadcast messages from other stations will now be rejected.

To block messages sent from all network stations, including those from the console, use the A option in the command, as shown here:

CASTOFF A

The CASTON command is used to return a workstation to its normal message receiving mode. Type the command on the command line as shown here:

CASTON

Playing Games

NSNIPES is a network game that can be played by one or more users. The object of the game is to shoot and destroy "snipes" and the factories that make snipes before being shot by the snipes. If you are playing against others, the object is to win the game by shooting other players as well.

There are two versions of the game. NSNIPES is played on systems with monochrome screens, and NCSNIPES is played on systems with color screens. The commands takes one of these forms:

NSNIPES *option*
NCSNIPES *option*

where *option* is replaced with a number between 1 and 10 to specify the skill level of the game. Increasing the skill level increases the number of snipes and how quickly they are produced.

The playing field is a maze, and the object is to shoot and destroy the snipes; if two or more players are playing the game, players may need to shoot other players as well. The following actions are available.

- Moving through the maze is accomplished by using the arrow keys on the keyboard.

- To move diagonally, press two arrow keys at once.

- To go faster, press the spacebar while pressing any of the arrow keys.

- To fire, press **A** to fire left, **D** to fire right, **W** to fire up, and **S** or **X** to fire down. To fire diagonally, press two keys at once.

- The game is stopped by pressing the CTRL-BREAK key combination.

Note: The game is limited to five players who must have Read, Write, Open, Create, and Delete rights in a given directory.

If two or more players want to play SNIPES in the same maze, they must map their default drives to the same directory on the same file server. One user executes the game by specifying the skill level after the NSNIPES or NCSNIPES command. Remaining users then enter the game by typing the NSNIPES or NCSNIPES command without a skill level, but from the same directory. The game is started after all users have pressed the ENTER key, unless there are five players, in which case the game automatically begins when the fifth player enters the command.

TWENTY

Printing with NetWare

How NetWare Printing Works
Printer Menu Utilities
Command Line Utilities for Printing
Console Printing Commands
The AUTOEXEC.SYS File

NetWare allows printing on a network to take place at a local printer attached to a workstation or at a network printer attached to the server. If a server printer is used, a print queue handles the print job. This chapter is about controlling network printing and print queues.

NetWare has three menu utilities designed for working with printers and print jobs: PRINTDEF, PRINTCON, and PCONSOLE. In addition, there are four NetWare command line utilities used to control printers and print jobs. These are CAPTURE, ENDCAP, NPRINT, and PSTAT. The functions of these menu utilities and command line utilities are outlined here:

PRINTDEF	Defines a printer and its special control codes
PRINTCON	Defines print-job configurations using the printers defined with PRINTDEF
PCONSOLE	Queues print jobs to printers using the printer configurations defined by PRINTCON
CAPTURE	Intercepts local printing and sends it to the server printers
ENDCAP	Ends the CAPTURE command

NPRINT   Prints files on file server printers

PSTAT   Displays information about network printers

How NetWare Printing Works

Use of the numerous printing commands available with NetWare demands an understanding of how the network handles printers, queues, and print jobs.

First, it is important to understand that printing can occur at a user's workstation, which requires no special commands or setup, or at the network server, which requires commands to redirect printing to the printers attached to the servers. In most cases the network supervisor establishes the network printing commands on workstations that do not have local printers, or informs users how to switch between local or network printing if the workstation does have a printer.

Note: Third-party applications are available to allow printing on the workstations of other users. In this way printers do not need to be localized at the server.

The CAPTURE command can be used to redirect printing at the workstation to printers attached to the server. A print file may be sent to a network printer with the PCONSOLE or NPRINT command. Here is an outline of the process and events that take place.

1. The user at the workstation issues the CAPTURE command to direct printing to the network server, or the commands are included in the user's log-in script. Alternatively, the user may invoke the PCONSOLE command to set up a network print job or use NPRINT to send a print job to a network printer.

2. The file is received by the server.

3. The server places the print job in the queue for the printer that will print the job (there may be several network printers). The print queue contains the names and numbers of each print job waiting to print. Supervisors and operators can rearrange the list of names

and numbers in the print queue to change the order of printing, if necessary.

4. The text of the print job is placed in a "spool" memory area. In this way, the users workstation can continue with other tasks and does not need to stand by with the print job information.

5. When a printer finishes one job, the next print job in the print queue starts.

Print Queues

Think of the print queue as a traffic cop that directs the jobs going to the printer. All print jobs are placed in the queue before printing. Some print jobs can be bumped and replaced by other print jobs. Print jobs also can be assigned to print at a later time, such as during off-hours, or they can be deleted by the users who create them or by supervisors and print- queue operators.

Now consider that a network server may have more than one printer. In turn, each printer must have its own print queue and spooler. When a network user decides to send a print job to the printer, one of the available printers must be selected. Under NetWare, each available printer on the server may be assigned more than one queue, which means that print jobs for a printer may accumulate in more than one queue. In addition, one print queue may be assigned to two or more printers. The next two sections describe the reasons why the network printers are set up in so many ways.

Note: If new, permanent print queues and spoolers need to be created other than the defaults made by NetWare, an AUTOEXEC.SYS file must be created so that the queues and spoolers are established every time the system starts. (The AUTOEXEC.SYS file is discussed later in this chapter.) Queues and spoolers established at the console level and not placed in the AUTOEXEC.SYS file will not be reestablished when the server is downed and started again.

Multiple Queues on One Printer

Multiple print queues often are set up when it is necessary to establish different queue features for each printer. For example, a supervisor could create a queue with a higher priority than other queues and then assign the use of that queue to managers. All print jobs sent to the queue by the managers would then be printed before any other print jobs. In another situation a queue could be created for rush jobs and then given the highest priority on the network.

Multiple Printers on One Queue

One queue can be assigned to more than one printer. This might be the case if a large number of print jobs are being sent by network users. As the queue receives print jobs, it sends them to whichever printer is not in use. For example, assume that all nonprioritized network users are given access to PRINTQ_3. This queue is set up to distribute print jobs to three similar high-speed printers. Jobs sent to PRINTQ_3 can be printed on either printer. Since the printers are identical, the user need not be concerned about the quality or compatibility of the print job with the printers. With three printers servicing the queue, users will not wait long for their print jobs.

Default Printer Settings

When a NetWare network is installed, printer numbers are given to each printer attached to the system. These numbers are used during printing operations to specify which printer should be used. The following default settings are made during the installation.

- One print queue is created for each printer attached to the server. A one-to-one relationship between printers and queues is established as follows:

    PRINTER0 = PRINTQ_0

    PRINTER1 = PRINTQ_1

    PRINTER2 = PRINTQ_2

- One spooler is created for each print queue.

- A default print-job configuration is created for each queue. This configuration prints one copy of a file with a banner (cover sheet) that contains the log-in name of the user. Additional print-job configurations can be created with PRINTCON.

- The group EVERYONE is given access to the print queues.

- The supervisor is assigned operator status to every queue. Operators are entitled to change the order of print jobs or delete print jobs within the queue.

Customizing Network Printing

In most cases, supervisors must perform some customization for network printing. The default settings can be changed or added to with the NetWare PRINTDEF, PRINTCON, and PCONSOLE menu utilities. The following changes can be made.

- New print queues can be created, and existing print queues can be changed.

- Network users can be assigned to use print queues.

- Print-queue privileges can be modified for each user.

- Print-queue operators can be created. Operators have the ability to change the order of queues or delete print jobs in queues.

- The printing capabilities of each printer can be controlled by defining various sets of control codes.

The NetWare printer menu utilities are covered in the section titled "Printer Menu Utilities." Before starting that section, you should become familiar with the AUTOEXEC.SYS file discussed next.

The AUTOEXEC.SYS File

Although queues and spoolers can be customized at any time with the console commands (covered in the last section of this chapter), the customizations are not permanent unless they are placed in the AUTOEXEC.SYS file. This file is read and its parameters are established every time the system is started. Changes to the printer configuration thus are made permanent.

When an AUTOEXEC.SYS file is created, NetWare no longer establishes its default printer settings, so you must include commands in the file not only to make your new changes but also to establish the default printing queues and spoolers, if you want to keep them.

The AUTOEXEC.SYS file can be created using either the DOS COPY CON command or the SYSCON utility. The file is explained in detail in the last section of this chapter. Be sure to create this file if you need to *permanently* alter the default settings.

Printer Menu Utilities

The NetWare menu utilities are used to customize the printing environment. The PRINTDEF utility defines the basic printer operations, PRINTCON builds print-job configurations using the printer configurations defined by PRINTDEF, and PCONSOLE manages print jobs.

PRINTDEF

The PRINTDEF utility is used to define network print devices and to define print forms.

Defining Print Devices

If you use applications that already are capable of accessing the functions of a printer, plotter, or other output device, you may not need to use PRINTDEF extensively. An application that is "device aware" usually contains a *print driver* designed specifically for your brand and model of printer, and is able to access the features and functions of that device with commands inside the program. For example, Microsoft Word comes with a print driver for the IBM ProPrinter. This driver allows you to set various print modes, such as boldface, underline, italics, double-wide, and many others in the text of a document. Microsoft Word then handles the task of setting the printer to print these various styles. In this way Microsoft Word is "aware" of the ProPrinter.

In some cases an application cannot set various modes on a printer. NetWare allows you to create your own print devices, assuming you know the special codes that must be sent to the printer to activate those modes. These codes usually are found in the printer owners manual.

NetWare now comes with 30 predefined definitions for the most popular printers to make this task easier. You can use PRINTDEF to load one of these existing drivers, if they match your output device, or you can create your own.

The following illustration shows the PRINTDEF main menu. Two options are available: the first is used to define print devices, and the second is used to define forms.

Select the first option to define a printer, and the following screen appears.

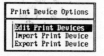

Select Import Print Device to import one of the predefined print devices, if one is available for your printer. When the Source Directory screen appears, change the path to indicate the PUBLIC directory, as shown here:

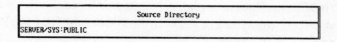

The Available .PDFs menu appears, as shown next:

Scroll through this list to find the driver that matches your printer. The drivers are given names that approximate printer brand names and model numbers. The following list will help you determine the brand code for your printer.

APP = Apple

CIT = Citizen

CITO = CItoh

DIAB = Diablo

EP = Epson

HP = Hewlett-Packard

IBM = IBM

NEC = NEC

OKI = Okidata

PAN = Panasonic

STAR = Star Micronics

TOSH = Toshiba

Select one device to add to your list of defined print devices. You can view this list and further edit the device by selecting Edit Print Devices from the Print Device Options menu. A screen similar to the following appears. In this screen, the Hewlett-Packard LaserJet and IBM ProPrinter II/XL devices have been imported.

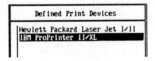

Highlight one of the devices so you can view or edit its current modes and functions. The following Edit Device Options screen appears.

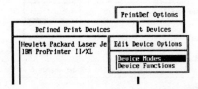

Device modes are sets of functions that cause the printer to perform a certain task, such as printing sideways or reinitializing the printer. The functions to make a printer perform these task are specific Escape codes found in the printers manual.

The following screen lists several predefined modes for the IBM ProPrinter driver.

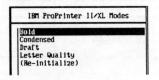

Later, when using the PRINTCON menu utility, you will be able to define the parameters for special print jobs. For example, you might want to create a print job the accounting department can use when printing accounting reports. In PRINTCON, you would first select a printer, such as the IBM ProPrinter, and then select one of the defined modes for that printer. Condensed mode would probably be selected to print checks.

Note: The modes you select apply to the whole document. It is not possible to apply them to individual parts of a document. This can only be done from within your applications programs, assuming they support the destination printer.

The next screen shows the Escape codes sent to the printer to initialize letter quality mode. This screen appears when you select Letter Quality from the previous screen.

```
┌─────────────────────────────────┬──────────────┐
│   IBM ProPrinter II/XL Modes     │ Def Options  │
│ ┌───────────────────────────────┼┬─────────────┴┐
│ │   Letter Quality Functions    ││ t Devices    │
│ │ ┌─────────────────────────────┼┼┬─────────────┴┐
│ │ │ letter quality              │││ vice Options │
│ │ │                             │└┼─────────────┬┘
│ │ │                             │ │ Modes       │
│ │ │                             │ │ Functions   │
│ │ │                             │ └─────────────┘
│ │ │                             │
└─┴─┴─────────────────────────────┘
┌──────────────────────────────────────────────────┐
│      letter quality Escape Sequence or Function   │
└──────────────────────────────────────────────────┘
<ESC>G
```

Some modes may consists of a chain of functions sent to the printer. For example, the next screen shows a list of functions sent to a Hewlett Packard LaserJet printer when Condensed is selected. Note that the bottom of the screen shows the Escape codes for the Pitch - 16-66 function.

```
┌─────────────────────────────────┬──────────────┐
│ Hewlett Packard Laser J... Modes │ Def Options  │
│ ┌───────────────────────────────┼┬─────────────┴┐
│ │      Condensed Functions      ││ t Devices    │
│ │ ┌─────────────────────────────┼┼┬─────────────┴┐
│ │ │ Reset                       │││ vice Options │
│ │ │ End-of-Line Wrap - Enable   │└┼─────────────┬┘
│ │ │ Orientation - Landscape     │ │ Modes       │
│ │ │ Pitch - 16.66               │ │ Functions   │
│ │ │ Vertical Motion Index - 5.4 │ └─────────────┘
└─┴─┴─────────────────────────────┘
┌──────────────────────────────────────────────────┐
│        Pitch - 16.66 Escape Sequence or Function  │
└──────────────────────────────────────────────────┘
<ESC>(s16.66H
```

If you press ESCAPE to the return to the Edit Device Options menu, you can select Device Functions to view a list of functions already defined for a printer. If you are using one of the drivers that came with NetWare, a list of predefined functions appears. The following screen shows a partial list of functions for the Hewlett-Packard LaserJet.

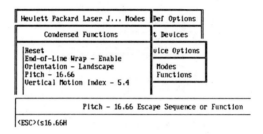

```
┌────────────────────────────────────────────────────┐
│       Hewlett Packard Laser Jet I/II Functions      │
│ ┌────────────────────────────────┬─────────────────┐│
│ │ Big Font                       │ <ESC>zz$3g      ││
│ │ Character Set - Line Draw      │ <ESC>(0B        ││
│ │ Character Set - Roman Extension│ <ESC>(0E        ││
│ │ Character Set - Roman-8        │ <ESC>(8U        ││
│ │ Character Set - USASCII        │ <ESC>(0U        ││
│ │ End-of-Line Wrap - Disable     │ <ESC>&s1C       ││
│ │ End-of-Line Wrap - Enable      │ <ESC>&s0C       ││
│ │ Font - Courier                 │ <ESC>(s3T       ││
│ │ Font - Helv2                   │ <ESC>(s4T       ││
│ │ Font - Letter Gothic           │ <ESC>(s6T       ││
│ │ Font - Linedraw                │ <ESC>(s0T       ││
│ │ Font - Lineprinter             │ <ESC>(s0T       ││
│ │ Font - Tms Rmn                 │ <ESC>(s5T       ││
│ │ Orientation - Landscape        │ <ESC>&l1O       ││
│ │ Orientation - Portrait         │ <ESC>&l0O       ││
│ │ Paper Source - Lower Tray      │ <ESC>&l4H       ││
│ │▼Pitch - 6                      │ <ESC>(s6H       ││
│ └────────────────────────────────┴─────────────────┘│
└────────────────────────────────────────────────────┘
```

These codes must be sent to a printer to establish various printing modes. You can combine these functions to create a specific printer mode. For example, you could build a mode to create lecture notes by combining the Big Font function with others such as Reset and End-of-Line Wrap. You can press F1 from the menu to display instructions for creating your own functions.

Defining Print Forms

A print form in NetWare is a paper form that you name. For example, payroll checks might be given the name CHECKS, while forms used by accounting might be called REPORTS. Each form is assigned a number. The number of lines that can be printed on the form is then specified, followed by the width of the form in characters-per-line. This will be enough information for NetWare to know how to perform page breaks. The form number is used when switching forms to make NetWare aware of the type of form currently in the printer. If a print job arrives at the server that requests a different form, NetWare knows that the forms need to be changed and notifies the print-queue operator.

When you select Forms from the PRINTDEF main menu, you will see a screen similar to the following:

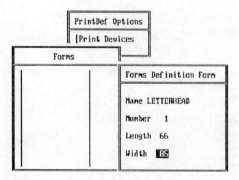

In this illustration, a form for letterhead stock is being defined. This form is a standard sheet, 8 1/2 by 11, with 66 lines down and 85 characters across. Initially this screen may be blank. By pressing INSERT, you can begin defining additional forms.

Remember that forms are defined so NetWare will know how to handle page breaks and page width. They are also used to inform NetWare when a new form has been installed in a printer. This is done with the CHANGE FORM TYPE MOUNTED IN PRINTER console command, described later in this chapter. If NetWare knows the number of the form currently in the printer, it can accept or reject new print jobs based on the form number requested. If a print job arrives that requests form 5, and NetWare knows form 3 is still mounted in the printer, it will inform the print-queue operator that a form change is necessary.

The supervisor or print-queue operators should define a form for each different type of paper or form that might be placed in printers. These can include normal 8 1/2-by-11 or 14-by-11 greenbar paper, paychecks, and accounting forms. The number of lines and the character width of these forms must be specified. Paper that is 11 inches long prints up to 66 lines. Paper 8 1/2 inches wide prints 85 characters across, and 14-inch-wide greenbar paper prints 140 characters across.

Exiting PRINTDEF

When all of the print devices and functions or forms have been defined, you can press ESCAPE to leave the PRINTDEF menu. The following screen appears.

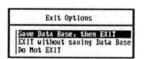

You must select Save Data Base. Then EXIT to save any additions or changes you have made in PRINTDEF.

PRINTCON

The PRINTCON utility creates customized print-job configurations, using the devices, functions, and forms created in PRINTDEF. Once a configuration is established, it is used by the PCONSOLE utility when lining up print jobs in the print queues. Print-job configurations are created to establish various printing parameters for jobs that are printed on a regular basis. Once the parameters are established in a configuration, they need not be specified every time the job is printed. Print-job configurations can be created for common printing tasks, such as month-end accounting reports, paychecks, and mailing labels.

To start the PRINTCON program and create or edit a print job configuration, enter this command:

PRINTCON

The PRINTCON main menu, titled the Available Options menu appears as shown here:

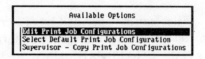

The first option creates or edits new configurations, the second selects which configuration will be used by default, and the third copies print-job configurations to other users.

Select Edit Print Job Configuration from the Available Options menu. The Print Job Configurations window that appears will be blank initially. Press INSERT to add a new configuration, giving it a name of your choice. After naming the new configuration and pressing ENTER, a screen similar to the following appears:

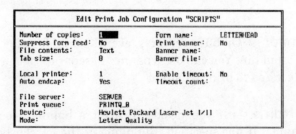

This screen has already been partially modified. The Hewlett-Packard LaserJet has been added as a printer in the Device field and Letter Quality has been selected for that printer in the Mode field. The fields are filled in with the printer and mode settings created in the PRINTDEF menu utility.

The following sections describe each of the fields in the configuration window. Once the fields are filled out according to the specifications of the print job, you can press ESCAPE to exit and save the configuration.

Number of Copies   You can enter from 1 to 65,000 copies to be printed.

Suppress Form Feed   Form feeds cause a sheet to be ejected after each print job. Enter **Yes** to suppress form feeds. If an application already performs this action, you should suppress form feeds to prevent an extra sheet from being ejected.

File Contents   Files can be specified as either Text or Byte Stream. Select Text when NetWare must interpret and format special formatting characters, such as tabs. Select Byte Stream if the application of origin can handle the formatting commands at the printer. Byte Stream is used with applications such as WordPerfect and Microsoft Word.

Tab Size   Use this field to specify the character width of tabs. You may specify a number from 1 to 18. The default is a tab 8 characters wide.

Form Name   Press ENTER to display a list of forms created with the PRINTDEF utility. These forms define the paper size in lines per page and characters of width. Select a form appropriate for the print job you are defining.

Print Banner   On busy servers, several print jobs may stack up in the printer output bin. You can use a banner to separate one print job from the next. Select Yes to print a banner.

Banner Name   If you decide to print a banner, you can specify a banner name. If not specified, the name of the currently logged user is printed on the banner.

Banner File   Text other than the name of the file being printed can be specified in this field. If left blank, the file name is printed on the banner.

Local Printer   Used with the CAPTURE command, this field can specify the local printer port from which to capture printer output.

Auto Endcap   Used with the CAPTURE command, Yes can be specified to cause printing of captured data when a program is exited or when the program closes the print device. If No is specified, the file is printed only after running the ENDCAP command.

Enable Timeout   Used with the CAPTURE command, Yes causes captured data to be sent to a print queue after the number of seconds specified in the Timeout Count field. If No is selected, printing performs according to the settings of the Auto Endcap field.

Timeout Count   The number of seconds of wait time from 1 to 1000 before queuing the saved file. The default is 5 seconds. You must specify a timeout count only if ENDCAP has not been used.

File Server   Press ENTER on the field to select a file server to use.

Print Queue   Press ENTER to select a print queue on the selected server.

Device   Press ENTER to select a print device as defined in the PRINTDEF menu utility.

Mode   Press ENTER to select a print mode as defined in the PRINTDEF menu utility.

Copying and Selecting Default Print-Job Configurations

You can select the default print-job configuration by making the second selection from the PRINTCON main menu. This displays each existing print job. Simply highlight the print job to be used by default and press ENTER.

Print jobs can be copied to users' mail directories so that the jobs in the configuration can be used every time they print. To copy the configurations, select the third option from the PRINTCON main menu and then press ENTER. You must specify the source user and target user to copy the file.

PCONSOLE

The PCONSOLE command is used to create and rename print queues, and assign queue operators. The PCONSOLE main menu is shown here:

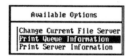

You can use this Available Options menu to change to a different file server or to view information about the current file server. The Print Queue Information middle selection is used most often to define new print queues and to add print jobs to print queues for printing.

The following illustration shows an example of a Print Queues screen that appears when Print Queue Information is selected from the main menu.

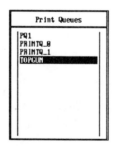

This screen shows the current print queues, but you can press INSERT to create a new print queue. Simply type the name of the new queue and press ENTER. It will be added to the list.

Once you create a queue, you must map it to a printer by specifying the print-queue ADD command in the console mode at the server, or by adding appropriate commands in the AUTOEXEC.SYS file (covered at the end of this chapter).

Note: The console QUEUE CREATE command can also be used to create a new print queue as covered later in this chapter.

When a queue is selected from the Print Queues screen, the following Print Queue Information menu is displayed.

From this menu you can add print jobs, check on the status of the queue, check on the currently attached server, view the print queue ID, and specify queue operators, servers, and users.

Adding, Viewing, or Editing Print Jobs

When you select Current Print Job Entries from the Print Queue Information screen, any existing print jobs are displayed, and you can select one of these jobs to view or to edit its parameters. You can edit or view a print job using the fields listed on the screen. You also can delete print jobs by highlighting the job and pressing DELETE.

To add new print jobs, press INSERT. At the prompt, enter the name of the directory containing the file to be printed. After specifying a directory, press ENTER to see a list of available files. Scroll through the list (or start typing the file name) to select the file you want to print, and press ENTER.

Note: Keep in mind that most programs will automatically add their print jobs to the print queue when you choose to print from within the program.

A list of print job configurations created with the PRINTCON menu utility appears as shown here. Select an appropriate configuration and press ENTER. The New Print Job to Be Submitted screen appears, as shown in the following illustration:

The New Print Job to Be Submitted screen appears. You can edit the parameters of the print job by altering the fields described in the following sections. Note that this menu can also be accessed by supervisors and print-queue operators who may want to change the status of a print job waiting in the queue. Also note that some of the fields will be filled in only if the print job has already been submitted and the window is open to view the status of a print job. Print jobs are considered submitted when the information on the screen has been filled out and the user escapes and saves the changes.

Print Job   The Print Job field contains the number of the print job, but only after it has been submitted.

File Size   This field defines the size of the submitted print job.

Client   This field shows who submitted the print job.

Description   The description of the print job is the file name, unless you enter a new description.

Status   The status of a print job is displayed, such as whether it is holding or currently being serviced.

User Hold   A print job can be put on hold, either when it is being created or after it has been submitted but is still waiting to print. Print jobs can be held so a user can print them all at one convenient time. If the printers are far away, all jobs can be held until the user is ready to stand by the printers.

Operator Hold   When you type **Yes** in this field, a queue operator can put a hold on a print job.

Service Sequence   The service sequence is the position of the print job in the queue.

Number of Copies   The number of copies to print can be selected.

File Contents   Files can be specified as either Text or Byte Stream. Select Text when NetWare must interpret and format special formatting characters, such as tabs. Select Byte Stream if the application of origin can handle the formatting commands at the printer. Byte Stream is used with applications such as WordPerfect and Microsoft Word.

Tab Size   If Text was selected in the File Contents field, specify the character width of the tabs.

Suppress Form Feed   If you want the printer to advance to the top of the next page after your print job, choose No in this field; otherwise select Yes to have the printer advance to the top of the next page.

Defer Printing   Select Yes in this field to print the job at a later time. If Yes is chosen, you must enter the target date and time.

Target Date   The date of deferred printing is specified in this field.

Target Time   The time of deferred printing is specified in this field.

Target Server   The target server can be specified in this field. Specify any server if a specific server is not required.

Form   Choose the form number as created in the PRINTDEF utility.

Print Banner   Choose Yes to print a banner.

Banner Name　　The name of the currently logged user will print on the banner unless other text is specified.

Banner File　　If other text is not specified in this field, the file name is printed on the banner.

Current Queue Status

The Current Queue Status window displays the number of entries in the queue and the number of print servers attached to the queue. The following operator flags on the menu can be changed by the supervisor or print-queue operators.

Users Can Place Entries in Queue　　If this flag is set to No, users cannot submit jobs to the selected queue.

Servers Can Service Entries in Queue　　If this flag is set to No, the print server cannot service the jobs in the queue until the flag is reset to Yes.

New Servers Can Attach to Queue　　If this flag is set to No, the print server cannot attach to the queue until the flag is reset to Yes.

Managing Print-Queue Operators, Servers, and Users

You can select either of the last three options on the Print Queue Information screen to add an operator, server, or user. Remember that a print-queue operator can change or delete print jobs for the currently selected queue. Other servers can be specified as capable of servicing the queue, and users can be added to a list of those able to use the print queue.

Select either of these options and press ENTER. A list of current operators, servers, or users appears. Press INSERT to add new candidates, or press DELETE to remove a selected operator, server, or user.

Command Line Utilities for Printing

There are four command line utilities with NetWare that can be used for printing: the CAPTURE and ENDCAP commands, which control whether printing occurs on local or network printers; NPRINT, which can send print jobs to network printers; and the PSTAT command, which is used to list the status of network print jobs.

CAPTURE

Many network applications are not designed specifically for network use. With such applications, print jobs are automatically sent to local printers, usually the parallel ports LPT1, LPT2, or LPT3. The CAPTURE command captures the data being sent to a local printer on the workstation and redirects it to network printers.

In its simplest form, the CAPTURE command can be invoked at the workstation when you enter **CAPTURE** just prior to entering an applications program that requires its printer output be sent to a network printer. This CAPTURE command automatically redirects printer output from LPT1 to the default network printer. The special options described in the following section enhance the capabilities of the CAPTURE command. Examples of using CAPTURE follow this section. Note that the ENDCAP command is used to end capturing and return printing to the local printer.

Options Used with CAPTURE

The following options can be included immediately following the CAPTURE command on the command line. In most cases, more than one option can be included with the command.

SH (SHow)   The SHow option is used to view the file server, the queue, and the printer that the local printing port (LPT) has been set to. This option cannot be used with any other CAPTURE option.

A (Autoendcap)   Include this option to send data to a network printer when, but not until, you exit an application. This option is useful if you want to save several different screens or files from the same application to the same network file.

NA (NoAutoendcap)　　This option prevents data from being sent to a network printer or file when entering or exiting an application.

TI (TImeout=*n*)　　This option enables the timeout feature. Replace *n* with a number from 1 through 1000 to represent the number of seconds between the moment you initiate printing and the moment the job is queued for printing. The default timeout is 0, which means that the timeout feature is disabled.

L (Local=*n*)　　Include this option to indicate which LPT port to capture. Replace *n* with 1, 2, or 3 to indicate LPT1, LPT2, or LPT3, respectively.

S (Server=*server*)　　Include this option along with the server name to indicate which server will be used to handle the print job.

J (Job=*job*)　　The name of a predefined print-job configuration can be specified with the Job option. Print-job configurations are defined with the PRINTCON utility.

P (Printer=*n*)　　The Printer option is used to indicate which network printer will be used for printing. Replace *n* with 0 through 4 to indicate one of the five network printers.

Q (Queue=*queue*)　　Include this option to indicate which queue the print job should be sent to. Replace *queue* with the name of the queue, such as PRINTQ_0 or PRINTQ_1.

F (Form=*form* or *n*)　　The Form option specifies the predefined form or form number, as defined by the PRINTDEF menu utility.

C (Copies=*n*)　　Copies specifies the number of copies of a print job to print. Replace *n* with a number from 1 to 256.

T (Tabs=*n*)   Use the Tabs option to specify the number of spaces to be used in tabs. The option is used for applications that do not have print formatters, which is rare.

NT (NoTabs)   Include this option only if an application does not have a print formatter (most applications do). This option ensures that all the tabs in your print job arrive at the printer unchanged.

NAM (NAMe=*name*)   The NAMe option specifies the username that appears on the upper half of a banner page. Replace *name* with the user's name if it is different than the log-in name of the current user.

B (Banner=*banner*)   A *banner* is a page with a word or phrase up to 12 characters long that is printed before documents. Banner pages identify the start of one print job and separate one print job from another in the bin of a printer. An underscore character must be used for spacing between words (for example, MY_PRINT_JOB).

NB (NoBanner)   Use the NoBanner option when you want to prevent banners from printing; for example, when several print jobs are not expected to be stacked in the "completed" bin of the printer and you don't want to waste paper on a banner.

FF (FormFeed)   The FormFeed option enables a form feed upon completion of the print job.

NFF (NoFormFeed)   The NoFormFeed option disables form feed upon completion of a print job.

CR (CReate=*filename*)   Include the CReate option to send data to a file instead of to a network printer. The file server, volume, and directory name should be included if the destination is other than the current directory.

K (Keep)   The Keep option is a safety feature. It is used when data is captured over several hours or more. This option ensures that the file server keeps all data it receives from a workstation, even if the workstation crashes. The server sends the data to a printer 15 minutes after a system crash. If the option is not used, the server discards any data received from the crashed workstation.

Using CAPTURE

The following examples represent the basic use of the CAPTURE command to capture printing on a network. Remember that the CAPTURE command should be entered before starting an application that uses a network printer. Also, use ENDCAP when network printing has finished to resume printing on a local printer.

Note: Subsequent CAPTURE commands override the settings of previous CAPTURE commands.

In the following example, local printing is redirected to network printer 2 using print job 2.

CAPTURE P=2 J=2

In the following command, any print jobs sent to LPT2 by the application are sent to network printer 1. Print jobs sent to LPT1 by the application are sent to the local printer as normal.

CAPTURE L=2 P=1

In this example, three copies are made of each print job sent to network printer 1.

CAPTURE P=1 C=3

In the next command, any print job sent to LPT2 in the applications program are sent to a special printer on the ACCTG server. All other print jobs are printed at the local printer as normal.

CAPTURE L=2 S=ACCTG

Data can be saved in a network file using the CReate option. In the following example, data is saved to a file called DATAHOLD on the F drive of the server. The NA (NoAutoendcap) option is used to disable the

Autoendcap option. This then allows the user to enter and exit applications without prematurely closing the file that is capturing data on the server. The option is often used to collect screen captures in a file.

CAPTURE CR=F:DATAHOLD NA

The current status of the LPT ports on a workstation can be listed by entering this command:

CAPTURE SH

The screen displays information similar to the following, depending on the options that are set.

LPT1: Capturing data to server ACCTG queue PRINTQ_1 (printer 1
    Capture Defaults:Enabled   Automatic Endcap: Enabled
    Banner :(None   Form Feed   :Yes
    Copies :1   Tabs   :8 spaces
    Form :0   Timeout Count   :2 seconds

LPT2: Capturing Is Not Currently Active.

LPT3: Capturing Is Not Currently Active.

ENDCAP

The ENDCAP command is used to end the capture of a workstations LPT ports established by the CAPTURE command. The form of the ENDCAP command is

    ENDCAP *option*

where *option* is one of the following:

L (Local=*n*)	Specifies the LPT port (either LPT1, LPT2, or LPT3) on which to end capturing. The *n* option is either 1, 2, or 3.
ALL	Ends the capture of all LPT ports on the workstation.

C (Cancel)	Ends capturing of the LPT1 port and discards any data without printing it.
CL (CancelLocal=*n*)	Ends the capture of the specified LPT port and to discard any data without printing it. The *n* option is replaced with 1, 2, or 3 to designate one of the LPT ports.
CALL (Cancel ALL)	Ends capturing on all LPT ports and discards any data without printing it.

Before entering an ENDCAP command, it is useful to list the current capture information with the following command:

CAPTURE SH

From the information listed, you can use an ENDCAP command to cancel the ports or printing processes you prefer. As an example, the following command ends capturing of the LPT2 printer port on the workstation:

ENDCAP L=2

To cancel the capture and delete any captured data that might be ready to print, enter the following command:

ENDCAP CL=2

PSTAT

The PSTAT command is used to view information about one or more network printers. The command lets you view information about a specific printer or printers on a particular server. The command takes the following form:

PSTAT *option*

where *option* is one of the following:

S (Server=*server*)   Allows the printer information about a particular server to be printed. Replace *server* with the name of the designated server.

P (Printer=*printer*)   Shows information about a particular printer. Replace *printer* with the number of the printer.

To view information about printers on all of the current files servers, enter this command:

PSTAT

A display similar to the following appears.

```
Server STARSHIP: Network Printer Information
Printer          Ready      Status     Form: number, name
0                On-Line    Active     0, unknown name
1                On-Line    Active     1, reports
```

The number of each printer is listed, along with its ready mode, which can be either On-Line or Off-Line; its current status, which can be either Active or Stopped; and the number of the currently loaded form. A stopped printer may be jammed or may have been stopped for servicing.

To view information about a specific printer, enter its printer number as shown in the following command, which lists printer 1:

PSTAT P=1

To view information about printers on another network, enter a command similar to the following, which lists printer information for the ACCTG server:

PSTAT S=ACCTG

To view information about a specific printer on another network, enter a command similar to the following, which lists printer information for printer 1 on the ACCTG server:

PSTAT S=ACCTG P=1

NPRINT

The NPRINT command is used to send files to a network printer. The CAPTURE command need not be active because NPRINT automatically sends to network printers, bypassing any local printers. Files sent to a server with NPRINT are placed in print queues and printed in the order received unless rearranged by the supervisor or queue operator.

Files sent by NPRINT must be ASCII files or print files to be printed properly. NPRINT does not have any special formatting tools, as most word processing programs do; therefore, the text of a file is printed exactly as it is stored. This is usually fine for straight ASCII text files, but it is not appropriate for files created by applications that may contain control codes and other formatting information that cannot be interpreted by NPRINT. Files created by applications can be "printed as files," however, which means the creating application sends all printing information to a disk file instead of the printer. The disk file then contains information that can be interpreted by the printer, and the NPRINT command can send the file to the printer at any time. In some cases, a print file can be created by one user for printing on another persons printer. The creating user must load a print driver for the receiving user's printer. A print file is then created and sent to the receiving user, who then uses NPRINT to print the file on his or her local printer. The file is printed correctly because it contains the correct formatting codes for that printer.

The NPRINT command takes the following form:

NPRINT *name options*

where *filename* is the name of the file to be printed and options is one or more of the options listed below. Note that *filename* must include the mapped drive letter or complete path specification of the file's location. A few examples of the NPRINT command are shown later.

Options Used with NPRINT

The following options can be included immediately following the NPRINT command on the command line. In most cases more than one option can be included with the command.

S (Server=*server*)   Include this option along with the server name to indicate which server will be used to handle the print job.

J (Job=*job*)   The name of a predefined print-job configuration can be specified with the Job option. Print-job configurations are defined with the PRINTCON utility.

P (Printer=*n*)   The Printer option is used to indicate which network printer will be used for printing. Replace *n* with 0 through 4 to indicate one of the five network printers.

Q (Queue=*queue*)   Include this option to indicate which queue the print job should be sent to. Replace *queue* with the name of the queue, such as PRINTQ_0 or PRINTQ_1.

F (Form=*form* or *n*)   The Form option specifies the predefined form or form number, as defined by the PRINTDEF menu utility. Replace *form* with the name of the form, or *n* with the number of the form.

C (Copies=*n*)   Copies specifies the number of copies of a print job to print. Replace *n* with a number from 1 to 256.

T (Tabs=*n*)   The Tabs option is used to specify the number of spaces to be used in tabs. The option is used for applications that do not have print formatters, which is rare.

NT (NoTabs)   Include this option only if an application does not have a print formatter (most applications do). This option ensures that all the tabs in your print job arrive at the printer unchanged.

NAM (NAMe=*name*)   The NAMe option specifies the user's name that appears on the upper half of a banner page. Replace *name* with a user's name if it is different than the log-in name of the current user.

B (Banner=*banner*)   A banner is a word or phrase up to 12 characters long that appears on the banner page of printed documents. Banner pages identify the start of one print job and separate one print job from another in the bin of a printer. Replace *banner* with the 12-character string you wish to use. An underscore character must be used for spacing between words (for example, MY_PRINT_JOB).

NB (NoBanner)   Use the NoBanner option when you want to prevent banners from printing; for example, when several print jobs are *not* expected to be stacked in the "completed" bin of the printer.

FF (FormFeed)   The FormFeed option enables a form feed upon completion of the print job.

NFF (NoFormFeed)   The NoFormFeed option disables form feed upon completion of a print job.

D (Delete)   The Delete option automatically erases the file after the printer has finished printing.

Examples of NPRINT

Files in the current default drive do not require a drive or path specification in order to be printed with NPRINT. In the following example, the file MYFILE.DOC is printed on the default network printer.

NPRINT MYFILE.DOC

If the file is in another mapped drive, such as drive G for example, the following command is used.

NPRINT G:MYFILE.DOC

Initially files are printed with the network printing defaults, which are as follows:

- Printer 0 is used by default.

- A banner page is printed that includes the currently logged in user's name.

- A form feed is performed at the end of the print job.

The NPRINT options are used to change the default settings of network printing. For example, the following command causes the file MYFILE.DOC to be printed on printer 2, using the LETTERS print-job configuration.

NPRINT MYFILE.DOC P=2 J=LETTERS

The next example inhibits the banner and form feed options.

NPRINT MYFILE.DOC P=2 J=LETTERS NB NFF

In this example, the file is deleted after it is printed.

NPRINT MYFILE.DOC P=2 J=LETTERS NB NFF D

Console Printing Commands

Most of the printing commands used at the console have several options and several different ways they can be used, so it is important to understand the commands before using them. Those who need to make permanent custom printer queues and spoolers must refer to this section. The AUTOEXEC.SYS file, which is used to execute console commands every time the server is booted, is covered at the end of this chapter.

To reach the console mode on nondedicated servers, type **CONSOLE** at the NetWare prompt.

The following abbreviations are used in the console commands. You can type the complete command or only the first letter.

P = PRINTER

Q = QUEUE

S = SPOOLER

To Add a Queue to the Printer

The ADD QUEUE TO PRINTER command is used to add an existing queue to a particular printer or to reroute a queue from one printer to another. The command takes the following form:

P *nn* ADD *queue-name* AT PRIORITY *xx*

or

P *nn* = *queue-name* AT PRIORITY *xx*

where P *nn* is the printer number and *queue-name* is the name of an existing print queue. AT PRIORITY *xx* is an option that can be used to specify the priority of the print job. The default priority is 1 if this is not specified.

Example

The following command adds the queue REPORTS to printer 3 with a priority level of 1.

P 3 ADD REPORTS AT PRIORITY 1

To Change the Form Type Mounted in the Printer

The following command can be used to tell the file server that a new form has been placed in the printer.

P *nn* FORM *xx*

where P *nn* is the printer number and FORM *xx* is the new form number. Forms are defined by the PRINTDEF utility.

For example, if the printer forms are changed to print payroll checks, the server must know a new type of form exists; otherwise it will attempt to print other print jobs on the checks. If the server knows the checks are installed, it will check the form number with those requested by new print jobs and act accordingly.

Example

Assume form 5 is a paycheck definition. The following command would inform the server that paychecks have been installed in printer 3.

P 3 FORM 5

To Change Queue Priority

A queue may hold several print jobs waiting to be serviced by the printer. Any print job can be moved to a higher or lower priority by the supervisor or queue operator. The command takes the following form:

Q *name* CHANGE JOB *nn* TO PRIORITY *xx*

where *name* is the print queues name and *nn* is the number of the job in the print queue determined by listing the queue. The queue can be listed by using the LIST QUEUE CONTENTS command described later in this section. The priority level (*xx*) is determined by the number of print jobs in the queue. If the print job is given priority level 1, it is printed first. If the print job is given a priority level higher than the number of jobs in the queue, it is placed last in the queue.

Example

To change the priority of a print job in the print queue REPORTS from position 1 to position 3, type the following command:

Q REPORTS CHANGE JOB 1 TO 3

To Change Spooler Mapping

The CHANGE SPOOLER MAPPING command can be used to map a spool to a different queue and takes the form

S *nn* TO QUEUE *name*

or

S *nn* = *name*

where *nn* is the spooler number and *name* is the name of the queue to map the spool to.

Example

To map spooler 3 to the REPORTS queue, type the following command:

S 3 TO REPORTS

Note that the word "QUEUE" is optional if a name conflict between any printer commands does not exist.

To Create a New Print Queue

New queues are often created to provide special features for different network users. When a new queue is created, the group EVERYONE is given rights to use the queue. The supervisor is given operator rights and the file server is given rights to service the queue.

Note: It is important that the queue be added to one or more printers by using the ADD QUEUE TO PRINTER command discussed earlier.

The command takes the following form:

Q *name* CREATE

where *name* is the name of the new queue to be created.

Example

To create a new queue called GRAPHICS, enter the following command:

Q GRAPHICS CREATE

To Delete All Jobs in a Queue

All print jobs in a queue can be permanently deleted using the DELETE ALL JOBS command. The command takes the form

Q *name* DELETE *

where *name* is the name of the print job queue to delete. The asterisk must be included at the end of the command to indicate that all jobs in the queue should be deleted.

Caution should be taken since all jobs are removed. To remove single print jobs, use the DELETE QUEUE JOB command described later.

Example

To delete the jobs in the REPORTS queue, issue the following command:

Q REPORTS DELETE *

To Delete a Queue from the Printer

A print queue can be removed from one printer and added to another with the DELETE QUEUE command. The queue is not lost—it can be added to another printer with the ADD QUEUE TO PRINTER command discussed earlier. The DELETE QUEUE command can be used to move a queue from a downed printer to a working one.

If it is necessary to permanently remove a queue, the supervisor should remove the commands that establish the queue in the AUTO-EXEC.SYS file.

The command takes the following form:

P *nn* DELETE QUEUE *name*

where *nn* is the number of the printer servicing the queue and *name* is the name of the queue. Note that QUEUE is optional if there are no name conflicts with other printer-related commands.

Example

The following command removes the REPORTS queue from being serviced by printer 2.

P 2 DELETE REPORTS

To Delete a Queue Job

A specific print-queue job can be deleted from a queue with the DELETE JOB command, which takes the following form:

Q *name* DELETE JOB *xx*

where *name* is the print queue name and xx is the print job number to be removed. To determine the job number, use the LIST QUEUE CONTENTS command described later in this section. When a job is removed from a queue, all other jobs advance forward in the queue.

Example

The following command removes job number 3 from the REPORTS queue:

Q REPORTS DELETE JOB 3

To Destroy a Print Queue

The QUEUE DESTROY command is used to remove all jobs in a queue, as well as the queue itself, for the current session. The command takes the following form:

Q *name* DESTROY

where *name* is the name of the queue to destroy.

To permanently remove the queue from the system, the printer commands used to establish the queue in the AUTOEXEC.SYS file must be removed by the supervisor.

Example:

The following command destroys the REPORTS queue:

Q REPORTS DESTROY

To Activate Form Feed

To advance the printer paper in a printer by one page, the FORM FEED command is used. The command takes the following form:

P *nn* FF

where *nn* is the printer in which paper is to be advanced.

Example

The following command advances the paper in printer 1 one sheet:

P 1 FF

To List a Printer's Queues

It is often necessary to list the queues serviced by a particular printer in order to determine the priority level at which each queue is being serviced. The LIST command takes the following form:

P *nn* Q

where *nn* is the number of the printer to list.

Example

The following command lists the queues for printer 1.

P 1 Q

A screen similar to the following will appear at the console.

Printer 1: Running   On-Line Form 0 mounted   Servicing 2 queues

Servicing REPORTS
        at priority 1
Servicing ACCTG
        at priority 2

To List All Print Queues

To list all queues serviced by all printers on the server, type **Q**. A screen similar to the following appears, assuming the server has the name COSMOS.

COSMOS Print Queues:

PRINTQ_0 1 queue jobs serviced by 1 printers
PRINTQ_1 2 queue jobs serviced by 2 printers
REPORTS 3 queue jobs serviced by 1 printers

The report conveniently lists the number of jobs in each queue and the number of printers servicing each queue.

To List the Current Spooler Mappings

The current spooler mappings for the file server are listed with the S (SPOOL) command. Spooler mappings are necessary for the NPRINT and CAPTURE commands to function properly. Spooler mappings are created in the AUTOEXEC.SYS file or automatically by the system to printers and queues.

A *spooler* is a memory location where a print job can be temporarily stored while it awaits printing. Spoolers are important on busy systems where most print jobs must wait for existing print jobs to finish. This allows users to continue using their workstations instead of waiting for the printer. All print jobs waiting in the spooler holding areas are managed by the queue in the order in which they are received, unless the order of the queue is rearranged.

To list the spoolers, type **S** at the console command line. Information appears similar to the following:

```
Spooler 0 is directed into PRINTQ_0
Spooler 1 is directed into PRINTQ_1
Spooler 2 is directed into REPORTS
```

To List Printer Status

The P (PRINTER) command is used to list the status of printers attached to the file server. Information on each printer is listed, including the status of each printer (on-line or off-line), the form number mounted in the printer, and the number of queues serviced by each printer.

Type **P** to see a screen similar to the following:

```
COSMOS is configured for 3 printers:

Printer 0: Running   On-Line Form 0 mounted  Servicing 1    Queues
Printer 1: Running   On-Line Form 3 mounted  Servicing 2    Queues
Printer 3: Running   On-Line Form 0 mounted  Servicing 2    Queues
```

To List Queue Contents

The contents of a queue can be listed with the LIST command. This command is useful when it is necessary to know the numbers of print jobs being serviced by the printer. These numbers are necessary to change the order of printing or to remove a print job from the queue.

The command takes the form

Q *name* JOBS

where *name* is the name of the print queue to list.

Example

The following command lists the jobs in PRINTQ_0.

Q PRINTQ_0 JOBS

A listing similar to the following appears.

Jobs currently in Print Queue PRINTQ_0:

Priority	User	File	Job	Copies
*1	Jack	APPEND.DOC	5	1
2	Jenny	APRRPRT.DAT	7	1

The asterisk indicates that Jack's APPEND.DOC file is currently being printed. The job number indicates that Jack's print job is the fifth job handled by the printer. The priority of each job is also listed.

To Mark the Top of the Form

The TOP OF FORM command is used to align continuous-feed, preprinted forms in a network printer. When the command is executed, the printer prints a horizontal line of asterisks, marking the position on the page where the printing will start. You can then adjust the paper accordingly.

The command takes the form

P nn MARK

where nn is the number of the printer that needs to be aligned. After the paper has been adjusted according to the mark, it may be necessary to issue the FORM FEED command to start at the top of the next form.

If a printer has trouble keeping a form aligned properly, you can interrupt printing with the STOP PRINTER command, realign the forms using the MARK TOP OF FORM command, and then restart the printer with the START PRINTER command. It may be necessary to issue the REWIND PRINTER command to reprint some pages that were not aligned properly.

Example

The following command prints an alignment mark on printer 1.

P 1 MARK

To Rewind the Printer

The REWIND command can be used to reprint pages of a print job that were printed incorrectly on the paper or that did not finish correctly because the printer was shut down or the power went out. This command is used in conjunction with STOP PRINTER, MARK TOP OF FORM, and START PRINTER.

The command takes the following form:

P *nn* REWIND *xx*

where *nn* is the printer number servicing the print job to be rewound and *xx* is the number of pages to back up for reprinting. If the file is not an ASCII file, or if you enter a number that exceeds the number of page breaks the file server has tracked (10 pages maximum), the job restarts from the beginning. If 0 is specified, printing restarts at the top of the current page. If nothing is specified, printing starts from the beginning of the job.

The current contents of the printer's hardware buffer may need to complete printing before the backtracked pages will start printing.

Example

To rewind printer 1 so it will reprint the last four pages, enter the following command:

P 1 REWIND 4

To Start the Printer

The START PRINTER command is used to restart a printer that has been stopped by the STOP PRINTER command. The command takes the form

P *nn* START

where *nn* is the number of the printer to start.

To Stop the Printer

The STOP PRINTER command is used to stop a printer that needs servicing, because, for example, paper is out of alignment or jammed or a printer ribbon needs replacement. The command takes the following form:

P *nn* STOP

where *nn* is the number of the printer to stop.

Note that the STOP PRINTER command stops the sending of data from the server. The printer may continue to print until its hardware buffer is depleted. A stopped printer can be restarted with the START PRINTER command.

The AUTOEXEC.SYS File

The AUTOEXEC.SYS file is used to store console commands that need to be executed every time the server is started. The file can be created using the SYSCON utility or with the DOS COPY CON command. It must be stored in the SYS:SYSTEM directory.

Any command needed to create custom print queues and spoolers must be placed in this file. Since multiple queues can be mapped to multiple printers, supervisors will find many reasons for placing queue creation commands in this file.

Keep in mind that if the AUTOEXEC.SYS file is created, NetWare does not create the default queues for existing printers. You must add commands to the AUTOEXEC.SYS file to create the old default settings as well as the new custom settings.

The following commands can be placed in an AUTOEXEC.SYS file in place of the default settings that would be made if the file didn't exist. The default settings are optional; you may want to map your own specially created print queues to the printers.

```
P 0 ADD PRINTQ_0
S 0 PRINTQ_0
P 1 ADD PRINTQ_1
S 1 PRINTQ_1
```

Refer to the ADD QUEUE TO PRINTER and CHANGE SPOOLER MAPPING commands discussed in the previous section for more information on mapping printers and spools.

As an example, assume that a company has a high-speed matrix printer and a laser printer attached to the file server. The matrix printer is to be used by the accounting department and the laser printer is to be used by management, as well as the personnel, marketing, and public relations departments. High-level management will be given high priority rights to both printers by mapping a print queue called TOPGUN to both. The matrix printer will be assigned a print queue called MATRIX, and the laser printer will be mapped to a printed queue called LASER.

The commands for the AUTOEXEC.SYS file are as follows:

```
Q TOPGUN CREATE
Q MATRIX CREATE
Q LASER CREATE
P 0 ADD TOPGUN AT PRIORITY 1
P 0 ADD MATRIX AT PRIORITY 2
S 0 PRINTQ_0
P 1 ADD TOPGUN AT PRIORITY 1
P 1 ADD LASER AT PRIORITY 2
S 1 PRINTQ_0
```

The first three commands create the new queues. Printer 0 is then mapped to TOPGUN with a priority level of 1 and to MATRIX with a priority level of 2. Printer 1 is then mapped to TOPGUN with a priority level of 1 and to MATRIX with a priority level of 2. The spoolers are also mapped with the S commands.

When the Q command is typed at the console level, the following descriptions for the print queues are displayed.

STARSHIP Print Queues:

MATRIX	0 queue jobs	serviced by 1 printers
LASER	0 queue jobs	serviced by 1 printers
TOPGUN	0 queue jobs	serviced by 2 printers

With this printer configuration, managers who have use of the TOPGUN queue are given high-priority printer service to the matrix printer or the laser printer. The accounting department can use only the matrix printer, and the remaining departments can use the laser printer.

Log-in Scripts

The Default Log-in Script
Creating or Changing Log-in Scripts
Log-in Script Identifier Variables
Log-in Script Commands
Log-in Script Examples

Log-in scripts are designed to establish the network environment when users first log in. A log-in script contains a set of commands that execute one after the other. In most cases log-in scripts contain mapping commands for drives and search drives, but you can also include commands to display greeting messages, attach the user to another server, or display a menu of selections.

There are three types of log-in scripts. The first type is the *default script,* which is used by NetWare if the system log-in script has not yet been created. This script sets up the basic drive mappings to the SYSTEM and PUBLIC directories. If you have been doing the examples in this book, you have already replaced the default script with a custom log-in script. An example of the default log-in script is given in a later section.

The second type of log-in script, the *system log-in script,* is designed to set various network parameters for all users. It is executed when anyone logs on the system, so it should contain commands that the supervisor considers necessary for all users. The supervisor must initially create the system log-in script, and is the only user who can alter it.

User log-in scripts can be written for each individual user. These scripts can contain commands for a specific user; for example, commands that establish group mappings or mappings to programs or data directories that only that user needs. Users can alter their own log-in scripts using the SYSCON utility.

Each server on a network can have its own system log-in script and user log-in scripts. When a user logs in to an addition server, the scripts are run on that server as well.

Note: It is recommended that supervisors perform all log- in functions in the system log-in script using generic commands. For networks with many users, it becomes too hard to edit and add functions to individual log-in scripts. Users can still edit their own log-in scripts as they see fit, however.

The Default Log-in Script

To understand how log-in scripts work, the commands in the default log-in script are explained here. You may want to create a log-in script with similar commands, so study the following script. Note that each line is numbered for reference; these numbers normally are not part of the log-in script. The log-in script commands discussed here will be covered in more detail later in this chapter.

```
1. WRITE "Good %GREETING_TIME, %LOGIN_NAME."
2. MAP DISPLAY OFF
3. MAP ERRORS OFF
4. Remark: Set 1st drive to most appropriate directory
5. MAP *1:=SYS:; *1:=SYS:%LOGIN_NAME
6. IF "%1"="SUPERVISOR" THEN MAP *1:=SYS:SYSTEM
7. Remark: Set search drives (S2 machine-OS dependent)
8. MAP S1:=SYS:PUBLIC; S2:=S1:%MACHINE/%OS/%OS_VERSION
9. Remark: Now display all the current drive settings
10. MAP DISPLAY ON
11. MAP
```

1. The first line uses the WRITE log-in script command to display a greeting message. The message uses two variables that start with the percent sign. These variable hold the variable "morning,"

"afternoon," or "evening" based on the current time. The log-in name is the name used by the user to log in.

2. The MAP DISPLAY OFF command is used to turn the display of drive mappings off during the log-in script. They are displayed by the MAP command at the end of the script after all drives have been mapped.

3. The MAP ERRORS OFF command is used to prevent error messages from displaying during the log-in process.

4. Line 4 is a remark that is not executed as a command but used only to help explain the log-in script to others who might edit it in the future.

5. The MAP command maps the first network drive to the user's personal directory. The asterisk is used with the number 1 to represent the first network drive. This option is used for workstations that run DOS 2. For DOS 3 and 4, the first network drive always is F, and it can be mapped to the user's personal directory, as you will see later.

6. If the user logging in is the supervisor, the sixth command maps the first drive to the SYS:SYSTEM directory.

7. Another remark.

8. The SYS:PUBLIC drive is mapped to search drive 1 and the DOS directory for the workstation is mapped to search drive 2.

9. Another remark.

10. Messages displayed by commands as they execute are made visible again with the MAP DISPLAY ON command

11. The current drive mappings are displayed.

Although your log-in scripts will perform functions similar to those of the default log-in script, the remainder of this chapter shows you how to improve on the default script to create scripts better-suited for your system.

Creating or Changing Log-in Scripts

Both the system and user log-in scripts are changed with the SYSCON menu utility. To change the system log-in script, select Supervisor Options from the main menu, and then select System Login Script from the next menu. Note that user log-in scripts are changed by selecting User Information from the SYSCON main menu. Login Script is then selected from the User Information window.

Once in the log-in script edit window, you can begin typing the commands you want to place in the script. Normal editing keys such as the arrow keys, HOME, END, and DEL keys can be used to make changes to the file. The F5 (Mark) key can be used to highlight a part of the text for deletion. After pressing F5, use the arrow keys to move through the text and highlight the portions you want to move, remove, or change. Text removed with the DEL key can be inserted elsewhere with the INS key.

Here are a few rules for working in the log-in script edit window:

- Only supervisors can edit the system log-in script, but users can create or edit their own scripts.

- Only specific log-in commands can be placed in the script. DOS commands can be included, but they must be preceded by a pound sign (#).

- Text in a command line cannot exceed 150 characters. For clarity, try to use only 78 characters, which is the width of the edit window.

- Only one command can be entered per line.

- The log-in script command must be the first word on the command line.

Press the F1 (Help) key to view several screens of log-in script help, including a list of editing keys, commands, and the special identifiers (%LOGIN_NAME, %MACHINE, OS_VERSION, for example) that can be used with many of the log-in script commands. Use the PGDN and PGUP keys to scroll through the help screens. You will find log-in scripts easy to create and edit if you use the help screens for reference.

Once a log-in script is complete, press the ESC key to return to the menu. You will be asked if you want to save changes.

Log-in Script Identifier Variables

The following variables can be used in many of the log-in script commands discussed in the next section. The variables have values that the system establishes during startup. Recall from Chapter 11 that a long machine name and short machine name can be specified in the SHELL.CFG file at each workstation. The SHELL.CFG file is read when the workstation attaches to the network and the variables set in the file are retained for use in the log-in scripts.

In log-in script commands like WRITE and MAP, the variables display messages or set operating system parameters for the specific workstation that has logged in. The majority of the variables are designed for the WRITE command, but they can be useful in other commands, as you will see in the next section. A percent sign is placed in front of the variable names when used with one of the log-in script commands. The percent sign is not required with some versions of the WRITE command, as explained later in this chapter.

Identifier variables provide an excellent way to make the system log-in script generic to all users. In this way the supervisor can more easily manage the log-in process for all users with one script, rather than tailoring individual log-in scripts for each user. A generic log-in script contains commands that use the following variables in MAP commands. Drives are mapped according the groups that users belong to. In this way the log-in script integrates with the trustee and group status of a user to create an environment that is easy for the supervisor to manage.

Note: For best results and to avoid problems, type all variables in uppercase at all times.

HOUR   Holds the current hour (1-12)

HOUR24   Holds the current hour in 24-hour time (00-23)

MINUTE	Holds the current minute (00-59)
SECOND	Holds the current second (00-59)
AM_PM	Holds the day or night specifier (am or pm)
MONTH	Holds the current month as a number (01-12)
MONTH_NAME	Holds the full name of the current month (January-December)
DAY	Holds the current day as a number (01-31)
NDAY_OF_WEEK	Holds the current week day number (1-7, Sunday is 1)
DAY_OF_WEEK	Holds the full name of the day of the week (Monday-Sunday)
YEAR	Holds the year in full format (1990, etc.)
SHORT_YEAR	Holds the short format of the year (89, 90, etc.)
LOGIN_NAME	Holds the current user's log-in name
FULL_NAME	Holds the current user's full name
STATION	Holds the number of the log-in workstation
P_STATION	Holds the 12-digit hex number of the physical workstation
GREETING_TIME	This variable is either "morning," "afternoon," or "night," according to the time of day
NEW_MAIL	When the optional NetWare mail system is used, this variable will be YES if mail exists in a user's mailbox

OS	Holds the workstation's operating system (PCDOS, MSDOS)
OS_VERSION	Holds the version of the workstations operating system (v3.3, v4.1, etc.)
MACHINE	The long machine name given to a workstation in the SHELL.CFG file with the command LONG MACHINE TYPE =
SMACHINE	The short machine name given to a machine by the SHELL.CFG file with the command SHORT MACHINE TYPE =
ERROR_LEVEL	A value indicating errors that have occurred; 0 indicates no errors

Log-in Script Commands

The following commands can be used in log-in scripts. Each command is explained in detail, along with a few examples. The last section of this chapter gives several examples of log-in scripts that use a combination of these commands.

ATTACH

Use the ATTACH command to attach to a different file server. The command takes the following form:

ATTACH *servername/username*; *password*

where *servername* is the name of the server to be attached to, *username* is the log-in name of the current user on the server, and *password* is the password required to gain access to the system.

You do not need to specify the names and passwords as part of the command, especially if the command is used in the system log-in script. If you do not specify variables, you receive the following messages:

Enter the server name:

Enter log-in name for server (fileserver):

Enter password for server (fileserver):

The variables should be included only in user log-in scripts to match the particular user's log-in name and password. In most cases the password should be left out of the script, since this may be changed often. If just the password is left out as a variable, the user is asked only for that variable when logging in.

In most cases a user issues the ATTACH command from the command line rather than in a log-in script. If a user needs to attach to a server on a regular basis for resource sharing, make the ATTACH command part of the user's personal log-in script. If all users need to have access to a server for resource sharing, place the ATTACH command in the system log-in script.

Novell recommends that users be given the same user name and password on each server they need to log in to for convenience. An additional advantage of using the same password on all servers is that if a password expires on one system, the log-in program asks for a new password and synchronizes it on all other file servers where the user has a user name and password.

Examples

In the following example the user is attached to the server ACCTG with the log-in name TED and the password TIREBITER:

ATTACH ACCTG/TED;TIREBITER

If you do not want to place the password in the log-in script, use the following command. The user will be asked for a password at log-in time.

ATTACH ACCTG/TED

BREAK

You can use the BREAK ON command in a log-in script if you need to stop the execution of its commands using CTRL-BREAK or CTRL-C. Use the BREAK OFF command to prevent a break in the log-in script. These commands are used if you place commands in the log-in script that may need to be prevented from processing under certain conditions. You can place the BREAK ON command at the beginning of a new log-in script for testing; then you can stop further commands from executing if a problem or error occurs.

The BREAK commands take the following forms:

BREAK ON

BREAK OFF

When BREAK ON is active, type-ahead keyboard input is not saved in the buffer.

COMSPEC

Use the COMSPEC command to specify to a workstation operating system where it can find a copy of the DOS COMMAND.COM file. This file must be read by the operating system when leaving most applications and returning to DOS.

If workstations are using different versions of DOS, you must create a directory for each different version. In most cases these directories branch from the PUBLIC directory. For example, the following directories are created for IBM DOS 3.3, Compaq DOS 4.1, and Tandon DOS 3.2:

SYS:PUBLIC\IBM33

SYS:PUBLIC\CPAQ41

SYS:PUBLIC\TAND32

Use a MAP command to map one of these directories to a search drive, then set the COMSPEC command to that search drive. Use the command LONG MACHINE TYPE in the SHELL.CFG file at each workstation to specify a machine name. This name then establishes which directory each workstation should use as a search drive for DOS. See Chapter 11 for more details.

The COMSPEC command takes the following forms:

COMSPEC = *n:COMMAND.COM

where n is the directory where the nth network drive maps. This is further explained under the MAP command.

Alternatively the command may take the form

COMSPEC = drive:COMMAND.COM

where *drive* is a local drive or mapped server drive.

The command also may be used as follows:

COMSPEC = Sn:COMMAND.COM

where Sn is the number of a previously mapped search drive.

Examples

These examples show the MAP commands that might be placed before each COMSPEC command in a log-in script.

In this example, the third network drive is mapped to a subdirectory of PUBLIC that matches the name specified in the identifier variable %MACHINE:

```
MAP *3:=SYS:PUBLIC\%MACHINE
COMSPEC = *3:COMMAND.COM
```

In the next example, COMSPEC is specified on the local A drive:

```
COMSPEC = A:COMMAND.COM
```

The next example is the most commonly used. A search drive is established for the subdirectory that branches from the PUBLIC directory holding the appropriate DOS files. The %MACHINE variable holds the name of the directory as specified in the workstation SHELL.CFG file (with the LONG MACHINE TYPE command).

```
MAP S3:=SYS:PUBLIC\%MACHINE
COMSPEC = S3:COMMAND.COM
```

DISPLAY and FDISPLAY

Use the DISPLAY and FDISPLAY commands to display the contents of text files during the processing of a log-in script. These text files can contain text to be read by users as they log on. Meeting announcements or server maintenance schedules are good examples of text you might display using the DISPLAY and FDISPLAY commands. An editor or word processor creates the text files outside of the log-in script editing screen. The DISPLAY and FDISPLAY commands can be used to display large screens of text in place of using the WRITE command, which is covered later.

Use the FDISPLAY command if the file contains control codes that are included by some word processors, such as WordStar. DISPLAY is used to display normal text files. Since FDISPLAY filters text files, it is preferable in most cases, although it may not be effective on text files created by some word processing programs. You should create the files to be displayed with an ASCII text editor, such as EDLIN. If you do create the files with a word processor, make sure to save them as straight text files.

A supervisor can use the DISPLAY and FDISPLAY commands in several ways. For example, the command DISPLAY DAILY.DOC can be placed in the log-in script. The supervisor then updates the DAILY.DOC file each day to give users the most up-to-date information about the server, meetings, or other information. The IF...THEN statement, which is covered later, can also be used to display messages for users only if they are members of a group or are logging in on specific workstations.

The commands take the following forms:

DISPLAY *path / filename*

FDISPLAY *path / filename*

where *path* is the full path to the file (or a mapped drive letter), and *filename* is the name of the text file created by an editor or word processing program.

Examples

The FDISPLAY command is used in all examples, since filtering of control codes in the text files is preferable in most cases. In the following command the file NEWS.DOC in the SYS:PUBLIC directory is displayed during the log-in script:

FDISPLAY SYS:PUBLIC\NEWS.DOC

The next example assumes a text file exists in a directory called SYS:NEWS for each day of the week. The identifier variable called DAY_OF_WEEK is used to display the appropriate file for each day of the week. Files such as MONDAY.DOC, TUESDAY.DOC, and so on can be created in the directory for each day and updated on a regular basis as required.

FDISPLAY SYS:NEWS\DAY_OF_WEEK.DOC

The next example uses the IF...THEN command to display a meeting schedule if the day of the week is Monday. In many cases you may have several commands to display files in your log-in scripts. The following command may follow the previous command example to display several messages based on the day of the week. Also keep in mind that the DISPLAY or FDISPLAY commands can be permanently left in the log-in scripts, assuming the external files they display are updated on a regular basis.

IF DAY_OF_WEEK = "MONDAY" THEN FDISPLAY SYS:NEWS\MEETINGS.DOC

The next example displays a message specifically related to those workstations logging in with the machine name of COMPAQ. Work-stations are given machine names with the statement LONG MACHINE NAME = in the SHELL.CFG file on their boot disk or directory.

IF MACHINE = "COMPAQ" THEN FDISPLAY SYS:NEWS\COMPAQ.DOC

DOS BREAK

Use the DOS BREAK command to specify that DOS commands can be interrupted with CTRL-BREAK or be CTRL-C. This command is different than the BREAK ON command, which is used to interrupt a log-in script.

The commands take the following forms:

DOS BREAK ON

DOS BREAK OFF

The default DOS BREAK is OFF. See your DOS manual for more information.

DOS SET

Use the DOS SET command to create variables that can be used in batch files after the log-in script has completed. The variables are used in many of the same ways that identifier variables are used.

The command takes the form

DOS SET name = "*value*"

where *name* is the name you want to give to a variable, and *value* is the value that will be held in the variable name. Note that value must be enclosed in double quotation marks. If you use backslashes, enter two to avoid conflicts since the backslash is used as a special programming character in NetWare commands.

Because NetWare has an extensive set of identifier variables, the DOS SET command may not be used much. On the other hand, it can be used to create variables from the NetWare identifier variables that can be used in DOS batch files or with the MENU utility, which is discussed in Chapter 22. For example, this command makes the NetWare identifier variable LOGIN_NAME equal to the DOS variable USER:

DOS SET USER = LOGIN_NAME

USER can then be used to customize batch files for each user logging on the system.

A DOS batch file could be created that logs users into their personal directory before starting an application. With a user's personal directory as the default directory, all files created and stored are placed in that directory. The commands for a batch file called GOWORD.BAT stored in the PUBLIC directory are

```
CD SYS:PUBLIC\%USER%
WORD
```

The DOS CD command changes to a user's personal directory, which branches from the SYS:USER directory. Microsoft Word is then started from the directory (this assumes a search drive has been mapped to the directory holding the WORD program files).

The variable USER that was defined in the log-in script is used in the CD command. It must be surrounded by percent signs and is replaced with the user's log-in name when the batch file is executed. Note that this technique will remap the current drive letter to that of the user's personal directory.

You also can use the DOS SET command for more generic purposes. In the following example the system prompt is set to display the current directory:

```
SET PROMPT = "$P$G"
```

$P displays the directory and $G displays the > sign, similar to the standard DOS prompt.

The SET command places variables in a memory area called the *environment space*. If too many variable are set, the environment space may become full. To increase the size of the environment space, place a command similar to the following in the CONFIG.SYS file on the boot disk or hard drive:

```
SHELL=COMMAND.COM/Exxx/P
```

This command increases the size of the environment space from 127 bytes to *xxx* bytes. Replace *xxx* with a suitable environment size, depending on the amount of space required by your new variables. The SHELL command is described in your DOS manual.

DOS VERIFY

Use the DOS VERIFY command to verify the reliability of file copies. Use this command if you are copying with the DOS COPY command. The NetWare NCOPY command performs automatic verifications. When VERIFY is on, file copying takes more time, but the copied files are compared with the original to ensure reliability. Each copied file on the destination is checked against its source file after each copy.

The commands take the following form:

DOS VERIFY ON

DOS VERIFY OFF

When you use DOS VERIFY ON, the operating system automatically verifies all copies made with the DOS COPY command. The default setting is OFF.

You can verify copies with each command by including the /V option after a COPY command. For best results use the NetWare NCOPY command whenever possible. It not only performs verifications automatically, but also is faster for multiple copies.

DRIVE

Use the DRIVE command in a log-in script to switch users to a particular mapped drive. Without the DRIVE command, users remain in drive F and the directory that it is mapped to in the log-in script. Drive F is the first network drive when DOS 3 or above is used. Before you log in, this drive is mapped to the LOGIN directory. If a different map is not specified, drive F remains mapped to the LOGIN directory.

In some log-in scripts, the user's personal directories are mapped to the first network drive, drive F, so that users are automatically placed in their personal directories. If drive F is mapped to a different directory, but you wish to initially place users in their personal directories, you can use the DRIVE command to switch to the drives mapped to those directories.

The DRIVE command takes the form

DRIVE *n*:

where *n* is a drive letter, or the form

DRIVE **n*:

where *n* is a drive number.

In the first form the command switches to a drive that was mapped earlier in the log-in script. In the second form the log-in script switches to the *n*th drive, as specified by a previous MAP command.

Example

In the following example, drive R is mapped to a directory where an accounting package is stored. Clerks who are only authorized to use the accounting package are switched to the drive with the command

DRIVE R:

EXIT

Use the EXIT command to stop the execution of the remaining commands in a log-in script. The command is usually used with an IF...THEN statement after a certain condition has been determined to be true or false. For example, you could place an EXIT command in the system log-in script that determines whether a user is a member of a group or not. This group might be called TEMPORARY and represent all temporary personnel for a company. Commands placed after the EXIT command would only be meant for regular employees. They might assign additional search drives or display company messages.

Note: You will need to place the PCCOMPATIBLE command in your log-in script if a non-IBM system is used.

The EXIT command takes either of the following forms:

EXIT

EXIT *"filename"*

The second form of the command can be used to execute a .COM, .EXE, .BAT, or DOS internal command such as DIR after exiting the log-in script. The command replaces *filename* between the quotation marks.

Examples

To stop a batch file, you can use the following command:

EXIT

The above form of the command has limited usage, but you can use it while you write and test a log-in script to exit the script before certain commands are actually executed.

Use the following form of the command in any log-in script to start a command line utility or batch file, or run a DOS command.

PCCOMPATIBLE
EXIT "MENU"

In this example, a batch file called MENU.BAT is executed. The PCCOMPATIBLE command also is executed before the command since the system is not an IBM system.

The most common way to use the EXIT command is after evaluating a certain condition with the IF...THEN command. The following command uses the temporary personnel example described earlier:

IF MEMBER OF "TEMPORARY" THEN EXIT "TEMPS"

TEMPS can be the name of a batch file that switches temporary personnel to a special data directory. It starts the applications program they are assigned to work with, such as a data base entry program.

Note that the EXIT command has some strict rules:

- The PCCOMPATIBLE command must be placed before the EXIT command for non-IBM systems.

- The command specified with EXIT must be located in a mapped search drive, which means you must include an appropriate MAP command before the EXIT command.

- The path to a command can be specified with the command, but the complete path and command cannot exceed 14 characters. The next rule also applies in this case.

- If backslashes are used with commands, they must be typed twice to differentiate them from backslashes used in other NetWare commands. A double backslash counts as a single character.

The following example illustrates how the previous command changes when you follow the rules:

```
PCCOMPATIBLE
IF MEMBER OF "TEMPORARY" THEN EXIT "\\PUBLIC\\TEMPS"
```

— External Program Execution

External commands can be executed from log-in scripts if the pound sign (#) is placed in front of the command. Parameters can also be used with the command in the same way they would be used if you execute the command from the prompt in the command mode. The path or mapped drive letter must be specified to run the command if it is not in either the default directory or the drive switched to with a previous DRIVE command.

The command takes the following form:

 # path / command parameters

where path must be specified if *command* is not in the current directory or default drive. *Parameters* can be specified as required by the command.

Each command must appear on a separate line, and the first character must be #. You should always try to place the commands after mapping drives and search drives, since you then can easily call the command from one of the mapped drives.

Since the log-in script is held in memory while the external program is running, the remainder of the script resumes execution when the external program ends or is exited. In this way the external program execution command is different than the EXIT command because the remainder of the log-in script is executed, whereas EXIT aborts the remainder of the log-in script.

Note: Users must have the proper rights (at least Read and Open) in the directories where programs are executed.

Examples

In the following series of commands, a program called INSET (a screen capture program) is executed during a user's log-in script. The script first maps drive J to the INSET directory and then switches to that drive using the DRIVE command. The INSET program is started with the third command and the fourth command switches the user back to drive F.

```
MAP J:=SYS:INSET
DRIVE J:
# INSET
DRIVE F:
```

One of the reasons for mapping and switching to the INSET directory is that the program must be started in the same directory that stores its supporting programs and startup files.

This example starts the PCONSOLE program when a print queue operator logs in with the user name POPS (Print console OPeratorS):

```
(starting log-in commands)
MAP INS S3:=SYS:PUBLIC
IF LOGIN_NAME = "POPS" THEN BEGIN
    # PCONSOLE
    END
(remaining log-in commands)
```

Additional commands can be placed after the END statement, and these commands will execute when the user leaves PCONSOLE. This is useful if the user has to use the system in a normal way. The SYS:PUBLIC directory is mapped as a search drive so the PCONSOLE program can be executed. This would be a normal command in any log-in script, but it must be placed before the PCONSOLE command in this batch file example. Notice the form of the IF...THEN BEGIN command, which allows multiple commands to be included between the BEGIN and END options. This will be covered under the IF...THEN statement.

When you use the routine shown in the previous example, the print-queue operator can get into the PCONSOLE program immediately to manage the printers and queues.

FIRE PHASERS

The FIRE PHASERS command can be used to generate sounds similar to Ronald Reagan's useless and expensive "star wars" program. Actually the sound alerts users to various conditions, such as the presence of mail when a mail system is used. For example, if users normally don't watch their screens during log-in, they may not realize an important message has been displayed. You can draw attention to the screen with the sound of PHASERS. Use PHASERS sparingly, however; users can become irritated by the sound.

The command takes the following form:

FIRE PHASERS *n* TIMES

where *n* is the number of times you want to fire the PHASERS.

Examples

The following command causes FIRE PHASERS to sound five times:

FIRE PHASERS 5 TIMES

On Mondays FIRE PHASERS could wake users up, as in the following example, which also includes a WRITE statement to display a message and a PAUSE command to pause the log-in script so users can read the message:

```
IF DAY_OF_WEEK = "Monday" THEN BEGIN
    WRITE "Wake up, it's Monday!"
    FIRE PHASERS 5 TIMES
    PAUSE
    END
```

The FIRE PHASERS command is executed after display of a message, and the whole series of commands is placed between IF...THEN and END statement.

IF...THEN

The IF...THEN command is one of the most useful commands for log-in scripts. It can be used to execute log-in script commands only when a specific condition is met. An IF...THEN command is used to evaluate the truth or equality of various conditions. Commands may then be executed, depending on how the condition evaluates.

You have already seen the IF...THEN command used with some of the other commands. For example, in the FIRE PHASERS command, the WRITE and FIRE PHASERS commands are executed if the day of the week is Monday.

The IF...THEN command takes the following forms:

IF *conditional(s)* THEN *command*

or

> IF *conditional(s)* THEN BEGIN
>
> *commands*
>
> *commands*
>
> END

In the first form the *conditional* argument is evaluated, and if true, the *command* following the THEN statement is executed. In the second example, if *conditional* is true, a series of *commands* are executed on one or more lines following a BEGIN statement until the END statement is encountered. If *conditional* is false, the commands are skipped, and processing of the log-in script continues with the commands that follow the END statement.

The IF...THEN command can evaluate the condition of one of the identifier variables listed earlier in this chapter. The following examples may help to explain how IF...THEN works. One or more commands are placed behind the THEN option in all cases.

```
IF DAY_OF_WEEK # "Monday" THEN ...
IF MEMBER OF "TEMPS" THEN ...
IF NOT MEMBER OF "TEMPS" THEN ...
```

The first example is similar to the statements used in the examples of FIRE PHASERS, except that the not-equal-to (#) specifier is used. The commands following THEN are executed only if the day of the week is not equal to Monday. In the second example, commands are executed if the user is a member of the group TEMPS. The third example is just the opposite of the second: commands are executed only if the user is *not* a member of the group TEMPS. Note that the first example uses an identifier variable (DAY_OF_WEEK), whereas the remaining examples use a special version of the IF...THEN command that determines membership in a group.

How to Use the IF...THEN Command

The IF...THEN command can be placed anywhere in a log-in script and can be used more than once. As mentioned earlier, there are two versions of the command. The first type is entered on one line and includes the command to be executed on the same line. The following example represents a single-line IF...THEN statement:

IF DAY_OF_WEEK = "Monday" THEN WRITE "Wake up, you!"

The second version is used for a block of commands placed on separate lines between BEGIN and END options. All commands between the BEGIN and END statement are executed if the IF...THEN statement evaluates as true. Each command must be typed on a separate line. In the following example, MAP commands are executed if a user is a member of the group MANAGERS. Indenting is used in the following example only to distinguish commands between BEGIN and END options. This technique is used often by programmers to set off subroutines.

IF MEMBER OF "MANAGERS" THEN BEGIN
    MAP H:=SYS:MGR-DATA
    MAP I:=SYS:ACCTDATA
    MAP INS S3:=SYS:MGR-PROG
    END

Since the mapped drives and search drives are only meant for managers, users who belong to the group MANAGERS will get the drive mappings. Other users can be given drive mappings of their own, depending on the groups they belong to.

Conditional Relationships

You can evaluate the following six relationships with the IF...THEN command:

Symbol	Relationship
=	Equal to
#	Not equal to
>	Greater than
<	Less than
>=	Greater than or equal to
<=	Less than or equal to

The word AND can be used to form compound conditionals, which are true only if the conditions joined by AND are both true. In the following example, the manager's news file is displayed if users belong to the MANAGERS group and if the day is Monday. Note that this command must be typed on one line.

```
IF MEMBER OF "MANAGERS" AND DAY_OF_WEEK = "Monday" THEN
FDISPLAY SYS:NEWS\MGRNEWS
```

Evaluating Command Line Parameters

The LOGIN command can include parameters that can be evaluated in the log-in script. These parameters are the server name, user name, and password, and each has a specific placement number on the command line known as a *parameter number*. For example, in the following LOGIN command

```
LOGIN STARSHIP/JOHN
```

STARSHIP is parameter %0 and JOHN is parameter %1. Unlike DOS parameters, the LOGIN command itself does not count as a parameter. You can now use these parameters in your log-in script.

The next example illustrates how you might use an IF...THEN command to log users in to multiple servers using command line parameters. Consider the following LOGIN command, in which the name of the ACCTG server is parameter %2:

```
LOGIN STARSHIP/JOHN ACCTG
```

If the following command is placed in the log-in script, the user will be attached to the ACCTG server by simply specifying the name of the server, as shown in the previous example.

```
IF %2 # " " THEN ATTACH %2
```

Note that the not-equal-to relationship is evaluated. If the user does not specify a name in the %2 position, the ATTACH command is not executed since the condition is false (%2 is blank and " " is also blank, making them equal; evaluating for not-equal makes the statement false).

   Note: Using command line parameters is not recommended in most situations. Their use can be quirky because users may not specify parameters every time they log in. An alternative is to use batch files that supply the parameters for the user, but they can expose the system to security risks. It is recommended that you use identifier variables whenever possible to execute commands based on the user's log-in name, group, or workstation.

Evaluating Group Membership Conditions

You can evaluate whether a user is or is not a member of a group using the special MEMBER OF or NOT MEMBER OF options with your IF...THEN commands. The commands take the following forms:

   IF MEMBER OF *"groupname"* THEN command

   IF NOT MEMBER OF *"groupname"* THEN *command*

where *groupname* is the name of the group the user belongs to and *command* is the command to execute if the user is a member (or is not a member). The following examples demonstrate how to use these commands on a single command line. They can also be used with block commands that use BEGIN and END.

```
IF MEMBER OF "SALES" THEN MAP T:=SYS:SALEDATA
IF NOT MEMBER OF "TEMPS" THEN MAP J:=SYS:USERNEWS
```

Evaluating Error-Level Conditions

Various command execution errors produce error codes that can be evaluated with an IF...THEN command. The "%ERROR_LEVEL" identifier variable holds the latest error code from a command that did not successfully execute. An error level of 0 always represents a successful command completion. Other error codes can be evaluated and commands or messages can be displayed if they are greater than 0.

The form of the command is similar to the following example, which exits to a batch file called ERRORS.BAT if a problem occurs:

```
IF "%ERROR_LEVEL"#"0" THEN EXIT "ERRORS"
```

Another way to use the command is to determine whether a file server is on-line before attempting to map drives to it. In the following example the ATTACH command is placed ahead of the IF...THEN statement. If the ATTACH command fails to attach to the ACCTG server, an error code other than 0 is produced and the commands following BEGIN are not executed.

```
ATTACH ACCTG
IF "%ERROR_LEVEL"="0" THEN BEGIN
    MAP I:=ACCTG/VOL1:DATA
    MAP INS S5:=ACCTG/VOL1:PROGRAM
    END
```

Note: The "%ERROR_LEVEL" identifier variable uses the last error code generated in the program by an ATTACH or # (External Program Execution) command. Make sure the last error code generated is appropriate for your log-in script.

INCLUDE

The INCLUDE command is used to make the log-in script execute an external set of commands, or subscripts. Programmers use subscripts to make large programs easier to use and create. Often-used code routines can be written to an external file, then included in a program by calling the file containing the code. The technique is used frequently when a set of code is used on a regular basis by many programs. The INCLUDE command is not useful for the system log-in script, but you might find it useful when developing numerous user log-in scripts.

The command takes the form:

INCLUDE *path \filename*

where *path* is the full path or drive specifier to the directory holding the external code file, and *filename* is the name of that file. You can nest INCLUDE statements up to ten levels deep.

Note: Users of INCLUDE files must have Open and Read rights in the directory where the files reside.

Example

In this example the file LOGIN2.DAT in the SYS:PUBLIC directory is included in the log-in script:

```
INCLUDE SYS:PUBLIC\LOGIN2.DAT
```

The INCLUDE command is of little use and adds confusion to log-in scripts. The system log-in script should be as integrated and generic as possible for maintenance purposes and should therefore not use the IN-CLUDE command.

MACHINE NAME

The MACHINE NAME command is used to set the machine name of a workstation to a specified name. Some programs written to run under PC DOS require the MACHINE NAME command. The name can include identifier variables and may contain up to 15 characters.

The command takes the form:

MACHINE NAME = *"name"*

where "*name*" is the name in quotation marks you want to assign to the machine.

Example

You can use the following command to assign a machine name of IBMPC to a machine:

MACHINE NAME = "IBMPC"

MAP

The MAP command is used extensively in log-in scripts to establish the mappings for all users or selected users. The IF...THEN commands can be used to map drives based on groups or other identifier variables. For more information on MAP, see Chapter 16, or refer to the examples at the end of this chapter.

Keep in mind that the MAP command can be used by itself to display the complete set of drive and search drive maps join at the end of a log-in script.

There are four additional MAP commands you can use in log-in scripts that are not covered elsewhere in this book.

MAP DISPLAY OFF   As drives are mapped in a log-in script, they are displayed on the screen. You can turn this display off to avoid screen clutter. Remember that a MAP command can be included at the end of the log-in script to display the final mappings to a user.

MAP ERRORS OFF   Errors encountered during a log-in script are not displayed if this command is used. In some cases IF...THEN commands that you need to use may produce errors, although the errors are not serious and processing continues with the next statement. You can use the MAP ERRORS OFF command to suppress the error messages. It is recommended that you not use this command until the log-in script has been completely tested and debugged.

MAP DISPLAY ON   Reverses the effect of the MAP DISPLAY OFF command.

MAP ERRORS ON   Reverses the effect of the MAP ERRORS OFF command.

These commands can be used anywhere within a log-in script; however, the OFF command must be used before the ON commands.

PAUSE

The PAUSE command is used to introduce a temporary stop in the log-in script. PAUSE is usually placed after a message is displayed. Simply type the command as it is. Processing continues when the user presses a key.

Example

In the following example, the PAUSE command is placed after the WRITE command.

```
WRITE "All users on this system are required to follow
software licensing rules and regulations."
PAUSE
```

PCCOMPATIBLE

The PCCOMPATIBLE command should be used if the EXIT command does not work properly. The command is designed for non-IBM systems and designates them as compatible machines.

Type the following command in the log-in script before any EXIT commands:

```
PCCOMPATIBLE
```

REMARK

The REMARK command can be used in a log-in script to include comments for your own use or for other users who may need descriptions of the routines in the script. Programs and scripts should always be documented as a courtesy to others who may need to manage and edit the file in the future. The command takes either of the following forms:

REMARK *text*

REM *text*

* *text*

; *text*

where *text* is the text to include in the remark. The REMARK command and text cannot reside with other commands on the command line.

The following command documents part of the MAP section of a log-in script:

REM The following MAP commands are for managers only

WRITE

The WRITE command is a frequently used command that displays text for users to read as the log-in script executes. It can also be used with the identifier variables in a number of ways.

The command takes either of the following forms:

WRITE "*text* "; *identifier*

WRITE "*text* %IDENTIFIER* "

where *text* between quotation marks follows the command and *identifier* is an identifier variable. You can also mix both text and identifier variables. The semicolon (;) is used to separate text from identifier variables if they both are not surrounded by quotation marks, as in the first command form. In the second form, both text and variable are surrounded by quotes. The identifier is in uppercase and begins with a percent sign. A semicolon is not required in this command form.

The following character strings can also be included in the command to perform specific tasks:

\r	Carriage return
\n	New line
\"	An embedded quotation mark
\7	A beep

The WRITE command can be used with any of the identifier variables listed earlier in this chapter. Enter each variable as shown, including the underscore characters. WRITE will replace the identifier variable with the text being held by the variable.

Two important rules to remember when using identifier variables within text strings are

- Use the semicolon to separate text from identifier variables, as shown here:

  WRITE "Good "; GREETING_TIME

- Identifier variables can be placed in text surrounded by quotation marks, as long as the variable is preceded by a percent sign and is typed in uppercase, as shown here:

  WRITE "Good %GREETING_TIME, %LOGIN_NAME"

Examples

The following example spaces down four lines, displays a greeting message for a user, then spaces down four more lines:

WRITE "\n\n\n\nGood %GREETING_TIME, %LOGIN_NAME\n\n\n\n"

In the next command, identifier variables are used to display month, day, and year. The percent sign and uppercase letters are used since the text is within quotes. Also the comma is used and will appear when the text is displayed.

WRITE "Today is %MONTH_NAME %DAY, %YEAR"

Log-in Script Examples

The following log-in scripts can be used as examples. The first script is the most basic and can be used on small networks where supervisors as well as users include most of the log-in commands in their personal log-in scripts, rather than the system log-in script. The system log-in script listed here sets only those parameters used by all users. Keep in mind that these scripts are only examples that can be adapted for your own use.Each line is numbered for reference; these numbers normally are not part of the log-in script.

```
1. SET PROMPT = "$P$G"
2. MAP F:=SYS:USERS\%LOGIN_NAME
3. MAP G:=SYS:PUB-DATA
4. MAP INS S1:=SYS:PUBLIC
5. MAP INS S2:=SYS:PUBLIC\%MACHINE
6. COMSPEC = S2:COMMAND.COM
```

The first command sets the system prompt to display the current directory. The second command maps drive F to the user's personal directory using the LOGIN_NAME identifier variable. Line 3 maps the PUB-DATA directory to drive G. Line 4 maps the first search drive to the SYS:PUBLIC directory. Note that the search drive is inserted with the INS command. This means that the user's current DOS path settings will be saved. Line 5 maps a DOS directory according to the long machine name specified in the SHELL.CFG file. The last line sets COMSPEC to the S2 search drive. This batch file is generic to all users since it establishes each user's personal directory and COMSPEC drive according to log-in name and machine type.

The following log-in script example simply adds features to line 5. The rest of the script is the same.

```
1. SET PROMPT = "$P$G"
2. MAP F:=SYS:USERS\%LOGIN_NAME
3. MAP G:=SYS:PUB-DATA
4. MAP INS S1:=SYS:PUBLIC
5. MAP INS S2:=SYS:PUBLIC\%MACHINE\%OS\%OS_VERSION
6. COMSPEC = S2:COMMAND.COM
```

Line 5 has been altered to accommodate large networks that may have many different types of DOS versions. In the first example, it was asumed that the long machine name described both the machine type and DOS version for networks that use only two or three different DOS types and versions. A network workstation may use IBM, Compaq, and AST DOS, in which case subdirectories called IBMDOS, CPAQDOS, and ASTDOS are created to branch from the PUBLIC directory. On a larger system, many different types and versions of DOS may exist at the workstations, so it may be necessary to create additional subdirectories, such as \PUBLIC\COMPAQ\MSDOS\V3.10 or \PUBLIC\COMPAQ\MSDOS\V3.30, to differentiate between the DOS versions. The altered version of line 5 uses identifier variables to create the search path to the version of DOS required by each workstation. The remaining variables describe the operating system. For example, Compaq DOS version 3.3 would cause line 5 to execute as follows:

```
MAP INS S2:=SYS:PUBLIC\COMPAQ\MSDOS\V3.30
```

If this method is used, you must create directories called COMPAQ, MSDOS, and V3.30, and then copy the DOS files into the V3.30 directory to get this command to work properly. Because of the number of directories, this method is not recommended. Instead, it is best to attempt a standardization of the DOS versions used at the workstations.

The next example is a system log-in script that adds various greeting messages and maps drives and search drives according to the groups users belong to. This log-in script places more emphasis on the use of the system log-in script rather than individual user log-in scripts. Keep in mind that it is best to let users manage their own personal log-in scripts, since this task can be too cumbersome for managers.

```
 1. WRITE "\n\n\n\nGood %GREETING_TIME, %LOGIN_NAME\n\n\n\n"
 2. SET PROMPT = "$P$G"
 3. MAP F:=SYS:USERS\%LOGIN_NAME
 4. MAP G:=SYS:PUB-DATA
 5. MAP INS S1:=SYS:PUBLIC
 6. MAP INS S2:=SYS:PUBLIC\%MACHINE
 7. COMSPEC = S2:COMMAND.COM
 8. IF MEMBER OF "TEMPS" THEN BEGIN
 9.       MAP F:=VOL1:ACCTDATA
10.       MAP S1:=VOL1:ACCTPROG
11.       EXIT "START"
12. IF MEMBER OF "MANAGERS" THEN BEGIN
13.       MAP H:=SYS:MGR-DATA
14.       MAP INS S3:=SYS:MGR-PROG
15.       END
16. IF LOGIN_NAME = "POPS" THEN BEGIN
17.       # PCONSOLE
18.       END
19. FDISPLAYSYS:NEWS\DAY_OF_WEEK.DOC
20. PAUSE
21. IF DAY_OF_WEEK = "MONDAY" THEN FDISPLAY SYS:NEWS\MEETINGS.DOC
22. PAUSE
23. IF MACHINE = "CPAQ" THEN FDISPLAY SYS:NEWS\CPAQ.DOC
24. PAUSE
25. DOS SET USER = LOGIN_NAME
26. PCCOMPATIBLE
27. IF P_STATION = "000025478525" THEN EXIT "FIX.BAT"
28. EXIT "MAIN"
```

This log-in script effectively uses group names to assign drive and search mappings to users according to the groups they belong to. Lines 8, 11, and 15 start commands that perform tasks only if the user is a member of a group. For example, the PCONSOLE command is executed in line 16 if the user signs in with the user name "POPS" (Print console OPeratorS). News and messages are then displayed with the commands in line 18 through 23. The PAUSE command is used to pause the screen for reading. Messages are displayed based on the day or the machine number. Line 24 sets the external variable USER to the user's log-in name so it can be used in batch files later in the session. Line 25 sets the PCCOMPATIBLE mode. Line 26 runs a special fix program for the station that matches the number shown in the IF...THEN command. The last command displays a main menu.

In line 8, personnel belonging to the TEMPS group are placed directly into an accounting program with the next three commands, and the rest of the log-in script is aborted. This assumes that the users who belong to this group are not regular employees of the company and should not view any of the messages or have any of the drive mappings that might be set in subsequent log-in script commands. The command in line 9 maps the data directory to their default drive, and line 10 maps a search drive to the accounting program. Line 11 starts the accounting program by first exiting the log-in script. In this way, the remaining log-in script commands do not execute for temporary personnel.

The messages displayed by the commands in lines 19 through 23 are kept in the SYS:NEWS directory and should be managed by the system supervisor. The meeting message files are updated according to the requests of different department managers. It is important for the supervisor to continually update messages displayed by the system log-in script.

The NetWare MENU System

Using MENU
Menu Example
Running MENU on Standalone Computers

NetWare has an extensive system for creating your own custom menus similar to those of the NetWare menu utilities like SYSCON, SESSION, and FILER. In this chapter, you will learn how to create menus for your own use as a supervisor or for network users with the NetWare MENU command.

Type the following command on the command line to see an example of a menu:

MENU MAIN

The MENU command executes commands in a text file called MAIN.MNU, which is stored in the SYS:PUBLIC directory. This menu comes with NetWare to help supervisors and users more easily access the NetWare menu utilities.

Note: The following files must be located in the SYS:PUBLIC directory for MENU to work:

MENUPARZ.HLP

MENU.EXE

MENUPARZ.EXE

If these files are not in the directory, they can be copied from the PUBLIC disks in the Novell NetWare disk set. MENU can also be run on standalone computers without the need to have NetWare running. Refer to the last section of this chapter for more details.

The following menu is displayed when you issue the MENU MAIN command:

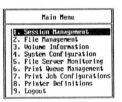

When you make a selection from the menu, the appropriate NetWare menu utility is started, unless you select the Logout option, which will log you out of the system. When you exit from the selected utility, the MAIN menu reappears so you can make additional selections. Press ESC to return to the normal command line.

Since the MAIN menu is of benefit to most NetWare users, you may want to display it every time the system is started. This can be done by placing a command at the end of the system log-in script, or at the end of the log-in script for users who should see the menu. By following these steps, you can include the command to display the menu at the end of the system log-in script:

1. Log in as the supervisor

2. Start the SYSCON menu utility

3. Select Supervisor Options from the SYSCON main menu

4. Select System Log in Script from the Supervisor Options menu

5. Include the PCCOMPATIBLE command if this is a non-IBM system or if you used the LONG MACHINE TYPE command in your SHELL.CFG file

6. Go to the last line of the script and type the following command:

    EXIT "MENU MAIN"

The EXIT log-in script command is covered in the previous chapter for those who need additional information. When a new user logs in, the menu is displayed. Note that the names of other menu files can be substituted for MAIN in the previous example.

The following section explains how the MAIN menu works and how to build menus of your own.

Note: The MENU command cannot be used from within a DOS batch file.

Using MENU

The MENU utility is a convenient way for supervisors as well as users to create menus that make often-used commands easier to access and use. Supervisors can create a menu designed especially for users, or a menu designed for supervisory and maintenance tasks. Users can also create their own menus to automate the tasks they perform on the system. The MENU command is so simple to use that most users will welcome the opportunity to customize their NetWare sessions.

You can create as many menus as you like, because each menu is a separate file that is run by typing the filename after the MENU command. Menu files must be *text-only* files that have a filename extension of MNU, unless you specify another extension when running the MENU command. Text-only files do not contain control codes or formatting characters commonly introduced by word processing programs. Use EDLIN, COPY CON or other basic editing programs, or make sure to save files created with word processing programs as text-only files.

You should create your menus in the PUBLIC directory; by default that is the directory in which MENU looks for the menu files if the specified menu is not in the current directory. However, one technique you can use to some advantage is to override the menu in the public directory by creating other menus with the same name in different directories.

Novell's MENU command is both easy to use and of infinite benefit to both users and supervisors. You can easily learn how to create striking, full-color menu systems with little effort. The rest of this chapter introduces you to the menu creation process. You can create the example menus presented here to help you learn how the whole process works. As you read through the chapter, menus become progressively more complex, but at the same time easy to comprehend. The example menu presented at the end of this chapter also is good for everyday use.

The MAIN menu discussed earlier is a relatively simple menu system. Each selection executes a single command that could just as easily be typed at the Novell command line. However, the menu saves you the trouble of having to remember the command to start each of the NetWare menu utilities and is useful to new users. Menus can also include complicated commands that you normally forget how to use or must type on a regular basis. In the example menu discussed at the end of this chapter, you will see how to run complex NDIR commands from menu selections.

Software applications can be started from menus. You can create a menu that lists each of the software packages available on a system. Users then easily select the package they want to use. You can also include commands to switch a user to a specific directory before the application starts so files will be stored in that directory.

Some menu selections can display *submenus,* which are overlapping menus that have additional selections. For example, a selection called Applications on the main menu may display a submenu that lists the software applications available on the network. Submenus help you categorize the menu selections you have and keep menus from becoming too cluttered with selections.

In general, MENU helps to speed up access to programs and the execution of commands. Complicated NetWare commands that normally require long and complex options to execute properly can be added as selections to menus. In this way you don't have to remember the options, and you don't have to retype them every time. A menu can be created for each user or for each type of task performed on the system. At the end of this chapter, you will see how to create a useful menu designed especially for both new and experienced users that will help them execute common NetWare commands and start applications.

The MAIN Menu Revisited

This section examines the MAIN menu so you can see how simple it is to put your own menus together. The contents of the MAIN.MNU file in the SYS:PUBLIC directory are listed here:

```
%Main Menu,0,0,3
1. Session Management
      Session
2. File Management
      Filer
3. Volume Information
      VolInfo
4. System Configuration
      SysCon
5. File Server Monitoring
      FConsole
6. Print Queue Management
      PConsole
7. Print Job Configurations
      PrintCon
8. Printer Definitions
      PrintDef
9. Logout
      !Logout
```

This file is a standard ASCII text file that can be edited with EDLIN or other text editors. When **MENU MAIN** is typed at the command line, each line of the file is read and interpreted by MENU to create the menu on the screen.

The lines of a menu file are categorized in one of four ways:

- The title of a menu or submenu

- The selections for a menu

- Commands to display submenus

- Commands executed when a menu selection is made

There are four rules for specifying how a line in a menu file should be categorized:

- The percent sign indicates a main menu title. The position and color palette of a menu can be specified at the end of the title using horizontal and vertical coordinates and color palette numbers.

- Menu selections are placed under menu titles and start at the left edge of the screen. Do not put spaces in front of a menu selection. The order of menu selections is not important because MENU places them in alphabetical order.

- Submenus are executed with a command that is indented or has at least one space in front of it and a percent sign. The submenu command causes the menu to jump to another part of the menu file that has the selections and commands for the submenu. The lines to define the submenus start in the same way as the main menu. The menu title is preceded by a percent sign and must match exactly the submenu command that called it.

- The commands that power menu selections are placed on the lines following the selection title in the text file and must be preceded by a space or tab, which designates it as a command.

Notice in the MAIN menu listing that the first line starts with a percent (%) sign, which designates it as the menu header. The header of the menu is Main Menu. You may want to start the menu at this time to inspect its menu heading and selections, or refer back to the previous illustration of the MAIN menu. In the MAIN.MNU listing, notice that each menu selection starts with a number and is left justified. The commands executed by each menu selection are directly beneath the selections and indented.

Note: Since the selections in MAIN.MNU are numbered, they retain their order when sorted by menu.

Planning and Creating Menus

You can begin creating your own menus immediately. Since the MENU.EXE file is located in the SYS:PUBLIC directory, you may want to switch to that directory to create your menu files, although it is not essential. Users may want to create menu files in their personal directories. If a user creates a second MAIN.MNU file in a personal directory, the second copy runs when that directory is the default, but the MAIN.MNU file in the SYS:PUBLIC directory executes if another directory is the default (unless the new default directory has its own MAIN.MNU file).

The following menu-planning information may help you organize what to place on a menu, when to use submenus, and how to determine who will get menu access.

Menu Planning

One of the first things to do when creating menus is to plan what they will do. The following sections will give you examples to work with, but you should be thinking about your own needs as you try out the examples. Many of the selections on the example menus can be substituted with selections that fit your own needs. The final example is designed to be useful for typical installations, except for the software applications window, which you change to match your own needs.

Recall that a main menu can have selections that display submenus. This is an important consideration in planning your menu system. As the supervisor, you could create one menu system for all users. This menu system could then separate programs, commands, and tasks into submenus. The main menu would list selections representing broad categories, such as Applications, NetWare Menu Utilities, NetWare Commands, Miscellaneous Utilities, and others.

You should also consider who will use the menu. Four different types of menu users are discussed here.

Supervisor   If a menu is for supervisory use only, you can include options that only the supervisor would use, such as the NetWare accounting, security, system repair, and diagnostics commands.

Users   If the menu is for users, you can include commands to make it easy for them to view their directory structure or the files they have on the system.

Groups   A menu might be created for a group of users. For example, temporary personnel might see a menu for starting a database file they are updating or for starting a word processing program to write letters. A group of managers might have a special menu that lists the applications only they use, as well as various network management tasks they have been assigned to perform.

Individual Users   An individual user might have a personal menu system they have created themselves to start their own applications or make tasks they perform easier to access.

New users to the network may require multiple submenus that lead them to various commands. Since the length of descriptions on the menu is limited, you may need to "lead" users to various commands by displaying more specific submenus with each selection. For example, a command that displays a user's files in a particular directory in sorted order may require several menu levels or categorization. The main menu might have a selection called Viewing Personal Information. The next level might have selections for viewing directories or for viewing files. At the "view-files" level, the user might then be able to select an option that displays files in various ways, such as by date, size, or filename.

Determine the categories your menu selections will fall into, and then create a main menu and submenus according to those categories. For example, an Applications selection at the main menu may display a submenu that lists Word Processing, Data Base Applications, and Spreadsheets selections. A submenu may exist for each of these categories because several different programs of the type listed are available on the network.

To plan a menu, write down the following:

- Who the menu is for: supervisor, users, groups, etc.

- What the menu will do. Will it be a main menu that encompasses all other menu tasks in submenus, or will it be a specific menu, such as the supervisors maintenance menu?

- Decide which selections will be placed on the main menu. Will they be directly executing commands, or will they display submenus? A mixture of both is common.

- Decide which program selections will be placed on the main menu or submenus.

- Categorize the programs to see if additional submenus are required to further group applications.

- Determine the commands you will need to execute each menu selection. In some cases several commands may be needed. Remember to include a PAUSE command if a listing is displayed, otherwise the user won't have time to read the listing since MENU immediately redisplays the menu after the commands have executed.

- Make sure users have the proper rights to use the menus or the programs they execute. If the selections switch users to other directories, make sure they have rights in those directories.

- When creating the commands, insert *variable requests* as needed. Variable requests ask users to enter the variables needed to produce the desired results from the commands.

- Plan the screen spacing and colors, if necessary, although MENU default settings can be used effectively.

Creating Menus

When creating menu files, remember to use a standard text editor such as EDLIN, or save files in text-only format. The menu file should be given a name that fits the use of the menu. Always give the menu file the extension MNU, unless you want to specify another extension when running the menu.

As an example, a menu called USER.MNU is created using the DOS EDLIN line editor. You can substitute the applications shown in this example to fit your needs. The User menu and its Applications submenu are shown in the following illustration:

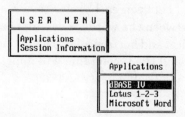

The completed USER.MNU file is shown here:

```
%U S E R M E N U,8,22,0
Session Information
        WHOAMI /A
        PAUSE
        USERLIST
        PAUSE
        MAP
        PAUSE
Applications
        %Applications
%Applications
Microsoft Word
        word
Lotus 1-2-3
        123
dBASE IV
        dbase
```

Start EDLIN with the following command:

```
EDLIN USER.MNU
```

You can refer to the DOS manual for details on using EDLIN. The asterisk is the EDLIN prompt and most of its editing commands are single-letter commands such as I (Insert) or L (List). At the asterisk, type **I** and press ENTER. Each line is numbered, and you can work with only one line at a time. On the first line, type the following text:

```
%U S E R    M E N U,8,22,0
```

Notice that the percent sign is used to indicate a menu header and that spaces were placed between each letter to spread the header out. Three spaces are used between the words. The numbers at the end of the menu determine its vertical and horizontal placement on the screen and its color.

Press ENTER and the second line will appear. Type the following on the line without indents, and press ENTER:

```
Session Information
```

On the third line, press TAB to create a command. A space character
can also be used. Type the following commands, making sure to press TAB
at the start of each line and ENTER at the end of each line:

```
WHOAMI /A
PAUSE
USERLIST
PAUSE
MAP
PAUSE
```

When the menu is run, these commands will be executed when you select
Session Information from the menu.

On lines 9 and 10, type the following header and command:

```
Applications
    %Applications
```

Do not type a space or press TAB before the header in line 9 since this will
be the heading for the Applications submenu. In line 10, press TAB and
type the percent sign to create the command for executing the Applications
submenu. When the menu is run, this command searches further in the
file for the menu header line %Applications, which in this case is the next
line. It is important that this line match exactly with the menu header you
will type in line 11.

On line 11, type the menu header for the submenu Applications. Type
the line exactly as shown here without a space or a tab before the percent
sign:

```
%Applications
```

You now can begin adding the selections for the menu. You can change
these to match the programs you want to run on your network. In the
following example, dBASE IV, Lotus 1-2-3, and Microsoft Word are used.
The commands to execute each application are included after the selection
name and indented with a tab to designate them as executable lines.

```
Microsoft Word
        word
Lotus 1-2-3
        123
dBASE IV
        dbase
```

At the end of the last line, press ENTER, then CTRL-BREAK to end the insert mode. At the EDLIN asterisk prompt, type **E** to end editing and save the menu. At the operating system prompt, type the following command to display the menu:

MENU USER

The first thing you may notice is that MENU has rearranged the order of the items on the menu from that typed in the USER.MNU file. MENU always sorts items in alphabetical order, as discussed in the next section.

Try each of the menu items to see how they work. With the Session Information selection, users can display information about their current session, such as trustee rights, other users, and current drive and search drive mappings.

Try running the software applications from the menu. After the application loads, exit the program and the menu should be restored. If you have problems running applications, refer to the "Running Software Applications from Menus" section of this chapter.

Menu Selection Order

MENU rearranges the items you place in MNU text files into alphabetical or numeric order when the menu file is processed. If you arrange the menu items in the order you prefer and then place numbers in front of each line, MENU keeps the order you used in the menu's text file.

As you have probably noticed from using other NetWare menu utilities, you can make selections on menus by typing the first few letters of a selection. In most cases you land on a selection by typing its first letter, but if two selections have the same first letter, you can type the second and third letter to get to the correct selection. When creating menus, keep in mind that you can use numbers to keep the selections in the order you want, or you can leave the numbers out to have MENU rearrange the order of the selections alphabetically.

If you don't like numbered selections, but you still want to keep the selections in the order you prefer, you must be creative with the names you use for the selections so MENU will keep them in the order you want. For example, if you wanted to keep two menu items together, create selection titles that start with the same first letter or word for each. Alternatively, you can create one- or two-letter codes for each menu item. This method is used in the software applications menu example at the end of this chapter.

Running Software Applications from Menus

If a software application is run from a menu, a search drive must be mapped to the application. The user will run the application from their current directory or mapped drive, unless you place commands in a menu selection that switch them to other directories. In the menu example at the end of this chapter, each software application has two selections. One switches users to their personal data directories and the other switches them to the appropriate public data directory before starting the program. In this way, files are stored in either one of these directories depending on the user's choice.

If a selection switches a user to another directory, they need Open, Create, Write, Read, Delete, and Search rights in that directory. The MENU program writes a temporary file to the directory that is deleted, so the Delete right is essential. Also note that some applications write temporary files as they execute in the directory where the program files exist, so users also may need Create and Write rights in the program directory.

Note: Do not include terminate-and-stay-resident (TSR) commands in your menus. Load these programs from the command line; otherwise, serious errors may occur.

Creating Submenus

A main menu can have submenus, and each submenu can have its own submenus, thus allowing for multilevel menu systems. When a submenu is to be displayed from a parent menu, an indented command preceded by a percent sign is used to call the submenu. The MENU program then searches the rest of the file for a line that exactly matches the command that called the submenu. The menu selections and commands for the submenu should immediately follow this line.

In the previous example the Applications submenu is called with the command %Applications. When MENU sees this command, it jumps to the line in the menu file that matches this command exactly. The same rules apply for defining submenus as apply for the main menu. The names of selections to be displayed on the submenu are listed and should not include preceding spaces or percent signs. The commands for each of these selections are on lines immediately following the names and are preceded by space characters or tabs.

Screen Placement of Menus

When multiple submenus will be displayed, you should consider the placement of the menus on the screen. If vertical and horizontal specifications are not made, MENU will automatically place each submenu on top of the parent menu. In some cases, you may want to stagger the menus so users can see each parent menu. The locations are specified as vertical and horizontal coordinates at the end of each menu header line. In the previous example, the menu placement for the USER MENU is 8,22, where 8 specifies the vertical and 22 the horizontal placement of the menus. The placement numbers are calculated using the following methods.

Vertical Placement   Vertical lines are counted from the top of the screen to the center of the menu. You must first determine how many lines your menu requires from top to bottom and then divide that number by two. Add that number to the number of lines you want between the top of the menu and the top of the screen.

Horizontal Placement

Horizontal placement is specified in characters or columns from left edge of the screen to the center of the menu. You must first determine the character width of your menu and then divide that number by two. Add that number to the number of columns you want between the left of the menu and the left screen border.

As an example, assume you have a menu that is 10 lines long and 20 characters wide. You want to place the top of the menu 5 lines down from the top of the screen and the left menu border 20 columns from the left screen border. The following formulas can be used to determine the vertical and horizontal placement numbers:

menu lines/2 + top-of-screen distance = vertical placement number

or

10/2 + 5 = 10

and

menu columns/2 + left-screen-distance = horizontal placement number

or

20/2 + 20 = 30

The menu header using these values would appear as

%A MENU HEADER,10,30,0

The last digit is the menu's color specification. If values are left out, MENU uses its default parameters, which center the horizontal and vertical placement. If a single value is left out, you must still insert the comma as a placeholder. In the following example, the default horizontal placement is used:

%A MENU HEADER,10,,0

Menu Variables

Variables can be used in your menu commands to request information from users, such as filenames, drive letters, and other information that can be used as options with commands. For example, you could place the NCOPY command in a menu and then ask for the source filename and destination filename. These names are inserted into numbered variables for use in the current command or subsequent commands within the same menu selection.

The @ symbol is used to request a numbered variable from the user. A remark or statement is typed in quotation marks following the variable. When the menu is run, the remarks appear in a box on the screen. When the user types the appropriate information in the box, it is saved in the variable for later use.

For example, the following command could be used to sort the user-specified directory in filename order, using the NDIR command with the SO FN option:

NDIR @1"Enter the drive letter or path" SO FN

The following window appears on the screen when a user selects the command:

```
Enter the drive letter or path: H:
```

If the user enters **H:** as shown, the following command is executed:

NDIR H: SO FN

This command lists the files of drive H in sorted filename order (SO FN). Note that the variable is inserted in the command exactly where the variable is used in the menu command.

In the next example, two variables are requested from the user for a COPY command. The first is the source filename and the second is the destination filename. You can then display the filenames with the NDIR command using the variables. The PAUSE command is used to pause the display before the menu is brought back to the screen.

```
COPY @1"Enter source name" @2"Enter destination name"
NDIR @1
NDIR @2
PAUSE
```

Note the following:

- There is a 100-character limit on the length of any command, so keep your variable messages short.

- Variables are saved only for the current group of commands under one menu selection heading. As soon as a new menu selection is made, previous variables are lost.

- Do not use the symbols @ or \ in your variable messages.

Menu Colors

If you want to select different colors for your menus, use the COLORPAL program covered in Appendix D to generate new menu color configurations.

Running and Testing Menus

You may need to run a menu several times before it works the way you want. Most of the problems can be easily fixed and have to do with omitted characters or incorrect command syntax. The following problems may occur:

- An error message may occur initially because MENU cannot run your menu script. Make sure the script was saved as an ASCII text file and that the first line starts with a percent sign and is a menu header.

- A selection may not be accessible because the command is left out or has incorrect syntax.

- A submenu may not be accessible because its parent selection name does not match the menu header exactly.

- A submenu may not contain selection options. Go back and add the options.

MENU displays several descriptive error messages you can use to debug your menu files.

Menu Example

The menu system shown in Figure 22-1 contains several submenus and menu techniques you may use when designing your own menu. Since the options on this menu are quite useful, you may want to create the entire menu for your system. Later you can make copies of the file and edit it for different menus. You can change the options in the applications submenu to fit the applications you have installed on your system.

This User menu is designed to provide useful information to all users on a system; therefore, it can be placed in the system log-in script. Figure 22-1 shows the submenus for the options on USER MENU where appropriate. Two options, Logout and User Session Information, execute commands directly.

The complete script file for the menu system is as follows:

```
%U S E R M E N U, 5, 20, 0
User Session Information
        WHOAMI /A
        PAUSE
        USERLIST
        PAUSE
        MAP
        PAUSE
Applications
        %Applications
Directory Listings
        %Display Directories
File Listings
        %File Listings for Current User
Printer Commands
        %Printer Commands
NetWare Utilities
        %NetWare Utilities
Logout
        !logout
%Applications
WP - Run Microsoft Word from Public Data Directory
        G:
        WORD
```

WU - Run Microsoft Word from Users Personal Directory
     F:
     WORD
DP - Run dBASE IV from Public Data Directory
     H:
     DBASE
DU - Run dBASE IV from Users Personal Directory
     F:
     DBASE
LP - Run Lotus from Public Data Directory
     I:
     123
LU - Run Lotus from Users Personal Directory
     F:
     123
%Display Directories
Complete System Directory Listing
     NDIR \ DO SUB
     PAUSE
Users Directory Listing
     NDIR \ DO SUB OW=%USER%
     PAUSE
Specific Directory & Subdirectory Listing
     NDIR @1"Drive/Path" DO SUB
     PAUSE
%File Listings for Current User
1. List All Current Users Files
     NDIR \ OW %USER% SO FN SUB FO
     PAUSE
2. List Current Users Files in Specified Directory
     NDIR @1"Drive/path" OW %USER% SO FN FO
     PAUSE
3. List Files in Subdirectories of Specified Directory
     NDIR @1"Drive/path" OW %USER% SO FN SUB FO
     PAUSE
4. List All Users Files Matching Specified "String"
     NDIR @1"Drive/Path" FN @2"String with wildcards" SO FN OW %USER% SUB FO
     PAUSE
5. List All Users Files Created Before Specified Date
     NDIR @1"Drive/Path" CR BEF @2"Date" SO FN OW %USER% SUB FO
     PAUSE

6. List All Users Files Created On Specified Date
    NDIR @1"Drive/Path" CR @2"Date" SO FN OW %USER% SUB FO
    PAUSE
7. List All Users Files Created After Specified Date
    NDIR @1"Drive/Path" CR AFT @2"Date" SO FN OW %USER% SUB FO
    PAUSE
8. Print Files Created Before Specified Date (Cleanup list)
    NDIR \ CR BEF @1"Date" OW %USER% SO CR SUB > DIRTEMP.DAT
    NPRINT DIRTEMP.DAT D
%Printer Commands
Show Current Printer Status
    PSTAT
    PAUSE
Show Current CAPTURE Status
    CAPTURE SH
    PAUSE
Set Network Printing On (CAPTURE)
    CAPTURE L=1 TI=2 NAM = %USER% NFF
Set Local Printing On (ENDCAP)
    ENDCAP L=1
%NetWare Utilities
Session Management
    Session
File Management
    Filer
System Configuration
    Syscon

You can easily locate the code for each submenu of this system by finding the lines with percent signs in the first character position. The code for the main menu starts at the top and goes through to the !logout command. This special command is used with the exclamation point to execute a system log-out.

Note in the main menu block that the User Session Information option directly executes the six commands that follow it. These are the WHOAMI, USERLIST, and MAP commands, with the PAUSE command placed between each to buffer the screen display. The remaining lines in this block display the menu selections and execute the jumps to other parts of the menu script. These are covered in the following sections under their header names.

Note: Keep in mind that the order of the menu selections in the menu script file are rearranged in alphabetical order by the MENU command.

Applications Submenu

The Applications submenu is displayed when a user makes the corresponding selection on the main menu. Locate the block of code that starts with %Application and ends with the 123 command just above the %Display Directories line. This code produces the Applications submenu shown in Figure 22-1. There are several interesting points here. First, the menu is sorted in the order of the codes placed before each menu item. These codes make it easy for a user to type the letter corresponding to the menu selection they want. Also note that the menu selections allow the user to work with either of the applications from their personal directory or the public directory. Looking at the code for each menu option, you can see that the command logs the user to the appropriately mapped drive. If this menu is to be generic, you must make sure that drive F always maps to a users personal directory and that drive G always maps to the public data directory.

Display Directories Submenu

The Display Directories submenu is used to display directory information, especially for the currently logged users. Take a look at the code section beginning with %Display Directories. Notice that three different versions of the NDIR command are used to display directories. Under the User Directory Listing option, a variable called %USER% is used to place the current users name behind the OWner (OW) option. This will list directories assigned to the current user. The %USER% variable is created in the system log-in script with the following command:

DOS SET USER = "LOGIN_NAME"

Be sure to include this command in your log-in script if you want to use the %USER% variable. It is also used in the file-listing submenu. The line under the Specific Directory & Subdirectory Listing selection requests the

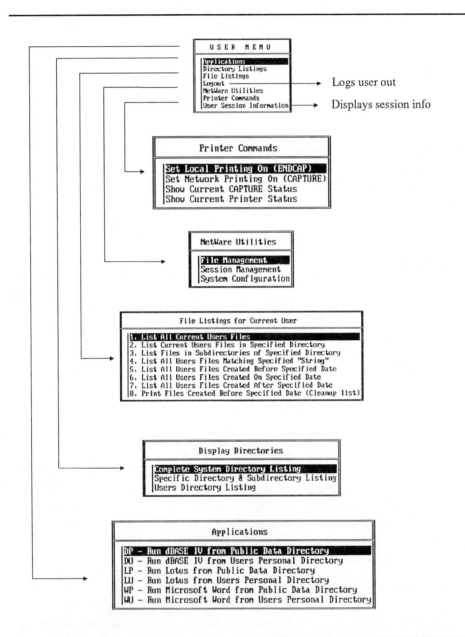

Figure 22-1. A composite of menus from the examples in this chapter

name of the drive or directory to be listed and places the name in the variable @1.

File Listing Menu

The lines in the script for the File Listing submenu start with the section in the text file that reads %File Listings for Current User. The NDIR command is used for each selection to display a list of files for the current user according to specific directories, matching strings, or dates. The selections are numbered so they appear in the specified order in the menu. In this way, the selections to list files by date are grouped together. The last command prints a list of files before a certain date, so users can delete old files from their personal directories or other directories.

Printer Commands Menu Selection

The Printer Commands menu includes a submenu with various printer commands for displaying the current status of a printer or queue, or for setting capture mode on or off. The code for the printer menu starts with the line %Printer Commands.

NetWare Utilities Menu Selection

The menu selection NetWare Utilities displays three of the available NetWare utilities. The commands, which start at the line NetWare Utilities in the menu file, are the same type of commands used in the main menu supplied with NetWare. You can add the other menu utilities to this menu if necessary.

Running MENU on Standalone Computers

MENU can be used on a hard-disk-based standalone computer; it does not require the NetWare operating system to run. You can use the utility to create convenient menus for your DOS environment. Copy the following files to a directory on your hard drive:

SYS$MSG.DAT

SYS$ERR.DAT

SYS$HLP.DAT

IBM$RUN.OVL

MENUPARZ.HLP

MENU.EXE

MENUPARZ.EXE

The file IBM$RUN.OVL must be renamed $RUN.OVL during the copy process or after the files have been copied.

Make sure the CONFIG.SYS file has at least the following parameter settings:

BUFFERS = 20

FILES = 30

NetWare's Accounting System

Accounting System Overview
Installing the Accounting System
Setting Accounting Charge Rates

NetWare's accounting system allows you to track the log-in and log-out activity of every user and thus to track how system resources are being used on the system. You can use this information to evaluate the quantity and quality of resources available to users. You can also use the accounting feature to monitor users' use of the resources and possibly charge them for their use. In most cases, educational institutions or time-sharing services would need to track a user's use of a system's resources and then charge the user for usage time.

Accounting System Overview

The accounting system is not initially installed when NetWare is brought up and running for the first time. The network supervisor must install the option before it begins tracking system usage. In most cases, this option should be selected because the information that is tracked can be very useful. Although accounting is typically associated with billing users for the time and resources they use on the system, NetWare's accounting system can provide other useful information.

If charge rates are not established, the accounting system still tracks user log-ins and log-outs in its most basic form. In addition, system usage is logged so supervisors can look at the usage logs at any time to determine exactly how resources are being used and by what users. Supervisors may use this information when considering the addition of new equipment and justifying their purchases with management. If it can be shown that a system is maximized, management is more likely to approve additional purchases.

The accounting system charges users for their time or resource they use with a point system. Points can have monetary value or they can be thought of as "tokens" or "game money" that users can spend. In this way a supervisor may allocate a certain number of points to a temporary user. If a user's points become depleted, the supervisor may freely grant the user more points, but at the same time the supervisor is made aware of the amount of time and system resources the temporary person is using. Points are like credit that can be limited or unlimited, depending on how the supervisor needs to manage the system.

Be careful when allocating points or placing limits on user's accounts. If users know they are reaching their limit, they may actually become less productive on the system. Never limit a system's resources when plenty are available since this may cut back on productivity. However, some networks may have a limited number of workstations for a large number of users. It may be beneficial to put limits on some user's accounts, as well as their access rights. In this way you can prevent users from wasting time on the system and at the same time, through the accounting reports, you can see how a system is being used.

An educational site is a good example of where the accounting system can be put to use. Students are given a certain amount of resources and charged for the resources they use. A report is produced on a regular basis (for example, at the end of each semester) and students are charged according to this report. Conversely, students may buy a block of usage time and space at the beginning of the school term. When the block runs out, they must buy more. Students who are aware of their limits will be more productive on the system and waste less of its resources.

Often it is hard to determine exactly what to charge for account usage or even to determine how much each resource is used. The best strategy is to establish a test period by installing the accounting feature right away, and then giving all users unlimited credit while you track their usage. At the end of the test period, you can check back with the accounting feature to see the usage of the system.

Types of Accounting

The accounting feature allows several different options to be used. Read through this section to determine which is right for your network. Keep in mind that the term "charges" does not necessarily refer to monetary charges. Charges can also be thought of as tracking units or "game money" that can help you get a handle on the amount of time and resources each user is using and the entire system is providing.

User log-in and log-out tracking is automatically selected when the accounting feature is installed. Whenever a user logs in or out of the server, an entry is made in the accounting file, but no charges are incurred.

Each user has an account of charges for the system resources they use. Each file server designated as a chargeable system makes entries into users' accounts. A special server designated only for printing might be another chargeable type of system.

Charges incurred by users fall into two main groups: those that use the servers' disk file space and those based on work performed by the server. If charges are to be made for the disk space, a rate must be established, and you as the supervisor must specify how often and at what times the file server should measure the disk space accessed by the user. Charges for the amount of work performed by a server can be put in one of four categories; you can charge using one or all of these methods:

- The amount of time a user is logged on the file server

- The amount of information read from the file-server disk

- The amount of information written to the file-server disk

- The number of requests made to the file server for services

These topics will be covered in more detail later. For now it's a good idea to get the accounting system started so you can begin a test period for tracking the usage of the system.

Installing the Accounting System

If NetWare has just been installed or you know the accounting feature has not yet been initialized, you can do so now. The accounting feature must be installed before it can track log-ins and log-outs, and before you can use it to charge users for resources.

Type the following command to start the SYSCON menu utility:

SYSCON

At the SYSCON main menu, select Accounting and press ENTER. In a moment, the following screen appears.

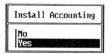

Select the Yes option to install the accounting feature on the current server, and then press ENTER.

Once the accounting feature is installed, the new Accounting menu appears as shown:

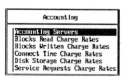

All accounting records will now be placed in a new file called NET$ACCT.DAT, which is stored in the SYS:SYSTEM directory for security reasons.

Removing the Accounting System

If you need to uninstall the accounting feature for any reason, you can select the Accounting Servers option from the menu to see a list of servers currently set up to perform accounting. Each of these servers must be removed before the option to remove the accounting system appears. Highlight each server, or use F5 (Mark) to select all servers; then press the DEL key. Once the servers are removed, a confirmation box appears asking if you want to remove the accounting feature. Highlight Yes and press ENTER to remove accounting.

Activating Accounting on Other Servers

The supervisor is allowed to establish a server's right to charge for its services. If you installed the accounting feature on a server, that server automatically is set to start charging for services.

If other servers exist, such as disk subsystems, you can establish accounting to track the usage of those systems as well. For example, another department may have a disk that holds accounting programs and data. You may want to authorize users in a department other than accounting to use this server and then track their usage. In this way you can track interdepartmental expenses or interdepartmental use of the accounting department's disk system, which may be required for security reasons.

Start the SYSCON menu utility and select Accounting from the main menu. At the Accounting menu select Accounting Servers. A menu similar to the following appears:

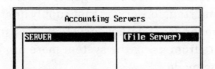

Press INS to display the Select Server Type menu, which shows the types of servers available. Highlight the type of server you want authorized to charge and press INS. In the Other Servers list, highlight the server you want to authorize to charge and press ENTER. Perform this step for each server, or user the F5 (Mark) key to select multiple servers at once. When you are done, press ESC to exit.

To revoke an existing accounting servers right to charge, use the DEL key to remove the server you no longer want to charge from the Accounting Servers menu.

Setting Accounting Charge Rates

You must determine the types of charges you want to make for services incurred by a user and the rate at which you want to charge the user for the services. In addition, you must set up an initial account balance and view the existing accounting information, either to help establish the initial rates or to bill users for usage.

Types of Charge Rates

The remaining selections on the Accounting menu are used to set the charge rates for the accounting feature. Each option is described in the following sections.

Blocks-Read Charge Rates

The Blocks Read option is used to set the charge rates for the amount of information read from the server drive. This is not the same as the charge for storing blocks on the disk, which is covered later under "Disk-Storage Time Charge Rates." Charges are specified in half-hour increments and are assigned per block read, with one block equal to 4096 bytes or 4K.

Each read from the drive is charged to the user's account. The Blocks Read option is important for servers that supply information to other users, such as an on-line service or database system. Keep in mind that this option may inhibit users from using the system more productively if they know charges are being made.

Blocks-Written Charge Rates

The Blocks Written option is similar to the Blocks Read option, except that users are charged for the amount of information written to the disk rather than read from the disk. Charges for blocks written to disk are not the same as charges for blocks of disk storage. Charges are specified in half-hour increments and are assigned per block written, with one block equal to 4096 bytes or 4K.

Each write to the drive is charged to the user's account. Be careful when using this option since some programs write to the disk continuously. You would be unfairly charging users of the program. In addition, users may be less productive if they know they are being charged for disk space. On the other hand, the feature may keep users from storing unnecessary files on the disk or induce them to remove old files.

Connect-Time Charge Rates

The Connect Time option charges users for the amount of time they are logged into the server. This option is the most obvious and easily understood charge for a user. It charges users for each half hour of connection time. It is important to consider the type of user and the resources available on the system before establishing this rate, however. If network usage is high, you may want to charge a higher rate to ensure that users do not tie up the system for too long, or that users are more efficient with the tasks they perform on the system. This may not be appropriate for some systems, however, especially if the system is new and there are many first-time users.

Disk-Storage-Time Charge Rates

The Disk Storage Time option allows you to set up charge rates for each block of disk storage. A block is 4096 bytes or 4K. A charge rate is established for every half-hour increment of disk storage used and is assigned on a block-day basis, which measures the number of blocks stored in a day.

If the network has limited disk storage, charges can be established to encourage users to be more efficient in the way they store files and to keep their storage area clear of unnecessary files.

Service-Request Charge Rates

The Service Request option is used to establish charge rates for use of the server in general. Every time a request is made to the server for any operation, the user is charged. Charge rates are specified in half-hour increments, and the user is charged per request received. Users are charged from the moment they log on to the moment they log off.

Establishing Charge Rates

Supervisors on each server can establish the charge rates for their server only. If your network uses a server controlled by another supervisor, charge rates on that server are controlled by its supervisor.

The ATOTAL command can be used to view the total usage for each service and can be used to help determine the charge rates for accounting. Supervisors should run this command after an initial test period to evaluate system usage before establishing the actual charge rates. The PAUDIT command is used to view the system accounting records in detail. Since the NET$ACCT.DAT file becomes quite large, you should view its contents periodically or compile it with the appropriate accounting application (available from third-party developers), and then remove it from the system. A new file will be created by the accounting system.

After viewing the accounting totals provided by the ATOTAL command, you should have a good idea how many services are being used. You can then begin establishing charges. Charges are calculated with the following formula:

$$\frac{\text{(Total you want to charge for a service)}}{\text{(Estimated total usage of a service)}} = \frac{\text{(Charge rate multiplier)}}{\text{(Charge rate divisor)}}$$

For example, assume you are trying to determine the charge rate for block reads and you have determined that 100,000 blocks were read. Now assume you have determined that this usage is typical and that $500 per week is sufficient income for it. Now assume that the points are equivalent to 1 cent. Convert the $500 weekly charge to cents to establish the proper multiplier/divisor formula, which would be calculated in the following way:

$$\frac{50,000}{100,000} = \frac{1}{2}$$

This is the ratio that will be placed in the charge screen for blocks read. Using the charge screen that appears when you select one of the Accounting menu charge rates options, you can establish different charge rates for each time of the day. An example is shown in the following illustration:

```
                                           Sun  Mon  Tue  Wed  Thu  Fri  Sat
              Blocks Read Charge Rates   8:00am  1    1    1    1    1    1    1
                                         8:30am  1    1    1    1    1    1    1
                                         9:00am  1    1    1    1    1    1    1
   Sunday                                 9:30am  1    1    1    1    1    1    1
   0:00 am To 0:29 am                    10:00am  1    1    1    1    1    1    1
                                         10:30am  1    1    1    1    1    1    1
   Rate  Charge     Rate  Charge         11:00am  1    1    1    1    1    1    1
    1  No Charge     11                  11:30am  1    1    1    1    1    1    1
    2                12                   12:00pm  1    1    1    1    1    1    1
    3                13                   12:30pm  1    1    1    1    1    1    1
    4                14                    1:00pm  1    1    1    1    1    1    1
    5                15                    1:30pm  1    1    1    1    1    1    1
    6                16                    2:00pm  1    1    1    1    1    1    1
    7                17                    2:30pm  1    1    1    1    1    1    1
    8                18                    3:00pm  1    1    1    1    1    1    1
    9                19                    3:30pm  1    1    1    1    1    1    1
   10                20                    4:00pm  1    1    1    1    1    1    1
         (Charge is per block)            4:30pm  1    1    1    1    1    1    1
```

Assigning Charges for Blocks Read, Blocks Written, Connect Times, and Service Requests

The charges for blocks read, blocks written, connect times, and service requests are all assigned in a similar way. Select either one of the rate options from the Accounting menu, and a screen similar to the previous illustration appears. The screen shows how much the file server charges for each request that is made by a workstation. The charge is shown for each half hour during the week, and you can vary the amount charged by supplying a different charge value. Charges are assigned by blocks of 4096 bytes.

To assign charge rates to a specific time of the day or week, press F5 (Mark) and use the arrow keys to highlight the exact area to be given a specific time charge. When the total area is highlighted, press ENTER. The following Select Charge Rate screen appears:

You can select the existing charge rate, which is No Charge, or you can define a new charge rate by selecting Other Charge Rate from the screen. The following New Charge Rate screen appears:

In this screen you can enter the multiplier/divisor rate you established for the particular service you have selected and the times you have selected. Using the previous example, you would enter **1** as the multiplier and **2** as the divisor.

Assigning Disk-Storage Charge Rates

Disk-storage rates are assigned according to how often the system should charge for the disk space used. For example, assume you have determined with ATOTAL that 500,000 blocks of space are being used, and you want to charge $1000 for that space. Assuming that each charge point is equal to 1 cent, the $1000 weekly charge is converted to 100,000. The following formula produces the multiplier and divisor required when setting charge rates:

$$\frac{100,000 = 1}{500,000 = 5}$$

You can now open the Disk Storage Charge Rate screen and assign the rate charges. This screen specifies how much the file server charges for each block (blocks are measured in 4096 bytes or 4K) of storage on the disk for one day. The file server checks the disk-storage space every half hour and charges for all the disk storage used in the last half hour according to the rate specified.

To assign charge rates to specific time of the day or week, press the F5 (Mark) key and use the arrow keys to highlight exactly the area to be given a specific time charge. When the total area is highlighted, press ENTER. The Select Charge Rate screen appears.

You can select the existing charge rate, which is No Charge, or you can define a new charge rate by selecting Other Charge Rate from the screen. The New Charge Rate screen appears. In this screen you can enter the multiplier/divisor rate you established for the particular service you have selected and the times selected. Using the example rate, you would enter **1** as the multiplier and **5** as the divisor.

Establishing a User's Account Balance

The supervisor may want to assign an account balance to each user to provide some limits on the amount of system resources they can use. Account balances can be unlimited if the supervisor only wants to monitor the use of the system for each user. Caution should be taken when assigning strict balances to users, because the system may log them out if their account balance is expended or comes close to a zero balance.

To assign account balances, start the SYSCON menu utility and select Supervisor Options from the main menu. Highlight Default Account Balance/Restrictions and press ENTER. Press DOWN ARROW to Account Balance at the bottom of the screen, and enter the default account balance you want to assign to users. The account balance should be specified in points, similar to those used on the accounting screen. In this way users are charged for each point according to the rates you specify, as discussed in the last section.

You can also specify additional credit by highlighting the options just below the Account Balance field. You can allow unlimited credit by highlighting Allow Unlimited Credit and entering **Yes**. You can assign a specified amount of credit by entering **No** in the Allow Unlimited Credit field and then entering a balance in the Low Balance Limit field. If you enter a negative number in the Low Balance Field, users still receive services until the charges have been used up. Entering a positive number in the field always leaves some value in the field. Users can then go to the supervisor and request additional services.

You can also assign account balances to individual users by selecting User Information on the SYSCON main menu, and then selecting a user from the User Names list and highlighting Account Balance from the User Information screen. The procedure for assigning an individual user balance is the same as described in the previous paragraphs.

Viewing the Accounting File

The ATOTAL and PAUDIT commands are used to view the accounting files. Supervisors must transfer to the SYS:SYSTEM directory or map a search drive to it before the commands can be executed. Both commands read and display information from the NET$ACCT.DAT file stored in the SYS:SYSTEM directory. ATOTAL lists totals only and can be used to view the way resources are used when establishing rates or determining new rate values.

The PAUDIT command is used to view the log-in and log-out activities of the server, or to view the resources that have been used. This file can be quite large, so the following command may be necessary to view it one page at a time. The first command redirects the screen display to a file.

PAUDIT > PAUDIT.DAT

The next command directs the file to the printer for hard copy print out:

NPRINT PAUDIT.DAT

The next command can be used to view the file one page at a time on the screen:

MORE < PAUDIT.DAT

After you have viewed the accounting information, you may want to delete the NET$ACCT.DAT file to open up space on the hard drive. The accounting system immediately begins to build a new file.

Note: Third-party applications are required to compile the accounting information into user billings. Check with your dealer for suitable applications.

Backing Up
And Archiving the Server

Back-Up Methods
Archiving to Local Drives with NetWare Commands
Archiving and Backing Up to Other Servers
with NetWare Commands
Archiving and Restoring from Local Drives
Archiving and Restoring to Network Drives

Blessed are the pessimists
for they have made back-ups
—Anonymous

We should all pause a few moments in silence for those users and supervisors who have lost data, and possibly their jobs as a result. Then take a few moments to consider the amount of data on your own server and the last time you backed it up. A week's worth of files and changes may be more valuable to your company than the entire LAN system put together, when you consider replacement costs and whether the data can even be replaced. It's enough to make you think about doing continuous real-time back-ups.

You might also want to consider what you would do if someone outright stole your file server, or if it were lost in a fire. Considering all this, there is no doubt that you should do back-ups. How and when you do these back-ups is the topic of this chapter.

One thing to get straight right away is the difference between archives and back-ups. In most cases, an *archive* is considered a permanent back-up to a specific media, whereas a *back-up* is a temporary back-up to a reusable media. To clarify, an archive might consist of data that is no longer required on the server, but must be kept for a number of years for accounting reasons. Back-ups are the nightly or weekly back-ups to disks or tapes. The media used for back-ups also points out the differences. Archives are made on more permanent physical media, such as optical disks, and then stored in an extremely safe area, such as a fireproof safe. Back-ups can be made to tape or disk, a media that wears out after a certain amount of usage but is inexpensive to replace. Since back-ups are performed almost continuously, it is necessary to replace the media often.

Although this chapter will concentrate mainly on back-ups, most of the commands and techniques covered here can also be used to make permanent archives of your data. Once an archive is made the data can be removed from the server hard drive to free up space.

Back-up Methods

There are several methods used to back-up the information on the server. The first is the back-up of files to disks and can be handled with the NetWare commands covered at the end of this chapter. Another method uses the NetWare commands to back-up server files to a hard drive or disks in a workstation. Other methods include back-up to tape systems, optical disks, and an archive server. Each back-up method will be covered in this section, except those using NetWare back-up commands. These will be covered in the final section of the chapter.

With any back-up method, you must establish a back-up strategy. Part of this strategy should include a test run of your back-ups, including a full restore to make sure you actually can use your server once it has been reestablished from the back-up sets. Here is a list of other things to consider:

- Back-ups should be created on two completely separate sets of disks or tapes. The sets should then be rotated every other day or week, depending on your strategy. In this way if one set is defective you can always revert to the previous set. The smaller the interval between back-ups, the less data you must reenter to restore the system to its pre-crash state.

- A back-up strategy should include a procedure to move back-up sets off-site in case of fire or other problems. Keep back-up sets in fireproof safes. Use multiple back-up sets so you can rotate sets to off-site locations. Keep in mind that some fireproof safes do not provide enough temperature protection to keep disks or tapes from warping or melting.

- A master back-up of the entire system should be created at regular intervals, for example, every Friday. Intermediate sets can then be created during the week. Only new files or files that have changed need to be backed up to the intermediate sets. This strategy makes disk back-up methods practical. Files created under NetWare have attributes that indicate whether they have not been backed up, such as new or changed files. You then can establish a strategy that backs up only these files, thus reducing back-up time and disk or tape requirements.

- Consider how a back-up set might be degraded. For example, a power outage during an actual back-up may render the back-up set useless; you would then need to rely on the most recent back-up set, assuming you have more than one.

- Be sure to back up hidden files, such as the NetWare bindery files NET$BIND.SYS and NET$BVAL.SYS. They reside in the SYS:SYSTEM directory and are normally hidden and kept secure from users other than the supervisor. The files contain user definitions such as names, passwords, group memberships, and so on. All back-up software should be "NetWare aware" and capable of backing up these hidden files. If not, use the LARCHIVE command discussed later in this chapter to copy the files to a disk or local hard drive.

- Be sure to keep track of exactly when the last back-up was made. Then you will know what data needs to be reentered prior to the system crash.

As previously mentioned, it is important to have a copy of the NetWare bindery files on hand. However, you should consider how secure your system will be if copies of these files are available outside the "domain" of the NetWare server. These files normally are stored under the full protection of the NetWare security system. It is important, therefore, to secure them from possible theft by those who may want to gain illegal access to your system by debugging the code in the files. Store these file back-ups in a safe and secure place.

Hard-Drive Back-up

The NetWare archiving commands give you the ability to back up to a hard drive on a workstation, which is a vast improvement over floppy-disk methods. You may want to consider dedicating a hard drive and workstation to this task. In addition, back-ups can be made to another server on the same network. This server allows you to completely switch to that server to run various applications and data if the primary server should go down. Methods for backing up to hard drives and other servers on the network are covered in the NetWare command section of this chapter.

Tape Back-up Systems

Tape systems that use cartridge and cassette-type media are increasingly popular due to their ease of use and integrity. They can be more practical than floppy-disk back-up methods because most network servers usually have high capacity drives that require too many disks to make reasonable back-ups.

Most tape back-up systems use a quarter-inch tape that comes in lengths of 600 to 1000 feet. Common tape formats include the DC600 streaming tape made popular by 3M. The DC600 cartridge can store 60MB to 150MB of data in a cartridge that fits in a jacket pocket. The maximum capacity of the tape is 320MB, using extended length tapes. Another common format, also standardized by 3M, is the DC2000 streaming tape. This tape cartridge is about the size of an audio cassette tape and stores 40MB, 60MB, or 80MB of data. The DC2000 is a little lower in cost than the DC600.

Still another method of tape back-up is the digital audio tape (DAT) which has storage capacities in the gigabyte range. The storage method used by DATs is different than that used by standard tapes such as the DC600 and DC2000 streaming tape methods. Streaming tape systems record all the way to the end of the tape on one track, and then reverse and record on the next track. This switch and reverse method is used for up to 32 tracks on a quarter-inch tape. DATs use a combination of tape and head movements to record, using a method called *helical scan.* Data is recorded in diagonal strips on the tape as it passes over a cylindrical drum containing several read-write heads. This method compresses data storage, which increases capacity and tape throughput simultaneously. Since data is compressed, it takes less time to scan a tape when you are trying to locate a file.

Most tape back-up systems make two different back-up methods available. The first is *image back-up,* which quickly copies everything on the hard drive exactly as it is stored, including file fragmentations, marked bad sectors, and files. *File-by-file back-ups* record files from the server to tape one file at a time. Fragmented files are gathered from their scatter blocks and written to the tape in a contiguous arrangement. File-by-file back-ups are preferable to image back-ups for two important reasons: you can restore single or multiple files and files can be restored to a new or replacement drive. Image back-up sets may write valuable data to marked bad blocks on the new drive, because the image is not aware of these bad blocks. Likewise, bad sectors from the original drive are restored to the new drive, even though the sectors on the new drive may not be bad.

When choosing or using tape back-up systems, make sure that the units back up the NetWare bindery and other hidden files, then make sure those files are stored in a safe, secure place. It also may be necessary to back up the system while files are in use. Find out how the tape system deals with open files, and then take appropriate action to ensure those files are backed up properly. A tape back-up system may wait until a file is closed before backing it up. Tape back-ups may also include timing software that lets you back up at a predefined time during off-hours. For example, the tape back-up could automatically take place at 3:00 AM.

Designate a user to be responsible for changing tapes and making them secure. This may include taking the tapes off-site. Also make sure tapes are replaced on a regular basis, because tapes are susceptible to stretching, aging, and other conditions. Date the tapes and throw them out after the manufacturer's recommended usage time has been exceeded.

Optical Disks

As mentioned previously, optical disk back-up is excellent for archiving of data files. The disks have a shelf life of many years and are not susceptible to problems inherent with magnetic media. Two types of technology are currently available: Write-Once-Read-Many (WORM) disks and Write-Many-Read-Many (WMRM) disks. Since optical disks have capacities in the gigabyte range, it may be a long time before a single disk is filled to capacity, so the WORM disk is a viable option for both back-ups and archiving strategies. Even a drive in the 300MB range can be completely backed up several times to a single optical disk. The WMRM disks may be more practical if your back-up strategy is oriented more to back-ups than archiving, since the disk can be written to and erased many times.

One thing to consider about both technologies is that they are slow. A typical file write to an optical disk may be slower than writing the same file to a floppy disk. However, the purpose of writing files to optical disks is different, which makes them viable. The process of "burning" data to the disk with the laser takes more time to write than traditional magnetic write methods. Recent drives are bringing the speed of writing data to a more acceptable level, but price is also a consideration.

Optical disks also provide an additional feature not available with traditional back-up and archiving methods. A single box with multiple-disk capability can be kept on-line, making vast amounts of data available to users at all times. Although this data may be slower to get at, it still is available to those users who need it. One drive is capable of holding up to 26 gigabytes of data on removable disks that can each hold 400MB. Disks can be changed in a matter of seconds, making additional on-line information available to users.

Archive Servers

Archive servers are full-sized computers with large hard drives. They are attached to the network as a server with the sole purpose of maintaining a constant back-up of the network file server in real time. To do this, archive servers work in the background, accessing and copying files from the server in the same way any user might access files. If files are opened, the archive server may skip them, only to return at a later time to back them up.

Back-up scripts can be created by supervisors and users who need sets of files backed up on a regular basis. These scripts can be designed to play at any time. For example, a user can start the back-up script after modifying a set of files, or designate an after-hours run- time for the script.

Since the archive server works continuously in the background, there is no need to down the server or make sure users are logged off to perform back-ups. The same is true when performing restores. A supervisor is called on less to assist with back-ups and restores because the script files provide all of the necessary commands users need to perform their own back-ups.

Archiving to Local Drives With NetWare Commands

The NetWare utilities described in this section are designed to help you back up and archive files from network directories to floppy disks, local hard drives, or directories on other servers attached to the network. The utilities can be executed from the command line.

Each of these commands except MACBACK will be described in the sections titled "Archiving and Backing Up to Other Servers with NetWare Commands." MACBACK is covered in *NetWare for Macintosh: Supervisor's Supplement*, a manual that comes with NetWare for Macintosh.

NCOPY—Network COPY

The NCOPY command can be used to back up data to another file server, if one is available on the system. This command is especially convenient since files can be quickly copied to another hard drive, as opposed to a directory on the same drive (NARCHIVE), local floppy disks, or hard drives (LARCHIVE). This method allows instant use of the files by simply switching to the destination drive or mapping a drive to it.

LARCHIVE—Local drive ARCHIVE

The LARCHIVE command is used to archive DOS files to local disk drives such as floppy disks or hard drives. The files can be restored with LRESTORE.

LRESTORE—Local drive RESTORE

This command restores files from local drives such as floppy disks and hard drives to network drives. The restored files must be files archived with LARCHIVE.

MACBACK

MACBACK allows back-up of Macintosh files on NetWare versions that support the Macintosh environment. Details of this file are supplied with the NetWare Macintosh support software.

NARCHIVE—Network ARCHIVE

This command is used to archive DOS files to network directories. It creates a log report called ARCHIVE.LOG. The related restore command is NRESTORE.

NRESTORE—Network RESTORE

The NRESTORE command is used to restore archived files to a network drive. The related archive command is NARCHIVE.

Archiving and Backing Up to Other Servers With NetWare Commands

Backing up files to another file server offers a quick and easy way to back up a main server on a regular basis. This can be done whenever files are changed, either daily or weekly. The files on the alternate server are immediately available for access. A restore is not required. In fact, the alternate server can be set up in the same way as the primary server. Assuming regular back-ups have been made from the primary to the alternate, users could switch to the alternate in an emergency and run programs and data on it with little down-time. Some reentry of data may be required for files that were not backed up since the last back-up, but back-ups can be as often as every hour, if necessary.

Note: The frequency of back-ups may be inhibited if files are in use. It may be possible to back up only during off-hours.

Supervisors can make it easy for users to manage their own back-ups by attaching the alternate server and mapping its directories in the system log-in script or in the user log-in script. Users can then use the NCOPY command to back up to the mapped drive with little knowledge that the drive is another server or the need to know the command syntax for accessing the server. Menus can even be created with specific back-up commands. These menus can be designed for each user or for the person who is in charge of back-ups. An example menu will be discussed later in this section.

The steps for backing up to other servers are as follows:

1. Attach to the appropriate file server with the ATTACH command.

2. If you have supervisor status on both servers, you won't have problems copying files from one server directory to another. If this routine is being established for another user, make sure the user has the appropriate rights to copy files from one server into the destination directory of another server. They need at least the Read, Write, and Create rights.

3. Map the destination directories on the attached server to which files will be backed up.

4. Issue the NCOPY commands.

The following series of commands could be used to back up a set of accounting data files on the primary server to a directory called SERVER2/ SYS:BACKUPS/ACCTG or the alternate server called SERVER2. Assume the source files are in a directory mapped to drive P on the primary server.

1. Issue the following ATTACH command for user FRED:

   ATTACH SERVER2/FRED

   Fred has all of the necessary rights in drive P and SERVER2/SYS:BACKUPS/ACCTG to perform the back-up.

2. The destination directory is mapped as drive Q with the following command:

   MAP Q:=SERVER2/SYS:BACKUPS/ACCTG

3. The NCOPY command is issued from drive P as follows:

   NCOPY P:*.* Q:

Automating Back-up

The entire back-up routine can be placed in a log-in script or included in a menu created with the MENU command.

For example, you could create a user called BACKUP. The BACKUP user name designates who is assigned to perform back-ups. The commands for performing the back-up are located in the log-in script for the user BACKUP so that the back-up commands are automatically executed when the user logs on. When the back-up is completed, the user is immediately logged off.

The following is an example of the series of commands you would place in the log-in script for BACKUP and assumes that the alternate server is already attached with commands in the system log-in script:

```
MAP P:=SERVER1/SYS:ACCTDATA
MAP Q:=SERVER2/SYS:BACKUPS/ACCTG
WRITE "Press any key to start the back-up."
PAUSE
#NCOPY P:*.* Q:
EXIT "LOGOUT"
```

The commands in the batch file are the same as those discussed earlier, except that they are immediately executed from the log-in script. The user BACKUP should have all the rights to the mapped P and Q directories. If the system log-in script executes drive mappings and other commands not intended for the BACKUP user, you can place the following command at the beginning of the system log-in script to prevent the execution of those commands when BACKUP logs on.

IF "LOGIN_NAME" = "BACKUP" EXIT

Note: In order for the EXIT command to work on non-IBM systems, the command PCCOMPATIBLE must be placed before it in the system log-in script, or the user log-in script.

Menu Utility for Backing Up to Other Servers

The MENU command can be used to create back-up menus for a user who logs in with the user name BACKUP. For example, a back-up menu with options similar to those in the following example could be created:

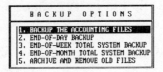

The user performing back-ups has several options to choose from, each of which is automated with the commands that can be placed in menu scripts. The MENU utility offers an excellent way for supervisors to automate the entire back-up process, including the use of screen messages made possible with the MENU variables. See Chapter 22 for more details on MENU.

Archiving and Restoring from Local Drives

The LARCHIVE and LRESTORE commands discussed here are used to back up and restore to local drives, which are the drives located in workstations.

LARCHIVE—Local drive ARCHIVE

The LARCHIVE utility archives files to a local disk drive that can be either a floppy disk or a hard drive. Keep the following in mind when you plan to use LARCHIVE:

- To back up to another volume on the current hard drive, use NARCHIVE.

- To back up to another server on the same network, use NCOPY.

- LARCHIVE does not back up Macintosh files. You must use the MACBACK utility for this; however, it is suggested that LARCHIVE be used before MACBACK. Likewise, LRESTORE should be used before restoring files with MACBACK. When planning your back-up strategies, you may want to consider placing Macintosh files in separate directories.

- The LARCHIVE command must be executed from a mapped drive that is the directory holding the files you want to back up.

- Anyone using the LARCHIVE command must have appropriate access rights in the source file directory. Users already have complete access rights to local destination drives, unless special file/directory-locking software is used on the workstation drives.

- The special security files NET$BIND.SYS and NET$BVAL.SYS located in the SYS:SYSTEM directory can only be backed up (and restored) by the supervisor or supervisor equivalent. These files must be backed up occasionally because they represent the entire security and user structure of the server.

The use of LARCHIVE can be categorized in a number of ways. For example:

- Files in only one directory can be backed up.

- A directory and some or all of its subdirectories can be specified for archiving.

- Files from various directories throughout the directory structure can be specified for archiving.

- Files in a specific volume can be specified.

The LARCHIVE command takes the following form:

LARCHIVE *path* [*mapped drive letter*] SYSTEM

where *path* or *mapped drive letter* is the name of the server directory that contains files to be backed up. The SYSTEM option is used to specify a complete system back-up. Unlike most NetWare command line utilities, which require various options and parameters on the command line, LARCHIVE asks the user for information as it runs. This is convenient for those who can't remember the command syntax.

Note: Since the LARCHIVE command is self-prompting and runs according to the way you answer various queries, LARCHIVE's options are covered under branching topics in the following discussion.

Follow these steps to back up files on a local drive:

1. To start LARCHIVE, type **LARCHIVE** on the command line. For this example, assume you are backing up files in a personal directory mapped to drive F.

2. The following display appears:

```
F:\USERS\JOHN>LARCHIVE
Advanced NetWare LARCHIVE V2.16b -- Archive DOS files to Local Disks
Copyright (c) 1987 Novell, Inc.  All Rights Reserved.

If you want to archive to a floppy disk drive (or other removable media),
   insert a new diskette NOW, before proceeding.

Enter the letter of the LOCAL disk drive on which to archive files:
```

You are asked to enter the local drive that will be *the* destination for the archived files. Type **B** to indicate floppy drive B, and press ENTER.

3. The display asks if you want a log report printed. The log report is a file named ARCHIVE.LOG that is created by LARCHIVE and is stored on the archive disk. A printed log report is useful as a catalog of the archive disk. When the disk is placed in storage, the report can be filed with it for future reference. The archive report is printed at the end of the LARCHIVE session on either the local printer or a network printer, whichever you prefer. If you select printing, the following display appears.

```
Do you want to print a log report of this session? (Y/N) Y
    Print to Local printer(L) or Network spooler(N)? (L/N) N
Select network printer: (0 - 1) 0
    Number of copies: (1-9) 1
```

The ARCHIVE.LOG file contains the date and time of the LARCH-IVE session, the directory path of each directory in the archive set, and a list of each archived file. You can print the ARCHIVE.LOG at any time using the NPRINT command.

4. The next prompt displayed by LARCHIVE is "Do you want to save directory rights and trustee lists? (Y/N)." Type **Yes** if you want to archive the maximum rights mask and the trustee list for each directory from which you archive files.

5. If you are logged in as the supervisor, the prompt "Do you want to archive the system's user and group definitions? (Y/N)" is displayed. Select this prompt to archive the server's security files NET$BIND.SYS and NET$BVAL.SYS in the SYS:SYSTEM directory. These files contain the lists of users, groups, passwords, security equivalences, full names, and ID numbers.

6. The next prompt to appear is "Select specific directories to be backed up?". If you want to select the specific directories to back up, type **Yes**. LARCHIVE displays the name of each directory and asks if you want to back it up. If you want to back up all directories, type **No**.

7. The next screen asks you what type of back-up mode you want to use for the directories. This may include all directories or the one you are selecting, depending on how you answered the last question.

   Select 1 to back up all files in all directories or the selected directory. Select 2 to back up only modified files. In some cases, you may have a third selection that allows you to back up specific files.

8. If you chose option 1 or 2 in the last step, you can then select specific files, ignore specific files, or back up all files. If you select option 1 or 2, you can enter a list of files to back up. The list can include wildcard characters and have up to 50 specifications. For example, the following list backs up all files that end in COM and EXE.

```
*.COM
*.EXE
```

9. Press ENTER to complete your selection. The LARCHIVE program backs up the files on the selected disk drive. When done, the message "Archive Session Completed" is displayed.

Using the LARCHIVE SYSTEM Option

The SYSTEM option allows you to archive files from various directories and subdirectories throughout the directory structure of the server. You must have supervisor's rights in order to perform a complete system back-up. If you are not a supervisor, you can only back up directories you have rights to.

To start a system back-up, type the following command:

```
LARCHIVE SYSTEM
```

Most of the prompts are similar to those discussed in the previous steps, so you may refer to those steps for assistance.

LRESTORE—Local drive Restore

Use the LRESTORE command to restore files previously archived with the LARCHIVE command. Before issuing the command, map a drive to the file server to which files should be restored. Be sure to include the volume specification if another volume is the target. Users of the command must have Open, Write, Create, Delete, and Search effective rights in the directory where files will be restored. You may want to print or view the ARCHIVE.LOG file created during the LARCHIVE process before restoring files.

The following steps will help you use the LRESTORE command.

1. At the system prompt, type **LRESTORE.**

2. At the prompt "Enter the letter of the LOCAL disk drive from which to restore files:" type the letter of the drive in which you have placed the archive disk.

3. When the prompt "Do you wish to restore security information with the directories? (Y/N)" appears, type **Yes** if you are logged on as the supervisor and you want to restore the security/bindery files. Type **No** if you don't want to restore the files, or press CTRL-BREAK to stop LRESTORE and then log on as the supervisor so you can restore the files.

4. At the prompt "Select Specific directories to be considered for restoration?", type **No** if you want to restore files to all directories and then go to step 5. Type **Yes** to restore files to specific directories. Then you are asked to enter the full names of directories to be restored. Follow the instructions on the screen.

5. The prompt "Specify files to restore to each selected directory? (Y/N)" appears. Type **Yes** to restore each file one by one. If you type **No,** all files are restored and you can skip to the last step.

6. If you typed **Yes** in the previous step, you are asked if you want to back up each directory in turn. Type **Yes** to restore the directory or **No** to go to the next directory.

7. If you typed **Yes** to one of the directory names, you are then asked if you want to restore all files to the directory. Type **Yes** to restore all files. If you type **No,** you are prompted with each filename, one by one.

8. Once the files are restored from all selected directories, you are asked if you want to restore from another disk. Type **Yes** to continue the LRESTORE session and restore files from other disks.

When the LRESTORE session is finished, the "Restore Session Completed" message appears and the DOS prompt returns.

Archiving and Restoring To Network Drives

The NARCHIVE and NRESTORE commands are used to back up to another volume and directory on the current server. The usefulness of these commands is limited since files backed up to the same physical hard drive, as well as the originals, would be lost if the drive were to crash. The commands can be used to place files that are not used often in other directories, or to simply rearrange the directory structure of a drive. You might also want to use the command to place old files out of the way for a period of time until they can be permanently moved to disk, tape, optical disk, or other media.

The operation of NARCHIVE and NRESTORE is functionally the same as LARCHIVE and LRESTORE, except that you are asked for the network volume you want to archive files from or restore files to.

Follow the prompts for LARCHIVE as covered in the previous section if you use NARCHIVE. When requested for the archive directory names, enter the full name, including the server and volume name if necessary, of the directories you want to archive files to.

When restoring files, follow the steps previously given for LRESTORE to respond to the instructions that appear.

System Console Commands

Messaging and Broadcasting
Downing the Server
Workstation-Related Commands
Network Status Commands
Disk-Related Commands

The console commands are entered at the file server to monitor and manage the network. NetWare console commands for controlling the printer were discussed in Chapter 20. This chapter discusses other console commands that can be used to monitor and control the activities of workstations on the network and the way the file server itself is being used.

Dedicated servers are always in the console mode, which is designated by the colon prompt, unless a console command such as MONITOR is running. Those using a nondedicated server as a workstation can type the following command at the server to enter the console mode:

CONSOLE

To return from the console mode to the DOS workstation, type the following command:

DOS

Many of the commands executed at the console, such as the DOWN command used to down the server, should be used only by the supervisor. Therefore, it is important to establish a supervisor log-in password as soon as the system is brought up and running. Many of the commands used at the console can be executed from the FCONSOLE menu utility at a workstation. Chapters 26 and 27 discuss the features of the FCONSOLE command in detail.

Messaging and Broadcasting

The following commands broadcast messages to all users or specific users. Messages should be broadcast before downing the server or disconnecting a workstation from the network.

BROADCAST

The BROADCAST command is used to send messages to every workstation that is currently logged in to the file server. Primarily, it notifies users when a change is to take place on the server or that the server will go down in a certain amount of time.

The command takes the following form:

BROADCAST *message*

where *message* can be a message up to 60 characters long and is not enclosed in quotes. For example, the following message, typed at the console colon prompt, warns users they must log out:

BROADCAST The server will be shut down in 10 minutes!!!

The message appears in line 25 of each user's display. To clear the message, the CTRL-ENTER key sequence can be pressed. If other messages have been sent, the next message is displayed immediately. Messages sent to the console can be cleared with the CLEAR MESSAGE command discussed next.

Note: Users who are logged into remote workstations over communications lines will not receive BROADCAST messages.

CLEAR MESSAGE

The CLEAR MESSAGE command clears messages from the message display area at the bottom of the screen. Invoke the command by typing

CLEAR MESSAGE

SEND

The SEND command sends console messages to specific workstations, unlike the BROADCAST command, which sends messages to all workstations.

The command takes the following form:

SEND *"message"* TO *station#,station#,...*

where *message* is a message up to 40 characters long to send to the workstations indicated by *station#*. More than one station number can be specified, each of which is separated by a comma. Note the following:

- The message must be within quotes.

- Messages are sent to only the stations specified.

- If stations are not specified, the message is sent to all stations.

The USERLIST command in the DOS mode can be used to list each user's workstation number.

Downing the Server

The DOWN command shuts down the file server. Various housekeeping tasks are taken care of before the server is shut down, such as writing the cache buffers to disk from memory. Always make sure users are logged off before issuing the command. You can use the BROADCAST command to display a message to users that all users should log off.

The command is issued by typing

DOWN

Because cache buffers may include important information in memory, a server should never be shut down by simply turning the power switch off. Use the DOWN command to write cache buffers, close all open files, and update the file allocation tables.

Workstation-Related Commands

The following commands can be typed at the server to monitor workstations, clear their connections, or prevent other users from logging on to the system. The commands may be used by the supervisor prior to or after servicing the server.

MONITOR

The MONITOR command displays the system monitor. The display keeps track of all activities at each workstation that is logged on to the server. MONITOR displays a list of files being used by each workstation. If a file cannot be accessed, the supervisor can scan the monitor list to see who is using it. MONITOR can also be used to view the currently logged workstations to determine if it is OK to shut down the system for servicing.

The MONITOR command takes the following form:

MONITOR *station-number*

where *station-number* is the number of a particular workstation to view. Since MONITOR shows only six workstations at a time, the *station-number* option is used only to position a six-panel display within the range of the workstation you specify. If a number is not specified, workstations 1 through 6 are displayed.

Note: The command may need to be re-executed occasionally to update the display.

Note: MONITOR should not be left on when not needed. It requires some of the server's processing time and may slow the system down slightly. Use the OFF command to turn MONITOR off.

At the top of the entire display is a list of the operating system version, server utilization, and the number of disk I/O's pending. Server utilization is a percentage of the file-server processor time used by network requests during the last second. The number indicates how close the file server is to having a full load. The display is updated once every second. The value of disk I/O's pending is the number of cache buffers that have been changed in the file server's memory but have not yet been written to disk.

Each box on the monitor display shows information for the workstation number listed in the upper-left corner of the box. The workstation number is followed by a colon and a space referred to as the *request area.* This area may display messages that indicate the most recent request the workstation has made of the file server. If a workstation has completed a task and all files have been released, this message area will display "End-of-Job."

The *transaction area* is the directory beneath the request area. When a workstation is not engaged in a transaction, this area is blank. "WAITING" may appear in this space if a workstation must wait for a file or a file record to be freed for use.

Beneath the request and transaction area is the *file and stat area.* This area displays the five most recently used files next to a number that represents the DOS task number. The stat heading may have the following indicators listed next to each file:

P   Located in the first column of letters. Indicates that other workstations cannot read the file.

R   Located in the second column of letters. Indicates that the workstation has the file open for a read.

P   Located in the third column of letters. Indicates that other workstations cannot write to the file.

W   Located in the fourth column of letters. Indicates that the workstation has the file open for a write.

Other status indicators may appear as follows.

Pers   Indicates that a file is logged but not locked

Lock   Indicates that a file is locked

If the file server is running SFT NetWare with the Transaction Tracking System (TTS) installed, the following indicators may appear:

T   Located in the first column of letters. Indicates that a transactional flagged file is open.

H   Located in the second column of letters. Indicates that a transactional file is on hold until the transaction is completed.

OFF

The OFF command is used to clear information from the console screen. It is also used to clear the MONITOR screen, which uses the server's processor time and can slow the operation of the system slightly if left on unattended. Invoke the command by typing

OFF

CLEAR STATION

The CLEAR STATION command stops the servicing of a workstation by the server. It normally is used when a workstation crashes but is still holding files open. The command takes the form

CLEAR STATION *nn*

where *nn* is the workstation number that can be determined by using the MONITOR command. For example, to clear workstation 3, you would type the following command at the console:

CLEAR STATION 3

When you issue the CLEAR STATION command, the file server closes all open files for the designated workstation and removes internal tables used by the server to track the station. Drive maps and other session settings are also lost. If a workstation crashes in the middle of a transaction or a file update, and the workstation was cleared, files may be saved incorrectly.

When a workstation is attached to two or more file servers and a drive is mapped to another file server, it is not necessary to reboot DOS and reload the NetWare shell to log in or attach to the file server where the CLEAR STATION command was issued. To log in again, switch to the mapped drive on the other server, and then execute the LOGIN or AT-TACH command to reconnect to the server where CLEAR STATION was issued. Note that the LOGIN or ATTACH command must be accessible, which may require the use of the DOS CD command to reestablish a mapped drive.

DISABLE LOGIN

The DISABLE LOGIN command prevents additional users from logging in to the server when you are attempting to bring it down for service. Invoke the command by typing

DISABLE LOGIN

Workstations already logged into the server will be able to continue working. Use the BROADCAST command to issue a warning to those users that you will be downing the server. To reenable log-in privileges, assuming the server was not brought down completely, issue the ENABLE LOGIN command.

ENABLE LOGIN

The ENABLE LOGIN command restores a workstation's log-in capability. The command normally is used after issuing a DISABLE LOGIN command to prevent new users from logging in so the file server can be serviced.

Invoke the command by typing

ENABLE LOGIN

You need not issue this command if the file-server power was completely reset. The system will be set to enable log-in whenever you bring it back up.

Network Status Commands

The following commands can be used by the supervisor to monitor or change the status of the server itself.

CONFIG

The console command CONFIG displays the hardware configuration for each network supported by the server. Each network interface card installed in the server constitutes a separate network.
Type the following command at the console colon prompt:

CONFIG

The network address, board address, hardware type, and hardware setting are displayed for each board in the server. Note that the hardware settings are not read from the board itself, but are assumed to be the settings made during installation. You may want to view the configuration information when installing additional network boards in the server to avoid hardware interrupt conflicts.

SET TIME

The SET TIME command is used to set the date and time on the file server. The command takes the following form:

SET TIME *month / day / year hour:minute:second* AM/PM

where *month/day/year* is the date and *hour:minute:second* is the time. Both may be set with one command or with separate commands. If only one parameter is set, the other remains unaffected. AM or PM must be specified, unless the time is entered in military format.

When setting the time, separate the hours, minutes, and seconds with colons. The minutes and seconds entry can be omitted; however, a colon must be typed after the hour. Times can be entered in either standard or military format.

TIME

The TIME command displays the time currently set on the server. Invoke the command by typing

TIME

NAME

The NAME command displays the name of the file server. Invoke the command by typing

NAME

The console screen displays the name of the file server in the following format:

This is Server *server name*

VAP

The VAP command displays a list of value-added processes (VAPs) currently loaded in the NetWare operating system. The commands used by each VAP are also listed.

VAPs are applications that run on top of the network operating system. They are loaded when the NetWare server is first started. VAPs normally are used to link third-party processes into the operating system.

These processes might be used to manage print servers or database servers. Invoke the command by typing

VAP

Disk-Related Commands

The following commands are used to monitor or alter the current disk configuration on the server.

DISK (Advanced NetWare Only)

The DISK command is functionally different for Advanced and SFT Net-Ware. If you are using SFT NetWare, refer to the next section.

The DISK command monitors the status of network disk drives and displays which drives are functioning normally and which are not. The command is entered as follows:

DISK

The status of all drives on the network are listed on the screen in two side-by-side blocks, which contain the following information:

- The first column has no heading. It contains the drive number for each drive. This number is used in error messages.

- The cha column indicates the drive channel.

- The con column indicates the controller number of the hard-disk controller board.

- The drv column indicates the physical drive number of the disk drive.

- The stat column indicates the status of the drive, using the following flags:

    "OK" is displayed if the drive is set up for Hot Fix.

"NO HOT" indicates that Hot Fix is not functioning on a disk set up for Hot Fix.

"OFF" indicates that the drive is not operating.

- The IO Err column indicates the number of input/output errors that have occurred on the drive and can be used as an indicator of the reliability of the drive.

- The Free column indicates how many blocks in the drive's Hot Fix Redirection Area are unused.

- The Used column indicates how many blocks have been used in the disk's redirection area.

DISK (SFT NetWare Only)

The DISK command is functionally different for Advanced and SFT NetWare. If you are using Advanced NetWare, refer to the previous section.

The DISK command for SFT NetWare has two variations. The first is used to view the status of drives on the network. The second lists all the volumes on the file server and indicates which physical drive holds each volume.

Type the following command to display the status of all drives on the network:

DISK

The screen displays the drive status in two side-by-side screens with the following headings:

- The first column has no heading. It contains the drive number for each drive. This number is used in error messages.

- The cha column indicates the drive channel.

- The con column indicates the controller number of the hard-disk controller board.

- The drv column indicates the physical drive number of the disk drive.

- The stat column indicates the status of the drive, using the following flags:

  "M-*xx*" indicates the drive is set for mirroring (or duplexing). The number that is displayed (represented here by *xx*) is the number of the other drive in the mirrored pair.

  "D-*xx*" indicates that the drive has been set for mirroring (or duplexing) and is now dead. The number after the D (represented here by *xx*) is the number of the other drive in the mirrored pair now operating without a mirror.

  "OK" is displayed if the drive is set up for Hot Fix but not mirroring or duplexing. A drive will register OK if its mirrored partner has been turned off, because the remaining drive continues to operate normally with Hot Fix.

  "NO HOT" indicates that Hot Fix is not functioning on a disk set up for Hot Fix.

  "OFF" indicates that the drive is not operating.

- The IO Err column indicates the number of input/output errors that have occurred on the drive and can be used as an indicator of the reliability of the drive.

- The Free column indicates how many blocks in the drive's Hot Fix Redirection Area are unused.

- The Used column indicates how many blocks have been used in the disk's redirection area.

The second variation of the DISK command is used to list all the volumes on the file server. This listing shows which physical drive contains each volume. If the volume's drive is one of a mirrored pair, the mirror drive also is indicated. The command is entered with the asterisk, as shown here:

DISK *

The listing shows the volume names, physical drive number, and the mirrored drive number. You can also type the following command to list information about a specific volume. This example lists information about the SYS volume:

DISK SYS

More detailed, self-explanatory information is displayed on the screen.

DISMOUNT

The DISMOUNT command changes a removable volume, such as a disk pack. Although the disk subsystem may contain a switch to physically remove the pack, the DISMOUNT command informs the operating system that the disk has been removed. The related command MOUNT mounts a removable volume. If a volume is already installed, the DISMOUNT command is used to remove the existing volume.

The command takes the form

DISMOUNT PACK *removable volume number*

where *removable volume number* is the number of the volume to be removed, if applicable. The PACK keyword is used to dismount disk packs. A pack may consist of several volumes, each of which is dismounted when the following command is used:

DISMOUNT PACK

Removable volumes should never be removed when they are being accessed by users. Physical damage to the drive may occur.

MOUNT

The MOUNT command is used to change a removable volume, such as a disk pack. After a disk subsystem has been physically mounted in the server or disk subsystem unit, the MOUNT command adds the volume to the server. The related command DISMOUNT removes a removable volume. If a volume is already installed, the UNMOUNT command must be used to remove the existing volume before the new volume can be mounted.

The command takes the form

MOUNT PACK *removable volume number*

where *removable volume number* is the number of the volume to be added if applicable. The PACK keyword is used to mount disk packs. A pack may consist of several volumes, each of which is mounted when the following command is used:

MOUNT PACK

Removable volumes should never be removed when they are being accessed by users. Physical damage to the drive may occur.

REMIRROR (SFT NetWare 286 Only)

Under SFT NetWare, two physical disks can be mirrored into one logical mirrored pair as a way to ensure continuous data integrity, protection, and backup. If one of the drives in the set goes bad, the second drive can be put into place or a new mirrored pair can be established. The UNMIRROR command, covered later in this chapter, disables a set of mirrored drives. The REMIRROR command covered here establishes a new set of mirrored drives.

In most cases one of the disks in a mirrored pair will go bad or begin to show signs of failure. The DISK command monitors the status of a drive. Referring back to the description of the DISK command covered previously, you should take note of the Used column in the Physical Disks Status and Statistics display to determine if a drive is beginning to show signs of wear. The stat column in the DISK display indicates mirrored drives with the designation M followed by the drive number.

Recall that the Used column indicates the number of blocks in the Hot Fix Redirection Area that are being used. As drives wear, sectors begin to fail (become incapable of safely storing data) and the Hot Fix feature redirects the data to blocks in the redirection area. Compare the number of used blocks with the number of blocks that still remain free, as listed in the Free column of the DISK display. The sum of the two columns indicates the total size of the redirection area. If the number of used blocks is approaching 50% of the redirection area, you should consider replacing the drive, especially if it has been in service for some time.

When the REMIRROR command is executed after a new physical drive has been installed, data on the currently operating drive is copied to the new drive. The drives become synchronized with each other once they both hold exactly the same volumes, directory structures and data. Mirroring or duplexing is then restored, and the system can be brought back into operation.

The REMIRROR command takes the following form:

REMIRROR *xx*

where *xx* is the number of the new drive to be remirrored.

Note: This discussion assumes the file server was downed between unmirroring the remirroring drives in order to replace the drive. If the drive was not replaced and the server was not downed, only changed data is updated to the mirrored drive when REMIRROR is executed.

Assume that the DISK command indicates "OK" in the stat column for disk 00. This means that the drive is currently operating on its own but was previously part of a mirrored pair. Disk 01 is showing the status of "D-00", indicating that it is currently dead. These conditions are normal after two drives have been disassociated with the UNMIRROR command.

After installing a new drive for drive 01, type the following REMIRROR command below to reestablish disk 01 as a mirror of disk 00:

REMIRROR 01

The following message is displayed:

Checking if the drive has been previously mirrored to the active drive.

The remirroring process continues with a message similar to the following:

Remirroring Drive 01
Beginning background copy of all allocated disk areas.

All of the data on drive 00 is copied to drive 01 in the background. You can execute the DISK command to follow the status of the remirroring process. The stat column will indicate "R" as a drive is remirrored and "M" when the remirroring has completed. You also see the following message on the file server console screen:

Re-mirroring successfully completed.

UNMIRROR (SFT NetWare 286 Only)

The UNMIRROR command removes a disk from a mirrored pair for servicing or replacement. The command can also shut down a drive in a mirrored pair for any reason. The command is used in conjunction with the REMIRROR command, which reestablishes a mirrored pair. Refer to REMIRROR for more details.

The UNMIRROR command takes the following form:

UNMIRROR *xx*

where *xx* is the number of the drive to shut down as indicated in the display presented by the DISK command. Refer to the stat column of the DISK display to determine mirrored drives, which are indicated with the "M" option.

For example, to shut down disk 01, which is mirrored to disk 00, execute the following command:

UNMIRROR 01

When the DISK command is executed, the newly unmirrored drive will appear in the stat column with the "D" option, which indicates it is a dead drive. You would also note that drive 00 is listed as "OK", which means it is a previously mirrored drive now operating only under the Hot Fix redirection feature.

NetWare Monitoring and Maintenance Commands

The FCONSOLE Command
NetWare System Repair Utilities
Managing the Transaction Tracking System
Changing the NetWare Configuration
Modifying NetWare Installation Options

This chapter will introduce you to the FCONSOLE command, as well as other utilities used by supervisors and system managers when monitoring and maintaining the network. In addition, the final part of the chapter covers NETGEN/ELSGEN, which will be of interest to those making changes to the NetWare operating system or the configuration of the server. Whenever the server's physical hardware is altered, you will need to run the NETGEN/ELSGEN program to update the operating system.

The FCONSOLE Command

Any user can use FCONSOLE, but a user's ability to access its functions will be limited, depending on whether he or she is the supervisor, a designated FCONSOLE operator, or a regular user. The FCONSOLE commands are typically used by the supervisor to monitor and maintain the file server and network. FCONSOLE can also be used by users to some extent to view the current condition of various aspects of the system and by FCONSOLE operators who have been assigned special rights in the

FCONSOLE utility. Many of the functions of FCONSOLE are similar to the console commands discussed in Chapter 25. However, FCONSOLE provides a more convenient and effective way of monitoring many different aspects of the network from any workstation, instead of from the server itself.

The FCONSOLE main menu is shown here:

FCONSOLE can be used to view current user connection information, view a file server's LAN-driver information, and view the version of NetWare running on the system. It can also be used to change file servers. System supervisors and FCONSOLE operators can use the menu utility to broadcast messages, purge salvage files, view more detailed current user connection information, view file and lock activity, view and alter the status of the file server, and view statistics about the file server's performance.

Note: The supervisor is the only user that can bring the server down with the Down File Server command on the FCONSOLE main menu.

All options available from the Statistics selection in the main menu are covered in the next chapter. These options display information designed for experienced network users and programmers. Supervisors and managers will be interested in using FCONSOLE to monitor the performance of the network through various memory management and disk-drive management techniques. Programmers will find the File/Lock Activity and Statistics options useful when writing advanced multiuser applications designed specifically to run on networks or when using the Transaction Tracking System (TTS). The information available through FCONSOLE can be used to write, test, and debug these programs.

Note: Console operators are assigned special rights to work with the FCONSOLE utility. Refer to Chapter 18 for information on designating users as FCONSOLE operators with the SYSCON menu utility.

The remaining portion of this section will discuss all FCONSOLE commands except those available from the File/Lock Activity and Statistics options. Information displayed by these options is of interest to programmers and advanced users and is covered in Chapter 27.

To start FCONSOLE, type this command from any directory:

FCONSOLE

The FCONSOLE main menu will appear, as shown previously. Keep in mind that FCONSOLE help information can be accessed from any location by pressing the F1 key.

Broadcasting Console Messages

The first option on the FCONSOLE menu is Broadcast Console Messages. This option can be used by the supervisor or by console operators to broadcast messages to all currently logged users. A message of up to 55 characters may be sent to users. After typing the message, press the ENTER key.

Messages will be displayed on line 25 of each user's workstation screen. Pressing CTRL-ENTER will clear the message. In most cases, this option is used to send messages to users before downing the file server.

Changing the Current File Server

Users can change to another file server by selecting the Change Current File Server option from the FCONSOLE main menu. When ENTER is pressed, a list of available file servers will appear. There are four ways to use this option:

- Press INS to log in to another file server. A list of servers will appear. You will then be asked to enter your user name and password in the normal way. The name of the file server will now appear in the File Server menu list. Use the next option to change to the server.

- Press ENTER to change to another file server. The screen heading will display the appropriate information for this server.

- To log out of a server, highlight the appropriate server from the Filer Server list and press the DEL key.

- You may wish to change to a different user name on a file server. To do so, press the F3 (Modify) key, type the name of the user you wish to change to, and press ENTER. You will be asked for the user's password if required.

Viewing Connection Information

When the Connection Information option on the FCONSOLE Available Options menu is selected, a list of current users is displayed in the Current Connections menu that appears. Each users connection number is listed on the menu, which is updated every two seconds as users log in and out.

Supervisors and FCONSOLE operators can select one or more currently connected user to display one of the menus shown next. If more than one of the users is selected with the F5 (Mark) key, the following display will appear:

If a single user is selected, the following display will appear. The options from the previous menu are included in this menu, along with additional options for viewing individual information for the selected user. These options are described in the following sections.

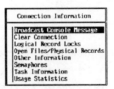

Broadcast Console Message

If several users were selected, you can use the Broadcast Console Message option to send messages to each of those users. If a single user was selected, the option will send a message to just that user. To send a message, type the message on the screen and press the ENTER key.

Clear Connection

Supervisors can clear a connection with the Clear Connection option. Connections may need to be cleared when a user's system has crashed and files are still open on the server. Supervisors may also clear a user for other reasons, such as security.

Logical Record Locks

The Logical Record Locks option is used to display all logical record locks for the currently selected user and the tasks using the locks. Logical record locks are used to control records in database files that are accessed by multiple users. When a record is locked by one user, others cannot access it. *Records* within databases are usually occupied by one set of information, such as the name, address, and other information for a single person in a database of many names. Logical record locking is a feature of interest to programmers and advanced users and are covered in Chapter 27.

Open Files/Physical Records

The Open Files/Physical Records option displays all files that are currently in use by the selected connection. It shows the status of files and any physical record locks the selected connection has in the files. To view the file status or physical record locks of a particular file, highlight the file and press ENTER. Open files and physical records are of interest to programmers and advanced users and are covered in Chapter 27.

Other Information

The Other Information option shows information about the connection, including which user is logged in, the network address of the station the user is logged in to, and the user's log-in time. The supervisor can use this information when sending messages, creating log-in scripts (with the P-MACHINE variable), and tracking the user's time on the system.

Semaphores

The Semaphores option is used to display a list of the semaphores a connection is using. Semaphores are used to limit how many tasks can use or change a resource at the same time, and to limit the number of workstations that can run a program at the same time.

A task uses a semaphore to request the use of a resource. If the resource is available, the task is allowed to proceed. If the resource is not available, the task is forced to wait until it is available. If a wait time is exceeded, an error message indicates that the resource is not available. Semaphores also prevent the maximum number of licensed users from accessing a program. Semaphores are of interest to programmers and advanced users and are covered in Chapter 27.

Task Information

The Task Information option shows which tasks are currently active at the selected connection's workstation and whether the workstation is waiting for a lock or a semaphore. These tasks are of interest to programmers and advanced users and are covered in Chapter 27.

Usage Statistics

When Usage Statistics is selected, a screen similar to the following will appear. The screen shows the total disk I/O and packet requests for the selected user. Supervisors may want to monitor this information to determine the resources used by a particular user, the application the user is running, or the workstation the user is using.

```
┌─────────────────────────────────────┐
│     Connection Usage Statistics     │
├─────────────────────────────────────┤
│ Connection Time:    11 Hours 15 Minutes │
│ Requests Received:            34,949 │
│ Disk Bytes Read:           2,666,466 │
│ Disk Bytes Written:           24,529 │
└─────────────────────────────────────┘
```

Shutting Down the File Server

The supervisor may down the file server using the FCONSOLE Down File Server option. If an attempt is made to down the server while files are still open, a warning message will appear. If the file server is brought down, any opened files will be closed automatically, and any unfinished transactions will be backed out.

Only supervisors may down the server. To down the server, select the option and press ENTER.

File/Lock Activity

The File/Lock Activity menu shows information about the use of files, locks, and semaphores, as well as transaction tracking information. This information is of interest to programmers and advanced users and is covered in the next chapter.

LAN Driver Information

The LAN Driver Information option displays information for the LAN drivers installed in the current file server. Since a server can have up to four installed network interface cards, up to four networks can be selected from the Select LAN Driver window that appears when LAN Driver Information is selected. Supervisors can view this information when installing new boards in order to prevent hardware conflicts. LAN information can also be useful when monitoring the efficiency or traffic on a particular network with other FCONSOLE commands.

When a LAN is selected, a screen similar to the following will appear:

```
                        LAN A Configuration
Network Address: 00454E44    Node Address: 640400454E44
LAN Board Type: AST-EtherNode
Configuration:   1
Hardware Option: IRQ = 5, IO = 300H, No DMA, ROM = CC00:0
```

The following describes each of the fields that appear on the LAN configuration window.

Network Address The network address is the address specified during the configuration of the NetWare operating system and should be the same as all other file servers connected to the same network.

Node Address The node address is the station address of the LAN board installed in the file server. No two network interface cards on the same network can share the same address. The node address is determined in one of three ways:

- Some network interface cards have "burned-in" node addresses that cannot be changed.

- Some boards set their own network node addresses.

- Some network boards allow users to set the node address.

LAN Board Type This field illustrates the name of the LAN board being used as specified during NetWare configuration.

Configuration The configuration option selected for the LAN is listed.

Hardware Option The interrupts, DMA channels, I/O addresses, or memory addresses are listed for the selected board. Other LAN boards installed in the server should not have these settings to avoid hardware conflicts. You can refer to this screen when installing new boards.

Purging Salvageable Files

The Purge All Salvageable Files option is used to permanently remove deleted files from the system. This option is used to eliminate the chance that another user could salvage deleted files.

When files are deleted, they are temporarily kept by the file server in a salvageable state and can be recovered with the SALVAGE command. With the Purge All Salvageable Files option, the disk space held by the files is released. Salvage files are also removed as other files are deleted or new files are created.

Note that each user maintains his or her own set of salvageable files. A link is established to both the user name and workstation being used when the files were deleted. Other users on other workstations will not affect the files that are salvageable by a user at his or her own workstation. Only the current user can salvage or affect the salvageability of the files.

Statistics

The Statistics option displays detailed information about the file server's performance. Only supervisors, supervisor equivalents, or console operators may view these options, which are discussed in the next chapter.

Status

The current status of the file server can be viewed or changed by selecting Status from the FCONSOLE main menu. The menu shown here will appear:

```
                    File Server Status

Server Date:  September 14, 1989   Time:  10:15:11 pm
Allow New Users To Login:  Yes
Transaction Tracking:  Not Available
```

Use the arrow keys to move among fields to make changes. Press the ENTER key after making changes, and then press ESC to save changes. The following fields are available.

Server Date and Time   The Server Date and Time fields can be changed by altering the information in the fields.

Allow New Users to Login   This field can be changed to No if you want to prevent further log-in on the system. This option is used if you plan to down the server. The option has the same effect as the console command DISABLE LOGIN.

Transaction Tracking   If a server supports TTS, this entry will show that it is enabled.

Version Information

The Version Information option on the FCONSOLE utility's main menu is used to view the current version number of NetWare running on the file server.

NetWare System Repair Utilities

The following utilities are used to make repairs or analyze problems with the NetWare operating system, its volumes, or its security system.

Repairing the Bindery with BINDFIX

The BINDFIX command is used to repair the bindery, which contains information about the users, user groups, queues, accounting charge rates, and other information important to the operation of the network. The bindery information is included in the files NET$BIND.SYS and NET$BVAL.SYS, which are hidden files in the SYS:SYSTEM directory.

The BINDFIX command is a utility used to correct the bindery files when they might possibly be corrupted. Problems such as the inability to delete or modify user names, passwords, and user rights indicate problems with the bindery files that can be repaired with BINDFIX. Error messages such as "Unknown server" may occur during spooling or errors referring to the bindery may be displayed. Run BINDFIX in such cases.

Before running the utility, make sure all users are logged off the system. BINDFIX shuts down the bindery files so users can't access them. It then rebuilds the bindery files and reopens them. Each task performed by BINDFIX is listed, and you will be asked if you want to delete the mail directories and trustee rights of users who have been deleted from the network.

Note: BINDFIX creates new NET$BIND.SYS and NET$BVAL.SYS files. The old files are renamed NET$BIND.OLD and NET$BVAL.OLD. Once the new bindery files are in place and working properly, you can remove the files with the .OLD extension. The "old" files can be restored if problems occur while rebuilding the bindery. The BINDREST utility, covered next, is used to restore the original bindery files.

To run BINDFIX, type the following command while logged in to the SYS:SYSTEM directory:

BINDFIX

The BINDFIX program will go through of series of checks as displayed in the following screen:

```
H:\SYSTEM>BINDFIX
Rebuilding Bindery.  Please Wait.
Checking for invalid nodes
Checking object's property lists.
Checking properties to see if they are in an object property list.
Checking objects for back-link property.
Checking set consistency and compacting sets.
Building avail lists and new hash tables.
There are 5 Object nodes and 3 Property Nodes free.
Checking user objects for standard properties.
Checking group objects for standard properties.
Checking links between users and groups for consistency.
Delete mail directories of users that no longer exist? (y/n): Y
Checking for mail directories of users that no longer exist.
Checking for users that do not have mail directories.
Delete trustee rights for users that no longer exist? (y/n): Y
Checking volume SYS.  Please wait.
Checking volume VOL1.  Please wait.

Bindery check successfully completed.
Please delete the files NET$BIND.OLD and NET$BVAL.OLD after you have verified
the reconstructed bindery.
```

You will be asked if you want to delete the directories of accounts that no longer exist. These directories branch from the SYS:MAIL directory. They do not include any personal directories you may have created for the user. You will then be asked if you want to delete the trustee rights for the user. If you answer Yes, BINDFIX will scan all mounted volumes and remove users that no longer exist from all trustee lists. Each volume is then checked.

If the BINDFIX command runs successfully, you will see a display similar to that at the bottom of the screen just shown. If the command is unsuccessful, the following message will appear:

Bindery check NOT successfully completed.

If the BINDFIX command is unsuccessful, you will need to run the BINDREST command to return the bindery to its original state.

Restoring the Bindery with BINDREST

The BINDREST command is used to return the NET$BIND.OLD and NET$BVAL.OLD files to their original bindery file status. The command cancels the new bindery files that were unsuccessfully completed and renames the .OLD files with the extension .SYS. To run the command, type it on the command line in the SYS:SYSTEM directory as shown here:

BINDREST

Repairing Volumes with VREPAIR

The VREPAIR utility is used to correct minor hard-disk problems at the volume level. The utility only affects the volumes you specify. The original data on the volumes is not destroyed.

Problems can occur on volumes when the file allocation table (FAT) becomes corrupted, due to defective media or a server that went down during a power loss. Undetected bad blocks can cause data loss. Major problems with a volume or an entire drive (remember, a drive can have more than one volume) may need to be repaired by completely backing up the data on the drive, reformatting the drive with the COMPSURF utility, and then restoring the data. COMPSURF will thoroughly analyze the disk surface for bad blocks and other problems. Part of this analysis destroys the data on the drive, so you must be sure you have a good backup set before proceeding.

Messages similar to the following will begin to appear as drive problems increase:

```
* WARNING * DISK READ ERROR, CANCEL MOUNT?
* WARNING * Sector xx DIR Table x Read Error on VOLUME name
* WARNING * Sector xx FAT Table x Read Error on VOLUME name
* WARNING * Directory sector xxx data mirror mismatch
* WARNING * FAT Table sector xxx data mirror mismatch
* WARNING * FAT Entry xxx multiple allocation in filename
WARNING: FATAL DIR ERROR ON VOLUME volume name DIR SECTOR xxx
WARNING: FATAL DIR ERROR ON VOLUME volume name FAT SECTOR xxx
Write Error: dir = xxx file = filename vol = volume name
```

Error messages may also appear at the workstation in the following form:

Warning: disk write error in file
Network Error: Physical I/O error during random/sequential read.

Note: Be sure to write down all error messages and error numbers in your network logs for future reference.

To run the VREPAIR utility, follow these steps:

1. Down the file server, making sure all users have first logged off before proceeding. The DOWN command can be issued from console mode with the FCONSOLE utility.

2. To restart the system, first spin up all external drives if they exist.

3. Reboot the server with DOS.

4. Insert the NetWare UTILEXE-2 disk if you have the 5 1/4-inch disk set, or the UTILEXE disk if you have the 3 1/2-inch disk set, into the floppy drive.

5. At the DOS prompt, issue the following command:

   VREPAIR

   You will then see the VREPAIR copyright messages, the number of cache buffers, and a list of drives on your system.

   Note: Keep in mind that mirrored or duplexed drives will appear as a single drive. Volume information is checked on the primary drive, and mismatches between the two mirrored drives are reported. Mismatches occur when data on the two drives is not the same.

6. Type the number of the drive you want to fix, and press ENTER. A list of volumes for the selected drive will then appear.

7. Type the number of the volume on the selected drive you want to repair.

   You can now specify the VREPAIR parameters, which specify whether to print a report of error conditions and corrections made, whether to test the volume for bad blocks, and whether to recover any "lost" blocks as a separate file. Lost blocks include data not identified in the file allocation table. They may contain valuable information that can be recovered to a temporary file for inspection and inclusion into new or existing files.

8. When the message "Do you want a printed report of any errors and corrections made?" appears, select Yes to print the report; otherwise, select No. If you plan to print a report, make sure you have a printer connected as network printer 0. It is recommended that you produce a printed copy of the VREPAIR report for future reference. The report should be filed with your network server's log sheets.

9. When the message "Do you want to test for Bad Blocks?" appears, you can answer Yes to test for bad blocks, but overall processing time will be increased.

10. When the message "Do you want to recover lost blocks as files?" appears, answer Yes if you want to attempt to rebuild files lost by the FAT. These are files that may not have been completely written to disk if the server went down. The data may be stored in blocks on the drive, but a corresponding entry is not available in the FAT. In most cases, you will want to recover the files and inspect them.

11. The final prompt will display the options you have selected and give you a chance to change them or continue with the VREPAIR tests. Select Yes to continue with the tests.

Once you have elected to continue with the tests, various messages will describe the progress of the tests as well as errors that have been detected and the actions taken to correct those errors.

If you have specified that lost blocks should be recovered, a message will appear for each lost block detected. It will indicate the file name that will be assigned to the recovered block and the directory path in which the file will be placed. The message "Abandon Error Report" will appear, to which you can answer Yes or No. Answering No will allow you to continue viewing the current sequence of error report messages, and answering Yes will abandon the current sequence of messages.

When VREPAIR has completed its analysis, the following prompt will be displayed:

Make corrections permanent [Yes or No]?

You should answer Yes to this prompt to make the corrections indicated in the previous error reports.

Once the corrections are made, you can select another volume or drive to repair or choose to exit VREPAIR by leaving the prompts blank and pressing the ENTER key. When exiting from the utility, you will see the following message:

VRepair complete.
Power off and back on to restart

Be sure to bring the server completely down, then start it up again before putting it back into service.

Managing the Transaction Tracking System

The Transaction Tracking System (TTS) is a system fault tolerance feature of SFT NetWare 286 that prevents database corruption if the system fails while transactional data is being written to database files. An entire sequence of database changes are viewed as a single transaction. Only when the entire sequence is completed does NetWare write the changes to disk. If the server should go down while changes are being made, NetWare "backs out" to the previous state before changes were made to the database, thus ensuring that the database is not corrupted.

In order to use TTS, you must first set the feature on. You must then give each database file that will use the TTS system a TTS file attribute. In some cases, the SETTTS utility must be used when running some programs with TTS.

Enabling and Disabling TTS

In most cases, the TTS system will already be running on a file server. However, it may be disabled if the volume designated for the backing out of transactions is full, or if TTS has been disabled by the supervisor. To enable TTS, type the following command at the server console:

ENABLE TRANSACTIONS

If you ever want to disable transactions to test software applications or speed up processing of transactional jobs on the server, type the following command:

DISABLE TRANSACTIONS

Flagging Files as Transactional

Each file that will be protected with the TTS feature must be flagged with the Transactional file attribute. This attribute can be set with the FLAG command or with the FILER menu utility. Both of these utilities are discussed in detail in Chapter 17. They are covered here briefly for your convenience.

Note: You must have Parental, Search, and Modify rights in the directory holding the file to receive the Transactional attributes.

Using FLAG

The FLAG command takes the following form for setting Transactional attributes:

FLAG *drive-or-path filename* T

where *drive-or-path* is the drive letter or complete path of the directory holding the file. The file is specified with *filename*. Wildcard characters (* and ?) can be used in the *filename* option to specify more than one file. The T option is used to mark the files with the Transactional attribute.

Note: Transactional files cannot be deleted or renamed. To delete or rename these files, you must first flag the files with the attribute NT (Nontransactional).

For example, to flag the MAILLIST.DBF file in the CUSTDATA directory, you would type the following command:

FLAG SYS:CUSTDATA\MAILLIST.DBF T

If the directory was mapped to drive R, you could also type

FLAG R:MAILLIST.DBF T

To unflag the file for renaming or deletion, the following command would be typed:

FLAG SYS:CUSTDATA\MAILLIST.DBF NT

Using FILER

To flag files as Transactional with the FILER utility, follow these steps:

1. Start FILER by typing the following command:

   FILER

2. Use the Select Current Directory option to switch to the directory holding the file to be flagged.

3. Use the File Information option on the FILER Available Topics menu to see a list of available files.

4. Highlight the file of choice, and press ENTER. You can mark more than one file with the F5 key.

5. Highlight the Attributes option in the File Information menu or highlight Set Attributes in the Multiple File Operations menu, and press ENTER.

6. Press INS to display the Other File Attributes window, highlight the Transactional attribute, and press ENTER. You will be asked to confirm the addition of the attribute to the files.

Changing the NetWare Configuration

Over time, you will probably need to make changes to the NetWare operating system. In most cases, these will be additions of hardware such as network interface cards, printers, and disk drives. You may also want to make changes to the operational characteristics of the operating system, such as its dedicated or nondedicated mode, printer configuration, or the way system resources are used. This section will outline the steps you need to take when reconfiguring and installing changes to NetWare.

Note: Before installing any new hardware in a server, it's a good idea to make sure the new hardware can coexist with existing equipment.

Most of the changes discussed here are made while running the NETGEN/ELSGEN utilities in configuration mode or installation mode, as discussed in Chapter 9, Chapter 10, and Appendix A. You may also need to refer to Chapter 11 for information on booting the server. Those performing the reconfiguration and installation should be familiar with NETGEN/ELSGEN, since this section only outlines the features that can be changed.

Note that one or more topics in this section may apply to the changes you want to make. You may need to refer to each section individually.

During reconfiguration and installation, NETGEN/ELSGEN will perform operations such as initializing newly added disks, installing Hot Fix on new disks, removing bad disk drives from the Master System Drive table, and restoring previously removed drives. The program can also make changes to the system configuration, volume, serial printer, and other parameters. You should be extremely careful when making changes to existing drives if you intend to keep the current data intact on the drive. If you elect to initialize or change the volume sizes on such drives, the data will be destroyed.

Note: Never make changes to an established network without proper backups. You might also consider establishing a second server as a duplicate before proceeding.

Starting NETGEN/ELSGEN

If you performed the installation of NetWare as outlined in Chapter 9, Chapter 10, and Appendix A, you will have a backup set of floppy disks, ready to perform a reconfiguration of the system. You can also use the hard disk or network drive methods discussed in those chapters. You should refer to Chapter 9 for instructions on copying the disks (if necessary) to determine the method and run mode you will use.

If you are modifying an installation that was made with the default settings, they are listed here:

Default System Configuration Parameters

Number of Open Files:	240
Number of Indexed Files:	5
Transaction Backout Volume:	SYS
Number of Transactions:	100
Limit Disk Space:	No

Default Volume Parameters

Volume Size:	Up to 255MB
Volume Name:	SYS, VOL1, VOL2, and so on
Cache the Directory:	Yes

Default Serial Printer Parameters

Baud Rate:	9600
Word Length:	8 bits
Stop Bits:	1 bit
Parity:	None
XON/XOFF Protocol:	No

Other Default Settings

Operating System:	TTS is set for SFT NetWare
Partition Table:	Entire disk for NetWare
Hot Fix Redirection	Approximately 2% of disk space

Remember that if you choose the default level of NETGEN/ELSGEN, the program will automatically select various default option settings. This discussion will concentrate on the custom installation modes, which should be selected if you plan to perform any of the following:

- Change the TTS level on SFT NetWare 286 Level II

- Choose a different configuration option for one or more of the LAN, disk, or other drivers you have selected for the file server

- Reload the NetWare operating system file without specifying a configuration

- Modify the partition table on the system hard disk

- Modify the Hot Fix redirection size

- Reinitialize the disk with new volume parameters
- Change any settings made using the default configuration and installation methods
- Change the network address
- Change the number of communication buffers
- Change the network printer configuration

Changing the Configuration With NETGEN/ELSGEN

After reentering NETGEN/ELSGEN, choose Select Network Configuration from the menu to begin the configuration process. You may be asked to insert several floppy disks, depending on the run method you are using. The options available from each menu are discussed in the following sections.

Changing the Operating System Level

To change the operating system level, select Set Operating System Options from the Available Options menu. If you are running SFT NetWare 286, you can select between an operating system that supports TTS or one that doesn't. TTS should be selected if you are running transaction-oriented applications such as database management systems or accounting packages. If you are running Advanced NetWare, you can select between dedicated or nondedicated mode for the operating system.

Resource Sets

Resource sets are used to help you avoid hardware conflicts when adding new equipment. A full explanation of resource sets is given in Chapter 9 and Appendix A. Appendix A explains the custom method of configuration and installation, which makes use of resource sets.

Resource sets allow you to specify in advance the equipment you have in your system. The specifications can include the interrupt lines, DMA lines, I/O addresses, and memory addresses. By specifying what lines and addresses existing hardware uses, NETGEN/ELSGEN will recommend settings for the boards and peripherals you are adding. If you decide to use resource sets, choose Select Resource Sets from the NETGEN/ELSGEN Available Options menu and follow the instruction in Appendix A for configuring the resources.

LAN Drivers

A common reason for changing the configuration of a server is to change or add network interface cards. This can be done to increase the performance of an existing LAN by splitting it between two separate interface cards, or to add a new type of interface board and network to the existing network.

To add LAN cards, choose Select LAN Drivers from the NETGEN/ELSGEN Available Options menu. You may then follow the procedures covered in Chapter 10 for configuring the boards. No two boards can share the same interrupts, lines, and addresses, so you will need to make switch settings or jumper changes to the boards as appropriate.

Each new LAN card attached to the server establishes a separate network. These networks are referred to as LAN A, LAN B, LAN C, or LAN D, depending on the number of boards you have installed. A maximum of four boards are allowed.

Disk Drivers

The Select Disk Drivers option is used to install or remove file-server disk coprocessor boards or third-party equivalent boards if you have Advanced NetWare or SFT NetWare. When a disk driver is added or removed, an entire hard-disk channel is affected. This change will also affect the Master System Drive table kept by NETGEN, which contains information about all the network hard disks, and will require that the operating system and file-server utilities be relinked and reconfigured. You may need to rerun the appropriate hard-disk configuration utility (DISKSET or its equivalent) to specify the new hard-disk configuration. Refer to your disk driver's manual for more installation information.

Other Drivers

The drivers required to run additional equipment may need to be loaded using the Other Driver Options selection on the NETGEN/ELSGEN Available Options menu. The process for loading these drivers is discussed in Chapter 10.

Selecting the New Configuration

After the LAN drivers, disk drivers, and other drivers have been selected, you must establish the configuration settings these boards will use. This is done through the Configure Drivers/Resources option, which is available when running custom mode. The menu that appears after choosing Configure Drivers/Resources will display options for each hardware component that may have more than one selectable configuration. Refer to Appendix A for details.

Changing the Network Addresses

It may be necessary to change the address of one of the networks installed in your server. This can be done by selecting Enter Server Information in the Configure Drivers/Resources menu. Whenever a new board is added, this option must be selected. It must also be run if you change from the dedicated to a nondedicated file server in Advanced NetWare. Each board in the server must have a unique network address; however, a board in a server may share the same network address as a board in another server connected to the same network.

Changing the Communications Buffer Size

Communications buffers are areas of memory set aside to hold network data packets arriving from workstations until the file server can process them. A higher number of buffers may be specified to increase the operational speed of the network, but the buffer space is deducted from the usable memory space of the server.

The default number of buffers is 40, but you can specify from 10 to 150 buffers. To determine the optimum number of buffers, start with 40, and then add one buffer for each additional workstation that is connected at any one time. To specify communications buffers, select Enter Server Information in the Configure Drivers/Resources option.

Regenerating the Operating System

After changing the options discussed in the previous section, you can regenerate the operating system. The process consists of linking and configuring, and is automatic if the default method is being used. If you are running the custom method, you may need to relink and reconfigure the operating system and the file server utilities by following the selections on the menu.

If you have added or deleted a driver, you will need to relink and reconfigure. The Link/Configure NetWare Operating System option will appear in the Network Generation Options menu. You should select this option and follow the instructions.

If you have added, deleted, or reconfigured a disk driver in your network configuration, certain file-server utilities must be relinked and reconfigured to communicate with the file server's disk drivers. Select Link/Configure File Server Utilities and Configure File Server Utilities from the Network Generation Options menu.

Additional options on the Network Generation Options menu may include Link/Configure Additional Utilities and Configure Additional Utilities. Select the first option if you have added or deleted "Other" drivers. If you have only changed the configuration option, select the second option.

Once the generation process is complete, you can exit NET-GEN/ELSGEN. You will be asked if you want to download the necessary files to floppy disk. This is important in order to carry the configuration files and information from the computer used to configure the server to the server where the installation will take place. You will be asked to insert each required disk.

Changing the Hard-Disk
Configuration with DISKSET

The DISKSET utility is used to add, remove, or replace any network hard-disk drives in a Novell disk coprocessor board channel. The utility is only used when working with disk coprocessor boards and is not appropriate when changing internal drives for AT-class machines or IBM PS/2 systems. Also, third-party disk channel interface boards will have their own configuration utilities. For more information on running the DISK-SET (DISK coprocessor SETup) utility, refer to the operating manual supplied with your coprocessor board.

Formatting and Testing Hard Disks
With COMPSURF

The NetWare COMPSURF (COMPrehensive SURFace analysis) utility is used to format and test hard-disk drives. The utility can be used to initially test drives or to reformat drives that are experiencing problems on the server. COMPSURF is a destructive program that will remove all existing data on a drive, so you should make sure you have backups of all existing data before proceeding.

An explanation of the COMPSURF utility is given in Chapter 10. You should refer to that chapter now for more information if you plan to reformat or configure a new drive.

Modifying NetWare Installation Options

This section is concerned with the installation phase of NET-GEN/ELSGEN, which is performed after the configuration options are selected, as discussed earlier. You should now be ready to reenter NETGEN/ELSGEN in the installation mode. Execute the NETGEN or ELSGEN command on the command line, and then choose Custom Installation to display the custom installation options.

Note: The information in this section may not apply to all versions of NetWare and only describes the methods used when running custom installation.

When the Custom Installation Options menu appears, you can proceed with the following sections.

Modifying the Hard-Disk Tables

You may find it necessary to modify the hard-disk partition table, Hot Fix redirection table, or the mirror table as described here. Note that the following options assume you are preparing a new disk or a disk that has been reformatted with COMPSURF.

- The partition table can be altered by selecting Modify Partition Table from the Custom Installation menu. Selecting this option will destroy existing data on the drive.

- The Hot Fix redirection table can be modified by selecting Modify Hot Fix Redirection Tables on the Custom Installation menu.

- The mirror table contains information about hard disks that are paired under the SFT NetWare operating system. You can set up a new mirrored/duplexed pair, or unmirror an existing mirrored/duplexed pair, by selecting Modify Mirror Tables from the Custom Installation menu.

Miscellaneous Maintenance

The topics in this section deal with the maintenance tasks that can be performed when Miscellaneous Maintenance is selected from the Custom Installation menu. These include setting the system and public files' load flags, changing the printers, changing the TTS parameters under SFT NetWare, and other options as covered in the following sections.

Setting the System Load Flag

If you are reconfiguring a NetWare operating system, you may not need to reload the operating system file (NET$OS.EXE). By selecting Load Operating System from the Miscellaneous Maintenance menu, you can change the system load flag.

There are three situations in which you need to load the system file:

- If you have changed the operating system file by adding new LAN drivers, disk drivers, or other drivers

- If you have reinitialized the server's hard drive, which destroyed the existing system files

- If you are upgrading the operating system from a previous version

When the Set Flag for Operating System Load option is set to Yes, the newly configured operating system file will be loaded to the server. If No is selected, the original file is left intact. Be sure to select No if you are *only* changing options on the Miscellaneous Maintenance menu.

Setting the System Load Flag

If you are reconfiguring a NetWare operating system, you may not need to reload the system, log-in, and public files, which can take some time and a considerable number of disk swaps. By selecting Load System and Public Files from the Miscellaneous Maintenance menu, you can change the status of the load flag.

There are two conditions in which you will need to load the system files:

- If you have reinitialized the server's hard drive, which destroyed the existing system files

- If you are upgrading the operating system from a previous version

When the Set Flag for System & Public Files Load option is set to Yes, the files are loaded to the server. If No is selected, the original files are left intact. Be sure to select No if you are changing *only* the options on the Miscellaneous Maintenance menu.

Changing the System Configuration Parameters

The system configuration parameters include the file-server name, the maximum number of open and indexed files, the TTS parameters (SFT NetWare only), and the Limit Disk Space option. Select System Configuration in the Miscellaneous Maintenance menu to display the current system configuration parameters. Through this menu, you can make the following changes:

- Change the file-server name. The name must be unique and can be from 2 to 45 characters long.

- Change the maximum number of open files. The peak number of files can be monitored with the FCONSOLE utility, as discussed in the next chapter. If the peak number of open files nears the configured maximum, you may want to increase the maximum number of open files.

- Change the maximum number of indexed files. An indexed file is one that is assigned the Indexed attribute. When the file is open, the server builds an index in memory of the file's location on disk to speed up reads and writes. The peak number of indexed files can be monitored in FCONSOLE, as discussed in the next chapter, and this number can be adjusted accordingly.

- Change TTS parameters (SFT NetWare only). The volume used as the Transaction Backout Volume can be changed, as can the number of transactions that are in progress (active) at a given time. The number of transactional files active at one time can be monitored with the FCONSOLE utility and adjusted accordingly.

- Change the disk space limitations: disk space can be limited for all network users by selecting Limit Disk Space. By selecting this option you will also need to set a limit on the number of users and groups (bindery objects). The number of bindery objects is the maximum number of users or groups that can be defined. The peak number of bindery objects can be monitored with FCONSOLE.

Changing Volume Information

Use the Volume Information option in the Miscellaneous Maintenance menu to change the volume name, the number of directory entries, and the caching parameters for any existing volume. The data in the volumes will not be damaged by changing these parameters. After selecting the volume to change, you can select and alter the following options:

- *Volume name.* The volume name can be between 2 and 15 characters long and must be unique.

- *Number of directory entries.* The number of directories, subdirectories, and files that can be created within the volume can be specified.

- *Cache option.* You can decide whether to cache the volume or not. In most cases, a cache is essential to disk performance, but it does require some system memory. You might decide not to cache if a server has many volumes but little memory. You might also turn the cache off on a volume used for archiving that has little disk activity.

Changing the Spooled Printer List

By selecting Printer Maintenance in the Miscellaneous Maintenance menu, you can change the list of spooled printers when you add or remove network printers. The parameters for the currently attached printers can also be changed.

A window will show the currently defined printers for each port of the file server. The definitions for each port can be altered by adding or changing a spooled printer number. Recall that spooled printer numbers can be 0 through 4, with 0 being the default printer. If you add or change a serial printer on the COM ports, you must also define the baud rate, word length, stop bits, parity, and Xon/Xoff protocol. These definitions should match the settings on your printer.

Exiting NETGEN/ELSGEN

After all changes have been made, you can select the Continue Installation option from the Installation Options menu. Answer the prompts appropriately. If the load flags for the system and public files were set, the installation will take longer and you will need to swap floppy disks. If these files are not being loaded, the reconfiguration will take about a minute or less. Once the reconfiguration is complete, you can exit NET-GEN/ELSGEN and reboot the server.

NetWare Performance
Monitoring and Analysis

The FCONSOLE Statistics Option
FCONSOLE Connection Information
File/Lock Activity

The FCONSOLE command is used by the supervisor to monitor and analyze the file server and network. FCONSOLE can also be used by users to some extent to view the current condition of various aspects of the system, and by FCONSOLE operators, who have been assigned special rights in the FCONSOLE utility. Most of the options used to view settings were covered in the previous chapter. This chapter is concerned with more technical aspects of the utility.

FCONSOLE is an advanced utility designed for experienced network users and programmers. Experienced users are those familiar with the terminology of networks and the functioning of network hardware on a technical level. Supervisors and managers will be interested in FCONSOLE to monitor the performance of the network through various memory, disk-drive, and network management techniques.

FCONSOLE is also of interest to programmers who are writing advanced multiuser applications designed specifically to run on networks. The information available through FCONSOLE can be used to write, test, and debug these programs.

This chapter describes the information available from the File/Lock Activity option and the Statistics option on the FCONSOLE main menu. Information for specific users available under Connection Information on the FCONSOLE main menu is also described.

The FCONSOLE Statistics Option

The Statistics option on the FCONSOLE Available Topics menu will give you detailed information about the file server and its performance. You will be able to view this information and possibly make changes to your network that will optimize its performance. The File Server Statistics menu is shown here. Note that when the menu first appears, the Summary option is highlighted. In many cases, this option will be most useful to those who need an encapsulated version of the statistics information. It is described first, followed by the other menu options in order.

```
                    ┌──────────────────────────────┐
                    ║       Available Options       ║
         ┌──────────────────────┬───────────────────┴──┐
         │ File Server Statistics│st Console Message    │
         ├──────────────────────┤Current File Server   │
         │Cache Statistics      │ion Information        │
         │Channel Statistics    │le Server             │
         │Disk Mapping Information│ck Activity           │
         │Disk Statistics       │ver Information        │
         │File System Statistics│ll Salvageable Files  │
         │LAN I/O Statistics    │ics                   │
         │Summary               │                      │
         │Volume Information    │   Information         │
         └──────────────────────┴──────────────────────┘
```

Summary Statistics

The Summary screen is reached by selecting Summary from the File Server Statistics menu. A screen similar to the following is displayed. Each option is discussed in the following paragraphs.

```
┌──────────────────────────────────────────────────────────────────┐
│                  File Server Statistics Summary                   │
├──────────────────────────────────────────────────────────────────┤
│ File Server Up Time:     0 Days  0 Hours  2 Minutes 21 Seconds    │
│ Number Of File Service Processes:     5  Current Server Utilization:    66%│
│ Disk Requests Serviced From Cache:  91%  Packets Routed:               0│
│ Total Packets Received:             727  File Service Packets:         5│
│ Total Number Of Cache Buffers:       29  Dirty Cache Buffers:          0│
│ Total Server Memory:            519,168  Unused Server Memory:     7,168│
│                                                                    │
│                        Maximum    Peak Used    Currently In Use    │
│ Routing Buffers:          40          5              0             │
│ Open Files:              244         17             16             │
│ Indexed Files:            0           0              0             │
│ Transactions:           N/A         N/A            N/A             │
│ Bindery Objects:        N/A         N/A            N/A             │
│ Connections:            100           1              1             │
│ Dynamic Memory 1:    16,384       1,970          1,448             │
│ Dynamic Memory 2:    26,812       4,552          4,490             │
│ Dynamic Memory 3:    47,104         708            100             │
└──────────────────────────────────────────────────────────────────┘
```

File Server Up Time   The amount of time the file server has been up since last booted.

Number of File Service Processes   The number of processes in the file server that can simultaneously service requests.

Current Server Utilization   This field indicates the percentage of time the file server's central processing unit is being used and is based on the idle time of the processing unit.

Disk Requests Serviced from Cache   A high percentage in this field indicates that the cache buffers are being used efficiently.

Packets Routed   The number of packets routed from one LAN to another in the last second.

Total Packets Received   The number of packets received by the server, including file service requests, packets to be routed, and packets destined for IPX sockets other than the file-service socket since the server has been up.

File Service Packets   The number of request packets for file service received by the server in the last second.

Total Number Buffers   The number of cache buffers in the file server, which is determined by available memory. Buffers can be increased by increasing the amount of memory.

Dirty Cache Buffers   The number of cache buffers in the file server that have updated data not yet written to disk. This data would be lost if the server crashed or the power went out.

Total Server Memory   The amount of memory available to the server.

Unused Server Memory   The amount of server memory in bytes not being used. This memory is fragmented into pieces too small to use.

The following information is listed at the bottom of the screen. The numbers in the Maximum, Peak Used, and Currently in Use columns can be used to evaluate the settings of the server. In most cases, if the Peak Used figures are near the Maximum figures, you should consider increasing the maximum figures using the NETGEN/ELSGEN utilities.

Routing Buffers   The number of routing buffers in the file-server configured during installation. These buffers are used to store incoming packets when file services are not available. They also store all packets being sent by the server, except replies to file service requests.

Open Files   The field shows the number of files that can be opened, the peak used and the number currently open.

Indexed Files   The field shows the maximum number of files that can be opened, the peak used, and the number of currently indexed files open.

Transactions   The field shows the maximum number of files that can be tracked, the peak number of files that have been tracked, and the current number of files being tracked. Transaction tracking is used to ensure data integrity for database files.

Bindery Objects   The field shows the maximum number of objects that can be created, as well as the peak and the current number in use if the disk space was limited during installation. Otherwise, N/A is displayed.

Connections   The field shows the maximum number of connections that can be made at one time, the peak, and the current connections.

Dynamic Memory 1   The figures show the amount of memory available in bytes in the first dynamic memory pool. For 80286 systems, this is the DGGROUP memory pool used for mapping directories as a temporary buffer while a file service request is being processed. The field is not configurable.

Dynamic Memory 2   The figures show the amount of memory available in bytes in the second dynamic memory pool. For 80286 systems, this is the memory pool used for keeping track of open files, file locks, and record locks. The amount of memory in this pool is configured during installation by setting the maximum number of files that can be open at the same time.

Dynamic Memory 3   The figures show the amount of memory available in bytes in the third dynamic memory pool. For 80286 systems, this is the memory pool used to track file-server and routing information. The field is not configurable.

Cache Statistics

The file server's disk-caching statistics can be viewed by selecting the Cache Statistics option in the File Server Statistics window. A screen similar to this one will appear:

```
                        Cache Statistics
 File Server Up Time:    8 Days  8 Hours  2 Minutes 52 Seconds
 Number Of Cache Buffers:        29   Cache Buffer Size:        4,896
 Dirty Cache Buffers:             8
 Cache Read Requests:         2,985   Cache Write Requests:       163
 Cache Hits:                  2,882   Cache Misses:               364
 Physical Read Requests:        325   Physical Write Requests:     58
 Physical Read Errors:            8   Physical Write Errors:        8
 Cache Get Requests:          3,839
 Full Write Requests:           109   Partial Write Requests:      54
 Background Dirty Writes:         8   Background Aged Writes:       37
 Total Cache Writes:             48   Cache Allocations:          353
 Thrashing Count:                 8   LRU Block Was Dirty:         11
 Read Beyond Write:               8   Fragmented Writes:            2
 Hit On Unavailable Block:        8   Cache Blocks Scrapped:        8
```

Disk caching is used to increase the performance of the server's hard drives by providing memory buffers for data read from the disk. The data in the buffers is held with the expectation that the user may request it later. Data retrieval from memory is faster than retrieval from the hard disk. If cache buffers are increased, there is more of a chance that requested data will be in cache memory, thus providing an increase in performance. However, an increase in buffers decreases the amount of memory available for other uses unless a suitable amount of memory is available. Using the Cache Statistics screen, you can determine whether you need to increase your server's memory.

Cache buffers may contain data that needs to be written to the disk as well. Because buffers may hold unwritten data, a server should always be shut down with the FCONSOLE or console DOWN commands to close out buffers properly.

The entries in the Cache Statistics screen are described in the following paragraphs.

Number of Cache Buffers   The number shown represents the number of cache buffers being used by the system and is determined by the memory size and other parameters configured on the file server. The higher this number is, the better the system performance will be. Cache buffers are allocated to memory that is left after other memory requirements have been fulfilled.

Cache Buffer Size   The cache buffer size is the amount of memory set aside for each buffer, which is always 4096 bytes, as established during NetWare installation. The total cache size is therefore 4096 multiplied by the number of cache buffers.

Dirty Cache Buffers   These are the number of buffers that currently contain data not yet written to disk. Changes made to data in the cache buffers is written to disk at the first opportunity as a background process.

Cache Read Requests   The number of times the cache buffer has been requested to read data from the disk is displayed in this field. The requested data may have been cached in memory already or may have been read from the disk.

Cache Write Requests   This entry contains a count of the number of times the disk-cache software was asked to write data to the disk. Data being written to the disk is always placed in a cache buffer and then written to the disk as a background task. This figure also includes figures from the Full Write Requests and Partial Write Requests fields.

Cache Hits   Cache hits are the number of times a request for a disk read could be read from data already available in a cache. This number should always be close to the number of combined read and write requests.

Cache Misses   This is the number of times a new cache block was created because the requested data was not in an existing cache block. This figure also includes the figures from the Cache Allocations and LRU Block Was Dirty fields.

Physical Read Requests   This figure indicates the number of times the cache software issued a request to a disk driver to read in a block of data.

Physical Write Requests   This figure indicates the number of times the cache software issued a request to a disk driver to write a block of data to disk. The figure includes the figures from the Total Cache Writes and Fragmented Writes fields.

Physical Read Errors   This is the number of times the disk driver failed when reading data from the disk.

Physical Write Errors   This figure represents the number of times the disk driver failed to write data to the disk.

Cache Get Requests   This figure is the number of times the cache software was asked to retrieve information from the disk. The figure is a combination of the figures in the Cache Read Requests and Cache Write Requests fields.

Full Write Requests   This is the number of times the cache software was instructed to write information to the disk, and the information exactly filled one or more 512-byte sectors on the disk. It indicates that the cache software was able to place the data in a cache buffer without first reading the data previously in the disk block.

Partial Write Requests   This is the number of times the cache software has been instructed to write information that did not completely fill a sector. The original data was placed in a cache buffer before new data could be written to the cache buffer.

Background Dirty Writes   The number of times a full cache block has been written to disk. Cache blocks are written to disk as soon as they are filled with data.

Background Aged Writes   The number of times a cache block partially filled with new data is written to disk. The block is written out because new data existed for 3 seconds, even though the block was only partially full.

Total Cache Writes   The number of cache buffers written to disk. Only writes in which the entire cache buffer was written are included.

Cache Allocations   The number of times a new cache block is created, not including allocations of cache buffers that were not dirty.

Thrashing Count   The number of times a cache block was not available when a new cache block needed to be allocated. This situation only occurs when cache blocks are full and in use; it is an indication that the system needs more memory.

LRU Block Was Dirty   This is the number of times a cache block already contained updated data that needed to be written to disk before new data could replace it in the cache.

Read Beyond Write   This is the number of times a read request asked for data in an already allocated cache block, but the existing data needed to be written to disk. When a cache block is being filled with new data by cache write requests and then a cache read request asks for data beyond the point the new data has been written to, the new data is read from the disk.

Fragmented Writes   This is the number of times updated cache information was written to disk with several write requests. When new data is written to the cache buffer and fills some but not all cache buffers, each group of sectors is written separately.

Hit on Unavailable Block   The number of times the requested disk block was cached in memory but was not available because it was being read from or written to the disk.

Cache Blocks Scrapped   This is the number of times a cache buffer was scrapped during allocation while another request was serviced.

Channel Statistics

The Channel Statistics option shows information about the operational status, configuration, and failure of disk channels. A channel is the pathway from the microprocessor and memory to the disk drives on the server. If more than one channel is available (Advanced and SFT NetWare only), you will be requested to select a channel before the Disk Channel screen, similar to that shown here, will appear:

```
                          Disk Channel 0
File Server Up Time:    0 Days  1 Hour  41 Minutes 14 Seconds
Status: Channel is running.
Synchronization: No one is using the channel.
Driver Type: 2. IBM AT hard disk controller or compatible  (001012)
Driver Version: 1.00
IO Addresses: 01F0h to 01F7h
Shared Memory Addresses:
Interrupts Used: 0Eh
DMA Channels Used:
Channel Configuration: AT controller  I/O base = 1F0h, Interrupt = 14
```

Up to five disk channels are possible if you have disk coprocessor boards (DCBs) installed. Up to four DCBs can be in use along with one internal hard-disk channel. The information in the Disk Channel display is updated every second. Each field is described here.

Status   The status of the channel is indicated as either running, stopping, stopped, or nonfunctional. If the message "Channel is running" appears, the channel is functioning normally. If the message "Channel is being stopped" appears, a failure has occurred during disk access and recovery is being attempted by the system. All disk access to this channel is being stopped. If the message "Channel is stopped" appears, the channel is currently under repair and no disk access is permitted. If the message "Channel is nonfunctional" appears, the disk channel is not working and should be checked or serviced. Make sure all cables are attached properly between the hard drive and the disk controller boards.

Synchronization A channel that is synchronized is one that is also being used by a non-NetWare process such as DOS. Some value-added processes (VAPs) also use synchronization to share the disk channels with NetWare. If the channel is not shared, the message "No one is using the channel" will appear. If channels are being shared, the following messages may appear:

NetWare is using the channel, someone else wants it.
Someone else is using the channel, NetWare does not need it.
Someone else is using the channel, NetWare needs it.
Someone else has released the channel, NetWare should use it.

Driver Type This field indicates the type of disk driver installed in the file server for the selected disk channel.

Driver Version This field indicates the version of the disk driver software.

I/O Address This field shows the I/O address the disk driver uses to control the selected disk channel. The field may be blank if the driver does not use I/O addresses to communicate with a channel's board.

Shared Memory Addresses This field may contain up to two shared memory addresses, but it will be blank if the disk channel does not use shared memory.

Interrupts Used This field contains up to two interrupts used by the disk driver to communicate with the disk channels. This field will be blank if the driver does not use interrupts.

DMA Channels Used   This field shows the direct memory access (DMA) channels the disk driver uses to communicate with the selected disk channel's board. Since not all drivers use DMA, the field may be blank.

Channel Configuration   This field displays the channel's current hardware configuration.

Disk Mapping Information

You can view and evaluate the current disk drive mappings by selecting Disk Mapping Information from the File Server Statistics menu. A screen similar to the following will appear when the option is selected:

```
                       Disk Mapping Information
File Server Up Time:    8 Days  2 Hours 38 Minutes 52 Seconds
SFT Support Level:      1            Pending I/O Commands:   8
Logical Disk Count:     1            Physical Disk Count:    1
Disk Channels  8) Active  1) Unused  2) Unused  3) Unused   4) Unused
              Logical Disk To Physical Disk Mappings
     Primary  Mirror          Primary  Mirror          Primary  Mirror
 8)  8       None        11)                      22)
 1)                      12)                      23)
 2)                      13)                      24)
 3)                      14)                      25)
 4)                      15)                      26)
 5)                      16)                      27)
 6)                      17)                      28)
 7)                      18)                      29)
 8)                      19)                      38)
 9)                      28)                      31)
18)                      21)
```

Each entry is explained in the following paragraphs.

SFT Support   The level of system fault tolerance (SFT) is shown in this field. A 1 will appear if you are using Advanced NetWare, and a 2 will appear if you are using SFT NetWare. Recall that Advanced NetWare has directory and file allocation table duplication, plus read-after-write verification and Hot Fix. SFT NetWare has the same features in addition to disk mirroring, duplexing, and the Transaction Tracking System (TTS).

Pending I/O Commands   This field indicates the number of disk access requests currently waiting in the disk queue. NetWare sequences the queue so that information closest to the disk head will be retrieved first, which provides more efficiency during disk access.

Logical Disk Count   If SFT NetWare is being used, this field will indicate the number of disks that users will actually "see" on the system when disk mirroring is in effect. Since mirrored pairs appear as one logical drive, the Logical Disk Count field will always count a mirrored pair as one, whereas the Physical Disk Count field (described next) will count them as two.

Physical Disk Count   The actual number of physical disk drives mounted in the system is shown, even though two drives may be listed as one mirrored pair in the Logical Disk Count field.

Disk Channels   This field indicates which disk channels are active, inactive, or failed. If a disk channel has failed, all disk drives attached to it will not be accessible.

Logical Disk to Physical Disk Mappings   The fields at the bottom of the screen show which physical disks are mapped to which logical disks. If the "None" message appears, no mirror exists and the primary drive will always be shown. If "Dead" appears, the drive has been shut down because it failed. If a disk is mirrored, the disk number used to mirror the primary drive is listed under the Mirror column. If the status of a disk is other than normal, the message "Disabled," "Remirroring," or "None" may appear under the Mirror column. A disabled disk can be remirrored with the REMIRROR command, discussed in Chapter 25. While a drive is being remirrored, the message "Remirroring" will appear. This indicates that data is being copied from the primary drive to the mirror drive so the drives will duplicate each other. Messages regarding the progress of the remirroring will be displayed.

Disk Statistics

The Disk Statistics options can be selected from the File Server Statistics menu to display information about the disk drives mounted in the file server. The fields of the screen show the drive type, channel information, Hot Fix information, disk size, and cylinder information, in addition to other information described in the following paragraphs.

If you have more than one physical disk, you will be requested to select one of the disks before the information screen appears:

```
┌──────────────────────────────────────────────────────────────────┐
│                         Physical Disk 0                            │
│ File Server Up Time:   0 Days  3 Hours  5 Minutes  8 Seconds       │
│ Disk Type:   0, IBM AT Hard Disk  "C"    type  033                 │
│ Non-Removable Drive                                                │
│ Disk Channel:   0   Controller Number:   0   Drive Number: 0       │
│ Controller Type: 0,                                                │
│ Drive Size (less hot fix area): 86,175,744 bytes                   │
│ Drive Cylinders:  1,022  Drive Heads:   5   Sectors Per Track:  34 │
│ IO Error Count:        0                                            │
│ Hot Fix Table Start: 21,039        Hot Fix Enabled                 │
│ Hot Fix Table Size:  678 blocks    Hot Fix Remaining: 667 blocks   │
└──────────────────────────────────────────────────────────────────┘
```

Disk Type   This field displays the make and model of the currently selected disk.

Disk Channel   This field displays the number of the disk channel to which the selected disk is attached.

Controller Number   This field shows the controller number on the disk channel used to access the drive.

Drive Number   This field shows the drive number on the controller for the selected drive.

Drive Size   This field shows the physical drive size in bytes and does not include the portion used for Hot Fix redirection, which is shown in the lower part of the menu.

Drive Cylinders   This field indicates the number of cylinders on the drive. Zero is shown if the server does not know the cylinder count.

Drive Heads   This field indicates the number of heads on the disk drive. Zero is shown if the server does not know the head count.

Sectors Per Track   This field indicates the number of 512-byte sectors on each track of the drive. The message "Varies" will appear if the track count varies between inside and outside tracks or if the server does not know what the sector count is.

I/O Error Count
This field shows the number of errors that have occurred while accessing the disk.

Hot Fix Table Start
This is the start block of the Hot Fix redirection table. The status of the Hot Fix is also shown. It may be enabled, disabled, or not available.

Hot Fix Table Size
This is the number of redirection blocks set aside on the disk for Hot Fix redirection. Some or all of these blocks may be in use.

Hot Fix Remaining
This is the number of redirection blocks still available in case of media failure. You must subtract this count from the Hot Fix Table Size figure, minus an extra 6, to determine how many blocks have been redirected.

File System Statistics

The File System Statistics screen, shown here, can be displayed by selecting the appropriate option from the FCONSOLE File Server Statistics menu. The table can help you determine if file use is being optimized and if the memory allocated to file creation is utilized properly.

```
                         File System Statistics
 File Server Up Time:   0 Days  3 Hours 21 Minutes 35 Seconds
 Configured Max Open Files:        244  Peak Files Open:             18
 Open Requests:                     48  Currently Open Files:        17
 Read Requests:                  3,761  Write Requests:             188
 FAT Sector Writes:                  9  Dirty FAT Sectors:            0
 FAT Write Errors:                   0  Fatal FAT Write Errors:       0
 FAT Scan Errors:                    0
 Configured Max Indexed Files:       0  Peak Indexed Files Open:      0
 Active Indexed Files:               0  Attached Indexed Files:       0
```

The following paragraphs explain the entries on the menu screen.

Configured Max Open Files
This field displays the maximum number of files that can be open simultaneously and is set with NET-

GEN/ELSGEN. You need to compare the count in the Peak Files Open field with this number. If the numbers are close together, you may want to increase the configured maximum number of open files using NETGEN/ELSGEN. If the Peak Files Open figure is far below the maximum files, you may want to consider decreasing the maximum number of open files.

Peak Files Open   This field shows the largest number of files the file server had open at one time since the server was brought up. The server should be kept on and used under normal conditions for a long time to get an accurate reading in this field. The figure can then be used to determine the maximum number of open files, as discussed in the previous paragraph.

Currently Open Files   This field shows the number of files currently open on the file server. Open files include those opened by the workstation and those opened by the operating system.

Open Requests   This field shows the number of requests for files received by the server since it was started.

Read Requests   This field shows the number of read requests received by the file server since it was started.

Write Requests   This field shows the number of write requests received by the file server since it was started.

FAT Sector Writes   This field shows the number of times the file server has written sectors with file allocation table (FAT) information.

Dirty FAT Sectors   This field shows the number of sectors waiting to be written to disk. The field indicates the number of file allocation table changes that will occur when the information is written.

FAT Write Errors   This field shows the number of failed file allocation table updates.

Fatal FAT Write Errors   This field shows the number of fatal errors that occur when the server can't write to the primary or backup file allocation table. Such errors are caused by disk media failure, or possibly cable problems between the drive and controller. Before downing the server, be sure to back up the existing data on the drive. Then check the system and drive. You may need to perform a COMPSURF on the drive or replace it.

FAT Scan Errors   This field shows the number of times an internally inconsistent state was detected in the file server. Call your authorized Novell dealer if a count appears in this field.

Configured Max Indexed Files   This field shows the maximum number of FAT indexed files that can be opened simultaneously. Files with the Indexed attribute have their disk locations held in memory for fast retrieval, which can be a benefit with large database files. The maximum number of indexed files is specified during the NETGEN/ELSGEN process. If the figure in the Peak Indexed Files Open field is close to the maximum indexed files count, you may want to consider increasing the maximum number by running NETGEN/ELSGEN again. You can also lower the number if the count is much less.

Peak Indexed Files Open   This field shows the maximum number of indexed files that have been active simultaneously since the file server was last started. The number can be compared with the count of maximum indexed files open, as discussed in the last paragraph.

Active Indexed Files   This field shows the current number of open indexed files.

Attached Indexed Files   This field shows the number of indexed files ready for indexing but not currently open. The index of the file is kept in memory so it doesn't need to be rebuilt.

LAN I/O Statistics

You can view the statistics of the network itself by selecting LAN I/O Statistics from the File Server Statistics menu. A screen similar to this will appear:

```
                          LAN I/O Statistics
File Server Up Time:    0 Days  3 Hours 56 Minutes 51 Seconds
Total Packets Received:          5,759  Packets Routed:            25
File Service Packets:            5,468  NetBIOS Broadcasts:         0
Packets With Invalid Slots:          0  Invalid Connections:        0
Invalid Sequence Numbers:            0  Invalid Request Types:      0
Detach With Invalid Slot:            0  Forged Detach Requests:     0
New Request During Processing:       0
New Attach During Processing:        0  Ignored Duplicate Attach:   0
Reply Canceled By New Attach:        0
Detach During Processing Ignored:    0
Reexecuted Requests:                 0  Duplicate Replies Sent:     0
Positive Acknowledges Sent:          0  File Service Used Route:    0
Packets Discarded Because They Crossed More Than 16 Bridges:     0
Packets Discarded Because Destination Network Is Unknown:        0
Incoming Packets Lost Because Of No Available Buffers:           0
Outgoing Packets Lost Because Of No Available Buffers:           0
```

The screen displays information about the traffic on the network and how busy it is. Most of the fields display information about how NetWare validates the connection to workstations and handles the request made by the workstations to the server. Requests may fail for various reasons, and a workstation may resend its request. NetWare may then send messages to the workstation to let it know that a request has been received and is being processed. In other cases, a workstation may crash, and then be reconnected while the server is working on its previous requests. NetWare then throws out old requests and begins reestablishing connections and handling new requests. The screen will show these activities, as explained in the next paragraphs.

Note: The numbers in the fields discussed here represent only the information available to the server since it was last started.

Total Packets Received   Indicates the number of packets received by the file server, including file-server requests, packets routed to another network, and packets sent to other IPX sockets in the server.

Packets Routed   The number of packets the server has routed to another network.

File Service Packets   The number of packets received for services at the file server.

NetBIOS Broadcasts   Shows the number of times the current file server has received a NetBIOS broadcast packet and has rebroadcast the packet on all other LANs to which it bridges.

Packets with Invalid Slots   Indicates the number of packets that have gone to the server with bad connection numbers.

Invalid Connections   These are packets that come in with a connection number that the file server has not allocated, or with a packet source address that does not match the address to which the connection was allocated. Invalid connections occur if a server is brought down while a workstation is still connected.

Invalid Sequence Number   The number of times the server received an incorrect sequence number from a workstation.

Invalid Request Types   The number of request packets received at the server with an unknown request type.

Detach with Invalid Slot   The number of times the file server has received a request to detach a workstation from connections not supported by the server.

Forged Detach Requests   The number of times the server ignored a detach request from a workstation whose connection number did not match the address of the station actually connected at that address.

New Request During Processing   The number of times a new request is received by the server while it is still processing a previous request. This occurs if a workstation resends a request to the server, but the server's response to the first request is already on its way to the workstation.

New Attach During Processing   The number of times the server receives a request to establish a connection from a station that it is processing a request for. This occurs if the workstation is rebooted. The connection is reestablished, and the previous request is rejected.

Ignored Duplicate Attach   The number of times the server received a packet that duplicated a request for a connection. This occurs if the workstation sends another connection request while the server is still processing the first.

Reply Canceled by New Attach   The number of times a reply to a request has been canceled. This occurs if a workstation sends another request while the server is still processing the first.

Detach During Processing Ignored   The number of times a request to terminate a connection has been received while a previous request is still being processed. The server ignores the request to detach.

Re-executed Request   The number of times the file server has reexecuted a request for a workstation, as when the reply to a first request is lost by the network.

Duplicate Replies Sent   The number of times the server was asked to reexecute a request but did not have to because the previous reply was in memory. A reply is a message saved in memory that can be resent if a workstation reissues the same request.

Positive Acknowledges Sent   The number of positive acknowledges sent by the file server. A positive acknowledge is sent whenever a station repeats a request that is currently being serviced. It lets the station know that the request has been received and is being processed.

File Service Used Route   The number of times file services were not available to service a request. The requests are put in a buffer to wait for an available file service process.

Packets Discarded Because They Crossed More Than 16 Bridges
The number of packets received by the file server that have already crossed 16 bridges. The packet is assumed lost or traveling in a circle and is discarded.

Packets Discarded Because Destination Network Is Unknown
The number of packets discarded because their destination network was not known to the server. This occurs when a workstation is not aware that a network is no longer accessible.

Incoming Packets Lost Because of No Available Buffers   Number of packets that could not be received because no more buffers were available.

Outgoing Packets Lost Because of No Available Buffers   Number of packets the server attempted to send but lost because routing buffers were not available.

Transaction Tracking Statistics

Networks running SFT NetWare will have the Transaction Tracking Statistics option on the File Server Statistics menu. You can select this option to view statistics about the file server's Transaction Tracking System. Recall that a transaction is a set of write operations that must be either wholly completed or backed out to their previous state. If the server goes down, the previous state of the transactions is resurrected and the database is restored to that condition. The entries on the Transaction Tracking Statistics menu are covered here.

Transaction Tracking Status   This field indicates whether the TTS is enabled or disabled.

Transaction Tracking Volume   This field indicates the name of the volume the server is using to store transaction files.

Configured Max Transactions   The maximum number of transactions the server can track simultaneously, as set during installation.

Peak Transactions   The maximum number of transactions active simultaneously since the server has been up. This number can be compared with the number in the Configured Max Transactions field to determine if the maximum needs to be increased or decreased.

Current Transactions   The number of currently tracked transactions.

Transactions Performed   The total number of transactions tracked by the TTS since the file server has been up.

Transactions Written   The number of transactions tracked by the TTS that caused data to be changed.

Requested Backouts   The number of backed-out transactions, which may occur if a workstation fails or requests a backout.

Unfilled Backout Requests   The number of transactions the TTS was instructed to back out, but could not because TTS was disabled.

Current Used Disk Space   The amount of disk space used by the TTS. If the disk space is filled, the TTS will not work.

Total File Extensions   The number of times a transaction caused a file to be extended and the extension required the allocation of a new disk block. The TTS must deallocate the disk block if a transaction backout is requested.

Total File Size Changes   The number of times transaction-tracked files have changed their file size since the file server was last brought up. This includes all size changes—even those that do not require allocating or deallocating a disk block.

Total File Truncations   The number of times transaction-tracked files have been truncated within a transaction. The TTS tracks all the information in the part of the file that was truncated so that it can be restored if a backout is requested.

Volume Information

The Volume Information screen shown here is available by selecting the appropriate option on the File Server Statistics menu. You will be requested to select the volume for which you wish to view information. The topics on the menu are discussed next.

```
                      Volume Information
File Server Up Time:     0 Days  7 Hours  1 Minute  30 Seconds
Volume Name:      SYS              Volume Number:        0
Volume Mounted:   Yes              Volume Removable:  No
Volume Hashed:    Yes              Volume Cached:     Yes
Block Size:       4,096            Starting Block:       4
Total Blocks:     12,800           Free Blocks:      3,494
Maximum Directory Entries:         3,712
Peak Directory Entries Used:       1,862
Current Free Directory Entries:    1,849
Logical Drive Number:     0
Volume Mirrored:          No
Primary Disk Number:      0        Mirror Disk Number:  N/A
```

Volume Name   The name of the selected volume.

Volume Number   The number of the selected volume. This is the number assigned by the server when the volume was mounted.

Volume Mounted   This field indicates whether the volume has been put into service.

Volume Removable   Removable volumes can be mounted or dismounted from the server. This field indicates the volumes status.

Volume Hashed   This field indicates whether the volume is hashed. A hashed volume has its directories indexed for faster file access.

Volume Cached   If the volume is cached, this field will indicate so.

Block Size   The size of the blocks on the volume are listed in this field.

Starting Block   The starting block number of the volume is displayed in this field.

Total Blocks   The size of the volume in blocks is displayed in this field.

Free Blocks   The number of directory blocks on the volume available for use are displayed in this field.

Maximum Directory Entries   The number of directories, files, salvage files, and trustee entries that can exist on this volume, as configured during installation, are displayed.

Peak Directory Entries Used   The highest-numbered directory entry in use by the volume.

Current Free Directory Entries   The number of directory entries currently available. Files, directories, salvage files, and trustee nodes use up directory entries.

Logical Drive Number   The logical number of the disk drive where the volume is located.

Volume Mirrored   This field shows whether the volume is mirrored on two physical disks.

Primary Disk Number   The number of the physical disk drive of the volume.

Mirror Disk Number   The number of the physical disk the volume is mirrored on, or N/A if mirroring is not used.

FCONSOLE Connection Information

Most of the options for the Connection Information selection of the FCONSOLE menu were covered in the previous chapter. This section provides information on four options in the Connection Information menu that deal with files, record locks and the task activity of the workstations. The options are

Logical Record Locks

Open Files/Physical Records

Semaphores

Task Information

Logical Record Locks

The Logical Record Locks option is used to display all logical record locks for the currently selected user and the tasks using the locks. Logical record locks are used to control records in database files used by multiple users. When a record is locked by one user, others cannot access it. Records within databases are usually occupied by one set of information, such as the name, address, and other information for a single person in a database of many names.

The menu that appears will display the lock and log status of a logical record, according to the options listed here.

Logged   The Logged status indicates the station has included the record in a list of records it wants to lock as a set. The records in the set cannot be used by other stations until the station releases them.

Locked Shareable   The Locked Shareable status indicates a station may lock the shareable record, but no other station can lock the record exclusively. This mode is most often used when reading data that should not be changed by other stations.

Locked Exclusively   A Locked Exclusively record cannot be locked by another station. The exclusive mode is used most often when the station is changing data and no other station should be reading or updating the data.

Being Held by the Transaction Tracking System   If a file is being updated that is "transaction tracked," the operating system will hold exclusive locks until the entire transaction has been completed. This allows the transaction to be backed out cleanly in the event of a component failure during the transaction.

Open Files/Physical Records

The Open Files/Physical Records option displays all files that are currently in use by the selected connection. It shows the status of files and any physical record locks the selected connection has in the files. To view the file status or physical record locks of a particular file, highlight the file and press ENTER. A menu will appear and you can select between File Status or Physical Record Locks.

If File Status is selected from the menu, one or more messages will describe the status of the selected file. If Physical Record Locks is selected, a window will list the physical record locks of the selected file. A physical record lock can prevent another station from accessing or changing a range of bytes (a record) in the file. Unlike a logical record lock, a physical record lock is enforced without the cooperation of other stations. Other stations attempting to access the file will be denied access. The lock status of the file will be displayed as described in the "Logical Record Locks" section of this chapter.

Semaphores

The Semaphores option is used to display a list of the semaphores a connection is using. Semaphores are used to limit how many tasks can use or change a resource at the same time, and to limit the number of workstations that can run a program at the same time.

A task uses a semaphore to request the use of a resource. If the resource is available, the task is allowed to proceed. If the resource is not available, the task is forced to wait until it is. If a wait time is exceeded, an error message indicates that the resource is not available. Semaphores also act to prevent the maximum number of licensed users from accessing a program.

When the Semaphore option is selected, a window will show the semaphore name, the task it is being used for, its open count, and its value. "Open count" indicates the number of connections that have this semaphore in use. "Value" limits the use of the resource and indicates how many users can access the resource at one time. A value of 0 indicates the resource is in use by the maximum number of allowed users. Negative numbers indicate that users are waiting to use the resource.

Task Information

The Task Information option shows which tasks are currently active at the selected connection's workstation and whether the workstation is waiting for a lock or a semaphore. The Connection Status and Active Status windows will appear when Task Information is selected.

The Connection Status window will display messages describing whether or not the connection is waiting on a physical record lock, file lock, semaphore, or logical record lock. If the Transaction Tracking System is used, the following messages will appear.

Normal   The task is using files, locks, or semaphores.

Explicit transaction in progress   The task has issued an explicit "begin transaction." All changes made by this task to files that are flagged Transactional are being tracked by the TTS so they can be backed out if a crash occurs.

Implicit transaction in progress   The task has locked a physical or logical record, causing the TTS to assume an implicit "begin transaction" call. All changes made by this task to the files that are flagged Transactional are being tracked by the TTS so they can be backed out if the station crashes.

Shared file set lock in progress   The task has issued a "begin shared file set transaction" call. All the files it had open are locked. When the shared file set transaction is finished, the files will be detached and no further access will be allowed until they are locked again. The TTS is not tracking changes.

Explicit transaction and shared file set lock in progress   Indicates the task has issued an explicit "begin transaction" call to the TTS, as well as a "begin shared file set transaction" call.

Implicit transaction and shared file set lock in progress   Indicates the task has locked a physical or logical record causing the TTS to assume an implicit "begin transaction" call. A "begin shared file set transaction" call has also been issued.

File/Lock Activity

The File/Lock Activity option on the FCONSOLE Available Options menu is used to show information about the use of files, locks, and semaphores. It also allows you to view information about the Transaction Tracking System (TTS). Only console operators or the supervisor may select this option.

The following menu will appear when the selection is made. If you are using SFT NetWare, the Current Transactions selection will also be available. Each option is discussed in the following sections.

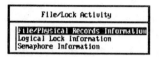

Current Transactions

The Current Transactions option displays the number of transactions currently being tracked by the Transaction Tracking System (TTS), along with the connections and tasks. The Current Transactions and Conn Task menu appear. Each entry is discussed here.

Transactions in Progress   The transactions that the server has finished but not yet written to disk and the transactions currently in progress are listed. If transactions are in progress, the connection and the task performing the transaction will be displayed in the second window.

New Transactions   The number of transactions that have been started in the last second.

Total Transactions   The number of transactions that have been tracked by TTS since the server was brought up.

Connection Number and Task Number   These numbers are displayed for each transaction in progress.

File/Physical Records Information

The File/Physical Records Information option is used to show all the connections using a file and the file's status. It also shows all physical record locks on the file. When the option is selected, you must enter the path of the file for which you want to view information. This can be done by typing or by using the INS key. When the directory has been specified, you then enter the name of the file and press ENTER.

At the File/Physical Records Information menu, you can choose to view either the file status or the physical records locks, as described in the following paragraphs.

File Status

Two windows appear when File Status is selected. The options on these first windows are described here.

Use Count   The number of connections using the file, including opening, logging, or locking a file.

Open Count   The number of connections that currently have the file opened.

Open for Read   The number of connections that currently have the file open for reading.

Open for Write   The number of connections that currently have the file open for writing.

Deny Read   The number of connections that have opened the file and requested that other stations not be able to open the file with Read privileges.

Deny Write   The number of connections that have opened the file and requested that other stations not be able to open the file for writing.

Status   Displays the locked status of the file.

The options on the second menu are as follows.

Connection Number and Task Number   Displays the connections using the file. The connection number, task number, lock status, and log status are displayed.

Status The lock status of the file is shown as locked exclusive, shared set lock, not locked, or held by TTS. Log status can be either logged or not logged.

Physical Records Lock

If Physical Record Lock is selected, a window will show all physical locks that any connection has on the selected file. The list is updated every two seconds. Physical record locks can prevent other stations from accessing or changing a range of bytes within the file. This lock is enforced without the cooperation of other stations, which will receive an "Access Denied" message when attempting to access the range of bytes.

The window lists the byte range (in hexadecimal) being locked, the number of connections using the range, and the lock status of the range.

Logical Lock Information

The Logical Lock Information option displays a set of windows that allow you to view all the connections using a specific logical record lock and the status of the lock. When the option is selected, you will be asked for the logical record name. After the name is typed and the ENTER key is pressed, two screens will appear. The first has the following entries.

Use Count The number of connections that have the logical record locked or logged.

Share Count The number of connections that have the logical record locked Shareable. If the count is zero, no connections have it locked Shareable.

Status The status of the record is displayed.

The second menu has the following entries.

Connection Number and Task Number The connections using the selected logical record, connection number, and task number are listed.

Status   The status of the file is displayed.

Semaphore Information

The Semaphore Information option displays information about a particular semaphore. Select the option from the File/Lock Activity menu to display a dual window with the following information.

Open Count   The number of connections that have the selected semaphore open for use.

Value   The current value of the semaphore. A negative value indicates the number of workstations waiting for the service of the semaphore. A positive value indicates free semaphores.

Connection   The connection number of the workstation using the semaphore.

Task   The number of the task using the semaphore.

Custom Installation Procedures

Modifying NetWare
Resource and Resource Set Management
Running Custom SHGEN
Running Custom NETGEN/ELSGEN Configuration
Running Custom NETGEN/ELSGEN Installation

This appendix is designed for those who need to run the SHGEN and NETGEN/ELSGEN programs in custom mode. System installers and integrators, as well as those with special needs, will find this appendix of use. If you need to alter the installation or upgrade from another version, you should also use this appendix. The following sections are provided:

- Modifying NetWare

- Resource and Resource Set Management

- Running Custom SHGEN

- Running Custom NETGEN/ELSGEN Configuration

- Running Custom NETGEN/ELSGEN Installation

These sections assume that you are familiar with the default installation mode, having run it at least once.

You may be referring to this section because the default installation procedures covered in Chapter 10 were insufficient for your needs and system configuration. The custom configuration and installation levels of SHGEN and NETGEN/ELSGEN allow you to choose LAN drivers that are not available on the LAN_DRV-.??? disks supplied with NetWare; you will be able to load driver files obtained from Novell or other manufacturers from disks. The custom level is also used when interrupts and address conflicts are likely to occur. You will be able to select from a wider variety of LAN driver options with the custom method.

Modifying NetWare

You can make modifications to a NetWare system that has already been installed by performing most of the configuration and installation steps discussed here and in Chapter 10, with a few exceptions. Do not make modifications to or initialize hard-drive volumes; this would destroy the existing data. You can make modifications to install additional boards, change addresses, change printer ports, and other features. A full list is provided at the end of Chapter 26.

When making a modification to the system, you may need to specify that the operating system and public files *not* be loaded. This can be done by setting the following flags to No:

- In the NETGEN/ELSGEN installation phase, from the Miscellaneous Maintenance menu, select Load Operating System and choose No.

- In the same Miscellaneous Maintenance menu, select Load System & Public Files and choose No.

If you change the size of volumes, COMPSURF the disk, initialize the disk, or perform other operations that drastically alter the server's hard drive, you will lose the data on the hard drive, so be careful when you make changes and always back up the volume beforehand. Make sure your backup software backs up the bindery files as well.

Resource and Resource Set Management

The custom configuration and installation method also accommodates the selection of other resources. Resources are non-NetWare-related hardware you may be installing in your workstations or servers. Most installable resources use the interrupts, I/O addresses, and memory addresses of the system they are being installed in. NetWare's resource management options give you the opportunity to specify, in advance, what lines and addresses these resources will use. SHGEN and NETGEN/ELSGEN can then keep track of the addresses in use and provide you with line and address information for the cards you are adding.

The resource management options that are available in SHGEN and NETGEN/ELSGEN should be considered tools to help you avoid hardware conflicts. The resource selections you make do not alter any hardware options themselves, as is the case with some PC installation programs that make changes to programmable ROM chips (PROMs). Specifying resources is a way of telling the configuration and installation programs which lines and addresses have been "spoken for." The configuration program then presents you with nonconflicting lines and addresses when configuring additional resources.

It is not necessary to use the resource management functions if you are installing components in IBM PS/2 systems. The IBM Reference disk that comes with each PS/2 is used to configure additional equipment for the computers and to prevent hardware conflicts.

Resource sets are collections of resources. The AT Compatible File Server resource, for example, consists of an auxiliary ROM chip, an AT hard-drive controller, and a floppy-drive controller. System integrators and installers may want to define resource sets for the type of equipment they install on a regular basis to speed up the configuration and installation process.

Resource Editing

The custom installation menus display the Edit Resource List and Edit Resource Sets options, as shown here. You can choose the first option to define a new resource. The second option is used to build resource sets. In order to be able to select any resource, it must be a member of a set, even if it is the only member of the set. Defining resources, then, involves two steps: Define the parameters that make up the resource, then place it in a resource set.

The following screen appears when Edit Resource List is selected. As you can see by the help screen at the bottom, resources can be edited, inserted, deleted, and marked (for marking groups).

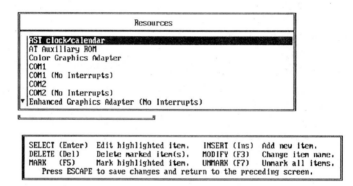

Pressing ENTER on any selection will display the Resource Configurations menu, which lists the possible configurations of one of the selected devices. In most cases there will only be one configuration, but the EGA adapter has two, one for attachment to a color/EGA monitors and one for attachment to monochrome monitors, as shown here:

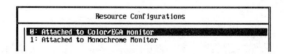

The name will often define the configuration, such as "0: IRQ=2, BASE I/O=300h, DMA=5, MEMORY=C000h." A Configuration Information menu similar to the following will appear when you select one of the configurations presented. This menu is for an Enhanced Graphics Adapter attached to a color/EGA monitor. It is on this menu that you specifically define the parameters of a particular board to be installed in the server.

```
┌─────────────────────────────────────────────────────────────┐
│ Configuration Information                  (Mode: Decimal)   │
├─────────────────────────────────────────────────────────────┤
│ Number of I/O Address Ranges:   2  Bus: Standard            │
│    Starting Address #1:   960     Range (bytes):        16   │
│    Starting Address #2:   976     Range (bytes):        16   │
│ Number of Memory Address Ranges: 2                           │
│    Starting Segment #1:   40960   Range (Paragraphs): 4096   │
│    Starting Segment #2:   47104   Range (Paragraphs): 2048   │
│ Number of Interrupt Lines:       0                           │
│    Interrupt Line #1:             Interrupt Line #2:         │
│ Number of DMA Lines:             0                           │
│    DMA Line #1:                   DMA Line #2:               │
└─────────────────────────────────────────────────────────────┘
```

Manufacturers or designers of special boards can create their own customized configurations for the boards they make by pressing INS at the Resources menu or at the Resource Configurations menus. You will be asked for the name of the new resource if INS was pressed at the Resources menu or the resource configuration name if INS was pressed at the Resource Configurations menu. Press ENTER to insert the new name in the menu, and then highlight the entry and press ENTER again to begin editing it. You can change most of the options on the Configuration Information menu to customize your new resource. When the configuration has been defined, remember to add the resource to a set, as described next.

Defining Resource Sets

A resource set is a collection of individual resources you have defined or resources that have already been defined by NetWare. A typical resource set might define all of the resources for a particular computer system. The Novell 286A file server is described here.

To build resource sets or add a newly configured resource to a set, select Edit Resource Sets from the SHGEN or NETGEN/ELSGEN main menu. Sets can have several different resources, as shown here for the Novell 286A file server:

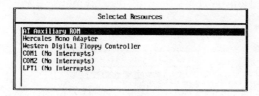

```
┌─────────────────────────────────────────────────────┐
│              Selected Resources                      │
├─────────────────────────────────────────────────────┤
│ AT Auxiliary ROM                                     │
│ Hercules Mono Adapter                                │
│ Western Digital Floppy Controller                    │
│ COM1 (No Interrupts)                                 │
│ COM2 (No Interrupts)                                 │
│ LPT1 (No Interrupts)                                 │
│                                                      │
└─────────────────────────────────────────────────────┘
```

To insert a new resource set, press the INS key at the Resource Sets menu. You will then be asked to name the new set. Once the new set appears on the main menu, you can select it, and then press ENTER at the Selected Resources menu to begin adding resources to the set. When you are done adding resources to the set, press ESC to return to the main menu. When you are exiting the SHGEN or NETGEN/ELSGEN programs, you will be asked if you want to save the new resource set definitions, to which you can answer Yes if you want to save them for future configurations.

Running Custom SHGEN

The SHGEN program creates the boot files IPX.COM and NET*x*.COM, which are used at the workstation to log on to the network. A specific set of these files is needed for each workstation that uses a different network interface card. A set will also be required for boards that have had their lines and addresses changed to avoid conflicts with other system resources. You will need to have a separate master shell disk ready for each SHGEN boot file set you create. This floppy disk should be capable of booting the version of DOS you intend to run at the workstations.

If you are running ELS NetWare Level II, start SHGEN by typing **SHGEN** on the command line. If you are running Advanced NetWare and SFT NetWare, you can start the program in custom mode by typing the following command. The N (New) option should only be used if you want to ignore settings made during previous sessions.

SHGEN -NC

After selecting the SHGEN custom configuration level and the run method from the initial menus, choose Select Shell Configuration from the Shell Generation Options menu. In a moment, the following screen will appear:

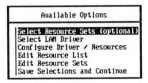

By choosing Select Resource Sets from this menu, you can begin to set aside the resources on the workstation you are configuring. The following menu appears after you press ENTER twice at the Select Resource Sets option:

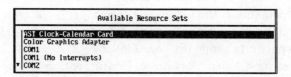

When a resource is selected, it will appear in the Selected Resource Sets window. If a resource you need is not on the list, you can create it with the Edit Resource List or Edit Resource Sets option from the main menu, as described in the first part of this chapter.

Next, you can choose the LAN driver to use in the workstation by choosing Select LAN Driver from the main menu. After choosing Select Available Items from the LAN Driver Options window, you can highlight the correct driver from the Available LAN Drivers menu. Press ESC to return to the Available Options menu.

Once the LAN driver has been selected, the Configure Driver/Resources option will appear in the Available Options menu. Select this option to make specific interrupt and address selections for the LAN driver. A screen similar to the following will appear:

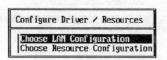

Selecting the Choose LAN Configuration option will display the Unconfigured Driver screen. Highlight the driver you wish to configure, and press ENTER. A screen similar to the following will appear:

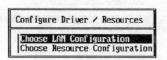

SHGEN presents a list of available configurations that have not been "spoken for" by the resources you selected earlier. Choose one of the configurations that matches the switch and jumper settings you can make on your LAN board. You may want to make those board settings while viewing the menu. If the interface board must be altered by mounting it in a computer and running a special program, write down the settings you have selected and change the board later.

Selecting Choose Resource Configuration from the Configure Driver/Resource menu will allow you to configure the resources you selected further. For example, the following screen appears if Enhanced Graphics Adapter was chosen in the Select Resource Sets option of the Available Options menu:

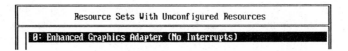

By pressing ENTER twice, you can select a color or monochrome configuration, as shown here:

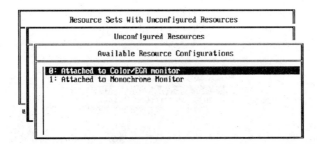

After making the appropriate selections, choose Save Selections and Continue from the main menu. Choose Yes if you want to continue the generation process. In a moment, the following screen will appear. Select Link NetWare Shell to proceed with the configuration as normal.

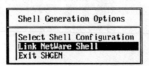

Running Custom NETGEN/ELSGEN Configuration

The custom level of NETGEN/ELSGEN provides the same added features for configuring your system that the custom level of SHGEN provides for changing the default levels. The additional items can be seen on the menu shown here, which is displayed when Select Network Configuration is selected:

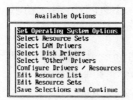

```
        Available Options
 Set Operating System Options
 Select Resource Sets
 Select LAN Drivers
 Select Disk Drivers
 Select "Other" Drivers
 Configure Drivers / Resources
 Edit Resource List
 Edit Resource Sets
 Save Selections and Continue
```

In the custom level, you can select resource sets and extended LAN driver options for the server, as well as edit your own resource lists and resource sets. Since the resource selection process is exactly the same for the NETGEN/ELSGEN program as it is for the SHGEN program, refer to the previous discussion on resource sets for more information.

To start the custom NETGEN level, type **NETGEN -C**, or type **NETGEN -CN** if you want to start a new session. If you are running ELSGEN, you can select the custom level from menus in the program. Follow these steps to configure the server operating system with custom options:

1. Select Set Operating System Options to select dedicated or non-dedicated mode or, if you are configuring SFT NetWare, to add the Transaction Tracking System (TTS).

2. Choose Select Resource Sets to specify the additional resources you plan to place in the server. The procedure for using this option is the same as that for SHGEN, so you can refer to the previous section for more details. You can also select Edit Resource List and Edit Resource Sets to configure you own resources, as de-scribed earlier.

3. Choose Select LAN Drivers to select the driver for the network interface card to be used in the server. Those configuring Advanced NetWare and SFT NetWare can select up to four separate LAN drivers for the server.

4. Choose Select Disk Drivers to select the disk drivers for the server.

5. Choose Select Other Drivers to select any additional drivers you need to load from disk.

6. Choose Configure Drivers/Resources to configure the drivers and resources you selected in the previous steps. The procedure is similar to that used in SHGEN.

7. Select Save Configuration and Continue to accept the drivers and resources you have selected and continue with the configuration.

In a moment, the Network Generation Options screen will appear, as shown here. You will need to select the linking and configuring options before exiting the configuration phase.

When you select the Exit option, you will be asked if you want to download

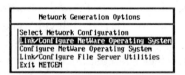

files to floppy disk if you are running the hard-drive configuration method. Select Yes and insert the appropriate disks when requested.

Running Custom NETGEN/ELSGEN Installation

The custom installation method of NETGEN is much more extensive than the default installation method. Advanced NetWare and SFT NetWare provide options for partitioning disks, and SFT NetWare provides options provide options for partitioning disks, and SFT NetWare provides options for creating mirrored or duplexed drives. The sections presented here for the custom levels of NETGEN and ELSGEN are as follows:

- Accessing ELSGEN Custom Options

- Accessing NETGEN Custom Options

- Setting Up Mirror Tables: SFT NetWare Only

- Partition Tables: Advanced NetWare and SFT NetWare Only

- Customizing Hot Fix: All NetWare Versions

- Setting the System Configuration

- Defining Hard-Drive Volumes

- The Miscellaneous Maintenance Menu

- Completing the NETGEN/ELSGEN Installation

Note: Be sure to install all network interface cards and other options in the server before continuing. Refer to Phase 3 installation options in Chapter 10 for more information.

Accessing ELSGEN Custom Options

To access the custom level of ELSGEN, start the program in the normal way from the floppy drive at the server by typing **ELSGEN**. If you are using the network-drive method, map a drive to the directory \GENER-ATE\NETWARE on the existing file server from the workstation that will become the new server, and then type **ELSGEN**.

When the ELSGEN Run Options menu appears, select the run method to use. (Do not select the Hard Disk option when performing the installation phase.) The Network Generation Options menu will appear. Select NetWare Installation to proceed with the installation. You will be asked to verify the hard-disk configuration, as discussed in Chapter 10, and then the Installation Options menu will appear. Choose Select Custom Installation Options. You may now continue with the following sections that pertain to ELSGEN custom options.

Accessing NETGEN Custom Options

To access the custom level of NETGEN, start the program in the normal way from the floppy drive at the server by typing **NETGEN - C**. If you are using the network-directory method, map a drive to the directory \GEN-ERATE\NETWARE on the existing file server from the workstation that will become the new server, and then type **NETGEN -C**. Do not select the N (New) option at this time.

When the NETGEN Run Options menu appears, select the run method to use. (Do not select the Hard Disk option, since the utility must read the information downloaded to disk in the configuration phase.) The Network Generation Options menu will appear. Select NetWare Installation to proceed with the installation. You will be asked to verify the hard-disk configuration, as discussed in Chapter 10, and then the Installation Options menu will appear. Choose Select Custom Installation Options. You may now continue with the following sections that pertain to NETGEN custom options.

Setting Up Mirror Tables: SFT NetWare Only

If two or more hard disks are installed in the server and you are running SFT NetWare, the Mirroring Options menu will appear. You can choose to establish a mirror pair if you want to take advantage of NetWare system fault tolerance options.

Drives can be paired for mirroring if they are on the same channel and duplexed if they are on different channels. These options are discussed in Chapter 9. Highlight Establish Mirror Pair from the menu, then decide which of the listed disks will be the primary drive in the pair.

Note: Once two disks are paired together, they will appear as a single disk and assume the drive name and information of the primary disk.

Partition Tables: Advanced NetWare And SFT NetWare Only

The Custom Installation menu may display the Modify Partition Table option. You can choose this option if you wish to allocate a specific portion of your hard disk's storage space to another operating system such as DOS.

Keep in mind that only one of the operating systems present on your hard drive can be operated at one time. Therefore, operating systems residing in other partitions must be started with boot disks.

It is not recommended that you establish a DOS partition, since it will drastically limit the disk space allocated to NetWare. This is because the DOS partition must be placed below a 32MB limit. At the same time, NetWare must start at cylinder 0, which means that NetWare would be limited to less than 32MB. NetWare cannot reside in an extended partition as DOS is capable of doing.

On the other hand, a DOS partition can increase the boot time required to start a NetWare server. The files to start the server can be placed in the DOS partition on the hard drive, where they will execute much faster.

If you decide to partition a disk, select the Modify Partition Table option. You will see a list of the file server's current drives along with the channels and controllers they are attached to. Highlight the drive you want to partition, and press ENTER. A blank partition table window will appear. You can press INS to begin creating the partitions for the drive. Partitions require the following information:

OS Type Name	Enter the name of the partition, such as NetWare, DOS or UNIX/XENIX.
Status	Enter the boot status of the partition. In most cases, you will want to make NetWare the bootable partition.
Start Cylinder	Enter the cylinder where the partition will begin.
End Cylinder	Enter the cylinder where the partition will end.

The NetWare partition must begin with cylinder 0, and DOS partitions cannot extend past the 32MB cylinder. This imposes some restrictions on the size of both NetWare and DOS partitions. In order to modify partitions, you will need to know how many cylinders your hard drive has and how many megabytes are available in each cylinder. You can initially determine how many cylinders are available on the drive by inserting at least one partition. Note the starting and ending cylinder categories. You will see an entry such as "(Max = 1021)." Divide this number by the total storage capacity of the drive. For example, 1021 (cylinders) divided by 86 (86MB) equals 12 cylinders per megabyte.

Once you know how many megabytes there are per cylinder, you can determine how many cylinders to allocate for NetWare (starting at cylinder 0) and other operating systems. Since DOS must reside in the first 32MB of the drive, you can determine the exact cylinders to use for the DOS partition.

Note that the DOS partition forces you to allocate a small NetWare partition since NetWare must start at cylinder 0 and stop somewhere before the 32MB cylinder so you can insert a DOS partition. The remainder of the drive can not be allocated to NetWare.

When selecting a partition, you are given the following options:

DOS 12-Bit FATs	Select this for disks up to 10MB in size.
DOS 16-Bit FATS	Select this for disks larger than 10MB in size.
Extended DOS	Select this if you have additional disk space available for DOS after the 32MB limit.
NetWare	Select this when creating the first partition.
Other	Select this for other operating systems. An OS indicator value will be requested, which you can obtain from the manufacturer or distributor of the operating system.

Note: Use the DOS FDISK and FORMAT commands to prepare the DOS partitions after NetWare has been installed and the NETGEN program completes. You must also start the server under NetWare before attempting to run the DOS programs.

After partitioning the drives, you may return to the Custom Installation menu. The Hot Fix Drives to Default option will appear on the screen. You should run this option, unless you want to customize the Hot Fix feature as discussed in the next section. Generally, you would select the NetWare defaults unless you want to minimize the amount of disk space used by the Hot Fix feature.

Customizing Hot Fix: All NetWare Versions

Choose the Modify Hot Fix Redirection Tables option from the Custom Installation screen to modify the Hot Fix tables. The Hot Fix Redirection area is a portion of the disk set aside to receive bad blocks from areas of the disk NetWare has determined are failing or are bad. The Hot Fix area is normally about 2% of the disk space.

The Hot Fix disk area can be modified if the disk is small and you want to minimize the area. If you are installing an older disk that has had a lot of previous use, you may want to increase the Hot Fix area to set aside additional redirection space for a larger number of bad blocks that will surely develop.

SFT NetWare users will need to consider changing the Hot Fix area based on the disk mirroring and duplexing options. If disk pairs used in mirroring and duplexing are of different sizes, you must set them to the same logical size so that they become a matched pair.

Highlight Modify Hot Fix Redirection Tables in the Custom Installation menu, and press ENTER. The screen will display the current Hot Fix table, showing channels, controllers, drives, logical size, and Hot Fix information. Highlight one of the drives in the listing and adjust the logical disk size to the amount of the disk space you want to allocate for storage. The remaining disk space will be used for Hot Fix. SFT NetWare users with mirrored or duplexed drives must set the paired drives' logical disk size exactly the same.

When the Hot Fix sizes have been set, record the setting on your network log sheets and press ESC.

Setting the System Configuration

After you set the options discussed in the previous sections, the System Configuration menu will appear. In custom installation mode, you can change options on this menu as discussed here:

File Server Name   Enter the name for the file server you are configuring. If other file servers will be attached to the network, be sure the name is different. The file-server name can be from 2 to 45 characters long.

Number of Open Files   This is the maximum number of files that can be open simultaneously on the file server. Each open file requires 100 bytes of overhead.

Number of Indexed Files   NetWare builds an index of a file's location in memory if it is marked as an Indexed file to increase the speed at which it can be accessed. Set the index to the number of large files, especially databases, that you intend to have open at any one time. For best results, accept the default and then run your system for a while to see if it is sufficient. You can always reconfigure the operating system at a later time.

Transaction Backout Volumes (SFT NetWare Only)   This field option will appear if you installed the Transaction Tracking System (TTS). Transaction tracking restores opened and modified records to their previous condition when a file server comes back on line after being shut down by a system failure. NetWare requires a certain amount of disk space to run TTS, and you must designate a volume as the backout volume. The disk must have sufficient free space (1MB is recommended) to maintain a copy of the largest transaction. Novell also recommends that the backout volume be on a different disk channel than the drive from which the transactions originate.

Number of Transactions (SFT NetWare Only)   NetWare users will be able to mark the files they want to protect with the TTS option by assigning them the Transactional file attribute. The default number of transaction files will display on the screen and can be adjusted if a larger number of transaction files will be open.

Limit Disk Space   The amount of disk space storage available to each user can be limited by specifying Yes in this field. If selected, you must set the number of bindery objects, as covered next.

Number of Bindery Objects   This option is used to set the number of users and groups on the file server if Limit Disk Space is set to Yes. The default setting will usually be appropriate; however, you can adjust the number. The number of bindery objects must be between 500 and 5000.

Once the System Configuration settings have been made, you can press ESC to move to the next screen.

Defining Hard-Drive Volumes

The custom installation method allows you to adjust volume sizes. The Volume Information screen will appear after you have configured the system. Press the INS key to make volume adjustments.

Volume Name   The first volume must be SYS. Each remaining volume should be named VOL1, VOL2, and so on.

Volume Size   The maximum size for any volume under NetWare 286 is 255MB. If only one volume is being defined, accept the default volume size. You can specify other volume sizes, but make sure the total of these volumes is equal to the disk size. Novell recommends that only one volume be selected per disk.

Number of Directory Entries   Directory entries are defined by the number of directory names, subdirectory names, and file names you will use on your system. The default setting should be sufficient unless you have reason to change it.

Cache the Directory   When a volume's directory is cached, a copy is kept in system memory to increase the speed of file searches. In most cases you should keep this option set to Yes unless your system is low on memory or the volume is being used for archive purposes with little disk I/O.

After setting the options just discussed, you can press ESC to move on to the next menu. A prompt will ask if you want to create the volumes just defined; you can answer Yes. If you answer No, you can restart the initialization process.

The Miscellaneous Maintenance Menu

After you complete the hard-disk initialization, the Miscellaneous Maintenance option will appear on the Custom Installation menu. The following menu is displayed when this option is chosen. The available options are described next.

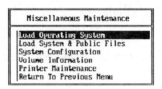

Load Operating System   This option sets a flag that directs the NETGEN/ELSGEN program to load the operating system files. Set this flag to Yes if this is the first time you are installing NetWare or if you have made changes that affect the operating system, such as adding a LAN card or other resource option. Set this flag to No if you are running NETGEN/ELSGEN after changing one of the options discussed in this section.

Load System & Public Files   This option sets a flag that directs the NETGEN/ELSGEN program to load the system and public files. Set this flag to Yes if this is the first time you are installing NetWare. Set this flag to No if you are running NETGEN/ELSGEN after changing an option and you do not wish to reinstall the files.

System Configuration   This option allows you to specify a different volume as the TTS backout volume. Refer to "Setting the System Configuration" earlier.

Volume Information   This option displays the volume information.

Printer Maintenance   This option allows you to define the printers to be attached to the server. A list of ports available on the server will appear. Highlight the port a printer is attached to, and refer to these instructions:

- Serial printers can be attached to COM1 or COM2. When one of these ports is selected, you must define the parameters for the port that match the printer. This includes the baud rate, word length, stop bits, parity, and Xon/Xoff protocol. Refer to your printer manual and the setting on the printer for this information. You must also specify a spooled printer number between 0 and 4. This is the number that the server will use to identify the printer. In most cases, the port assigned to printer number 0 will be the default printer.

- The only parameter required for parallel printer ports is the spooled printer number they will use. This is the number that the server will use to identify the printer. In most cases, the port assigned to printer number 0 will be the default printer.

Return to Previous Menu   Use this option to return to the Custom Installation menu to continue with the installation.

Completing the NETGEN/ELSGEN Installation

After reviewing or making changes according to the custom installation options described, you can complete the NetWare installation. Simply highlight the Continue Installation field in the Installation Options menu.

Gateway and Remote Connection Installation

Generating External LAN Bridges with BRGEN
Configuring and Operating a Remote Workstation
Starting the Bridge
Bridge Console Commands
Starting a Remote Workstation

This chapter covers the installation of NetWare external LAN bridges using Advanced NetWare and SFT NetWare. Recall that external bridges are made in workstations, whereas internal bridges are made in file servers. If you are installing an internal bridge, you can refer to the normal NETGEN/ELSGEN procedures covered in Chapter 10 and Appendix A. An internal bridge is simple to install: simply specify up to four different LAN drivers for each card (and network) you plan to install. External bridges require additional software at the workstation, which is configured by following the steps in this appendix.

Advanced NetWare and SFT NetWare can be connected to another LAN, a remote LAN, or a remote workstation. Recall from Chapter 6 that a connection to another LAN may be made to extend the area of an existing LAN or to connect to a LAN that uses different topologies and interface cards. A remote LAN is one that may be some distance from the existing LAN and may require telephone lines or other transmission media to make the connection. A remote workstation is a single PC at a remote location that connects to the LAN through typical modem connections.

Generating External LAN Bridges With BRGEN

The procedures for starting the BRGEN bridge generation program, selecting the run level (floppy-disk, hard-disk, or network- drive method), and selecting the configuration method (default or custom) are similar to the procedures used for the NETGEN/ELSGEN programs, as discussed in Chapter 10 and Appendix A. The operation of the menus is also similar. This section will only cover the custom configuration method for BRGEN.

The BRGEN program creates a file called BRIDGE.EXE that should be copied to the boot disk used to start the external bridge. If the external bridge has a hard drive, you should copy this file to the root directory of the hard drive if it is a bootable drive.

Starting BRGEN

To begin, you will need to locate the following disks, and then refer to the "Floppy-Disk Method" or "Hard-Disk or Network-Drive Method" sections that follow. You should make copies of the disks listed here.

5 1/4-inch Disk Set	3 1/2-inch Disk Set
BRGEN-1	BRGEN-1
BRGEN-2	BRGEN-2
BRGEN-3	LAN_DRV_.001
LAN_DRV_.001	LAN_DRV_.002
LAN_DRV_.002	

Floppy-Disk Method

If you are running BRGEN from floppy disk, insert the disk labeled BRGEN-1 in drive A. Place the AUXGEN disk in drive B if the drive is available. Type **BRGEN -N** (use -N only if you want a new session and do not want to save settings made in a previous BRGEN session). When the System Configuration Method window appears, you can choose the method you want to run, but only the custom configuration method is covered here. You can now jump ahead to "Running BRGEN."

Hard-Disk or Network-Drive Method

If you are running BRGEN from a hard disk or over a network, you will need to copy the files from the disks listed earlier to the hard drive. First, move to the \GENERATE\NETWARE directory and create directories for each of the disks listed earlier. Next, copy the contents of the disks to each of the respective directories. Note that the numeric portion of the LAN_DRV_.001 and LAN_DRV_.002 disk names should be typed as a file-name extension and separated by a period. For example, type **MD LAN_DRV_.001** to create the directories.

After copying the disks to directories, copy the contents of the BRUTILS disk into the \GENERATE\NETWARE\BRGEN-1 subdirectory. Next, copy the BRGEN.EXE and IBM$RUN.OVL files from the BRGEN-1 disk to the \GENERATE\NETWARE directory of the hard drive.

To start the BRGEN program, make sure you are in the \GENERATE\NETWARE directory if you are using the hard-disk method. If you are using the network-drive method, map a drive to this directory. Type **BRGEN -N** (use -N only if you want a new session and do not want to save settings made in a previous BRGEN session). When the System Configuration Method window appears, you can choose a run method (only the custom configuration method is covered here).

Running BRGEN

After you start the BRGEN program and select the Custom Configuration option, the following menu will appear:

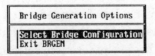

Choose Select Bridge Configuration to continue. In a moment, the Available Options menu will appear, as shown next. You can select the bridge type, resource sets, and LAN drivers with this menu. Resource sets can be selected in the same manner as described in Appendix A. You can also edit resource lists and sets.

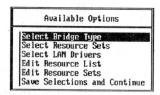

Selecting the Bridge Type

External bridges can be either dedicated or nondedicated. A dedicated bridge is an external workstation that is used for the sole purpose of bridging networks or remote workstations. A nondedicated bridge can still be used as a network workstation, but it is susceptible to failure if the software running on it should lock up. This would bring down the bridge and prevent access to it by others. Dedicated bridges are less likely to fail because they are not functioning as workstations. They are also faster since their resources are dedicated to serving the bridge. The choice of dedicated or nondedicated mode is made when you start the bridge with the BRIDGE command, as you will see later. For now, you must select a bridge type based on whether the bridge will run in dedicated or nondedicated mode.

Choose Select Bridge Type from the menu to display the following screen:

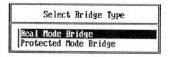

A dedicated bridge must be run in real mode, regardless of the computer type being used for the bridge. A nondedicated bridge can be run in either real or protected mode. Select the option that is best for your external bridge. You can then begin the resource selection process as covered next.

Protected-Mode Bridge   A protected-mode bridge will accommodate up to 8MB of memory, which provides enough room to run value-added processes (VAPs) on the bridge. A VAP is an additional NetWare application that runs on top of the network operating system. These applications are linked into the NetWare operating system and executed while the

bridge is running. The Macintosh VAP is an example. If you plan to install more than one VAP, you should choose protected-mode bridging and install at least 2MB of memory.

Real-Mode Bridge   The real-mode bridge uses the standard 640K base memory of most DOS machines, but you will be limited to running only one or two VAPs.

Selecting Resources

Resource selection is the same for BRGEN as it is for NETGEN/ELSGEN, as discussed in Appendix A. Recall that resource selection is designed to help you prevent line and address conflicts with the boards and devices in your system before actually installing them. You can use the Edit Resource options to create any resources not available on the list provided. This is also covered in Appendix A.

Selecting LAN Drivers

LAN drivers are selected by choosing the Select LAN Driver option from the menu. You will have the opportunity to choose up to four different devices. The BRGEN screen looks like this when two networks and one remote LAN using the IBM ASYNC driver are selected:

```
                      Selected LAN Drivers
 A: 3Com 3C503 EtherLink II  V3.00EC (881104)
 B: NetWare RX-Net  V1.00 (881010)
 C: IBM ASYNC (COM1/COM2)  V1.00 (888888)
```

Be sure to select the remote communications driver last.

Configuring the Resources and Drivers

Once resources and LAN drivers have been selected, they must be configured before proceeding. Choose the Configure Drivers/Resources option from the menu. You will then see a menu for configuring either the LAN drivers or the resource drivers. Step through each menu, pressing the ENTER key on each item to select an available configuration. A screen similar to the following will appear when you select one of the LAN drivers in the Unconfigured LAN Drivers window. Highlight one of the available configurations and make sure the board dip-switch setting and jumpers are configured in the same way.

```
                    Available LAN Configurations

  0: I/O = 330h, INT = 4, RAM = C800, BNC
  1: I/O = 350h, INT = 5, RAM = CC00, BNC
  2: I/O = 250h, INT = 3, RAM = D800, BNC
  3: I/O = 200h, INT = 2, RAM = DC00, BNC
  4: I/O = 300h, INT = 3, RAM = C800, BNC
  5: I/O = 310h, INT = 2, RAM = CC00, BNC
  6: I/O = 330h, INT = 4, RAM = D800, BNC
  7: I/O = 350h, INT = 5, RAM = DC00, BNC
```

You can select resource options in the same way. Refer to Appendix A for additional instructions on using these menus, since they function in the same way as the SHGEN and NETGEN/ELSGEN menus.

Assigning Network Addresses

The Configure Drivers/Resources window contains the Set Network Addresses option. Select this option to set the addresses for each of the boards you have selected, as shown here. Type the network address for each card that coordinates with the rest of your network. You can also change the number of communications buffers used by the bridge. The range is from 10 to 150 and should be set according to the amount of memory your system has. Use the default if you are operating with standard 640K of memory.

```
                     Network Information

  A: 3Com 3C503 EtherLink II  V3.00EC (881104)
        Network Address: 1
  B: NetWare RX-Net  V1.00 (881010)
        Network Address: 2
  C: IBM ASYNC (COM1/COM2)  V1.00 (880808)
        Network Address: 3
  Communication Buffers: 40
```

Press ESC after assigning network addresses and buffers. You can review the setting by selecting Review Selected Configuration. To continue with the bridge generation, proceed to the next step.

Generating the Bridge

Once all of the options are set, select Save Selections and Continue from the Available Options menu. You will be asked to confirm the configuration. Selecting No will allow you to go back and make further changes. If you select Yes and have edited resources, you will be asked if you want to save them.

After you select the option for continuing, the following menu will appear. Highlight Link Bridge to complete the bridge generation.

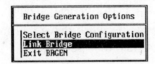

When the linking process is complete, the BRIDGE file required to start an external bridge will exist. You can now exit the BRGEN program by selecting the Exit BRGEN option.

Configuring and Operating
A Remote Workstation

After running the BRGEN program to configure the external bridge for remote communications, you can run the ARCONFIG program to specify the configuration of the remote communications board. Follow the commands that pertain to your system to start the program.

Starting ARCONFIG: Floppy-Disk Method

If you are running the floppy-disk method, insert the BRUTILS disk into drive A and BRGEN-2 (3 1/2-inch format) or BRGEN-3 (5 1/4-inch format) into drive B if it is available. If you are using 3 1/2-inch disk formats, type the following to start the program:

ARCONFIG BRGEN-2:BRIDGE.EXE

If you are using 5-1/4 inch disks, type the following to start the program:

ARCONFIG BRGEN-3:BRIDGE.EXE

Now skip to the "Configuring the Remote Bridge" section.

Starting ARCONFIG, Hard-Disk And Network-Drive Methods

Switch to the \GENERATE\NETWARE directory if you are using the hard-disk method, or map the \GENERATE\NETWARE directory to a drive if you are using the network-drive method. If you have a BRGEN-3 directory and the 5 1/4-inch disk set, type

BRUTILS\ARCONFIG BRGEN-3:BRIDGE.EXE

Otherwise, type

BRUTILS\ARCONFIG BRGEN-2:BRIDGE.EXE

Configuring the Remote Bridge

The first screen to appear will depend on the number of remote communications drivers you specified in the BRGEN program. If more than one driver was configured, you will be asked to select the LAN driver to configure. If only one driver exists, the following menu will appear:

Select Configure Bridge Server, and the Edit Bridge window will appear:

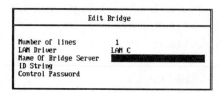

The Number of Lines entry should be 1, unless you are using a special board such as the Novell WNIM board that has up to four communications lines. The LAN driver should match that selected in the BRGEN program. Type the name of the bridge server, using an easily identifiable name such as a city or address. Next, type in an uppercase ID string. This string is optional but is useful for security. It must exactly match the ID string assigned at the remote workstation. Finally, enter a password for this station if you need password security. Press ESC to leave the menu, and choose Yes to the save prompt.

After the bridge has been configured, perform the following steps to configure the line it uses. If several communications lines are being used, you will need to perform these steps for each line. Select Configure a Particular Line from the main menu, and press ENTER. You may be asked to select a line. The following screen will appear. You can then fill out the screen, as described next.

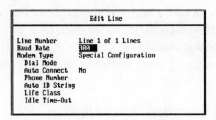

- Press ENTER in the Baud Rate field to see the available baud-rate selections, and then choose a rate that matches your modem.

- On the Modem Type field, press ENTER to select between Hayes Compatible or Special Configuration. Select Special Configuration if your modem is not Hayes-compatible or if you need to configure a remote connection in other ways. For example, you can configure a leased line, a satellite transceiver connection, or any other hardware that stays in a communication-ready state at all times.

- At the Auto Connect field, you can select Yes to have the bridge automatically establish communications when booted. ENTER the phone number if you selected a Hayes-compatible modem in the last step.

- At the Dial Mode field, select Pulse or Touch Tone.

- At the Phone Number field, enter the phone number of the remote location the modem will dial. A modem initialization string may precede the phone number. If an outside-line access number is required (usually 9), type the number followed by a comma before the phone number.

- At the Auto ID String field, type the ID string for the remote workstation. This number must match exactly the ID string given to the bridge.

- At the Life Class field, select whether the line will remain continuous, as is common with leased lines, or will be timed, which specifies the number of minutes the line waits before terminating after the last packet is sent. The number of minutes is specified in the Idle Time-Out field.

When done, press ESC to exit, and then choose Yes to save the configuration or No to go back for changes. If other lines need to be configured, such as those for WNIM boards or other multiport communications boards, repeat these steps for each line. When you are done, press ESC to complete the configuration. You may need to repeat the entire process if you are using more than one remote driver.

Configuring the Remote Workstation

You should have created the necessary workstation startup files and master boot disks for the remote workstation in the SHGEN configuration process covered in Chapter 10 and Appendix A. You are now ready to configure the remote workstation shell for the type of connection you will be making. The following procedure is used to assign the workstation ID, baud rate, and modem type.

The first step is to give the remote workstation master boot disk a disk label with the DOS LABEL command. The name given to the disk can be the city or address of the workstation.

Next, insert the BRUTILS disk in drive A, or change to the \GEN-ERATE\NETWARE\BRUTILS directory if you are using the hard-disk method. If possible, insert the remote workstation disk in another available drive. Map the \GENERATE\NETWARE\BRUTILS directory if you are using the network-drive method. Type the following command to start the configuration, where *label* is the disk label you gave the workstation disk in the previous step:

ARCONFIG *label*:IPX.COM

The Edit Shell menu will appear. Fill out the fields on the menu as described here.

- At the ID String field, type the optional ID string for the workstation in uppercase. It must exactly match the ID string you specified when configuring the bridge software for this workstation.

- At the Workstation ID field, type an easily recognizable ID that matches the user, city, or address of the workstation.

- At the COM Port field, select the port used for communications.

- At the Baud Rate field, press ENTER and select an appropriate baud rate to match the modem at the bridge.

- At the Modem Type field, you can select either a Hayes modem or a special configuration. Special-configuration modems can be configured as leased lines, satellite transceivers, or other hardware that maintains a communication-ready state at all times.

If a Hayes-compatible modem was selected, you are given the opportunity to enter a modem string and phone number. Modem strings are listed in the modem manual and include P for pulse modem and T for touch tone modems. If an outside-line access number is required (usually 9), type it followed by a comma before the phone number to be called by the modem.

Press ESC when you are done, and select Yes to save the changed fields or No if you want to make additional changes. Press ESC to leave the ARCONFIG program when done.

Starting the Bridge

To prepare to start the bridge from a floppy-disk system, format a bootable floppy disk with the version of DOS you will be using, and then copy the

BRIDGE.EXE file from the BRGEN-2 or BRGEN-3 disk or subdirectory. If the bridge has a bootable hard drive, copy the BRIDGE.EXE file to the root directory of the hard drive. If the bridge is a protected-mode bridge, you must also copy the CONSOLE.COM file from the BRUTILS disk or directory onto the boot disk or hard drive. If you are running a non-dedicated bridge, copy the NET*x*.COM file created during the SHGEN configuration process in Chapter 10 or Appendix A so you can start NetWare and run the bridge as a workstation.

If value-added processes (VAPs) are being installed in a dedicated bridge, copy the VAP files to the boot disk or hard drive. Then create a file called XBRIDGE.CFG that contains instructions for loading the VAP, as outlined in the instruction manual for the VAP. Two additional commands for VAPs can be included in the file, as outlined here.

- The VAP WAIT command instructs the server to wait before automatically loading the VAPs. The command has the format

  VAP WAIT *xxx*

  where *xxx* is the number of seconds (from 10 to 360) to wait.

- The VAP DISK command allows loading of VAPs from an internal hard disk or a second floppy drive. The command takes the form

  VAP WAIT *path*

  where *path* is the drive letter and directory path to search.

Starting a Dedicated Bridge

After booting the system, type **BRIDGE** on the DOS command line. In a moment, the Novell copyright message will appear, and then the colon prompt, which indicates the bridge is in dedicated mode.

Starting a Nondedicated Bridge

Nondedicated servers are started by specifying the amount of memory to allocate to the bridge task, with a minimum of 180K of memory. Enter the command BRIDGE *xxx,* where *xxx* is the amount of memory to allocate. When the DOS prompt appears on the screen, enter the NET*x* command to load the NetWare shell. You may then operate the workstation as normal.

Bridge Console Commands

The following commands can be executed at the colon prompt for bridges running in console mode. Dedicated bridges always run in this mode. For nondedicated bridges, type **CONSOLE** at the DOS prompt to switch to console mode. Console commands can be used to view the bridge configuration, list loaded VAPs, and down the server, among other things. The following commands are available and are discussed in Chapter 25, "System Console Commands."

CONFIG	Displays information about the operating system's hardware configuration for each network supported by the bridge
CONSOLE	Used to select console mode when running a nondedicated bridge
DOS	Used to return to the DOS command line from console mode on nondedicated servers
DOWN	Brings the bridge down; always use this command when shutting down a bridge
MONITOR	Displays the version number of the NetWare bridge software
OFF	Clears the bridge console screen
VAP	Displays a list of value-added processes currently loaded into the NetWare operating system

Starting a Remote Workstation

To start a remote workstation, make sure the LAN you intend to connect to is running and that the bridge is ready to connect with your call. You should copy the NetWare LOGIN.EXE file to the remote workstation disk or hard drive to make the log-in process faster.

Start the workstation in the normal way with the remote workstation boot disk, or start it from the hard drive. Type the following commands at the DOS prompt:

```
IPX
NETx
```

where NET*x* is either NET2, NET3, or NET4, depending on your DOS version. You can now log in to the network in the normal way as covered in the text.

Note: If a special configuration modem is being used, you may need to initialize the modem and establish the connection before running the IPX and NET*x* program with a special communication program provided by the manufacturer.

Operating the Workstation

Communication from remote locations over phone lines is a slow and cumbersome process, but you can enhance server access by running NetWare utilities and commands from the local drive. In addition, you should run all software applications from a local drive. The communications line should only be used to access data or files that can be accessed only from the network itself.

Supervisors should supply users of remote workstations with a disk that contains the NetWare utilities and software programs they will need to operate a remote connection efficiently. Ideally, the remote workstation should have a hard drive to store all of these programs and files. To execute utilities and programs from the local drive, map that drive as the first search drive. For example, local hard drive C is mapped as search drive 1 with the following command:

```
MAP INSERT SEARCH1:=C:
```

The NetWare LCONSOLE utility allows you to change the parameters of the remote workstation while it is running. You may want to copy this command from the BRUTILS disk to the locally mapped drive. The LCONSOLE command is executed by typing **LCONSOLE** at the DOS prompt. The following options are available:

- Get Status displays the current status of the selected connection.

- Establish Connection allows connection to a new remote bridge.

- Terminate Connection ends the current session.

- Reset Modem resets the selected line.

Installing ELS NetWare Level I

ELS NetWare Level I is a four-user network system that is designed to run on a nondedicated server using one of the following servers and networks:

PC/AT-Class 80286 servers:

RX-Net, using either NetWare RX-Net or Standard Micro-systems ARCNET PC-100 network interface cards. Refer to Chapter 6 or your NetWare dealer for information on these networks.

Ethernet, using either NetWare NE-1000 or 3Com 3C501 network interface cards. Refer to Chapter 6 or your NetWare dealer for information on these networks.

IBM Personal System/2 servers:

IBM PCN Broadband Adapter II/A network card. The IBM PCN Adapter II is used in non-microchannel systems used as workstations. Contact your IBM dealer for more information.

IBM PCN Baseband Adapter II/A network card. The IBM PCN Adapter II is used in non-microchannel systems used as workstations. Contact your IBM dealer for more information.

NetWare ELS Level I needs to be ordered in the disk size (5 1/4- or 3 1/2-inch) appropriate for your server. All file servers must have a minimum of 640K base memory and 512K extended memory. It is recommended that all workstations have 640K of memory.

Installing ELS NetWare Level I

The following instructions will give you an overview of the installation process. There is only a slight difference between the installation for AT-class servers and IBM PS/2 microchannel servers, which will be described in the text.

Prepare the Disks

Make duplicates of the entire disk set that comes with NetWare by using the DOS DISKCOPY command. Do not use the COPY command, since it does not copy the electronic disk label on each disk. This label is required during the installation process.

If you are using the 5 1/4-inch disk set for AT-class machines, the following disks will be included for each network interface board supported by NetWare:

OS_RX-NET

OS_NE-1000

OS_3C501

You will use only one of these disks, depending on the type of network hardware you are using. After making the working copies, place the originals in a safe place.

Installing Network Hardware

ELS NetWare Level I will only accept specific interrupts and line addresses for each of the network interface boards it uses. The following sections will help you make those settings. You should refer to the manual for each board to determine exactly which switches to change to make the settings described.

If you have boards to install other than those for the network, install them now before proceeding, then run any SETUP programs required by the computer to initialize those boards. Instructions for running SETUP programs should be included with the computer's documentation.

It is recommended that you use the same boards for all stations in the network. You cannot mix Ethernet and RX-Net (or ARCNET) boards within the same LAN. You cannot mix broadband and baseband network interface cards when setting up a network using IBM PS/2 computers. If you plan to place the boards in diskless workstations, make sure you have purchased the remote reset PROMs to install on the boards. These PROMs are usually available as optional items.

Refer to Chapter 6 for instructions on installing each of the different types of network topologies.

Novell NE-1000 Network Interface Card

The Novell NE-1000 network interface cards must be set to the following switch settings:

Base memory address = D000h

Base I/O address = 300h

Interrupt = 3

Direct memory access (DMA) = none

Be sure to enable Remote Reset if the remote reset boot PROMs are installed and you plan to place the board in a diskless workstation; otherwise, make sure the option is disabled.

3Com 3C501 Network Interface Card

The 3Com 3C501 network interface cards must be set to the following switch settings:

Base memory address = D000h

Base I/O address = 300h

Interrupt = 3

Direct memory access (DMA) = 3

Be sure to enable Remote Reset if the remote reset boot PROMs are installed and you plan to place the board in a diskless workstation; otherwise, make sure the option is disabled.

RX-Net and ARCNET Network Interface Cards

The Novell RX-Net and Standard Microsystems ARCNET PC-100 network interface cards must be set to the following switch settings:

Base memory address = D000h

Base I/O address = 2E0h

Interrupt = 2

Be sure to enable Remote Reset if the remote reset boot PROMs are installed and you plan to place the board in a diskless workstation; otherwise, make sure the option is disabled.

Each RX-Net board must be set to a separate network address. Set each board in turn, and make sure that each board has a separate and distinct address.

IBM Broadband and Baseband Network Interface Cards

The installation of both broadband and baseband network interface cards is the same; however, there are two types of IBM broadband adapters and two types of baseband adapters. These are categorized by those that fit in standard PC- and AT-style systems with the standard interface bus, and those designed for IBM PS/2 microchannel bus computers. Both are covered here.

If you are installing an IBM Broadband Adapter II or IBM Baseband Adapter in a PC- or AT-style machine, place the jumpers over pins 1 and 2 on jumper blocks W1, W4, W5, W6, and W7.

If you are installing an IBM Broadband Adapter II/A or an IBM Baseband Adapter/A in an IBM Personal System/2 computer, you will make board settings by running a setup and configuration program instead of making physical board settings. Locate the Personal System/2 Reference disk that comes with your system. After installing the network interface card, start the system with the Reference disk and select Y when the message "Automatically configure the system" appears on the screen.

Installing NetWare ELS Level I

You can begin installing NetWare on the designated server once the network interface cards have been set and installed in the computer. During the installation, you will be asked to swap disks as the load procedure continues. Those installing NetWare for non-IBM systems should have the OS_RX-NET, OS_NE-1000, or OS_3C501 disk ready, depending on the type of hardware installed in the server.

Note: The following procedure formats the hard drive. Make sure you have made proper backups of any existing data you wish to save before proceeding.

Boot the designated server with the DOS version you plan to use on the server. Place the NetWare Start disk in drive A, and then make drive A the default drive and type the following command:

START

Follow the prompts on the screen, inserting the appropriate disks when requested. The START program will test and prepare the drive, a process that will take approximately 30 minutes to complete. You will be informed if the drive test was successful or not. If unsuccessful, contact your dealer for hardware assistance.

When the message "Insert your Operating System (OS) diskette in drive A:" appears, place the NetWare OS_*xxxxxx* disk in the drive that matches the hardware you have in the system. If you are setting up an IBM system, this disk will be the OS_PCN2 disk.

After you insert the disk and press any key, the NetWare shell will load. To change to the first network drive, type the following:

F:

At the DOS prompt, type the following to log in to the NetWare server:

LOGIN SUPERVISOR

You are now logged in to the file server as the network supervisor and can continue by reading Chapter 12. Keep in mind that ELS NetWare Level I does not have all of the features of more advanced NetWare operating systems. Refer to your NetWare owner's manual for specific information regarding each of the commands covered in this book.

Downing the Server

NetWare servers should always be brought down with proper procedures to ensure that all open files are closed and written to disk. Never turn the server computer off without following the steps outlined here.

1. All users should log out of NetWare by quitting their applications and then typing the following command:

   LOGOUT

2. Go to the NetWare server and place the OS_PCN2 (IBM systems), OS_RX-NET, OS_NE-1000, or OS_3C501 disk in drive A, depending on the network hardware installed. Log on to drive A.

3. Type the following command to get into console mode:

   CONSOLE

4. At the console colon prompt, type the following command to down the server:

   DOWN

In a moment, a message will indicate that you can turn the server off.

Starting the Server

1. Create a bootable DOS disk using the FORMAT command and the /S option, which places the DOS boot files on the disk.

2. Copy all the files on the OS_PCN2 (IBM systems), OS_RX-NET, OS_NE-1000, or OS_3C501 disk (depending on the network hardware configuration you are using) to the new boot disk.

3. Rename the file BOOT.BAT on the new boot disk with the following command:

   RENAME BOOT.BAT AUTOEXEC.BAT

4. Start the server using the new boot disk.

5. Type the following command to switch to the first network drive:

   F:

6. Type the following command to log in to the server:

   LOGIN

Creating Workstation Boot Disks

This section covers the steps required to create boot disks for workstations with floppy drives.

1. Create a bootable DOS disk with the FORMAT command and the /S option, which places the DOS boot files on the disk.

2. Copy the files in the appropriate directory on the SHELL-1 disk that matches your network hardware to the new disk. The following directories exist on the disk:

   3C501

   RXNET

NE1000

PCN2

The example command shown here illustrates how to copy the files in the RXNET directory to new disk, assuming the new disk is in drive A and SHELL-1 disk is in drive B:

COPY B:\RXNET A:

3. The files included in the copy include the AUTOEXEC.BAT file, which contains commands to connect to the network.

 Note: If you need NetBIOS to run some IBM programs, include the NETBIOS command before the ANET3 command in the AUTOEXEC.BAT file.

4. To log on to the network, start the workstation with the new disk. At the A prompt, type **F:** to switch to the first network drive and type **LOGIN** to begin the log-in procedure.

Creating Remote Reset Files on the Server

If you have installed non-IBM network interface cards with remote reset PROMs, you will need to create the appropriate files on the server to boot the diskless workstations. The files on the server "mimic" physical disk drives for the workstations.

 Note: Part of this procedure must be performed on a system that has a physical floppy drive.

1. Create a new formatted disk with the following command. Do not format a high-capacity disk for this task.

FORMAT B: /1/8/S

2. Locate the SHELL-1 disk and copy the ANET3.COM file from the directory on the disk that matches the hardware components you have installed in your network. The directories on the SHELL-1 disk are listed here.

3C501

RXNET

NE1000

PCN2

3. Since the disk will be used to create the disk "image" for the remote workstation, it should contain any programs or files you want to load at the workstation, such as the CONFIG.SYS or AU-TOEXEC.BAT file. Create those files now on the new disk. The following AUTOEXEC.BAT file can be created:

```
COPY CON AUTOEXEC.BAT
PROMPT $P$G
ANET3
F:NETBIOS
F:
LOGIN
^Z <Enter>
```

4. Connect to the network using a workstation that has at least one floppy-disk drive. Switch to drive F and log in as the supervisor. Then type the command

```
MAP F:=SYS:LOGIN
```

5. Insert the NetWare Install disk into drive A, and then make drive A the default drive.

6. Type this command to start the boot file creation process:

```
DOSGEN
```

7. You will see a display of information regarding the remote reset boot disk. When the message "Is this correct (Y or N)" appears, insert the new remote reset disk in drive A and type **Y** to start the process. After the remote reset file has been created, the message "Generation successfully complete" will appear.

8. Locate the SHELL-1 disk and copy the NETBIOS.COM file from the directory on the disk that matches the hardware components you have installed in your network to the F: drive on the server (the LOGIN directory). The directories on the SHELL-1 disk are listed here.

3C501

RXNET

NE1000

PCN2

The INSTALL Utility

The INSTALL utility is a software tool you can use to modify the file server as listed here. The utility is located on the Install disk.

- Initialize new server hard drives
- Create or edit a partition on a hard drive
- Reinitialize a hard drive
- Change the cache block size
- Change the maximum number of files that can be open at one time on the network
- Change the name of the file server
- Attach or detach printers
- Modify volume directories
- Remove a hard drive from the system

The INSTALL utility is run by first bringing the server down, as discussed in a previous section, and then booting DOS at the server and starting the utility by typing the following command at the A prompt after inserting the Install disk:

INSTALL

You will see a list of options as described earlier. Select one of the options, and follow the instructions on the screen.

The COLORPAL Menu Utility

COLORPAL Rules
Changing or Adding Color Palettes

The COLORPAL menu utility is used to create new color schemes for menu utilities, such as SYSCON, FILER, and SESSION. COLORPAL can also be used to create new color schemes. The default color palettes are initially set to blue backgrounds with white letters. If you change the default color palette, you will permanently change the color scheme of all the NetWare menu utilities, so it is suggested that you experiment with COLORPAL by creating your own palette files in directories other than SYS:PUBLIC.

THE COLORPAL menu utility is used to manage all palettes, which are numbered starting with palette 0. The first five palettes are the default palettes used by the NetWare menu utilities. If you change the color schemes for palettes 0 through 4, you will change the default colors for these utilities. You can create your own color palettes starting with palette 5. Your custom menus can use any of your custom palettes by including the palette number as a parameter on the menu header line in the menu text file, as discussed in Chapter 22.

The main color table used by COLORPAL is located in the file IBM$RUN.OVL in the SYS:PUBLIC directory. Any changes made with COLORPAL are stored in this file, assuming you make the changes while logged in to the SYS:PUBLIC directory.

A P P E N D I X   D

COLORPAL Rules

When menus are run, they will automatically use the color schemes specified by the IBM$RUN.OVL file in the SYS:PUBLIC directory, if that is the only color palette file stored on the server. However, menus will first look for an equivalent IBM$RUN.OVL file in the current default directory before using the one in SYS:PUBLIC. Menu utilities will then start searching through the mapped search drives for other palettes. The following rules apply:

- An altered version of IBM$RUN.OVL can be placed in any directory. Menus executed from that directory will use the altered version of IBM$RUN.OVL.

- An altered version of IBM$RUN.OVL can be placed in any directory that is mapped as the first search drive. Menus will then use this altered file before resorting to the IBM$RUN.OVL file in the SYS:PUBLIC directory. Note that this rule assumes the current default directory does not have an IBM$RUN.OVL file.

- You can specify a short machine type other than IBM in the SHELL.CFG file of a workstation to use a different color palette file during a session. For example, if the command

  SHORT MACHINE TYPE = AST

  is included in the SHELL.CFG file, NetWare will use a file called AST$RUN.OVL for its color palette specifications during the workstation session. Only the station booting with this SHELL.CFG file is affected. The AST$RUN.OVL file can coexist with the IBM$RUN.OVL file in the SYS:PUBLIC directory.

- Whenever you run COLORPAL from the SYS:PUBLIC directory, alterations are made to the default IBM$RUN.OVL file. To create custom palettes, simply run COLORPAL from another directory. COLORPAL will automatically place an altered version of the IBM$RUN.OVL file in the new directory. When menus are run from that directory, the colors of the altered palette file will be used.

- You can add additional palettes to the default IBM$RUN.OVL file in the SYS:PUBLIC by specifying palettes greater than 4. These palettes can then be called from your custom menu utilities by specifying the palette number as a parameter on a menu header line, as described in Chapter 22.

- Workstations running monochrome monitors are rarely affected by the COLORPAL settings. However, some monochrome monitors running on composite color video adapters may be unreadable. If this is the case, you should specify the CMPQ$RUN.OVL file in the SYS:PUBLIC directory for these stations by placing the following command in the SHELL.CFG file of the workstation:

  SHORT MACHINE TYPE = CMPQ

  The CMPQ$RUN.OVL file is designed for monochrome systems that may be affected by the contrast and intensity of the normal color palette file.

Default Color Palette

The default color palettes used by the NetWare menu utilities are the first five palettes specified in the IBM$RUN.OVL file. These palettes are listed here, along with the specific NetWare menus they affect.

Palette 0 affects lists, menus, and normal text.

Palette 1 affects main headers and screen backgrounds.

Palette 2 affects help screens.

Palette 3 affects error messages.

Palette 4 affects Exit and Alert menus.

Changing or Adding Color Palettes

Recall that a color palette is a color scheme used by the NetWare menu utilities or your own menu utilities. The first five color palettes in the IBM$RUN.OVL file are used by the NetWare menu utilities. If you change these palettes, you will permanently change the color of the utilities. This section will concentrate on adding additional color palettes that can be used by your custom menu, as discussed in Chapter 22.

You can start COLORPAL from the SYS:PUBLIC directory to make changes to the default IBM$RUN.OVL file, or you can start COLORPAL from another directory to create a new version of IBM$RUN.OVL in the current directory. Menus run from the current directory will then use the new color palette file instead of the one in the SYS:PUBLIC directory. This section will assume that you are logged in to the SYS:PUBLIC directory and are adding new palettes to the default color file.

To start the COLORPAL utility, type the command shown here while logged in to the SYS:PUBLIC directory:

COLORPAL

The menu will list the current palettes in order. The NetWare default palettes 0 through 4 are listed first. Press the INS key to add a new color palette. Color palette 5 will be added to the list of defined palettes.

To edit the new color palette, highlight it and press the ENTER key. When the Edit Attribute window appears, you will see a list of attributes you can change for color palette 5. These attributes are described here:

- Background Normal is the field on which menu titles and text are displayed.

- Background Reverse is the color of the highlight bar.

- Foreground Intense is the highlight for the text and borders of currently active menu options.

- Foreground Normal is the color of normal text and border displays.

- Foreground Reverse is the color of text covered by the highlight bar.

The Color Palette window shows how the various color attributes actually appear prior to making changes. This window will reflect any color changes made as you proceed.

To make changes, highlight the selection you want to change and press ENTER. A list of possible colors will appear. This list will be more extensive for foreground menu colors than for background colors. The current color is highlighted. Simply highlight a new color and press ENTER.

You can repeat this procedure for each menu attribute. When you are done, press ESC to exit from the menu and be sure to answer Yes to save any changes you have made.

Additional Novell Programs
And Services

Btrieve
Xtrieve
XQL
Novell Services
Training Courses

The following products and services are available from your authorized Novell dealer or directly from Novell.

Btrieve

Btrieve is a complete, key-indexed file management system than can be used with any programming language for high-performance file handling and improved programming productivity. Btrieve's fault-tolerant processing guarantees data integrity without additional programming. Based on the b-tree indexing method and implemented with cache buffers, Btrieve delivers fast, maintenance-free operation. The following features are available:

- Access speed does not degrade with database growth.

- Files expand dynamically as records are added.

- It is written in assembly language.

- It is based on the b-tree file-indexing system.

- Applications written for one version of Btrieve execute correctly with all other versions.

- Variable-length records can contain over 64,000 bytes, and fixed-length records can contain up to 4090 bytes.

- Data encryption methods are available.

- File-level password protection is available.

- Read-after-write verification is available.

- Btrieve can be quickly and easily incorporated into program development using BASIC, Pascal, COBOL, and C.

Xtrieve

Xtrieve is a menu-driven data retrieval system with a flexible, easy-to-use Report Writer option. Designed for application developers and value-added resellers (VARs), Xtrieve can provide an end-user interface to Btrieve applications.

System developers can customize Xtrieve to display command menus, help files, and error messages for their specific applications. Xtrieve allows users to catalogue, retrieve, analyze, and update information in databases. The system is menu-driven and has a relational interface. It also includes an extensive report-writing capability.

XQL

XQL is a relational database management system designed for programmers using COBOL, BASIC, Pascal, or C. It allows users to access their databases with the ease of Structured Query Language (SQL). In addition, XQL frees an application from physical file characteristics by providing true relational capabilities with data independence, data descriptions, data integrity, and security. XQL reduces programming time, enhances application capability, and improves performance.

XQL features include the following:

- An interactive SQL editor that allows users to test each statement before embedding it in an application

- Built-in transaction control and record locking with automatic file recovery upon system failure, assuming SFT NetWare is being used

- Variable-length records

- Maximum file size, up to the maximum size supported by the operating system

- Data independence through the ability to request data by field name

- Automatic query optimization with b-tree indexes

- Data validation on input with the specifications of ranges, character lists, and value lists

- Password security for read/write access at every level down to the field level

Novell Services

Novell offers several services to NetWare users, as described here. For additional information, contact your Novell dealer.

On-Line Information Services

Novell offers an on-line information service known as NetWire. This service allows users to access a wide range of information, including program files for downloading and a technical bulletin board. Updated programs, operating system shell drivers, utility programs, patches, and fixes can be downloaded at any time, day or night. Technical bulletin boards are available for review, allowing users to search for information in a technical database that is continuously updated by both Novell and its users.

NetWare is available as a subscription by contacting your authorized Novell dealer. A few of the features available are listed here:

- Novell technical bulletins since November 1985
- Software-enhancement program files
- Bulletin board questions and answers
- Hardware/software compatibility lists
- Novell press releases
- Novell company information, including financial information
- Novell training schedules and course offerings

On-Site Service

Novell Services Division offers on-site services to keep networking systems performing at maximum efficiency. On-site service agreements are available to ensure that LANs will perform at consistently high standards. Services are available during the standard principle period of maintenance (PPM), which is 8 A.M. to 5 P.M., Monday through Friday, excluding holidays. Options are available for extended maintenance. All prices are for 12-month service agreements; payments can be made monthly, quarterly, or annually.

Novell Services Division also offers a site preparation, cable, and network installation component called Installation Services. This package ensures that your installation will be performed by skilled service personnel familiar with NetWare and the needs of a LAN. A consulting service is also available to help with initial system design and configuration, as well as planning and installation.

NetWare Care

NetWare Care is a utility that permits network users to see how the network is operating, quickly determine the configuration of networks, and evaluate the performance of servers and workstations. The package offers the following features:

- Error monitoring
- Performance information compilation
- Point-to-point communications testing
- Internetwork testing
- Graphic display of the network, including node addresses, names, and services available

Service Response System

The Service Response System (SRS) is a comprehensive support system designed for large companies that desire to maintain their computer systems privately, or large resellers who want to enhance their ability to provide support for their customers. SRS consists of two modules: a call-handling and routing system called the Incident Management System (IMS), and an extensive information database called the Novell Technical Information Database (TID).

Consulting Services

Novell Services Division provides a key service for the large or complex network by providing consulting services. This is offered by the Novell Advanced Technical Services (ATS) group. Services offered include initial system design and configuration, as well as planning and installation.

Training Courses

Novell offers a wide range of training courses for end users, system managers, installers, and service personnel. Training takes place at various Novell education centers around the country. For more information, contact the Novell Utah Education Center, your authorized Novell dealer, or your nearest Novell Center.

Computer-Based Training

Novell offers a line of computer-based training (CBT) courses that can be taken at your on-site facilities. CBTs are designed for those who find it difficult to fit traditional classes into their schedule. Travel, hotel, meal, and tuition expenses are eliminated, especially if many users need to be trained. Since the CBT courses are purchased, they can be used over and over again at the installation site.

CBTs are available on floppy disk and will run on any IBM PC/AT-compatible system with a minimum of 285K of memory and a color graphics monitor. Currently, "NetWare User Basics" and "NetWare System Management" courses are available.

Programmer's Courses

Novell offers training courses at its education centers for those who are programming in the NetWare LAN environment. The courses familiarize programmers with the NetWare environment and assembly language principles required to use Advanced NetWare function calls. Methods for converting single-user products to multiuser programs are also presented, as well as methods for creating applications that take advantage of the distributed-processing environment.

Apple II®	Apple Computer, Inc.
AppleShare®	Apple Computer, Inc.
AppleTalk®	Apple Computer, Inc.
Arcnet®	Datapoint Corporation
Etherlink™	3Com Corporation
Ethernet®	Intel Corporation
IBM®	International Business Machines Corporation
IBM® LAN Program®	International Business Machines Corporation
IBM® PC®	International Business Machines Corporation
IBM® PC Network Program®	International Business Machines Corporation
IBM® System 34, 36, 38®	International Business Machines Corporation
Intel®	Intel Corporation
LaserWriter®	Apple Computer, Inc.
Macintosh®	Apple Computer, Inc.
Microsoft®	Microsoft Corporation
Microsoft® Networks®	Microsoft Corporation
Microsoft® Windows™	Microsoft Corporation
NetWare®	Novell Corporation
NetWare SFT®	Novell Corporation
Novell®	Novell Corporation
PostScript®	Adobe Systems, Inc.
Sniffer®	Network General
3Com™	3Com Corporation
Token-Ring®	International Business Machines Corporation
UNIX®	AT&T

TRADEMARKS

731

FOCUS ON GRAMMAR

An **ADVANCED** Course for Reference and Practice

VOLUME A

Focus on Grammar

An **ADVANCED** Course for Reference and Practice

SECOND EDITION

Jay Maurer

Longman

FOCUS ON GRAMMAR: AN **ADVANCED** COURSE FOR REFERENCE AND PRACTICE, **VOLUME A**

Pearson Education, 10 Bank Street, White Plains, NY 10606

Editorial director: Allen Ascher
Executive editor: Louisa Hellegers
Director of design and production: Rhea Banker
Development editor: Margaret Grant
Production manager: Alana Zdinak
Managing editor: Linda Moser
Production editor: Robert Ruvo
Senior manufacturing manager: Patrice Fraccio
Manufacturing manager: David Dickey
Photo research: Beaura Kathy Ringrose
Cover design: Rhea Banker
Cover image: *Frost, Penpont, Dumfriesshire,
    3 December 1989.* Copyright © Andy Goldsworthy
    from his book *A Collaboration with Nature,*
    Harry N. Abrams, 1990.
Text design: Charles Yuen
Text composition: Preface, Inc.
Illustrators: Moffitt Cecil: p. 246; Ronald Chironna: p. 15; Brian Hughes:
    p. 48; Jock MacRae: pp. 58, 102, 221; Don Martinetti: pp. 41, 42; Paul
    McCusker: pp. 49, 50, 74, 90, 93, 94, 150, 166, 170, 171, 207, 234, 242,
    249, 250; Dusan Petricic: pp. 2, 9, 29, 73, 77, 78, 87, 88, 131, 148, 152,
    182, 211, 230.
Photo credits: See p. xv.

ISBN 0-201-38310-1

6 7 8 9 10—CRK—05

CONTENTS

APPENDICES

ABOUT THE AUTHOR

Jay **Maurer** has taught English in binational centers, colleges, and universities in Portugal, Spain, Mexico, the Somali Republic, and the United States. In addition, he taught intensive English at Columbia University's American Language Program. He was also a teacher of college composition and literature for sixteen years at Santa Fe Community College and Northern New Mexico Community College. He is the co-author of the three-level *Structure Practice in Context* series, co-author of the five-level *True Colors* series, and co-author of the *True Voices* video series. Currently he writes and teaches in Seattle, Washington. *Focus on Grammar: An Advanced Course for Reference and Practice*, Second Edition, has grown out of the author's experiences as a practicing teacher of both ESL and college writing.

INTRODUCTION

THE **FOCUS ON GRAMMAR** SERIES

Focus on Grammar: An Advanced Course for Reference and Practice, Second Edition, is part of the four-level *Focus on Grammar* series. Written by practicing ESL professionals, the series focuses on English grammar through lively listening, speaking, reading, and writing activities. Each of the four Student Books is accompanied by an Answer Key, a Workbook, an Audio Program (cassettes or CDs), a Teacher's Manual, and a CD-ROM. Each Student Book can stand alone as a complete text in itself, or it can be used as part of the series.

BOTH CONTROLLED AND COMMUNICATIVE PRACTICE

Research in applied linguistics suggests that students expect and need to learn the formal rules of a language. However, students need to practice new structures in a variety of contexts to help them internalize and master them. To this end, *Focus on Grammar* provides an abundance of both controlled and communicative exercises so that students can bridge the gap between knowing grammatical structures and using them. The many communicative activities in each unit enable students to personalize what they have learned in order to talk to each other with ease about hundreds of everyday issues.

A UNIQUE FOUR-STEP APPROACH

The series follows a unique four-step approach. In the first step, **grammar in context**, new structures are shown in the natural context of passages, articles, and dialogues. This is followed by a **grammar presentation** of structures in clear and accessible grammar charts, notes, and examples. The third step is **focused practice** of both form and meaning in numerous and varied controlled exercises. In the fourth step, **communication practice**, students use the new structures freely and creatively in motivating, open-ended activities.

A COMPLETE CLASSROOM TEXT AND REFERENCE GUIDE

A major goal in the development of *Focus on Grammar* has been to provide Student Books that serve not only as vehicles for classroom instruction but also as resources for reference and self-study. In each Student Book, the combination of grammar charts, grammar notes, and expansive appendices provides a complete and invaluable reference guide for the student.

THOROUGH RECYCLING

Underpinning the scope and sequence of the series as a whole is the belief that students need to use target structures many times in many contexts at increasing levels of difficulty. For this reason, new grammar is constantly recycled so that students will feel thoroughly comfortable with it.

COMPREHENSIVE TESTING PROGRAM

SelfTests at the end of each part of the Student Book allow for continual assessment of progress. In addition, diagnostic and final tests in the Teacher's Manual provide a ready-made, ongoing evaluation component for each student.

THE **ADVANCED** STUDENT BOOK

Focus on Grammar: An Advanced Course for Reference and Practice, *Second Edition,* is divided into ten parts comprising twenty-five units. Each part contains grammatically related units, with each unit focusing on a specific grammatical structure or related groups of structures.

In this advanced-level text, some structures are grouped together because of their related application to writing. The infinitive of purpose, for example, is taught together with participial phrases because both kinds of structures function adverbially. But, more importantly, they have similar applications to the acquisition of two important concepts: sentence combining and avoiding dangling modifiers.

Each unit has one or more major themes relating the exercises to one another and providing a context that serves as a vehicle for the structures. All units have the same clear, easy-to-follow format:

GRAMMAR IN CONTEXT

Grammar in Context presents the grammar focus of the unit in a natural context. The texts, all of which are recorded, present language in various formats. These include newspaper and magazine articles, stories, conversations, and other formats that students encounter in their day-to-day lives. In addition to presenting grammar in context, this introductory section raises student motivation and provides an opportunity for incidental learning and lively classroom discussions. Topics are varied, ranging from birth order, marriage, money, and humor to cloning, sports, and compassion. Each text is preceded by a pre-reading activity called **Questions to Consider**. These pre-reading questions are intended to create interest, elicit student knowledge about the topic, help point out features of the text, and lead students to make predictions about the reading.

GRAMMAR PRESENTATION

This section is made up of grammar charts, notes, and examples. The grammar **charts** focus on the form of the unit's target structure(s). The clear and easy-to-understand boxes present each grammatical form in all its combinations. These charts provide students with a clear visual reference for each new structure.

The grammar **notes** and **examples** that follow the charts focus on the meaning and use of the structure(s). Each note gives a clear explanation of the grammar point and is always accompanied by one or more examples. BE CAREFUL! notes alert students to common ESL / EFL errors. Usage Notes provide guidelines for using and understanding different levels of formality and correctness. Reference Notes provide cross-references to related units and the Appendices.

FOCUSED PRACTICE

The exercises in this section provide practice for all uses of the structure presented in the Grammar Presentation. Each Focused Practice section begins with a recognition exercise called **Discover the Grammar**. Here, the students are expected to recognize the form of the structure with its meaning and often to explain why alternate forms could or could not be substituted. This activity raises awareness of the structures as it builds confidence. Occasionally, creative activities such as writing endings to stories complete this section.

Following the Discover the Grammar activity are exercises that practice the grammar in a controlled, but still contextualized, environment. The exercises proceed from simpler to more complex. There is a large variety of exercise types including fill-in-the-blanks, matching, multiple choice, question and sentence formation, and editing (error analysis). Exercises are cross-referenced to the appropriate grammar notes so that students can review the notes if necessary. As with the Grammar in Context section, students are exposed to many different written formats, including letters, postcards, journal entries, news articles, stories, and conversations. Some exercises are art-based, providing a rich and interesting context for meaningful practice. All Focused Practice exercises are suitable for self-study or homework. A complete **Answer Key** is provided in a separate booklet.

COMMUNICATION PRACTICE

The exercises in this section are intended for in-class use. The first exercise is **Listening**. Having had exposure to and practice with the grammar in its written form, students now have the opportunity to check their aural comprehension. They hear a variety of listening formats, including conversations, radio announcements, interviews, and phone recordings. After listening to the tape (or hearing the teacher read the tapescript, which can be found in the Teacher's Manual), students complete a task that focuses on either the form or the meaning of the structure. It is suggested that students be allowed to hear the text as many times as they wish to complete the task successfully.

The listening exercise is followed by a variety of activities that provide students with the opportunity to use the grammar in open-ended, interactive ways. Students work in pairs, small groups, or as a whole class in surveys, information gaps, discussions, games, and other problem-solving activities. Every unit gives students an opportunity to write an essay especially formulated to elicit practice of the unit's structures using the unit's theme. Finally, a **Picture Discussion** in each unit enables students to apply their mastery of structure. The subjects of the Picture Discussion range from reproductions of famous paintings to cartoons to drawings.

REVIEW OR SELFTEST

After the last unit of each part, there is a review feature that can be used as a self-test. The exercises in this section test the form and use of the grammar content of the part. These tests include questions in the format of the Structure and Written Expression sections of the TOEFL®. An **Answer Key** is provided after each test.

FROM GRAMMAR TO WRITING

At the end of each part, there is a writing section called From Grammar to Writing. This feature is designed to help students bridge the gap between writing in the ESL / EFL classroom and the less controlled writing they may need to do outside of class, whether in everyday or academic settings. These optional units occur after the SelfTests and focus on such writing issues as the sentence; subject-verb and pronoun-antecedent agreement; topic sentences; parallelism; avoiding fragments, run-on sentences, and comma splices; punctuating adjective clauses; writing direct and indirect speech; and unity, support, and coherence. Although these writing issues are not solely ESL / EFL related, they are highly important to the ESL / EFL student who wants to write successfully.

In most of the From Grammar to Writing units, the topic presented is related to the grammar content of the part just concluded. For example, the second writing unit on parallelism naturally and logically accompanies the gerund and infinitive part, since mixing gerunds and infinitives in a series is a common parallelism error. Two units deal with important issues in the structuring of a composition: writing good topic sentences and ensuring that a piece of writing is unified and coherent and has enough supporting details to make the writer's point. A new feature of the From Grammar to Writing units in this edition is a final writing section called **Apply It to Your Writing.** In this activity, students apply the principles they have just learned in a short composition and then work with a partner to edit each other's work.

APPENDICES

The Appendices provide useful information, such as lists of common irregular verbs, phrasal verbs, spelling rules, and names of countries. The Appendices can help students do the unit exercises, act as a springboard for further classroom work, and serve as a reference source.

NEW IN THIS EDITION

In response to users' requests, this edition has:

- new and updated texts for Grammar in Context
- a new easy-to-read format for grammar notes and examples
- rewritten grammar notes
- cross-references that link exercises to corresponding grammar notes
- authentic reading selections in most units
- more photos and art
- information gaps and games
- a vocabulary development component called Understanding Meaning from Context

SUPPLEMENTARY **COMPONENTS**

All supplementary components of *Focus on Grammar, Second Edition* —the Audio Program (cassettes or CDs), the Workbook, and the Teacher's Manual—are tightly keyed to the Student Book. Along with the CD-ROM, these components provide a wealth of practice and an opportunity to tailor the series to the needs of each individual classroom.

AUDIO PROGRAM

All of the Grammar in Context texts and all of the Listening exercises as well as other selected exercises are recorded on cassettes and CDs. The symbol appears next to these activities. The scripts appear in the Teacher's Manual and may be used as an alternative way of presenting these activities.

WORKBOOK

The Workbook accompanying *Focus on Grammar: An Advanced Course for Reference and Practice, Second Edition,* provides a wealth of additional exercises appropriate for self-study of the target grammar of each unit in the Student Book. Most of the exercises are fully contextualized. Themes of the Workbook exercises are typically a continuation or a spin-off of the corresponding Student Book unit themes. There are also ten tests, one for each of the ten Student Book parts. These tests have questions in the format of the Structure and Written Expression section of the TOEFL®. Besides reviewing the material in the Student Book, these questions provide invaluable practice to those who are interested in taking this widely administered test.

TEACHER'S MANUAL

The Teacher's Manual, divided into five parts, contains a variety of suggestions and information to enrich the material in the Student Book. The first part gives general suggestions for each section of a typical unit. The next part offers practical teaching suggestions and cultural information to accompany specific material in each unit. The Teacher's Manual also provides ready-to-use diagnostic and final tests for each of the ten parts of the Student Book. In addition, a complete script of the Listening exercises is provided, as is an answer key for the diagnostic and final tests.

CD-ROM

The *Focus on Grammar* CD-ROM provides individualized practice with immediate feedback. Fully contextualized and interactive, the activities broaden and extend practice of the grammatical structures in the reading, listening, and writing skill areas. The CD-ROM includes grammar review, review tests, and all relevant reference material from the Student Book. It can also be used alongside the *Longman Interactive American Dictionary* CD-ROM.

CREDITS

PHOTOGRAPHS

Grateful acknowledgment is given to the following for providing photographs:

p. 17 Scott Cohen—AP/World Wide Photos; **p. 27** UPI/Corbis; **p. 33** Corbis; **p. 34** Photofest; **p. 70** Atalante/Gamma Sport—Liaison Agency, Inc.; **p. 116** SuperStock, Inc.; **p. 118** Richard E. Hill/Visuals Unlimited; **p. 135** Robert Bores—AP/World Wide Photos; **p. 196** 20th Century Fox—AP/World Wide Photos/Paramount Pictures Corporation, Inc.; **p. 233** AP/World Wide Photos; **p. 244** Corbis.

THE STORY BEHIND THE COVER

The photograph on the cover is the work of **Andy Goldsworthy**, an innovative artist who works exclusively with natural materials to create unique outdoor sculpture, which he then photographs. Each Goldsworthy sculpture communicates the artist's own "sympathetic contact with nature" by intertwining forms and shapes structured by natural events with his own creative perspective. Goldsworthy's intention is not to "make his mark on the landscape, but to create a new perception and an evergrowing understanding of the land."

So, too, *Focus on Grammar* takes grammar found in its most natural context and expertly reveals its hidden structure and meaning. It is our hope that students everywhere will also develop a new perception and an "evergrowing" understanding of the world of grammar.

ACKNOWLEDGMENTS

Writing the SECOND EDITION of this book has been even more fun and challenging than it was the first time around. I'm indebted to many people who helped me in all kinds of different ways. Specifically, though, I want to express my appreciation and gratitude to:

- **My students** over the years.

- **Joanne Dresner**, for her confidence and encouragement.

- **Joan Saslow**, for her perceptive suggestions in the early stages.

- **Sylvia Bloch**, for her research help. She was terrific.

- **Laura McCormick**, for her help with permissions.

- **Irene Schoenberg**, for her friendship and moral support.

- **Robert Ruvo**, for his excellent and sharp-eyed production editing.

- The **CONSULTANTS**, for their invaluable suggestions: **Marcia Edwards Hijaab**, Henrico County Schools, Richmond, Virginia; **Kevin McClure**, ESL Language Center, San Francisco; **Tim Rees**, Transworld School, Boston; **Allison Rice**, Director of the International English Language Institute, Hunter College, New York; **Ellen Shaw**, University of Nevada, Las Vegas. This book wouldn't be what it is without them.

- **Luis Humberto Beze**, **Patricia C. Fleury**, **Luiz Claudio Monteiro**, and other teachers at the Casa Thomas Jefferson in Brasilia, for their many good suggestions for the new edition.

- **Joyce Munn**, International English Language Institute, Hunter College; **John Beesy**, Fordham University ESL Institute; **Eric Glatt**, Center for English Studies, Manhattan; and their students—for their feedback and their valuable suggestions for the new edition.

- **Flo Nyberg** and **Lena Dubinets**, for their help with Russian recipes.

- That genius, whoever he or she is, who came up with the joke about the genie that has been floating around in cyberspace for some time now. Ditto for the unknown authors of the bumper stickers.

- **Greg Stought**, for finding the joke about the girls and the lipstick.

- **Louisa Hellegers**, for her confidence and excellent direction of the whole project. Many thanks.

- **Margo Grant**, for being a topnotch and jolly editor. Sure was fun working with you.

- Above all, to my best friend.

J.M.

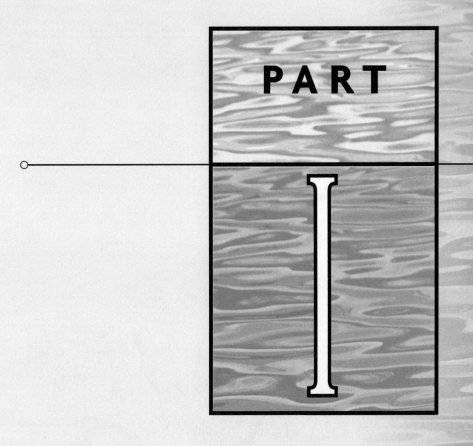

PART

I

TENSE AND TIME

1 PRESENT AND FUTURE TIME

GRAMMAR **IN CONTEXT**

QUESTIONS TO CONSIDER

1. Where do you like to travel?

2. Look at the cartoon. When you travel, do you ever bargain to get a better price?

3. Is it fair to try to get a lower price for an item, or is it better to pay the price the seller wants?

Read an article about learning how to bargain.

WORLD TRAVELER

It's a Bargain

BY TAMMY SAMUELSON

In an open-air market in Turkey, a tourist is admiring the beautiful oriental rugs on display. She finds one she likes and asks the price. "One thousand dollars," the vendor says. She knows she shouldn't pay the full price, so she says "six hundred." "Nine hundred," the vendor counters. The woman throws up her hands in mock frustration and walks away. The vendor goes after her. Not long afterwards both vendor and buyer agree on eight hundred dollars, a 20 percent reduction. Both vendor and customer are smiling and happy. They've just participated in a ritual that has existed for centuries, all over the world: bargaining.

So you're visiting another country this year? You already have your tickets, and you leave next Tuesday at 4 P.M. A week from now you'll be relaxing in the sunshine or visiting famous landmarks. By the end of the summer, you'll have been traveling for several weeks, and it'll be time to think about bringing back some souvenirs for friends and family. Souvenirs cost money, though, so maybe if you do some bargaining, you'll be able to get some good buys. . . . What? You don't know how to bargain? You're afraid to? Relax. In my capacity as *Times* travel editor, yours truly has been making trips abroad since 1995, and bargaining is one thing I've learned how to do. In this week's column I'm going to give you some tips on how to perform this most enjoyable activity.

Many people are used to paying fixed prices for items and are reluctant to bargain. Some may be afraid to hurt the vendor's feelings by offering too low a price. Others are afraid of being assertive. Some may even avoid bargaining because they want to give the impression they can afford anything. Bargaining is not too big a deal in some countries, but even in North America, a certain kind of bargaining goes on whenever someone goes to a yard or garage sale and tries to get the seller to lower the price. In most parts of the world, though, bargaining is a way of life. Vendors expect you to bargain and will be disappointed if you don't. Here are some bargaining tips.

First tip: Find out how much something is worth. When you bargain with someone, the object of the game is not to beat the vendor. It's to pay a fair price for whatever you want to buy. So do some research. Get a good idea of the general price range for an item. That way you'll be able to bargain with confidence.

OK. You've been doing your research. Now you know how much things cost, so you can go shopping.

Second tip: Never accept the first offer. You'll need to make a counter-offer when the vendor announces the price. Remember: The vendor expects this.

Third tip: Treat the vendor with respect. Remember that, while the bargaining experience should not be a competition, it should be a game. Stick to your guns, but have fun with the process. If the vendor insists it's impossible to go any lower on the price, show him or her how much money you have. But be polite.

Fourth tip: Be prepared to walk away if you don't get a fair price. Don't get angry. Just make it clear that you're not going to buy if the vendor doesn't come down. If he doesn't, start to walk away. As soon as you do this, he will most likely come running after you.

The final tip: Be sure to wear sunglasses. For centuries people of many cultures have regarded the eyes as "the windows of the soul." If you're nervous or intimidated, this will show in your eyes. Wear dark glasses to conceal your anxiety. You'll feel more confident if you do.

So, are you persuaded? Feel a little more confident, or at least a little less nervous? If you go home without having experienced bargaining, you'll have missed out on one of life's most interesting experiences. Give it a try. Have a great trip and have no fear! ⏺

Source: Based on Rich Beattie, "How to Bargain for Anything . . . Anywhere," *Travel Holiday,* September 1998, pp. 56, 58, 60.

UNDERSTANDING MEANING FROM CONTEXT

Circle the letter of the choice closest to the meaning of each italicized word or phrase from the reading.

1. The woman throws up her hands in *mock* frustration and walks away.

   a. pretended   **b.** good   **c.** true

2. They've just participated in a *ritual* that has existed for centuries, all over the world: bargaining.

   a. discussion   **b.** cultural practice   **c.** law

3. Many . . . *are reluctant to* bargain.

   a. really want to   **b.** really love to   **c.** don't really want to

4. *Stick to your guns,* but have fun with the process.

   a. Take your guns with you   **b.** Don't change your position   **c.** Pretend to shoot someone

5. Wear dark glasses to conceal your *anxiety*.

   a. interest   **b.** worry   **c.** anger

GRAMMAR **PRESENTATION**
PRESENT AND FUTURE TIME

PRESENT TIME: IN GENERAL; NOW

SIMPLE PRESENT

Souvenirs **cost** money.

	PRESENT PROGRESSIVE		
SUBJECT	**AM / IS / ARE**	**BASE FORM + -ING**	
A tourist	**is**	**admiring**	the beautiful oriental rugs on display.

PAST TO PRESENT TIME: FROM A TIME IN THE PAST UNTIL NOW

	PRESENT PERFECT		
SUBJECT	**HAS / HAVE**	**PAST PARTICIPLE**	
This ritual	**has**	**existed**	for centuries.

	PRESENT PERFECT PROGRESSIVE		
SUBJECT	**HAS / HAVE BEEN**	**BASE FORM + -ING**	
Yours truly	**has been**	**making**	trips abroad since 1995.

FUTURE TIME: A TIME IN THE FUTURE (GENERAL OR SPECIFIC)

	WILL	
WILL	**BASE FORM**	
You**'ll**	**need**	to bring back some souvenirs.

	BE GOING TO	
BE GOING TO	**BASE FORM**	
I'm going to	**give**	you some tips on bargaining.

	FUTURE PROGRESSIVE		
	WILL BE	**BASE FORM + -ING**	
A week from now you	**'ll be**	**relaxing**	in the sunshine.

SIMPLE PRESENT: A SCHEDULE OR TIMETABLE

You **leave** next Tuesday at 4 P.M.

PRESENT PROGRESSIVE: AN ALREADY-ARRANGED ACTION OR EVENT			
	AM / IS / ARE	**BASE FORM + -ING**	
So you	**'re**	**traveling**	abroad this summer?

TWO ACTIONS IN THE FUTURE
You**'ll need** to make a counter-offer when the vendor **announces** the price.

FUTURE TIME: BEFORE A CERTAIN TIME IN THE FUTURE

FUTURE PERFECT			
	WILL HAVE	**PAST PARTICIPLE**	
You	**will have**	**missed**	out on one of life's most interesting experiences.

FUTURE PERFECT PROGRESSIVE		
WILL HAVE BEEN	**BASE FORM + -ING**	
By the end of the summer, you**'ll have been**	**traveling**	for several weeks.

NOTES

EXAMPLES

1. Use the **simple present** to show actions, events, or states that happen habitually or as a general rule.

We also use the **simple present** to narrate events in sequence.

- Souvenirs **cost** money.
- Vendors **expect** you to bargain.

- A tourist **finds** a beautiful rug and **asks** the price.
- "One thousand dollars," the vendor **says.**

2. Use the **present progressive** to show actions, events, or states that are in progress at the moment (not finished).

▶ **BE CAREFUL!** Stative verbs are not usually used in the progressive. These verbs include *have* (= possess), *believe, own, want, like, need, know, love.* See Appendix 2 on page A-2 for a list of common verbs usually used statively. When stative verbs occur in the progressive, they generally have different meanings. Look at the examples in the next column.

- A tourist **is admiring** the beautiful oriental rugs on display.

- I **have** a blue Toyota Camry. *(possess)*
- We**'re having** dinner now. *(eating)*

3. The **present perfect** and the **present perfect progressive** connect the past and the present. Use them to express states or actions that began in the past and continue until now. Include *for* or *since* and a time expression. Remember that *for* is used to show an amount of time and *since* shows a starting point.

- Bargaining is a ritual that **has existed for** centuries. *(an amount of time)*
- Yours truly **has been making** trips abroad **since** 1995. *(a starting point)*

▶ **BE CAREFUL!** Use the present perfect, not the simple present, for actions or events that began in the past and are continuing now.

- I've **been** here for three months now. NOT ~~I'm here for three months now.~~

4. Use *will* to show a future state, action, or event decided on at the moment of speaking.

- You'll **need** to make a counter-offer when the vendor announces the price.

Will is used in the progressive to describe an action that will be in progress at a certain time in the future.

- A week from now you'll **be relaxing** in the sunshine or **visiting** famous landmarks.

5. *Be going to* usually shows a planned future. Use it to express a state, action, or event already planned before the moment of speaking.

- In this week's column, I'm **going to give** you some tips on how to perform this most enjoyable activity.

6. We can use both *will* and *be going to* when we say what we think will happen in the future.

- I think I'll **enjoy** the trip.
- I think I'm **going to enjoy** the trip.

▶ **BE CAREFUL!** Use *will*, not *be going to*, to express an unplanned future action.

- Call me next week. Maybe I'll **be** free. NOT ~~Maybe I'm going to be free.~~ (*Maybe* shows that the situation is unplanned.)

▶ **BE CAREFUL!** Use *be going to*, not *will*, to talk about a future situation that is already developing.

- Look at those dark clouds! It's **going to rain**. NOT ~~It will rain.~~

NOTE: Both *will* and *be going to* can be used informally in the progressive to show a planned future action.

- I'll **be studying** tonight.
- I'm **going to be studying** tonight.

7. You can use the **present progressive** to express a future event or action that has already been arranged.

- So you**'re visiting** another country this year?

8. The **simple present** can be used to show a future state, action, or event that is part of a schedule or timetable.

▶ **BE CAREFUL!** Use the simple present as future <u>only</u> to show something that is part of a schedule.

- You **leave** next Tuesday at 4 P.M.

9. Look at this sentence. It contains an independent clause and a dependent clause.

Many dependent clauses begin with words such as *if, when, before, after, as soon as,* and *until.*

When a dependent clause talks about a future time, use the simple present in the dependent clause and the future with *will* or *be going to* in the independent clause. Both verbs are future in meaning. The simple present shows the first future action, and the future shows the second future action.

▶ **BE CAREFUL!** Don't use the future with *will* or *be going to* in the dependent clause. Use it in the independent clause.

- independent clause
  You'll need to make a counter-offer
  dependent clause
  when the vendor announces the price.

- dependent clause
  As soon as you **walk** away,
  independent clause
  the vendor **will** most likely **come running** after you.

- When we get to Italy, we'll rent a car. NOT ~~When we will get to Italy, we'll rent a car.~~

10. Use the **future perfect** to show a state, action, or event that will happen before a certain time in the future.

You can also use the **future perfect** in the progressive.

NOTE: The **future perfect** is often used with *by* and *by the time.*

- If you go home without having experienced bargaining, **you will have missed out** on one of life's most interesting experiences.

- By the end of the summer, you**'ll have been traveling** for several weeks.

- **By the time** we finish our trip, we**'ll have visited** eighteen countries.

FOCUSED PRACTICE

1 DISCOVER THE GRAMMAR

Part A

1. List the verbs in the first paragraph of It's a Bargain. What verb tense is being used to tell the story? Why do you think that tense is being used?

2. In the last line of paragraph 1, what tense is the verb phrase "has existed"? Why is that tense used in that sentence?

3. In paragraph 2, the future is expressed in three different ways. Underline the verbs and label the ways.

Part B

Look again at some of the sentences from It's a Bargain. *On the lines provided, write the events in the order in which they will happen. Do not include imperatives (commands).*

1. You already have your tickets, and you leave next Tuesday at 4 P.M.

   First: ___You already have your tickets._____

   Second: ___You leave next Tuesday at 4 P.M._____

2. Maybe if you do some bargaining, you'll be able to get some good buys.

   First: _____

   Second: _____

3. You'll need to make a counter-offer when the vendor announces the price.

   First: _____

   Second: _____

4. Just make it clear that you're not going to buy if the vendor doesn't come down.

   First: _____

   Second: _____

5. As soon as you do this, he will most likely come running after you.

   First: _____

   Second: _____

6. If you go home without having experienced bargaining, you'll have missed out on one of life's most interesting experiences.

   First: _____

   Second: _____

2 A POSTCARD HOME

Connie Osborne is traveling in Europe. Complete her postcard to her friend Evelyn with the correct forms of the verbs below.

write	visit	shine	stay	love	be	go

London Towers Hotel

Hi Evelyn,   Sunday, July 19

    Well, I _____ in
                1.
London for a week now, and the sun
_____ every day since I got here. What a
        2.
surprise. I _____ my favorite museums
                3.
and all the usual attractions. Went to the British Museum
yesterday and had a great time. Also went to the Tower of
London. I love those guides in their funny hats.
    I _____ in a bed and breakfast, which is really
            4.
nice, but it's also pretty expensive, so I _____ to a
                                    5.
hostel tonight.
    The British people are so friendly and helpful!
And I really _____ the accent.
                6.
I _____ again soon.
        7.
                    Best,
                        Connie

To:

Britain 22p

Evelyn Nordin
5502 SW 99th St.
Seattle, WA 98136
        USA

3 DID YOU DO ANY BARGAINING?

Answer each of the following questions according to your own experience. Then work with another student. Compare your answers.

1. Have you ever traveled to another country?

2. Did you do any bargaining while you were there?

3. Have any of your friends ever given you tips on how to bargain?

Now imagine that you're going to bargain in an open-air market tomorrow.

4. If a vendor does not give you a fair price when you try to bargain, how do you think you'll react?

5. Do you think you'll be nervous or intimidated when you try to bargain? If so, why?

6. When you have been nervous or intimidated in the past, how have you reacted?

❹ THE FLEA MARKET

*Work with a partner. Decide which sentences Student A and Student B say. Mark the sentences **A** or **B**. Then write them in the order of a dialogue. Read the dialogue aloud with your partner.*

_____ Take it easy. We'll be there in a few minutes. We'll have arrived as soon as we cross the big bridge coming up. See it?

_____ I'll have developed a splitting headache by the time we get there if you don't stop complaining.

_____ Next time you go to the flea market, I'm staying home!

_____ Well, excuse me for living!

_____ Just stop making all that noise!

_____ We're really late. By the time we get to the flea market, they'll have sold all the best items. Those antique vases I love will be all gone.

_____ Yes. But we're already an hour late. We'll have missed all the best bargains.

_____ Next time we're going to leave home two hours earlier. That way, even if we get lost, we'll still have time to get some good bargains. You know how I love to bargain.

❺ A WORLD TRAVELER

Read the article about John Clouse. At the time the article was written, Clouse had visited more countries than anyone else in the world. Complete the passage by choosing the correct forms of the verbs in parentheses.

TRAVEL   Section 6

This Man's Been Nearly Everywhere

John Clouse _____ the thickest,
        1. (have)
most dog-eared passport in the world. Turn to page 16 of the *1996 Guinness Book of World Records* and you _____ the reason.
                           2. (find)
He _____ the record for traveling
    3. (hold)
to all 192 of the globe's sovereign countries, and to all but six of the non-sovereign or other territories that existed in early 1996.

Clouse, who has spent about $1.25 million roaming from A to Z in the past 40 years, says he travels for the love of it, not to outrun anybody else who may be keeping a list. He is now down to just three remote islands to visit.

Clouse _____ his journeys since
            4. (continue)
making the record book, and has not only visited every country in the world, but some two or

three times. Now he _____ on the

5. (focus)

remaining three islands.

"Yeah, I'm trying to finagle my way to three places: the Paracel Islands, owned by China in the South China Sea," he says. "And on two occasions the weather has kept me away from reaching Bouvet, an island in Norwegian Antarctica. No. 3 is Clipperton, a French island about 700 miles west of Acapulco."

Clouse says he _____ East Africa.

6. (love)

"It's one of the most beautiful places in the world," he says. "In Kenya and Tanzania the weather is gorgeous almost every day, and Lake Nyasa must be what the garden of Eden looked like."

After all his traveling he says, "I

_____ there are evil empires and evil

7. (not believe)

people. Yes, there are some bad leaders in the world, but seeing people as individuals has taught me that they are all basically alike. You can be in some terrible place and someone will extend hospitality to you."

Clouse _____ light, with a small

8. (travel)

suitcase, and seldom _____ first class.

9. (go)

His complete collection of *National Geographic* magazines is his main source for research.

Clouse began his traveling adventures just after

World War II when severe frostbite in the war sent him to England for recovery, then to Paris and other parts of Europe.

"I thought, boy, this is the life," he says of his travels then. "And when I got out of law school and was making a little money, I started to travel." Years ago he stopped taking photos and now

_____ a journal of his travels.

10. (keep)

He has crossed the Atlantic Ocean at least 100 times, and the Pacific Ocean 40 or 50 times. His 18-year-old son, Chauncey, had visited over 100 countries by the time he was 5 years old. But for now, it is not "like father like son."

"We _____ about seven miles across

11. (live)

the river from Kentucky," says Clouse. "My son would not go those seven miles . . . He'd say, sorry, Dad, I've got something else to do."

Clouse concludes that the right attitude is synonymous with the lightness of his suitcase. "Travel without a lot of mental baggage," he says. "Try not to go with preconceived notions that the

place _____ dirty or hostile, and if it

12. (be)

_____, go with the flow and make the

13. (be)

best of it.

"Learn a few words like please and thank you," he suggests. "That really _____ people."

14. (please)

6 UNDERSTANDING MEANING FROM CONTEXT

Mark the following sentences **True (T), False (F),** *or* **Impossible to know (I)**
based on the reading in Exercise 5.

Part A

_____ **1.** Clouse will have visited the six remaining territories by the year 2001.

_____ **2.** Clouse has been traveling all these years because he wants to break the world records.

_____ **3.** Clouse's son will accompany him to the last three remote islands.

_____ **4.** Clouse's son has been visiting all the countries with his father.

_____ **5.** Clouse has done all his research on the Internet.

_____ **6.** Clouse has always tried to develop preconceived notions about a place before his visit.

_____ **7.** According to Clouse, if you travel as he has, you will no longer categorize the people of a country as all good or all bad.

Part B

Now look again at these three sentences. Circle the letter of the choice that best explains the meaning of each italicized phrase. Explain the reason for your choice.

1. Clouse *will have visited* the six remaining territories by the year 2001.

    a. visited before the time mentioned   **b.** has already visited before now

_____

2. Clouse's son *has been visiting* all the countries with his father.

    a. visited once   **b.** has visited and is continuing to visit

_____

3. *Clouse has done all his research* on the Internet.

    a. the research is now finished   **b.** the research will be continued

_____

7 BY THIS TIME NEXT YEAR . . . Grammar Note 10

Tell a partner what new place(s) you will have visited by this time next year. Then tell your partner what you will have accomplished within five years. Use the future perfect.

      EXAMPLE:
      By this time next year, I **will have visited** Mexico City.
      Within five years, I **will have graduated** from college, **gotten** a good job, . . .

8 EDITING

Find and correct the thirteen mistakes in present and future verb usage in the following composition.

 Travel Log

           I am writing these words in English because I ~~am needing~~ *need* the practice. At this moment I am on an airplane over the Pacific Ocean, on my way to a year of study at New York University in the United States. I am looking forward to being there, but I am also a little afraid. What will I find when I will get to America? Will the Americans be arrogant and violent? Will I make any friends? Am I happy?

           These were the words I wrote in my diary on the airplane last month. But I'm here for a month now, and I've found that things are a lot different from what I expected. I've found that the majority of people here are friendly. They are going out of their way to help you if you need it.

           On television, the news programs are speaking a lot about bad events like accidents, murders, diseases, and fights. But I don't see as much violence in my life as I do on television. I have not been mugged and I no worry all the time about my safety.

           Two of the ideas I had about the United States, however, are seeming to be true. One is that Americans aren't paying much attention to rules. One of my best American friends says, in fact, "Rules are made to be broken." The other idea I had is about the American family. In Japan the family is very important, but some Japanese people are thinking that the family means nothing in the United States. I'm not knowing if this is true or not. But I think it might be true, since my American friends almost never are mentioning their parents or their brothers and sisters. Anyway, I am going to have a chance to see a real American family. I'm going with my roommate Susan to spend Thanksgiving break with her family in Pennsylvania. When I will see her family, I will understand more!

COMMUNICATION PRACTICE

9 LISTENING

The Fosters, a family from England, are traveling in Canada. Listen to their conversation. Then listen again and mark the following sentences **True (T)** *or* **False (F)**.

_____ **1.** Tim is still in bed.

_____ **2.** The Fosters are going to the mall this morning.

_____ **3.** Amy and Tim want to go to the museum.

_____ **4.** Dad thinks the children can learn something at the museum.

_____ **5.** The Fosters are on the tour bus now.

_____ **6.** The Fosters will miss the bus if they don't hurry.

_____ **7.** Amy and Tim like tours.

_____ **8.** Tim thinks it's always important to learn new things.

_____ **9.** Amy and Tim would rather go to the museum by themselves than go on a tour.

_____ **10.** The Fosters will go to the mall before they go on the tour.

10 GROUP GUESSING GAME: A VACATION SPOT

Get into groups of four to six. Choose a vacation spot that you might like to visit. Use the Internet or go to the library to get information about the place. Then talk about your place to the class, describing it and telling what you'll do there, but don't say the name of the place. The rest of the class must guess the vacation spot.

11 ESSAY

Divide into groups of four. Look back at This Man's Been Nearly Everywhere.

Clouse says, "I don't believe there are evil empires and evil people. Yes, there are some bad leaders in the world, but seeing people as individuals has taught me that they are all basically alike. You can be in some terrible place and someone will extend hospitality to you."

Do you agree with Clouse? Why or why not? Give examples to support your viewpoint from your own experiences.

Write a short essay (one or two paragraphs) expressing your response to the quote by Clouse. Give examples from your own experience to support your viewpoint.

12 PICTURE DISCUSSION

Talk with a partner about the picture. What has happened? Do you think the father will have fixed the car by nightfall? Do you think the other car is slowing down in order to help?

2 PAST TIME

GRAMMAR **IN CONTEXT**

1. What do you understand by the term "arranged marriage"?

2. Would you rather find your own person to marry or have someone else select that person for you?

3. Do you think an arranged marriage is likely to be a happy marriage?

Read an article about an unusual marriage that took place recently.

LIFESTYLES

A Marriage Made on the Internet?

How many Americans have ever considered asking friends or relatives to select their future spouse for them? Not very many, apparently. Yet this is exactly what David Weinlick did.

Weinlick had apparently been considering marriage and had known for a long time that he was going to get married on June 13, 1998. Where the wedding would take place and who would be invited he already knew. He just didn't know who he would be marrying. You see, he hadn't met his bride yet.

It all started four years ago. Friends would repeatedly ask Weinlick, an anthropology student at the University of Minnesota, when he was going to tie the knot.

He got tired of these questions, so he just picked a date out of the blue: June 13, 1998. As this date kept getting closer and closer, Weinlick, twenty-eight, knew he had to do something. His friend Steve Fletcher came up with the idea of a democratic selection process. Weinlick liked the idea, so he advertised for a bride on the Internet on a Bridal Nomination Committee Web site.

He devised an application form and asked friends and relatives to interview the candidates and select the winner. They did this at a "bridal candidate mixer" before the ceremony on the day of the wedding.

Weinlick's friends and relatives took the request quite seriously.

Internet Marriage

Though Weinlick wasn't sure who his bride would be, he did want to get married. He said he thinks commitment is important and that people have to work at relationships to make them successful. Weinlick's sister, Wenonah Wilms, said she thought that all of the candidates were nice but that she was looking for someone really special. Wilms added that it was important for her brother to marry someone who would fit into family celebrations like at Christmas.

So who won the election? It was Elizabeth Runze, a pharmacy student at the University of Minnesota. Runze hadn't met Weinlick before she picked up a candidate survey on the Monday before the wedding. They talked more when Runze turned in the survey about her career plans and hobbies the next day. After her selection, Runze said the day was the most incredible she had ever experienced.

Weinlick was happy, too. After the selection the groom said the plan turned out almost exactly as he had hoped.

By the time the wedding day rolled around, Weinlick had prepared everything: the rings, the musicians, his tuxedo, and the reception afterwards. The two took their vows at the Mall of America in Minneapolis while about 2,000 shoppers looked on from the upper levels of the mall.

Runze's parents support the marriage. Runze's mother said her daughter was taking the whole event seriously. She predicted the couple's marriage would be long-term.

Weinlick's father wasn't so positive. He said he admired his son's independence and wished him well but wasn't really happy about the wedding, adding that he thought it was a case of treating a serious step too lightly.

From all accounts, the newlyweds are doing well. Weinlick and Runze's union qualifies as an "arranged marriage," a phenomenon which has never had much currency in America. Arranged marriages are common in many other parts of the world, though, or at least they used to be. Maybe they're not such a bad idea.

Sources: Based on information in "A Match Made in the Mall: Minnesota Anthropology Student Weds Bride Chosen by Family and Friends," *Dallas Morning News,* June 14, 1998, p. 7A, copyright: The Associated Press; "Here Come the Bridal Candidates; Society: Friends of 28-year-old will vote to select his mate. As election day nears, Dad is not so sure of the plan," Home Edition, *Los Angeles Times,* June 8, 1998, p. A-19.

UNDERSTANDING MEANING FROM CONTEXT

Make a guess about the meaning of each italicized word or phrase from the reading. Write your guess in the blank provided.

1. Friends would repeatedly ask Weinlick . . . when he was going to *tie the knot.*

   _____

2. He got tired of these questions, so he just picked a date *out of the blue.* . . .

   _____

3. After the selection, the *groom* said the plan turned out almost exactly as he had hoped.

   _____

4. The two *took their vows* at the Mall of America in Minneapolis.

   _____

5. Weinlick and Runze's union qualifies as an "arranged marriage," a phenomenon which has never *had much currency* in America.

   _____

GRAMMAR **PRESENTATION**
PAST TIME

PAST TIME: A TIME IN THE PAST (GENERAL OR SPECIFIC)

SIMPLE PAST
Weinlick's father **admired** his son's independence and **wished** him well.

PAST PROGRESSIVE			
SUBJECT	WAS / WERE	BASE FORM + -ING	
Weinlick's sister	**was**	**looking for**	someone really special.

USED TO + BASE FORM
Arranged marriages **used to be** common in many parts of the world.

WOULD + BASE FORM
Friends **would** repeatedly **ask** Weinlick when he was going to tie the knot.

PAST TIME: A TIME IN THE PAST (INDEFINITE)

PRESENT PERFECT
How many Americans **have** ever **considered** asking friends or relatives to select their future spouse for them?

PAST TIME: BEFORE A TIME IN THE PAST

PAST PERFECT			
SUBJECT	HAD	PAST PARTICIPLE	
Weinlick	**had**	**known**	for a long time that he was going to get married on June 13, 1998.

PAST PERFECT PROGRESSIVE			
SUBJECT	HAD BEEN	BASE FORM + -ING	
Weinlick	**had** apparently **been**	**considering**	marriage.

PAST TIME: AFTER A TIME IN THE PAST BUT BEFORE NOW

	WAS / WERE GOING TO	BASE FORM	
FUTURE IN THE PAST			
Weinlick had known for a long time that he	**was going to**	**get**	married on June 13, 1998.

	WOULD	BASE FORM	
FUTURE IN THE PAST: *WOULD*			
He knew where the wedding and who	**would** **would**	**take place** **be**	invited.

	WOULD	BASE FORM + -ING
FUTURE IN THE PAST: *WOULD BE + -ING*		
He just didn't know who he	**would**	**be marrying**.

NOTES

1. Use the **simple past** to express a state, event, or action at a specific time in the past or a general time in the past.

2. Use the **past progressive** to express an action that was in progress (not finished) at a time in the past.

3. Use the **present perfect** (*have / has* + past participle) to express a state, event, or action at an indefinite time in the past.

▶ **BE CAREFUL!** Don't use the present perfect with a past time expression.

EXAMPLES

- Weinlick **liked** the idea, so he **advertised** for a bride on the Internet.

- Weinlick's sister said she **was looking for** someone really special.

- How many Americans **have** ever **considered** asking friends or relatives to select their future spouse for them?

- Weinlick **got** married **several months ago**.
  NOT ~~Weinlick has gotten married several months ago.~~

Notice the difference between the simple past and the present perfect. The simple past is the definite past. The present perfect is the indefinite past.

- The two **took** their vows at the Mall of America in Minneapolis. (definite—a specific time)
- Arranged marriage **has** never **had** much currency in America. (indefinite—no specific time)

4. Use the **past perfect** (*had* + past participle) to show a state, event, or action that happened before a certain time in the past.

Use the **past perfect** with the past tense to show which of two past states, events, or actions happened first. The **past perfect** is often used with *by* or *by the time*.

- Weinlick **hadn't met** his bride yet. *(He had not met her before he set the wedding date.)*

- By the time the wedding day rolled around, Weinlick **had prepared** everything. *(First he prepared everything; then the wedding day rolled around.)*

5. Use **used to** + base form to show a habitual state, event, or action that was true in the past but is no longer true.

- Arranged marriages **used to be** common in many countries. *(They're not very common anymore.)*

6. You can also use **would** + base form to express actions or events that occurred regularly during a period in the past.

▶ **BE CAREFUL! Used to** and **would** are similar in meaning when they are used to express past actions. They can be used interchangeably in many situations. However, only **used to** can show past location, state, or possession.

- Friends **would** repeatedly **ask** Weinlick when he was going to get married.

- We used to have a summer home. NOT ~~We would have a summer home.~~

7. Use **was / were going to** or **would** + base form to describe a state, event, or action that was planned in the past (before now). Sentences with **was / were going to** or **would** are sometimes called **future in the past**. See Note 5, page 39 for a discussion of sequence of tenses.

- Weinlick had known for a long time that he **was going to get** married on June 13, 1998.
- He knew where the wedding **would take place** and who **would be** invited.
- He just didn't know who he **would be marrying**.

FOCUSED PRACTICE

① DISCOVER THE GRAMMAR

Part A

1. *Find three examples of* **would** *+ verb in the unit opener,* A Marriage Made on the Internet? *Do they show a future in the past or a habitual action in the past?*

_____

2. *List the simple past tense irregular verbs in the opener. Write the present form of each one next to the past tense.*

_____

3. *Find a sentence that shows two past actions, one happening before the other. Write the word that says which one happened first.*

_____

Part B

Look again at some of the sentences from A Marriage Made on the Internet?
Write the earlier-occurring state or action on the left and the later-occurring state or action on the right.

1. Weinlick . . . had known for a long time he was going to get married on June 13, 1998.

earlier	**later**
Weinlick had known for a long time	he was going to get married on June 13, 1998.

2. He just didn't know who he would be marrying.

earlier	**later**

3. Friends would repeatedly ask Weinlick . . . when he was going to tie the knot.

earlier	**later**

4. Runze hadn't met Weinlick before she picked up a candidate survey on the Monday before the wedding.

earlier	**later**

5. By the time the wedding day rolled around, Weinlick had prepared everything . . .

earlier	**later**

2 **DO OPPOSITES ATTRACT?**　　　　　　Grammar Notes 1, 3

Complete the story with the correct past forms of the indicated verbs. Use contractions with pronoun subjects.

Ellen Rosetti and Mark Stevens ___have been married___ for almost a year now. Their
　　　　　　　　　　　　　　　　　1. (be married)

marriage almost _____, though. They _____ on a blind date
　　　　　　　2. (not happen)　　　　　　　　　　　　3. (meet)

when Jennifer's friend Alice _____ two extra tickets for a concert. At first
　　　　　　　　　　　　4. (have)

Jennifer _____ Mark was the most opinionated man she'd ever met. A
　　　　5. (think)

couple of weeks after the concert, Mark _____ and _____
　　　　　　　　　　　　　　　　6. (call up)　　　　　　　　7. (ask)

Ellen out. Ellen _____ to say no, but something _____ her
　　　　　　　8. (want)　　　　　　　　　　　　　　9. (make)

accept. After that, one thing _____ to another. Today Mark says, "Ellen is
　　　　　　　　　　　　10. (lead)

unique. I _____ anyone even remotely like her."
　　　　11. (never / meet)

　　　Ellen says, "At first glance you might have trouble seeing how Mark and I could be

married. In certain ways, we're as different as night and day. I'm an early bird; he's a night

owl. He's conservative; I'm liberal. He loves sports, and I can't stand them. I guess you

might say we're a case of opposites being attracted to each other. But in other ways we're

not so different. For one thing, we both love to travel. We _____ three
　　　　　　　　　　　　　　　　　　　　　12. (take)

fantastic trips since we _____ the knot. The other thing is that we love to
　　　　　　　　13. (tie)

talk. I can't tell you how many fascinating conversations we _____. There
　　　　　　　　　　　　　　　　　　　　　　14. (have)

_____ lots of times when we _____ all night talking."
　　　15. (be)　　　　　　　　　　　　16. (stay up)

Maybe opposites do attract.

3 THE REST IS HISTORY

This is the story of how Jim Garcia and Jennifer O'Leary met. The sentences are out of order. On a separate piece of paper, rewrite them in a paragraph or two in chronological order, using the past and past perfect as appropriate. Combine sentences as needed. Then compare what you have written with a partner. Here are two possible beginning sentences:

A: Jim Garcia and Jennifer O'Leary got married six months ago.

B: Jim Garcia and Jennifer O'Leary had gone to high school together and had been good friends.

About a year ago, both Jennifer and Jim returned to their home town.

Jennifer accepted.

Jim and Jennifer got married six months ago.

Jennifer went away to college.

Jim asked Jennifer for a date.

The rest is history.

Jim Garcia and Jennifer O'Leary had gone to high school together and had been good friends.

Jim and Jennifer graduated and went their separate ways.

Jim went into the military.

Jim and Jennifer ran into each other in the drugstore.

Jim and Jennifer fell in love.

4 BEFORE AND AFTER

Jim Garcia and Mark Stevens both got married fairly recently. Fill in the blanks in their conversation with the correct forms of **used to** *or* **would** *and the indicated verbs. Use* **would** *if possible. Contract* **would** *if it occurs with a pronoun.*

MARK: So, Jim, how does it feel to be an old married man? Been about six months, hasn't it?

JIM: Yep. It feels great. It's a lot different, though.

MARK: Yeah? How so?

JIM: Well, I guess I'd say I _____used to have_____ a lot more freedom. Like on Saturdays,
　　　　　　　　　　　　　　　　1. (have)

for example. I _____ until eleven or even noon. Then when I got up
　　　　　　　　　2. (sleep)

my buddies and I _____ out for breakfast at a restaurant. Now
　　　　　　　　　　3. (usually go)

Jennifer and I get up at eight at the latest. She's really an early bird. And I either

make her breakfast or she makes it for me. And then on Saturday nights I

_____ on a date and stay out till all hours of the night. Now it's just
　　　　4. (go)

the two of us. Sometimes we go out on Saturday nights, and sometimes we don't.

MARK: Does that bother you?

JIM: You know, it doesn't. Life actually _____ kind of lonely. It's not
　　　　　　　　　　　　　　　　　　　　5. (be)

anymore. What about you? Have things really changed?

MARK: They sure have. For one thing, the neighborhood is totally different. Remember the

apartment I _____ in, right north of downtown? Well, Ellen and I
　　　　　　　6. (live)

just bought a house in the suburbs. That's a trip, let me tell you.

JIM: I'll bet.

MARK: Yeah. My weekends _____ my own. I _____ all day
　　　　　　　　　　　　　7. (be)　　　　　　　　　　　8. (spend)

Saturday working on my car or going mountain biking. Now I have to cut the grass

and take care of the yard.

JIM: So would you change anything?

MARK: Sure wouldn't. You know how everyone says how great it is to be single? Well, that

_____ my attitude too. Not now. Now I'd say "been there, done that."
　　　　9. (be)

JIM: Me too. I wouldn't change a thing.

---

⑤ PLANS AND EXPECTATIONS　　　　　　　　　　**Grammar Note 7**

*Before Jim got married, he jotted down some of his plans and expectations. Now
that he's married, he's looking at them. Some of them came true, and some didn't.
Jim is telling Mark about his thoughts. Write Jim's sentences. Use the indicated
future-in-the-past constructions:* **was / were going to** + *verb or* **would** + *verb.*

(continued on next page)

Column A

1. "I think it'll be quite a while before we have any children."

2. "I think I'll probably feel just a little bit trapped."

3. "I think that we're going to live in an apartment."

4. "I expect that there won't be as much money to spend."

5. "I hope that we'll be happy."

6. I'm sure that we're going to have a lot of fun together."

7. "I don't think I'll be seeing as much of my buddies."

8. "I figure that we're going to be taking a lot of trips."

Column B

I thought it would be quite a while before we had any children,

but that's not true. Our first baby is due in four months.

_____

_____

but I haven't felt that way at all.

_____

_____

and we do.

_____

_____

but that's not true. Jennifer really knows how to keep our lifestyle economical.

_____

and we are. Tremendously.

_____

and we do.

_____

and I don't. That's OK, though.

_____

but we haven't taken any, yet.

6 DEAR ANN

Read the excerpt from Ann Landers' advice column. Complete the advice column with the correct form of the indicated verbs.

Ann Landers

Dear Ann: My husband and I _____were_____ recently married.
1. (be)
Our wedding _____ beautiful, but there
2. (be)

_____ one problem. We _____ 17 no-shows
3. (be)   4. (have)
and four surprise guests. Two days before the wedding, we

_____ give the caterers the exact number of guests. After
5. (have to)
that, we _____ billed no matter how many no-shows there
6. (get)

_____. That means we _____ for 13 extra
7. (be)   8. (pay)
meals that nobody _____.
9. (eat)

   I understand that sometimes an emergency comes up, but we _____ over $330
10. (waste)

on those no-show dinners. The four extra guests _____ to be no problem because
11. (turn out)

of the no-shows, but generally, surprises are not welcome. What if those 17 people had shown up

and we didn't have enough dinners? It would have been a nightmare.

   It is simply good manners to let the hostess know if you are coming or not. And if the number

of people in your party _____, she should be informed about that, too. When you
12. (change)

RSVP, the information you give the hostess is what the cost of the event is based on. Wedding

receptions aren't cheap these days, and paying for no-shows is a terrible waste.

   Am I expecting too much from guests? If so, please tell me.   —*San Diego*

Dear San Diego: You are not expecting too much. Letting the hostess know whether you

are coming is no more than common courtesy. Not having enough food because some

inconsiderate people _____ to let you know they were coming is a major
13. (not bother)

embarrassment. A response card and stamped envelope are well worth the extra expense.

I recommend them.

Source: Ann Landers, *Seattle Post-Intelligencer,* October 6, 1998, p. F-2. Permission granted by Ann Landers and Creators Syndicate.

Now discuss the letter with a partner. Do you agree with Ann Landers' advice? Why or why not?

7 EDITING

Read Jennifer Garcia's diary entry. Find and correct the nine errors in verb constructions.

May 20

Dear Diary,

    I just had to write today. It's our six-month anniversary. Jim and I ~~are~~ ^{have been}

married six months as of today. So maybe this is the time for me to take stock of

my situation. The obvious question is whether I'm happy I get married. The

answer is "Absolutely." When I remember what my life has been like before we get

married, I realize now how lonely I've been before. Jim is a wonderful guy. Since we

both work, we take turns doing the housework. He's really good about that.

When we have been dating, I wasn't sure whether or not I'm going to have to do

all the housework. But I had not to worry. Today we split everything 50/50. The

only complaint I have is that Jim snores at night. When I told him that, he only

says, "Well, sweetie, you snore too." I don't believe it. But if this is our only

problem, I guess we're pretty lucky.

    Well, Diary, I would have a long and tiring day. It's time to go to sleep. I'll

write again soon.

Jennifer

COMMUNICATION PRACTICE

8 LISTENING

Listen to the news broadcast. Then listen again and mark the following sentences **True (T)** *or* **False (F)**.

True **False**

❏ ❏ **1.** According to the broadcast, this is the first parachute wedding that has ever taken place.

❏ ❏ **2.** The bride and groom have known each other for four years.

❏ ❏ **3.** This was the first parachute jump for Yang and Hammer.

❏ ❏ **4.** Yang and Hammer had intended to get married while bungee-jumping.

❏ ❏ **5.** By the time Yang and Hammer landed, they were married.

❏ ❏ **6.** Yang and Hammer were able to find a minister who agreed to marry them while bungee-jumping but decided not to because it was too expensive.

❏ ❏ **7.** This is the most unusual wedding ceremony Reverend Martinez has ever performed.

❏ ❏ **8.** To date, Martinez has made several parachute jumps.

❏ ❏ **9.** Reverend Martinez once married a couple on horseback.

❏ ❏ **10.** Martinez intends to do more parachute jumping.

Do you take this woman to be your lawfully wedded wife?

UNUSUAL WEDDINGS

I now pronounce you husband and wife.

❾ INFORMATION GAP: BETTER THAN IT USED TO BE

Working with a partner, complete the text. Each of you will read a version of the same story. Each version is missing some information. Take turns asking your partner questions to get the missing information.

Student A, read the story about Jack Strait. Ask questions and fill in the missing information. Then answer Student B's questions.

Student B, turn to page 32 and follow the instructions there.

EXAMPLE:

A: What kind of company did he use to work for?

B: He used to work for a large, impersonal company.
How long would he be on the road?

A: He would be on the road for two or three weeks at a time.

Jack Strait's life is quite different now from the way it used to be. He used to work for

_____ company. His job required him to do a lot of traveling. He would be on

the road for two or three weeks at a time. It was always the same: As soon as he pulled in

to a town, he would look for _____. The next morning he'd leave his business

card at a lot of different establishments, hoping that someone would agree to see him. If

he'd been lucky enough to arrange an appointment in advance, he'd show them

_____. Occasionally they would buy something; most often they wouldn't.

Jack's marriage began to suffer. He missed his wife a lot, but there wasn't much he

could do about the situation. And when he was on the road, he hardly ever saw his

children. He would try to call them _____ if he had a spare moment, but

usually it was so late that they had already gone to bed. They were growing up without

him. Finally, his wife laid down the law, saying, "Why should we even be married if we're

never going to see each other?" Jack decided she was right. He took a risk. He quit his job

and started his own business. Things were difficult at first, but at least the family was

together.

That was five years ago. Things have changed a lot since then. Jack and his family used

to live in a small apartment. Now they own a house. Life is good.

Compare your story with your partner's. Are they the same? Now discuss these questions: What did Jack's occupation use to be? Is it important to take risks in life as Jack did? Can you think of an example of a risk you have taken in your life?

10 ESSAY

Write three or four paragraphs about how marriages used to be arranged and how young people would meet their future mates when your parents were young. Ask an older person you know how it was.

11 PICTURE DISCUSSION

With a partner, discuss this picture. Describe the situation. What is happening? Approximately how long do you think these people have been married? Do you think their relationship is less interesting or satisfactory than it used to be, or is it just different? Present your opinions to the class.

Source: Printed by permission of the Norman Rockwell Family Trust. Copyright © 1930 the Norman Rockwell Family Trust.

INFORMATION GAP FOR STUDENT B

Student B, read the story about Jack Strait. Answer Student A's questions. Then ask your own questions and fill in the missing information.

EXAMPLE:

A: What kind of company did he use to work for?

B: He used to work for a large, impersonal company.
How long would he be on the road?

A: He would be on the road for two or three weeks at a time.

Jack Strait's life is quite different now from the way it used to be. He used to work for a large, impersonal company. His job required him to do a lot of traveling. He would be on the road for _____. It was always the same: As soon as he pulled in to a town, he would look for a cheap motel to stay in. The next morning he'd leave _____ at a lot of different establishments, hoping that someone would agree to see him. If he'd been lucky enough to arrange an appointment in advance, he'd show them his samples. _____ they would buy something; most often they wouldn't.

Jack's marriage began to suffer. He missed his wife a lot, but there wasn't much he could do about the situation. And when he was on the road, he hardly ever saw his children. He would try to call them in the evenings if he had a spare moment, but usually it was so late that they had already gone to bed. They were growing up without him. Finally, his wife laid down the law, saying, "Why should we even be married if we're never going to see each other?" Jack decided she was right. He took a risk. He quit his job and started his own business. Things were difficult at first, but at least the family was together.

That was five years ago. Things have changed a lot since then. Jack and his family used to live _____. Now they own a house. Life is good.

Compare your story with your partner's. Are they the same? Now discuss these questions: What did Jack's occupation use to be? Is it important to take risks in life as Jack did? Can you think of an example of a risk you have taken in your life?

Past, Present, and Future

GRAMMAR IN CONTEXT

QUESTIONS TO CONSIDER

1. Would you like to have a personal robot in your home that would work for you?

2. What are some of the advantages and disadvantages of technology around the house?

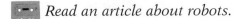 *Read an article about robots.*

My Friend the Robot

Technology marches on. What we only dreamed about yesterday is a reality today. What we dream about today will become a reality tomorrow—or, at the rate things are going, maybe this evening. Did you know, for example, that there are now computers that can operate underwater? Soon there will be computers that we can wear. There is now computer-controlled plastic surgery. And then there are robots. Twenty years ago, hardly anyone thought personal computers would become common in the home, but they have. Robots may now be at the stage that personal computers were twenty years ago. The development of the personal robot may be the next big technological advance, and some are predicting that within twenty years, home robots will have become as common as PCs are today.

Robots that looked like vaguely humanoid, walking tin cans used to be the staple of science fiction writers. Czech writer Karel Čapek gave us the word "robot" in his play *R.U.R.*, *Rossum's Universal Robots*, in 1921. Čapek coined the term from *robota*, which means "forced labor" or "drudgery." The robots in Čapek's play eventually destroyed mankind because they had learned to love

continued ▶

and hate. Today, though, most visualize robots not as threatening creatures but as beneficial machines that are helping us with our work, especially unpleasant drudgery.

Computer science professor Gregory Dudek recalls how bulky and awkward computers were when they first appeared and how they've been getting much smaller and more efficient. He predicts the same kind of development for the personal robot, saying, "That's the kind of change we're looking for in the robot industry. I don't think it will happen in the next two years, but in the next five or ten, certainly."

The commercial robot is already a reality. For years, industry has been using robots in factories. Different kinds of robots have started to appear in catalogues and in robot specialty shops. What will the personal robots of the future look like and do? They probably won't resemble humans as much as they do today, and they'll almost certainly be much smaller. Researchers envision small robots that will come out at night to do things like vacuum and mop the floors, eat up dirt and insects, and wash the windows.

However, many researchers see future robots as much more than just mechanical workers that perform the tasks we don't want to do. Many see them as companions. Consider robotic pets, for example. The Sony Corporation has developed a robotic dog that wags its tail, fetches a ball, and responds to human commands. Researchers at the Georgia Institute of Technology have been developing a mobile robot called Pepe, short for "personal pet." Its makers hope that future users will regard it more as a friend or companion than as a robot. Wouldn't you like to have a robot pet that does what you want, but you wouldn't have to feed it or take it to the vet to get its shots?

Another use of robots is as waiters or servants. Does this sound unbelievable? It isn't. In London's Yo! Sushi restaurant, there are robots that prepare food, serve drinks, warn customers to get out of their way, and make funny statements like, "Life is a never-ending circuit."

Robots will probably never replace humans. Wouldn't it be nice, though, to have companions who will do our drudgery for us, be there when we wish, speak when spoken to, listen attentively to everything we say, and not talk back?

UNDERSTANDING MEANING FROM CONTEXT

Circle the letter of the choice closest in meaning to each italicized word or phrase from the reading.

1. Robots that looked like vaguely humanoid, walking tin cans used to be the *staple* of science fiction writers.

   a. main product   **b.** mechanical device   **c.** home

2. Čapek *coined* the term from "robota," which means "forced labor" or "drudgery."

   a. bought   **b.** created   **c.** imagined

3. Today, though, most visualize robots not as threatening creatures but as beneficial machines that are helping us with our work, especially unpleasant *drudgery*.

   a. easy, enjoyable work   **b.** creative work   **c.** boring, difficult work

4. Computer science professor Gregory Dudek recalls how *bulky and awkward* computers were when they first appeared and how they've been getting much smaller and more efficient.

   a. small and easy to handle   **b.** expensive and difficult to obtain   **c.** large and hard to handle

5. The Sony Corporation has developed a robotic dog that wags its tail, *fetches* a ball, and responds to human commands.

   a. gets and brings back   **b.** takes away   **c.** chews

GRAMMAR **PRESENTATION**
CONTRASTING TENSES: PAST, PRESENT, AND FUTURE

PAST TIME

SIMPLE PAST: DEFINITE

Czech writer Čapek **gave** us the word "robot" in his play *R.U.R.* in 1921.

PRESENT PERFECT: INDEFINITE

Personal computers **have become** common in the home.

SIMPLE PAST AND PAST PERFECT: TWO PAST ACTIONS

Robots **destroyed** mankind because they **had learned** to love and hate.

PRESENT TIME

SIMPLE PRESENT: IN GENERAL

Technology **marches** on.

PRESENT PROGRESSIVE: NOW

That's the kind of change we**'re looking for** in the robot industry.

PRESENT PERFECT: FROM A TIME IN THE PAST UNTIL NOW

Professor Stern **has worked** at the university all his adult life.

FUTURE TIME

FUTURE WITH *WILL*

Personal robots **won't resemble** humans as much as they do today, and they**'ll** almost certainly **be** smaller.

FUTURE PERFECT: BEFORE A TIME IN THE FUTURE

Some are predicting that within twenty years robots **will have become** as common in the home as PCs are today.

FINISHED ACTION

PRESENT PERFECT			
SUBJECT	*HAS / HAVE*	**PAST PARTICIPLE**	
General Robotics	**has**	**developed**	a robot dog named Pepe.

UNFINISHED ACTION

PRESENT PERFECT PROGRESSIVE			
SUBJECT	*HAS / HAVE BEEN*	**PRESENT PARTICIPLE**	
General Robotics	**has been**	**developing**	advanced robots for years.

SIMPLE AND PROGRESSIVE FORMS: ALL OR PART OF AN ACTION

ALL OF AN ACTION: SIMPLE FORM
Sony Corporation has developed a robotic dog that **wags** its tail and **fetches** a ball.

PART OF AN ACTION: PROGRESSIVE FORM
That robot dog **is wagging** its tail.

VERBS USED STATIVELY AND ACTIVELY

STATIVE USE
We **have** a personal robot at our house.
The food **tastes** delicious.

ACTIVE USE
The children **are having** a good time playing with their personal robot.
The chef **is tasting** the stew that he's making.

SEQUENCE OF TENSES

TENSE AND TIME
Most people **visualize** robots as beneficial creatures that **will help** us with our work. Twenty years ago hardly anyone **thought** personal computers **would be** common in the home.

NOTES	EXAMPLES

1. With certain verbs, the **present perfect** and the **present perfect progressive** are similar in meaning. Speakers often use the progressive to suggest a shorter or more temporary action. They often use the simple form to suggest a longer or more permanent action.

- John Brown **has been working** at General Robotics for a year.
- Professor Stanley **has worked** for a robotics firm for over twenty years.

If the word *always* is in the sentence, we can only use the simple form.

- Professor Stanley **has always worked** in robotics.
  NOT ~~Professor Stanley has always been working in robotics.~~

In another use, the progressive and the simple forms are very different in meaning. Only the simple form can be used to describe actions that are finished.

- General Robotics **has developed** a robot dog. (a finished action)

The progressive form is used to describe actions that are still in progress.

- General Robotics **has been developing** advanced robots for years. (an unfinished action)

---

2. Remember that we use simple forms to describe finished actions or states and actions in general.

- The Sony Corporation has developed a robotic dog that **wags** its tail, **fetches** a ball, and **responds** to human commands. (actions in general)

We use progressive forms to describe actions in progress.

- That's the kind of change we**'re looking for** in the robotics industry. (action in progress)

3. Verbs used **statively** show conditions or situations that exist. Verbs used **actively** show action. Some verbs are basically stative and are rarely used actively (= to depict an action that is happening). Examples of these are *want, need, like, own, know,* and *belong.*

- Professor Stanley **knows** a lot about robots.
  NOT ~~Professor Stanley is knowing a lot about robots.~~

Other verbs are often used statively but are sometimes used actively (= to depict an action happening). When they are used in this way (usually in the progressive), they often take on different meanings. Examples of these are *have* (= eat or drink), *be* (= behave), *think* (= work mentally), and the sense verbs *see, hear, taste, feel,* and *smell.*

- Everyone **will have** a personal robot. *(will possess)*
- We**'ll be having** dinner at a restaurant. *(will be eating)*
- Helen **is** a serious person. (state of being)
- Helen **is being** silly today. *(behaving)*
- The food **tastes** delicious. (state)
- The cook **is tasting** the soup. (action)
- I **think** technology is wonderful. *(My opinion is . . .)*
- Jim **is thinking** carefully. *(working mentally)*

4. Remember that the word **there** shows the **existence** of something. It can be used in the past, present, and future. It is used with simple, not progressive, forms and usually with the verb *be.*

- In a Sushi restaurant in London, **there are** robots that serve drinks.
- **There have been** a lot of technological advances in the last twenty years.
- Didn't **there use to be** a factory on this lot?
- **There were** a lot of people working there.

5. When verbs in the same sentence are in the same general time frame, we usually keep them in the same sequence: past with past; present or present perfect with present or future.

- Twenty years ago, hardly anyone **thought** personal computers **would be** common in the home.
- The Sony Corporation **has developed** a robotic dog that **wags** its tail, **fetches** a ball, and **responds** to human commands. (same general time frame)

When verbs in the same sentence are in different time frames, they are usually not in the same sequence.

- Robots **may** now **be** at the stage that personal computers **were** twenty years ago. (different time frames)

FOCUSED PRACTICE

1 DISCOVER THE GRAMMAR

Part A

1. *Paragraph 1:* Read part of the last sentence in paragraph 1: "within twenty years, home robots will have become as common as PCs are today." Does "will have become" mean *will be in the process of becoming* or *will already be*?

2. *Paragraph 2:* "The robots . . . destroyed mankind because they *had learned* to love and hate." What tense is the verb phrase "had learned"? Why is it used here?

3. *Paragraph 3:* Find and list the simple present tense verbs and the present progressive verbs. Then find the one present perfect progressive verb. Can you explain the difference in meaning among these three different types of verb phrases?

4. *Paragraph 5:* Look at the sentences with "has developed" and "have been developing." What is the difference in meaning between the two sentences?

5. *Paragraph 5:* List the simple present tense verbs. What does this tense signify in these sentences?

Part B

Look again at these sentences from My Friend the Robot. *Then circle* **True (T)** *or* **False (F)**, *according to the meaning of each sentence.*

1. . . . some are predicting that within twenty years, home robots will have become as common as PCs are today.

   Ⓣ F   Home robots will become common before twenty years have passed.

2. The robots in Čapek's play eventually destroyed mankind because they had learned to love and hate.

   T F   The robots destroyed mankind before they learned to love and hate.

3. Computer science professor Gregory Dudek recalls how bulky and awkward computers were when they first appeared and how they've been getting much smaller and more efficient.

   T F   They are still getting smaller and more efficient.

4. For years, industry has been using robots in factories.

   T F   Industry has finished using robots in factories.

5. The Sony Corporation has developed a robotic dog that wags its tail, fetches a ball, and responds to human commands.

   T F   The company is still developing this robot.

6. Researchers at the Georgia Institute of Technology have been developing a mobile robot called Pepe, short for "personal pet."

   T F   The company is still developing this robot.

② IN THE YEAR 2012

It is the year 2012. Look at the pictures. Complete the paragraph with the
appropriate forms of the verbs in the box.

| smell | be | think | have | taste | help |

It's almost dinnertime. Herkimer the robot

__is tasting__ the soup to see if it's ready.
   1.

Joshua and Jane are hungry. The food

_____ delicious.
   2.

Mr. and Mrs. Bellotti are relaxing. Mrs. Bellotti

_____ some flowers Mr. Bellotti has just
   3.

brought home.

The Bellottis _____ dinner. Everyone
                        4.
_____ the food _____
        5.   6.
delicious.

It's later in the evening. Joshua _____ a
                                          7.
test tomorrow in mathematics. Right now he

_____ trouble finishing his last
        8.
homework problem. Herkimer _____
                                        9.
Joshua. He _____ about the solution to
                10.
the problem.

Now it's bedtime. Jane _____ usually
                                11.
very cooperative. Tonight she _____
                                        12.
difficult. Helena the robot _____ a
                                    13.
hard time getting Jane to brush her teeth.

---

③ WE'VE COME A LONG WAY   **Grammar Note 4**

*Think of a grandparent or an older person you know. Interview that person,
asking these questions. Then record the answers, using* **there** + *the appropriate
form of the verb* **be** *on the lines below. Share the interview with the class.*

   1. In your opinion, what advances in technology have there been in the past fifty years
   that you find amazing?

   _____

   2. What change has there been in your life as a result of these advances in technology?

   _____

3. What problems or difficulties did there use to be in your life that no longer exist because of technology?

_____

4. What new inventions do you think there will or might be in our homes fifty years from now?

_____

5. What's the best new invention there ever was, as far as you're concerned?

_____

4 EDITING

Herkimer is one of the new multilingual robots that speak several languages. However, he has problems with English verb tenses. Find and correct the nine errors in verb usage in his journal entry.

April 15; 5:42 P.M.

    My owners, Mr. and Mrs. Bellotti, ~~were purchasing~~ *purchased* me a week ago. However, they didn't bring me to their home until yesterday, so I have only been knowing them for one day.

    There have been two of us robots in the household, myself and my co-robot, who is named Helena. Helena lived here for several months. She and I are having different responsibilities. Her principal responsibilities are the care of Jane, the daughter, and the household cleaning. My principal responsibilities are the care of Joshua, the son, and the preparation of the family's meals.

    So far today I have been preparing breakfast and lunch. The family liked their breakfast very much. They said the food was delicious. For the last hour I have prepared dinner, and it will be ready soon.

    Later this evening I will helping Joshua with his mathematics homework. Joshua thinks mathematics is difficult. I'm thinking Joshua needs more self-confidence.

COMMUNICATION PRACTICE

5 LISTENING

*Read the statements. Then listen to the news broadcast. Circle **True (T)** or* **False (F)** *according to the statements in the broadcast.*

T F   **1.** Personal robots have not been available until now.

T F   **2.** Ready Robotics' new personal robot will be cheaper than previous robots.

T F   **3.** Robert the Robot has already gone into production.

T F   **4.** Researchers have been working on Robert the Robot for five years.

T F   **5.** The company expects to sell a million units of Robert the Robot before the end of the year.

T F   **6.** The problem of the woman in Manitoba was that her personal robot ran away.

T F   **7.** When Parker found the robot, it was vacuuming the floor.

T F   **8.** Parker had washed her dishes before going to bed.

T F   **9.** The robot washed the dishes and then mopped the floor.

T F **10.** The robot that Parker found was friendly.

6 INFORMATION GAP: RENEGADE ROBOTS

Working with a partner, complete the following newspaper article. Each of you will read a version of the article. Each version is missing some information. Take turns asking your partner questions to get the missing information.

Student A, read the article below. Ask questions and fill in the missing information. Then answer Student B's questions.

Student B, turn to page 46 and follow the instructions there.

EXAMPLE:

A: What happened to Marsha Jacobs at four o'clock in the morning?

B: She was awakened at four o'clock in the morning.
Where did she think she was?

A: She thought she was in the Twilight Zone.

DALLAS MORNING NEWS   Section 3

Robots Answer Mystery Summons

BY MARILYN SCHWARTZ
STAFF WRITER

DALLAS—Marsha Jacobs _____ at four o'clock in the morning. She thought she was in the Twilight Zone.

"It was like _____," Mrs.

Jacobs explained. "There was this funny, shuffling noise. I looked up and couldn't believe what I was seeing.

"The inflatable robot we got for Christmas _____. The scary part was that the remote control that operates the unit was in the den. That robot _____."

The incident didn't end at the Jacobs' north Dallas home. All over the city, inflatable butler robots _____.

"I got a call at midnight last week," explained Jesse Summers. "It was my sister's security patrol company. My sister _____, and they had my number to call in case of an emergency."

The sister's burglar alarm was ringing. Summers met the security men and _____ to check the problem.

"I didn't know whether to laugh or scream," said Summers. "There was no intruder, just my sister's inflatable robot walking around. I mean it was eerie."

One of the security men gave him a disgusted look. He told Summers that was the second time in a month a robot had set off an alarm system.

Jim Smith of Plano, Texas, says his robot _____ during Christmas dinner.

"I thought my son was playing a trick with the remote control," Smith said. "He thought _____. We stopped laughing when we discovered the remote control was turned off in the den."

So who are you going to call when a robot comes to life?

Source: Marilyn Schwartz, "Robots Answer Mystery Summons," *The Dallas Morning News.* Reprinted with permission of *The Dallas Morning News.*

7 ESSAY

Overall, would it be positive or negative to have a household robot? Write an essay of two or three paragraphs, expressing your opinion about what you think might or might not happen if household robots become common.

8 PICTURE DISCUSSION

With a partner, talk about the cartoon. Explain the meaning of each statement. What has already happened? Will the man be able to defeat his robot friend in the next game?

WHAT IF YOUR ROBOT PAL IS SMARTER THAN YOU ARE?

ROBOTMAN © NEA. Reprinted by permission.

INFORMATION GAP FOR STUDENT B

Student B, read the article below. Get information from Student A. Ask questions and fill in the missing information. Answer Student A's questions.

EXAMPLE:

A: What happened to Marsha Jacobs at four o'clock in the morning?

B: She was awakened at four o'clock in the morning.
Where did she think she was?

A: She thought she was in the Twilight Zone.

DALLAS MORNING NEWS   Section 3

Robots Answer Mystery Summons

BY MARILYN SCHWARTZ
STAFF WRITER

DALLAS—Marsha Jacobs was awakened at four o'clock in the morning. She thought she was in _____.

"It was like a bad movie or a nightmare," Mrs. Jacobs explained. "There was this funny, shuffling noise. I looked up and couldn't believe _____.

"The inflatable robot we got for Christmas was heading straight for our bed. The scary part was that the remote control _____ was in the den. That robot was walking by itself."

The incident didn't end at the Jacobs' north Dallas home. All over the city, inflatable butler robots seemed to be coming to life.

"I _____ at midnight last week," explained Jesse Summers. "It was my sister's security patrol company. My sister was out of town, and they had my number to call in case of an emergency."

The sister's burglar alarm _____.

Summers met the security men and entered the house to check the problem.

"I didn't know whether to laugh or scream," said Summers. "There was no intruder, just my sister's inflatable robot walking around. I mean it was eerie."

One of the security men gave him a disgusted look. He told Summers that was the second time in a month _____.

Jim Smith of Plano, Texas, says his robot just walked into his dining room during Christmas dinner.

"I thought my son _____ with the remote control," Smith said. "He thought I was doing the same thing. _____ when we discovered the remote control was turned off in the den."

So who are you going to call when a robot comes to life?

Source: Marilyn Schwartz, "Robots Answer Mystery Summons," *The Dallas Morning News.* Reprinted with permission of *The Dallas Morning News.*

REVIEW OR SELFTEST

I. *Sherry, Akiko, and Lisa are spending the school year in an international exchange program in Spain. Complete their conversation with their friends, using **would** or **will** and correct forms of **be going to** (was / were going to or is / are going to). Use **will** or **would** if **be going to** is not specified.*

SHERRY: I wonder where Jaime and Demetrios are. Demetrios said

_____*they'd be*_____ here by 12:30. It's already 12:45.
<u>1. (they / be)</u>

AKIKO: Well, when I talked to Jaime this morning he told me he

_____ stop at the post office to mail a package. That's
<u>2. (be going to)</u>

the only thing I can think of.

LISA: These men! They can never be anywhere on time. We

_____ miss the train if they don't come soon.
<u>3. (be going to)</u>

SHERRY: What about lunch? Did Jaime say _____ bring
<u>4. (he / be going to)</u>

sandwiches?

AKIKO: No, he says _____ at a restaurant near the castle.
<u>5. (we / eat)</u>

. . . Oh, here they come. . . . At last! Where have you guys been?

_____ a new leaf and not be late anymore?
<u>6. (you / be going to / turn over)</u>

That's what you said.

JAIME: Well, we promised that _____ not to always be late!
<u>7. (we / try)</u>

We're working on it. Oh, by the way, Igor is coming after all. He says

_____ a later train and meet us at three o'clock. OK,
<u>8. (he / take)</u>

ladies, time's a-wasting. Let's get on the train!

II. *Complete the conversations with **used to** or **would**. Use **would** if possible.*

1. A: _____*Didn't you use to smoke*_____ ?
<u>a. (not / you / smoke)</u>

B: Yeah, I _____ , but I quit six months ago.
<u>b.</u>

A: Good. I _____ smoke, too. It was terrible. When I was a

_____c._____

serious smoker, I _____ smoke two packs a day. I'm glad

_____d._____

I stopped.

2. A: When I was a child, my family spent every summer at a lake in the mountains.

We kids _____ a hike every morning. In the afternoon, we

_____e. (take)_____

_____ swimming.

___f. (go)___

B: Yeah, our summers were like that, too. My parents _____ a

____g. (own)____

cottage on the beach. They sold it after we grew up, but when I was ten and eleven,

we _____ every July there. Ah, those were the good old days!

___h. (spend)___

Life _____ carefree. Now it's just hectic.

___i. (be)___

III. *The Mendozas are visiting Italy as part of a tour. Today is the morning of July 20.
Look at their itinerary. Then complete the sentences, using the correct verb tense
forms and pronouns.*

Fred and Alice Mendoza	**Itinerary**	**Italy Trip, July 15–23**

July 15: Arrive at Rome airport; check in at hotel in Rome

July 16: Tour Vatican City, including the Sistine Chapel

July 17: Day trip to Pompeii; return to Rome to spend
   the night

July 18: Visit other attractions in Rome: the Colosseum, the
   Forum, the Trevi Fountain; stay in Rome that night

July 19: Take train to Venice; arrive in Venice late afternoon

July 20: Take walking tour of Venice in the morning;
   take gondola ride in the afternoon; tour
   St. Mark's Cathedral; take evening train to
   Florence; arrive early morning

July 21: Tour Florence

July 22: Another day touring
   Florence; late afternoon:
   take train to Pisa; spend
   the night there

July 23: Tour Pisa. Return to Rome
   late afternoon; take 9:00
   P.M. evening flight to
   return home

1. The Mendozas _____have been_____ in Italy since the night of July 15.
   (be)

2. They _____ the first four nights in Rome.
   (stay)

3. On their first full day in Rome, _____ Vatican City.
   (tour)

4. Since arriving in Italy, _____ Pompeii, the Colosseum, the Trevi Fountain,
   (also see)
   the Forum, and some of Venice.

5. Right now it's 11:00 A.M. _____ around Venice since 9:00 this morning.
   (walk)

6. _____ a gondola ride yet.
   (take)

7. Tonight _____ the train to Florence.
   (take)

8. _____ in Florence early tomorrow morning.
   (arrive)

9. _____ two days in Florence and one night in Pisa.
   (spend)

10. By late afternoon on July 23, _____ to Rome.
    (return)

11. _____ home at 9:00 P.M. on the twenty-third.
    (fly)

IV. *Look at the pictures. Complete each pair of sentences with a simple verb form in one sentence and a progressive verb form in the other. Use the verbs* **develop,** **taste, be, have,** *and* **write.**

1. Mr. Schoenberg's students _____ usually
   a.
   well behaved. Today, for some reason, they

   _____ difficult.
   b.

2. Amy Tanaka is a novelist. She _____ five
   a.
   novels. She _____ a sixth novel since last
   b.
   October and expects to complete it in July.

3. The employees of Excelsior Computer

_____ their annual holiday party
<u>a.</u>

this evening. They always _____ it
<u>b.</u>

sometime in December.

4. Excelsior Computer _____ an
<u>a.</u>

amazing new software program since last

summer and expects to release it in four months.

In the past ten years the company

_____ fifteen major software
<u>b.</u>

programs.

5. Helen Hammond _____ the stew
<u>a.</u>

she's been making. It _____ terrible.
<u>b.</u>

V. *Circle the letter of the one word or phrase that is <u>not</u> correct.*

1. Just before the telephone <u>rang</u>, I <u>was hoping</u> someone <u>called</u> to   A B Ⓒ D
                                A   B   C

<u>suggest</u> going somewhere.
D

2. Igor <u>doesn't go</u> with us to Toledo today; <u>he's</u> <u>staying</u> home because he   A B C D
               A   B   C

<u>has to</u> finish a term paper.
D

3. By the time <u>you'll</u> <u>get</u> to Manila, <u>I'll</u> <u>have returned</u> to Barcelona.   A B C D
                      A   B   C   D

4. After I <u>got up</u> this morning, I <u>went</u> out, <u>was doing</u> the shopping, and   **A B C D**
     A   B   C

   <u>cleaned</u> up the apartment.
     D

5. I <u>hope</u> dinner <u>is going to</u> <u>be</u> ready soon. <u>It's smelling</u> delicious!   **A B C D**
    A   B   C   D

6. <u>I didn't even think</u> there <u>would be</u> a party. Akiko and Jaime   **A B C D**
        A   B

   <u>have done</u> a great job of <u>organizing</u> last night's get-together.
    C   D

7. The plane <u>has</u> just <u>taken off</u> when I <u>realized</u> that I <u>had given</u> my   **A B C D**
         A   B   C   D

   parents the wrong arrival date.

8. Demetrios <u>was</u> surprised when he <u>received</u> an "A" on the exam   **A B C D**
          A   B

   because he <u>thought</u> he <u>will fail</u> it.
        C   D

9. When the professor <u>asked</u> me where my homework <u>was</u>, I <u>told</u> him   **A B C D**
              A   B   C

   <u>I already turned</u> it in.
     D

10. We <u>haven't</u> <u>been visiting</u> Venice for more than a year, so I <u>think</u>   **A B C D**
      A   B   C

   <u>we'll be going</u> there.
     D

VI. *Go back to your answers to Part V. Write the correct form for each item that you believe is incorrect.*

1. would call

2. _____

3. _____

4. _____

5. _____

6. _____

7. _____

8. _____

9. _____

10. _____

▶ **To check your answers, go to the Answer Key on page 56.**

From Grammar to Writing
The Sentence

In English a sentence must have at least one **independent**, or **main**, clause. A main clause must have a subject and its verb—a verb that shows person, number, and time. Only one type of main clause has no subject: an imperative sentence. In imperative sentences, the subject *you* is understood. (Note that *Let's dance* is a kind of imperative sentence. *You* is understood to be included in the meaning of *Let's*.)

A main clause does not depend on another clause to be fully understood.

Other clauses are said to be **dependent**. Dependent clauses have a subject and a verb, but they are dependent on another clause to be fully understood.

Look at the following sentences. The complete subjects are underlined once and the complete verbs twice.

> **Examples:**
>
> Sherry and her friends are students.
>
> They are spending a year studying in Spain in an exchange program.
>
> All the students in the program arrived a month ago.
>
> Most of them will stay for the entire year.
>
> Sherry's sister Martha has received three letters from her.
>
> The letters were written over a period of three months.
>
> Write soon.
>
> Are exchange programs good learning experiences?

The following word groups are not sentences.

Sherry sitting and writing a letter. (no verb)

Were taking the train to Barcelona. (no subject)

Such an exciting year. (no subject or verb)

Because she was afraid of heights. (dependent clause)

Which was a beautiful building. (dependent clause)

1 *On the line below each of the following word groups, write* **sentence** *if the group is an independent clause. If the word group is not a sentence, write* **not a sentence** *and explain why by writing* **no subject**, **no verb**, **no subject and no verb**, *or* **dependent clause**.

1. Sherry at the library doing research.

   not a sentence—no verb

2. All afternoon.

3. Akiko and Lisa were at home.

4. Has been an exciting year.

5. A worthwhile experience meeting students from many nations.

6. They would do it again.

7. Which they had always wanted to do.

8. Think about this question.

2 *Read the following paragraph. You will find eight sentences and nine groups of words that are not sentences. On the lines provided, write the eight sentences.*

In late December. Sherry, Akiko, and Lisa took a one-day trip to Barcelona. Not knowing anyone there. They stayed in a youth hostel for a very reasonable price. On their one day in the city. They visited the Sagrada Familia, Gaudí's famous cathedral. Which was unfinished when Gaudí died and is still unfinished. All three girls were impressed by the cathedral's beauty. And decided to climb to the top instead of taking the elevator. Nearing the top, Akiko began to feel vertigo and had to start down again. Sherry and Lisa continued climbing. Even Sherry, who had done a great deal of mountain climbing in Canada. Felt nervous and unprotected at the summit. Both she and Lisa agreed that the view was magnificent. And the climb worth it. The three decided to return to Barcelona. As soon as they could.

(continued on next page)

1.   Sherry, Akiko, and Lisa took a one-day trip to Barcelona. _____

2. _____

3. _____

4. _____

5. _____

6. _____

7. _____

8. _____

The first word of a sentence begins with a capital letter. A sentence ends with some punctuation, most commonly a period, a question mark, or an exclamation point. Sometimes a sentence ends with a semicolon or colon. When one sentence ends with a semicolon or colon, the first word of the next sentence does not need to be capitalized. In sentences containing quotations, quotation marks come <u>after</u> commas and periods.

EXAMPLES:

Who knows the answer?

French food is very delicious; **i**t is known all over the world.

That's Don's problem: **h**e never wants to do anything adventurous.

"When you're traveling in England," our travel agent said, "I recommend staying in bed and breakfasts."

3 *Read and study the following paragraph. It contains seventeen sentences. Find the seventeen sentences and insert initial capitalization and end punctuation in the appropriate places. Do not add or eliminate any commas.*

Last summer when my wife and I were traveling in Morocco, we had one of the most interesting bargaining experiences ever. we were in an open air market in Rabat, and I really wanted to buy a Moroccan jilaba, a long, heavy, ankle-length garment there were several different shops where jilabas were sold, but Helen and I were drawn to one shop in particular, why I don't know I tried one jilaba on it fit perfectly, and I knew it was the one I wanted, so I asked the merchant how much it was he said it was $200 now I've always been intimidated by the prospect of bargaining, so I was ready to pay his price Helen took me aside, however, and said, "That's too much he expects you to bargain" when I said I couldn't bargain, she told me that bargaining was part of the game and that I should offer him $100 I sighed, tried to swallow the lump in my throat, and croaked "$100" he smiled and said "$150," whereupon I said "$110" he looked offended and shook his head Helen grabbed my hand, and we started walking away I thought that was going to be the end of the experience, but then the merchant came running after me, saying "$125, Sir" I ended up buying the jilaba for that amount, and I still have it since then I've never been afraid to bargain

4 APPLY IT TO YOUR WRITING

One of the best ways to avoid sentence fragments is to read what you have written aloud, for your voice will usually tell you where one sentence ends and another begins. Write a paragraph or two about an experience you have had while traveling. Read your paragraph aloud to discover whether you have any sentence fragments. Then work with a partner. Your partner will read your paragraph aloud, and you will read your partner's. Try to discover and correct any sentence fragments.

PART
I

REVIEW OR SELFTEST
ANSWER KEY

NOTE: In this answer key, where the contracted verb form is given, it is the preferred form, though the full form is also acceptable. Where the full verb form is given, it is the preferred form, though the contracted form is also acceptable.

I.
2. was going to
3. 're going to
4. he was going to
5. we'll eat
6. Weren't you going to turn over
7. we'd try
8. he'll take

II.
b. used to
c. used to
d. 'd
e. would take
f. 'd go
g. used to own
h. 'd spend
i. used to be

III.
2. stayed
3. they toured
4. they've also seen
5. They've been walking
6. They haven't taken
7. they're taking
8. They'll be arriving / They'll arrive
9. They're spending / They're going to spend / They'll be spending
10. they'll have returned
11. They fly / They're flying

IV.
1. a. are
   b. 're being
2. a. has written
   b. has been writing
3. a. are having
   b. have
4. a. has been developing
   b. has developed
5. a. is tasting
   b. tastes

V.
2. A   5. D   8. D
3. A   6. C   9. D
4. C   7. A   10. B

VI.
2. isn't going (to go)
3. you
4. did
5. It smells
6. did
7. had
8. would fail / was going to fail / had failed
9. I'd (I had) already turned
10. visited

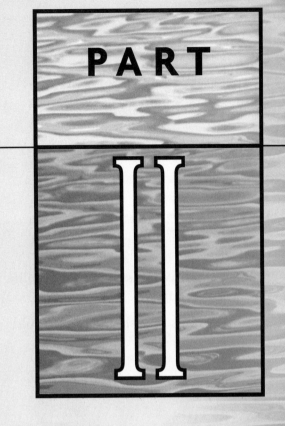

PART

II

MODALS

4 MODALS: NECESSITY

GRAMMAR **IN CONTEXT**

QUESTIONS TO CONSIDER

1. Look at the cartoon. What is the mother telling her son to do? Is this a practice in your culture?

2. What are some things that should and shouldn't be done in your culture?

What We **Should** and **Shouldn't** Have Done

BY TRAVEL EDITOR TIM LARSON

SIX MONTHS AGO my company sent me to work at our branch office in Japan. My Japanese co-workers have been friendly and gracious, and last week one of them invited my wife and me to his house for dinner. We were honored to be invited, and the food was delicious. But even though Masayuki and Yukiko, his wife, were most polite and friendly and never gave an indication that anything was wrong, we felt a bit uncomfortable about the evening. I decided to ask my friend Junichi about it. He's lived both in Japan and Canada, so he knows the differences between the two cultures. He gave me a lot of pointers. Now we know what we should and shouldn't have done.

The first tip was about taking off our shoes. We knew that you're supposed to take off your shoes when you enter a Japanese home, so we did. We didn't know we were supposed to arrange them so they'd be pointing toward the door when we left so that we'd be able to put them on without having to turn around. But this wasn't a big mistake, Junichi said.

The second pointer was about gifts. Helen and I knew you're supposed to take a gift to a Japanese home. Masayuki and Yukiko seemed a little shocked, though, when we pulled the present out of a plastic bag and said, "We thought you'd like this Canadian CD. It's rock and roll." Junichi chuckled and said, "Well, you should have wrapped the CD. It's OK to bring it in a plastic bag, but the gift itself has to be wrapped. And you mustn't say anything about it. Just give it to your hosts. The main problem, though, was the gift itself."

"You mean we should have taken something different?"

"Yes. A rock and roll CD isn't really an appropriate gift."

"Well, what should we have taken?"

"Maybe a box of chocolates. Or you could have taken some flowers."

After that I told Junichi about what happened before dinner. Masayuki and Yukiko had invited us to sit down for some tea and snacks. The tea was delicious, but we had trouble eating the raw sushi. I was able to finish mine, but Helen couldn't finish hers. Masayuki and Yukiko seemed a little puzzled. Junichi chuckled again and said, "Well, in Japan, it's considered impolite to leave half-eaten food on a plate."

> *"Well, in Japan, it's considered impolite to leave half-eaten food on a plate."*

"You mean you've got to eat everything that's offered to you?" I asked.

"You don't have to. But if you take something, you must finish it."

After we ate, Helen asked Yukiko if she could help her in the kitchen. This is the way we do things back in Canada, but Junichi says you shouldn't in Japan. According to the rules of

(continued on next page)

Japanese culture, visitors aren't allowed to go into the kitchen. The other thing you probably shouldn't do, he says, is praise pictures or ornaments in the house. If you do, your Japanese hosts might feel they have to give the object to you. Fortunately, we didn't do that.

At the end of the evening, Masayuki asked us if we'd like to have another drink. We thought it wouldn't be polite to say no, so we accepted and stayed for another half hour. Finally we felt that we absolutely had to leave, so when Masayuki invited us to have another drink, I said, "We'd really like to, but it's late. We'd better get going, or we won't be able to get up in the morning." Masayuki and Yukiko seemed relieved.

Junichi said, "That's what you should have done in the first place. When a Japanese host invites you to have a drink at the end of the evening, you should refuse gently. Otherwise you could be there all night."

I asked what he thought we might do to rectify the situation. "Shall we invite them over?" I asked. He said, "Yeah, you ought to do that. Just remember all the things I've told you. But don't invite them to an informal, western-style party with a lot of loud music. Just make it a simple dinner for the four of you."

Good advice, I thought. What really struck me is how much we all have to learn about other cultures.

Source: **Based on information in Rex Shelley,** *Culture Shock: Japan* (Portland, OR: Graphic Arts Publishing, 1993).

UNDERSTANDING MEANING FROM CONTEXT

Make a guess about the meaning of each italicized word or phrase from the reading. Write your guess in the blank provided.

1. He gave me a lot of *pointers*.

_____

2. The other thing you probably shouldn't do is *praise* pictures or ornaments in the house.

_____

3. I asked what he thought we might do to *rectify* the situation.

_____

4. What really *struck* me is how much we all have to learn about other cultures.

_____

GRAMMAR **PRESENTATION**
MODALS: NECESSITY

DEGREE OF NECESSITY

ABSOLUTELY NECESSARY; OBLIGATORY

If you take something, you absolutely **must finish** it.

The gift itself **has to be** wrapped.

If you express admiration for objects in the house, your hosts might feel they **have to give** the object to you.

You mean you**'ve got to eat** everything that's offered to you?

You **don't have to take** everything that's offered to you.

And you **mustn't say** anything about it.

Finally we felt that we absolutely **had to leave**.

EXPECTED

We knew that you**'re supposed to take off** your shoes when you enter a Japanese home, so we did.

We didn't know we **were supposed to arrange** them so they'd be pointing toward the door when we left.

STRONGLY ADVISED

We**'d better get going**, or we won't be able to wake up in the morning.

ADVISED

You probably **shouldn't praise** pictures or ornaments in the house.

Yeah, you **ought to do** that.

You **should have wrapped** the CD.

Shall we **invite** them over?

SUGGESTED

Then Helen asked Yukiko if she **could help** her in the kitchen.

I asked what he thought we **might do** to rectify the situation.

Or you **could have taken** some flowers.

NOTES	EXAMPLES

1. *Can, could, shall, should, may, might, will, would, must, ought to,* and *had better* are **modals**. They are special auxiliary verbs that behave differently from other verbs.

- Helen asked Yukiko if she **could help** her in the kitchen.
- You **mustn't say** anything about it.
- **Shall** we **invite** them over?

2. In general, modals are restricted in their use. There are **modal-like expressions** with similar meanings to replace them. Note these:

must	*have to*
should	*be supposed to*
can / could	*be able to*
may	*be allowed to*

- You **must finish** everything on your plate. / You **have to finish** everything on your plate.
- You **should take** a gift. / You**'re supposed to take** a gift.
- Helen **couldn't finish** her sushi. / Helen **wasn't able to finish** her sushi.
- You **may not enter** the kitchen. / You**'re not allowed to enter** the kitchen.

3. The modals and modal-like expressions *must, have to, have got to, had better, be supposed to, should, ought to, might,* and *could* show degrees of **necessity**, with *must* as the strongest and *could* as the weakest.

- You **must finish** everything on your plate. (very strong—a rule)
- You **should take** a gift. (less strong—a good idea)
- You **could take** some flowers. (even less strong—It would be a nice action, but there are other possibilities.)

4. *Must, have to,* and *have got to* are similar in meaning. *Must* is more formal. Use it to show very strong **obligations** that can't be escaped.

- If you take something on your plate, you **must** finish it.

Have to is used in all tenses and situations.

- Your hosts might feel that they **have to give** you the object.

Have got to is informal and is used mostly in conversation. It is rarely used in the negative. *Have to* is used instead.

- You mean you**'ve got to eat** everything that's offered to you?
- No, you **don't have to**.

Note the two negatives of *must*. They are very different in meaning. *Mustn't* means "necessity not to do something." *Don't / doesn't have to* means "no necessity to do something."

- When you present a gift, you **mustn't say** anything about it. *(It's necessary not to do this.)*
- You **don't have to eat** everything that's offered to you. *(It's not necessary to do this.)*

Use *will have to* to show **future necessity**.

- We**'ll have to invite** them over to our house.

Use *had to* to show **past necessity**.

- We felt we **had to leave**. *(We felt it was necessary.)*

▶ **BE CAREFUL!** Don't use *must have* + participle to show past necessity. Use *had to* instead.

- We **had to leave**.
  NOT ~~We must have left.~~

5. *Should* and *ought to* are similar in meaning and are equivalent in most situations. They mean "it would be a good idea if . . ." Use them to offer advice. *Should* is more theoretical. *Ought to* is used more to offer a specific suggestion that may be followed. *Ought to* is rare in questions and negatives, where it is usually replaced by *should*.

- You **should refuse** gently. *(a good idea in theory)*
- You **ought to invite** them over. *(an actual suggestion that I am making for you to follow)*

6. Note the difference in meaning between *should* and *must*. Use *must* (or *have to* or *have got to*) to express an obligation that can't be escaped. Use *should* (or *ought to*) to give advice. Remember that advice is a good idea but does not have to be followed.

- You **must take off** your shoes when you enter a Japanese house. *(a rule of Japanese culture)*
- You **should take** candy or flowers as a gift. *(a good idea, but these are not the only two things that can be taken)*

7. *Had better* is stronger than *should* and *ought to*. Use it to show a warning that something bad or negative will happen if the advice isn't followed.

- We**'d better get going**, or we won't be able to wake up in the morning.

▶ **BE CAREFUL!** Since *had better* is a strong expression, it can seem rude or impolite if not used correctly. It is usually used by people who have authority over other people or with people we know very well.

- Jim, if you're going to the Carlsens' house for dinner, you**'d better take** a gift of some sort.

  OK, Mom. Good suggestion.

8. Use *be supposed to* to show a **strong expectation**. *Be supposed to* is used only in the present and past. In the past, the affirmative suggests that the expectation didn't happen. The negative suggests that the expectation did happen.

- We knew that you**'re supposed to take off** your shoes when you enter a Japanese home, so we did.
- We didn't know we **were supposed to arrange** them so they'd be pointing toward the door when we left. *(We didn't do this.)*
- We **weren't supposed to mention** the gift we'd brought. *(We did mention it.)*

Notice the difference in meaning between *be supposed to* and *have to / had to*.

Be supposed to shows an expectation, but *have to / had to* shows an obligation.

- We **were supposed to take** flowers. *(That was the expectation, but we didn't do it.)*
- We **had to leave** when he offered us a second drink. *(That was the obligation. We did.)*

9. Use *should have* and *ought to have* + past participle to express **advice** about past situations. *Should have* and *ought to have* suggest that the action did not happen. *Shouldn't have* suggests that it did.

- That's what you **should have done** the first time. (*That's what you **ought to have done** the first time.*)

10. Use *might* or *could* to talk about polite, not-too-strong **suggestions**.

- I asked what we **might do** to rectify the situation. (*I asked what we **could do** to rectify the situation.*)

11. Use *might have* and *could have* + past participle to make polite **suggestions** about a **past opportunity**. They are similar in meaning. In this sense, *might have* and *could have* in an affirmative sentence mean that the action didn't happen.

- You **could have taken** some flowers. (*This is my suggestion. It was an opportunity, but it didn't happen.*)

12. *Shall* is sometimes used in questions to ask about another person's **opinion** about a course of action. It is used only with *I* or *we*. When *shall* is used with *we*, it is often followed by a sentence with *let's*. In this meaning, *shall* is somewhat similar to *should*.

This is the only common use of *shall* in North American English.

- **Shall** we **invite** them over? (*What's your opinion about this idea?*)

13. Use *could* to show **past ability**. Don't use it in the affirmative to talk about a single (finished) action in the past. Use *was / were able to* instead.

In the negative, *was / were able to* and *could* are interchangeable.

- I **was able to finish** my sushi. NOT ~~I could finish my sushi.~~

- Helen **couldn't finish** her sushi.
  OR
- Helen **wasn't able to finish** her sushi.

FOCUSED PRACTICE

1 DISCOVER THE GRAMMAR

Look again at some of the sentences from What We Should and Shouldn't Have Done. *Each sentence can be said in a similar way. Circle the letter of the choice that is similar in meaning.*

1. We knew that you're supposed to take off your shoes when you enter a Japanese home, so we did.

   (a.) You should take off your shoes when you enter a Japanese home.

   b. You could take off your shoes when you enter a Japanese home.

2. "Well, you should have wrapped the CD."

   a. You might have wrapped the CD.

   b. You were supposed to wrap the CD.

3. "Or you could have taken some flowers."

   a. You might have taken some flowers.

   b. You should have taken some flowers.

4. "You mean you've got to eat everything that's offered to you?" I asked.

   a. You mean you're supposed to eat everything that's offered to you?

   b. You mean you have to eat everything that's offered to you?

5. After we ate, Helen asked Yukiko if she could help her in the kitchen.

   a. Helen asked Yukiko if she might help her in the kitchen.

   b. Helen asked Yukiko if she should help her in the kitchen.

6. According to the rules of Japanese culture, visitors aren't allowed to go into the kitchen.

   a. Visitors may not go into the kitchen.

   b. Visitors would not go into the kitchen.

7. And you mustn't say anything about it.

   a. You don't have to say anything about it.

   b. You had better not say anything about it.

8. If you do, your Japanese hosts might feel they have to give the object to you.

   a. Japanese hosts might feel they must give the object to you.

   b. Japanese hosts might feel they should give the object to you.

9. When a Japanese host invites you to have a drink at the end of the evening, you should refuse gently.

   a. You must refuse gently.

   b. You ought to refuse gently.

10. "Shall we invite them over?" I asked.

    a. Should we invite them over?

    b. Will we invite them over?

11. He said, "Yeah, you ought to do that."

    a. You're supposed to do that.

    b. You should do that.

2   **SHOULD WE LEAVE A TIP?**   Grammar Notes 1, 2, 3

Masako, a visiting exchange student, is talking to her American friend Jane.
Complete their conversation with items from the box. Use each item once.

could have left	should we have left	don't have to leave	had to worry
should you leave	you're supposed to do	were supposed to leave	expected to do
I ought to leave	~~are you supposed to leave~~		

JANE: Hi, Masako. How are things going?

MASAKO: Really well. But there's something I wanted to ask you about.

JANE: OK. What?

MASAKO: Tipping. I just don't understand it. <u>Are you supposed to leave</u> a tip everywhere
                                      1.

      you eat? This is really bothering me. I've never _____
                                                  2.

      about this before. We don't tip in Japan.

JANE: You don't?

MASAKO: No. You're not really _____ that. It's all included in the
                                        3.

      service charge.

JANE: Tell me more. Have you had a problem with this?

MASAKO: Yeah. Last week a Chinese friend of mine and I had dinner at a restaurant. We

      knew we _____ a tip, but we didn't know how much.
                              4.

JANE: How much did you leave?

MASAKO: About twenty-five percent. _____ more?
                                              5.

JANE: Wow! Twenty-five percent. That's a lot. The service must have been really good.

MASAKO: Actually, it wasn't. The waiter was pretty rude . . . and slow.

(continued on next page)

JANE: Well, if you're really not satisfied with the service, you

_____ anything.
6.

MASAKO: So how much _____ if you're satisfied?
7.

JANE: Between fifteen and twenty percent. Fifteen is the usual.

MASAKO: Hmm. OK. Now here's another question. I'm confused about what

_____ if you're sitting at a lunch counter instead of at a
8.

table. Do you leave anything?

JANE: It's a nice gesture. Why do you ask?

MASAKO: Yesterday I had lunch at a cafeteria counter. There was a waitress who was really

nice and polite. I felt like _____ her something.
9.

JANE: Did you?

MASAKO: No.

JANE: Well, you _____ something. Maybe five to ten percent.
10.

MASAKO: Oh. OK. Next time I will.

❸ SHOULDS AND SHOULDN'TS   Grammar Notes 2, 3, 5, 6

Look again at What We Should and Shouldn't Have Done. *Write seven sentences
about what Bob and Helen* should have done *and* shouldn't have done.

> **EXAMPLE:**
> They should have wrapped the CD.

1. _____

2. _____

3. _____

4. _____

5. _____

6. _____

7. _____

4 **DEAR MISS MANNERS** **Grammar Notes 4, 5, 11, 12**

Part A

Read Miss Manners' advice column. As you read, take note of the italicized expressions.

MISS MANNERS RESCUES CIVILIZATION

Christmas Presents

DEAR MISS MANNERS,

This year, my company sent me a gift box containing, among other things, ham, bacon, and sausage. Last year, I received a whole smoked turkey. I have been a vegetarian for over four years and am offended even by the sight of such frivolous expense of life. But I don't want to offend my company superiors, and I know that all employees receive the same gift, so it might not be fair to make exceptions for just me. But how can I prevent this from happening next year, and what *do I do* with the corpses in the freezer? *Should I send* a thank you note?

GENTLE READER,

Unless you work for a grocery wholesaler, it seems foolish of your employer to spend money on presents which *could have been put* into a Christmas bonus. This being a business relationship, not a friendship, the company can hardly be expected to know what would please each individual, as demonstrated by the fact that even a conventional food item was offensively unsuitable in your case.

It seems equally futile to try to explain your individual preferences in the minimal thank you note appropriate for an impersonal gesture. If you *must, Miss Manners suggests you thank them* for the food "which, as a vegetarian, I do not eat, but which I have donated to the homeless." Just don't count on this being remembered next year, when someone else may be assigned to send out silly presents.

Source: From **MISS MANNERS RESCUES CIVILIZATION: FROM SEXUAL HARASSMENT**, FRIVOLOUS LAWSUITS, DISSING AND OTHER LAPSES IN CIVILITY by Judith Martin. Copyright © 1996 by Judith Martin. Reprinted by permission of Crown Publishers, Inc.

Now rewrite each of the italicized phrases with a modal or modal-like expression having a similar meaning. Go over the answers as a class. Then discuss possible answers to questions 1 and 2.

1. What *do I do* with the corpses in the freezer?

   What should I do with the corpses in the freezer?

2. *Should I send* a thank you note?

   _____

3. It seems foolish of your employer to spend money on presents that *could have been put* into a Christmas bonus.

   _____

4. If you *must* . . .

   _____

5. *Miss Manners suggests that you thank them* for the food . . . [Hint: Eliminate "Miss Manners." Use "you" as the subject.]

   _____

Part B

Discuss the letter with a partner. Do you agree or disagree with Miss Manners'
suggestions?

5 EDITING

Read the letter that Jason, who is traveling in East Africa, sent to his sister. Find
and correct the eleven errors in modals or modal-like expressions.

May 15

Dear Emily,

    have written

    I know I should ~~write~~ sooner, but I just won't be able to find the time. This package deal that

Steve and I got was so cheap, and we've been so many places! We've been having some

amazing adventures. We climbed Mount Kilimanjaro! Yes, really! It took five days. We went to a

hotel in Arusha, Tanzania, and hired a group of Tanzanian men to take us up to the top and

down again. That's the only way anyone is allowed climb the mountain these days. You can't

just go up on your own. It takes three days to climb up and two to come back down.

    We stayed in a little cabin each night. On the third night, we were at 15,000 feet, and it

was really cold. We went to bed at sunset so that we can get up at 2 A.M. to attempt the

summit. I was so cold I must put on all my clothes in my sleeping bag. I was glad to get up so I

could have gotten warm.

    It took three hours to climb to the top, and both Steve and I had our own guide. I could make

it to the top, but Steve wasn't able to because he had altitude sickness. Too bad. But what an

experience it was to be at the top! I felt like I was the king of the world. Anyway, we couldn't

meet any nicer guys than the ones who carried our stuff. I heard that you're suppose to tip

them if you feel they've given you good service, so of course we were glad to do that.

    After Kilimanjaro we took a bus to Ngorongoro Crater. We rode a Land Rover down into the

crater to see the animals. We were able see lions, rhinos, giraffes, and hundreds of zebras.

Fantastic. You and Jennifer ought to have come next summer if you can save up the money.

Maybe you can get a special deal like we did.

    Well, enough for now. We're flying to Nairobi tonight,

and then it's on to Cairo and then Turkey. I'll write again

when I have time. Love to Mom and Dad.

          Love,

          Jason

COMMUNICATION PRACTICE

6 LISTENING

Listen to the telephone conversation.

Then listen again. Circle the item that correctly completes each statement.

1. Jason (sent / didn't send) his parents a postcard.

2. Jason and Steve (went / didn't go) to Cairo.

3. Jason and Steve (were able to / were not able to) get another flight to Cairo a few days later.

4. It (was necessary / wasn't necessary) to leave early to get to the airport.

5. Emily thinks Jason (should / shouldn't) go to the embassy.

6. Jason (wrote down / didn't write down) his passport number.

7. You (must have / don't have to have) identification to get a new passport.

8. The embassy (has been able to / hasn't been able to) prove Jason's identity.

9. Jason (wants / doesn't want) Emily to fax him a copy of his passport application.

7 INFORMATION GAP: WHY WON'T THEY WAIT ON US?

Working with a partner, complete the story. Each of you will read a version of the same story. Each version is missing some information. Take turns asking your partner questions to get the missing information.

Student A, read the story below. Ask questions and fill in the missing information. Then answer Student B's questions.

Student B, turn to page 75 and follow the instructions there.

> **EXAMPLE:**
> **A:** Where were the married couple traveling?
> **B:** They were traveling in eastern Europe.
>   What was the first problem?
> **A:** The first problem was finding accommodations.

A married couple were traveling in _____. Up until they had entered this particular country, they had been having a wonderful time. Now, however, everything seemed to be going wrong. The first problem was finding accommodations. They were supposed to stay at _____, but when they arrived at the hotel, they discovered that there was no record of their reservation, so they had to spend their first night at the train station. The next day, after several hours of looking, they

(continued on next page)

were finally able to get a room at a hotel _____. There were two rooms available: one very expensive room with one king-sized bed, and another inexpensive one with only one small twin bed. Since they were on a tight budget, they decided they'd better take the inexpensive room.

The second problem had to do with communication. In other countries they had been able to use _____. Here very few people were able to speak those languages. Since the couple didn't speak the native language of the country, it was hard to make themselves understood.

The third problem involved food. After spending hours finding accommodations, they were starving, so they went into an elegant restaurant. They sat down at a table and were soon brought menus. When they looked at them, however, _____ _____. The husband said he thought they should have at least brought along a phrase book. They hadn't done that, though, so they didn't know what to order.

Time passed. Other people were being served, but none of the waiters would _____. They began to get quite frustrated. They noticed that a boy about ten years old seemed to be listening to their conversation. Just when they were at their wits' end, the boy got up and came over to their table. "Excuse me," he said. "I couldn't help hearing you talk about your problem. No one has come and taken your order because you have to _____. Then they'll take your order." The husband and the wife were both astonished but grateful to the boy. The wife asked, "How is it that your know our language? You speak it very well." The boy said, "Oh, I lived in your country for three years. I learned it there." Then the boy asked, "Shall I help you order? I can translate the menu for you." The couple were even more grateful and thanked the boy heartily.

When they got back to their own country, their friends asked them what they had liked best about the trip. The wife said, "Well, we both think _____ _____. Everything went wrong at first, but the whole thing is engraved in our memories. We won't forget it. At some point, everybody should have the kind of trip where things don't go right. That's when you learn things. Maybe that's what people mean when they say travel is broadening."

8 SMALL GROUP DISCUSSION: IS IT OK IN YOUR CULTURE?

Divide into groups of four. Decide individually whether each of the following behaviors is required, advised, or allowed in your culture or another culture you are familiar with. Check the appropriate boxes. Then discuss the results with the others in your group.

	must	should	mustn't	shouldn't	don't have to
a. take a gift when invited to someone's house	❏	❏	❏	❏	❏
b. ask how old someone is	❏	❏	❏	❏	❏
c. smoke without asking permission	❏	❏	❏	❏	❏
d. hug friends when you see them	❏	❏	❏	❏	❏
e. shake hands when you meet someone	❏	❏	❏	❏	❏
f. take off your shoes when you enter a house	❏	❏	❏	❏	❏
g. offer to pay your share when someone invites you to a restaurant	❏	❏	❏	❏	❏
h. ask how much someone weighs	❏	❏	❏	❏	❏
i. ask what someone does (as an occupation)	❏	❏	❏	❏	❏
j. leave a tip in a restaurant	❏	❏	❏	❏	❏
k. call people by their first name	❏	❏	❏	❏	❏

9 ESSAY

Write a short essay (two to three paragraphs) about a situation that you had to deal with or are still facing—a problem like Jason's in the dialogue. Tell what you should or could have done (past) or what you should, could, or ought to do (future).

10 PICTURE DISCUSSION

With a partner, discuss this picture, saying as much as you can. Describe the situation. How must the woman and her children be feeling? Consider the family from another country. What do you think they should or shouldn't have done? How should they be behaving? What could they do to reduce the discomfort of the woman and her children?

INFORMATION GAP FOR STUDENT B

Student B, read the story below. Answer Student A's questions. Then ask your own questions and fill in the missing information.

> **EXAMPLE:**
> **A:** Where were the married couple traveling?
> **B:** They were traveling in eastern Europe.
> What was the first problem?
> **A:** The first problem was finding accommodations.

A married couple was traveling in a small country in Europe. Up until they had entered this particular country, they had been having a wonderful time. Now, however, everything seemed to be going wrong. The first problem was _____.
They were supposed to stay at the Grand State Hotel, but when they arrived at the hotel, they discovered that there was no record of their reservation, so they had to spend their first night at _____. The next day, after several hours of looking, they were finally able to get a room at a hotel far from the center of town. There were two rooms available: one very expensive room with one king-sized bed, and another inexpensive one with only one small twin bed. Since they were on a tight budget, they decided they'd better _____.

The second problem had to do with communication. In other countries they had been able to use French, German, and Spanish. Here _____ were able to speak those languages. Since the couple didn't speak the native language of the country, it was hard to make themselves understood.

The third problem involved food. After spending hours finding accommodations, they were starving, so they went into an elegant restaurant. They sat down at a table and were soon brought menus. When they looked at them, however, they could hardly understand a word. The husband said he thought they should have at least brought along _____. They hadn't done that, though, so they didn't know what to order.

Time passed. Other people were being served, but none of the waiters would come and take their orders. They began to get quite frustrated. They noticed that a boy about ten years old seemed to be listening to their conversation. Just when they were at their wits' end, the boy got up and came over to their table. "Excuse me," he said. "I couldn't help

(continued on next page)

hearing you _____. No one has come and taken your order because you have to go and pay for your meal first. Then they'll take your order." The husband and the wife were both astonished but grateful to the boy. The wife asked, "How is it that your know our language? You speak it very well." The boy said, "Oh, I lived in your country for three years. I learned it there." Then the boy asked, "_____? I can translate the menu for you." The couple were even more grateful and thanked the boy heartily.

When they got back to their own country, their friends asked them what they had liked best about the trip. The wife said, "Well, we both think the most memorable part was visiting that little country. Everything went wrong at first, but the whole thing is engraved in our memories. We won't forget it. At some point, everybody should have _____ _____. That's when you learn things. Maybe that's what people mean when they say travel is broadening."

MODALS: CERTAINTY

GRAMMAR **IN CONTEXT**

QUESTIONS TO CONSIDER

1. Why don't cats like to swim?

2. Why are baby boys usually dressed in blue and girls in pink?

3. Why are there so few women pilots?

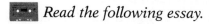 *Read the following essay.*

THE REALLY IMPORTANT QUESTIONS IN LIFE

A couple of weekends ago I had a dinner party at my house, and the after-dinner conversation time was the perfect opportunity for Sally to tell us all about the new things she'd learned. Sally is one of those people who collect all kinds of information that's certainly interesting but may not be very useful. True to form, Sally announced, "Guess what I found out?"

We all groaned, for we knew what was coming next.

"What, Sally? " I said tolerantly.

"Well, I've been reading this fascinating book called *Imponderables*. You know, puzzling questions that you can't explain precisely but that we all wonder about? I found out some really neat things. Want to hear about them?"

"Everybody'd better get themselves some soda and a snack," I said. "This could take a while."

"OK. Here's the first thing I learned. Now, I'm going to ask you these questions, and we'll see how many you can answer. Ready?"

"Ready!" we all chorused.

"OK. First question. Why don't cats like to swim?"

(continued on next page)

"They must be afraid of water," Scott said. "Or at the very least, they must not like it much."

"That can't be the reason," Nan said. "It's too obvious."

"Nan's right," Sally answered. "Everyone thinks cats are afraid of water. But that's not it."

"It might be because they're lazy. They know they'll have to clean their coats," Mary volunteered.

"Right on, Mary!" Sally said. "That's pretty much it. Cats are fanatics about keeping themselves clean. And they *are* basically lazy. They don't like to swim because they know it'll take too long to get their coats clean and dry."

"OK," I said. "Not bad. What's your next question?"

"Next question: Why in some cultures do people dress baby boys and baby girls in different colors? And why boys in blue and baby girls in pink? You've got to go back in history to answer this one."

"Hmm," Marilyn mused. "I don't know about why pink and blue specifically, but they might have started using different colors just to tell boys and girls apart."

"That's absolutely right. They did," Sally answered. "And so what about blue and pink?"

"Well," said Jim, "They may have thought that certain colors were luckier than others. Is that part of it?"

"Yep. People thought that babies needed to be protected from evil spirits. And they thought blue was the strongest color because it was the color of the sky, and the sky was associated with heaven."

"But," Jim said, "why did boys get the blue?"

"That's easy enough to answer," Nan said. "They must have felt boys had more status, so they got the strongest color. They really couldn't have chosen any other color if blue was the strongest."

"That's it," said Sally. "As for girls, it's not so clear. But people in those times must not have thought that evil spirits would bother girls, because it was several centuries before girls got their own color. When girls did get a color, it was because legend taught that girls were born inside of pink roses."

"Very interesting," said Bob. "What else, Sally?"

"Why are there so few women pilots on commercial airplanes?"

"There may not be enough jobs to go around," I said.

"No, that's not it. There are lots of jobs."

"Easy," said Marilyn. "It's got to have something to do with gender stereotypes. People have traditionally thought that women aren't capable of flying airplanes."

"That's part of it," Sally said. "But there's more to it than that."

"Could it have something to do with military experience?" Jim queried. "Back when they started, there might not have been enough women with the right training."

"Yes," Sally answered. "In the early days of commercial airlines, a lot of pilots were hired because they had military flying experience, especially in combat. Women didn't have combat experience, so very few of them were chosen. If they were chosen, they had to have experience in flight school."

Nan said, "But now that a lot more women are in the military, that should change, right? I mean, women can go into combat now."

"Right," said Sally. "In fact, some experts think that women actually have an advantage over men because they make better pilots. It may take a while, but it'll change."

"You know, Sally," Nan asked, "I think I want to read this book. Where can I get hold of it?"

"You ought to be able to find it at that big bookstore downtown. Or you might even find it in the supermarket. But I'll lend you my copy if you can't."

"Great," Nan said.

Source: Based on information in David Feldman, *Imponderables: The Solution to the Mysteries of Everyday Life* (New York: William Morrow, 1986, 1987).

UNDERSTANDING MEANING FROM CONTEXT

Circle the letter of the choice closest in meaning to each italicized word or phrase from the reading.

1. *True to form,* Sally announced, "Guess what I found out?"

   a. Telling the truth   **b.** Speaking formally   **c.** As she usually does

2. We all groaned, *for* we knew what was coming next.

   a. because   **b.** although   **c.** besides

3. "They don't like to swim because they know it'll take too long to get their *coats* clean and dry."

   a. paws   **b.** fur   **c.** surroundings

4. "Women didn't have *combat* experience, so very few of them were chosen."

   a. military   **b.** supervisory   **c.** fighting

GRAMMAR **PRESENTATION**
MODALS: CERTAINTY

DEGREE OF CERTAINTY: PRESENT AND PAST

				SPEAKER IS ALMOST CERTAIN
It	must has to 's got to	have	something to do with cultural stereotypes.
They	must not	like	it much.
That	can't	be	the reason.
They	must have	felt	boys had more status.
People	must not have	thought	spirits would bother girls.
They	can't have couldn't have	chosen	any other color if blue was the strongest.

				SPEAKER IS LESS CERTAIN
It	may might could	take	a while, but it'll change.
He	could	be	wondering when things will change.
There	may not might not	be	enough jobs to go around.
They	may have	thought been	that certain colors were luckier than others. wondering what colors were luckier.
	might have	started	using different colors just to tell boys and girls apart.
There	may not have might not have	been	enough women with military training.

DEGREE OF CERTAINTY: FUTURE

SPEAKER IS QUITE SURE
But now that a lot more women are in the military, that **should change**, right?
You **ought to be able to** find it at that big bookstore downtown.

SPEAKER IS LESS SURE BUT CONSIDERS SITUATION POSSIBLE			
It	**may** **might** **could**	take	a while, but it'll change.

NOTES

EXAMPLES

1. The modals and modal-like expressions *must, have to, have got to, may, might, can't, couldn't, should,* and *ought to* express degrees of **certainty**. They are used when a speaker is speculating about something based on logic and facts as understood by the speaker.

Remember that models are used in progressive as well as simple forms.

When we want to state a fact we are absolutely—100 percent—sure of, we don't use modals.

- This information is interesting but **may not be** very useful. (a degree of certainty)

- They may have been wondering which colors were luckier.

- This information is interesting but **is not** useful. (certainty—no use of modals)

2. Use *must* when you are speculating and are almost sure.

Have to and *have got to* are also used to show **near certainty**.

- Cats **must be** afraid of water.
- They **must have felt** boys had more status.

- It**'s got to have** something to do with gender stereotypes.

3. Use *can't, can't have, couldn't,* and *couldn't have* when you feel that it is **impossible** to conclude otherwise.

- That **can't** be the reason.
- They **couldn't have used** any other color besides blue.

4. Use *may, might,* or *could* when you are less sure but think that a situation is at least possible.

- There **may not be** enough jobs to go around.
- It **might be** because they're lazy.
- **Could it have** something to do with military experience?
- There **might not have been** enough women with the right training.

5. Use *should, ought to, may, might,* and *could* to express **future probability**. *Should* and *ought to* express a greater degree of certainty. *May, might,* and *could* express a lesser degree.

- But now that a lot more women are in the military, that **should change**, right?
- You **ought to be able to find** it at that big bookstore downtown.
- Or you **might** even **find** it in the supermarket.

6. Note the two different meanings of *could have* + participle.

- They **could have started** using different colors just to tell boys and girls apart.
  (It's possible they did this. I'm not sure.)
- You **could have called** me.
  (You didn't—a missed opportunity.)

FOCUSED PRACTICE

1 DISCOVER THE GRAMMAR

Look again at some of the sentences from The Really Important Questions in Life. *For each item, circle the letter of the choice that is similar in meaning.*

1. "This could take a while."

   a. This may take a while.

   b. This should take a while.

2. "That can't be the reason."

   a. That couldn't be the reason.

   b. That must not be the reason.

3. "It might be because they're lazy."

   a. It could be because they're lazy.

   b. It must be because they're lazy.

4. ". . . they might have started using different colors just to tell boys and girls apart."

   a. They could have started using different colors . . .

   b. They must have started using different colors . . .

5. "They may have thought that certain colors were luckier than others."

   a. They might have thought that certain colors were luckier than others.

   b. They must have thought that certain colors were luckier than others.

6. "But people in those times must not have thought that evil spirits would bother girls . . ."

   a. It's probable that they thought this.

   b. It's possible that they thought this.

7. "It's got to have something to do with gender stereotypes."

   a. It might have something to do with gender stereotypes.

   b. It must have something to do with gender stereotypes.

8. "You ought to be able to find it at that big bookstore downtown."

   a. You might be able to find it there.

   b. You should be able to find it there.

9. "Or you might even find it in the supermarket."

   a. You may be able to find it there.

   b. You should be able to find it there.

2 WHERE'S HARRY?

Read the conversation. Complete it with modal constructions from the box.

must have	might be	~~may have had to~~	should be
must have been visiting	could be working	~~could have gotten~~	might be meeting

BLAKE: I wonder what's keeping Harry. He's usually on time for office parties. I

suppose he _____could have gotten_____ stuck in traffic.

     1.

SAMANTHA: Yeah, that's a possibility. Or he _____ work late. I've never

     2.

known him to be late to a party.

BLAKE: You know, I've always felt there's something a little puzzling—or even

mysterious—about Harry.

SAMANTHA: What makes you say that?

BLAKE: Well, he never says much about his past. He's really an interesting guy, but I

don't know much about him. For all I know, he _____ an

     3.

international spy.

SAMANTHA: I think I know what you mean. Or he _____ as a

     4.

government agent.

BLAKE: Something tells me this is a case of *cherchez la femme.*

SAMANTHA: What does that mean?

BLAKE: It means "look for the woman." I figure he _____ a

     5

girlfriend that he doesn't want us to know about.

SAMANTHA: Yeah, maybe so. You know, now that I think of it, he always leaves work early

on Friday afternoons. I see him go to the parking garage about 4:00, and it

always seems like he's trying not to be seen. He _____ his

     6.

secret love somewhere.

[*The doorbell rings.*]

BLAKE: Oh, wait a minute. There's the doorbell. Everyone else is here. That

_____ him.

     7.

HARRY: Hi, folks. Sorry I'm late. Had some business to take care of.

SAMANTHA: Business, huh. You mean romantic business?

HARRY: Romantic business? What are you talking about?

BLAKE: We figure you _____ your lady love. After all, we see you
8.
leave early every Friday afternoon.

HARRY: Pretty funny. Well, there is a lady, and I love her. But it's not what you think.

SAMANTHA: What is it, then?

HARRY: My mother. She's eighty-eight years old and she lives in a retirement center.

I go and see her every Friday.

---

3 THE TUNGUSKA EVENT   Grammar Notes 1, 2, 5

Read about a strange occurrence in Siberia in 1908.

THE TUNGUSKA EVENT

On June 30, 1908, in the Tunguska area of central Siberia, a momentous event took place, the cause of which remains unexplained to this day. The calm of the summer morning was suddenly destroyed by an object which plowed erratically through the sky and crashed into the ground, exploding on impact with a force of 10 to 15 megatons of energy. Eyewitnesses in the nearby town of Vanovara said the explosion of the object, whatever it was, left an illuminated trail in the sky many kilometers in length and a mushroom-shaped cloud over the scene. In the town of Kansk, 800 kilometers away, an engineer stopped his train because he thought some of the train cars had exploded. The shock wave from the explosion was recorded as far away as London. The impact caused immense devastation: Most of the trees within 20 kilometers of the point of impact were knocked down, and in the vicinity of the impact point, windows were broken and roofs torn off houses. The Angara, a major river of the area, flooded. Villages and herds of reindeer, along with 500,000 acres of pine forest, were obliterated.

> a momentous event took place, the cause of which remains unexplained to this day

One would assume that scientists, government officials, and other interested parties would have made it a high priority to investigate the explosion. It wasn't until 1927, though, that an official investigation was conducted. One of the most puzzling facts to emerge from the investigation was that no crater was discovered at the impact site. Researchers theorized that there had been a crater and that it was now simply buried beneath a swamp.

Twenty years later, a geologic expedition ascertained that no crater in fact existed, suggesting that the blast hadn't been caused by the impact of a meteor. The expedition recorded further evidence of the great devastation wrought by the blast, including the fact that toppled trees were discovered radiating outward from the center of the explosion. However, there were still trees standing at the center of the blast area, indicating that the

(continued on next page)

explosion had taken place from immediately above. Tests made on botanical specimens from the area showed great and quick tree growth, perhaps caused by radiation. To some investigators, this suggested the same kind of nuclear explosion as took place in Hiroshima during World War II.

Today there are a number of explanations given as to the possible cause of the Tunguska Event. The most widely accepted one is that a 10,000-ton remnant of Encke's Comet entered the earth's atmosphere at a very high speed, burned up during entry, and crashed onto the earth's surface, causing a fireball and a shock wave but not creating a crater. Other explanations include the possibility of the impact of an errant black hole or the crashing of an alien space ship. The jury is still out.

Source: Based on information in www.kent/net/paranormal/places/tungus/index.html.

Now look back at the article. Write sentences with past modals about the Tunguska blast, using the prompts given. Choose the more appropriate modal in each case.

1. People who observed the blast _____must have been_____ astonished.
　　　　　　　　　　　　　　　　　(should / must) be

2. The blast _____ people and animals living near the impact point.
　　　　　　　(must / might) kill

3. Because they found no crater, scientists assumed that it _____ a
　　　　　　　　　　　　　　　　　　　　　　　　　(should / could) not be
meteor that caused the blast.

4. Today, a widely accepted explanation is that a comet _____ over the
　　　　　　　　　　　　　　　　　　　　　　　　　(must / should) explode
earth's surface.

5. Another explanation is that a black hole _____ the earth.
　　　　　　　　　　　　　　　　　　　　(must / might) hit

6. Still another explanation is that an alien space ship _____ in
　　　　　　　　　　　　　　　　　　　　　　　　　(may / ought to) crash and explode
the blast area.

7. Some people wonder if the Tunguska blast _____ a nuclear explosion.
　　　　　　　　　　　　　　　　　　　　　　　(could / must) be

4 EDITING

Read the following student essay. Find and correct the nine errors in the use of modals.

Why We Itch

　　　　　　　　　　　　　　　　might
One ~~must~~ think that with all the scientific progress that has been made in the last

century, researchers would be able by now to answer this very simple question: Why do

we itch? Unfortunately, scientists can't answer this question with any certainty. They

simply don't know.

There are some clear cases involving itching. If a patient goes to her doctor and complains of terrible itching and the doctor finds hives or some other kind of rash, the doctor might say that she must eaten something that didn't agree with her—or that she might been stung or bitten by some insect. This kind of case can be easily diagnosed. Most itching, however, does not have obvious causes.

Here's what scientists do know. Right under the surface of the skin there are sensory receptors that register physical stimuli and carry messages to the brain. These receptors detect pain and let the brain know about it. If there is a high level of physical stimulation to the body, this stimulation might reported it to the brain as pain. If the level of physical stimulation is low, the sensors might be report it as itchiness.

There has been a lot of speculation about the function of itching. Some researchers theorize that the function of itching may to warn the body that it is about to have a painful experience. Others theorize that early humans might developed itching as a way of knowing that they needed to take vermin and insects out of their hair. Still others believe that itching could a symptom of serious diseases such as diabetes and Hodgkin's disease.

One of the most interesting aspects of itching is that it may have be less tolerable than pain. Research has shown, in fact, that most people tolerate pain better than itching. Many will allow their skin to be painfully broken just so they can get rid of an itch.

Source: Based on information in David Feldman, *Imponderables: The Solution to the Mysteries of Everyday Life.*
(New York: William Morrow, 1986, 1987).

COMMUNICATION PRACTICE

5 LISTENING

Listen to a discussion in a biology class. Then listen to certain sentences again. Circle the letter of the sentence that gives the correct information about what each speaker says.

1. **a.** It's impossible that it was me on the tape.

    b. It's possible that it was me on the tape.

2. **a.** There's probably a mistake.

    b. There's possibly a mistake.

3. **a.** The students might have had this experience before.

    b. It's almost certain that the students have had this experience before.

4. **a.** According to Professor Stevens, it would be a good idea for the students to figure out the answer.

    b. According to Professor Stevens, the students will probably be able to figure out the answer.

5. **a.** Allison thinks it's probably because we hear the sound in different ways.

    b. Allison thinks it's possibly because we hear the sound in different ways.

6. **a.** Bart thinks it's possibly because the sound travels through different substances.

    b. Bart thinks it's almost certainly because the sound travels through different substances.

7. **a.** Kathy believes that it's certain that it's a combination of the two things.

    b. Kathy believes that it's possible that it's a combination of the two things.

8. **a.** Darren thinks the sound others hear must be the real sound.

    b. Darren thinks the sound others hear could be the real sound.

9. **a.** Kathy thinks the sound we hear should be the real sound.

    b. Kathy thinks the sound we hear has to be the real sound.

10. **a.** Professor Stevens is sure that internal hearing is more real than external hearing.

    b. Professor Stevens is almost certain that internal hearing is more real than external hearing.

6 SOLVE THE PUZZLE

Work with a partner to solve these riddles. Using past modals, suggest several possible solutions to each puzzle—from most likely to least likely—and label them accordingly.

1. On November 22, 1978, an eighteen-year-old thief broke into a lady's house and demanded all her money. She gave him all she had: $11.50. The thief was so angry that he demanded she write him a check for $50. Two hours later the police caught the thief. Why?

2. A dog owner put some food in a pan for her cat. Then, because she didn't want her dog to eat the cat's food, she tied a 6-foot rope around his neck. Then she left. When she came back, she discovered that the dog had eaten the cat's food. What happened?

3. A young girl named Michelle decided to ride her bicycle from her own town to a town 10 kilometers away. After a while she reached a crossroads where she had to change direction. She discovered that the signpost with arrows pointing to different towns in the area had blown down. She didn't know which road was the right one. Nevertheless, she was able to figure out which road to take. What do you think she did?

4. Roy Sullivan, a forest ranger in Virginia, had seven experiences in his life in which he was struck by a powerful force. Two times his hair was set on fire. He had burns on his eyebrows, shoulder, stomach, chest, and ankle. Once he was driving when he was hit and was knocked 10 feet out of his car. What do you think happened to him?

Sources: For riddle 1: Eric Elfman, Almanac of the Gross, Disgusting, and Totally Repulsive (New York: Random House, 1994); for riddles 2 and 3: Louis G. Cowan, The Quiz Kids, Questions and Answers (Akron, Ohio: Saalfield Publishing, 1941); for riddle 4: Ann Elwood and Carol Orsag Madigan, The Macmillan Book of Fascinating Facts (New York: Macmillan, 1989).

7 SMALL GROUP DISCUSSION

Form groups of four. Look back at The Tunguska Event. *Which explanation do you think is the most likely? Which do you like best? Discuss your opinions with your partners. Report your opinions to the class.*

8 ESSAY

Write a paragraph or two in which you attempt to answer one of the following questions. You can make your paragraphs serious or humorous.

- Why don't we ever see baby pigeons?
- Why do we cry at happy endings?
- Why do women wear such uncomfortable shoes?
- Why are cities warmer than their outlying areas?

Source of topics: David Feldman, Imponderables: The Solution to the Mysteries of Everyday Life (New York: William Morrow, 1986, 1987).

9 PICTURE DISCUSSION

With a partner, discuss this picture. Describe the situation, saying as much as you can. Why do you think the house is such a mess? Where do you think the teenagers' parents are? Have they been gone a short time or a long time? Do you think the parents will be back soon?

REVIEW OR SELFTEST

I. *Complete the letter to a columnist and the columnist's response with the correct tense forms of the indicated modals and modal-like expressions. Make the modals negative where necessary, and include necessary subject pronouns.*

Dear Pamela:

My wife, Jeaninne, and I invited a Japanese colleague to dinner last week.

We had invited her before, but she'd ___had to decline___ because of other
　　　　　　　　　　　　　　　　　1. (have to / decline)

commitments. Finally, _____. Things were going well at
　　　　　　　　　　　2. (be able to / come)

first. Yoko, my co-worker, seemed a little nervous, but that was

understandable. I thought she was probably trying to remember how

_____ when you visit an American home. She brought a
3. (be supposed to / act)

beautifully wrapped present, which my wife just _____ right
　　　　　　　　　　　　　　　　　　　4. (have to / open)

away. Yoko _____ that very much, because she looked upset.
　　　　5. (must / like)

I thought maybe in Japan _____ the paper. Maybe
　　　　　　　　　　6. (be supposed to / tear)

_____ it off gently and fold it, or something. Anyway, my
7. (be supposed to / take)

wife tore it off with a flourish and pulled out a box of excellent chocolates.

She _____ until after dinner, but she insisted on passing
　　　8. (could / wait)

them around and having everyone eat some of them. Before dinner! Yoko was

embarrassed. She said she _____ something else for a gift.
　　　　　　　　　　　　9. (should / bring)

　　Pamela, what went wrong? It think it was all Jeaninne's fault.

　　　　　　　　　　　　　　　　　　　　　Puzzled in Pittsburgh

Dear Puzzled:

　　You _____ anybody for this problem. It's a clear case
　　　　10. (have to / blame)

of cultural misunderstanding. What you _____ is that
　　　　　　　　　　　　　　11. (must / understand)

in Japan when someone takes a gift to a friend's house, the friend

_____ it in front of the visitor. It is more polite to wait until
12. (should / open)

(continued on next page)

later to open it, so it _____ something of a shock to your Japanese friend
13. (may / be)

to see your wife make such a big scene. That's not what one _____ in
14. (be supposed to / do)

Japan.

Don't be too concerned about it. I'm sure your friend will understand when you explain

to her and apologize.

Pamela

II. *Read the story. Replace each underlined expression with a modal or modal-like
expression having the same or a similar meaning. Write your answers on the lines
below.*

One of the most puzzling experiences I've ever had happened last winter. It was one of

those typical dark and stormy nights that you read about in mystery novels. Sitting on the

sofa in the living room, I <u>could hear</u> thunder and see an occasional flash of lightning.
1.

It <u>had to have been</u> at least 1:00 A.M. I was reading a mystery novel that was so exciting
2.

I <u>couldn't put it down</u>. Suddenly the phone rang, startling me out of my wits. I picked up
3.

the receiver, muttering to myself something like, "Who <u>can that be</u> at this hour of the night?
4.

<u>Someone probably died</u>." But no. There were a few seconds of silence; then a low,
5.

disembodied voice said, "Help me. Help me." "Who are you?" I asked. "Who is this?" No

answer. The phone went dead.

The next morning it all seemed like a bad dream. I was troubled enough by the

experience to tell my friend Josh about it. "It <u>may have just been</u> a crank call," he said.
6.

"Or it <u>might have been</u> one of your friends playing a joke on you."
7.

"What <u>do you think I should do</u>?"
8.

"Do? Why do anything? It won't happen again."

It did happen again, though, the following night. At precisely 1:12 A.M. (I looked at my

watch this time) the phone rang again, waking me out of a sound sleep. The same deep,

disembodied voice was on the other end of the line. I responded in the same way, but the

voice just said, "Help me, help me." Then there was silence, and the line went dead as

before.

The next day I told Josh about it again. "I still say <u>it's got to be</u> some friend of yours
9.

playing a joke. Don't you recognize the voice?"

"Not at all," I said. "It <u>can't be</u> anyone I know."
10.

"Well, call the phone company. <u>They'll probably have</u> an idea about what to do."
11.

I never did call the phone company, for some reason. This experience went on for the

next five nights. At precisely 1:12 A.M., the phone would ring, and I would pick it up, only

to hear the same thing. "Help me, help me." After that, it stopped. Since then I haven't

stopped wondering if I <u>should have called</u> the police.
12.

I wonder if it <u>could really have been</u> someone who needed help. Or was it just a
13.

trickster? <u>Maybe I'll never find out</u>.
14.

1. _was able to hear_   8. _____

2. _____   9. _____

3. _____   10. _____

4. _____   11. _____

5. _____   12. _____

6. _____   13. _____

7. _____   14. _____

III. *Look at the pictures. Write a sentence using the suggested modal or modal-like
expression to describe each situation, making sure to put the verbs in the correct
tense.*

1.

(should)

They should all be

wearing their seat belts.

2.

(must)

_____

_____

(continued on next page)

3.

(had better)

_____

4.

(be supposed to)

_____

5.

(might)

_____

6.

(could)

_____

7.

(may)

_____

_____

8.

(should)

_____

_____

IV. *Circle the letter of the one word or phrase in each sentence that is <u>not</u> correct.*

1. I think we <u>ought</u> <u>look into</u> a nice guided tour—that is, if we <u>can find</u>   Ⓐ **B** **C** **D**

      A   B

one that <u>won't bankrupt</u> us.

    D

2. Fortunately, I <u>could get</u> a scholarship to attend college; otherwise,   **A B C D**
A

I never <u>could have</u> <u>afforded</u> <u>to go</u>.
B   C   D

3. You <u>had better</u> <u>to set</u> your alarm if you expect to <u>be able to</u> <u>wake up</u>   **A B C D**
A   B   C   D

on time.

4. The only thing I <u>can think</u> of as to why Joe isn't here is that he   **A B C D**
A

<u>might have</u> <u>have to</u> <u>work</u> late.
B   C   D

5. Do you think I <u>shall</u> <u>take</u> a gift to the party today, or do you think   **A B C D**
A   B

I <u>might</u> <u>be able to wait</u> until Saturday?
C   D

6. They <u>might not</u> <u>had</u> <u>been</u> injured in the accident if they had been   **A B C D**
A   B   C

<u>wearing</u> their seatbelts.
D

7. We <u>ought to</u> <u>take</u> some extra cash along on the trip, but we absolutely   **A B C D**
A   B

<u>don't have to</u> <u>forget</u> our passports.
C   D

8. Joe called to say that he <u>won't be able to</u> make it by seven o'clock, but   **A B C D**
A   B

he <u>must</u> <u>manage to get</u> here by eight.
C   D

9. <u>You'll be</u> <u>supposed to</u> to fertilize your rose bushes if <u>you expect</u> them   **A B C D**
A   B   C

<u>to produce</u> any flowers.
D

10. I suppose Amy <u>could have</u> <u>had to</u> stay late at the office, but she told   **A B C D**
A   B

me she <u>didn't</u> <u>had to</u> work tonight.
C   D

V. *Go back to your answers to Part IV. Write the correct form for each item that you believe is incorrect.*

1. <u> ought to   </u>   **6.** _____

2. _____   **7.** _____

3. _____   **8.** _____

4. _____   **9.** _____

5. _____   **10.** _____

▶ **To check your answers, go to the Answer Key on page 99.**

PART II

FROM GRAMMAR TO WRITING TOPIC SENTENCES

A common way of organizing an essay or other piece of writing in English is to begin with a topic sentence. A topic sentence is a general sentence which covers the content of the entire paragraph. All the supporting examples and details of the paragraph must fit under this sentence. It is usually the first sentence in the paragraph. Look at this paragraph from the essay "The Tunguska Event":

> Today there are a number of explanations given as to the possible cause of the Tunguska Event. The most widely accepted one is that a 10,000-ton remnant of Encke's Comet entered the earth's atmosphere at a very high speed, burned up during entry, and crashed onto the earth's surface, causing a fireball and a shock wave but not creating a crater. Other explanations include the possibility of the impact of an errant black hole or the crashing of an alien space ship. The jury is still out.

The topic sentence for this paragraph is "Today there are a number of explanations given as to the possible cause of the Tunguska Event." This sentence tells the reader what to expect in the paragraph: some explanations about the causes of the Tunguska explosion.

 Look at this paragraph. It contains many supporting details but no topic sentence. Read the paragraph. Then circle the letter of the best topic sentence for the paragraph.

For one thing, you should always remove your shoes when you enter a Japanese home, and you should leave them pointing toward the door. Another suggestion is to make sure that you bring a gift for your Japanese hosts, and to be sure to wrap it. A third recommendation is to be appreciative of things in a Japanese house, but not too appreciative. Finally, remember that when you sit down to eat, you do not have to accept every kind of food that you are offered, but you are expected to finish whatever you do put on your plate.

Choices

  a. Visiting a Japanese home is very enjoyable.

  b. Taking a gift is very important when you visit a Japanese home.

  c. There are a number of things to keep in mind when you visit a Japanese home.

  d. When you visit a Japanese home, be sure not to eat too much.

---

2 *Read the following paragraph. Then look at the four variations of possible topic sentences. Which one is the best? Why? What is wrong with each of the other choices?*

One reason is that when commercial flights began, all pilots were male. Men were hired because they had flight experience obtained in combat. Women, not having been in combat, had no flight experience. A second reason is simply prejudice: The powers in the airline industry presumably believed the stereotype that there are certain jobs that women cannot do as well as men. A third reason is inertia and the status quo—flying has mostly been a male-dominated profession since it began, and it takes time to change things. Eventually we will see more and more female commercial airline pilots, but for the present, old ideas die hard.

Choices

  a. Why there are so few women commercial pilots today.

  b. There are three principal reasons why there are so few women commercial pilots today.

  c. Women pilots in aviation.

  d. Men are still prejudiced about women's capabilities.

---

3 *Look at each of the following sets of details. For each set, write an appropriate topic sentence.*

  1. _____

    a. For one thing, there's almost always a traffic jam I get stuck in, and I'm often late to work.

    b. Also, there's not always a parking place when I do get to work.

    c. Worst of all, I'm spending more money on gas and car maintenance than I would if I took public transportation.

  2. _____

    a. One is that I often fall asleep when watching the TV screen, no matter how interesting the video is.

    b. Another is that watching movies is basically a social experience, and I'm usually alone when I watch videos.

    c. The main reason is that the TV screen, no matter how large it is, diminishes the impact that you get when watching a movie on the big screen.

(continued on next page)

3. _____

   a. Nothing spontaneous usually happens on a guided tour, but I've had lots of spontaneous things happen when I've charted my own vacation course.

   b. Tour guides present you with what they think is interesting, whereas when you are in charge of your own vacation, you do what you think is interesting.

   c. Unplanned vacations can often be cheaper than guided tours.

4. _____

   a. Cats don't bark and wake up the neighbors or bite the mailman.

   b. Dogs have to be walked at least two times a day, but cats handle their own exercise.

   c. Cats eat a lot less than dogs.

   d. You can't leave your dog at home when you take a vacation, but you can leave your cat if a friend or neighbor will come and feed it.

4 APPLY IT TO YOUR WRITING

Write a paragraph of several sentences about one of the following topics, a similar topic that interests you, or a topic suggested by your teacher. Make sure that your paragraph has a topic sentence. Then share your work with three or four other students. Read each others' paragraphs. Point out strengths and offer suggestions.

Topics
- an annoying habit
- the best part of the day
- night owls vs. early birds
- the ideal vacation
- a societal problem
- expectation vs. reality

Review or SelfTest
Answer Key

I.
2. she was able to come
3. you're supposed to act
4. had to open
5. must not have liked
6. you're not supposed to tear
7. you're supposed to take
8. could have waited
9. should have brought
10. don't have to blame
11. must understand
12. shouldn't open
13. may have been
14. is supposed to do

II.
2. must have been
3. wasn't able to put it down
4. could that be
5. Someone must have died
6. It might have just been / It could have just been
7. may have been / could have been
8. do you think I ought to do / shall I do
9. it has to be / it must be
10. couldn't be
11. They should have / They ought to have
12. ought to have called
13. might really have been / may really have been
14. I may never find out / I might never find out

III. Possible Answers:
2. They must have forgotten to put gas in the tank.
3. They'd better slow down.
4. Drivers are supposed to carry their driver's license with them.
5. Jerry might have missed his flight. / Jerry might have decided to take a different flight.
6. Jerry could have called his parents to tell them what he was going to do.
7. It may rain.
8. They should have brought their raincoats and umbrellas. / They shouldn't have tried to play tennis today.

IV.
2. A	5. A	8. C
3. B	6. B	9. A
4. C	7. C	10. D

V.
2. was able to get
3. set
4. had to
5. should / ought to
6. have
7. mustn't
8. should
9. You're
10. have to

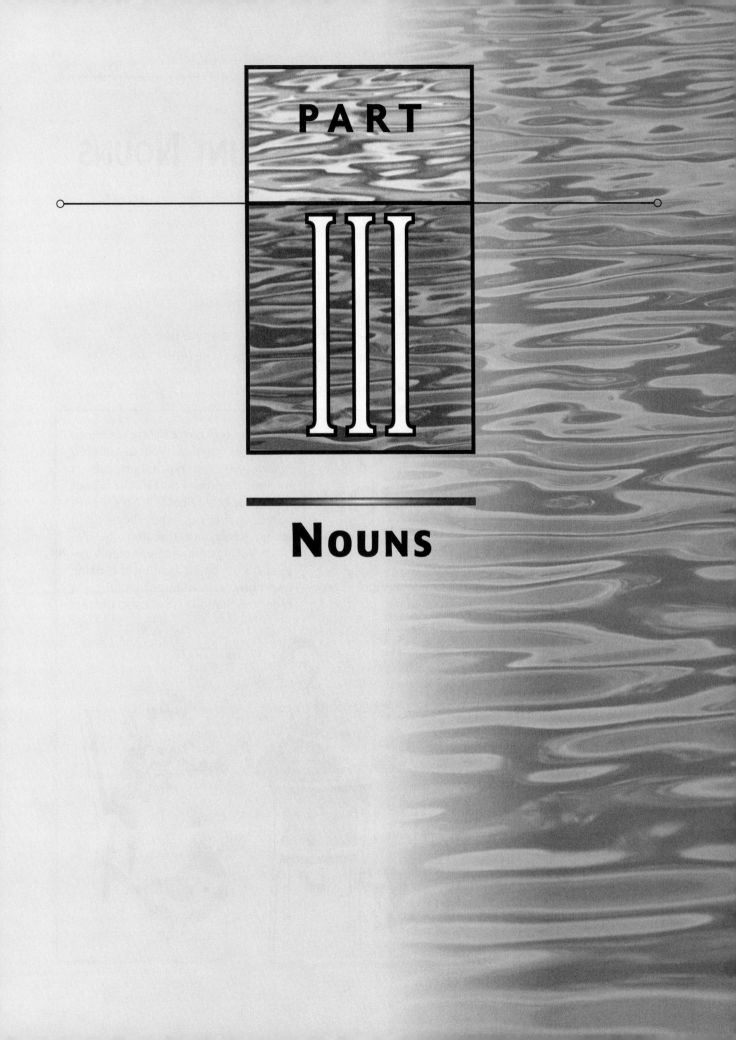

PART

III

NOUNS

COUNT AND NON-COUNT NOUNS

GRAMMAR **IN CONTEXT**

QUESTIONS TO CONSIDER

1. What foods of cultures other than your own do you like?

2. What are some ways that people use food in their culture?

Read an article about fusion cooking.

TIME FOR FUSION

Think, now. Are you tired of the same old meals, tired of eating your own cooking? Weary of the fare at fast-food establishments? Can't stomach another plate of bland, home-cooked pasta? Here's a piece of advice: It's time you discovered fusion. No, I'm not talking about nuclear fusion. I'm talking about fusion cooking. What is it? It's a phenomenon that has swept the world in recent years and threatens to displace boring and tasteless meals forever. It's the amalgamation of cooking traditions from different cultures—a blending that takes the best, tastiest

EAT YOUR VEGETABLES.

elements of one culture's cooking and mixes them with the best elements of others.

There are many kinds of fusion cooking, of course, but Pacific Rim fusion, or East–meets–West, is paramount. In her *Terrific Pacific Cookbook,* Anya Von Bremzen, an authority in the field of cuisine, talks about Pacific Rim fusion. According to Von Bremzen, "The great culinary traditions of Europe and Asia, long distant and remote, each exotic to the other, have blended, fused, and overlapped—sometimes with seismic effects. The heartland of this new cuisine is a great loop of countries strung like a necklace around the edges of the seemingly endless Pacific Ocean." Foods and flavors which would have been unheard of in the past—coconut, ginger, lemon grass, curry, tropical fruit—are fast becoming the norm in the American home kitchen. However, the movement is not all in one direction. While Americans have gotten more into such things as noodles and curry, Asian people are beginning to embrace pasta and enchiladas. With a little effort, you can learn to bring your meals out of the dull and commonplace and into the realm of the exciting and delicious.

But wait a minute, you say. It takes a lot of work to prepare good, tasty Asian food, doesn't it? Not really. Fusion meals can be prepared easily. In a matter of minutes, a little bit of work will transform your meal into a work of art.

Nowhere is this fusion more apparent than in Hawaii, which, appropriately enough, is one of those crossroad places that bridge cultures. Hawaiians have taken elements of the food traditions of the peoples of Polynesia, Japan, China, Portugal, Okinawa, Korea, Southeast Asia, and even New England and have created a new cuisine known simply as "Local Food." In Hawaii, no one group sets the cultural tone. The population is one-third Pacific Islander, one-third Asian, and one-third Caucasian, and Local Food is a synthesis of the favorites of these groups. Established as a phenomenon after World War II, Local Food usually has rice as the center of the meal, more meat than Asians usually eat, and fewer fruits and vegetables. It's the kind of food you can get at lunch wagons and small eateries—not what you would find at a classy restaurant. A common meal might include Japanese white rice topped by several different meats, such as beef teriyaki, Chinese pork, or curry, perhaps accompanied by macaroni salad and some kind of vegetable.

Rachel Laudan, an authority on Hawaiian cuisine, is amazed by the ways in which Hawaiian people use food. It brings people together and helps them communicate. "Laudan describes Local Food, along with the local pidgin language, as the glue that holds the diverse ethnic groups together and sets them apart from outsiders," says writer Judith Pierce Rosenberg.

Hawaiian Local Food may be a microcosm of the future. We're surely going to see more of fusion cooking in the new millennium. Not only does it allow us to escape from the monotony of choices at fast-food restaurants, but it also allows us to eat more healthfully. And perhaps fusion cooking symbolizes something more than just tastier meals. Perhaps it represents the advent of the shrunken world and the world culture whose outlines we are just beginning to be able to recognize. ⏱

Sources: Based on Anya Von Bremzen, *Terrific Pacific Cookbook* (New York: Workman Publishing, 1995); Judith Pierce Rosenberg, "Hawaii's 'Local Food': A Fusion of Ethnic Flavors," *Christian Science Monitor,* June 3, 1998, p. 14.

UNDERSTANDING MEANING FROM CONTEXT

Part A

Make a guess about the meaning of each italicized word or phrase from the reading. Write your guess in the blank provided.

1. *Weary* of the fare at fast-food establishments?

   _____

2. Weary of the *fare* at fast-food establishments?

   _____

3. With a little effort, you can learn to bring your meals out of the dull and commonplace and into the *realm* of the exciting and delicious.

   _____

4. Hawaiian Local Food may be a *microcosm* of the future.

   _____

Part B

Answer the questions about other vocabulary from the reading.

5. The word *cuisine* is used many times in the reading, along with its more common synonym. What word is a synonym of *cuisine*?

   _____

6. Look at this sentence from the reading:

   > It's the amalgamation of cooking traditions from different cultures—a blending that takes the best, tastiest elements of one culture's cooking and mixes them with the best elements of others.

   The word *amalgamation* has a synonym in this sentence. What word means something similar to *amalgamation*?

   _____

GRAMMAR **PRESENTATION**
COUNT AND NON-COUNT NOUNS

NON-COUNT NOUNS IN "COUNTABLE" FORM	
NON-COUNT NOUN	**"COUNTABLE" FORM**
I'll have **tea**.	I'll have **a cup of tea**.
You need **advice**.	Let me give you **a piece of advice**.
We're having **meat** for dinner.	There are **several different meats** in this dish.
Fruit is nutritious.	Hawaiian food has **fewer fruits** and vegetables than Asian food.
Let's play **tennis**.	Let's play **a game of tennis**.

USES OF NON-COUNT NOUNS	
NON-COUNT NOUNS IN "MASS" USE	**NON-COUNT NOUNS IN "COUNT" USE**
It takes **work** to prepare a meal.	Your meal is **a work** of art.
I want some **coffee**.	Please bring us **two coffees**.
Wine is produced in France.	Chablis is **a white wine**.
This food needs some **spice**.	Turmeric and cardamom are **two spices** that originated in India.
The sun provides **light**.	She saw **two lights** shining in the sky.

NOTES

EXAMPLES

1. Nouns are names of persons, places, and things. There are two types of nouns: **proper nouns** and **common nouns**. **Proper nouns** are names of particular persons, places, or things. They are usually unique.	• Akira Kurosawa, São Paulo, the Golden Gate Bridge
Common nouns refer to people, places, or things but are not the names of particular individuals.	• book, courage, heart, rhinoceros, vegetable, water

2. There are two types of common nouns: **count nouns** and **non-count nouns**. **Count nouns** name things that can be counted.

- one woman, nine planets

Non-count (or **mass**) **nouns** name things that cannot be counted in their normal sense because they exist in a "mass" form. Non-count nouns in their normal meaning are not preceded by *a* or *an*, though they are often preceded by *some* and *the*.

- I bought rice.
  NOT ~~I bought a rice.~~
- Let me give you **some advice**.
  NOT ~~Let me give you an advice.~~

A **non-count noun** is normally followed by a **singular verb**.

- **Corn is** grown there.
  NOT ~~Corns are grown there.~~
- **Rice feeds** millions.
- **Physics seems** complicated.

3. Notice the following categories of non-count nouns and examples of them. See Appendix 5 on page A-4 for a more complete list of non-count nouns.

Abstractions	• advice, behavior, chance, energy, evil, fun, good, happiness, honesty, love
Activities	• bowling, dancing, football, hiking, soccer, tennis
Diseases	• AIDS, cancer, malaria, measles
Elements	• gold, magnesium, plutonium, silver
Foods	• beef, fruit, meat, rice, wheat
Gases	• air, carbon dioxide, oxygen, smoke
Liquids	• coffee, gasoline, soda, water, wine
Natural phenomena	• aurora borealis, cold, electricity, ice, light, lightning, rain, snow, thunder
Occupations	• construction, nursing, teaching
Particles	• dust, pepper, salt, sand, sugar
Subjects	• astronomy, business, English, history, Japanese, physics, science, Spanish
Others	• choice, equipment, furniture, news

4. We frequently make **non-count nouns countable** by adding a phrase that gives them a form, a limit, or a container. See Appendix 6 on page A-5 for a more complete list of phrases for counting non-count nouns.

NON-COUNT NOUN	**"COUNTABLE STATE"**
furniture	• a piece of furniture
lightning	• a bolt (*flash*) of lightning
meat	• a piece of meat
rice	• five grains of rice
sand	• a grain of sand
tennis	• a game of tennis
thunder	• a clap (*bolt*) of thunder
water	• a cup of water

5. Many non-count nouns are used in a countable sense without the addition of a phrase (such as "a piece of"). When they are, they can be preceded by *a / an* and can occur in the plural. Compare the following **non-count nouns** in **mass use** and **count use**.

MASS USE	**COUNT USE**
I ate **meat** for dinner.	• Different **meats** are available at the supermarket. (*types of meat*)
We need to take **water** along on the camping trip.	• There are carbonated and uncarbonated mineral **waters**. (*brands of mineral water*)
TV is both good and bad.	• Yesterday we bought **a TV**. (informal for *television set*)
Too much **salt** in the diet can be unhealthful.	• The mixture contains **a salt**. (*a type of chemical compound*)
I drink **coffee** every morning.	• Please bring us **three coffees**. (informal for *three cups of coffee*)
France produces **wine**.	• Cabernet Sauvignon is **a wine** produced in France.

(continued on next page)

It takes **work** to prepare an elegant meal.	• Your meal is **a work** of art.
Light is essential for the growth of crops.	• There's **a light** in the window.
Many events seem governed by **chance**.	• I had **a chance** to talk with Sarah. (*an opportunity*)
I have no **money**.	• The state will use tax **moneys** to fund the project. (*amounts of money from different tax sources*)

6. **BE CAREFUL!** When non-count nouns occur alone or are preceded by *some*, they denote things that don't have any particular boundaries.	• I drank **some soda**. (*no particular amount*) • **Work** can be exhausting. (*work in general*)
When non-count nouns are preceded by *a* or *an*, they acquire a boundary and are limited in some sense. A discrete amount or limit is suggested.	• I drank **a soda**. (*a discrete amount— probably a can or glass*) • *Don Quixote* is **a literary work**. (*a single literary work, contained in a book*)

7. Study the following **non-count nouns ending in -s** and **irregular plural count nouns**. See Appendix 4 on page A-4 for a list of irregular plurals.	• **mathematics, economics, physics** (non-count nouns ending in *-s*) • **criterion, phenomenon, nucleus** (singular count nouns) • **criteria, phenomena, nuclei** (irregular plural forms) • **cattle** (a plural form only; no singular form exists)

8. **BE CAREFUL!** In its normal usage, the word *people* is a **plural**, denoting "more than one person." In this meaning, it does not have a singular form. The word *people* meaning a particular group of human beings or particular groups of human beings can have a singular and a plural form.	• Hawaiian **people** use food in unusual ways. (*Hawaiian people in general*) • Hawaiians have taken elements of the food traditions of many **peoples** and have created a new cuisine. (*many different ethnic groups*)
The word *cattle* (= a group of cows) is a collective plural. There is no singular form.	• Ranchers raise **cattle**. (*cows*)

FOCUSED PRACTICE

 DISCOVER THE GRAMMAR

Look again at these two paragraphs from Time for Fusion. *You will find thirteen non-count nouns and twenty-three count nouns. Circle the count nouns and underline the non-count nouns as used in the exercise. Do not include proper nouns (any words capitalized). Count usages of words only once.*

There are many (kinds) of fusion cooking, of course, but Pacific Rim fusion, or East–meets–West, is paramount. In her *Terrific Pacific Cookbook*, Anya Von Bremzen, an authority in the field of cuisine, talks about Pacific Rim fusion. According to Von Bremzen, "The great culinary traditions of Europe and Asia, long distant and remote, each exotic to the other, have blended, fused, and overlapped—sometimes with seismic effects. The heartland of this new cuisine is a great loop of countries strung like a necklace around the edges of the seemingly endless Pacific Ocean." Foods and flavors which would have been unheard of in the past—coconut, ginger, lemon grass, curry, tropical fruit—are fast becoming the norm in the American home kitchen. However, the movement is not all in one direction. While Americans have gotten more into such things as noodles and curry, Asian people are beginning to embrace pasta and enchiladas. With a little effort, you can learn to bring your meals out of the dull and commonplace and into the realm of the exciting and delicious.

But wait a minute, you say. It takes a lot of work to prepare good, tasty Asian food, doesn't it? Not really. Fusion meals can be prepared easily. In a matter of minutes, a little bit of work will transfer your meal into a work of art.

 BLENDING **Grammar Notes 3, 5**

Part A

Read more about fusion cooking. Complete the article with words from the box.

menu	rolls	foods	ways	rules	century
~~food~~	cuisines	chefs	spices	flavoring	

COPLEY NEWS SERVICE, SAN DIEGO, CA   AUGUST 5, 1998   F5

"Fusion" Cooking Melds Cultures and Tastes
BY CHARLYN FARGO

Fusion _____*food*_____ can be called the blending of flavors and _____ as completely
              1.   2.

and effectively as the melding of America, and it is a celebration of the country's multiculturism.

Under the old French _____ of cooking, certain _____ were always
                                      3.   4.

prepared certain ways. Those rules have been changed. Egg _____ don't have to include only
                                                    5.

Chinese cabbage and shrimp. Plum sauce isn't just used in Chinese cuisine but to give the foods an

Asian _____.   *(continued on next page)*
           6.

And not just Asian. Mexican, Caribbean, Cuban—they all work to influence regional cuisine in

_____ not previously considered. On the West Coast, the cuisine of East and West have
　　　　7.

flourished side by side for more than a _____, since the California gold rush propelled
　　　　　　　　　　　　　　　　　　8.

San Francisco's first significant Asian immigration.

But it's only in the past two decades that inventive _____ have begun to blend the
　　　　　　　　　　　　　　　　　　　　　　　9.

cooking styles of East and West.

Norman Van Aken, chef and owner of Norman's in Miami and the author of *Norman's New World

Cuisine,* is credited as the father of "new world" cuisine and with coining the term "fusion cuisine."

For Van Aken fusion cuisine began more than ten years ago when he was working in Key West, Florida.

He began drawing on tropical flavorings along with _____ and seasonings from Cuba,
　　　　　　　　　　　　　　　　　　　　　　10.

the Bahamas, and the Old South for his food. His _____ was filled with items such as
　　　　　　　　　　　　　　　　　　　　11.

lobster enchiladas, rum and pepper-painted grouper (the sauce includes rum, peppercorns, cloves, and

soy sauce) and yucca-stuffed crispy fish.

His new world cuisine—with the flavors of the Bahamas and Cuba melded with Florida's

produce—is just one of many cuisines considered fusion.

Source: Charlyn Fargo, "Fusion Cooking Melds Cultures and Tastes," Copley News Service (San Diego, CA),
August 5, 1998, p. F5.

Part B

Work with a partner to answer these questions.

1. Could "foods" be a correct answer for item 1 in Part A? Why or why not?

   _____

2. Could "food" be a correct answer for item 4 in Part A? Why or why not?

   _____

3. Could "flavorings" be a correct answer for item 6 in Part A? Why or why not?

   _____

4. Could "spice" be a correct answer for item 10 in Part A? Why or why not?

   _____

3 **COMMUNITY BULLETIN BOARD**

The new interactive websites on the Internet give people information about entertainment, cultural events, and the weather. Fill in the blanks in the bulletin board messages, choosing from the forms given. Refer to Appendices 5 and 6 on pages A-4 and A-5 for help in completing this exercise if necessary.

Community Bulletin Board for August 25, 2002

_____Rain_____ is in the forecast for this afternoon and early evening. Don't worry,
1. (Rain / A rain)

though; it will be light rain, not at all like the heavy _____ which have been
2. (rains / rain)

falling in the Midwest this week.

Community Bulletin Board for August 25, 2002

Poet Jefferson Saito will give _____ of his poetry tonight in the Burlington
3. (reading / a reading)

Civic Center. He describes his latest book of poems as _____ in
4. (work / a work)

_____.
5. (progress / a progress)

Community Bulletin Board for August 25, 2002

On Tuesday afternoon at four o'clock at City Hall, Professor Helen Hammond, who has

written _____ of the space program, will lead _____ on the
6. (history / a history)   **7. (talk / a talk)**

exploration of _____ in the twenty-first century at _____ when
8. (space / a space)   **9. (time / a time)**

we seem to be running out of funding for the space program.

(continued on next page)

Community Bulletin Board for August 25, 2002

If you haven't made reservations for the annual Labor Day picnic, _____ is

10. (a time / time)

running short. _____ on the remodeling of Patton Pavilion, where the picnic will

11. (Work / A work)

be held, is almost complete. All residents of Burlington are of course invited, but you must have a

ticket, which will cover the price of dinner. The menu will include fish, meat, and pasta as

possible main courses. _____ and _____ are complimentary.

12. (Soda / A soda)   13. (milk / a milk)

Adult participants may purchase _____, including Columbia Merlot,

14. (wine / a wine)

_____ produced in the eastern part of the state.

15. (a red wine / red wine)

Community Bulletin Board for August 25, 2002

On Friday evening at 8:00 P.M. in the Civic Auditorium, Professor Mary Alice Waters will present

a program on the Xhosa, _____ of southern Africa. Professor

16. (indigenous people / an indigenous people)

Waters will show _____ about marriage customs of the Xhosa and other

17. (a film / film)

_____ of the southern third of the African continent.

18. (people / peoples)

---

4 A WORK OF ART

*Work with a partner. Take turns asking questions using items in the box. Each
partner asks and answers six questions.*

a work of art	fruits	a game of . . .	a piece of advice
spices	pieces of furniture	a TV	a wine
tax moneys	peoples	a people	cuisines

EXAMPLES:

PARTNER A: Tell me something that you consider **a work of art**.

PARTNER B: I consider Van Gogh's painting *Starry Night* **a work of art**.

PARTNER B: How many pieces of furniture . . . ?

PARTNER A: There are eight . . .

5 EDITING

Find and correct the eleven errors involving count and non-count nouns in the letter.

⁓ Sugar Loaf Mountain   Rio de Janeiro, Brazil ⁓

April 15

Dear Kids,

Your mom and I are having a wonderful time in Brazil. We landed in Rio de Janeiro on Tuesday as scheduled and made it to our hotel without any problems. On Wednesday we walked and sunbathed on Copacabana and Ipanema beaches. The only
                                                                         sand
problem was that I dropped my camera and got ~~sands~~ in it, and now it's not working. Actually, there's one other problem: we don't have enough furnitures in our hotel room. There's no place to put anything. But everything else has been great. We went to a samba show, and even though it was geared for tourist, it was a lot of fun.

The Brazilian people is very friendly and helpful. On Friday we had a flight to São Paulo scheduled for 9:00 A.M., and we missed the bus and couldn't get a taxi. But we were saved by one of the hotel employee, who gave us a ride to the airport. We got there in the nick of time. Now we're in São Paulo. It's an exciting place, but I can't get over the traffics. It took two hours to get from our hotel to the downtown area. Yesterday we had lunch at a famous restaurant where they serve feijoada, a typical Brazilian foods. It had so many spice in it that our mouths were on fire, but it was delicious. Tonight we are going to have dinner at another restaurant where they serve all kinds of meat. They raise a lot of cattles in Brazil, and meat is very popular. This restaurant is one of the most famous ones.

The other thing about Brazil that's really interesting is the amount of coffee the Brazilians drink. They have little cups of coffees several times a day—called caffezinho. We tried it; it's very strong and sweet.

That's all for now. Your mom hasn't had a time to go shopping yet, which is good. You know how much I hate shopping.

Love,
Dad

COMMUNICATION PRACTICE

6 LISTENING

Read the statements. Then listen to the cooking show.

1. Flo's pelmeni is a _____ dish. (national origin)

2. The principal meat ingredient of pelmeni is _____. (type of meat)

3. Other types of meat that can be used in making pelmeni are _____.

4. The meat mixture is contained in balls made of _____.

5. Pelmeni generally contains only one vegetable: _____.

6. The meat mixture contains _____. (part of eggs)

7. Pelmeni balls are cooked by _____. (method of cooking)

8. The pelmeni balls are finished cooking when _____.

9. At banquets in the home country, _____ are made. (number of individual balls of pelmeni)

10. One person can easily eat at least _____ pelmeni balls. (number)

Now listen again. Complete the statements.

7 INFORMATION GAP: A GRAIN OF SAND

Student B, turn to page 117 and follow the instructions there. Student A, read statements 1–6 aloud. Student B will read the best completion for each statement, including a phrase from the box below in each statement. Then reverse the process for items 7–12.

| a speck of | a piece of | a grain of | a bolt of / a flash of | a branch of |
| an article of | a clap of | a game of | a current of | a herd of |

Student A's statements

1. An individual particle of a cereal grown in warm and wet areas is called . . .

2. A collection of bovine mammals is called . . .

3. A continuing flow of electrons is termed . . .

4. A small piece of a very fine, sometimes powdery material is termed . . .

5. A particular staging of an athletic competition played on an outdoor field and using a round ball is called . . .

6. A subcategory of that science which deals with the study of planets, stars, and galaxies is called . . .

Student A's completions

g. thunder

h. clothing

i. sand

j. lightning

k. furniture

l. advice

Dictation

Now listen to the sentences. On a separate sheet of paper, write each sentence in full.

8 ESSAY

Write an essay of two or three paragraphs about the best or worst meal experience you have ever had. Your essay can be serious or funny. Describe the kind of meal it was and what was good or bad about it.

❾ PICTURE DISCUSSION

Working with a partner, look carefully at this photograph for a few minutes. Talk to your partner about all the foods you see. Then close your books and together try to remember as many details as possible. Compare your findings with those of other students.

INFORMATION GAP FOR STUDENT B

Listen as Student A reads each statement (1–6). Read aloud the best completion for each statement including a phrase from the box below. Then read statements 7–12. Student A will read the best completion for each statement.

a speck of	a piece of	a grain of	a bolt of / a flash of	a branch of
an article of	a clap of	a game of	a current of	a herd of

Student B's completions

a. soccer

b. astronomy

c. rice

d. cattle

e. electricity

f. dust

Student B's statements

7. A statement of recommended behavior is . . .

8. An individual particle of a material produced by the disintegration of stone and rocks is called . . .

9. A single discharge of electrical current between clouds or between clouds and the earth is . . .

10. A single movable structure on which one sits or sleeps is called . . .

11. An item worn to cover the body is called . . .

12. An instance of loud sound usually accompanying lightning is . . .

DEFINITE AND INDEFINITE ARTICLES

GRAMMAR **IN CONTEXT**

QUESTIONS TO CONSIDER

1. What is an example of an environmental problem that you consider serious?

2. Do you think people exaggerate the seriousness of hazards to the environment?

3. How can serious environmental problems be remedied?

Read the story and think about the environmental issues raised.

Once Upon a Time . . .

ONCE UPON A TIME there was a green and beautiful planet. It was the third planet out from a yellowish sun in a stellar system in a relatively remote part of the galaxy. Members of the Galactic Council knew that the planet was between 4 and 5 billion years old, but no one was sure exactly how long life had existed there.

The Galactic Council had been watching Green, as they called it, for millennia. It was a responsibility of the Council to observe and monitor all planets that harbored life in an effort to predict which ones might destroy themselves. Thus the Council could intervene if it had to. Each planet had its own watcher, and Planet Green's was Ambassador Gorkon. His job was to visit Green and investigate thoroughly. On this occasion Gorkon was making his report to Mr. Xau, the president of the Galactic Council.

President Xau said, "Well, Gorkon, you're late getting back. There must have been something serious happening to keep you on Green for so long."

Gorkon responded, "Yes, sir. I had to stay longer to be absolutely sure of my calculations. Affairs are not going well there. I'm afraid that if Green doesn't change its ways immediately, the planet won't be able to support life, and life won't endure there. Green is now on a destructive path. There used to be clean air and water, but now there's pollution everywhere. The acid rain that's caused by the pollution in the atmosphere has killed plants and some animals. In some large cities you can hardly see the sky, and the land is full of garbage and toxic waste dumps. They're cutting down beautiful rain forests in the southern hemisphere. They've been releasing some very dangerous chemicals—fluorocarbons, we would call them—into the atmosphere, and a hole in the ozone layer has developed over the southern polar cap. You're aware how dangerous ultraviolet radiation can be. If something isn't done, the amount of radiation in the atmosphere will be very dangerous and even lethal within twenty or thirty years. It could happen even sooner."

The president looked sad and asked, "Is that the only serious problem?"

Gorkon responded, "Unfortunately not. Several individual nations on Green have developed the bomb and other deadly weapons. So far they've avoided using the weapons against each other, and right now there's a sort of uneasy peace, but there's no guarantee it's going to last. The saddest thing that's happening on Green, though, is the extinction of species. Some have already died off entirely, and many more species are endangered—like wolves and tigers. Environmentalists are making efforts to save the whale and the panda, but it's mostly a case of too little too late. You know what happens to a planet when its species start to die off."

"Yes, of course," said the president. "We've got to stop that. Well, shall I call the Council into executive session?"

"Yes, Mr. President," said Gorkon. "Right away. I'm afraid we're going to have to interfere. If we don't, Green may not last much longer. We wouldn't want to see them suffer the same fate as Earth did."

UNDERSTANDING MEANING FROM CONTEXT

Read each sentence and study the italicized word or phrase. Then answer the vocabulary questions.

1. It was a responsibility of the Council to observe and monitor all planets that *harbored* life in an effort to predict which ones might destroy themselves.

   What verb in the fourth paragraph has the same general meaning as

   harbored? _____

2. I'm afraid that if Green doesn't change its ways immediately, life won't be able to *endure* there.

   What word in the final paragraph has a similar meaning to *endure*?

   _____

3. If something isn't done, the amount of radiation in the atmosphere will be very dangerous and even *lethal* within twenty or thirty years.

   What verb in the same paragraph is closest in general meaning to

   lethal? _____

4. The saddest thing that's happening on Green, though, is the *extinction* of species.

   What verb in the same paragraph has the same general meaning as

   extinction? _____

5. I'm afraid we're going to have to *interfere*.

   What verb in the second paragraph has a similar meaning to *interfere*?

   _____

6. We wouldn't want to see them *suffer the same fate* as Earth did.

   What is the meaning of the phrase *suffer the same fate as*?

   _____

GRAMMAR **PRESENTATION**
ARTICLES

THE: DEFINITE ARTICLE

FOR COUNT NOUNS

Members of **the Galactic Council** knew that **the planet** was between 4 and 5 billion years old.

Several individual nations on Green have developed **the bomb**.

FOR NON-COUNT NOUNS

The acid **rain** that's caused by **the pollution** in the atmosphere has killed plants and some animals.

A / AN: INDEFINITE ARTICLE

FOR SINGULAR COUNT NOUNS

Green is now on **a** destructive **path**.

It was **a responsibility** of the Council to observe and monitor all planets that harbored life in **an effort** to predict which ones might destroy themselves.

ZERO ARTICLE

FOR PLURAL COUNT NOUNS

The land is full of garbage and toxic waste **dumps**.

They're cutting down beautiful rain **forests** in the southern hemisphere.

FOR NON-COUNT NOUNS

. . . but now there's **pollution** everywhere.

You're aware how dangerous ultraviolet **radiation** can be.

FOR PROPER NOUNS

The Galactic Council had been watching **Green**, as they called it, for millennia.

President Xau said, "Well, **Gorkon**, you're late getting back."

Planet Green's [watcher] was **Ambassador Gorkon**.

NOTES	EXAMPLES
1. A **noun** or **noun phrase** is **definite** when the speaker and listener both know which specific person, place, or thing is being talked about. Use the **definite article**, *the*, with singular and plural count and non-count nouns that are definite for you and your listener.	• They're cutting down beautiful rain forests in **the southern hemisphere**. • So far they've avoided using **the weapons** against each other.
2. A noun is also definite when it represents something that is **unique**.	• There is a hole in **the ozone layer**. (*There is only one ozone layer.*) • **The president** needs to do something. (*There is only one president.*)
3. An adjective can often make a noun represent something unique. Some examples of such adjectives are *right*, *wrong*, *first*, *only*, and the comparative and superlative forms of adjectives.	• Is that **the only** serious **problem**? • **The saddest thing** that's happening on Green is the extinction of species.
4. A noun or noun phrase can be made definite by context.	• In some large cities you can hardly see the sky, and **the land** is full of garbage and toxic waste dumps.
5. When a speaker or listener does not have a particular person, place, or thing in mind, the noun representing it is indefinite. Use the **indefinite article**, *a / an*, with indefinite singular count nouns.	• You know what happens to **a planet** when its species start to die off. (*any planet—no particular planet in mind*)

6. A noun is often indefinite the first time a speaker mentions it. It is usually definite after the first mention.	• Several individual nations on Green have developed the bomb and other lethal **weapons**. • So far they've avoided using **the weapons** against each other. (second mention of *weapons*)
7. Use **zero article** (= no article) with plural count nouns and non-specific non-count nouns.	• **Affairs** are not going well there. (*affairs in general*) • . . . now there's **pollution** everywhere.
8. Use zero article before the names of people or their titles.	• **Gorkon** was making his report to **Mr. Xau**. • **President Xau** said, "Well, **Gorkon**, you're late getting back." • Planet Green's [watcher] was **Ambassador Gorkon**.
9. A noun is **generic** when it represents all members of a class or category of persons, places, or things. Generic nouns can be singular or plural count nouns. Note these three ways of using count nouns generically. These patterns are approximately the same in meaning *when used to classify or define* something. Non-count nouns can also be used generically.	• Many more species are endangered—like **wolves** and **tigers**. (zero article + count noun) OR • Many more species are endangered—like **the wolf** and **the tiger**. (definite article + singular count noun) OR • Many more species are endangered—like **the wolves** and **the tigers**. (definite article + plural count noun) • You're aware how dangerous ultraviolet **radiation** can be. (zero article + non-count noun)

(continued on next page)

10. BE CAREFUL! In statements where you are <u>not</u> classifying or defining with a generic noun, you may <u>not</u> use *a / an* in front of the noun.

- Environmentalists are making efforts to save **the whale** and **the panda**.

  OR

- Environmentalists are making efforts to save **the whales** and **the pandas**.

  OR

- Environmentalists are making efforts to save **whales** and **pandas**.
  NOT ~~Environmentalists are making efforts to save a whale and a panda.~~

11. The definite article, *the*, is used with the names of some countries and many geographical features or regions.

See Appendices 7 and 8 on pages A-5 and A-6 for lists of these countries and regions.

- There are environmental problems in **the United States**.
- Camels are native to **the Middle East**.

FOCUSED PRACTICE

 DISCOVER THE GRAMMAR

Look again at some of the sentences from Once Upon a Time *on page 118. Circle the letter of the sentence that describes the meaning of each sentence from the text.*

1. It was the third planet out from a yellowish sun.

    a. We know how many suns there are.

    (b.) We don't know how many suns there are.

2. Members of the Galactic Council knew that the planet was between 4 and 5 billion years old.

    a. There was one Galactic Council.

    b. There was more than one Galactic Council.

3. It was a responsibility of the Council to observe and monitor all planets that harbored life.

    a. The Council had one responsibility.

    b. The Council had many responsibilities.

4. They're cutting down beautiful rain forests in the southern hemisphere.

    a. They're cutting down some of the rain forests in the southern hemisphere.

    b. They're cutting down all of the rain forests in the southern hemisphere.

5. A hole in the ozone layer has developed over the southern polar cap.

    a. There is one ozone layer.

    b. There is more than one ozone layer.

6. A hole in the ozone layer has developed over the southern polar cap.

    a. There is one polar cap.

    b. There is more than one polar cap.

7. Several individual nations on Green have developed the bomb.

    a. They have developed one particular type of bomb.

    b. They have developed bombs in general.

8. Environmentalists are making efforts to save the whale and the panda.

    a. They're trying to save a particular whale and a particular panda.

    b. They're trying to save all whales and all pandas.

9. You know what happens to a planet when its species start to die off.

    a. This sort of thing can happen to all planets.

    b. This sort of thing can happen to one planet only.

2 JULY BREAKS RECORD   Grammar Notes 1–7, 10

Part A

Read the article. Insert **a**, **an**, *or* **the** *where necessary. If no article is needed, leave a blank.*

USA TODAY, Sunday, August 2, 1998   Section 9

July Breaks Worldwide Temperature Record

⊕ Global Warming   BY TRACI WATSON

WASHINGTON—July was __the__ world's
1.
warmest month on record, and 1998 is on
track to become _____ planet's hottest
2.
known year, data reported Monday shows.

_____ temperatures in each of the
3.
past 15 months have broken global highs
for that month. But July was distinctive in
another way: Its average of 61.7 degrees
Fahrenheit was more than half a degree
higher than that of July 1997, the planet's
previous warmest month, according to the
National Climatic Data Center in Asheville,
North Carolina. Scientists say the increase,
0.6 degrees, is unusually large.

"It would be hard to ignore that something's going on—and that something is
global warming," Vice President Gore said
Monday in announcing the data.

Last year was the hottest year measured since reliable data collection began
in the late 1800s.

Gore has held _____ series of news
4.
conferences to focus _____ attention on
5.
_____ global warming, one of his pet
6.
causes. And the weather is working in his
favor.

_____ heat wave slammed North
7.
Texas with 29 consecutive days of triple-
digit temperatures in July and August.
_____ heat is blamed for 126 deaths in
8.
the state.

Heat in _____ Middle East has killed
9.
52 people and sickened hundreds, according to The Associated Press. Even Egyptians,
used to toiling in the desert, have taken to
working at night to avoid 100-degree daytime heat that has persisted for three
weeks. Temperatures have hit 122 degrees
in Kuwait, where pools have equipment to
chill the water.

Temperatures soared to 100 in Paris on
Monday, and even higher elsewhere in

France. Locals and _____ tourists splashed
                    10.
in fountains near the Eiffel Tower and the
Louvre.

Some scientists suspect that the new
records are due partly to the El Niño
weather phenomenon and partly to global
warming. But a few say the higher temperatures are part of the normal climate cycle.

Most scientists agree that global warming, the gradual rise in worldwide temperature over the past century, is caused by so-
called greenhouse gases. These gases are
emitted by _____ cars, factories, and
             11.
power plants. They rise into _____
                               12.
atmosphere and trap heat.

Some climate experts predict that

continued global warming could bring
more floods, more droughts, and higher sea
levels that would inundate coastal areas.

But scientists caution that it is impossible to link global warming to any given
abnormal weather event.

Gore has long been one of the most
prominent voices calling for action against
global warming. He was the primary supporter in the White House of an international treaty to slow global warming that
was written in December 1997 in Kyoto,
Japan.

That treaty has been greeted with skep-
ticism in the Senate, which must ratify it for
_____ United States to take part.
  13.

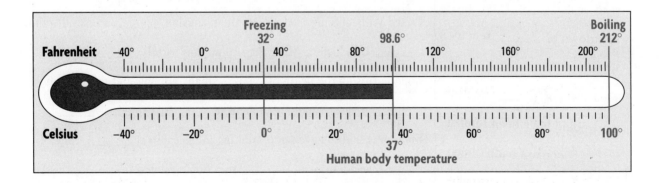

Part B

Work with a partner. Partner A, explain the reasons for your choices in items 2–7.
Partner B, explain the reasons for your choices in items 8–13.

3 DISASTERS

Here are some notable environmental disasters that have occurred in this century.
*Insert **a**, **an**, or **the**, where necessary. Leave a blank where no article is required.*

Disaster at Sea: Many Lives Lost

APRIL 16, 1912. ___The___ *Titanic,* _____

_{1.}   _{2.}

British steamer, sank in _____ North

_{3.}

Atlantic last night after hitting _____

_{4.}

iceberg, disproving its builders' claims that

it couldn't be sunk.

Partial Meltdown at Three Mile Island

On March 28, 1979, _____ worst

_{5.}

nuclear accident ever to occur in

_____ United States took place at

_{6.}

the Three Mile Island nuclear reactor

in Pennsylvania. _____ causes

_{7.}

were _____ equipment failure and

_{8.}

_____ human error, leading

_{9.}

to a loss of coolant in _____

_{10.}

reactor and _____ partial

_{11.}

meltdown of _____ reactor's

_{12.}

nuclear core. _____

_{13.}

meltdown of _____ nuclear

_{14.}

core could have been total. If

_____ coolant hadn't been

_{15.}

lost, _____ accident might

_{16.}

not have happened.

Chernobyl Damage Wider Than Previously Reported

DETAILS ARE FINALLY EMERGING. On April 26, 1986,

_____ fires and explosions following _____

_{17.}   _{18.}

unauthorized experiment caused _____ worst accident

_{19.}

in _____ history of nuclear

_{20.}

power at the nuclear power plant in Chernobyl, Ukraine.

At least thirty-one people were killed in _____ disaster

_{21.}

itself, and _____ radioactive material

_{22.}

was released into the atmosphere. Approximately 135,000

people were evacuated from _____ vicinity. Scientists

_{23.}

warned of _____

_{24.}

MASSIVE OIL SPILL IN ALASKA

MARCH 24, 1989. _____ oil tanker *Exxon Valdez* struck Bligh Reef in

_{26.}

Prince William Sound, Alaska, tonight, causing _____ worst oil spill in

_{27.}

_____ U.S. history. More than 10 million barrels of _____ oil were

_{28.}   _{29.}

spilled, causing the death of _____ many animals and resulting in

_{30.}

_____ great environmental damage. _____ captain of _____

_{31.}   _{32.}   _{33.}

Valdez was said to have been drinking in his cabin at _____ time of

_{34.}

_____ accident, with _____ ship being piloted by _____ first

_{35.}   _{36.}   _{37.}

mate, who was inexperienced. Exxon agreed to pay for _____ cost of

_{38.}

cleaning up _____ spill. It was determined that _____ captain, rather

_{39.}   _{40.}

than _____ first mate, should have been piloting _____ vessel.

_{41.}   _{42.}

Source: Some information taken from *The World Almanac and Book of Facts 1999* (Mahwah, NJ: Primedia Reference, 1998), pp. 228, 236.

 **EDITING**

Read the following composition about genetic engineering and the environment.
It contains twelve errors in the use of articles. Find and correct the errors. Some
of the errors are made more than once.

Genetic Engineering and the Environment

People say we are now able to perform genetic engineering. I am
against this for several reasons. First, it is dangerous to tamper with
~~the~~ nature because we don't know what will happen. We could upset
the balance of the nature. For example, people are against the
mosquito because it carries a malaria. Suppose we change the DNA of
the mosquito so that it will die off. That will stop a malaria, but it will
upset the balance of the nature because certain other species depend
on the mosquito. If we destroy it, these other species won't be able to
survive. This will have serious effect on environment.

Second, genetic engineering will take away people's control over their
own lives. Suppose scientists develop the capability to isolate gene for
violent behavior and they eliminate this gene from future generations.
This may eliminate violence, but I believe that behavior is matter of
choice, and this type of genetic engineering will eliminate choice. It will
make people behave as someone else has determined, not as they have
determined, and it will take away an individual responsibility.

Third, genetic engineering will remove chance from our lives. Part
of what makes the life interesting is unpredictability. We never know
exactly how someone, or something, is going to turn out. It's fun to
see what happens. As far as I am concerned, we should leave genetic
engineering to Creator.

COMMUNICATION PRACTICE

5 LISTENING

Read the statements. Then listen to the conversation between a husband and a wife.

1. **a.** The Indian tribe wants to kill all whales.
   (b.) The Indian tribe wants to kill some whales.

2. **a.** The standoff is between all environmentalists and all Indians.
   b. The standoff is between some environmentalists and some Indians.

3. **a.** The newspaper article supports the environmental point of view in general.
   b. The newspaper article supports a particular environmental point of view.

4. **a.** The husband supports all Indians.
   b. The husband supports a particular group of Indians.

5. **a.** The husband thinks the Indians should be able to kill all whales.
   b. The husband thinks the Indians should be able to kill some whales.

6. **a.** The wife believes in saving some whales.
   b. The wife believes in saving all whales.

7. **a.** The wife thinks it's cruel to hunt all whales.
   b. The wife thinks it's cruel to hunt some whales.

8. **a.** Some cattle are domestic animals.
   b. All cattle are domestic animals.

9. **a.** The wife thinks all whales are intelligent.
   b. The wife thinks some whales are intelligent.

10. **a.** The husband thinks we should consider the viewpoint of all Indians.
    b. The husband thinks we should consider the viewpoint of a particular group of Indians.

Now listen again. Then circle the letter of the sentence that correctly conveys the information in the conversation.

6 INFORMATION GAP: YOUR ENVIRONMENTAL QUOTIENT

Work with a partner to find out your Environmental Quotient (EQ). How much do you know about the environment and the world of nature? Student B, turn to page 134 and follow the instructions there. Student A, read the five sentence beginnings below. Student B will read aloud the best completion for each statement. Then reverse the process. Where necessary, circle the choice that uses the correct article or zero article.

Student A's prompts

1. (The environment / Environment) is . . .

2. A primate is . . .

3. A cetacean is . . .

4. A marsupial is . . .

5. (The ozone layer / An ozone layer) is . . .

Student A's completions

Student A, read the best completion for each sentence aloud. Circle the correct article or zero article where necessary.

f. a tailless Australian marsupial living in and feeding on (a eucalyptus tree / the eucalyptus tree).

g. compounds of (fluorine and carbon / the fluorine and carbon) used industrially to lubricate and refrigerate.

h. (a member / the member) of an order of animals that bear their young alive.

i. a form of oxygen with (the distinctive odor / a distinctive odor).

j. the upper portion of (atmosphere / the atmosphere) above 11 kilometers.

Now determine your EQ and your partner's EQ.

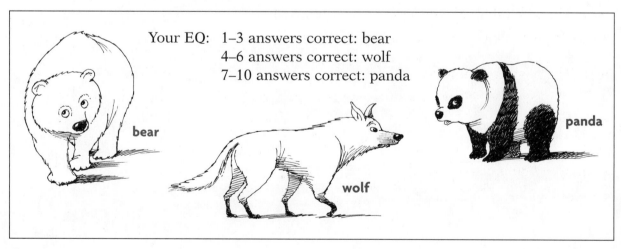

Your EQ: 1–3 answers correct: bear
4–6 answers correct: wolf
7–10 answers correct: panda

bear

wolf

panda

7 ESSAY

Choose an environmental issue that you consider important, and write an essay of two or three paragraphs on it. Say why you think the issue is important and what should be done about it. Choose one of these issues or your own idea.

Possible Issues

- saving endangered animals

- improving air quality

- improving water quality

- getting rid of nuclear weapons

- disposing of garbage

- ensuring the supply of clean water

8 PICTURE DISCUSSION

Examine the chart of geologic time on page 133. With a partner, choose one period of time that interests you and research that period on the Internet (if you have access to a computer, or in printed resource materials if you don't). One informative website you may wish to visit is www.ucmp.berkeley.edu. You can specify a particular period that you want information about:

www.ucmp.berkeley.edu./paleozoic

www.ucmp.berkeley.edu./mesozoic

www.ucmp.berkeley.edu./cenozoic

Then prepare a short lecture about the period you chose (with illustrations, if possible) to present to the class.

Outline of the earth's history

This geological time scale outlines the development of the earth and of life on the earth. The earth's earliest history appears at the bottom of the chart, and its most recent history is at the top.

Era	Period	Period or epoch and its length	Beginning (years ago)	Development of life on the earth	
Cenozoic Era	Quaternary Period	Holocene Epoch $11\frac{1}{2}$ thousand years	$11\frac{1}{2}$ thousand	Human beings hunted and tamed animals; developed agriculture; learned to use metals, coal, oil, gas, and other resources; and put the power of wind and rivers to work.	Cultivated plants
		Pleistocene Epoch 2 million years	2 million	Modern human beings developed. Mammoths, woolly rhinos, and other animals flourished but died out near the end of the epoch.	Human beings
	Tertiary Period	Pliocene Epoch 3 million years	5 million	Sea life became much like today's. Birds and many mammals became like modern kinds and spread around the world. Humanlike creatures appeared.	Horses
		Miocene Epoch 19 million years	24 million	Apes appeared in Asia and Africa. Other animals included bats, monkeys, and whales, and primitive bears and raccoons. Flowering plants and trees resembled modern kinds.	Apes
		Oligocene Epoch 10 million years	34 million	Primitive apes appeared. Camels, cats, dogs, elephants, horses, rhinos, and rodents developed. Huge rhinoceroslike animals disappeared near the end of the epoch.	Early horses
		Eocene Epoch 21 million years	55 million	Birds, amphibians, small reptiles, and fish were plentiful. Primitive bats, camels, cats, horses, monkeys, rhinoceroses, and whales appeared.	Grasses
		Paleocene Epoch 10 million years	65 million	Flowering plants became plentiful. Invertebrates, fish, amphibians, reptiles, and mammals were common.	Small mammals
Mesozoic Era		Cretaceous Period 80 million years	145 million	Flowering plants appeared. Invertebrates and amphibians were plentiful. Many fish resembled modern kinds. Dinosaurs with horns and armor became common. Dinosaurs died out.	Flowering plants
		Jurassic Period 68 million years	213 million	Cone-bearing trees were plentiful. Sea life included shelled squid. Dinosaurs reached their largest size. The first birds appeared. Mammals were small and primitive.	Birds
		Triassic Period 35 million years	248 million	Cone-bearing trees were plentiful, as were fish and insects. The first turtles, crocodiles, and dinosaurs appeared, as did the first mammals.	Dinosaurs
Paleozoic Era		Permian Period 38 million years	286 million	The first seed plants—cone-bearing trees—appeared. Fish, amphibians, and reptiles were plentiful.	Seed plants
	Carboniferous Period	Pennsylvanian Period 39 million years	325 million	Scale trees, ferns, and giant scouring rushes were abundant. Fish and amphibians were plentiful. The first reptiles appeared. Giant insects lived in forests where coal later formed.	Reptiles
		Mississippian Period 35 million years	360 million	Trilobites had nearly died out. Crustaceans, fish, and amphibians were plentiful. Many coral reefs were formed.	Amphibians
		Devonian Period 50 million years	410 million	The first forests grew in swamps. Many kinds of fish, including sharks, armored fish, and lungfish, swam in the sea and in fresh waters. The first amphibians and insects appeared.	Fish
		Silurian Period 30 million years	440 million	Spore-bearing land plants appeared. Trilobites and mollusks were common. Coral reefs formed.	Corals
		Ordovician Period 65 million years	505 million	Trilobites, corals, and mollusks were common. Tiny animals called graptolites lived in branching *colonies* (groups).	Graptolites
		Cambrian Period 39 million years	544 million	Fossils were plentiful for the first time. Shelled animals called trilobites, and some mollusks, were common in the sea. Jawless fish appeared.	Trilobites
	Precambrian Time Almost 4 billion years (?)		$4\frac{1}{2}$ billion (?)	Coral, jellyfish, and worms lived in the sea about 1,100 million years ago. Bacteria lived as long ago as $3\frac{1}{2}$ billion years. Before that, no living things are known.	Bacteria

Source: From *THE WORLD BOOK ENCYCLOPEDIA*, © 2000, World Book, Inc. By permission of the publisher.

INFORMATION GAP FOR STUDENT B

Student B, read aloud the best completion for each sentence that Student A reads. Circle the correct article or zero article where necessary. Then read the sentence beginnings below.

Student B's completions

a. (the member / a member) of an order of mammals including dolphins, porpoises, and whales.

b. the part of the atmosphere that normally has high ozone content and that blocks ultraviolet radiation from entering the lower atmosphere.

c. the collection of physical, biological, and climatological surroundings in which earth organisms live.

d. (member / a member) of a higher order of mammals which includes apes and human beings.

e. a member of a group of lower mammals having (a pouch / the pouch) on the abdomen.

Student B's prompts

Student B, read the next five prompts aloud.

6. Fluorocarbons are . . .

7. (A stratosphere / The stratosphere) is . . .

8. Ozone is . . .

9. A koala is . . .

10. A mammal is . . .

MODIFICATION OF NOUNS

GRAMMAR **IN CONTEXT**

QUESTIONS TO CONSIDER

1. What is the difference between hoping for something to happen and expecting it to happen? Discuss this with your classmates.

2. In your experience, does what you expect to happen usually happen? Give an example.

3. How can expectations be a negative force? How can they be a positive force?

Read an article about expectations from Pocket Digest.

The Expectation Syndrome

I Hope for It, but I Don't Expect It

by JESSICA TAYLOR

PICTURE THE SCENE: It's the seventeenth Winter Olympics in Lillehammer, Norway. Dan Jansen, a famous American speed skater, is about to compete in the 500-meter race. This is the fourth Olympics he has participated in. In the first three races, he failed to win any medals. This will be his last Olympic competition, so the pressure is on. About halfway through the 500, one of Dan's skates catches a rough spot on the ice, and this slows him down. He wins no medal at all. Three days later Dan competes in the 1000-meter race. Everyone knows this is his last chance for a medal. Some observers have already written him off. Dan starts off well. As he is coming around a turn, though, his skate again hits a rough spot on the ice, and he almost falls. Will the outcome be the same? He says to himself that he's just going to keep skating and let what happens happen. In effect, he "casts his fate to the winds" and ceases to worry about the outcome. The result? Dan sets a world record and wins the gold medal. ▶

speed skater Dan Jansen

Picture another situation: Your two best film-buff friends have seen the reissued *Star Wars*, but you haven't seen it yet. They rave about its superb color photography and awesome special effects. They applaud its basically serious and even profound treatment of the age-old conflict between good and evil. They say it's the best American movie of the last half of the century. When you go to see it, though, you're disappointed. You don't find it as excellent as everyone has been saying. In fact, you consider it just another action-adventure flick.

These situations illustrate what we might call "the expectation syndrome," a condition in which events do not turn out as we feel they ought to. Children often do not meet their parents' career expectations of them. Athletes do not always win what people expect them to win. Great literature doesn't always seem as good as it should. I asked psychiatrist Robert Stevens whether there is an actual scientific basis for the negativity of expectations or whether this is merely a philosophical question, an unpleasant, frustrating irony of the human condition.

STEVENS: Well, what we're really talking about here, I think, is the immense power of the mind. For example, there is a documented medical phenomenon called "focal dystonia," which is an abnormal muscle function caused by extreme concentration. Somehow, when

> In effect, they're **letting their expectations control them.**

athletes are concentrating too hard, they "short circuit" certain brain functions and miss the basket, don't hit the ball, or lose the race. In effect, they're letting their expectations control them. So there's a physiological counterpart to what the mind manifests.

POCKET DIGEST: Have you ever had any experience with this phenomenon in your personal, everyday life?

STEVENS: Yes, I think I have. We're learning more about the human brain all the time. It seems that the mind has immense power for both positive and negative things. Let me give you an example from skiing. There are days when, as a cautious, high-intermediate skier, I stand at the top of a steep, icy slope, plotting my every move down the course, fearing that I'll fall. Sure enough, I do fall. Other days I feel different. My expectations are miles away. I ski well and don't fall. When we focus excessively on goals, our expectations tend to take over and our mind places us outside the process. On the other hand, when we concentrate on the process instead of the goal, we're often much more successful. Have you heard the phrase "trying too hard"?

POCKET DIGEST: Very interesting. What would be your recommendation about expectations, then?

STEVENS: Well, all I've been able to come up with so far is that it's better to hope for things than to expect them.

UNDERSTANDING MEANING FROM CONTEXT

Circle the letter of the choice closest in meaning to each italicized word or phrase from the reading.

1. Your two best *film-buff* friends have seen the reissued "Star Wars."

   a. film producer   **b.** film lover   **c.** film star

2. They *rave about* its superb color photography and awesome special effects.

   a. report about   **b.** are crazy about   **c.** talk enthusiastically about

3. In effect, he *"casts his fate to the winds"* and ceases to worry about the outcome.

   a. trusts that the winds will be favorable   **b.** waits for favorable winds   **c.** just takes his chances

4. So there's a *physiological* counterpart to what the mind manifests.

   a. emotional   **b.** physical   **c.** psychological

5. So there's a physiological counterpart to what the mind *manifests*.

   a. discloses   **b.** conceals   **c.** maintains

GRAMMAR **PRESENTATION**
MODIFICATION OF NOUNS

ADJECTIVE MODIFIERS		
	MODIFIER(S)	**HEAD NOUN**
Dan Jansen is	a **famous American** speed	skater.
He won in in	a **gold*** the **1000**-meter the **seventeenth** Winter	medal race Olympics.

NOUN MODIFIERS		
	MODIFIER(S)	**HEAD NOUN**
Dan Jansen is	a famous American **speed**	skater.
He won in in	a **gold*** the 1000-**meter** the seventeenth **Winter**	medal race Olympics.

ADJECTIVE AND NOUN MODIFIERS OF THE SAME HEAD NOUN		
	MODIFIER(S)	**HEAD NOUN**
Your	**two best film-buff**	friends have seen the reissued *Star Wars*.
They rave about its and	**superb color** **awesome special**	photography effects.

*The word *gold* can be considered a noun or an adjective, depending on whether it refers to the material or the color.

NOTES	**EXAMPLES**

1. Nouns can be modified both by adjectives and by other nouns. **Adjective and noun modifiers** usually come before the noun they modify. The noun that is modified is called the **head noun**.	• Dan Jansen, a **famous American**
	    adjective modifier
	  noun modifier
	  speed skater, is . . .

2. When there is more than one modifier, the modifiers generally occur in a fixed order. The following list shows the order that adjectives most often follow*. This order is not invariable and can be affected or changed by the emphasis a speaker wishes to give to a particular adjective. It is unusual for head nouns to have more than three modifiers.

POSITION	TYPE OF MODIFIER	
1	determiners	• a, an, the, this, that, these, those, my, your, Allison's
2	possessive amplifier	• own
3	sequence words	• first, second, tenth, next, last
4	quantifiers	• one, two, few, little, much, many, some
5	opinions or qualities	• ugly, beautiful, dull, interesting, intelligent, wonderful, disgusted, interested
6	size, height, or length	• big, tall, long, short
7	age or temperature	• old, young, hot, cold
8	shapes	• square, round, oval
9	colors	• red, blue, pink, purple
10	nationalities, social classes, or origins	• American, Brazilian, Japanese, eastern, upper-class, lower-middle-class, scientific, historic, mythical
11	materials	• wood, cotton, denim, silk, glass, stone

*Although many authors have developed lists explaining the order of modifiers, the author wishes to acknowledge particularly Thomas Lee Crowell, *Index to Modern English* (New York: McGraw-Hill, 1964).

3. The examples in the right-hand column illustrate modifier order as listed in Note 2. When a noun has two or more modifiers from the same category, their order is difficult to prescribe.

determiner	sequence word	quantifier	head noun
• **the**	**first**	**three**	competitions

determiner	opinion or quality	age	
• **that**	**interesting**	**old**	lady

determiner	size	shape	color	
• **a**	**big**	**round**	**red**	ball

determiner	opinion or quality	age	origin	
• **that**	**beautiful**	**old**	**Russian**	vase

determiner	opinion or quality	age	material	
• **those**	**fragile**	**old**	**porcelain**	vases

4. Noun modifiers always come before the nouns they modify.

- A **house guest** is a guest who is visiting and staying in someone's house.
- A **guest house** is a small house for guests to stay in.

When there are both adjective and noun modifiers, the noun modifiers come closest to the head noun.

- Jansen is a **famous American speed** skater.

5. Compound modifiers are constructed of more than one word. Here are two common kinds of compound modifiers.

a. number + noun

- She has a **ten-year-old** daughter.
  (She has a daughter who is ten years old.)

b. noun + past participle

- It's a **crime-related** problem.
  (It's a problem related to crime.)

When compound modifiers precede a noun, they are always hyphenated.

▶ **BE CAREFUL!** Note how the plural word in this phrase becomes singular when it comes before the noun.

- It's a race of 500 **meters**.
- It's a 500-**meter** race.
  NOT ~~It's a 500-meters race.~~

6. When a noun has **two or more modifiers**, commas separate only those of equal importance. To decide whether modifiers are of equal importance, place *and* between them. If the meaning of the new phrase is logical, the adjectives are equally important and need to be separated by a comma. If the meaning with *and* is not logical, the adjectives are not equally important and are not separated by a comma.

- a **cautious, high-intermediate** skier
  (A *cautious and high-intermediate skier* sounds logical.)
- an **abnormal muscle** function
  (An *abnormal and muscle function* does not sound logical.)

7. **BE CAREFUL!** In written English, it is generally recommended to have no more than two nouns together. Using too many nouns together can be confusing. Look at the examples. Is Jerry a student who won an award for painting portraits? Is Jerry a painter who won an award for painting students? Is the award given by the students?

To avoid confusing sentences like this, break up the string of nouns with prepositional phrases or rearrange the modifiers in some other way.

There is no similar problem with adjective modifiers.

- Jerry Jones won the **student portrait painter** award.

- Jerry Jones won the award for painting portraits of students.

  OR

- Student Jerry Jones won the award for painting portraits.

- The clever little brown-and-white fox terrier impressed us all.
  (All the adjectives clearly modify *fox terrier*.)

FOCUSED PRACTICE

1 DISCOVER THE GRAMMAR

*Examine the following sentences from the article that opens this unit or related to the article. Circle all head nouns that have noun or adjective modifiers. Underline adjective modifiers once and noun modifiers twice. Underline only those modifiers that come before the noun. Do not underline determiners in this exercise (**a, an, the, this, that, my, your,** etc.).*

1. It's the <u>seventeenth</u> <u><u>Winter</u></u> (Olympics) Lillehammer, Norway.

2. Your two best film-buff friends have seen the reissued *Star Wars*.

3. They rave about its superb color photography and awesome special effects.

4. They applaud its basically serious and even profound treatment of the age-old conflict between good and evil.

5. Children often do not meet their parents' career expectations of them.

6. I asked Robert Stevens whether there is an actual scientific basis for the negativity of expectations.

7. There is a documented medical phenomenon called "focal dystonia," which is an abnormal muscle function caused by extreme concentration.

8. Can we generalize this phenomenon beyond the sports arena into common, everyday occurrences?

9. I stand at the top of a steep, icy slope, plotting my every move down the course.

10. This skiing example illustrates the basic problem of expectations.

11. Right now we're really in the elementary stages of biological and psychiatric brain research.

2 READING ALOUD Grammar Notes 5, 6

Pam and Alan Murray have taken their son Joshua to Charles Tanaka, a reading specialist, because Joshua cannot read aloud in class. Complete the sentences in their conversation with compound modifiers, using the phrases in parentheses to create a hyphenated phrase.

DR. TANAKA: Joshua, tell me about your problems with reading.

JOSHUA: Well, I get frustrated in my reading class. It's only

_____ a fifty-minute period _____, but to me it seems like a year. This
1. (a period that lasts fifty minutes)

semester our teacher gives us oral reading assignments every day. She used to call on me to read aloud and I would freeze up, even if it was only

_____. Now she doesn't call on me anymore.
2. (an assignment that is one paragraph long)

DR. TANAKA: But you don't have any problem with silent reading?

JOSHUA: Nope. I can read _____ in a day or two. I love to
3. (a book that is 300 pages long)

read to myself.

PAM: And his reading comprehension is excellent!

DR. TANAKA: Uh-huh. Pam and Alan, how long has this been going on?

ALAN: Since Josh started the first grade—he's twelve now, so it's been

_____ for him and for us.
4. (an ordeal that has lasted six years)

DR. TANAKA: Any idea how this started?

PAM: Well, I definitely think it's _____. Joshua lisped
5. (a problem related to stress)

when he started school. He pronounced all his "s" sounds as "th" sounds.

That might have had something to do with it.

JOSHUA: Yeah! The other kids would laugh at me when I tried to read aloud and get

the "s" sounds right. It just got worse and worse until I couldn't read

anything out loud.

DR. TANAKA: Uh-huh. There is another possibility. Maybe this is just

_____. You might need glasses. Let's test your
6. (a problem related to eyesight)

vision. Look at that eye chart on the wall and say the letters on the fifth line.

JOSHUA: [reads] X-Z-Q-A-M-W.

DR. TANAKA: OK. Now the seventh line.

JOSHUA: [reads] P-S-R-B-N-F.

DR. TANAKA: Hmm. OK, now the bottom two lines. Look carefully. They make a sentence.

JOSHUA: [reads] "Night was falling in Dodge City. The gunslinger walked down the

street wearing _____."
7. (a hat that holds ten gallons)

DR. TANAKA: Very good! I think I understand. It sounds like you have what we call

_____. You're anxious about being asked to
8. (anxiety induced by performance)

perform, and you expect to read poorly aloud, so you do. But you just

(continued on next page)

showed me you can read fine out loud when you're not thinking about it. I

distracted you when I told you I wanted to test your eyes.

JOSHUA: Wow! No kidding?

DR. TANAKA: That's right. It's not going to be that hard to help you, either. I've got

_____ that should have you reading perfectly—if
9. (a program that takes two months)

you're game to try it. What do you think?

JOSHUA: I sure am. When can we start?

3 **PARTY EXPECTATIONS**   Grammar Notes 2, 3, 5, 6

*Bill and Nancy, a young married couple, are going to attend a party at the home
of Nancy's new boss. They are trying to dress for the occasion and aren't sure
what is expected, and Nancy is very worried about making a good impression.
Unscramble the sentences in their conversation.*

BILL: This is _____a formal office party_____, isn't it? What if I wear
                         1. (party / office / formal / a)

_____?
2. (tie / my / silk / new)

NANCY: That's fine, but don't wear _____ with it.
                                    3. (shirt / purple / ugly / that / denim)

People will think you don't have _____.
                                4. (clothes / any / suitable / dress-up)

BILL: So what? Why should I pretend I like to dress up when I don't?

NANCY: Because there are going to be _____, and I have
                                       5. (people / business / a lot of / important / there)

to make _____. It's my job, remember? I don't
        6. (impression / a / intelligent / , / good)

want people to think I have _____ for a
                            7. (dresser / unstylish / a /, / sloppy)

husband, which of course you're not. Humor me just this once, OK, Sweetie?

Hmm . . . I wonder if I should wear _____ or
                                   8. (round / my / earrings / sapphire / blue)

_____.
9. (green / oval / ones / emerald / the)

[Later, at the party]

NANCY: Hi, Paul. This is Bill, my husband.

PAUL: Welcome. Bill, I'm glad to know you. You two are

_____ to arrive. Help yourselves to snacks.
10. (guests / two / first / our)

There are _____. Please make

       11. (sandwiches / excellent / some / tomato and fresh mozzarella cheese)

yourselves at home. You know, Nancy, I'm sorry I didn't make it clear that this isn't

_____. You two really look great, but I hope you

       12. (elegant / party / dress-up / , / an)

won't feel out of place.

BILL: Thanks. By the way, Paul, I really like _____

       13. (beautiful / shirt / purple / denim / that)

you're wearing. Where did you get it?

---

4 EDITING

Every week or two, medical student Jennifer Yu writes in her computer diary.
Find and correct the thirteen modification errors here.

Dear Diary:

    It's 12:00 midnight, the end of ~~day a long~~ ^*a long day*^. My two first weeks of school medical are

over, and I'm exhausted but exhilarated! I'm so glad I decided to go to medical school. It was

definitely right the decision. I'm not completely sure yet, but I think I want to go into

psychiatry child clinical because I love working with children.

    Yesterday our child psychology class visited a hospital local where disturbed children

many go for treatment. I expected to see a lot of boys and girls acting out, but most of them

were pretty quiet and relaxed. They just looked like they needed some personal attention.

    Today in our class medical surgery we had a teacher student, male young a intern who

was filling in for professor our usual. It was really interesting to get viewpoint a student

on things.

    Only the thing I don't like about medical school is the tasteless cafeteria food! I'm going

to have to start taking lunch my own brownbag.

    Well, Diary, it's time for me to get some sleep. I hope this new computer program works

correctly. I'll write again soon.

COMMUNICATION PRACTICE

5 LISTENING

Joshua Murray is working on his reading program with Dr. Tanaka. Listen to their conversation.

Comprehension

Mark **True, False**, or **I don't know** for each sentence.

	True	False	I don't know
1. The first session will last only thirty minutes.	❏	❏	❏
2. Joshua likes his own voice.	❏	❏	❏
3. A growth spurt often occurs during adolescence.	❏	❏	❏
4. Joshua is thirteen years old.	❏	❏	❏
5. Joshua is afraid of reading orally.	❏	❏	❏
6. The phrase that Joshua will say to distract himself will not be difficult to remember.	❏	❏	❏
7. In the story Joshua reads, people feel lonely.	❏	❏	❏
8. The people in the story have three dogs.	❏	❏	❏
9. Large, warm, and furry dogs can keep you warm on a cold night.	❏	❏	❏

Optional Dictation

Now listen again and fill in the blanks. Place commas between adjectives when the speaker pauses, and be sure to hyphenate compound modifiers.

1. Our first meeting is only going to be _a thirty-minute session_____ .

2. We don't want to make this _____ .

3. I feel like _____ .

4. And I feel like I have _____ .

5. You're just going through _____ .

6. It happens to _____ .

7. The key to getting you over this _____

   is to distract you from thinking about how well you're doing.

8. Let's think of _____

   that you can keep in the back of your mind.

9. "It was _____."

10. "It promised to be one of _____."

11. What's _____?

12. It's a night that's so cold that you need _____

to sleep with to keep you warm.

6 TAPE DISCUSSION

1. How does Joshua feel at the end of the conversation?

2. How can developmental problems like Joshua's affect a person's life? Do you know any examples you can share with the class?

3. If you had a friend with a similar problem, what advice would you give?

7 INFORMATION GAP: BASEBALL

Work with a partner.

Student A: Add a noun or adjective modifier to each definition and read it to Student B. Student B has ten seconds to identify what you are referring to. If Student B doesn't understand, repeat your sentence. Then listen to Student B's definitions.

Student B, turn to page 151 and follow the instructions.

EXAMPLE:
STUDENT A: They can throw a baseball at _____high_____ speeds.
STUDENT B: Baseball pitchers.

Definitions

1. He hits the ball with a _____, smooth stick.

2. He wears a _____ mask to protect his face.

3. Mark McGwire holds the record for hitting the most of these in _____

season.

4. To hit a home run, a batter has to run around the _____ bases and land

on this.

5. This is _____ name for a baseball field.

(continued on next page)

Answers

  1. the batter

  2. the catcher

  3. home runs

  4. home plate

  5. the diamond

⓼ A POEM

 Read and think about the poem. Think particularly about how the poem deals with the question of expectations.

CASEY AT THE BAT

By Ernest L. Thayer

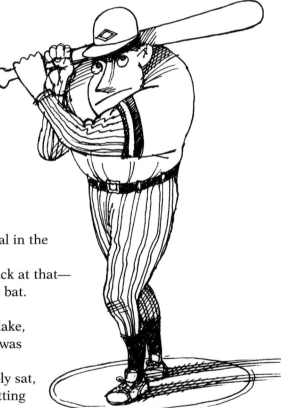

The outlook wasn't brilliant for the
  Mudville nine that day;
The score stood four to two, with but
  one inning more to play;
And so, when Cooney died at first, and
  Barrows did the same,
A sickly silence fell upon the patrons
  of the game.

A straggling few got up to go in deep despair.
The rest clung to that hope which springs eternal in the
  human breast;
They thought, if only Casey could but get a whack at that—
We'd put up even money now, with Casey at the bat.

But Flynn preceded Casey, as did also Jimmy Blake,
And the former was a pudding, while the latter was
  a fake;
So upon that stricken multitude grim melancholy sat,
For there seemed but little chance of Casey's getting
  to the bat.

But Flynn let drive a single, to the wonderment of all,
And Blake, the much despised, tore the cover off the ball;
And when the dust had lifted, and men saw what had occurred,
There was Jimmy safe at second and Flynn a-hugging third.

Then from the gladdened multitude went up a joyous yell;
It bounded from the mountain-top, and rattled in the dell;
It struck upon the hillside, and recoiled upon the flat,
For Casey, mighty Casey, was advancing to the bat.

There was ease in Casey's manner as he stepped into his place,
There was pride in Casey's bearing, and a smile on Casey's face.
And when, responding to the cheers, he lightly doffed his hat,
No stranger in the crowd could doubt 'twas Casey at the bat.

Ten thousand eyes were on him as he rubbed his hands with dirt,
Five thousand tongues applauded when he wiped them on his shirt;
Then while the writhing pitcher ground the ball into his hip,
Defiance gleamed in Casey's eye, a sneer curled Casey's lip.

And now the leather-covered sphere came hurtling through the air,
And Casey stood a-watching it in haughty grandeur there;
Close by the sturdy batsman the ball unheeded sped.
"That ain't my style," said Casey. "Strike one," the umpire said.

From the benches, black with people, there went up a muffled roar,
Like the beating of the storm-waves on a stern and distant shore;
"Kill him! Kill the umpire!" shouted someone in the stand.
And it's likely they'd have killed him had not Casey raised his hand.

With a smile of Christian charity great Casey's visage shone;
He stilled the rising tumult; he bade the game go on;
He signalled to the pitcher, and once more the spheroid flew,
But Casey still ignored it, and the umpire said "Strike two."

"Fraud!" cried the maddened thousands, and the echo answered, "Fraud!"
But a scornful look from Casey, and the audience was awed;
They saw his face grow stern and cold, they saw his muscles strain,
And they knew that Casey wouldn't let that ball go by again.

The sneer is gone from Casey's lip, his teeth are clenched in hate,
He pounds with cruel violence his bat upon the plate;
And now the pitcher holds the ball, and now he lets it go,
And now the air is shattered by the force of Casey's blow.

Oh, somewhere in this favored land the sun is shining bright,
The band is playing somewhere, and somewhere hearts are light;
And somewhere men are laughing, and somewhere children shout;
But there is no joy in Mudville—mighty Casey has struck out.

Source: Historybuff.com/library

Discussion

1. What does this poem show about expectations?

2. Why do you think Casey struck out?

9 ESSAY

Have you ever expected something to happen and it didn't? You didn't win the game, get an A, win the election, and so on. Write two or three paragraphs telling what happened. Try to explain why it happened. Did it have anything to do with the expectation syndrome?

10 PICTURE DISCUSSION

Select one student who likes to draw to go to the board. (This person does not look at the picture.) Then study the picture of the dining room and describe it in as much detail as you can to the student standing at the board. The student at the board draws the dining room, based on your descriptions. When that student has finished drawing, discuss what is out of place or unusual about what the student at the board has drawn.

INFORMATION GAP FOR STUDENT B

Listen to Student A read the definitions. You have ten seconds to guess the items your partner is referring to. If you do not understand, Student A will repeat the definition.

Add a noun or adjective modifier to each definition and read it to Student A. Student A has ten seconds to identify what you are referring to. If Student A doesn't understand, repeat your sentence.

EXAMPLE

STUDENT B: This _____keen-eyed_____ person stands behind the catcher and decides whether or not the ball thrown is a strike.

STUDENT A: The umpire.

Definitions

1. This is a _____-member group of players.

2. This happens when a batter takes a _____ swing and misses the ball.

3. This is the name for a one-_____ hit.

4. This is the name for a two-_____ hit.

5. This is the name for a three-_____ hit.

Answers

1. a baseball team

2. a strike

3. a single

4. a double

5. a triple

QUANTIFIERS

GRAMMAR **IN CONTEXT**

QUESTIONS TO CONSIDER

1. Do you pay for most things with cash or with credit cards?

2. What would be the advantages and disadvantages of living in a cashless society?

Read an article about money.

What's Happening to Ca$h?

A major event took place on January 1, 1999. The Euro made its debut in most of the countries of the European Union. What is the Euro? It's a single currency that, by the year 2002, will replace most of the individual European currencies—like the German mark, the French franc, and the Spanish peseta. The debut of the Euro seems destined to accelerate a trend that has been developing for many years now: the movement toward the cashless society.

Not all of the countries of the European Union are using the Euro. Britain, Sweden, and Denmark, for the time being at least, are maintaining their own currencies. Even so, the Euro will have a great many significant effects not only on European finance but also on that of the world in general. There won't be any Euro coins and bills for a

while, but people will be able to use either checks or debit and credit cards to make a lot of their purchases. The European phenomenon will accelerate the trend worldwide to use less cash and more "electronic" money. Is this positive or negative? Or is it just neutral, neither a good nor a bad thing?

Are there any advantages to cash? Yes, of course. Suppose, for example, that you are walking down a street and you remember that you need to buy some flowers. You see a flower vendor, and you suddenly decide that this is the time to buy a dozen roses. So what do you do? Write a check, or pull out your debit or credit card? At this writing, few flower vendors take checks, and even fewer take plastic. Most of them prefer cold, hard cash. If you've got a little money with you, you simply pull out a few bills, hand them to the vendor, and happily walk away with your flowers. Pretty easy, huh? It wouldn't be that easy without cash.

Or suppose you're at an athletic event—a soccer match, a basketball game, or a volleyball tournament. Suddenly you realize you're hungry. You walk out to the concession stand to buy a couple of hot dogs. How would that work in a cashless society? Can you imagine pulling out a credit or debit card to pay for a hot dog? So cash has its advantages.

Of course, cash has a good many disadvantages as well. For one thing, it's easy to be robbed. For another, cash is heavy. Carrying a lot of coins can make holes in your pockets. It's inconvenient to take a great deal of money with you to pay for large purchases. Imagine trying to carry enough cash to pay for a house, or a car—or even a sofa.

Now there are also a number of advantages to electronic money. Think about it. You're traveling in Europe. Anyone who did this in the past knows that it was a bit of a pain to have to learn a new money system every time you crossed a border. Now, however, Euro prices are standardized, and you don't have to worry about whether a certain amount of your money will bring a different rate each time it's changed into a different local currency. What if things were that way everywhere? Wouldn't it be simpler?

Then there's the matter of bill paying. Traditionally, most people in North America have paid their bills with checks. Recently, however, a trend has developed to have bills paid automatically. Japanese people have been doing this for years. In Japan, payment for such things as heat, electricity, and water is handled by automatic electronic deduction from a bank account. It's much easier than having to write several different checks to several different agencies. And since it's automatic, people don't have to worry about whether they've forgotten to pay their bill.

Of course, there are certain disadvantages to electronic money, too. Some people have little use for plastic cards, saying that using them encourages us to live beyond our means. Others say that using electronic money places too much control of our personal finances in the hands of strangers. Mistakes are easily made.

The jury is still out on whether the trend toward less and less use of cash is good or bad. What seems clear is that it's definitely on its way.

UNDERSTANDING MEANING FROM CONTEXT

Circle the letter of the choice closest in meaning to each italicized word or phrase from the reading.

1. The Euro *made its debut* in most of the countries of the European Union.

   a. had a significant effect   **b.** made its first appearance   **c.** was proposed

2. The debut of the Euro *seems destined to* accelerate a trend that has been developing for many years now.

   a. it's possible that it will   **b.** it's probable that it will   **c.** it's unfortunate that it will

3. You walk out to the *concession stand* to buy a couple of hot dogs.

   a. food and drink stand   **b.** vending machine   **c.** restaurant

4. Some people have little use for plastic cards, saying that using them encourages us to *live beyond our means*.

   a. spend more money than we have   **b.** spend money responsibly   **c.** spend very little

5. *The jury is still out on* whether the trend toward less and less use of cash is good or bad.

   a. There are court cases to decide   **b.** It's obvious   **c.** It's not yet clear

GRAMMAR **PRESENTATION**
Quantifiers of Nouns

QUANTIFIERS USED WITH SINGULAR COUNT NOUNS

It was a bit of a pain to have to learn a new money system **every** time you crossed a border.

. . . whether a certain amount of your money will bring a different rate **each** time it's changed into a different local currency . . .

You can use **either** currency in this country.

Or is it just neutral, **neither** a good nor a bad thing?

QUANTIFIERS USED WITH PLURAL COUNT NOUNS

. . . you simply pull out **a few** bills . . .

. . . **few** flower vendors take checks . . .

. . . and even **fewer** take plastic.

. . . a trend that has been developing for **many** years now . . .

. . . the Euro will have **a great many** significant effects . . .

Of course, cash has **a good many** disadvantages as well.

It's much easier than having to write **several** different checks to **several** different agencies.

Now there are **a number of** advantages to electronic money.

You walk out to the concession stand to buy **a couple of** hot dogs.

. . . you suddenly decide that this is the time to buy **a dozen** roses.

People will be able to use **either** checks or credit and debit cards to make some of their purchases.

Of course, there are **certain** disadvantages to electronic money, too.

QUANTIFIERS USED WITH NON-COUNT NOUNS

If you've got **a little** money with you . . .

Some people have **little** use for plastic cards . . .

The European phenomenon will accelerate the trend to use **less** cash and **more** electronic money.

It's inconvenient to take **a great deal of** money with you to pay for large purchases.

Others say that using electronic money places too **much** control of our personal finances in the hands of strangers.

. . . it was **a bit of** a pain to have to learn a new money system every time you crossed a border.

QUANTIFIERS USED WITH NON-COUNT NOUNS AND PLURAL COUNT NOUNS

NON-COUNT NOUNS

I've got **a lot of** (**lots of**) cash on me.

She has **no** money at all.

The European phenomenon will accelerate the trend worldwide to use **less** cash and **more** electronic money.

The children have already spent **most of** their allowance.

I need **some** financial advice.

I've got **plenty of** plastic but no cash.

None of the work is finished.

Did you save **any** money?

All of the cash has been spent.

Imagine trying to carry **enough** cash to pay for a house, or a car . . .

PLURAL COUNT NOUNS

Carrying **a lot of** (**lots of**) coins can make holes in your pockets.

I have **no** credit cards with me.

We made **more** purchases on this year's vacation than last year's.

The Euro made its debut in **most of** the countries of the European Union.

. . . you remember that you need to buy **some** flowers.

Plenty of us are credit card junkies.

None of the bills have been paid.

Do you take **any** credit cards?

Not **all** (**of**) the countries of the European Union are using the Euro.

I have **enough** financial problems to see a consultant.

NOTES

EXAMPLES

1. Quantifiers state precisely or suggest generally the amount or number of something. English has many expressions to quantify nouns and pronouns. These are comprised of phrases or single words that come before the noun or pronoun.

- You suddenly decide that this is the time to buy **a dozen** roses.

- Are there **any** advantages to cash?

2. Certain quantifiers are used with singular count nouns; others are used with plural count nouns; others are used with non-count nouns; and still others are used with count and non-count nouns.

a. *Each, either, every,* and *neither* are used with singular count nouns.

- It was a pain to learn a new money system **every** time you crossed a border.
- Or is it **neither** a good nor a bad thing?

b. *Both (of), a bunch (of), a couple (of), either of, neither of, a few (of), fewer (of), a great many (of), a good many (of), many (of), a number of,* and *several (of)* are used with plural count nouns.

- It's much easier than having to write **several** different checks to **several** different agencies.
- The Euro will have **a great many** significant effects.

c. *A bit of, a great deal of, less, little (of), a little (of),* and *much (of)* are used with non-count nouns.

- It was **a bit of** a pain to have to learn a new money system every time you crossed a border.

d. *All (of), any (of), enough (of), half (of), a lot of, lots of, most of, no, none, none of, some (of),* and *(ten) percent (of)* are used with non-count nouns and plural count nouns.

- Not **all (of)** the countries of the European Union are using the Euro.
- I spent **all (of)** my money.
- The Euro made its debut in **most of** the countries of the European Union.
- My son spent **all (of)** his allowance.

(continued on next page)

3. Many quantifiers appear in phrases with the preposition *of*. The *of* is used when the speaker or writer is specifying particular persons, places, things, or groups.

When speakers or writers make general statements, having no particular persons, places, or things in mind, they use quantifiers without *of*.

- **Most of** the countries of the European Union are using the Euro.
  (*The speaker has in mind a group of countries.*)

- **Most people** don't really understand finance.
  (*people in general—no specific group*)

4. In **spoken affirmative sentences**, native speakers usually prefer *a lot of* or *lots of* to *much* and *many*, which sound more formal. However, *much* and *many* are often used in negative sentences and in questions.

- Carrying **a lot of coins** can make holes in your pockets.
- Do you have **much cash** with you?
- Do you have **many** credit **cards**?

5. Note the characteristics of *some* and *any*. Use *some* with plural count nouns and non-count nouns in affirmative statements.

Use *any* with plural count nouns and non-count nouns in negative statements.

Use both *some* and *any* in questions. *Any* is generally preferred in negative questions.

- You need to buy **some flowers**.
- We need to take **some money** with us.

- There won't be **any** Euro **coins**.
- I don't have **any cash** on me.

- Are there **any** advantages to cash?
- Are there **some** advantages to cash?

6. Note that when *any* is used in affirmative statements it doesn't quantify. It refers to an unspecified person, place, or thing.

- **Any** of these currencies can be used in Europe.

7. Note the difference between *less* and *fewer* and between *amount* and *number*. *Less* and *amount* are used with non-count nouns, while *fewer* and *number* are used with count nouns.

- The European phenonmenon will accelerate the trend to use **less cash** and more electronic money.
- Even **fewer [vendors]** take plastic.
- . . . whether a certain **amount of** your **money** will bring a different rate each time it's changed . . .
- Now there are also **a number of** advantages to electronic money.

8. Note the difference between *a few* and *few*, *a little* and *little*.

- You simply pull out **a few** bills.
  (You pull out some bills.)
- **Few** vendors take checks.
  (Not many vendors take checks.)
- If you've got **a little** money with you . . .
  (If you've got some money with you . . .)
- Some people have **little** use for plastic cards.
  (Some people don't have much use for plastic cards.)

9. **BE CAREFUL!** The quantifiers *some of, any of, most of, half of, (ten) percent of,* and *none of* can be followed by a singular or a plural verb, depending on the noun before the verb.

- **Most of** the money **has** been spent.
- **Most of** the European Union countries **are** using the Euro.

FOCUSED PRACTICE

1 DISCOVER THE GRAMMAR

Look again at some of the sentences from What's Happening to Cash? *In each case, say whether or not the word in parentheses could be used to replace the italicized word or phrase without changing the meaning or creating an incorrect sentence. If not, explain why.*

1. Even so, the Euro will have *a great many* significant effects. (many)

2. There won't be *any* Euro coins and bills for a while. (some)

3. Are there *any* advantages to cash? (some)

4. You remember that you need to buy *some* flowers. (any)

5. At this writing, *few* flower vendors take checks . . . (a few)

6. . . . and even *fewer* take plastic. (less)

7. If you've got *a little* money with you . . . (little)

8. . . . you simply pull out *a few* bills. (few)

9. Of course, cash has *a good many* disadvantages as well. (a great many)

10. Carrying *a lot of* coins can make holes in your pockets. (many)

11. Some people have *little* use for plastic cards. (a little)

12. The jury is still out on whether the trend toward *less and less* use of cash is good or bad. (fewer and fewer)

2 SAVING FOR A TRIP   Grammar Notes 2–5, 7, 9

Married couple Ron and Ashley Lamont are trying to save money for a trip to Europe. They are examining their budget. Fill in the blanks in their conversation with expressions from the box. You will use each expression once.

some	the amount of	plenty of	most of
both of	~~a lot of~~	the number of	fewer
less	one of	both	much
neither one of	many	every	

ASHLEY: Honey, we're still spending _____a lot of_____ money on things we don't really

1.

need. After I pay the bills, we're going to have _____ cash left over

2.

than we did last month. And we were supposed to be saving for the trip to

Europe, remember? If we don't start saving more money, we won't be able to go.

RON: What have we bought that we don't need?

ASHLEY: That new exercise machine, for one thing. _____ us has used it more

          3.

than two or three times since we bought it. We could get a year's membership at

the athletic club for _____ money that it cost and still have money

          4.

left over.

RON: You mean _____ us could get a membership?

          5.

ASHLEY: No, _____ us could. That's what I'm saying. The machine cost $300,

          6.

and memberships are $100 each. Let's sell the thing and start going to the athletic

club.

RON: Hmm . . . maybe you're right. What else?

ASHLEY: Well, we're spending more than ten dollars a month extra on those premium

cable channels. We'd have _____ channels to choose from if we cut

          7.

back to the basic coverage, but we don't watch _____ TV anyway.

          8.

RON: Yeah, you're right. . . . And based on _____ times we've actually used

          9.

it, I'd say we could get rid of call waiting on the phone. Even though it hasn't

happened very _____ times, _____ my friends say they

          10.   **11.**

hate it when they call and then another call comes in while we're talking.

ASHLEY: Uh-huh. Let's cancel it, then. And one more suggestion. We should

_____ start taking a brownbag lunch to work instead of going out at

          12.

noon. If we did these four things, we'd have _____ money left over

          13.

_____ month that could go into our trip fund.

   14.

RON: Oh, no! Not my lunches with the boys! Lunchtime is when I get to see them.

ASHLEY: Invite the boys over to play _____ volleyball. Then think of Paris.

                      15.

3 **THE EURO**

Read the following article about the Euro. Then work with a partner. Together, complete the text with appropriate quantifiers. Discuss your selections.

TRAVEL GUIDE

TRAVELERS WILL BENEFIT FROM EURO

LONDON (AP)—Trying to keep track of expenses while traveling around Europe can feel like a never-ending math test, converting every price into dollars. Make a mistake, and you might get fleeced like a Shetland sheep.

The creation of the Euro, a common currency for _____eleven_____ European nations,
1.
will bring short-term headaches to travelers, but _____ long-term benefits.
2.
The headaches stem from the fact that _____ actual Euro notes or coins
3.
will be available until 2002, even though the Euro will officially exist in bank accounts beginning January 1.

You should be able to charge purchases on your credit card in Euros in _____
4.
places, especially tourist destinations, but _____ cash transactions will have
5.
to be made in local currencies.

Two Prices

During the three-year transition before the Euro fully takes over, travelers will see _____ goods with two prices, one
6.
in local currency and the equivalent in Euros.

More math mayhem? Perhaps not.

You'll still have to fork over francs to get what you want in France, but the Euro number can be useful for comparing prices across borders and for figuring out dollar equivalents.

Because the eleven currencies will have permanently fixed rates against the Euro, you no longer have to keep track of eleven exchange rates, just one: the dollar–Euro rate. No more dividing _____ price by
7.
1,600 in Italy and 5.6 in France.

What's more, the Euro's value is expected to be fairly close to the dollar's, meaning a lot _____ long division and a welcome
8.
relief for the mathematically challenged.

Comparison Shopping

Comparison shopping across the borders will be a snap. A hotel room in Paris for 850 francs might seem like a bargain compared with one that costs 225,000 lire in Rome. But not when you see that the Paris room is 130 Euros vs. 115 Euros for the one in Italy.

Some people who travel frequently to Europe are already looking forward to the Euro, even if it means seeing double on _____ price tags for three years.
9.

Richard Schroeter, an agricultural trade consultant based in Washington, says the Euro should be "a real plus" for frequent travelers to Europe such as himself.

"It gets very confusing figuring out how _____ things cost. Trying to go from
10.
shopping in Belgium to shopping in Italy is quite a change," Schroeter said. "Now, it's as if you were traveling through the United States and every state had a different currency."

Source: The Associated Press, *CBS Market Watch Report,* December 30, 1998.

4 EDITING

Read the following excerpt from the president's speech to the nation. Find and correct the eight errors in his speech which the proofreader did not find.

"MY FELLOW CITIZENS. We're at a time in our history when we need to make some real sacrifices. Recent presidents have made a great many pledges they didn't keep. You may not like everything I tell you tonight, but you deserve to hear the truth. On the economy, we've made ᵃlittle progress, but we still have a great deal more to do, so there are several things I'm proposing. First, I want to raise taxes on the very wealthy because a few of them are really paying their share. Second, the amount of middle-class people shouldering an unfair share of the tax burden is too great, so I'm asking for a tax cut for the middle class. If I'm successful, most of you in the middle class will be paying ten percent less in taxes next year, though few of you in the higher-income brackets might see your taxes rise little. How do I intend to make up the lost revenue? The problem with the national income tax is that there are much loopholes in the current law which allow any people to avoid paying any taxes at all. My additional plan is to replace the lost revenue with a national sales tax, which is fairer because it applies to all people equally. Third, we have no money to finance health care reform, and we've made a little progress in reducing pollution and meeting clean air standards. Therefore, I am asking for a fifty-cent-a-gallon tax on gasoline. With a great many more people using mass transit, and with the amount of additional revenue, we will be able to finance our new health care program and help the environment at the same time."

COMMUNICATION PRACTICE

5 LISTENING

Jack Andrews, who is three months behind on his loan payments, is talking on the telephone with Nancy Grant, the loan officer at his bank.

Comprehension

Listen to their conversation. Write **True (T)** *or* **False (F)** *next to each statement.*

_____ **1.** Jack can't pay the bank right away.

_____ **2.** Jack has always made his payments on time.

_____ **3.** Jack will earn more money in his new job than he did in his old job.

_____ **4.** At first, Nancy doesn't want to recommend an extension of Jack's time to pay.

_____ **5.** Jack has to pay something right away, or Nancy will turn his account over to a collection agency.

_____ **6.** Nancy says Jack has to make his full payment immediately.

_____ **7.** Jack asks for a lot of time to come up with some money.

_____ **8.** Nancy can help Jack a lot even if he doesn't make a payment.

Optional Dictation

Now listen again and fill in the blanks in the text.

(telephone rings)

GRANT: United Central Bank. This is Nancy Grant speaking. May I help you?

ANDREWS: Hello, Ms. Grant? This is Jack Andrews.

GRANT: Oh, yes, hello, Mr. Andrews. What can I do for you?

ANDREWS: I wanted to ask if I could have ___a little more time___ on this month's

payment.
                                                          1.

GRANT: OK. Let me just look at your file. Hmm . . . well, we've received

_____ for three months, and your file shows that
            2.

_____ have been made on time since you took out the loan.
         3.

I'm sorry, but I can't recommend _____.
                                              4.

ANDREWS: I know, Ms. Grant, but I just started a new job. I'll be earning

_____ than I did in my last position, but I won't be getting
5.

paid for a month.

GRANT: Well, Mr. Andrews, we try to be helpful here, but we do have

_____ that we have to uphold. There's _____
6.   7.

I can do at this point. In fact, I'm going to have to turn your account over to a

collection agency if you don't pay at least _____ on your
8.

outstanding balance.

ANDREWS: Could I have just _____ to try to come up with
9.

_____? I'm sure I can arrange something if I can have just
10.

_____.
11.

GRANT: _____ would you need?
12.

ANDREWS: How about ten days?

GRANT: All right, Mr. Andrews. If you can make a payment within ten days, we'll reopen

your account. I can't do _____ for you otherwise.
13.

ANDREWS: Thank you, Ms. Grant.

6 THE NUMBERS GAME

*Look at the exchange chart. Play in teams of four to six students. Team B, turn to
page 167. Team A asks Team B the six questions that appear on page 166. Then
Team B asks Team A six questions. Score points.*

CURRENCY LAST TRADE	U.S. $ N/A	Aust $ Jan 8	U.K. £ Jan 8	Can $ Jan 8	DMark Jan 8	FFranc Jan 8	¥en Jan 8	SFranc Jan 8	Euro Jan 8
U.S. $	1	0.6348	1.645	0.6614	0.5929	0.1768	0.009013	0.7195	1.159
Aust $	1.575	1	2.591	1.042	0.934	0.2785	0.0142	1.133	1.826
U.K. £	0.608	0.386	1	0.4021	0.3605	0.1075	0.00548	0.4375	0.7049
Can $	1.512	0.9598	2.487	1	0.8964	0.2673	0.01363	1.088	1.753
DMark	1.687	1.071	2.774	1.116	1	0.2981	0.0152	1.214	1.955
FFranc	5.657	3.591	9.304	3.742	3.354	1	0.05099	4.07	6.559
¥en	111	70.43	182.5	73.38	65.78	19.61	1	79.83	128.6
SFranc	1.39	0.8823	2.286	0.9192	0.824	0.2457	0.01253	1	1.611
Euro	0.8625	0.5475	1.419	0.5705	0.5114	0.1525	0.007774	0.6206	1

Team A's Questions:

1. Andrew has 10,000 pounds in his savings account. Roberta has 10,000 dollars in hers. In terms of absolute value, who has less money?

2. The Euro is currently trading at $1.16 to the dollar. Will it take fewer dollars or fewer Euros to purchase something?

3. A tourist from France and another tourist from Germany both want to buy the same item. Will it take more francs or more marks to make the purchase?

4. A tourist from Canada wants to buy something in the United States. She has $400 Canadian. The price is $350 U.S. Will she have enough money?

5. Will it take fewer Swiss francs or French francs to purchase an item?

6. A tourist from Japan is traveling in Europe and has only traveler's checks in denominations of 1,000 yen. He wants to buy something that costs one Euro. How much money will he have to change?

7 ESSAY

Have you ever had a problem figuring out the currency when you visited another country? Did you perhaps tip the waiter $10 instead of $1 by mistake? Did something amusing happen? Something not so funny? Write two or three paragraphs telling your story.

8 PICTURE DISCUSSION

Talk with a partner. Explain what is happening. What is the problem? What would you do if you were in this situation?

THE NUMBERS GAME FOR TEAM B

*Look at the exchange chart. Play in teams of four to six students. Team A asks
Team B six questions. Then Team B asks Team A six questions. Score points.*

CURRENCY LAST TRADE	U.S. $ N / A	Aust $ Jan 8	U.K. £ Jan 8	Can $ Jan 8	DMark Jan 8	FFranc Jan 8	¥en Jan 8	SFranc Jan 8	Euro Jan 8
U.S. $	1	0.6348	1.645	0.6614	0.5929	0.1768	0.009013	0.7195	1.159
Aust $	1.575	1	2.591	1.042	0.934	0.2785	0.0142	1.133	1.826
U.K. £	0.608	0.386	1	0.4021	0.3605	0.1075	0.00548	0.4375	0.7049
Can $	1.512	0.9598	2.487	1	0.8964	0.2673	0.01363	1.088	1.753
DMark	1.687	1.071	2.774	1.116	1	0.2981	0.0152	1.214	1.955
FFranc	5.657	3.591	9.304	3.742	3.354	1	0.05099	4.07	6.559
¥en	111	70.43	182.5	73.38	65.78	19.61	1	79.83	128.6
SFranc	1.39	0.8823	2.286	0.9192	0.824	0.2457	0.01253	1	1.611
Euro	0.8625	0.5475	1.419	0.5705	0.5114	0.1525	0.007774	0.6206	1

Team B's Questions

1. A tourist has 100 Canadian dollars and 100 Australian dollars. He wants to change them into French francs. Will he get more francs for the Canadian money or for the Australian money?

2. In a duty-free shop at an airport, a tourist sees two items she would like to buy. One costs two French francs, and the other costs two Swiss francs. Which item costs less?

3. Two tourists came back from a trip to Europe. One had 100 German marks. The other had 100 Australian dollars. In terms of absolute value, who had more money?

4. A tourist had only 1,000 yen. He wanted to buy something that cost 20 U.S. dollars. Did he have enough money?

5. Will it take fewer British pounds or U.S. dollars to purchase something?

6. A German tourist wants to buy something that costs 10 Australian dollars. He has only traveler's checks in denominations of 10 marks each. How many traveler's checks will he have to change?

REVIEW OR SELFTEST

I. *Complete each item with* **a / an** *or* **the**. *Leave a blank if no article is needed.*

CYCLONES

According to ____the____ National Weather Service, _____ cyclones
                  1.   **2.**

are _____ areas of circulating winds that rotate counterclockwise in
       3.

_____ Northern Hemisphere and clockwise in _____ Southern
  4.   **5.**

Hemisphere. They are generally accompanied by some kind of _____
                                                    6.

precipitation and by _____ stormy weather. _____ tornadoes and
               7.   **8.**

_____ hurricanes are _____ types of cyclones, as are _____
  9.   **10.**   **11.**

typhoons, which are _____ storms that occur in _____ western
              12.   **13.**

Pacific Ocean.

_____ hurricane is _____ cyclone that forms over _____
 14.   **15.**   **16.**

tropical oceans and seas and has _____ winds of at least seventy-four
                        17.

miles _____ hour. _____ hurricane rotates in _____ shape
      18.   **19.**   **20.**

of _____ oval or _____ circle. _____ hurricanes can cause
   21.   **22.**   **23.**

_____ great environmental damage. _____ Hurricane Andrew,
 24.   **25.**

which hit _____ coasts of Louisiana and southern Florida in August
       26.

1992, caused _____ extreme devastation. In terms of _____
         27.   **28.**

environmental damage, _____ Hurricane Andrew is one of _____
               29.   **30.**

most devastating hurricanes ever to hit _____ United States. Fourteen
                    31.

people died because of _____ Andrew's effects.
            32.

II. *Each of the following sentences contains one error in the use of articles. Correct each sentence by rewriting each incorrect phrase.*

1. One of the best things we can do to help the environment is to encourage the recycling.

. . . to encourage recycling.

2. Bats are mammals, not the birds.

_____

3. An orangutan is anthropoid ape dwelling in the jungles of Borneo and Sumatra.

_____

4. The Mesozoic era was third of the four major eras of geologic time.

_____

5. Jurassic period was the period of the Mesozoic era when dinosaurs were present and birds first appeared.

_____

6. The Milky Way galaxy is galaxy to which the sun and the solar system belong.

_____

7. The meltdown is an inadvertent melting of a nuclear reactor's core.

_____

8. The movie *The China Syndrome* dramatizes a theoretical disaster hypothesizing the meltdown of nuclear reactor so total that the earth would be penetrated by radioactive material.

_____

9. Rain forests in South America are being cleared to make fields for raising the cattle.

_____

10. The acid rain is rain with higher-than-normal acidity caused by pollution.

_____

III. *Look at the pictures. Write a sentence under each picture, in which the indicated noun is used in a count sense, either with **a / an** or in the plural.*

1. (light)

There's a light in the window.

2. (furniture)

3. (work)

4. (advice)

5. (people)

6. (spices)

7. (lightning)

_____

_____

8. (wine)

_____

_____

IV. *Complete the conversations by putting the noun modifiers in the correct order.*

1. A: It feels like _____ a sweltering summer day _____ here, even though it's spring.
       a. (sweltering / a / day / summer)
    What's the weather like where you are?

   B: Here it feels like _____. I envy you.
              b. (chilly / day / a / winter / late)

2. A: What do you think of _____?
              a. (satin / pink / new / my / tie)

   B: It makes you look like _____.
              b. (European / young / handsome / a / businessman)

3. A: We were finally able to build _____. It's just
              a. (brick / own / our / new /house)
    what we've always wanted.

   B: It sounds great. Maybe we could do the same. We feel like we're living in

    _____.
              b. (hovel / little / dirty / old / a)

V. *Complete the conversations with the correct quantifiers, choosing from the items given.*

1. A: Let's get off this freeway. There's just too _____ much _____ traffic.
              a. (much / many)

   B: Yeah, let's. The _____ of people driving is incredible. I've never seen
              b. (amount / number)
    this _____ cars.
          c. (much / many)

2. A: Can you bring soda to the picnic? I don't have _____.
              a. (some / any)

   B: Yeah, I think I've got _____ left over from the party.
              b. (some / any)

3. A: How do you feel about your new job? Do you have as _____
a. (much / many)

responsibilities as you used to?

B: The job is great. I have about the same _____ of work
b. (amount / number)

to do as before, but I have _____ stress and _____
c. (less / fewer)   d. (less / fewer)

problems.

4. A: How do you think you did on the test? I think I did _____ better
a. (little / a little)

than last time—maybe even _____ better. What about you?
b. (a lot / many)

B: Well, I think I probably made _____ mistakes, but I have the feeling
c. (few / a few)

I did well overall.

5. A: Mr. President, do you think _____ of your proposed legislation will
a. (much / many)

be passed by Congress during this session?

B: Yes, I think _____ of our proposals will be approved. We're
b. (a great deal / a great many)

not taking _____ for granted, though. We still have
c. (nothing / anything)

_____ work to do.
d. (a great deal of / a great many)

A: The polls say that there's _____ support nationwide for your
e. (little / a little)

military program. Isn't that going to hurt you?

B: Not in the long run, no. _____ of the voters actually support the
f. (Few / A few)

military system the way it is now. I think we'll be successful.

VI. *Circle the letter of the one word or phrase in each sentence that is not correct.*

1. The journey from Los Angeles to San Diego is a three-hours trip if   A B Ⓒ D
   A   B   C
   the traffic isn't heavy.
   D

2. The chief executive officer of the company I work for lives in   A B C D
   A   B
   beautiful condominium in a ten-story building.
   C   D

3. Plan to build a comprehensive monorail system is a   A B C D
   A   B   C
   citizen-initiated proposal.
   D

4. One of <u>the most famous inventions</u> in <u>the history</u> of <u>humankind</u> is   **A B C D**
　　　　　_A　　　　　　　　　　_B　　　　　_C

　　<u>a wheel</u> .
　　　_D

5. The <u>two first</u> films shown in last weekend's film series were   **A B C D**
　_A　_B

　　<u>the most popular ones</u> in <u>the series</u>.
　　　　　_C　　　　　　　　_D

6. <u>The extinction</u> of <u>the dinosaurs</u> is still <u>a matter</u> of debate in   **A B C D**
　　　_A　　　　　_B　　　　　　　_C

　　<u>scientific community</u>.
　　　　　_D

7. Vancouver, <u>the largest city</u> in <u>Canadian Southwest</u>, is   **A B C D**
　　　　　　　_A　　　　　　_B

　　<u>the closest major Canadian port</u> to <u>the Far East</u>.
　　　　　　　_C　　　　　　　　_D

8. When Sarah was a child, she disliked <u>peas</u>, <u>carrots</u>, <u>bean</u>, and   **A B C D**
　　　　　　　　　　　　　　　　_A　　_B　　_C

　　<u>most other vegetables</u>.
　　　　　_D

9. <u>The Wheelers'</u> <u>ten-years-old daughter</u>, Melanie, was born in   **A B C D**
　　　_A　　　　　　_B

　　<u>the city of Rotterdam</u> in <u>the Netherlands</u>.
　　　　　_C　　　　　　　_D

10. Ralph is in <u>the intensive care ward</u> of <u>the city hospital</u> after being   **A B C D**
　　　　　　　　_A　　　　　　　　_B

　　struck by <u>a lightning</u> on <u>a camping trip</u>.
　　　　　　_C　　　_D

VII. *Go back to your answers to Exercise VI. Write the correct form for each item that you believe is incorrect.*

1. ___three-hour___   **5.** _____   **8.** _____

2. _____   **6.** _____   **9.** _____

3. _____   **7.** _____   **10.** _____

4. _____

▶ *To check your answers, go to the Answer Key on page 180.*

PART III

FROM GRAMMAR TO WRITING
AGREEMENT

When we speak of agreement in English, we are referring to agreement in number and gender. Agreement in number is the matching of singulars with singulars and plurals with plurals. Agreement in gender is the matching of masculine with masculine and feminine with feminine. There are two types of agreement: subject-verb agreement and pronoun-antecedent agreement.

Every sentence in English can be divided into two parts: the subject and the predicate. The subject is a person, place, or thing about which a statement is made. The predicate is the statement, and it always contains the verb. Subjects and verbs of English sentences must agree in number. In the following sentences, the complete subject is underlined once and the complete predicate is underlined twice.

Birds chirp.

Koalas live in Australia.

The men at Ron's office like to play volleyball.

Nadia and Phil López are trying to save money.

The danger of credit cards is that they encourage us to live
   beyond our means.

To determine the complete subject of a sentence, ask a *who* or *what* question. The answer to that question will be the complete subject.

The man on the train reminded Penny of her father.

Who reminded Penny of her father? **The man on the train.**
   (complete subject)

The increasing extinction of plant and animal species is
   alarming.

What is alarming? **The increasing extinction of plant and
   animal species.** (complete subject)

1 *Underline the complete subject in each of the following sentences.*

1. <u>Five of my best friends</u> are coming over tonight to play volleyball.

2. The Siberian tiger and the blue whale are endangered species.

3. That man who is sitting at the mahogany desk is our loan officer.

4. Relatively few adults or teenagers are able to handle credit cards wisely.

5. The expectation that we will like well-known works of art, literature, or music can detract from our appreciation of them.

There is one word in the complete subject that controls the verb (or auxiliary) in the sentence. To determine this main subject, find the word that the other words modify. In the following sentences, the main subject is underlined.

My blue silk <u>necktie</u> is gorgeous.

Our first three <u>attempts</u> were unsuccessful.

Notice that the main subject of a sentence is never located in a prepositional phrase (a phrase beginning with a preposition and ending with a noun or pronoun—e.g., *on the table*). In the following sentences the prepositional phrases are underlined, the main subject is circled, and an arrow is drawn between the simple subject and the verb.

(One) <u>of my best friends</u> has five credit cards.

(Both) <u>of my brothers</u> are behind on their car payments.

The (fate) <u>of the blue whale</u> is unclear.

(Either) <u>of the plans</u> is worthwhile.

(None) <u>of the proposals</u> has much merit.

(Neither) <u>of the skaters</u> is expected to win a gold medal.

2 *Circle the main subject in each of the following sentences, and draw an arrow between it and the verb.*

1. A (list) of available jobs was posted on the office bulletin board.

2. Much of what you were told was inaccurate.

3. Neither of those two politicians is in favor of cutting taxes.

4. None of the work has been completed satisfactorily.

5. Very little of this work can be done by one person working alone.

6. The singing of that famous Australian opera star is uplifting.

Be careful with the word ***there***. Even though ***there*** is often the grammatical subject of a sentence, it is linked to a word later in the sentence that controls the verb. In the following sentences, an arrow connects the word ***there*** and the noun it is linked to. Note the underlined verb.

There ~~are hundreds of animals on the~~ Endangered Species list.

There ~~have been many en~~vironmental disasters in the last twenty years.

There <u>is</u> a large, fierce dog guarding the house.

3 *Choose the correct verb to complete each sentence.*

1. There _____ has _____ never been an environmental disaster of this magnitude.
      (has / have)

2. There _____ many reasons why I am against the use of nuclear power.
      (is / are)

3. There _____ always a rational explanation for his behavior.
      (isn't / aren't)

4. There _____ been fewer business mergers this year than last.
      (has / have)

5. There _____ a lot of demonstrators present at the environmental rally.
      (was / were)

6. There _____ any elegantly dressed people at the party. Everyone was
      (wasn't / weren't)

wearing blue jeans.

Compound subjects are those in which the subject is composed of more than one item. They are often connected by *and*.

Ron and Ashley are going to join a health club. (two subjects—*Ron, Ashley*)

The blue whale, the timber wolf, and the whooping crane need our protection. (three subjects: *whale, wolf, crane*)

Sometimes words appear to be compound subjects, but they really constitute a single phrase made up of two items acting as a unit. These take a singular verb.

Bacon and eggs is a high-cholesterol but nourishing meal.
   (*Bacon and eggs is a single dish.*)

The owner and manager of the bank is Mr. Bates.
   (*Mr. Bates is one person who has two roles.*)

4 *Choose the correct verb to complete each sentence.*

1. Both the whale and the grizzly bear _____*need*_____ federal protection.
    (needs / need)

2. Bipolar disorder and schizophrenia _____ two serious mental disorders.
    (is / are)

3. The director and star of the film _____ Robert Redford.
    (was / were)

4. Liver and onions _____ a meal detested by many children.
    (is / are)

5. Mathematics _____ often considered a difficult subject.
    (is / are)

Pronoun agreement is similar to subject-verb agreement. In formal English, pronouns agree in number and gender with their antecedents.

> All the **students** brought **their** books to class on the first day. (*Their* agrees with *students*.)

> **Jack** ate **his** lunch quickly. (*His* agrees with *Jack*.)

> **Martha** stopped by to see **her** mother after class. (*Her* agrees with *Martha*.)

> Each of **us** needs to bring **our** own ideas to the meeting. (*Our* agrees with *us*.)

In informal English, usage is somewhat different. The words *everyone / everybody, anyone / anybody, someone / somebody, no one / nobody,* and *a person* are often used with plural forms. Look at these examples.

Formal	Informal
Everyone drove **his** (**her / his or her**) car to the picnic.	**Everyone** drove **their** own car to the picnic.
If you see **anyone** from our office, tell **him** (**her / him or her**) to see me.	If you see **anyone** from our office, tell **them** to see me.
All the **employees** came, didn't **they**?	**Everybody** came, didn't **they**?

BE CAREFUL! Use these plural forms only in informal (conversational) English. Use the correct singular forms in writing and formal speech.

Sometimes it is possible to make a sentence correct for formal English by changing the subject to the plural:

> **Everyone** brought **their** own lunch.   All the **employees** brought **their** own lunch.

5 *Complete each of these sentences with correct forms for formal and for informal English.*

Formal	Informal

1. Does everyone have _____

1.

book with him?

2. No one knows _____ own

3.

destiny.

3. If any of the performers shows up,

send _____ to my office.

5.

4. A person needs to have

_____ priorities straight.

7.

Does everyone have _____

2.

book with them?

No one knows _____ own

4.

destiny.

If any of the performers show up,

send _____ to my office.

6.

A person needs to have

_____ priorities straight.

8.

Subjects connected by *either / or* and *neither / nor* behave differently from compound subjects. The subject that is closer to the verb determines whether the verb is singular or plural.

> Either the **president** or his cabinet **members are** responsible for this environmental policy. (two subjects: *president, members; members* is closer to the verb and forces the plural verb *are*)

> Neither the **members** of the city council nor the **mayor supports** more real estate development. (two subjects: *members, mayor; mayor* is closer to the verb and forces the singular verb *supports*)

Note that if we reverse the order of the above sentences, the verb changes.

> Either the cabinet **members** or the **president is** responsible for this environmental policy.

> Neither the **mayor** nor the **members** of the city council **support** more real estate development.

Pronouns whose antecedents are nouns connected by *either / or* and *neither / nor* behave in the same way. The noun closer to the pronoun determines the correct pronoun.

> Neither **Susan** nor **the Johnsons** enrolled **their** children in that school. (*The Johnsons* is closer to the pronoun and forces *their*.)

---

6 *Choose the correct verb or pronoun in the following sentences.*

1. Either Bob Ashcroft or the Mendozas _____are_____ going to host this year's party.

(is / are)

2. Neither pollution nor other atmospheric phenomena _____ thought to be

(is / are)

related to the unusual weather we've been having.

3. Neither the local environmentalists nor the mayor _____ a plan that will
(has / have)

satisfy everyone.

4. Either major credit cards or a check _____ an acceptable means of payment.
(is / are)

5. Neither Venus nor the outer planets _____ a breathable atmosphere.
(has / have)

6. Neither my daughters nor my son owns _____ own car.
(their / his)

 *The following letter to the editor of a newspaper has twelve errors in
subject-verb agreement and pronoun-antecedent agreement. Find and
correct the errors. Use forms that are correct for formal English.*

Editor, The Times

    Many parts of our once-beautiful city is *(are)* starting to look like mini garbage dumps.
You will recall that legislation requiring recycling within the city limits were passed last
year, and the mayor and other local politicians encourages us to recycle, but in my
apartment complex there is no bins for recycling. The result is that people take no
responsibility for his own actions, and everyone tosses their trash and recyclables
(glass, plastic bottles, cans, etc.) right in with the food that is being thrown away.
Neither the manager of the complex nor the owners of the building has bought any
new containers for the items that are supposed to be recycled. So what else can
everyone do but mix their trash together? Either the manager or the owners is
responsible for breaking the law here. Not us! Meanwhile, trash cans in the downtown
area is overflowing with garbage, and vacant lots all around the city is littered with
soda cans, broken glass, and paper. The owner and publisher of your newspaper,
Stanford Black, have always been a supporter of a clean environment. I urge your
paper to take leadership in solving this problem.

8 APPLY IT TO YOUR WRITING

*Interview someone about his or her family or some close friends. Ask about
brothers, sisters, children, activities, and so on. Then write a paragraph of
five or six sentences summarizing what the person said. Make sure that you
have correct subject-verb and pronoun-antecedent agreement. Write the
paragraph twice: once for those forms correct in formal English, and once
for forms used in informal English. Exchange papers with a partner. Edit
each other's paragraphs. Then rewrite your paragraphs, if necessary, and
submit them to your teacher.*

PART III

REVIEW OR SELFTEST
ANSWER KEY

I.

2. no article	**18.** an
3. no article	**19.** A
4. the	**20.** the
5. the	**21.** an
6. no article	**22.** a
7. no article	**23.** no article
8. no article	**24.** no article
9. no article	**25.** no article
10. no article	**26.** the
11. no article	**27.** no article
12. no article	**28.** no article
13. the	**29.** no article
14. A	**30.** the
15. a	**31.** the
16. no article	**32.** no article
17. no article	

II.

2. . . . not birds.
3. An orangutan is an anthropoid ape . . .
4. The Mesozoic era was the third . . .
5. The Jurassic Period . . .
6. The Milky Way galaxy is the galaxy . . .
7. A meltdown is . . .
8. . . . hypothesizing the meltdown of a nuclear reactor.
9. . . . raising cattle.
10. Acid rain is . . .

III. Possible Answers

2. Several pieces of furniture are for sale.
3. *A Thousand Cranes* is a work of literature by Yasunari Kawabata.
4. The mother is giving her son a piece of advice.
5. The Shan are a people of Myanmar.
6. Curry, rosemary, oregano, and thyme are spices.
7. The tree was hit by a bolt of lightning.
8. Rioja is a wine produced in Spain.

IV.

1. b. a chilly late-winter day
2. a. my new pink satin tie
   b. a handsome young European businessman
3. a. our own new brick house
   b. a dirty little old hovel

V.

1. b. number	**b.** a lot
c. many	**c.** a few
2. a. any	**5. a.** much
b. some	**b.** a great many
3. a. many	**c.** anything
b. amount	**d.** a great deal of
c. less	**e.** little
d. fewer	**f.** Few
4. a. a little	

VI.

2. C	**5.** B	**8.** C
3. A	**6.** D	**9.** B
4. D	**7.** B	**10.** C

VII.

2. a beautiful condominium
3. The plan
4. the wheel
5. first two
6. the scientific community
7. the Canadian Southwest
8. beans
9. ten-year-old daughter
10. lightning / a bolt of lightning

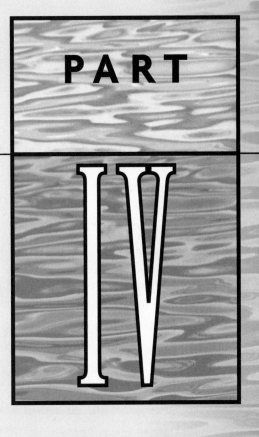

PART IV

ADJECTIVE CLAUSES AND PHRASES

ADJECTIVE CLAUSES: REVIEW AND EXPANSION

GRAMMAR **IN CONTEXT**

QUESTIONS TO CONSIDER

1. If you could select one adjective that best describes your personality, what adjective would it be?

2. Is there anything to be gained by classifying people into personality types or placing yourself in a personality category? If so, what?

Read an article about personality types.

WHAT TYPE ARE YOU?

Suppose you attend a party where there are several people you know well. The hosts have a new party game. They ask everyone to take five minutes and compare each person to a flower. Which flower would you choose for each person? For that matter, which flower would you choose for yourself? Are you the kind of person who resembles a sunflower, open to the world most of the time? Or are you more like a four o'clock, someone who only opens up at special moments?

This may sound like just a fun activity, something which is suitable only for get-togethers or for amusing yourself. But there is actually a science of identifying personality types. Personality identification grew out of the work of Swiss psychologist Carl Jung and the studies of two American women, Katharine Briggs and her daughter, Isabel Briggs Myers. After considerable study of Jung's work, Briggs and her daughter developed a system in which they formulated four personality dimensions and sixteen different personality types. This test, which has been refined many times over the decades, has been validated by the millions of people who have taken it. What follows is a brief description of what has come to be known as the Myers-Briggs test. Take a look at it. As you're reading about these categories, try to place yourself into one or more of them.* You may learn something about your friends, co-workers, and loved ones, and yourself.

The first dimension is a familiar one: extrovert or introvert. This category has to do with the way in which people direct their energy. An extrovert is basically a person whose energies are activated by being with others. An introvert is basically a person whose energies are activated by being alone. Mary is a good example of an extrovert. She's the kind of person whom others consider shy, but there's no correlation between shyness and either introversion or extroversion. At a party, once Mary meets some people she feels comfortable with, she starts to open up and get energized. Her friend Bill is the opposite. Bill isn't shy at all, but after he's been at a party for a while, he's weary and ready to go home. He finds the conversation interesting enough but is just as likely to be imagining a time when he was hiking alone in the mountains.

The second dimension of personality is sensor or intuitive. This category has to do with the kind of information we notice and remember easily. Sensors are practical people who notice what is going on around them. They rely on past experiences to make determinations. Intuitives are more interested in relationships between things or people. They tend to be imaginative and to focus on what could be. Jack and Barbara, who have been married for years, are good examples of these types. At a party, Jack, whose parents own a sofa company, notices immediately that their hosts have bought a new sofa and asks the hosts where they bought it. Barbara is much less interested in the sofa and more interested in the strained way their hosts are talking with each other. Did they have a fight? Jack is the sensor and Barbara the intuitive here.

The third personality dimension is thinker or feeler. This category has to do with the way in which we come to conclusions. Thinkers are those who tend to make decisions objectively and impersonally on the basis of what makes sense and what is logical. Feelers make decisions based on their own personal values and how they feel about choices. Helen and Gary are good examples. They've just gone to a bank to apply for a loan. The loan officer tells them that they owe too much on their credit cards and that they'll have to pay off their debt before they can borrow money. This makes perfect sense to Helen, which leads us to classify her as a thinker. Gary's reaction is quite different. The loan officer, by whom Gary feels criticized, is only trying to do his job. Gary takes his comments personally, which is why he is to be considered a feeler.

The fourth category is judger or perceiver. This dimension has to do with the kind of environment that makes us feel most comfortable. Judgers are people who prefer a structured and predictable environment. They like to make decisions and have things settled. Perceivers are more interested in keeping their options open, preferring to experience as much of the world as possible. Tim and Samantha are good examples of these types. Tim, who always has a plan for everything, gets impatient with Samantha when he calls and asks

*To learn more about personality type and to determine your type, visit *www.personalitytype.com*.

(continued on next page)

WHAT TYPE ARE YOU?

her for a date. Tim wants things to be nailed down; Samantha wants to keep her options open and flexible.

So now we're left with this question: What good is the ability to pigeonhole people, or ourselves, for that matter? It certainly doesn't give us any magic powers or tools for dealing with people. But it can give us insight. It can help us understand others better, and perhaps minimize or at least reduce conflict. Best of all, it can help us to understand ourselves.

Source: Adapted from "What's Your Personality Type?" *New Woman.* August 1998, pp. 68–71, by Barbara Barron-Tieger and Paul D. Tieger, authors of *Do What You Are, Nurture by Nature,* and *The Art of SpeedReading People.*

UNDERSTANDING MEANING FROM CONTEXT

Make a guess about the meaning of each italicized word or phrase from the reading. Write your guess in the blank provided.

1. This test, which has been *refined* many times over the decades, has been validated by the millions of people who have taken it.

_____

2. Barbara is much less interested in the sofa and more interested in the *strained* way their hosts are talking with each other.

_____

3. Tim wants things to be *nailed down*; Samantha wants to keep her options open and flexible.

_____

4. What good is the ability to *pigeonhole* people, or ourselves, for that matter?

_____

5. But it can give us *insight*.

_____

GRAMMAR **PRESENTATION**
ADJECTIVE CLAUSES: REVIEW AND EXPANSION

IDENTIFYING ADJECTIVE CLAUSES

WHO

Are you the kind of person **who resembles a sunflower**, open to the world most of the time?

THAT

This dimension has to do with the kind of environment **that makes us feel more comfortable**.

WHOM

She's the kind of person **whom others consider shy**.

WHEN

He is likely to be imagining a time **when he was hiking alone in the mountains**.

WHERE

Suppose you attend a party **where there are several people you know well**.

WHICH

This may sound like just a fun activity, something **which is suitable for get-togethers**.

WHOSE

An introvert is basically a person **whose energies are activated by being alone**.

PREPOSITION + WHICH

This category has to do with the way **in which people direct their energy**.

PREPOSITION + WHOM

He finds the people **with whom he's talking** interesting.

DELETED RELATIVE PRONOUN

Suppose you go to a party where there are several people **(whom / that) you know well**.

NONIDENTIFYING ADJECTIVE CLAUSES

WHO

Jack and Barbara, **who have been married for many years**, are examples of these types.

WHOM

The loan officer, **by whom Jack feels criticized**, is only trying to do his job.

WHICH

This test, **which has been refined many times over the decades**, has been validated by the millions of people who have taken it.

WHOSE

Jack, **whose parents own a sofa company**, notices immediately that his hosts have bought a new sofa.

NONIDENTIFYING ADJECTIVE CLAUSE MODIFYING AN ENTIRE PRECEDING IDEA

This makes perfect sense to Helen, **which is why we can classify her as a thinker**.

NOTES

1. Adjective clauses are **dependent clauses** that modify nouns and pronouns. They are introduced by the relative pronouns *who, whom, whose, that*, and *which*, or by *when* and *where*. Sentences with adjective clauses can be seen as a combination of two sentences.

2. Adjective clauses that are used to identify (distinguish one person or thing from another) are called **identifying** (also called **restrictive**, **defining**, or **essential**).

EXAMPLES

- Sensors are persons. Sensors are practical and notice what is going on around them.
- Sensors are persons **who are practical and notice what is going on around them**.

- Judgers are people **who prefer a structured and predictable environment**. (The clause *who prefer a structured and predictable environment* identifies which kind of people are judgers.)

3. An adjective clause that is not used to identify something but simply adds extra information is called **nonidentifying** (or **nonrestrictive**, **nondefining**, or **nonessential**).

- Jack and Barbara, **who have been married for years**, are good examples of these types. (The clause *who have been married for years* doesn't identify the people we are talking about. The names *Jack* and *Barbara* do that. This clause simply adds extra information about Jack and Barbara.)

Punctuation note: Nonidentifying adjective clauses are enclosed by commas. Identifying adjective clauses have no commas around them.

Pronunciation note: When spoken, identifying adjective clauses have no pauses before or after them. Nonidentifying clauses do have pauses when spoken.

- The man who is sitting in the first row is married to Barbara. (identifying—no pauses)
- Jack, who is sitting in the first row, is married to Barbara. (nonidentifying—pauses)

See From Grammar to Writing after Part IV, page 214, for more information about punctuation of adjective clauses.

---

4. Like all clauses, adjective clauses contain subjects and verbs. The **relative pronouns** *who*, *which*, and *that* are used as subjects.

- Are you **someone who only opens up at special moments**? (*Who* is the subject of the clause verb *opens*.)
- This may sound like just a fun activity, something **which is suitable only for get-togethers**. (*Which* is the subject of the clause verb *is*.)
- This dimension has to do with the kind of environment **that makes us feel most** comfortable. (*That* is the subject of the clause verb *makes*.)

▶ **BE CAREFUL!** Do not use a double subject pronoun in an adjective clause.

- Judgers **are people who prefer a structured and predictable environment**.
  NOT ~~Judgers are people who they prefer a structured environment~~.

(continued on next page)

5. The **relative pronouns** *whom*, *that*, and *which* are used as objects in adjective clauses.

- She's the kind of person **whom others consider shy**. (*Whom* is the direct object of the verb *consider*.)

- Once Mary meets some people **that she feels comfortable with**, she starts to open up. (*That* is the object of the clause preposition *with*.)

- This category has to do with the way **in which people direct their energy**. (*Which* is the object of the clause preposition *in*.)

▶ **BE CAREFUL!** It is common in conversation to omit the relative pronoun *who*, *whom*, *which*, or *that*. This can only be done, however, if the relative pronoun is an object. You cannot omit the relative pronoun if it is the subject of a clause.

- Once Mary meets some people
  may be omitted
  (that) she feels comfortable with . . .

                           may not be omitted
- Sensors are people **who are practical and notice what is going on around them**.
  NOT ~~Sensors are people are practical and notice what is going on around them.~~

6. *Who* and *whom* are used to refer to persons, not things. *That* can be used to refer to both persons and things and is considered more informal than *who* or *whom* when it is used to refer to people. *Which* is used to refer only to things.

Which and *that* are used interchangeably in identifying clauses.

In **nonidentifying clauses**, only *which* is usually used.

- Thinkers are those **who / that tend to make decisions objectively and impersonally**.
  NOT ~~Thinkers are those which tend to make decisions objectively and impersonally.~~

- This dimension has to do with the kind of environment **that / which makes us feel most comfortable**.

- This test, **which has been refined many times over the decades**, has been validated by the millions of people who have taken it.
  NOT ~~This test, that has been refined . . .~~

7. *Whom* is considerably more formal than *who* and is appropriate for formal writing and careful speech. *Who* is appropriate elsewhere. (Although *who* is used as a subject in adjective clauses, it is often used as an object in conversational speech.)

- She's the kind of person **whom others consider shy**. (formal)

- She's the kind of person **who others consider shy**. (less formal, conversational—*who* is used as an object)

8. In conversation and informal writing, native speakers commonly place the preposition in an adjective clause at the end of the sentence, and they often omit the relative pronoun.

- Once Mary meets some people **she feels comfortable with** . . . (informal, conversational)
- Once Mary meets some **people that she feels comfortable with** . . . (slightly more formal)
- Once Mary meets some people **who she feels comfortable with** . . . (a bit more formal)
- Once Mary meets some people **whom she feels comfortable with** . . . (even more formal)
- Once Mary meets some people **with whom she feels comfortable** . . . (the most formal)

9. The **relative pronoun *whose*** is used to introduce an adjective clause in which a possessive is needed. *Whose* does not appear without a following noun in an adjective clause.

- An extrovert is basically a person **whose energies are activated by being with others**.

10. Adjective clauses can be introduced by *when* and *where*. Adjective clauses with *when* describe a time; adjective clauses with *where* describe a place.

- He is just as likely to be imagining a time **when he was hiking alone in the mountains**.
- Suppose you attend a party **where there are several people you know well**.

11. The **relative pronoun *which*** can be used informally to introduce a clause that modifies an entire preceding idea. In this situation, *which* must be preceded by a comma. This type of sentence is used in conversation and informal writing but not generally in formal writing. In formal writing, a noun is added before *which*.

- This makes perfect sense to Helen, **which leads us to classify her as a thinker**. (The clause *which leads us to classify her as a thinker* modifies the entire preceding idea: that "this makes perfect sense to Helen.")
- This makes perfect sense to Helen, **a fact which leads us to classify her as a thinker**.

FOCUSED PRACTICE

 DISCOVER THE GRAMMAR

Part A

Look again at the following sentences adapted from What Type Are You? *In each case, say whether or not the italicized relative pronoun could be rewritten according to the suggestion in parentheses without creating a different meaning or an incorrect sentence. Explain why or why not.*

1. Are you the kind of person *who* resembles a sunflower, open to the world most of the time? (that)

2. This may sound like just a fun activity, something *which* is suitable only for get-togethers or for amusing yourself. (who)

3. She's the kind of person *whom* others consider shy . . . (delete the relative pronoun)

4. He finds the conversation interesting enough but is just as likely to be imagining a time *when* he was hiking alone in the mountains. (where)

5. This category has to do with the kind of information we notice and remember easily. (add the relative pronoun *that* before *we*)

6. Sensors are people *who* are practical and notice what is going on around them. (whom)

7. Jack and Barbara, *who* have been married for years, are good examples of these types. (that)

8. Jack takes the comment personally, wondering what he did wrong, *which* is why he would be classified as a feeler. (that)

9. Tim, *who* always has a plan for everything, gets impatient with Samantha when he calls and asks her for a date. (that)

10. In the decades since, this test has been refined many times and has been validated by the millions of people *who* have taken it. (delete the relative pronoun)

Part B

Find three sentences in the reading in which the relative pronoun has been deleted. How could these sentences be said with a relative pronoun?

1. _____

2. _____

3. _____

② PEOPLE IN THE OFFICE   Grammar Note 11

Dolores Atwood, a personnel officer for a publishing company, is writing an evaluation of the employees in her department who are being considered for promotion. Write adjective clauses with **which** *to modify entire preceding ideas.*

LOOK BOOKS Personnel Evaluation   CONFIDENTIAL

Elaine Correa has only been with us for a year but is definitely ready for promotion,

___which is not surprising___ given the glowing recommendations she got from her last employer.
   1. (not / be surprising)

   Burt Drysdale has proven himself to be a team player, _____
                                                    2. (I / find / somewhat amazing)

considering the fact that he rubbed everyone the wrong way at first. I do recommend him for promotion.

   Alice Anderdoff, on the other hand, is not performing up to expectations,

_____ because I was the one who recruited her. I don't believe she
        3. (bother / me)

should be considered for promotion at this time.

   Mel Tualapa is a very congenial employee, _____, but he can't
                                        4. (be / what everyone / like / about him)

be promoted yet because he's only been with us for six months.

   Lately, Tom Curran has often been ill and consistently late to work, _____
                                                              5. (be / mystifying)

because he was such a model employee at first. I don't recommend him at this time.

---

③ FORMAL AND INFORMAL   Grammar Notes 1, 2, 4–8, 11

Read the following two descriptions. The first is a spoken report by a head attorney to her team of lawyers. The second contains the same information but is a formal written description. Complete the spoken report with informal adjective clauses, omitting the relative pronoun if possible and using contractions. Put the verbs in the correct tenses. Complete the written report with formal adjective clauses. Do not omit the relative pronoun, and put prepositions at the beginning of clauses in which they occur. Do not use contractions.

Spoken Report

Our client is a guy ___who's been in trouble___ for minor offenses, but I don't think he's a
              1. (have / be / in trouble)

murderer, _____ I feel comfortable defending him. He served time
        2. (be / why)

in the penitentiary from 1997 to 1999, and according to all the reports he was a person

_____. Since he got out of jail in 1999, he's had a good employment
   3. (the other prisoners / look up to)

(continued on next page)

record with Textrix, an electronics company _____. The

                4. (he / be working / for)

psychological reports on him show that when he was in prison he was a person

_____ well balanced and even tempered, _____

   5. (the psychiatrists / consider)   6. (be / why)

I don't think he's guilty.

Written Report

Our client is a man _____ for minor offenses, but I do not believe

       7. (have / be / in trouble)

that he is a murderer, _____ feel comfortable in defending him.

       8. (a fact / make me)

He served time in the penitentiary from 1997 to 1999, and according to all the reports

he was a person _____. Since he was released from prison in

     9. (the other prisoners / respect)

1999, he has had a good employment record with Textrix, an electronics company

_____. His psychological profile suggests that when he was in

   10. (for / he / be working)

prison he was a person _____ well balanced and even tempered,

       11. (the psychiatrists / consider)

_____ believe that he is not guilty.

  12. (evidence / make me)

④ EDITING

Read the letter from a college student to his parents and correct the eight errors in relative pronouns in adjective clauses.

Dear Mom and Dad,   September 28

    Well, the first week of college has been hectic, but it's turned out OK. My advisor is a lady

who

~~she~~ is also from Winnipeg, so we had something who we could talk about. Since I haven't

decided on a major, she had me take one of those tests show you what you're most interested

in. She also had me do one of those personality inventories that they tell you what kind of

person you are. According to these tests, I'm a person whom is an extrovert. I also found out

that I'm most interested in things involve being on the stage and performing in some way, who

doesn't surprise me a bit. I always liked being in school plays, remember? I signed up for two

drama courses. Classes start on Wednesday, and I'm getting to know the other guys which live

in my dormitory. It's pretty exciting being here.

    Not much else. I'll call in a week or so.

                                     Love,

                                     Al

COMMUNICATION PRACTICE

5 LISTENING 1

Listen to the conversation. Then listen again and circle the letter of the sentence which correctly describes what you heard.

1. **a.** Bob took the job because it pays well.
   b. Bob took the job because he likes the work.

2. **a.** Paperwork makes Bob angry.
   b. The fact that Bob has been assigned to do a lot of paperwork makes him angry.

3. **a.** Bob is irritated because his co-worker is a passive-aggressive type of person.
   b. Bob is irritated because he wasn't consulted before being assigned to his co-worker.

4. **a.** Jennifer is surprised that Bob is disgruntled.
   b. Jennifer is surprised that Bob took the job.

5. **a.** His feelings about his co-workers are making Bob wonder about himself.
   b. The fact that Bob didn't investigate the company is making him wonder about himself.

6 TAPE DISCUSSION

How can you deal with a co-worker you are not getting along with? Talk with a partner. Share your views with the class.

7 LISTENING 2

Read and listen to the following excerpts from a telephone conversation that Al had with his parents. Then circle the letters of the sentences that correctly describe the meanings of certain sentences that you heard.

1. **a.** There is one supervisor.
   b. There is more than one supervisor.

2. **a.** All of Al's roommates are from Canada.
   b. Some of Al's roommates are from Canada.

3. **a.** Al has one English class.
   b. Al has more than one English class.

4. **a.** Al has one history class.
   b. Al has more than one history class.

(continued on next page)

5. a. There is one group of girls.

    b. There is more than one group of girls.

6. a. Al has one advisor.

    b. Al has more than one advisor.

8 INTERACTION

Work with a partner. On a separate piece of paper, complete this questionnaire, once for yourself and once in relation to the personality traits you perceive your partner to have. Then compare your answers.

1. I would rather spend Friday or Saturday night

    a. at a party with a group of people.   **b.** at home alone.

2. I am basically

    a. outgoing.   **b.** reserved or shy.

3. In general I'd say I am

    a. easy to get to know.   **b.** not so easy to get to know.

4. In general, I am closer to being

    a. a creative person.   **b.** a practical person.

5. In general, I

    a. appreciate constructive criticism.   **b.** dislike constructive criticism.

6. I think it's more important to

    a. always tell the truth, no matter the consequences.   **b.** avoid telling the whole truth if necessary to keep from hurting someone's feelings.

7. Basically, I prefer

    a. to be the leader.   **b.** to let someone else be the leader.

8. I usually

    a. take a long time to make a decision.   **b.** make a decision quickly.

9 ESSAY

Consider again the personality categories which have been mentioned in this unit, and choose the one which you believe fits you the best. Write an essay of three or four paragraphs showing why you fit the category. Include several examples from your own experience.

OR

Visit the Keirsey Web site at http://www.keirsey.com/cgi-bin/keirsey/newktsa.cgl *and take the Keirsey Temperament Sorter II test online. Then study the results. Write an essay in which you explain why you feel the test is accurate or inaccurate regarding your personality.*

10 PICTURE DISCUSSION

Look at this picture as a reflection of a time and a place. What was it like? How are the people dressed? How do they relate to each other? Describe the picture, using adjective clauses whenever appropriate.

Georges Seurat, French, 1859–1891, *A Sunday on La Grande Jatte*—1884–86.
Oil on canvas, 1884–86, 207.6 × 308 cm. Helen Birch Bartlett Memorial Collection, 1926.224.
Photograph ©1999, The Art Institute of Chicago, All Rights Reserved.

EXAMPLE:
The woman **who is standing in the center of the picture** is holding her daughter's hand very tightly.

ADJECTIVE CLAUSES WITH QUANTIFIERS; ADJECTIVE PHRASES

GRAMMAR **IN CONTEXT**

QUESTIONS TO CONSIDER

1. Do you like movies? What do you look for in a movie? Do you see movies primarily for entertainment, or do you want a film to be something morc?

2. Which kind of movie do you like better—one in which you already know what is going to happen, or one in which you don't know what is going to happen?

Read the movie review.

TITANIC

by Dartagnan Fletcher

All the fanfare surrounding James Cameron's blockbuster movie *Titanic* was rubbing this reviewer the wrong way. When *Titanic* had first been released I'd resisted seeing it because, to be frank, I just didn't feel like watching 1,500 people drown. I was even more turned off when I heard James Cameron accept his Academy Award for Best Direction: "Tonight I'm the king of the world." "How arrogant can a person be?" I wondered. The next day at my desk at the newspaper, I jotted down ten reasons why I shouldn't have to see *Titanic* and write a review of it, all of which I eventually threw away when my wife dragged me to the picture. It's a good thing she did. Arrogance aside, Cameron, director of many well-known movies, including *Terminator I* and *II* and *True Lies*, has done it again. I was quite pleasantly surprised. My advice to you is this: Go and see it. Anyone interested in cinema should experience this film.

Titanic, said to have cost at least $200 million to make, is well on its way to becoming the highest-grossing movie of all time. Before seeing the picture I was aware that many people have gone back again and again to see it, and I wondered why. "It must be because of the special effects," I said to myself. There's much more to *Titanic* than special effects, however. What really makes the picture work is the story-within-the-story framework. As the film opens, we focus on a modern-day treasure hunter who has mounted an expedition in which divers will attempt to recover a famous and very valuable necklace reported to have gone down with the *Titanic* when it sank on April 16, 1912. The expedition just happens to be televised, and the telecast just happens to be watched by a 101-year-old woman who not only was on the *Titanic* but who has the necklace. Before we know it, the woman and her granddaughter have joined the expedition, at which time they proceed to tell everyone what it was really like the night of the disaster. Once the old lady begins telling her tale, the film proceeds in flashbacks of her recollections.

One of *Titanic's* strengths is its full panoply of actors, most of whom distinguish themselves. Leonardo DiCaprio plays Jack Dawson, the young man on the ship who meets and rescues Rose DeWitt Bukater (a young woman played by Kate Winslett) from an impending marriage about which she is despairing. There's an interesting chemistry between DiCaprio and Winslett. Gloria Stewart does a wonderful job of playing Winslett's character at the age of 101. Particularly effective is Kathy Bates, who plays the role of Molly Brown of unsinkable Molly Brown fame. But the real standout for this reviewer is Billy Zane, who plays to perfection the role of Rose's incredibly arrogant and stuffy fiancé whom, of course, Rose does not marry in the end.

(continued on next page)

TITANIC (continued)

Watching a movie like this, one is faced with the inevitable question that has been asked many times: Is it more suspenseful to know the end of a story or not to know the end of it? I come down on the side of the former. We all know what happened when the *Titanic* sank: 1,500 people died. Somehow, knowing the outcome makes the suspense greater. Once we have gotten to know the characters, our knowledge of their ultimate fate makes the experience of watching their story play out all the more poignant. Still, if you're James Cameron making a blockbuster movie, the fact remains that 1,500 people died in the disaster, in which case you've got to figure out how not to make the film a downer. I mean, you can't just end it with 1,500 dead people slipping beneath the water, can you? Cameron had to find a way to end *Titanic* in an uplifting fashion, and he did. I'll leave it to you to find out how he does it.

By the way, I must assure my readers that I will not be a member of that group responsible for destroying the pleasure of many moviegoers by divulging the secret of what happens to the necklace. Find out for yourself by going and seeing the movie. Rumor has it, though, that with *Titanic's* reissue, the lines to get in are long, in which case you might want to take along a sleeping bag and a picnic lunch. The wait will be worth it. Rating: $3\frac{1}{2}$ stars out of a possible ★★★★.

UNDERSTANDING MEANING FROM CONTEXT

Circle the letter of the choice closest in meaning to the italicized word or expression from the reading.

1. All the *fanfare* surrounding James Cameron's blockbuster movie *Titanic* was rubbing this reviewer the wrong way.

    a. confusion   **b.** celebration   **c.** music

2. All the fanfare surrounding James Cameron's blockbuster movie *Titanic* was *rubbing this reviewer the wrong way*.

    a. irritating this reviewer   **b.** helping this reviewer   **c.** puzzling this reviewer

3. One of *Titanic's* strengths is its full *panoply* of actors . . .

    a. collection   **b.** impressive arrangement   **c.** acting ability

4. Billy Zane . . . plays to perfection the role of Rose's incredibly arrogant and *stuffy* fiancé . . .

    a. interesting   **b.** boring   **c.** intelligent

5. Once we have gotten to know the characters, our knowledge of their ultimate fate makes the experience of watching their story play out all the more *poignant*.

    a. annoying   **b.** difficult to comprehend   **c.** emotionally powerful

GRAMMAR **PRESENTATION**
ADJECTIVE CLAUSES WITH QUANTIFIERS; ADJECTIVE PHRASES

ADJECTIVE CLAUSES WITH QUANTIFIERS

One of *Titanic's* strengths is its full panoply of actors, **most of whom distinguish themselves**.

The next day at my desk at the newspaper, I jotted down ten reasons why I shouldn't have to see *Titanic* and write a review of it, **all of which I eventually threw away** when my wife dragged me to the picture.

Rumor has it, though, that the lines to get into *Titanic* are long, **in which case you might want to take along a sleeping bag and a picnic lunch**.

ADJECTIVE PHRASES

Anyone **interested in cinema** should experience this film.

Titanic, **said to have cost at least $200 million to make**, is well on its way to becoming the highest-grossing movie of all time.

Cameron, **director of many well-known movies, including *Terminator I* and *II* and *True Lies***, has done it again.

NOTES

EXAMPLES

1. Certain **nondefining adjective clauses** follow the pattern quantifier + preposition + relative pronoun *whom* or *which*. These relative pronouns refer to an earlier head noun.

- One of *Titanic's* strengths is its full panoply of actors, **most of whom distinguish themselves**. (*Whom* refers to the head noun *actors*.)

2. Another adjective clause of this type is made with just a preposition and a relative pronoun. Sentences with *of whom* and *of which* are rather formal and more common in writing than in speech.

- Jack Dawson meets and rescues Rose DeWitt Bukater from an impending marriage **about which she is despairing**.

Sometimes a noun can appear instead of a quantifier.

- Cameron has directed many famous movies, **examples of which** are *Terminator I* and *II* and *True Lies*.

▶ **BE CAREFUL!** Remember that we use *whom* to refer to people and *which* to refer to things.

- One of *Titanic's* strengths is its full panoply of actors, **most of whom** distinguish themselves.
  NOT ~~most of which distinguish themselves.~~

3. The adjective phrase *in which case* is used to introduce a clause. Use this phrase when you could restate the phrase by saying *in that case, in that situation, if that is the case,* or *if that happens*. The relative pronoun *which* refers to an idea described earlier in the sentence.

- Rumor has it that lines to get into the movie are long, **in which case** you should take along a sleeping bag and a picnic lunch. (*In which case* can be restated as "If it is the case that the lines are long . . .")

4. Remember that a **phrase** is a group of words which doesn't have a subject and a verb. Adjective clauses, both defining and nondefining, are commonly reduced to adjective phrases. Speakers and writers do this when they want to achieve an economy of language while maintaining clarity of meaning.

- Anyone **who is interested in cinema** should experience this film.

- Anyone **interested in cinema** should experience this film. (The relative pronoun *who* and the verb *is* are deleted, leaving a defining phrase modifying *anyone*.)

5. There are two ways of reducing an adjective clause to an adjective phrase.

a. If the adjective clause contains a form of the verb *be*, delete the relative pronoun, the form of *be*, and any accompanying auxiliaries.

- I will not be a member of that group [that is] **responsible for destroying the pleasure of many moviegoers by divulging the secret of what happens to the necklace**.

- *Titanic*, [which is] **said to have cost at least $200 million to make**, is well on its way to becoming the highest-grossing movie of all time.

b. If the adjective clause does not contain a form of the verb *be*, delete the relative pronoun and change the verb to its present participial form.

- *Titanic*, **which stars** Leonardo DiCaprio and Kate Winslett, is on its way to becoming the highest-grossing movie of all time.

- *Titanic*, **starring** Leonardo DiCaprio and Kate Winslett, is on its way to becoming the highest-grossing movie of all time.

FOCUSED PRACTICE

 DISCOVER THE GRAMMAR

Part A

Look again at the movie review. Find three adjective clauses containing **which** *and one containing* **whom** *and write them on the lines provided. Then write the noun referred to by each of these relative pronouns.*

1.   which I eventually threw away. noun: reasons

2. _____

3. _____

Part B

On the lines provided, write six adjective phrases which have been reduced from adjective clauses by deleting the verb **be***. Then write each phrase as a clause by restoring the verb* **be***.*

1.   all of the fanfare surrounding James Cameron's blockbuster movie.

    all of the fanfare that is surrounding James Cameron's blockbuster movie.

2. _____

_____

3. _____

_____

4. _____

_____

5. _____

_____

6. _____

_____

Part C

Look at this sentence. Rewrite it as two sentences by changing the adjective phrase with **including** *to a separate sentence.*

Cameron is the director of many well-known movies, including *Terminator I* and *II*.

_____

_____

2 FILM TRIVIA

Complete the following statements about movies, writing adjective clauses in the form **quantifier + preposition + relative pronoun**.

1. Mel Gibson and Danny Glover, <u>both of whom starred in the *Lethal Weapon* movies</u>,
(both / star / in the *Lethal Weapon* movies)
also acted together in *Maverick*.

2. Sean Connery, Roger Moore, and Timothy Dalton,

_____, come from Britain, while
(all / have / play / the role of James Bond)
Pierce Brosnan, the newest Bond, is Irish.

3. *Star Wars, The Empire Strikes Back,* and *Return of the Jedi,*

_____, are the middle three films in a
(all / have / earn / over $100 million)
projected nine-part series.

4. *Saving Private Ryan* and *Schindler's List,*

_____, have been critical as well as
(both / direct / by Steven Spielberg)
financial successes.

5. Walt Disney's animated productions,

_____, are known worldwide.
(most / be / loved by children)

6. Roberto Benigni and Wim Wenders,

_____, are both highly regarded
(neither / be / very / very well-known to mass American audiences)
European film directors.

3 POPULAR MOVIES

Complete each sentence with a nonidentifying adjective phrase for each film mentioned.

1. *E.T.,* _____ directed by Steven Spielberg _____, was the top-earning film
(direct / by / Steven Spielberg)
until it was toppled by the reissued *Star Wars* and by *Titanic*.

2. *Jurassic Park,* _____, is the fourth-
(base / on / Michael Crichton's novel)
biggest moneymaking film of all time.

3. *The Sound of Music,* _____, is the
(star / Julie Andrews and Christopher Plummer)
top-grossing nonanimated musical film.

4. *Dances with Wolves,* _____, is the
(direct and produce / by / Kevin Costner)
top-grossing western film.

5. *Star Wars, The Empire Strikes Back,* and *Return of the Jedi,*

_____, were conceived, written, and
(feature / Harrison Ford, Carrie Fisher, and Mark Hamill)
produced by George Lucas.

④ MOVIE GENRES   Grammar Notes 2–5

*Combine each pair of sentences about types of movies into a single sentence with
an adjective clause or phrase.*

1. Many recent science fiction films have been huge financial successes. They include
Jurassic Park, Independence Day, and *Men in Black.*

Many recent science fiction films, including Jurassic Park, Independence Day, and

Men in Black, have been huge financial successes.

2. Comedies have continued to be extremely popular and very successful financially.
Recent examples of them are *There's Something about Mary, Mrs. Doubtfire,* and
Liar, Liar.

_____

_____

3. Musical animated films have also become very popular. They include *The Lion King,
Pocahontas,* and *The Hunchback of Notre Dame.*

_____

_____

4. It looks as though sequels to big movie hits may lose their appeal. In that case,
moviemakers will be forced to become more creative.

_____

_____

⑤ EDITING

Read the letter and correct the ten errors involving adjective clauses and phrases.
Delete verbs or change relative pronouns where necessary, but do not change
punctuation or add relative pronouns.

Malibu Manor
BED AND BREAKFAST

July 15

Dear Eric,

Diana and I are having a great time in Los Angeles. We spent the first day at the

beach in Venice and saw where *Harry and Tonto* was filmed—you know, that movie

a few years ago ~~starred~~ *starring* Art Carney and an orange cat? Yesterday we went to

Universal Studios and learned about all the cinematic tricks, most of them I wasn't

aware of. Amazing! The funny thing is that even though you know that an illusion

is presented on the screen is just an illusion, you still believe it's real when you see

the movie. Then we took the tram tour around the premises and saw several actors

working, some of them I recognized. I felt like jumping off the tram and shouting

"Would everyone is famous please give me your autograph?" In the evening we

went to a party at the home of one of Diana's friends, many of them are connected

with the movie business. I had a really interesting conversation with a fellow works

in the industry who claims that a lot of movies are made these days are modeled

conceptually after amusement park rides. Just like the rides, they start slowly and

easily, then they have a lot of twists and turns are calculated to scare you to death,

and they end happily. Pretty fascinating, huh? What next?

Sorry to babble on so much about the movies, but you know what an addict

I am. Anyway, I may be coming back a day early, in that case I'll call and let you

know so that you can pick me up at the airport.

Love you lots,

Jean

COMMUNICATION PRACTICE

6 LISTENING

Listen to the TV film reviewer give her weekly review. Then listen again to certain of the reviewer's sentences. For each numbered item, respond **T (True)** *or* **F (False)** *to indicate if it correctly restates the sentence that you heard.*

_____ **1.** The film festival can be seen this holiday weekend.

_____ **2.** None of these great movies has been shown in more than a decade.

_____ **3.** *Fargo* is based on a murder case created by director Joel Coen.

_____ **4.** *Fargo* is about a car salesman who is kidnapped because of his debts.

_____ **5.** The reviewer believes that it was right for *Forrest Gump* to win the award for best picture.

_____ **6.** *Forrest Gump* makes the reviewer cry.

_____ **7.** The reviewer thinks that you shouldn't see *Evita* if you don't like musicals.

_____ **8.** *Evita* was directed by Madonna.

_____ **9.** Michael J. Fox was responsible for launching *Back to the Future*.

_____ **10.** The reviewer says black-and-white movies are not pretty.

_____ **11.** All who regard themselves as serious movie junkies must see *Casablanca*.

7 A REVIEW OF *THE LION KING*

Read this capsule movie review.

MOVIE REVIEW

The Lion King
(1994) **C-88m.**

Rating: ★★★	**Directors:** Roger Allers, Rob Minkoff.

Voices of: Jonathan Taylor Thomas, Matthew Broderick, James Earl Jones, Jeremy Irons, Moira Kelly, Miketa Calame, Ernie Savella, Nathan Lane, Robert Guillaume, Rowan Atkinson, Madge Sinclair, Whoopi Goldberg, Cheech Marin, Jim Cummings.

A lion cub raised to take his father's place someday as king of the jungle is sabotaged by his evil uncle—and lives in exile until he realizes his rightful place in the circle of life. With distant echoes of BAMBI, this entertaining Disney cartoon feature (highlighted by a chart-topping and Oscar-winning music score by Hans Zimmer) has dazzling scenics, some show-stopping animation, and outstanding voice work—but drama so intense (and comedy so hip) it's not really for very young viewers. [G]

Source: "The Lion King," copyright © 1997 by Leonard Maltin, from *LEONARD MALTIN'S TV MOVIES AND VIDEO GUIDE* by Leonard Maltin. Used by permission of Dutton Signet, a division of Penguin Putnam, Inc.

Discussion

Is violence in children's movies and / or literature appropriate? Violence and threatening situations are part of the world of children's literature—consider Little Red Riding Hood, Jack and the Beanstalk, *and so on. Why do you think this is so? Discuss as a class.*

8 INFORMATION GAP: A MOVIE REVIEW

Working with a partner, complete the text. Each of you will read a version of a review of the film Schindler's List. *Each version is missing some information. Take turns asking your partner questions to get the missing information.*

Student A, read the review of Schindler's List. *Ask questions and fill in the missing information. Then answer Student B's questions.*

Student B, turn to the Information Gap on page 208 and follow the instructions there.

EXAMPLE:

A: Whom did Schindler save?

B: He saved more than 1,000 Polish Jews.
Whom did they manufacture crockery for?

A: For the German army.

MOVIE REVIEW
Schindler's List
(1993) **C/B&W-195m.**

Rating: ★★★★ **Director:** Steven Spielberg. **Starring:** Liam Neeson, Ben Kingsley, Ralph Fiennes, Caroline Goodall, Jonathan Sagalle, Embeth Davidtz, Malgoscha Gegel, Shmulik Levy, Mark Ivanir, Beatrice Macola.

Staggering adaptation of Thomas Keneally's best-seller about the real-life Catholic war profiteer who initially flourished by sucking up to the Nazis, but eventually went broke saving the lives of more than 1,000 _____ by employing them in his factory, manufacturing _____ for the German army. Filmed almost entirely on location in Poland, in gritty b&w, but with a pace to match the most frenzied Spielberg works, this looks and feels like nothing Hollywood has ever made before. The three central characters rate—and receive—unforgettable performances: Neeson, who's towering as _____; Kingsley, superb as his Jewish accountant (and conscience); and Fiennes, who's frightening as the odious _____. Outstanding screenplay by Steven Zaillian and _____ by Janusz Kaminsky. Spielberg's most intense and personal film to date. Seven _____ include Best Picture, Director, Adapted Screenplay, and Original Score (John Williams).®

⑨ GROUP DISCUSSION

Divide into groups of six to eight and discuss the pros and cons of one of the following issues. For the first item (the rating system), prepare carefully for the discussion by doing some research, either by going to the library or by using the Internet. For the second item, you can speak from your own experience. Share the main points of your discussion with the class as a whole.

1. The rating system for films should be strengthened / should be left as it is.

2. Movies have / have not become too violent.

⑩ ESSAY

Write your own movie review in an essay of three or more paragraphs. Choose a film that you liked or disliked, but try to be objective in your review. Read your review to the class and answer any questions your classmates might ask about the movie.

⑪ PICTURE DISCUSSION

Talk with a partner. What is happening here? Why are the teenagers protesting? What is the theater policy? What do you think the reporter is saying? Write her statements.

_____

_____

_____

Student B, read the review of Schindler's List. *Answer Student A's questions.*
Then ask your own questions and fill in the missing information.

EXAMPLE:

A: Whom did Schindler save?

B: He saved more than 1,000 Polish Jews.
Whom did they manufacture crockery for?

A: For the German army.

 **MOVIE REVIEW**
Schindler's List
(1993) **C/B&W–195m.**

Rating: ★★★★ **Director:** Steven Spielberg.
Starring: Liam Neeson, Ben Kingsley, Ralph Fiennes, Caroline Goodall, Jonathan Sagalle, Embeth Davidtz, Malgoscha Gegel, Shmulik Levy, Mark Ivanir, Beatrice Macola.

Staggering adaptation of Thomas Keneally's best-seller about the real-life Catholic war profiteer who initially flourished by sucking up to the Nazis, but eventually went broke saving the lives of more than 1,000 Polish Jews by employing them in his factory, manufacturing crockery for _____. Filmed almost entirely on location in _____, in gritty b&w, but with a pace to match the most frenzied Spielberg works, this looks and feels like nothing Hollywood has ever made before. The three central characters rate—and receive—unforgettable performances: Neeson, who's towering as Oskar Schindler; Kingsley, superb as _____ (and conscience); and Fiennes, who's frightening as the odious Nazi commandant. Outstanding _____ by Steven Zaillian and cinematography by Janusz Kaminsky. Spielberg's most intense and personal film to date. Seven Oscars include Best _____, Director, Adapted Screenplay, and Original Score (John Williams).®

Source: "Schindler's List," copyright © 1997 by Leonard Maltin, from *LEONARD MALTIN'S TV MOVIES AND VIDEO GUIDE* by Leonard Maltin. Used by permission of Dutton Signet, a division of Penguin Putnam, Inc.

REVIEW OR SELFTEST

I. *Read the paragraphs and underline all of the adjective clauses.*

Recently at work I had an experience that proved to me the truth of that old adage: Things may not be what they seem. The experience involved two people I work with in my secretarial job. The first, whom I'll call "Jennifer," is one of those sunny types who always greet you in a friendly manner and never have an unkind word to say. The second, whom I'll call "Myrtle," is the type who rarely gives compliments and can sometimes be critical. Between the two of them, I thought Jennifer was the one who was my friend. Myrtle never seemed to care much for me, which is why I didn't seek out her friendship. I learned, though, that I had been reading them wrong.

About two months ago, some money was stolen from someone's purse in the office. It happened on an afternoon when all three of us, Jennifer, Myrtle, and I, were working together. Our boss, who tends to jump to conclusions, questioned the three of us and said that someone whose name he wouldn't reveal had implicated me in the theft. Jennifer, whom I expected to stand up for me, hemmed and hawed and said she didn't know where I'd been at the time of the theft, which was a lie. Myrtle, however, spoke up and said she knew I couldn't have been the one who had stolen the money because she and I had been working together all afternoon. The boss accepted her statement, and that ended the unpleasantness, and it also ended my friendship with Jennifer. I found out later that she wanted my job. I don't know whether or not she was the one who took the money, but I do know that the old proverb that tells us not to judge a book by its cover has some truth in it. Myrtle and I have been friends ever since.

II. *Read the sentences, which form a narration. Circle the correct relative pronoun for each sentence.*

1. John and Kathleen Carter, (that / who) got married about a year ago, recently bought a new house.

2. The neighborhood (that / in which) they have been living is a somewhat dangerous one.

3. The neighborhood (that / who) they are moving into is much safer.

4. Their new house, (that / which) they bought quite cheaply, does need some fixing up.

5. However, they will be receiving some help from their neighbors, most of (who / whom) they like.

6. The Ibarguens, (who / whom) live next door to them, have volunteered to lend their tools.

7. The Travantis, (who / whom) live across the street from John and Kathleen, have promised to help them put in a new lawn.

8. The Ibarguens, (who / whose) daughter is the same age as Mackenzie, John and Kathleen's daughter, are helping Mackenzie make new friends.

9. Kathleen, (that / who) works for a county hospital, will still have to commute to work.

10. John, (whom / whose) company is nearby, will be able to walk to work.

III. *Read the sentences, which form a narration. Put the relative pronoun in parentheses if it can be omitted. Do not omit relative pronouns if they are subjects.*

  1. On our trip to Europe last summer, we met a lot of people (whom) we liked.

  2. One of the most interesting was a young man from Italy who was named Cosimo.

  3. We were hitchhiking outside Florence. Cosimo, who was on his way home from Pisa, stopped and picked us up.

  4. The car that he was driving was a 1982 Volkswagen.

  5. Cosimo took us to his house, which was not far from downtown Pisa, and invited us to stay for a few days.

  6. He also introduced us to a group of people that we felt very comfortable with.

  7. We were scheduled to go to Switzerland next, so Cosimo gave us the address of a cousin of his who lived in Bern.

  8. We had such a wonderful time in Italy and Switzerland that we decided to go back next year, which will cost money but will be worth it.

IV. *Complete each sentence with a nonidentifying* **which-** *clause that modifies the first clause. Add necessary pronouns and verbs.*

  1. Frannie needs to stay home to reenergize herself,

    <u>which is why she can be considered an introvert.</u>
                (why / an introvert)

  2. Jonathan becomes energized when he is around other people,

    _____

                (why / an extrovert)

3. Sensors are practical people who notice what is going on around them,

_____.

(why / past experiences to make determinations)

4. Intuitives are interested in relationships between things or people,

_____.

(the fact that / what could be than what is)

5. Judgers are people who prefer a structured and predictable environment,

_____.

(preference for making decisions and having things settled)

V. *Write a sentence containing an adjective clause describing the indicated people. Punctuate the clauses correctly, paying attention to whether the clauses are identifying or nonidentifying. Use* **who**, **whom**, **whose**, **that**, **which**.

1. The man ___who is talking with the receptionist has brought his daughter to the dentist___.

2. The girl _____.

3. The boy _____.

4. The man _____.

5. The poster _____.

6. The poster _____.

7. The woman _____.

8. The woman _____.

VI. *Circle the letter of the one underlined word or phrase which is not correct in each sentence.*

1. George Lucas, <u>whose</u> work <u>including</u> *Star Wars, The Empire Strikes*
            A   B

   Back, and *Return of the Jedi* and <u>who</u> <u>has become</u> a world-famous
                           C   D

   movie director and producer, is directing more *Star Wars* films.
       A Ⓑ C D

2. Previously married couple Kenneth Branagh and Emma Thompson,

   <u>both</u> <u>of which</u> are well-known internationally, appeared together
    A   B

   while still married in films <u>directed</u> by Branagh, <u>including</u> *Henry V*
                          C   D

   and *Peter's Friends*.
       A B C D

3. Police <u>in Charleston</u> are investigating a crime <u>that</u> <u>was committing</u>
          A   B   C

   yesterday evening between 11:00 P.M. and midnight at the city art
       A B C D

   museum, <u>which</u> is located on Fifth Avenue.
           D

4. Detective Amanda Reynolds, <u>who</u> is the chief investigating officer in the
                          A
       A B C D

   case, says <u>that</u> the police have no suspects yet but are focusing on tips
          B

   <u>suggest</u> <u>that</u> the theft may have been an inside job.
     C   D

5. Al, <u>whom</u> is a freshman at the university, is pleased with his college
       A
       A B C D

   living situation because he likes <u>the people</u> <u>he</u> is rooming <u>with</u>.
                         B   C   D

6. His courses, <u>none</u> <u>of which</u> are easy, are all classes <u>requiring</u> a
            A   B   C
       A B C D

   considerable amount of study, <u>that</u> is why he has joined a study group.
                          D

7. Textrix, <u>the company</u> <u>for that</u> Alex works, tends to employ people
            A   B
       A B C D

   <u>who are</u> self-starters and <u>who have</u> at least ten years of experience in
     C   D

   the field.

8. Alicia, <u>an extrovert loves</u> working with people and <u>who can</u> also work
           A   B
       A B C D

   independently, had many accomplishments in her last job, <u>which is</u> why
                                              C

   I think she's <u>the person we should hire</u>.
                D

9. The lines <u>to get into</u> *Star Wars: The Phantom Menace,* <u>a movie</u> <u>directed</u> **A B C D**
            A   B   C

    by George Lucas, may be long, <u>in that case</u> I would recommend going
                                             D

    to a matinee screening.

10. Jaime, <u>who</u> has been employed for ten years at a company <u>that</u> stresses **A B C D**
            A

    team-building and cooperative effort, is a person <u>who</u> has learned to
                                            C

    value <u>the people with he works</u>.
             D

VII. *Go back to your answers to Exercise VI. Write the correct form for each item that you believe is incorrect.*

    1.   includes   _____   **6.** _____

    2. _____   **7.** _____

    3. _____   **8.** _____

    4. _____   **9.** _____

    5. _____   **10.** _____

▶ **To check your answers, go to the Answer Key on page 217.**

FROM GRAMMAR TO WRITING
PUNCTUATION OF ADJECTIVE CLAUSES

Remember that the two types of adjective clauses are identifying and nonidentifying. Identifying adjective clauses identify or give essential information. Nonidentifying clauses give additional or nonessential information.

> **EXAMPLES:**
> I saw three movies last week. The movie that I liked best was *You've Got Mail*.

The adjective clause **that I liked best** is identifying because it says which movie I am talking about. If the clause were removed, the sentence would not make complete sense.

> The movie was *You've Got Mail*.

Therefore, the clause is essential for the sentence's meaning.

> *Casablanca*, **which contains the famous song** "As Time Goes By," is considered a film classic.

The nonidentifying clause **which contains the famous song "As Time Goes By"** adds more information about *Casablanca*. This clause, however, is not used to identify. If it were removed, the sentence would still make sense.

> *Casablanca* is considered a film classic.

In speech, identifying clauses have no appreciable pauses before or after them. Therefore, they are not enclosed in commas when written. Nonidentifying clauses, on the other hand, do have pauses before and after them. Therefore, they are enclosed in commas.

> **EXAMPLES:**
> A person who needs others to become energized is an extrovert. (identifying; no commas)
> James, who comes alive when he feels comfortable with the people around him, is an extrovert. (nonidentifying; commas)

If you are unsure whether a clause is identifying or nonidentifying, try reading it aloud. The natural pauses made by your voice will help you to determine whether or not the clause needs to be enclosed in commas.

1 *Punctuate the following sentences containing adjective clauses. They form a narration.*

1. Tom and Sandra who have been married for more than twenty-five years are both outgoing people.

2. Tom who is clearly an extrovert loves meeting new people.

3. Sandra who is very quick to make friends loves to have friends over for dinner.

4. Tom and Sandra have two married sons both of whom live abroad.

5. The son who is older lives with his family in Britain.

6. The son who is younger lives with his family in southern Italy.

7. Tom and Sandra own a house in the city and one in the country. The one that they spend most of their time in is in the city.

8. The house that they spend summers in is located in Vermont.

Like clauses, adjective phrases are also identifying or nonidentifying, depending on whether they add essential or extra information.

EXAMPLES:
The postwar director most responsible for putting Italian cinema on the map is Federico Fellini. (identifying; no commas)

Federico Fellini, the director of such classics as *8 1/2*, died in 1994. (nonidentifying; commas)

2 *Punctuate the following sentences containing adjective phrases.*

1. A film produced by George Lucas is almost a guaranteed success.

2. A film directed by Steven Spielberg is likely to be a blockbuster.

3. *Life Is Beautiful* directed by Roberto Benigni and starring Benigni and his wife has become well known all over the world.

4. Many Canadians including Donald Sutherland and Michael J. Fox are major international film stars.

5. The Universal Studios located in California was established decades ago.

6. The Universal Studios located in Florida was established much more recently.

❸ *Punctuate the following letter containing adjective phrases and clauses.*

September 30

Dear Mom and Dad,

Thanks for bringing me down here to the University last Sunday. Classes didn't start until Wednesday, so I had a few days to get adjusted. I'm signed up for five classes: zoology, calculus, English, and two history sections. It's a heavy load, but they're all courses that will count for my degree. The zoology class which meets at 8:00 every morning is going to be my hardest subject. The history class that I have in the morning is on Western Civilization; the one in the afternoon is on early United States history. Calculus which I have at noon every day looks like it's going to be easy. Besides zoology, the other class that's going to be hard is English. We have to do a composition a week.

   I like all of my roommates but one. There are four of us in our suite including two girls from Texas and a girl from Manitoba. Sally who is from San Antonio is great; I feel like I've known her all my life. I also really like Anne the girl from Manitoba. But Heather the other girl from Texas is kind of a pain. She's one of those types of people who never tell you what's bothering them and then get hostile. All in all, though, it looks like it's going to be a great year. I'll write again in a week or so.

Love,

Vicky

❹ APPLY IT TO YOUR WRITING

Bring to class a detailed photograph from a magazine, a newspaper, or your own collection. In class, write a paragraph of eight to ten sentences describing the picture. Include a number of adjective clauses in your paragraph, making sure to use at least one identifying and one nonidentifying adjective clause. Exchange your paper with a partner. Read each other's paragraphs aloud and make suggestions if necessary. Check for correct punctuation.

REVIEW OR SELFTEST
ANSWER KEY

PART IV

I. I work with in my secretarial job

whom I'll call "Jennifer"

who always greet you in a friendly manner and never have an unkind word to say

whom I'll call "Myrtle"

who rarely gives compliments and can sometimes be critical

who was my friend

which is why I didn't seek out her friendship

when all three of us, Jennifer, Myrtle, and I, were working together

who tends to jump to conclusions

whose name he wouldn't reveal

whom I expected to stand up for me

which was a lie

who had stolen the money

who took the money

that tells us not to judge a book by its cover

II.
2. in which
3. that
4. which
5. most of whom
6. who
7. who
8. whose
9. who
10. whose

III.
2. no change
3. no change
4. (that)
5. no change
6. (that)
7. no change
8. no change

IV. Possible Answers:
2. which is why he can be termed an extrovert
3. which is why they often rely on past experiences to make determinations
4. which is indicated by the fact that they tend to focus more on what could be than on what is
5. which is shown by their preference for making decisions and having things settled

V. Possible Answers:
2. The girl, whose father is talking to the receptionist, doesn't want to visit her dentist.
3. The boy, whose mother is reading him a story, is named Jerry.
4. The man who is looking at one of the posters has a bad toothache.
5. The poster that is to the left of the receptionist's desk is about gum disease.
6. The poster that is to the right of the receptionist's desk is about brushing properly.
7. The woman who is reading a story to her son is wearing an enormous hat.
8. The woman who is reading a magazine has her dog with her.

VI.
2. B
3. C
4. C
5. A
6. D
7. B
8. A
9. D
10. D

VII.
2. of whom
3. was committed
4. suggesting
5. who
6. which
7. for which
8. an extrovert who loves
9. in which case
10. the people with whom he works / the people he works with

217

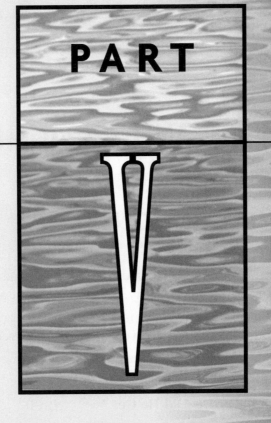

PART

V

PASSIVE VOICE

THE PASSIVE:
REVIEW AND EXPANSION

GRAMMAR **IN CONTEXT**

QUESTIONS TO CONSIDER

1. Many people find unsolved mysteries fascinating. Do you enjoy hearing about them? Why? Do you know of any unsolved mysteries?

2. Some people think there is a need for mystery in life, for things to remain unexplained. Do you agree or disagree?

3. Why do people sometimes sympathize with criminals and want them to get away with their crimes?

Read the article Did He Get Away with It?

DAILY NEWS

Did He Get Away with It?

A lot of crimes never get solved. The case of Dan Cooper is one that hasn't been. It was the evening before Thanksgiving, late November 1971. On a short flight between Portland and Seattle, a flight attendant was handed a note by a mysterious middle-aged man dressed in a dark suit. The flight attendant thought he was making a romantic advance, so she slipped the note into her pocket. The man leaned closer to her, saying, "Miss, you'd better look at that note. I have a bomb." A bit later he opened his briefcase so that she could see several red cylinders and a lot of wires within. The man, who used the alias "Dan Cooper," was demanding $200,000,

four parachutes, and a plane that would fly him to Mexico.

The plane proceeded to Seattle with none of the other passengers even aware that it was being hijacked. The other passengers got off the plane, and "Cooper" got what he was demanding. He received the $200,000, all in twenty-dollar bills that had been photo-copied by FBI agents so that they could easily be identified later. Then the plane was refueled and took off for Mexico.

A few minutes later, Cooper ordered the flight attendant to go to the cockpit and stay there. As she was leaving, she noticed him trying to tie something around his waist—presumably the bag of money. Then he opened the plane's rear stairway and jumped out of the plane. The crew felt pressure bumps which were probably caused by Cooper's jumping off the stairway. When Cooper jumped, into wind and freezing rain, the air temperature was seven degrees below zero. He was wearing no survival gear and only loafers on his feet.

Cooper has not been seen or heard from since that night. Who was Cooper? Did he get away with his escapade? Or did he get killed in the process of trying to commit the perfect crime?

Authorities speculate that Cooper landed near Ariel, a small town near the Columbia River north of Portland. Only one real clue has been discovered. Eight and a half years later, in 1980, an eight-year-old boy who was digging in a sandbank unearthed $5,800 of Cooper's loot. The money was only a few inches below the surface of the earth, but it had been eroded so badly that only the picture and the serial numbers on the bills were visible. Rotting rubber bands were found along with the money, indicating that the cash must have been deposited there before the bands fell apart. Since then, the area has been searched thoroughly, but no trace of Cooper has been found.

So what really happened? Many investigators believe that Cooper had to have been killed by the combination of the weather conditions and the impact of his fall. If this is true, though, why have none of the man's remains ever been discovered? Is more information known about this case than has been released? Have knowledgeable people been prevented from discussing the case? Is Cooper's body lost in some inaccessible area of the wilderness area into which he jumped, or is he living a luxurious life under an alias in some unknown location and driving a Rolls-Royce? Did he have the $5,800 buried by an accomplice in order to throw authorities off the track? Or did he bury it himself? In Ariel, the small town near where he might have landed, Cooper has become a legend. His story has been depicted in books and articles and even a movie. Patrons of a tavern in Ariel still celebrate the anniversary of the hijacking every year. The bar's owner, Dona Elliot, says, "He did get away with it . . . so far." Others don't think so. Jerry Thomas, a retired soldier who has been working independently on the case, thinks Cooper didn't survive the fall and that eventually his body will be found. "I know there is something out here," he says. "There has to be."

The mystery goes on.

Sources: Based on information in Mark McGwire, "15 Minutes of Fame," *Biography Magazine*, September 1998; and Richard Severn, "D. B. Cooper: Perfect Crime or Perfect Folly?" *Seattle Times*, November 17, 1996.

UNDERSTANDING MEANING FROM CONTEXT

Read each sentence. Think about the meaning of each italicized word or expression. Then answer each question.

1. The man, who used the *alias* "Dan Cooper," was demanding $200,000, four parachutes, and a plane that would fly him to Mexico.

   Was "Dan Cooper" the man's real name or a false name?

   _____

2. Did he *get away with his escapade*?

   Does the question ask whether Cooper succeeded in his plan or

   abandoned his plan? _____

3. Eight and a half years later, in 1980, an eight-year-old boy who was digging in a sandbank *unearthed $5,800 of Cooper's loot*.

   Did the boy find the money above ground or below ground?

   _____

4. *Rotting* rubber bands were found along with the money, indicating that the cash must have been deposited there before the bands fell apart.

   What was the condition of the rubber bands found along with the

   money? _____

GRAMMAR **PRESENTATION**
THE PASSIVE: REVIEW AND EXPANSION

SIMPLE PRESENT		
SUBJECT	**BE (OR GET)**	**PAST PARTICIPLE**
Some mysteries	**are**	**solved** easily.
A lot of crimes never	**get**	**solved**.

PRESENT PROGRESSIVE

Cooper's case **is** still **being investigated**.

SIMPLE PAST		
SUBJECT	**BE (OR GET)**	**PAST PARTICIPLE**
Some think Cooper	**was**	**killed** when he jumped from the plane.
Some think Cooper	**got**	**killed** when he jumped from the plane.

PAST PROGRESSIVE

The plane proceeded to Seattle with none of the other passengers even aware that it **was being hijacked**.

PRESENT PERFECT

Cooper has **not been seen or heard from** since that night.

PAST PERFECT

He received the $200,000, all in twenty-dollar bills that **had been photocopied** by FBI agents.

FUTURE

Jerry Thomas thinks Cooper didn't survive the fall and that eventually his body **will be found**.

MODALS AND MODAL-LIKE EXPRESSIONS

Rotting rubber bands were found along with the money, indicating that the cash **must have been deposited** there before the bands fell apart.

Many investigators believe that Cooper **had to have been killed** by the combination of the weather conditions and the impact of his fall.

PASSIVE CAUSATIVE

Did he **have** the $5,800 **buried** by an accomplice in order to throw authorities off the track?

NOTES	EXAMPLES
1. Passive sentences are formed with the verbs *be* (*am, are, is, was, were, be, been, being*) or *get* (*get, gets, got, gotten, getting*) plus a past participle.	• The plane **was refueled** and took off for Mexico. • A lot of crimes never **get solved**.
▶ **BE CAREFUL!** Only **transitive verbs**, those that take one or more objects, can be made passive. **Intransitive verbs** (verbs which do not take objects) cannot be made passive.	• People **have found** no trace of Cooper. (transitive—can be made passive) • No trace of Cooper **has been found**. (passive) • The plane **proceeded** to Seattle. (intransitive—cannot be made passive)

NOTES	EXAMPLES
2. In general, the **active voice** is considered stronger than the **passive voice**. Writers often prefer the active to the passive voice. In academic writing, however, the passive is frequently used. In writing and speaking, there are three instances in which the passive voice is recommended.	
a. When we don't know or don't care who performed the action.	• Then the plane **was refueled** and took off for Mexico.
b. When we want to avoid mentioning who performed the action.	• **Have** knowledgeable people **been prevented** from discussing the case?
c. When we want to focus on the receiver instead of the performer of the action.	• Cooper **had to have been killed** by the combination of the weather conditions and the impact of his fall.

NOTES	EXAMPLES
3. We often omit the *by* phrase in passive sentences if we consider it undesirable or unnecessary to mention the performer.	• Why **have** none of the man's remains ever **been discovered**?

4. Most commonly, the **direct object** in an active sentence becomes the subject in a passive sentence.

However, it is common for an **indirect object** to be the subject of a passive sentence.

- active   direct object
  Cooper **hijacked the plane**.
- passive
  The plane was hijacked by Cooper.
- direct object
  Cooper **handed** a note **to the** indirect object **attendant**.
- **The attendant was handed** a note by Cooper.

5. The passive with *get* is more informal than the passive with *be*. It is conversational and is characteristic of informal writing.

The *get*-passive sometimes is used to emphasize action and to focus on what happens to someone or something.

- If Cooper survived, will he ever **get caught**?

- Did Cooper **get killed** when he jumped from the plane?

6. *Get* and *have* are used to form the **passive causative**. Use the passive causative to talk about services that people arrange for someone else to do.

The **passive causative** can occur with or without a *by* phrase, but we often omit the *by* phrase.

- Perhaps Cooper **got** his hair **dyed** before the hijacking to disguise himself.

- **Did** Cooper **have** the $5,800 buried by an accomplice?

7. Review the formation and use of the passive in modal constructions.

- The 20-dollar bills had been photocopied by FBI agents so that they **could** easily **be identified** later.

FOCUSED PRACTICE

1 DISCOVER THE GRAMMAR

Part A

Look again at the opening reading, Did He Get Away with It? *You will find 24 passive constructions. Underline them. Then look at Grammar Note 2 on page 224. Write* **a**, **b**, *or* **c** *above each passive construction to show what kind of passive it is.*

   1. get *a* solved

Part B

   Listen to the excerpt from the radio mystery show "Phantasma." Then listen again as you read the "Phantasma" script. Circle all passive constructions with **be** *or* **get.**

Midnight. Earlier the city was blanketed by a nearly impenetrable mist, the perfect environment for a crime to be committed. Now the streets are getting pelted by violent raindrops. No one is about. On the sixty-seventh floor of a massive office building, the door to an executive suite of offices lies ajar. Inside, the main room is dimly lit. A man's body lies crumpled near the windows. An hour ago he got hit by a heavy object. The carpet around him is slowly getting stained by blood. A perfect crime has been committed. Or has it? A spark of life remains in the man. His life can be saved if help arrives soon. The perpetrator is now far from the scene, sure that he is going to be paid handsomely for his work. He is certain that the man was killed by the blow to his head, and he is convinced that his murderous actions were not noticed. He believes that his whereabouts are unknown. He is wrong! Phantasma knows who the perpetrator is and where he is. Phantasma knows all! Ha ha ha ha ha ha ha!

Part C

Complete the "Phantasma" story. Write an ending of three or four sentences. Use at least one passive in your ending. Read your ending to the class.

_____

_____

_____

_____

_____

❷ THREE FAMOUS MYSTERIES

Fill in the blanks in the following article with passive constructions with **be** *and the indicated verbs in the correct tenses.*

Three Unsolved Mysteries Continue to Fascinate

So you think there are no more mysteries, that all mysteries __are solved__
1. (solve)
in time? Think again. The pages of history teem with mysteries that _____.
2. (never crack)
Consider, for example, the case of the brigantine ship *Mary Celeste*. The ship had left New York for Italy in 1872 and _____
3. (later sight)
floating erratically east of the Azores. No one _____ on board, though
4. (find)
everything else on the ship _____
5. (determine)
to be in order, and there was no indication why the *Mary Celeste* _____. In
6. (abandon)
fact, tables _____ for afternoon
7. (apparently set)
tea. One theory speculates that the ship _____ by an impending explo-
8. (threaten)
sion that _____ by fumes from
9. (cause)
her cargo of alcohol. That theory, however,

_____.
10. (never prove)

A second perplexing mystery is that of Amelia Earhart, the famous aviator who in the twenties and thirties _____
11. (consider)
the quintessential example of the rugged female individual. Earhart flew across the Atlantic with two males in 1928 and set a record for a cross-Atlantic flight in 1932. In 1937 she embarked on her most ambitious plan, a flight around the world. Earhart began her flight in Miami in June and _____ only by Fred
12. (accompany)
Noonan, her navigator. They reached New Guinea and left for Howland Island in the South Pacific on July 1. After that, no radio reports or messages of any kind _____. No remains of her plane
13. (receive)
_____ by naval investigators.
14. (locate)
Did she simply attempt the impossible? _____ when her
15. (she and Noonan / simply kill)
plane ran out of fuel and crashed in the Pacific? Or could something else have happened? No one really knows.

A third unsolved mystery has to do with monsters—lake monsters, that is. Everyone knows about Nessie, the famous creature that is supposed to inhabit Loch Ness in Scotland.

(continued on next page)

Not too many people are yet aware, however, of the monster who is said to live in the Great Lake at Ostersund in central Sweden. This mystery _____. Over four
16. (still investigate)
thousand sightings _____ of
17. (report)
Nessie, the Scottish beast, but the resident of the Great Lake, if he exists, _____
18. (only spot)
175 times in 400 years. The monster, who

_____ Storsjoeodjuret in Swedish,
19. (name)

_____ as being 15 to 20 feet long,
20. (describe)
gray, green, or red in color, with a head like a dog or fish. In 1998, the lake

_____ in a search for clues.
21. (comb)
Storsjoeodjuret _____, but Adrian
22. (not see)
Shine, the noted investigator of the Loch Ness monster, is optimistic, saying about the search that "It was inconclusive but encouraging." More investigations _____
23. (undertake)
in the future.

For the time being, at least, the riddle of the *Mary Celeste*, the fate of Amelia Earhart, and the existence of the Swedish lake monster will have to remain mysterious.

Sources: Adapted from Kenneth C. Davis, *Don't Know Much About History* (New York: Avon Books, 1990) and "Swedish Lake Monster Eludes Search Party," *Dallas Morning News,* August 17, 1998, p. 14A.

③ JOYCE'S DIARY Grammar Note 5

*Read the following diary entry. Fill in the blanks with forms of the **get**-passive.*

Dear Diary,   March 15

This has been a strange day. I __got woken up__ by a phone call at five o'clock this
                                     1. (wake up)
morning. When I answered the phone, I heard music in the background, and there

was just the click of someone hanging up. I wouldn't think anything of it except that

this is the fifth time I've _____ out of bed like this. It has me worried.
                                2. (roust)
Am I just _____ by some "friend" with a weird sense of humor, like my
          3. (harass)
friend Harriet? She _____ periodically by practical jokers. Or am I
                     4. (bother)
going to _____ by someone who's been watching me and my apart-
         5. (rob)
ment? Tomorrow I'm going to _____ on the doors just in case. I'm also
                             6. (the locks / change)
going to call the telephone company. I just hope I don't _____ again
                                                         7. (disturb)
tomorrow morning. I need a good night's sleep.

                                                                                      Joyce

4 **EDITING**

Read the following script for a radio bulletin about a hit-and-run accident. In order to strengthen the writing, change all the sentences except the ones that are underlined from passive to active or from active to passive. Write the sentences in the order that makes the most sense.

<u>A hit-and-run accident occurred this evening at approximately 8:45 P.M.</u> The intersection of Fourth and Madison was being crossed by an eight-year-old boy.[1] A blue Toyota Corolla hit him.[2] Massive injuries were sustained by the boy.[3] Paramedics took him to Harborview Medical Center.[4] They are caring for him in the intensive care ward.[5] <u>His condition is critical.</u> The sheriff asks anyone with information about the accident to contact the sheriff's office at 444-6968.[6] They are offering a reward.[7]

1.   An eight-year-old boy was crossing the intersection of Fourth and Madison.

2.   _____

3.   _____

4.   _____

5.   _____

6.   _____

7.   _____

COMMUNICATION PRACTICE

5 LISTENING

Some animals have been stolen from the city zoo. Listen to the conversation between police detective Harry Sadler and zoo administrator Lane Akimura. Then listen again. Circle the letter of the sentence that gives correct information about what happened.

1. **a.** The janitor found the keeper.

   b. The keeper found the janitor.

2. **a.** Akimura examined the keeper.

   b. A physician examined the keeper.

3. **a.** The keeper had been drugged.

   b. The keeper had been hit.

4. **a.** It takes two weeks to see turtles.

   b. Two turtles were taken two weeks ago.

5. **a.** The police were notified about the first theft.

   b. The police weren't notified about the first theft.

6. **a.** The zoo expansion has been completed.

   b. The zoo expansion hasn't been completed.

7. **a.** Voters haven't yet approved the zoo expansion.

   b. Voters have already approved the zoo expansion.

8. **a.** First the animals eat. Then the food preparation area is cleaned.

   b. First the food preparation area is cleaned. Then the animals eat.

9. **a.** Detective Sadler will check the janitor's references himself.

   b. Detective Sadler will ask someone else to check the janitor's references.

6 INFORMATION GAP: A MYSTERY ENTITY

Student A, read clues 1–4 to Student B. Student B will complete the clues. Switch roles after item 4. Then put the clues in the correct order and decide what the mystery item is.

Student B, turn to page 233 and follow the instructions there.

Student A's Prompts

1. I was born, or maybe I should say I was created . . .

2. An all-night card game . . .

3. I was created by . . .

4. The "hero" type of me gets its name . . .

Student A's Conclusions

5. . . . have been known by my name since then.

6. . . . some slices of meat between two slices of bread.

7. . . . is shaped like a submarine.

8. . . . so he ordered a snack to be delivered to the gambling table.

9. . . . that I'm being eaten somewhere in the world this very minute.

 7 "RAFFLES" GANG HITS PALACES OF VENICE

Read the London Daily Telegraph *account of a contemporary unsolved mystery.*
Then respond **True (T)**, **False (F)**, *or* **Don't Know (DK)**.

LONDON DAILY TELEGRAPH

"Raffles" Gang Hits Palaces of Venice

EUROPEAN WIRE SERVICE—A gang of thieves is stripping Venice's finest palaces of paintings and artifacts worth millions of rands. The gang, known as the "Raffles of the Rialto," appears to have inside knowledge of which palaces are equipped with burglar alarms and which are unoccupied at any particular time.

In the biggest of a string of heists so far, the gang made off just over a week ago with the only oil painting still in private hands by the Venetian Old Master Canaletto, estimated to be worth about R11.35 million.

The 65m by 13m signed canvas, *Il Fonteghetto dela Farina,* was spirited away from the collection of the late Count Alvise Guistiniani. It was the most celebrated work in the collection.

The thieves also took a valuable map of Venice and other treasures from a palace in the Dorsoduro when the Count's adopted daughter was out. The palace had no alarm.

Before departing, the robbers added insult to injury by drinking the owner's champagne in antique Murano glasses.

The Canaletto was reportedly not even insured. Days before it was stolen, the thieves paid a visit to the house next door belonging to Italy's ambassador to London, Paolo Galli, which cost his family dearly.

On this occasion, the gang emptied the entire first floor of the palace, taking the family silver valued at about R946,000. The break-in was discovered by his daughter Francesca when she returned from a holiday.

Two other similar robberies took place in September,
(continued on next page)

"Raffles" Gang

including one in Palazzo Mocenigo. The palace was once the ancestral home of Count Alvise di Robilant, the former Sotheby's director bludgeoned to death in an unsolved case early last year, and was where Lord Byron lived when he wrote *Don Juan*.

Investigators piecing together the clues last week said they believed they could be dealing with a group of professionals who were working on commission and knew the city "to perfection." "These people are too clever and too well informed for words," an investigator said. "It's as though they had a plan of Venice where every palace minus an alarm was clearly indicated."

Source: © Telegraph Group Limited, London, 1999.

Comprehension

_____ **1.** "Raffles" is the Italian word for "gang."

_____ **2.** Priceless paintings and other art works are being cleaned out of Venice's finest palaces.

_____ **3.** The thieves were daring enough to drink brandy in antique glasses at one of the palaces.

_____ **4.** The palaces that were robbed were all outfitted with new alarm systems.

_____ **5.** One of the palaces that were robbed was the home of Sotheby's director, who was murdered in an unsolved case last year.

_____ **6.** The work of the thieves led police to call them amateurs.

Small Group Discussion

In groups of four, discuss these questions.

1. Why do you think the Canaletto was not insured?

2. Why do you think the palace from which the painting was stolen had no alarm?

3. How could the gang who stole the painting have such complete knowledge of Venice and knowledge of which palaces were unoccupied and without alarms?

8 ESSAY

Write an essay describing an unsolved mystery in the area where you live. It could be a murder, someone's disappearance, or some strange natural phenomenon. Describe what the mystery is and how it might have been caused. Offer some possible solutions to the mystery.

9 PICTURE DISCUSSION

This is a photograph of one group of crop circles which have been found in grain fields in England. There is still no officially accepted explanation of how these circles were made, or by whom. Form groups of four. Describe the circles in as much detail as possible. Then speculate as to how they might have been made. Use the passive whenever appropriate.

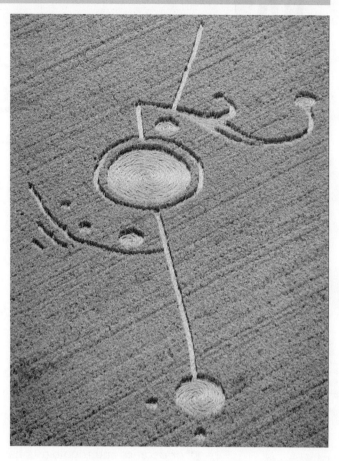

EXAMPLE:
The grass in the circles **has been flattened** by some force.

INFORMATION GAP FOR STUDENT B

Choose one of the phrases 1–4 to complete each clue that Student A reads. Switch roles after item 4. Then put the clues in the correct order and decide what the mystery item is.

Student B's Conclusions

1. . . . because of the hero-sized appetite that's needed to eat me.

2. . . . at 5 o'clock in the morning on August 6, 1762.

3. . . . was being played at a gambling table.

4. . . . an Englishman named John Montagu, the fourth earl of the place I was named after.

Student B's Prompts

5. The snack ordered by my creator was composed of . . .

6. It's almost certain . . .

7. My creator was hungry but too busy to leave the game, . . .

8. Two slices of bread with a filling between them . . .

9. And the submarine type of me . . .

13

REPORTING IDEAS AND FACTS WITH PASSIVES

GRAMMAR **IN CONTEXT**

QUESTIONS TO CONSIDER

1. Look at the illustration. What does it show? What is happening here?

2. What do you think the illustration means? Discuss your answer with a partner before you read the story.

Read an article about an unusual tribe of people.

The Strangest of Peoples

THE SHRINE ROOM

For decades anthropologists have been studying strange and unusual peoples all over the world. One of the strangest peoples of all is a group called the Nacirema, a legendary tribe living in North America.

The territory of the Nacirema is located between the Canadian Cree and the Tarahumare of Mexico. On the southeast their territory is bordered by the Arawak of the Caribbean. Relatively little is known of the origin of this people, though they are said to have come from somewhere east. In fact, the Nacirema may be related to certain European peoples.

Nacirema people spend a great deal of time on the appearance and health of their bodies. In Nacirema culture the body is generally believed to be ugly and likely to decay. The only way this decay can be prevented is through participation in certain magical ceremonies. In every Nacirema house there is a special shrine room dedicated to this purpose. Some Nacirema houses have more than one shrine room. In fact, it is felt in Nacirema culture that the more shrine rooms a family has, the richer it is.

What is in the shrine room? The focal point is a box built into the wall. Inside the box is a large collection of magical potions, medicines, and creams. Below the box is a small font from which water is obtained. Every day each member of the Nacirema family enters the shrine room, bows to the chest, and receives magic, holy water from the fountain.

Women whose heads have been baked are regarded as beautiful.

Several rituals in Nacirema culture are performed by one sex or the other, but not by both. Every morning, for example, a Nacirema man places a magic cream on his face and then scrapes and even cuts his face with a sharp instrument. A ritual performed only by women involves a barbaric ceremony in which the women bake their heads in small ovens for an hour or so. Women whose heads have been baked are regarded as beautiful.

In Nacirema culture, the mouth is considered one of the most important parts of the body. The Nacirema are fascinated by the mouth and believe that its condition has an important and supernatural effect on all social relationships. The daily body ritual involves an activity which would be considered disgusting in some cultures. It is reported that the Nacirema actually insert into their mouths a stick on one end of which are animal hairs covered with a magical paste! They then move these sticks back and forth in their mouths in highly ritualized gestures.

Among the most important individuals in the culture are practitioners named "holy-mouth-people." Naciremans visit these practitioners once or twice a year. The holy-mouth-people possess excellent sharp instruments for performing their magic ceremonies. They place these instruments in the mouths of the Naciremans. If there are any holes in the teeth, they are enlarged by the use of these tools. Then a supernatural substance is placed in each hole. It is said that the purpose of this practice is to prevent decay in the teeth and to help the Nacirema people to make friends and find spouses.

Another very important person in Nacirema culture is the "listener," a witch doctor who has the power to get rid of the devils in the heads of people who have been bewitched. Naciremans believe that parents bewitch their own children, especially while teaching them the secret toilet rituals, and that the listeners must "unbewitch" them. It is also believed that the secret to getting rid of these devils in their heads is simply to talk about them, usually while reclining on a sofa.

Much more research is needed in order to understand this strange people.

Clearly, the Nacirema are a magic-inspired tribe. Much more research is needed in order to understand this strange people.

Source: Adapted from Horace Miner, "Body Ritual among the Nacirema," *American Anthropologist* 58:3, June 1956.

UNDERSTANDING MEANING FROM CONTEXT

Circle the letter of the choice closest in meaning to the italicized word or phrase from the reading.

1. In every Nacirema house there is a special *shrine room* dedicated to this purpose.
   - **a.** place for doing work
   - **b.** place for practicing religious ceremonies
   - **c.** place for relaxing

2. Below the box is a small *font* from which water is obtained.
   - **a.** body of water
   - **b.** source of water
   - **c.** container of water

3. They then move these sticks back and forth in their mouths in highly *ritualized* gestures.
   - **a.** ceremonial
   - **b.** energetic
   - **c.** athletic

4. Naciremans believe that parents *bewitch their own children* . . .
   - **a.** criticize their own children
   - **b.** teach their own children
   - **c.** place their children under magical control

COMPREHENSION

1. Is this article serious, or is it supposed to be funny?

2. On what does the author seem to think too much of the Nacirema people's time is spent?

3. What are the magical ceremonies that are practiced by the Nacirema?

4. What is the special ritual that is performed by the Nacirema man every morning?

5. What is the special ritual that is performed by the woman?

6. Is the description of the shrine room amusing to you? Why is it funny?

7. What is your response to the author's descriptions of the Nacirema's tribal customs?

8. Pick out a few details of the descriptions that are particularly funny to you. Share them with the class to see if they are seen as humorous by everyone.

9. By whom is the story told? What do you think that person's culture might be like? Would it be different from that of the Nacirema?

GRAMMAR **PRESENTATION**
REPORTING IDEAS AND FACTS WITH PASSIVES

PASSIVE

In Nacirema culture the body **is** generally **believed** to be ugly and likely to decay.

STATIVE PASSIVE

The territory of the Nacirema **is located** between the Canadian Cree, the Tarahumare of Mexico, and the Arawak of the Caribbean.

REDUCED PASSIVE

One of the strangest peoples of all is a group **called** the Nacirema, a legendary tribe living in North America.

NOTES

EXAMPLES

1. There are two types of **passive constructions**: action passives and non-action passives. Action passives show actions. Non-action passives show ideas, beliefs, opinions, findings, and facts.	• A supernatural substance action passive **is placed** in each hole. non-action passive • The mouth **is considered** one of the most important parts of the body.
2. Non-action passives are often used in reporting the news and in academic discourse. We use them to create an impartial and objective impression by removing the speaker or writer somewhat from the idea.	• Little **is known** about the origin of this strange people.
3. Speakers and writers can create an even greater distance between themselves and the idea by starting the sentence with *It*.	• **It is felt** that the more shrine rooms a family has, the richer it is.

4. Non-action passives are made from *be* + past participle. They are not made from *get*.	• The Nacirema people **are said** to have come from somewhere east.

5. Non-action passives frequently used to report ideas, beliefs, and opinions include *think, consider, regard, say, allege, believe, claim,* and *suggest*.	• Women whose heads have been baked **are regarded** as beautiful.
These passives can take a *by* phrase.	• Women whose heads have been baked **are regarded by Naciremans** as beautiful.
Passive sentences of this type can be converted to the active voice.	• **Naciremans regard** women whose heads have been baked as beautiful.

6. Passive sentences that express the opinions and beliefs of others are often followed by infinitives.	• In Nacirema culture the human body **is** generally **believed to be** ugly and likely to decay.

7. Stative passives are a kind of non-action passive. They are often used to report facts. Examples of stative passives include *be located* (*in, at,* etc.), *be found* (*in, at,* etc.), *be made up of, be divided* (*into, by,* etc.), *be related to*.	• The Nacirema territory **is located** between the Canadian Cree, the Tarahumare of Mexico, and the Arawak of the Caribbean.
Stative passives cannot take a *by* phrase and cannot be converted to the active voice. There is no performer of an action.	• The Nacirema **may be related to** certain European peoples. (no *by* phrase or active sentence possible)

8. Notice how some passive constructions can be reduced from full passives by deletion of *be* and the relative pronouns *who, which,* or *that*.	• One of the strangest peoples of all is a group **(that is) called** the Nacirema.

FOCUSED PRACTICE

 DISCOVER THE GRAMMAR

Part A

Look again at the opening reading, The Strangest of Peoples. *Find five action passives and five non-action passives. Write them in the blanks provided.*

Action Passives	**Non-Action Passives**
can be prevented	is located

Part B

Look at these two sentences from The Strangest of Peoples. *Could they be rewritten with a* **by** *phrase? Could they be rewritten in the active voice? Why or why not? Explain on the lines provided.*

1. In Nacirema culture, the mouth is considered one of the most important parts of the body.

2. In fact, the Nacirema may be related to certain European peoples.

Part C

Look again at The Strangest of Peoples. *Find the six reduced passives and rewrite them as full passives.*

1. a group called the Nacirema / a group that is called the Nacirema

2.

3.

4.

5.

6.

2 MYTH, LEGEND, OR REALITY?   Grammar Notes 1, 2, 4–7

Read the following article about past cultures. Complete the sentences with passive constructions, using the indicated verbs.

W🌐RLD REVIEW

Where do we draw the lines among myth, legend, and reality? How much is true and how much invented? What happens to groups or cultures when they disappear? What happens to their people? We decided to explore some of these questions.

First let's consider the saga of the ancient pueblo people of the U.S. Southwest. They ____are called____ the Anasazi by the Navajo
    1. (call)
people, a term which means "ancient ones," and though their origin _____,
                                2. (not know)
they _____ to have settled about
      3. (think)
A.D. 100 in the Four Corners area, where today the corners of the states of Arizona, Utah, Colorado, and New Mexico come together. They _____ to have
                            4. (know)
developed subsistence agriculture and to have built impressive cities and spectacular cliff dwellings. About the year 1300, however, something happened to the Anasazi.

They abandoned their dwellings and migrated to other locales such as the Rio Grande Valley in New Mexico and the White Mountains in Arizona.

Today it _____ by many
          5. (assume)
anthropologists that the Anasazi are the forebears of present-day pueblo peoples in the Southwest. The question remains, however: What brought an end to their flourishing culture? Drought? Incursions by unfriendly tribes? Can certain present-day Native Americans of the Southwest _____ as the descendants of
    6. (regard)
the Anasazi? Or did the Anasazi actually disappear?

Next, let's turn our attention to the story of Atlantis, the famed "lost continent" which _____ to have existed in the
    7. (say)
Atlantic Ocean. Supposedly Atlantis _____ west of the Strait of
    8. (locate)
Gibraltar, which _____ the
                    9. (call)

Pillars of Hercules by the Greeks. Is Atlantis a myth, or does it have a basis in reality? Plato wrote about Atlantis in two of his dialogues, describing it as a fabulous island larger than Libya and Turkey put together. Atlantis _____ by Plato to have

10. (believe)

existed about nine thousand years before his era. The Atlanteans _____ to

11. (repute)

have conquered many lands around the Mediterranean and _____ to

12. (say)

have become evil and greedy in the process. Their island or continent _____

13. (suppose)

to have sunk into the sea after being hit by earthquakes. Was there really an Atlantis? Were the survivors of the catastrophe really the ancestors of the present-day Basques, as _____ by certain twentieth-

14. (claim)

century tale-spinners? Is the Atlantis story just an entertaining legend invented by Plato? Or, if Atlantis was real, is the problem simply that it existed so long ago that wisps of its memory are all that remain? The legend of Atlantis _____ by many present-

15. (think)

day scholars to have been influenced by reports of the disaster on the island of Thira, north of Crete in the Mediterranean Sea. Thira was destroyed about 1500 B.C. by volcanic eruptions and accompanying earthquakes, which also devastated civilization on nearby Crete. Is the Thira disaster the basis for the Atlantis legend, or do the descendants of Atlanteans walk among us? The answer _____.

16. (not / yet / know)

③ EDITING

Read the following student essay about a creature that may or may not be real. Find and correct the ten errors in passive constructions. Some passive constructions have more than one error.

The Snowman

Every area of the world has its own legends, and Asia is no different. One of the most famous is the Abominable Snowman, or yeti, of the Himalayas. Is yeti just a legend that is ~~believe~~ *believed* because people want strange things to be real, or does he really exist?

Yeti said to be a huge creature—perhaps as tall as eight feet. His body is suppose to be covered with long, brown hair. He said to have a pointed head and a hairless face that looks something like a man's. And it is claiming that he lives near Everest, the highest mountain in the world.

Sightings of yeti have reported for centuries, but he was made know to the rest of the world only in 1921. In that year, members of an expedition to climb Mt. Everest saw very large tracks in the snow that looked like prints of a human foot. No conclusive evidence of Yeti's existence was found during that expedition, but interest stimulated. Other expeditions were made. In 1951, explorer Eric Shipton led a search in which some gigantic, human-appearing tracks were found. One again, yeti himself was not seen. In 1969, Sir Edmund Hillary, who along with Tenzing Norkay first climbed Mt. Everest, mounted another expedition, this time with the intention not only of seeing yeti but of capturing him. Once again, tracks were discovered, but that was all. Hillary apparently decided eventually that the tracks might simply be normal animal tracks enlarged by the daytime melting of the snow. In 1964, Boris F. Porshev, a Russian scientist, said that he believed that yeti actually existed. He theorized that yeti is a surviving descendant of Neanderthal man, a creature who thought to have lived 25,000 to 75,000 years ago. Porshev has never been able to see an actual yeti, however.

The mystery continues. Does yeti really exist, or do people just want to believe he exists? It seems to me that there must be more to this mystery than just melted tracks. Centuries of reports by Himalayan sherpas must mean something. Besides, other yeti-type creatures have reported—most notably, Bigfoot in North America. Time will tell, but in the meantime, perhaps we shouldn't be so quick to dismiss the Abominable Snowman as nothing more than an entertaining story.

Source: Based on information in Kenneth B. Platnick, "Yeti," in *Great Mysteries of History* (New York: Dorset Press, 1971).

COMMUNICATION PRACTICE

4 LISTENING 1

Listen to the news bulletin. Then listen again and mark the following statements **True, False,** *or* **I don't know** *based on what you heard.*

	True	False	I don't know
1. The earthquakes are said to have registered a nine on the Richter scale.	❏	❏	❏
2. The epicenter of the quakes was located in the Pacific Ocean.	❏	❏	❏
3. The exact number of drowned people is known.	❏	❏	❏
4. It is certain that severe flooding has occurred inland.	❏	❏	❏
5. The citizens of the country should head for low areas.	❏	❏	❏
6. The country struck by earthquakes is very large.	❏	❏	❏
7. The citizens of this country are calm, gentle, and law-abiding.	❏	❏	❏
8. The time is the present day.	❏	❏	❏

5 LISTENING 2

Comprehension

Listen to the TV quiz game. Match these items to complete each statement.

_____ **1.** Homer

_____ **2.** Siddartha Gautama

_____ **3.** Simón Bolívar

_____ **4.** Anastasia Romanova

_____ **5.** Plato

a. was thought to have been murdered in the 1917 Russian revolution.

b. is thought to have created the story of Atlantis.

c. is known as the father of Buddhism.

d. is considered the father of South American democracy.

e. is thought to have been the author of the *Iliad* and the *Odyssey*.

Optional Dictation

Now listen again, completing the sentences with passive constructions.

He _____was called_____ the Liberator and _____ the father of South
         1.   **2.**

American democracy.

He _____ the author of the *Iliad* and the *Odyssey*. However, it
      3.

_____ for certain whether he was one specific person or a composite of
    4.

many people.

His *Dialogues* _____ today all over the world. He _____ in
           5.   **6.**

Greece in 427 B.C. Some people say that the myth of Atlantis _____ by him.
                                                      7.

Born in India, he _____ as the father of Buddhism, a religion that
               8.

_____ by many people in Asia.
    9.

She _____ in the 1917 revolution. It _____ persistently
        10.

_____ that this one daughter somehow survived the assassination attempt
    11.

and eventually made her way to America.

---

❻ GROUP GUESSING GAME

*Divide into groups of four to six. Using passive
constructions, prepare five or more statements about any
famous figure you choose: a political or religious leader,
an author, an explorer, an inventor, and so on. The other
students in your group will try to guess who the figure is.
Make the first statements less obvious than the later ones.*

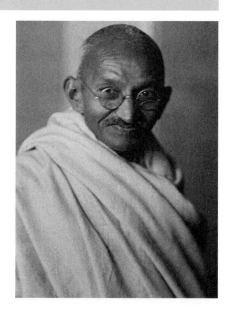

> **EXAMPLES:**
> 1. He **was called** "great soul" by his followers
>   and admirers.
> 2. In his time, he **was revered** for, among
>   other things, his efforts in favor of the
>   untouchables.
> 3. He **is known** today as the father of the
>   nonviolent movement called passive
>   resistance.

4. He **is regarded** as the principal force behind the achievement of India's independence.

5. In the world today he **is considered** one of the greatest religious leaders of all time.

Answer: Mohandas (Mahatma) Gandhi

 THE NACIREMA

Read more about the Nacirema.

The focal point of the shrine is a box or chest which is built into the wall. In this chest are kept the many charms and magical potions without which no native believes he could live. These preparations are secured from a variety of specialized practitioners. The most powerful of these are the medicine men, whose assistance must be rewarded with substantial gifts. However, the medicine men do not provide the curative potions for their clients, but decide what the ingredients should be and then write them down in an ancient and secret language. This writing is understood only by the medicine men and by the herbalists who, for another gift, provide the required charm.

The charm is not disposed of after it has served its purpose, but is placed in the charm-box of the household shrine. As these magical materials are specific for certain ills, and the real or imagined maladies of the people are many, the charm-box is usually full to overflowing. The magical packets are so numerous that people forget what their purposes were and fear to use them again. While the natives are very vague on this point, we can only assume that the idea in retaining all the old magical materials is that their presence in the charm-box, before which the body rituals are conducted, will in some way protect the worshipper.

The focal point of the shrine is a box or chest which is built into the wall.

Source: Horace Miner, "Body Ritual among the Nacirema," *American Anthropologist*, 58:3, June 1956.

Now, with a partner, decide what these items really represent:

the charm-box   herbalists

the medicine men   magical packets

 ESSAY

Imagine that you are writing a description like the Nacirema story about the people of your own country. Write two or three paragraphs. Describe some habits that you think other people would find amusing, or describe them in an amusing way as in the Nacirema story. Have fun!

9 PICTURE DISCUSSION

Divide into several groups and study this map of the East Asian region. Discuss what you know about the history, culture, peoples, and geography of this area. Then, as a group, prepare a set of questions with passive voice about some of the facts you discussed. Each group should take a turn asking questions of the other groups. Score points.

REVIEW OR SELFTEST

I. *Complete the conversations with* **be** *or* **get** *passive forms and the indicated verbs. Use* **be** *unless* **get** *is specified.*

1. A: Where ___was the missing child found___ ?
　　　　　　　　a. (the missing child / find)

　　B: She _____ walking barefoot along
　　　　　　　b. (discover)

　　Stinson Beach.

2. A: How do you think the team is going to do this year?

　　B: Pretty well, except that I'm sure they'll

　　_____ by Central University.
　　　(get / beat)

3. A: What happened to your car?

　　B: It _____ by a truck—a small one,
　　　　　　　(get / hit)

　　fortunately.

4. A: Mary, _____ for six months.
　　　　　a. (we / getting / overcharge)

　　B: I think we ought to _____. I've heard the
　　　　　　　　　b. (have / the company / investigate)

　　same complaint from the neighbors.

5. A: Why are these floors so dirty? _____
　　　　　　　　　　　　　a. (they / not / clean)

　　every day?

　　B: Normally, yes, but somehow the cleaning

　　_____ this morning.
　　　b. (not / get / do)

6. A: Please don't give food to the animals. They

　　_____ on a special diet.
　　　a. (feed)

　　B: OK. Will we be able to see the animals

　　_____ while we're here at the zoo?
　　　b. (getting / feed)

　　A: Yes. _____ at four o'clock today.
　　　　　c. (they / will / feed)

II. *Read the newspaper article. Rewrite the six numbered sentences, changing passive verb forms to the active and active verb forms to the passive. Eliminate all* **by** *phrases in passive sentences. Do not change intransitive verbs, and do not change the quotation.*

<u>It is said by local citizen Ronald Mason that his lesson has been learned by him</u>. On
1.
Tuesday, Mason was in a hurry to get to a job interview. <u>His motorcycle was parked by</u>
2.
<u>him in a handicap parking space</u>. <u>When Mason came out of the interview, it was</u>
(2. continued)   **3.**
<u>discovered by him that someone had removed his motorcycle from the handicap spot</u>.
(3. continued)
<u>Someone had placed it upside down in the pool of the adjacent fountain</u>. <u>People had</u>
4.   **5.**
<u>noticed no one in the area</u>. <u>After recovering his motorcycle, it was said by Mason</u>, "I'll
(5. continued)   **6.**
never do that again. I deserved what I got."

1. Local citizen Ronald Mason says that he has learned his lesson.

2. _____

3. _____

4. _____

5. _____

6. _____

III. *Fill in the blanks in the paragraph with passive forms of the indicated verbs.*

Consider the situation of the mysterious "lost colony" established by Sir Walter Raleigh

in 1585 on the Outer Banks of what is now North Carolina. It _____is felt_____
1. (feel)

today that the plan for the settlement, which _____ on Roanoke Island,
2. (locate)

was ill conceived from the start. Geographical conditions were not favorable, and the local

tribes were not friendly. In 1590 all of the colonists _____ by explorers to
3. (find)

have vanished, leaving behind only some refuse and the word *Croatoan*, the name of a

nearby island, written on a tree. What happened to the colonists? No one knows for sure,

but today they _____ to have been killed or carried away by neighboring
4. (assume)

peoples.

Today it _____ by some that at least a few of the colonists were
5. (believe)

absorbed into local tribes. In fact, descendants of the original native inhabitants of the

area claim Raleigh's colonists as their ancestors. If this is true, the people of the lost

colony _____ lost at all, for their genes live on in those descendants.
6. (not / should / consider)

Source: Adapted from Kenneth C. Davis, *Don't Know Much About History?* (New York: Avon Books, 1990), pp. 13–14.

IV. *Look at the pictures. For each picture, write a passive sentence with **be** or **get**. Use **be** unless **get** is specified, using the suggested prompts.*

1.

Mrs. O'Reilly (get / catch)

Mrs. O'Reilly is going to get
caught for speeding if
she doesn't slow down.

2.

Mrs. O'Reilly (get / stop)

_____

_____

_____

3.

Two months ago (tear down)

_____

_____

_____

4.

Now (build)

_____

_____

_____

5.

Mrs. Platt (have / repair)

_____

_____

6.

Once a month / Mr. Platt
(get / cut and trim)

_____

_____

7.

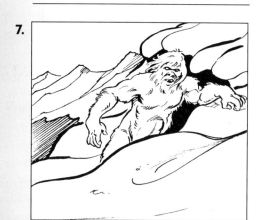

The yeti / the Himalaya Mountains
(think / live)

_____

_____

8.

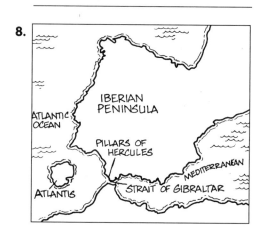

The lost continent of Atlantis /
Atlantic Ocean / Strait of Gibraltar
(say / be located)

_____

_____

_____

V. *Read the sentences in the news broadcast. Circle the letter of the one underlined word or phrase that is not correct.*

This is news to the hour on KXYZ.

1. The Hawaiian island of Kahoolawe <u>has</u> just <u>being</u> <u>hit</u> <u>by</u> a tsunami,
                                   A   B   C D   A **B** C D

or tidal wave.

2. The tsunami <u>were</u> <u>caused</u> <u>by</u> an earthquake <u>centered</u> in the Pacific   **A B C D**
                       A   B   C   D

Ocean south-southeast of Midway Island.

3. Damage on Kahoolawe <u>is</u> <u>say</u> <u>to</u> <u>be</u> extensive.   **A B C D**
                         A   B   C   D

4. In Central Africa, a breakthrough <u>is</u> <u>being</u> <u>report</u> involving resumption   **A B C D**
                                 A   B   C

of the <u>stalled</u> peace talks.
     D

5. These talks <u>were</u> <u>been</u> <u>held</u> last week <u>between</u> the leaders of Tintoria   **A B C D**
                 A   B   C   D

and Illyria.

6. They <u>have been</u> <u>broken off</u> <u>when</u> the president of Illyria <u>stormed</u> out   **A B C D**
            A   B   C   D

of the first face-to-face meeting.

7. The Secretary-General of the United Nations <u>says</u>, "We <u>must</u> <u>get</u> these   **A B C D**
                                    A   B   C

talks <u>start</u> again."
      D

8. In fact, it <u>is</u> <u>rumored</u> that the talks <u>are be</u> <u>resumed</u> next week in   **A B C D**
               A   B   C   D

Switzerland.

9. The new space station that <u>is being</u> <u>sponsored</u> by the seven-nation   **A B C D**
                             A   B

consortium <u>will</u> <u>launch</u> next week from Woomera Field in Australia.
             C   D

10. The station <u>will</u> <u>be</u> <u>staff</u> by astronauts from each of the seven   **A B C D**
                   A   B   C

<u>participating</u> nations.
    D

That's news to the hour from KXYZ.

VI. *Go back to your answers for Exercise V. Write the correct answer for each item you believe to be incorrect.*

1. _____been_____   6. _____

2. _____   7. _____

3. _____   8. _____

4. _____   9. _____

5. _____   10. _____

▶ *To check your answers, go to the Answer Key on page 256.*

PART V

FROM GRAMMAR TO WRITING
PARALLELISM

Parallelism (also called parallel structure) is an important feature of English that makes our speaking, and especially our writing, easier to understand. To make speech or writing parallel, put all items in a series in the same grammatical form.

> **EXAMPLES:**
>
> Over the weekend I **bought a new car**, **painted the living room**, and **planted a garden**. (All three verbs in the predicate are in the simple past and in the active voice.)
>
> The prisoner **was arrested**, **taken** to the police station, and **booked** and **fingerprinted**. (All three verb phrases are in the passive voice.)
>
> My favorite hobbies are **skindiving**, **reading**, and **playing the guitar**. (All three subject complements are gerunds or gerund phrases.)
>
> Children in this program are not allowed **to watch television** or **to eat junk food**. (The two complements are infinitive phrases.)

We will concentrate in this unit on parallelism with nouns and articles and with active or passive voice. See *From Grammar to Writing* after Part VII, page 342, for a discussion of parallelism with gerunds and infinitives.

In writing sentences that contain a series of nouns and articles, you can place the article before each noun or before the first noun only. However, it is more common to place the article before each noun.

> **EXAMPLES:**
>
> On her shopping trip, Mrs. Figueroa bought **a** book, **a** dress, and **a** CD.
>
> OR
>
> On her shopping trip, Mrs. Figueroa bought **a** book, dress, and CD.
>
> NOT
>
> ~~On her shopping trip, Mrs. Figueroa bought a book, dress, and a CD.~~

1 *Read the following paragraph and correct the five errors in parallel structure with nouns and articles.*

Rolleen Laing poured herself a second cup of coffee as she ate her breakfast, which consisted of a fried egg, ^an^ orange, and a piece of dry toast. She was sixty-two years old and had been successful as a university professor, writer of detective fiction, and an amateur detective. Just then the telephone rang. It was Harry Sadler, a local police detective. Ever since Rolleen had helped Harry crack a murder case several years previously, she had been called in as an unofficial consultant on several cases. She had helped Harry solve cases involving a hit-and-run victim, a murdered television executive, and, most recently, koala stolen from the city zoo.

"Hi, Rolleen. This is Harry. You're needed on another case. It's a robbery this time. Some thieves broke into the art museum and stole a Van Gogh, Picasso, Gauguin, and a Matisse. Meet me at the museum at 10:00, OK?"

In sentences with the passive voice, the auxiliary may be repeated each time or before the first item only. If the parallel items are short, the auxiliary is generally not repeated.

> The prisoner **was arrested**, **tried**, and **found** innocent.

If the parallel items are long, the auxiliary is generally repeated for the sake of clarity.

> The mythical nation of Atlantis **is said** to have existed about twelve thousand years ago, **is thought** to have been located in the Atlantic Ocean west of the Strait of Gibraltar, and **can be regarded** as a thematic source of many present-day legends of lost peoples.

Notice the following nonparallel sentence with two phrases with the passive voice and one with the active.

> The evidence was taken to the crime lab, a team of biochemists analyzed it, and used in a criminal trial.

To put this sentence in parallel structure, change the middle item to the passive voice, eliminating the word *it*.

> The evidence **was taken** to the crime lab, **analyzed by a team of biochemists**, and **used** in a criminal trial.

2 *Each of the following sentences contains an error in parallelism involving active or passive voice. In each case, one item is nonparallel with the others. Correct the nonparallel item.*

1. Yeti is described as a huge creature, ~~is~~ said to have long, brown hair, and is thought to live in the Himalayan Mountains.

2. According to historical records, the American outlaw Billy the Kid was known as a fearless gunfighter, was hunted by the law, and killed in a gunfight.

3. Anthropologists speculate that the Anasazi might have been attacked by unfriendly tribes, decimated by crop failures, or drought might have driven them away.

4. After Amelia Earhart's airplane was lost, naval investigators searched for debris, interviewed residents of South Pacific islands, but no trace of Earhart and Noonan was found.

5. According to legend, the continent of Atlantis was struck by devastating earthquakes, inundated by floods, and the ocean swallowed it up.

3 *Read the following paragraph about the Judge Crater mystery. Correct the three errors in parallelism with active or passive voice.*

On the evening of August 6, 1930, Judge Force Crater, a wealthy, successful, and good-looking New York lawyer, disappeared without a trace. Earlier in the evening he had been seen with friends at a Manhattan restaurant. At 9:10 P.M. he left the restaurant, hailed a taxi, and ~~was driven~~ *drove* away. No one ever saw or heard from him again. It was ten days before he was even reported missing. On August 16, his wife called his courthouse, the secretary was asked about his whereabouts, and learned that he was probably off on political business. This news reassured Mrs. Crater somewhat, but when he still hadn't turned up by August 26, a group of his fellow judges started an investigation. A grand jury was convened, but its members could not come to any conclusion as to what had happened to Judge Crater. They theorized that the judge might have developed amnesia, run away voluntarily, or been a crime victim. His wife disagreed with the first two possibilities, holding that he had been murdered by someone in the Tammany Hall organization, the political machine that controlled New York City at the time. The mystery remains unsolved to this day. He could have been killed by a Tammany Hall hiree, a girlfriend could have murdered him, or kidnapped by an organized crime group. He might in fact have suffered from amnesia, or he might have planned his own disappearance. Reports of Judge Crater sightings have continued to surface over the last sixty years.

Source: Adapted from E. Randall Floyd, *Great American Mysteries* (Little Rock: August House Publishers, 1990).

4 APPLY IT TO YOUR WRITING

Write a paragraph of six to ten sentences on one of the following topics. Use the passive voice where appropriate.

- An accident or natural disaster that you have witnessed or heard about

- An unsolved mystery that you are aware of

- An unusual or mysterious experience you have had

In your paragraph, include at least one sentence containing verbs in the passive voice in parallel structure. Also include at least one sentence containing a series of nouns in parallel structure. Exchange papers with a partner. Discuss each other's paper and then rewrite your paragraph if necessary. Submit your paragraph to your teacher.

REVIEW OR SELFTEST
ANSWER KEY

I.
- **1b.** was discovered
- **2.** get beaten
- **3.** got hit
- **4a.** we've been getting overcharged
- **4b.** have the company investigated
- **5a.** Aren't they cleaned
- **5b.** didn't get done
- **6a.** are fed
- **6b.** getting fed
- **6c.** They'll be fed

II.
- **2.** He parked his motorcycle in a handicap parking space.
- **3.** When Mason came out of the interview, he discovered that his motorcycle had been removed from the handicap spot.
- **4.** It had been placed upside down in the pool of the adjacent fountain.
- **5.** No one had been noticed in the area.
- **6.** After recovering his motorcycle, Mason said, "I'll never do that again. I deserved what I got."

III.
- **2.** was located
- **3.** were found
- **4.** are assumed
- **5.** is believed
- **6.** should not be considered

IV. Possible Answers
- **2.** Mrs. O'Reilly got stopped by a police officer.
- **3.** Two months ago this old building was being torn down.
- **4.** Now a new stadium is being built here.
- **5.** Mrs. Platt is going to have her toaster repaired.
- **6.** Once a month, Mr. Platt gets his hair cut and his beard trimmed.
- **7.** The yeti is thought to live in the Himalaya Mountains.
- **8.** The lost continent of Atlantis is said to have been located in the Atlantic Ocean west of the Strait of Gibraltar.

V.
- **2.** A
- **3.** B
- **4.** C
- **5.** B
- **6.** A
- **7.** D
- **8.** C
- **9.** D
- **10.** C

VI.
- **2.** was
- **3.** said
- **4.** reported
- **5.** being
- **6.** were
- **7.** started
- **8.** are going to be / will be
- **9.** be launched
- **10.** staffed

APPENDICES

1 Irregular Verbs

Base Form	Simple Past	Past Participle
arise	arose	arisen
awake	awoke / awaked	awaked / awoken
be	was, were	been
bear	bore	borne
beat	beat	beaten / beat
become	became	become
begin	began	begun
bend	bent	bent
bet	bet	bet
bite	bit	bitten
bleed	bled	bled
blow	blew	blown
break	broke	broken
bring	brought	brought
broadcast	broadcast / broadcasted	broadcast / broadcasted
build	built	built
burn	burned / burnt	burned / burnt
burst	burst	burst
buy	bought	bought
cast	cast	cast
catch	caught	caught
choose	chose	chosen
cling	clung	clung
come	came	come
cost	cost	cost
creep	crept	crept
cut	cut	cut
deal	dealt	dealt
dig	dug	dug
dive	dived / dove	dived
do	did	done
draw	drew	drawn
dream	dreamed / dreamt	dreamed / dreamt
drink	drank	drunk
drive	drove	driven
eat	ate	eaten
fall	fell	fallen
feed	fed	fed
feel	felt	felt
fight	fought	fought
find	found	found
fit	fitted / fit	fitted / fit
flee	fled	fled
fling	flung	flung
fly	flew	flown
forbid	forbade / forbad	forbidden / forbid
forget	forgot	forgotten
forgive	forgave	forgiven
forgo	forwent	forgone
freeze	froze	frozen

Base Form	Simple Past	Past Participle
get	got	gotten / got
give	gave	given
go	went	gone
grind	ground	ground
grow	grew	grown
hang	hung / hanged*	hung / hanged*
have	had	had
hear	heard	heard
hide	hid	hidden / hid
hit	hit	hit
hold	held	held
hurt	hurt	hurt
keep	kept	kept
kneel	knelt / kneeled	knelt / kneeled
knit	knit / knitted	knit / knitted
know	knew	known
lay	laid	laid
lead	led	led
leap	leaped / leapt	leaped / leapt
leave	left	left
lend	lent	lent
let	let	let
lie (down)	lay	lain
light	lighted / lit	lighted / lit
lose	lost	lost
make	made	made
mean	meant	meant
pay	paid	paid
prove	proved	proved / proven
put	put	put
quit	quit / quitted	quit / quitted
read / riʸd /	read / rɛd /	read / rɛd /
rid	rid / ridded	rid / ridded
ride	rode	ridden
ring	rang	rung
rise	rose	risen
run	ran	run
saw	sawed	sawed / sawn
say	said	said
see	saw	seen
seek	sought	sought
sell	sold	sold
send	sent	sent
set	set	set
sew	sewed	sewn / sewed
shake	shook	shaken
shave	shaved	shaved / shaven
shear	sheared	sheared / shorn

*hung = hung an object
hanged = executed by hanging

(continued on next page)

Base Form	Simple Past	Past Participle	Base Form	Simple Past	Past Participle
shine	shone / shined**	shone / shined **	strike	struck	struck / stricken
shoot	shot	shot	swear	swore	sworn
show	showed	shown / showed	sweep	swept	swept
shrink	shrank / shrunk	shrunk / shrunken	swell	swelled	swelled / swollen
shut	shut	shut	swim	swam	swum
sing	sang	sung	swing	swung	swung
sink	sank / sunk	sunk	take	took	taken
sit	sat	sat	teach	taught	taught
slay	slew	slain	tear	tore	torn
sleep	slept	slept	tell	told	told
slide	slid	slid	think	thought	thought
sneak	sneaked / snuck	sneaked / snuck	throw	threw	thrown
speak	spoke	spoken	undergo	underwent	undergone
speed	sped / speeded	sped / speeded	understand	understood	understood
spend	spent	spent	upset	upset	upset
spill	spilled / spilt	spilled / spilt	wake	woke / waked	waked / woken
spin	spun	spun	wear	wore	worn
spit	spat / spit	spat / spit	weave	wove / weaved	woven / weaved
split	split	split	weep	wept	wept
spread	spread	spread	wet	wet / wetted	wet / wetted
spring	sprang / sprung	sprung	win	won	won
stand	stood	stood	wind	wound	wound
steal	stole	stolen	withdraw	withdrew	withdrawn
stick	stuck	stuck	wring	wrung	wrung
sting	stung	stung	write	wrote	written
stink	stank / stunk	stunk			
strew	strewed	strewn			

**shone = intransitive: The sun shone brightly.
shined = transitive: He shined his shoes.

2 Common Verbs Usually Used Statively

Example:
She **seems** happy in her new job.

Appearance	Emotions	Mental States		Perception and the Senses	Possession	Wants and Preferences
appear	abhor	agree	hesitate	ache	belong	desire
be	admire	amaze	hope	feel	contain	need
concern	adore	amuse	imagine	hear	have	prefer
indicate	appreciate	annoy	imply	hurt	own	want
look	care	assume	impress	notice	pertain	wish
mean (= signify)	desire	astonish	infer	observe	possess	
parallel	detest	believe	know	perceive		**Other**
represent	dislike	bore	mean	see		cost
resemble	doubt	care	mind	sense		include
seem	empathize	consider	presume	smart		lack
signify (= mean)	envy	deem	realize	smell		matter
	fear	deny	recognize	taste		owe
	hate	disagree	recollect			refuse
	hope	disbelieve	remember			suffice
	like	entertain (= amuse)	revere			
	love	estimate	see (= understand)			
	regret	expect	suit			
	respect	fancy	suppose			
	sympathize	favor	suspect			
	trust	feel (= believe)	think (= believe)			
		figure (= assume)	tire			
		find	understand			
		guess	wonder			

1. ABILITY

can	I can speak French.
could	She could talk when she was a year old.
was / were able to	Henry was able to get a scholarship.
will be able to	Sarah will be able to buy a new house.

2. ADVICE

should	You should study harder.
ought to	You ought to sing in the choir.
should have	You should have acted sooner.
ought to have	We ought not to have said that.
had better	You'd better do something fast.
shall	Shall I continue? *

3. CERTAINTY: PRESENT AND PAST

must	He's not here. He must be on his way.
must have	I must have forgotten to pay the bill.

4. CERTAINTY: FUTURE

should	They should be here by nine.
ought to	That ought to help the situation.

5. EXPECTATION: PRESENT AND PAST

be to	You are to report to the traffic court on April 1.
	He was to be here by nine.
be supposed to	A person accused of a crime is supposed to have a speedy trial.
	The boys were supposed to feed the pets.

6. FUTURITY

will	He will do it.
shall	I shall never travel again. **
be going to	They are going to visit us.
be about to	The bell is about to ring.

7. HABITUAL ACTION: PAST

used to	I used to procrastinate, but I don't anymore.
would	When I was a child, we would spend every summer at our beach cabin.

8. HABITUAL ACTION: PRESENT AND FUTURE

will	Many people will gossip if given the chance.

9. IMPOSSIBILITY: PRESENT AND PAST

can't	This can't be happening.
couldn't	She couldn't be here. I heard she was ill.
can't have	They can't have arrived yet. It's a two-hour trip.
couldn't have	They couldn't have bought a car. They didn't have any money.

10. LACK OF NECESSITY: PRESENT AND PAST

don't have to	We don't have to leave for work yet.
didn't have to	Frank didn't have to work yesterday.
needn't	You needn't rewrite your essay.
needn't have	She needn't have bothered to call. Mary wasn't home.

11. NECESSITY: PRESENT AND PAST

must	Everyone must pay taxes.
have to	She has to have surgery.
have got to	We've got to do something about the situation.
had to	John had to fly to New York for a meeting.

12. NECESSITY NOT TO

mustn't	You mustn't neglect to pay your car insurance.

13. OPPORTUNITY

could	We could go to the park this afternoon.
could have	You could have done better in this course.

14. POSSIBILITY: PRESENT AND PAST

may	He may be sick.
may have	Zelda may have saved enough money.
might	I might go to the play; I'm not sure.
might have	The money might have been stolen.
could	Frank could be on his way.
could have	They could have taken the wrong road.

15. PREFERENCE

would rather	Martha would rather stay home tonight than go to the play.

16. WILLINGNESS (VOLITION)

will	I'll help you with your homework.

*The use of *shall* in a question to ask another's opinion or direction is the only common use of *shall* in American English.

**Shall* used to express futurity is rare in American English.

4 Irregular Noun Plurals

Singular Form	Plural Form	Singular Form	Plural Form	Singular Form	Plural Form
alumna	alumnae	fish	fish, fishes**	people	people ****
alumnus	alumni	foot	feet	phenomenon	phenomena
amoeba	amoebas, amoebae	genus	genera	(no singular form)	police*****
analysis	analyses	goose	geese	policeman	policemen
antenna	antennae, antennas	half	halves	policewoman	policewomen
appendix	appendices, appendixes	index	indexes, indices	postman	postmen ***
		knife	knives	protozoan	protozoa, protozoans
axis	axes	leaf	leaves		
basis	bases	life	lives	radius	radii
businessman	businessmen	loaf	loaves	series	series
businesswoman	businesswomen	louse	lice	sheaf	sheaves
calf	calves	mailman	mailmen ***	sheep	sheep
(no singular form)	cattle	man	men	shelf	shelves
child	children	millennium	millennia, millenniums	species	species
crisis	crises			thesis	theses
criterion	criteria	money	moneys, monies	tooth	teeth
datum	data	moose	moose	vertebra	vertebrae, vertebras
deer	deer	mouse	mice		
dwarf	dwarfs, dwarves	octopus	octopuses, octopi	wife	wives
elf	elves	ox	oxen	woman	women
fireman	firemen*	paramecium	paramecia		

```
   * Also: firefighter, firefighters
  ** fishes = different species of fish
 *** Also: letter carrier, letter carriers, postal worker, postal workers
**** Also: person, persons; a people = an ethnic group
***** Also: police officer, police officers
```

5 Common Non-Count Nouns

Abstractions		Activities		Ailments	Solid Elements	Gases
advice	inertia	badminton	golf	AIDS	calcium	carbon dioxide
anarchy	integrity	baseball	hiking	appendicitis	carbon	helium
behavior	love	basketball	reading	cancer	copper	hydrogen
chance	luck	biking	sailing	chicken pox	gold	neon
choice	momentum	billiards	singing	cholera	iron	nitrogen
decay	oppression	bowling	skating	diabetes	lead	oxygen
democracy	peace	boxing	soccer	flu (influenza)	magnesium	
energy	pollution	canoeing	surfing	heart disease	platinum	
entertainment	responsibility	cards	talk	malaria	plutonium	
entropy	slavery	conversation	tennis	measles	radium	
evil	socialism	cycling	volleyball	mumps	silver	
freedom	spontaneity	dancing	wrestling	polio	tin	
fun	stupidity	football		smallpox	titanium	
good	time			strep throat	uranium	
happiness	totalitarianism			tuberculosis (TB)		
hate	truth					
hatred	violence					
honesty						

FOODS	LIQUIDS	NATURAL PHENOMENA	OCCUPATIONS	PARTICLES	SUBJECTS	MISCELLANEOUS
barley	coffee	air	banking	dust	accounting	clothing
beef	gasoline	aurora australis	computer	gravel	art	equipment
bread	juice	aurora borealis	technology	pepper	astronomy	furniture
broccoli	milk	cold	construction	salt	biology	news
cake	oil	electricity	dentistry	sand	business	
candy	soda	fog	engineering	spice	chemistry	
chicken	tea	hail	farming	sugar	civics	
fish	water	heat	fishing		computer	
meat		ice	law		science	
oats		lightning	manufacturing		economics	
pie		mist	medicine		geography	
rice		rain	nursing		history	
wheat		sleet	retail		Latin	
		smog	sales		linguistics	
		smoke	teaching		literature	
		snow	writing		mathematics	
		steam	work		music	
		thunder			physics	
		warmth			psychology	
					science	
					sociology	
					speech	
					writing	

6 Some Common Ways of Making Non-Count Nouns Countable

ABSTRACTIONS
a piece of advice
a matter of choice
a unit of energy
a type *or* form of entertainment
a piece *or* bit of luck

ACTIVITIES
a game of badminton, baseball, basketball,
   cards, football, golf, soccer, tennis, etc.
a badminton game, a baseball game, etc.

FOODS
a grain of barley
a cut *or* piece of beef
a loaf of bread
a piece of cake
a piece *or* wedge of pie
a grain of rice
a portion *or* serving of—

LIQUIDS
a cup of coffee, tea
a gallon *or* liter of gasoline
a can of oil
a can *or* glass of soda
a glass of milk, water, juice

NATURAL PHENOMENA
a drop of rain
a bolt *or* current of electricity
a bolt of lightning
a clap *or* bolt of thunder

PARTICLES
a speck of dust
a grain of pepper, salt, sand, sugar

SUBJECTS
a branch of accounting, art, astronomy,
   biology, business, chemistry, civics,
   economics, geography, literature,
   linguistics, mathematics, music, physics,
   psychology, science, sociology, etc.

MISCELLANEOUS
an article of clothing
a piece of equipment
a piece *or* article of furniture
a piece of news *or* a news item *or* an item
   of news
a period of time

7 Countries Whose Names Contain the Definite Article

The Bahamas
The Cayman Islands
The Central African Republic
The Channel Islands
The Comoros
The Czech Republic

The Dominican Republic
The Falkland Islands
The Gambia
The Isle of Man
The Leeward Islands
The Maldives (the Maldive Islands)

The Marshall Islands
The Netherlands
The Netherlands Antilles
The Philippines
The Solomon Islands
The Turks and Caicos Islands

The United Arab Emirates
The United Kingdom (of Great
   Britain and Northern Ireland)
The United States (of America)
The Virgin Islands
The Wallis and Futuna Islands

8 Selected Geographical Features Whose Names Contain the Definite Article

GULFS, OCEANS, SEAS, AND STRAITS

The Adriatic Sea
The Aegean Sea
The Arabian Sea
The Arctic (Ocean)
The Antarctic (Ocean)
The Atlantic (Ocean)
The Baltic Sea
The Black Sea
The Caribbean (Sea)
The Caspian Sea
The Coral Sea
The Gulf of Aden
The Gulf of Mexico

The Gulf of Oman
The Indian (Ocean)
The Mediterranean (Sea)
The North Sea
The Pacific (Ocean)
The Persian Gulf
The Philippine Sea
The Red Sea
The Sea of Japan
The South China Sea
The Strait of Gibraltar
The Strait of Magellan
The Yellow Sea

MOUNTAIN RANGES

The Alps
The Andes
The Appalachians
The Atlas Mountains
The Caucasus

The Himalayas
The Pyrenees
The Rockies
   (The Rocky Mountains)
The Urals

RIVERS

The Amazon
The Colorado
The Columbia
The Danube
The Euphrates
The Ganges
The Hudson
The Indus
The Jordan
The Mackenzie
The Mekong
The Mississippi
The Missouri
The Niger
The Nile

The Ob
The Ohio
The Orinoco
The Po
The Rhine
The Rhone
The Rio Grande
The St. Lawrence
The Seine
The Tagus
The Thames
The Tiber
The Tigris
The Volga
The Yangtze

OTHER FEATURES

The Equator
The Far East
The Gobi (Desert)
The Middle East (Near East)
The North Pole
The Occident
The Orient
The Panama Canal
The Sahara (Desert)
The South Pole
The Suez Canal
The Tropic of Cancer
The Tropic of Capricorn

9 Common Verbs Followed by the Gerund (Base Form of Verb + -ing)

Example:
Jane **enjoys playing** tennis and **gardening**.

abhor
acknowledge
admit
advise
allow
anticipate
appreciate
avoid
be worth
can't help
celebrate

confess
consider
defend
delay
deny
detest
discontinue
discuss
dislike
dispute
dread

endure
enjoy
escape
evade
explain
fancy
feel like
feign
finish
forgive
give up (= stop)

imagine
keep (= continue)
keep on
mention
mind (= object to)
miss
necessitate
omit
permit
picture

postpone
practice
prevent
put off
recall
recollect
recommend
report
resent
resist

resume
risk
shirk
shun
suggest
support
tolerate
understand
urge
warrant

10 Common Verbs Followed by the Infinitive (To + Base Form of Verb)

Example:
The Minnicks **decided to sell** their house.

agree
appear
arrange
ask
attempt
beg
can / can't afford
can / can't wait
care
chance
choose

claim
come
consent
dare
decide
demand
deserve
determine
elect
endeavor
expect

fail
get
grow (up)
guarantee
hesitate
hope
hurry
incline
learn
manage

mean (= intend)
need
offer
pay
prepare
pretend
profess
promise
prove
refuse

remain
request
resolve
say
seek
seem
shudder
strive
struggle
swear

tend
threaten
turn out
venture
volunteer
wait
want
wish
would like
yearn

Verbs Followed by the Gerund or Infinitive without a Change in Meaning

attempt	can't bear	continue	like	prefer	regret
begin	can't stand	hate	love	propose	start

 Verbs Followed by the Gerund or the Infinitive with a Change in Meaning

forget	go on	quit	remember	stop	try

forget
I've almost **forgotten meeting** him. (= At present, I can hardly remember.)
I almost **forgot to meet** him. (= I almost didn't remember to meet him.)

go on
Jack **went on writing** novels. (= Jack continued to write novels.)
Jack **went on to write** novels. (= Jack ended some other activity and began to write novels.)

quit
Ella **quit working** at Sloan's. (= She isn't working there anymore.)
Ella **quit to work** at Sloan's. (= She quit another job in order to work at Sloan's.)

remember
Velma **remembered writing** to Bill. (= Velma remembered the activity of writing to Bill.)
Velma **remembered to write** to Bill. (= Velma wrote to Bill. She didn't forget to do it.)

stop
Hank **stopped eating**. (= He stopped the activity of eating.)
Hank **stopped to eat**. (= He stopped doing something else in order to eat.)

try
Martin **tried skiing**. (= Martin sampled the activity of skiing.)
Martin **tried to ski**. (= Martin tried to ski but didn't succeed.)

13 Verbs Followed by Object + Infinitive

Example:
I **asked Sally to lend** me her car.

advise	choose*	expect*	hire	order	persuade	teach	want*
allow	convince	forbid	invite	pay*	remind	tell	warn
ask*	encourage	force	need*	permit	require	urge	would like*
cause							

*These verbs can also be followed by the infinitive without an object.
Example:
I **want to go**.   *or*   I **want Andy to go**.

14 Common Adjectives Followed by the Infinitive

Example:
I was **glad to hear** about that.

afraid	curious	disturbed	fascinated	hesitant	pleased	reluctant	surprised
alarmed	delighted	eager	fortunate	impossible	possible	right	touched
amazed	depressed	easy	frightened	interested	prepared	sad	unlikely
angry	determined	ecstatic	furious	intrigued	proud	scared	unnecessary
anxious	difficult	embarrassed	glad	likely	ready	shocked	willing
astonished	disappointed	encouraged	happy	lucky	relieved	sorry	wrong
careful	distressed	excited	hard	necessary			

Common Adjective + Preposition Expressions

These expressions are followed by nouns, pronouns, or gerunds.

Example:
I'm not **familiar with** that writer.

accustomed to	careful of	furious with	nervous about	sick of
afraid of	concerned with / about	glad about	obsessed with / about	slow at
amazed at / by	content with	good at	opposed to	sorry for / about
angry at / with	curious about	guilty of	pleased about	suited to
ashamed of	different from	happy about	poor at	surprised at / about / by
astonished at / by	excellent at	incapable of	ready for	terrible at
aware of	excited about	intent on	responsible for	tired from
awful at	famous for	interested in	sad about	tired of
bad at	fascinated with / by	intrigued by / at	safe from	used to
bored with / by	fed up with	mad at (= angry at,	satisfied with	weary of
capable of	fond of	angry with)	shocked at / by	worried about

 Common Inseparable Phrasal Verbs

Example:
We **got rid of** our old furniture.
We **got rid** of it.

advise against	come out	get behind	let up	run across
apologize for	come over	get by (on)	listen in on	run into
approve of	come through	get even (with)	listen to	run out of
back out (of)	come to	get in	live up to	run through
bear up	come up	get into	look after	stand up to
be familiar with	come upon	get off	look at	stick to
believe in	come up with	get on	look back on	stoop to
brush up (on)	complain about	get out of	look down on	succeed in
carry on (with)	count on	get over	look for	take after
catch up (on)	cut down on	get rid of	look forward to	take care of
catch up (with)	deal with	get through	look like	talk about
choose between / among	do without	get through to	look out for	think about
come about	dream about / of	get through with	look up to	try out for
come across	feel like	get to know	make up (= become	turn into
come along	fill in for	get up (= rise)	friendly again)	turn out for
come apart	follow up on	give up on	make up for	turn up (=appear
come around	get about	go back on	miss out (on)	suddenly)
come between	get after	go in for	object to	wait for
come by	get ahead	go through	part with	walk out on
come down with	get along (with)	hurry up to	plan on	watch out for
come in	get around	insist on	put up with	wonder about
come into	get away (with)	keep up with	rely on	work up to
come off	get back	laugh at	resort to	write about

17 Common Separable Phrasal Verbs

Example:
I **figured out** the answer.
I **figured** the answer **out**.
I **figured** it **out**.

bring about	drop off	make up (= invent)	stir up
bring along	figure out	make up one's mind	take away
bring around	fill out	(= decide)	take back
bring in	fill up	mix up	take off (= remove)
bring on	find out	pay back	take on
bring over	get across	pick up	take over
bring through	give away	put across	take up
bring up	give back	put away	think over
call off	give up	put off	try on
call up	hand out	put on	try out
clear up	have on	put out	turn down
cut off	hold up	run by / past	turn off
cut up	look over	set aside	turn on
do over	look up	show off	turn up (=increase the volume)

18 Coordinating Conjunctions

Example:
We went to the party, **but** we really didn't have a good time there.

and	but	for	nor	or	so	yet

19 Common Subordinating Conjunctions: Single Words and Phrases

after	before	in spite of the fact that	such . . . that
although	despite the fact that	no matter if	though
as	due to the fact that	no matter whether	till
as if	even if	on account of the fact that	unless
as long as	even though	once	until
as many as	even when	plus the fact that	when
as much as	however (= the way in which)	provided (that)	whenever
as soon as	if	providing (that)	whereas
as though	if only	since	whether (or not)
because	inasmuch as	so that	while
because of the fact that	in case	so . . . that	

20 Transitions: Single Words and Phrases

A. TO SHOW AN "AND" RELATION	**B. TO SHOW A "BUT" RELATION**	**C. TO SHOW A "WHY / BECAUSE" RELATION**	**D. TO SHOW A TIME / SEQUENCE RELATION**	
additionally	actually	accordingly	after this / that	in the meantime
again	anyhow	arising out of this / that	afterwards	just then
along with this / that	anyway	as a result	an hour later (several	meanwhile
also	as a matter of fact	because of this / that	hours later, etc.)	next
alternatively	at any rate	consequently	at last	on another occasion
as a matter of fact	despite this / that	for this / that reason	at the same time	previously
besides	even so	hence	at this moment	second(ly)
by the way	however	in consequence	before this / that	then
finally	in any case	in such an event	briefly	third(ly) (fourth,
first	in either case	in this / that case	first(ly)	fourthly, etc.)
for example	in spite of this / that	on account of this / that	from now on	to resume
for instance	instead (of this / that)	otherwise	henceforth	to return to the point
furthermore	nevertheless	then	hitherto	to summarize
in addition	nonetheless	therefore	in conclusion	under the
incidentally	on the contrary	this / that being so	in short	circumstances
indeed	on the other hand	thus	in sum	until then
in fact	rather	to this end	in summary	up to now
in other words	still		in the end	
in the same way				
likewise				
that is				

21 Verbs and Expressions Followed by the Subjunctive (Base Form)

Examples:
We **demand that** he **do** it.
It is **essential that** he **do** it.
The professor **suggested that** we **read** his book.

ask*	it is desirable that	it is required that	propose
demand	it is essential that	move (= formally propose in a	recommend
insist	it is important that	meeting)	request*
it is advisable that	it is mandatory that	order*	suggest
it is crucial that	it is necessary that	prefer*	urge*

* These verbs also take the form verb + object pronoun + infinitive:
   We ask that she be present.   *or*   We ask her to be present.

22 Expressions That Can Be Followed by Unreal Conditional Forms

as if	as though	if only	it is time	what if	would rather (that)

Examples:
She acts **as if (as though)** she were president.
If only I **had** more time.
It's time we left.
What if we **had** a million dollars?
I'd rather (that) we **didn't** stay.

INDEX

This Index is for the full and split editions. All entries are in the full book.
Entries for Volume A of the split edition are in black. Entries for Volume B are in color.